Protecting Historic Architecture and Museum Collections from Natural Disasters

Protecting Historic Architecture and Museum Collections from Natural Disasters

Edited by
Barclay G. Jones, Ph.D.

Butterworths
Boston London Durban Singapore Sydney Toronto Wellington

Figures appearing on pages 149, 150, 153 and 154 are reprinted
with permission of John Wiley & Sons, Inc.

Library of Congress Cataloging-in-Publication Data

Protecting historic architecture and museum collections
   from natural disasters.

   Includes bibliographies and index
   1. Cultural property, Protection of.   2. Cultural
property, Protection of—United States.   3. Antiquities
—Collection and preservation.   4. United States—
Antiquities—Collection and preservation.   I. Jones,
Barclay G.
CC135.P76   1986   363.6′9   86-6159
ISBN 0-409-90035-4

Butterworth Publishers
80 Montvale Avenue
Stoneham, MA 02180

10 9 8 7 6 5 4 3 2 1

Printed in the United States of America

Table of Contents

Preface

Important structures deteriorate and collapse; valuable papers and books mildew and burn; precious objects become damaged or broken. We watch with dismay the slow attrition of our cultural heritage. We devote much time, energy and money to maintaining, conserving and restoring the structures and artifacts we value, and we wish we could do more to save them. However, many of the things we treasure are lost not through the slow processes of exposure but through the quick violence of natural disasters from which they were inadequately protected.

Earthquakes, volcanic eruptions, landslides, tornados, hurricanes, floods and other disasters cause terror in everyone. Reports of them seize our appalled attention at frequent intervals. We react with shock at the awesome destruction shown vividly by the media, and we respond with horror at the plight of the victims. We are less frequently aware of the often great losses to the cultural heritage of structures and artifacts. Nevertheless, catastrophic events are probably the greatest single cause of attrition.

The toll from natural disasters has been enormous during the past generation alone. We have responded with heroic rescue efforts, and many conservators of architecture and artifacts have gained invaluable experience in salvaging and recovering elements that might otherwise have been completely lost. By recording what has been learned and making it available to others, future losses may be reduced through more knowledgeable protection, prevention and emergency response.

To call attention to the threats of natural disasters and the wisdom of preparing for them, and to record and disseminate experience gained in coping with catastrophes, the papers which follow were commissioned in the execution of a project. The project on The Protection of Historic Architecture and Museum Collections from Earthquakes and Other Natural Disasters was undertaken by the Architectural Research Centers Consortium, Inc., a federation of the research components of colleges of architecture at three dozen universities throughout the United States. In addition to providing a forum for promoting research as an element of architectural education, the Consortium also engages in projects to carry out research or disseminate research findings. The project was supported by the National Science Foundation through grant number PFR8007116. James L. Haecker, the Executive Director of the Consortium, served as the Project Manager and Barclay G. Jones, Professor of City and Regional Planning at Cornell University, served as Principal Investigator.

An informal advisory committee was established to review the outline and plan of the project and to assist in identifying appropriate experts to contribute papers. Much of the success of the project is attributable to the substantial amounts of time, interest, expert advice and other service the members of the committee generously gave to the effort. The committee consisted of Dr. Ernest Allen Connally of the National Park Service, U.S. Department of the Interior; Ms. Ann Hitchcock, Chief Curator, National Park Service, U.S. Department of the Interior; Russell V. Keune, AIA, then the Senior Vice President of the National Trust for Historic Preservation; James C. Massey, then President of the Historic House Association of America; Hugh C. Miller, AIA, Chief Historical Architect, National Park Service, U.S. Department of the Interior; Dr. Henry A. Millon, Dean, Center for Advanced Study in the Visual Arts, National Gallery of Art; and Paul N. Perrot, then Assistant Secretary for Museum Programs, Smithsonian Institution.

The purpose of the project was to produce a handbook consisting of papers by expert individuals which would serve as a useful guide for professionals engaged in the preservation of our cultural heritage, whether artifacts or structures. An integral part of the plan for carrying out this work was to convene the contributors at a seminar at which they would present their papers to each other and to the public. Revised versions of the papers could incorporate comments and discussion from the seminar. The seminar was held March 29–30, 1982, in the Auditorium of the National Academy of Sciences in Washington. Organizations which lent their support by sponsoring the seminar were AAM-ICOM, the Advisory Board on the Built Environment of the National Research Council-National Academy of Sciences, the American Association of Museums, the American Institute of Architects, the American Institute for Conservation of Historic and Artistic Works, the Association for Preservation Technology, the Committee on the History and Heritage of American Civil Engineering of the American Society of Civil Engineers, the Historic House Association of America, the National Park Service, the National Trust for Historic Preservation, the Smithsonian Institution and US/ICOMOS. Their support contributed greatly to the success of the meeting. Dr. Bates Lowry, Director of the National Building Museum, gave the support of the museum by making the Old Pension Building available for a reception and dinner session. The staff of the National Academy of Sciences, particularly Harold Foleck, Audio Visual Manager, and Mrs. Nancy Geasy, Assistant Manager, Meetings Office, provided superb technical support so that the seminar went smoothly at every step.

Michael L. Joroff, then the President of the Architectural Research Centers Consortium, Inc., gave enthusiastic interest and expert support throughout the project. Dr. Frederick Krimgold, then the Program Manager for the project in the National Science Foundation, participated in the planning sessions and contributed from his expert command of the subject matter at every stage of the project. Ralph W. Rose served as Professor Jones's assistant and contributed to every aspect throughout the period of the project from the planning stages through preparing the manuscript for publication. He compiled the bibliographies, and his participation truly constitutes collaboration. Polly Haecker assisted the Project Manager in innumerable ways at every stage of the study. Jonathan Gitlin helped to edit the final manuscript, and Beverly Kisner typed and prepared it for publication. Martha Garrison prepared the index.

SECTION ONE

Destruction of the Cultural Heritage by Earthquakes and Other Natural Disasters

Experiencing Loss

Barclay G. Jones

PRESERVING THE WORLD CULTURAL HERITAGE

Since World War II interest in the cultural heritage represented by documents, artifacts and structures has increased enormously throughout the world. Accompanying this surge of interest has been a greater awareness of the irreplaceable value of objects which inform us about past cultures and societies and record their evolution to the present. Consequently, there has been a growing worldwide concern with surveying, documenting, recording, protecting, preserving and restoring architectural and engineering works and historic and cultural artifacts.

Enormous sums have been spent on projects as far removed as the restoration of the major historic structures in Leningrad from the depredations of the siege of that city in World War II, the rescue launched in 1963 of the temples of Abu Simbel from the rising waters of Lake Nasser behind the Aswan High Dam [Gerster, 1969], and the painstaking reconstruction of the Stupa at Borobudur neglected since the area was deserted following earthquakes and volcanic eruptions in 1006. [Morton, 1983] The heroic efforts to protect Venice and London from subsidence and sea surges are remarkable. [Judge, 1972] The moveable sea barrier erected between 1974 and 1982 across the Thames at Woolwich is an extraordinary engineering feat. [Wholey, 1982; Starbird, 1983]

We have devised elaborate mechanisms for preserving and protecting the heritage. We have directed much attention to the threats of destruction by the natural elements such as decay, subsidence, air pollution and other forms of attrition. Many of the public efforts and much of the legislation that has been enacted is intended primarily to prevent destruction by human agents through neglect, demolition for replacement by more modern items, theft, vandalism, and acts of war. We have excellent documents to assist us in these tasks. [Tillotson, 1977] In contrast, we have given relatively little attention to the threat of losses as the result of natural

3

disasters, and only a few works on preservation deal specifically with this danger. [Feilden, 1982, pp. 117-129]

DESTRUCTION BY NATURAL DISASTERS

We are all quite aware, when we think about it, which apparently is not often enough, that natural disasters have been the cause of destruction that has obliterated much of the most valuable elements from our past. For example, we admire the torso as an art form and associate it with modern sculptors such as Rodin, Mailiol and Brancusi and with Greek and Roman works from antiquity. We seldom consciously acknowledge that the ancient works that provided the inspiration for modern efforts were not designed as torsos but are the major remains of complete figures, the limbs of which were undoubtedly snapped off in earthquakes or were broken when the statues were toppled. (Figures 1.1, 1.2)

We know that the seismic history of the civilized world has been active and violent. We acknowledge that disasters preserve and create as well as destroy: that some of the best preserved Roman artifacts, paintings and architecture we have were buried in Pompeii and Herculaneum in the devastating volcanic eruptions of August 24, 25, 79 AD; that the undisturbed ruins of the largest intact Roman provincial city, Jerash, are available to us because it was abandoned for 1100 years after the violent earthquake in the Jordan Valley of January 18, 746; and that the handsome baroque center of the city of Dubrovnik is a consequence of the rebuilding after the catastrophic earthquake of April 6, 1667, which killed two-thirds of the population. [Judge, 1982; Browning, 1982; Carter, 1972] We regret the losses, but we seldom think systematically about the enormity of the toll over the centuries.

RECENT LOSSES

Our ability to forget can be graphically illustrated simply by considering the losses from the major events of the last 20 years. The earthquake on July 26, 1963, that struck Skopje destroyed many historic buildings, damaged the Mosque of Mustapha Pasha, and did great damage to the Kursumli Han, an ancient caravansary that housed the archaeological museum. Later that same year considerable damage was done to historic structures by the floods resulting from the collapse of the Vaiont Dam on the Piave River in northern Italy that was a consequence of earthslides on October 10, 1963.

Probably the most extensive devastation of historic structures, of works of art and museum collections in the recent past occurred three years later when the flood of the Arno River struck Florence on November 4 and 5, 1966. [Judge, 1967; Klein, 1969] The Ponte Vecchio

4

Figure 1.1. Los Angeles, California: Forest Lawn Memorial Park, Marble Copy of Michelangelo's David.

Figure 1.2. Los Angeles, California: Forest Lawn Memorial Park, Marble Copy of David Showing Destruction Caused by Earthquake of February 9, 1971.

was damaged as were Ghiberti's bronze doors of the Baptistry of the Duomo and Andrea del Sarto's fresco in San Salvi, Cimabue's "Crucifixion" at San Croce, frescoes by Uccello, Botticelli, Lorenzetti and Martini. Archives and furniture were damaged or destroyed in the Strozzi Palace; ancient musical instruments were lost in the Bardini Museum, scientific instruments in the Museo delle Scienze, armor at the Bargello, and the Etruscan collection at the Museo Archeologico. A hundred and thirty thousand photographic negatives were among the losses of the Uffizi Gallery; and there was tremendous damage to the state archives, 6000 volumes at the Opera di Duomo, 250,000 volumes at the Gabinello Vieusseux, 14,000 volumes at the Jewish Synagogue, 36,000 volumes at the Geography Academy, the entire collection at the Music Conservatory, and 1,300,000 volumes in the Biblioteca Nazionale. [Horton, 1967; Cornell, 1976, p. 148] Salvage, cleaning, repair and restoration was a horrendous undertaking and provided invaluable experience to a generation of experts who devised many of our best current conservatorial methods.

Two years later, Hurricane Camille of August 18, 1969, did much damage to the Jefferson Davis Shrine in Biloxi, Mississippi, and the collections of documents, pictures, costumes, uniforms and other artifacts in the museum on the ground floor of the beachfront mansion. [Organ and McMillan, 1969] The subsequent Hurricane Frederick on September 12, 1969, damaged a number of historic structures in Mobile, Alabama. In the earthquake that struck Peru on May 31, 1970, the archaeological museum in Huaras was damaged. (Figure 1.3) On February 6, 1971, an earthquake did enormous damage to the historic structures that composed the ancient hill town of Tuscania, north of Rome. Three days later in the United States the earthquake of February 9, 1971, in the San Fernando Valley in California severely damaged 5 rooms of the Villa Adobe on Olivera Street in Los Angeles, the oldest building in that city.

A year and a half later the floods produced by the rains resulting from Hurricane Agnes on June 22 and 23, 1972, severely damaged the collection of the Corning Glass Museum, [Martin, 1977] and many collections of historic furniture, archives and artifacts the full length of the Susquehanna River Basin. These included extensive damage to the Heisey House, the headquarters and museum of the Clinton County Historical Society, at Lock Haven, Pa., and the Wyoming Historical and Geological Society at Wilkes Barre. Lesser damage was done to the Golden Plough Tavern and the General Gates House in York, Pa., and several other museums. While the Fort Pitt Museum was flooded and suffered much damage, the collections were saved. [Whipkey, 1973]

The same year many historic structures including the cathedral and the Presidential Palace were completely destroyed or severely damaged along with their contents in the devastating earthquake and subsequent fire in Managua, Nicaragua, on December 24, 1972. (Figure 1.4) Less than a year later on August 28, 1973, the earthquake that struck the states of Puebla, Veracruz, and Oaxaca in Mexico damaged 200 important colonial churches, many beyond repair. [Cornell, 1976]

Figure 1.4. Managua, Nicaragua: Bust of Ruben Dario Thrown From Pedestal by Earthquake of December 23, 1972. EERI.

Figure 1.3. Huaras, Peru: City Street After Earthquake of May 31, 1970. University of Colorado.

The Xenia, Ohio Tornadoes that swept eleven states on April 3, 1974 destroyed historic homes and public structures in many communities. [Boone, 1974]

Large scale devastations of historic structures and artifacts resulted from the severe earthquake of May 6, 1976, in the Friuli district in northeastern Italy. [Pichard, Ambrayseys and Ziogas, 1976; Schwartzbaum, Silver and Grissom, 1977] Many cities, towns and villages suffered considerable damage causing the effect on historic structures and artifacts to be extremely widespread. Subsequent earthquakes on the 11th and 15th of September further damaged structures weakened in the first shock and undid much of the salvage and repair work that had been initiated. On March 4, 1977, the earthquake in Romania, while it caused only moderate damage to the museum buildings in Bucharest, severely damaged the museum collections and contents, particularly the Ethnographic collection. The museum contains the largest collection of works by Constantin Brancusi but fortunately none of these were lost. Historic structures in the countryside outside the capital city received substantial damage. [Ambraseys, 1977] Much less publicized is the fact that extensive damage was done to historic structures in northern Bulgaria that were affected by the same tremor. [Brankov, 1983] An ironic event was the July 1977 flood which destroyed the Johnstown Flood (May 31, 1889) Museum in Johnstown, Pennsylvania.

A tornado on April 10, 1979 did extensive damage to the museum at Wichita Falls, Texas. [Glass, et. al., 1980] The earthquake of April 15, 1979, that struck Montenegro damaged many historic buildings in Kotor, a city which had been severely struck by the same earthquake that devastated Dubrovnik in 1667. [Petrovski and Paskalov, 1981] The moderate earthquake of November 6, 1979, in Greece produced no casualties and little damage but caused serious cracks in the Parthenon, the loss of a large number of amphorae in the Acropolis Museum and caused the National Museum in Athens to be closed for a number of months. The Campania Basilicata earthquake in southern Italy November 23, 1980, did tremendous amounts of damage to the historic structures that gave the towns and villages of that countryside its character. [Lagorio and Mader, 1981] (Figures 1.7, 1.8) Much of the same area suffered that had been devastated in the Naples–Bari earthquake of July 23, 1930. It was the worst disaster in southern Italy since the tremors that leveled Messina and Reggia December 29, 1908, and the Neapolitan earthquake of 1857.

While accounts can be found, it is necessary to dig rather deeply to determine the losses from many natural disasters. There are usually few reports in the press about the loss of cultural artifacts. Media coverage focuses on loss of life and the personal tragedies of the survivors. [Scanlon and Alldred, 1982] Few accounts of the crash on March 1, 1962 into Jamaica Bay of an American Airlines Boeing 707 bound from Kennedy Airport for Los Angeles that cost the lives of 95 people noted that 15 paintings and 5 drawings by Arshile Gorky bound for a West Coast exhibition were lost. [Cornell, 1976] The owners and proprietors of collections of artifacts and buildings are seldom inclined

Figure 1.5. Antigua Guatemala, Guatemala: Damage to Ruins of Cathedral of San Augustin by Earthquake of February 4, 1976. USGS.

Figure 1.6. Mixco Viejo, Guatemala: Damage to Mayan Site by Earthquake February 4, 1976. USGS.

9

Figure 1.7. Campania, Italy: Destruction of Hill Town by Earthquake of November 23, 1980. National Academy Press.

Figure 1.8. Valvano, Italy: Collapse of Church Caused by Earthquake of November 23, 1980. National Academy Press.

to publicize their losses. We do not have a really clear picture of the devastation to our cultural heritage through natural events in the recent, let alone the remote, past.

PREVENTIVE MEASURES IN RESPONSE TO LOSS

Indeed, it seems remarkable that anything at all has survived from the past. But there is clear evidence that at many times in many places, people recognized the possibilities of natural disasters and took preventive measures to mitigate their effects. In particular, inhabitants of the earthquake-prone regions of the eastern Mediterranean appear to have developed aseismic building techniques as early as the Mycenean Age. [Schaar, 1974] Similar methods, called xylodesia, survive today in vernacular systems of construction. [Porphyrios, 1971] As is natural, we learn from experience, and disasters lead to devising new measures to safeguard lives, buildings and possessions. The great fire that destroyed most of London north of the Thames that raged for four days after it broke out on September 1, 1666 led to the banning of wooden construction and overhanging gables. The rebuilt city had wider thoroughfares to serve as firebreaks. Among the losses in the fire were St. Paul's Cathedral, 87 parish churches, 6 chapels, the Royal Exchange, the Customs House and the Guildhall. [Cornell, 1976] After the devastating earthquake in Sicily on January 11, 1693, the Spanish Viceregal government proposed reconstruction plans for cities that provided more open spaces for refuge and streets less likely to be impassable with rubble. [Tobriner, 1980] The earthquake and tidal wave that devastated Lisbon on November 1, 1755 led not only to reconstruction planning schemes to reduce the vulnerability of urban areas but also aseismic building designs and measures to reduce the spread of fire. [Tobriner, 1980] The Marquess de Pombal initiated the first scientific investigation of earthquakes, and the analysis of effects throughout Europe by the English physicist John Mitchell led to the first crude theory of wave motion. [Cornell, 1976] A generation later the series of extremely destructive earthquakes in Calabria led the government to the planning of towns less vulnerable to devastation and to the promotion of extremely sophisticated building methods. [Tobriner, 1983]

RENDERING EXPERIENCE INTO KNOWLEDGE

Perhaps we too will respond to the substantial number of disastrous events over the past 20 years by learning better how to protect, minimize damage, rescue, salvage and restore. But there is some urgency if we are to assimilate and transmit this knowledge. Many people have been involved in emergency measures during these events and in conservation and recovery operations after them and

11

have acquired as a consequence tremendous funds of experience. Experts have gained knowledge at enormous expense not only in human time and effort but also in material losses. Important documents and source materials have been produced. But too frequently, there is little written record readily available of the actions that they took, the successes they had, and the methods and procedures that they learned. It is immensely important that this information not be lost but be collected and codified and made readily available. It should be extremely useful in helping people to anticipate the kinds of impacts disasters may have on them and their possessions and take appropriate preventive and preparatory measures to mitigate them. It will also provide a deep source of experience that will help experts and knowledgable people in the future to prepare themselves for the kinds of actions they will have to undertake in the event they find themselves in a disaster. This exchange and dissemination of experience and information should be invaluable in protecting elements of the heritage from destruction and in facilitating their salvage, conservation and reconstruction. If less of our heritage is lost through catastrophic natural events in the next period, the exercise will have been rewarding.

REFERENCES

Ambraseys, Nicholas N. "The Romanian Earthquake of 4 March 1977." Disasters. Volume I, Number 3, 1977, pp. 175–177.

Boone, C. F. The Ohio Tornadoes April 3, 1974. Lubbock, Texas: C. F. Boone, Publisher, 1974.

Brankov, Georgi Jordanov. Vrancea Earthquake in 1977. Its After-Effects in the People's Republic of Bulgaria. Sofia: Publishing House of the Bulgarian Academy of Sciences, 1983.

Browning, Iain. Jerash and the Decapolis. London: Chatto & Windus, 1982.

Carter, Francis W. Dubrovnik (Ragusa) A Classic City-State. London: Seminar Press, 1972.

Cornell, James. The Great International Disaster Book. New York: Charles Scribner's Sons, 1976.

Feilden, Bernard M. Conservation of Historic Buildings. London: Butterworth Scientific, 1982.

Gerster, Georg. "Abu Simbel's Ancient Temples Reborn." National Geographic. Volume 135, Number 5, May 1969, pp. 724–744.

Glass, Roger I., Robert B. Craven, Dennis J. Bregman, Barbara J. Stoll, Neil Horowitz, Peter Kerndt, Joe Winkle. "Injuries from the Wichita Falls Tornado: Implications for Prevention." Science. Volume 207, Number 4432, February 15, 1980, pp. 734–738.

Horton, Carolyn. "Saving the Libraries of Florence." Wilson Library Bulletin, Volume 41, June 1967, pp. 1034–1043.

Judge, Joseph. "Florence Rises from the Flood." National Geographic. Volume 132, Number 1, July 1967, pp. 1-43.

Judge, Joseph. "Venice Fights for Life." National Geographic. Volume 142, Number 5, November 1972, pp. 591-631.

Judge, Joseph. "On the Slope of Vesuvius a Buried Roman Town Gives Up Its Dead." National Geographic. Volume 162, Number 6, December 1982, pp. 686-693.

Klein, Richard M. "The Florence Floods." Natural History. Volume LXXVIII, Number 7, August-September 1969, pp. 46-55.

Lagorio, Henry J. and George G. Mader. Earthquake in Campagnia Basilicata, Italy, November 23, 1980. Berkeley, California: Earthquake Engineering Research Institute, July, 1981.

Martin, John H., Ed. The Corning Flood: Museum Under Water. Corning, New York: The Corning Museum of Glass, 1977.

Morton, W. Brown, III. "Indonesia Rescues Ancient Borobudur." National Geographic. Volume 163, Number 1, January 1983, pp. 126-142.

Organ, Robert M. and Eleanor McMillan. "Aid to a Hurricane-Damaged Museum (Biloxi)." Bulletin of the American Group-IIC, Volume 10, Number 1, October 1969, pp. 31-39.

Petrovski, Jakim and Trifun Paskalov, Eds. The Montenegro, Yugoslavia, Earthquake of April 15, 1979. Publication No. 65 of the Institute of Earthquake Engineering and Engineering Seismology. Skopje, Yugoslavia: IZIIS, November, 1981.

Pichard, Pierre, Nicholas N. Ambraseys, and G. N. Ziogas. The Gemona di Friuli Earthquake of 6 May 1976. UNESCO Serial No. FMR/CC/SC/ED/76/169, UNESCO Restricted Technical Report No. RP/1975/2,222,3. Paris: UNESCO, 1976.

Porphyrios, Demetrius Thomas Georgia. "Traditional Earthquake-Resistant Construction on a Greek Island." Journal of the Society of Architectural Historians. Volume XXX, Number 1, March 1971, pp. 31-39.

Scanlon, T. Joseph and Suzanne Alldred. "Media Coverage of Disasters: The Same Old Story." Social and Economic Aspects of Earthquakes. Barclay G. Jones and Miha Tomazevic, Eds. Ithaca, New York: Program in Urban and Regional Studies, Cornell University, 1982.

Schaar, Kenneth W. "Traditional Earthquake-Resistant Construction: The Mycenaean Aspect." Journal of the Society of Architectural Historians. Volume XXIII, Number 1, March 1974, pp. 80-81.

Schwartzbaum, Paul M., Constance Silver and Carol A. Grissom. "Earthquake Damage to Works of Art in Ariculi Region of Italy." Journal of the American Institute of Conservation. Volume 17, Number 1, 1977, pp. 9-16.

Starbird, Ethel A. "That Noble River, the Thames." National Geographic. Volume 163, Number 6, June 1983, pp. 750-791.

Tillotson, Robert G. Museum Security. Paris: International Council of Museums and American Museums Association, 1977.

Tobriner, Stephen. "Earthquakes and Planning in the 17th and 18th Centuries." Journal of Architectural Education. Volume XXXIII, Number 4, Summer 1980, pp. 11-15.

Tobriner, Stephen. "La Casa Baraccata: Earthquake-Resistant Construction in 18th Century Calabria." Journal of the Society of Architectural Historians. Volume XLII, Number 2, May 1983, pp. 131-138.

Whipkey, Harry E. After Agnes: A Report on Flood Recovery Assistance by the Pennsylvania Historical and Museum Commission. Harrisburg, Pennsylvania: Pennsylvania Historical and Museum Commission, 1973.

Wholey, Jane. "Saving London from an Impending Threat of Flood." Smithsonian. Volume 13, Number 5, August 1982, pp. 78-87.

Protection of Our Cultural Heritage
Against Natural Disasters

Dr. Bernard M. Feilden, C.B.E., F.R.I.B.A.

INTRODUCTION

Protection of our cultural heritage against natural disasters falls within the field of Conservation Studies, but not one of us has a full grasp of all the problems. It is extremely valuable to draw many skills together to exchange ideas and pool experience. Conservation is a multidisciplinary activity controlled by one methodology and guided by a theory which has taken centuries to evolve.

Prevention of decay or damage is the highest form of conservation. I am hopeful that by discussing our problems and submitting to friendly criticism that we will establish communication between each of the separate disciplines working in the field of conservation of historic architectural and museum projects. I will touch upon some of the vast number of considerations that must be taken into account in this enormous topic. Many of these subjects will be developed at greater length in other papers later in this volume.

Undoubtedly the theory that prevention is better than cure is correct, but it is difficult to apply, human nature being what it is. We all hope that a disaster won't happen, and we all go about our business of caring for cultural heritage without developing the management techniques to make it in people's interest to prepare for foreseeable risks. The ultimate 100 year flood may come tomorrow as it did on November 4, 1966 in Florence, where if the risks had been assessed much needless damage could have been prevented. There are cycles of intense earthquakes and whilst the exact date of the Friuli earthquake could have not been predicted, had strengthening measures been applied two or three years in advance, many lives could have been saved.

What sort of disasters do we have to consider? Floods take the greatest toll of human life, earthquakes probably damage the cultural heritage most and are often followed by fire and water damage, as well as tidal waves, particularly in the Pacific Ocean, or landslips such as the one that engulfed a whole town in Peru. UNDRO in its publications puts the protection of our cultural heritage as its lowest

15

priority. After the protection of human life and structures, such as hospitals, which advance that purpose, protection of the cultural heritage should be the second priority as it cannot be replaced. In fact, if we do protect our historic buildings we will also save lives. But objects matter too, and even less attention is given them. The problem of designing special earthquake resistant mounts and display cases for valuable objects in museums has, as far as I know, scarcely been touched upon, and would be a worthy one for research in detail. It is good to note that some of the later papers in this volume deal with this subject.

FLOODS

As mentioned above, floods probably cause more loss of life than other major disasters but, in general, need not damage cultural property if the risks are properly assessed and prior action taken. However, there are rare cases of almost unpredictable floods, like Hurricane Agnes that flooded the Corning Museum or like the one on the high veld of South Africa which was caused by a flash storm over a wide flat area creating a raging torrent which half buried a township in gravel. Some floods are turned into disasters by manmade actions, for instance a new bridge may block the ice flows on a river and so cause an unexpected flood in a low lying area.

However, the climatologist can predict the height of floods much more accurately than the seismologist can predict earthquakes, because engineering hydrology is a much more developed science, and there are sufficient observations to permit the laws of statistical prediction to apply.

Floods have two main causes which may sometimes be combined, intense rain and melting snow with ice, which may form a jam against a bridge or other impediment to the flow of the river. It is necessary to know the rainfall characteristics of a river basin. For the United States maps are available to show the amounts of water, which are based on calculations, likely to be received in 30 minutes, 1, 2, 3, 6, 12, and 24 hours within periods of 1, 2, 5, 10, 25, 50 or 100 years. Using these estimates it is possible to have the flood flow calculated using a run off coefficient, c, multiplied by rainfall intensity, i, over the duration of concentration time of the basin whose catchment area is A. The flood flow $q = ciA$. [Griffiths, p. 105] The run off coefficient may be changed, as for example when forests are cleared and land drainage improved in the interests of the agricultural lobby.

Storage reservoirs reduce flood hazards unless they themselves fail for some reason, possibly due to earthquakes. Indeed, large storage reservoirs induce earthquakes in zones previously imagined to be free from this hazard. The recent earthquake in Egypt has been attributed to the Aswan High Dam. Flood control reservoirs can be used to reduce a flow downstream, but if a second flood comes while the reservoir is still full from the first flood, its value is lost. But if there is adequate climatological data of the time distribution of rainfalls of flooding intensity, this risk can be calculated.

Forecasting sea and river conditions requires reliable information concerning present and future conditions of weather which emphasizes the role of meteorology in this field. A clearing center for meteorological information is essential so that the information available on rainfall, snow depth and intensity, and air temperatures can be assessed. To be effective this requires good communications.

Sea floods depend on the tides, for which relatively accurate predictions are available. The wind, which can easily add 2 meters to the height of a spring flood in the North Sea and 6 meters in the Bay of Bengal, must not be forgotten. As the tide flows along the coast in a recognized pattern, one station can warn others if a flood tide is expected. Waves originating in earthquakes under the sea, called tsunami, as high as 20 meters (66 feet) have been recorded. A warning center for the Pacific Ocean has been established in Hawaii.

With the amount of information available, it is possible to protect most cultural property from flood hazards, where they exist, by the simple expedient of placing any vulnerable object above the level of the highest predictable floods. This includes all organic materials, furniture, paintings, books and archives. If this is not absolutely possible, only the amount of material that can be moved in the anticipated warning time should be allowed at lower levels. In siting new museums the flood hazard must be considered. [Building Research Establishment Digest, 1972]

The hazard of rainfall penetrating a building and causing the structure and contents to decay must not be forgotten—although it is entirely preventable by good design and regular maintenance. In passing it should be said that higher standards are required for museums and historic buildings, and the local climate needs study. The greatest rainfall in one minute was 31 mm recorded at Unionville, Maryland, USA and in one day 187 cm at Cilaos, Reunion Island. [Griffiths, 1976, p. 15] Unfortunately standard climatic data mainly give averages, and we are interested in extremes. Each city has a different profile for its most intense storms, and it is essential that the rainwater disposal system will deal with these, otherwise irreparable damage will be done. The capacity of the rainwater disposal system can be calculated easily, but allowance must be made for the higher standards required for historic buildings and museums.

GEOLOGICAL MOVEMENT

Slow geological movements of the soil up, down and sideways may also be classified as natural disasters although their effects are very slow. The famous Iron Bridge at Coalbrookdale, symbol of the beginning of the Industrial Revolution, was built over the river Severn which follows a geological fault. This fault closed the distance between the two abutments and caused severe distress to the inflexible cast iron of the bridge. Hopefully, the movement has been stopped by an immensely strong reinforced concrete strut under the river bed. Another example is the gradual sinking of the Dalmatian Coast and Venice which is estimated at 1 mm per year.

EARTHQUAKES

Earthquakes cause immense damage to cultural property. They are, however, blamed for things within man's control as a large proportion of the damage is preventable, even if buildings are not made completely earthquake resistant. Prevention is achieved by regular inspections, establishing a maintenance strategy which would include strengthening the weak points of the typical construction of historic buildings.

Earthquake prediction has progressed so much that it can tell us where the hazards are greatest and show a likely pattern of events and the frequency of major earthquakes: for example, every 50 years in the foothills of the Himalayas or every 70 years in the Friuli district. Even if short term prediction were accurate, it is more likely to be useful in saving life than historic buildings and their contents, as it would take more than a few hours to take preventive action.

Since the art of designing to resist earthquakes is still in relative infancy using codes based on gross simplifications with horizontal loadings or base shearing as the design criteria for new buildings, it is the considered opinion of experienced engineers and scientists that such codes should not be applied to historic buildings which are of a very different structural typology.

There is great difficulty in assessing the performance of historic buildings under earthquake conditions, indeed calculation may be virtually impossible due to the number of variables and unknown factors. Japan and the United States pioneered full scale induced vibration tests on tall buildings, and recently the Building Research Establishment in the United Kingdom has produced equipment sufficiently portable and accurate enough to analyze the dynamic performance of historic buildings. This may be a major breakthrough and save many historic buildings from ill advised interventions or even destruction because of non-compliance with an irrelevant earthquake engineering code.

Preventive action for each historic building against earthquakes is a special study. Each building is an individual on a site with a specific seismic spectrum. Present day codes are of variable quality, and if applied by unimaginative engineers may result in more damage in an earthquake or lead to the destruction of a building by the Code in advance of a possible earthquake. Observation, experience and judgment aided by science are the essentials for a correct approach to this difficult problem, which must be guided by the principles of conservation and respect for the "values" in the building.

The seismic spectrum for any particular site will take local ground conditions into account such as soil types, the slope of sedimentary soils, the existence of any bedding planes and their angle of slope, horizontal changes in soil types, the depth of the soil over bedrock and the typography of the bedrock including ridges and deposited soils. [Dowrick, 1977] Water content and the level of water table are most important, for with a water table less than 8 meters (26 feet) depth there is a danger of soil liquefaction in an earthquake. Such an investigation is expensive, but certainly justified if one is siting a new national or state museum in an earthquake zone or studying how to strengthen a major historic building. How much use can be made of this information for protecting an historic building depends on the building itself and the ability of its engineers and architects.

In general terms, insurance companies have the shrewdest estimate of the hazards from earthquakes and other natural disasters. The maps produced by Munich Re, together with their handbook are most useful. It is understood that ICOMOS proposes to add an overprint with the density of cultural heritage, but this raises the difficult question of evaluating cultural heritage. It is suggested that this map should be widely circulated so that the museum curators and architects responsible for the cultural heritage would have some idea of their hazards and could use this information as a spur to preventive action. Both Friuli and Basilicata Campania were shown as very high risk areas on the map.

Naturally, high risk areas should be given priority, but sometimes the worst earthquakes occur at intervals of centuries in lower risk zones. I suspect that the Jordan valley may be one such area: certainly Petra and Jerash in particular suffered from disastrous earthquakes in the 8th century when the latter city's life was extinguished.

Examination of earthquake damage shows three main aspects:

(1) Damage due to the unequal action of the foundation soil.
(2) Damage due to the inherent defects in traditional construction.
(3) Damage due to the lack of maintenance and decay of materials.

The two latter causes can be prevented to a large degree using simple measures to strengthen the structure and repair weaknesses. Thinking dynamically is essential. Most historic buildings are stiff, their construction being weak in tension; so simple methods of introducing tensile reinforcement are best although sophisticated methods of drilling and post-tensioning also have their uses. An outline of the multi-professional methodology of repair to earthquake damage is given in Appendix A. It is essential that all the professionals involved should visit the site together.

In thinking dynamically the form of the building must be considered. Simple rectangular shapes are best while projecting wings, attached towers and even buttresses are vulnerable to shear. If elements can be separated so that they can act in their separate modes, so much the better as in this way actual battering will be avoided. However, in general the strategy must be to tie the elements of a building together to prevent battering during an earthquake. Roof rafters must be tied to the wall plate, the wall plate to the wall, with strengthening at corners, partitions and floors, used as diaphragms, must be tied to the walls. Weaknesses above and below windows and over doors need strengthening with tensile reinforcement. Chimneys and gables present special problems again requiring tensile reinforcement which, if inserted vertically from foundations to eaves, can greatly strengthen a building. Combined with insertion of tensile reinforcement one can use the techniques of grouting which can achieve spectacular strengthening without altering the appearance of the building, so preserving its historical and architectural values.

All this is empirical but practical stuff; but no one can yet calculate what intensity or magnitude of earthquake an old historic building will resist. We know however that if such strengthening is applied to the large number of simple buildings which comprise the majority of our historic centers that lives will be saved and the damage to the buildings substantially reduced. We must remember that many of these buildings, in their prime, also resisted several earlier earthquakes.

Recording historic buildings and their contents fully and methodically is desirable on any account, but in earthquake zones it is vital and should be given the highest priority. Computerized methods seem inevitable but one system only should be used for planning and architectural studies which must include the objects within the building. Photogrammetric techniques are invaluable for recording both buildings and their contents. If there is a disaster, it is much easier to repair or reconstruct a building or an object such as a piece of statuary that has been properly recorded.

OTHER NATURAL DISASTERS

We must also consider frost, snow, high winds, driving rain, tornados, and hurricanes. As historic buildings have a longer life expectancy than others, the design codes are often inadequate as is generally the case for rain disposal and wind loads. Particulates, smoke, dust and sand are a nuisance but can scarcely be regarded as disasters unless a historic building is threatened by advancing sand dunes.

Lightning is also a hazard and the protective insulation requires regular maintenance if it is not to become a liability. The lightning conductor invented by Benjamin Franklin has saved many a building from damage and outbreak of fire. Whether or not a historic building should be fitted with a lightning conductor depends on the following factors:

(1) The cultural and economic value of the building and its contents.
(2) The record of previous strikes on the building.
(3) The size, shape and height of the building.
(4) The location and surroundings of the building.
(5) The general assessment of the risk in the geographical location of the building.
(6) Whether the lightning conductor will be maintained regularly. (At least annually for a museum with valuable contents.)

Some disasters such as geological settlements or the lowering of the ground water table creep up on us imperceptibly and may be manmade rather than natural, so where do we draw the line? Both London and Venice have sunk due to industry drawing off vast quantities of water so becoming severe flood risks. Water extraction also caused alarm for the stability of the Leaning Tower of Pisa.

Is fire a natural disaster? Sometimes yes if the cause is outside normal hazards, otherwise it is preventable and generally man made. Yet as the predisaster planning to prevent fire is so similar to that for purely natural hazards, fire should also be included in our consideration, although most fires can be prevented.

PLANNING

Administrative measures such as town planning are important in both the predisaster and recovery situations. However reports on what actually happened during a disaster indicate that considerable improvements could be made in post disaster operations, if there had been predisaster planning. The aim should be to establish communication and understanding between key people before the event. The military are generally called in because they are mobile and have good communication networks. There is a need to allocate on a permanent basis one officer to a particular area so that those responsible for cultural property can establish a working relationship.

Town planning methodology should be a great help in reconstruction after a natural disaster, but unless the plans are ready before hand and are regularly updated the effect of town planning procedures can be negative because of the uncertainties, blight and delays caused by waiting for the plans to be formulated. While the displaced occupants wait for the plan, their damaged houses disintegrate due to rain, wind and frost.

In planning terms a disaster is also an opportunity to implement overdue changes and environmental improvements. The problem, however, is that the disaster may change demographic projections and the economic base of the community so the "disaster plan" may have to assess the effect of various possibilities. This in itself will be useful input into the long term plan, as it will tend to minimize the damage inflicted when the predicted disaster occurs. In planning,

21

geological faults and flood plains must obviously be avoided. Unfortunately much good agricultural land lies in areas liable to flooding or, as in the Coromandel and Bengal, to inundation by a tidal surge. In the report on the cyclone of November 19, 1977 when a 6 meter wave surged over a large area of Coromandel it was found that the solidly built ancient temples provided the only safe refuges. This example introduces the principle that if one can not achieve absolute protection against possible disasters at least sufficient refuges should be provided.

Some of the kinds of changes that may have been wrought by a disaster and that may influence the range of possibilities that can be incorporated into a long term plan have been identified by Professor Jones.

> The seismic event will also have substantial impact on the social, economic and political system depending upon a number of factors. The interrelationships between people and between people and the environment they inhabit in the impacted region will have changed. Past relationships may no longer exist at all, and new relationships may have been created . . . .
>
> Many of the landscape features may have changed drastically. Earth slides and rock slides may have changed the character of large areas and eliminated many physical elements. Subsidence, fault displacement, the devastation of sea surges and tsunami may have substantially altered the landscape and destroyed many of the modifications that had been made by the population to make it productive and useful for their purposes. Among the features that may have been radically changed are waterways, water impoundments, estuaries and natural harbors . . . . Both occupied and unoccupied structures will have suffered. The failure of both will have caused effects on the human population and the artifacts that are so necessary to the operation of the system. [Jones, 1980]

The opportunities a disaster presents a planner to carry out long-needed changes have also been considered by Jones. He too recognizes the negative effects town planning can have if it causes uncertainties and delays in the reconstruction process.

> Planning can assist the reconstruction and recovery basically in three ways. First, it can increase the efficiency and rapidity with which reconstruction occurs. Second, it can help to guide the reconstruction process so that the rebuilt socio-economic system is less vulnerable to the disruptions of seismic events than it was before the disaster. Third, and quite the most important, it can help to see that the reconstruction efforts and the immense investments in rebuilding that are made are carried out in

22

such a way as to promote the development of the region in an optimal fashion.

It is immediately apparent that there are obvious conflicts between these three objectives. The most efficient and rapid way of restoring the stricken community may leave it equally vulnerable as before and impede its development. Reducing the vulnerability of the reconstructed community to seismic disasters may make the recovery period substantially longer and the process less efficient. It can also be carried out in such a way as to impede growth and development. Carrying out reconstruction with the primary purpose of promoting development may delay the recovery process inordinantly and reduce its efficiency extensively. It also may result in a new system which is even more vulnerable certainly in terms of higher levels of economic loss than the previous community. Likewise pursuing any two of the three objectives could seriously jeopardize the achievement of the third. With such inherent conflicts between the objectives, obviously trade-offs will have to be made, and these must be given thoughtful consideration.

. . . Everything that is done in the reconstruction process must conform in a very profound way with the nature of the existing system in the region and the trends of its evolution. Otherwise the activities are likely to be counterproductive and lead to less than optimal results. They will be alien to the character of the region and, therefore, destructive of it. A methodology for planning for the reconstruction of stricken regions needs to be delineated. The task that has just been described may seem entirely too complex and require too much study and research over too long a period of time to be at all useful in the exigencies of a reconstruction process. That is not the case. We have enough understanding of regional social and economic systems that we can come to understand their essential features fairly rapidly. Sufficient information is available for many areas to make the necessary study rather simple and, for most regions, to bring it well within the range of accomplishment. [Jones, 1980]

Obviously there should be a prepared disaster plan for each area with a high risk. There should also be a check list of the items which will be required immediately after the disaster so that organizations wishing to help can give something useful. Plastic sheeting for temporary weatherproofing, bricks, blocks and cement as well as strutting and shoring materials including ajustable steel props are all necessary aids to the emergency works. Speed is the essence of the operation in case there is a second earthquake.

23

Buildings have been dealt with at some length because if a building collapses the contents inevitably suffer. Along with civic hospitals, museums should be given the highest priority for strengthening against earthquakes. Now we must consider the contents. What can be done to make earthquake resistant mounts for objects or shock proof showcases strong enough to resist falling plaster, or how to prevent statuary from shearing off at the ankles?

The objects themselves will need a hospital if there is an earthquake. A weatherproof warehouse with fumigation facilities and a mobile laboratory and deep freezers would be invaluable. The account of the Corning Flood gives a valuable case history and some preparatory recommendations are given in Appendix B, while pre-disaster plans in general are dealt with elsewhere in this volume.

CONCLUSION

Insurance companies have an exact idea of the incidence of disasters, but their policies are expensive and don't replace the irreplaceable object or historic building with their compensation. The best insurance is a policy of regular inspection with formal reporting and strategic maintenance programs for buildings, supported by a clear definition of the responsibilities of architects and museum curators for objects in their care. This means that professionals in the field must be made aware of the risks to our cultural heritage. To make our policy of prevention more effective we should identify any factors for damage which are in our power to minimize and should take necessary action.

The action must not destroy the emotional, cultural and social values in the historic building or object, and should make its message clearer to the beholder. In natural disasters the emotional values of identity, continuity as well as the symbolic and spiritual value of buildings and objects are very important. If the cultural values, be they artistic, archaeological, architectural, documentary, historic, scientific, townscape or landscape, are lost, the community is the poorer so these should be preserved. The social functional and economic values of the buildings and museum objects is of course well defined, and must be saved. In any project the conservation team of Town Planner, Architect, Engineer, Art Historian, and Conservator must meet on the site and agree on the order of priorities relevant in each case. Action must be guided by theory. We must study the practicalities of any given situation with as many alternative solutions as possible and then choose "the least bad one" according to theory. Then the damage caused by the natural disaster will be minimized.

REFERENCES

The School of Planning and Architecture. Cyclones and Building Behaviour. New Delhi: Buduas Press, 1980.

Jeary, A. P. "Vibration Tests of Structures at Varied Amplitudes." Garston, England: Building Research Establishment, 1981.

Jeary, A. P. "A Chronological Bibliography of Full Scale Induced Vibration Tests on Tall Buildings." Note 88/80. Garston, England: Building Research Establishment, 1980.

Griffiths, John F. Applied Climatology, 2nd Edition. Oxford: Oxford University Press, Oxford, 1976.

"Repair of Flood Damaged Buildings." Building Research Establishment Digest 152, H.M.S.O., April 1972.

Dowrick, Donald J. Earthquake Resistant Design. London: John Wiley & Sons, 1977.

Jones, Barclay G. "Planning for Reconstruction of Earthquake Stricken Communities." Proceedings of the P.R.C.-U.S.A. Joint Workshop on Earthquake Disaster Mitigation Through Architecture, Urban Planning and Engineering, Beijing, China: Office of Earthquake Resistance, State Capital Construction Commission, P.R.C., November 2-6, 1981, pp. 240-255.

Martin, John H. The Corning Flood: Museum Under Water. Corning, New York: The Corning Museum of Glass, 1977.

APPENDIX A
PRINCIPLES OF STRUCTURAL INTERVENTIONS TO HISTORIC BUILDINGS IN EARTHQUAKE ZONES

1. Analyze the "values" in the Building.

    (A) Emotional   –Continuity Identity
                                     –Symbolic Spiritual

    | (B) Cultural | –Artistic | –Architectural |
    | | –Art | –Documentary |
    | | –Historical | –Scientific |
    | | –Archaeological | –Townscape |
    | | –Landscape | |

    | (C) Use | –Economic | –Functional |
    | | –Social | –Political |

    These must be respected.

2. Analyze the structural system.
    This should not be changed.

    –How many previous earthquakes has it withstood?
    –Were any of these greater than Modified Mercalli IX?
    –Study records of past repairs and alterations, if these can be found.

3. Inspect the whole building and its surroundings.
    List all visible defects.

4. Review the causes of decay: slow, rapid or man–made.

5. Decide how the structural system is 'working'.
    a) the whole   b) the elements   c) the materials.

    –What and where are the critical parts?
    –Study the dynamic behaviour of the building.

    Which parts are likely to dissociate themselves, e.g., chimneys, gables, balconies, towers, roof tiles and beams? Which elements cause stress concentrations, e.g., doors, windows? Is the structure tied together, e.g., cross walls and floors and roofs? What are the typical defects of the vernacular or traditional construction?

    Are there inequalities in the ground supporting the building, which will cause different modes of vibration? Is there a danger of liquefaction of the soil due to high ground water level, likely to cause a landslip? What is the quality of the workmanship?

6. Having understood the building in its totality, consider what other experts can assist with investigation and advice: engineers, soil mechanics specialists, materials scientists, archaeologists and art historians.

   Note: the key experts must make a <u>joint</u> inspection and discussion together at the building.

7. Is a new use proposed? Does this impose new structural requirements? Is is sympathetic to the building and its values?

8. Outline all alternative possibilities for action.

   -Review techniques which increase the tensile strength without altering the dynamics of the structural system (which would introduce new and possibly unforeseeable effects). Develop special techniques for long shot drilling, grouting and reinforcement of masonry where necessary.

9. Consider the evidence in the structure requiring the proposed actions. Consider the past performance of the building.

10. Review the advantages and disadvantages of at least two probable courses of action in the light of the theory of conservation. Are the values in correct order of priority? Is the minimum intervention proposed necessary? Does the scheme prejudice future interventions?

APPENDIX B
PLANNING TO PROTECT AN INSTITUTION AND ITS COLLECTIONS

Few libraries, museums, or historical societies have the prescience to develop a plan for the handling of a disaster—a disaster which may never come and which the odds indicate will happen to someone else. Unfortunately, institutions do suffer damage from fire, water, or extremes of nature, and when no plan for handling such emergencies is available, the loss will be greater than necessary. The following considerations may help in drafting a plan for specific situations.

A. INSURE

Be certain that insurance coverage is complete and covers the collection, equipment and building—as well as office furniture, restoration of files, costs of temporary relocation, and the myriad expenses involved in returning to the status quo before the disaster.

The first step in planning is to locate an insurance agent who can help to provide the proper coverage for all aspects of the institution's activities and holdings. Advice can be sought from local insurance representatives or from the appropriate professional organizations such as The American Library Association, The American Association of Museums, The American Association of State and Local History, or other pertinent organizations.

Working with an insurance expert is essential, for few professionals in museum or library work know the intricacies of proper coverage. The kind of records needed to estimate damage or loss to prove a claim are most important if an adequate settlement is to be reached. The details on which claims might be based must be well documented: records of the date of acquisition, source, original cost, current replacement values, and so forth must be readily available, for there will be no time to develop such details after a disaster when the struggle to maintain services and to restore the collection must go on concurrently.

Insurance coverage should be considered not only in terms of replacement costs but in terms of restoration costs as well. A price can be set for replacing a standard dictionary, but what is the restoration cost or loss-of-value factor if a nineteenth-century pamphlet or unique Venetian goblet is damaged or destroyed? What is the value of staff time in replacing a damaged or destroyed catalogue of holdings or in reconstructing files and records?

B. KEEP AND DUPLICATE APPROPRIATE RECORDS

The accession records, shelf list, or catalogue of collections are among the most important holdings of an institution, sometimes more important after a disaster than the items they represent. No proper inventory, no adequate claim of loss can be carried out without adequate and available data when catastophes occur.

Such data should include a complete description of the object, with size, condition, etc., date of acquisition, source, provenance (where applicable), or original cost, current replacement value (this can be of assistance as well in adjusting insurance coverage as values increase or if de-accessioning of duplicates is under consideration), number of pages (books), number of plates illustrations (color, black and white), and other pertinent information.

Not only must documentation be complete and up-to-date, but it must be available—which implies duplicate copies. A complete catalogue is of little help if the only copy is destroyed in the disaster. All key records should be available on microfilm and copies should be stored far away from the institution's headquarters so that they will not be lost also. Storage in a bank vault is not good enough—if the bank is in the same disaster-prone area as the institution. Duplicate records may be kept in the general area, but a master microfilm should be stored, preferably in a commercial archival storage vault where proper humidity control is available. Such storage firms can usually produce duplicate copies of masters if such are needed. Information on such facilities can be obtained from the National Microfilm Association.

Once the records of all holdings have been microfilmed, an annual filming of new records should be undertaken to keep the records complete. Often this means keeping an additional accession card to be used for the filming at the end of the year. Periodically (every five or ten years) it would be well to remicrofilm the master records so as to provide one master duplicate file which can replace the original master microfilm and its five or ten supplements.

C. FORMULATE A PLAN

A plan for handling a disaster should be developed in consultation with or review by the entire staff of the institution so that each person knows his area of responsibility and to whom he reports during the emergency (the emergency chain of command may differ from the formal system of report). It should be in writing, available to all staff, and should be reviewed annually for up-dating or change.

The plan's priorities should outline action to be taken during specific disasters. If flood, hurricane, or tornados threaten, there may be time to take preventive action. Fire or burst pipes necessitate different responses, naturally. Thus it is well to divide the plan into three parts:

Actions to be taken prior to a disaster
Actions to be taken during a disaster
Actions to be taken after the disaster

These three aspects are covered in the following pages. Some of the types of disaster which should be anticipated include:

Bomb Threat	Gas Leak	Riot
Earthquake	Flood	Panic
Explosion	Water Damage	Power Failure
Plane Crash	High Wind	Accidents or illness on
Fire	Hurricane	premises

John H. Martin, Editor. <u>The Corning Flood: Museum Under Water.</u> Corning, N.Y.: The Corning Museum of Glass, 1977, p. 54.

APPENDIX C
STRUCTURAL INTERVENTIONS IN HISTORIC BUILDINGS

Experienced engineers and architects met together at ICCROM in Rome, to discuss an appropriate technology for the conservation of historic buildings.

Their ideas are summarized below. To some, these may seem revolutionary, to some reactionary and to some the obvious lessons of history.

The official "Code of Practice" approach to historic building is virtually rejected.

The functional value of traditional materials such as lime mortar, is recognized again and the Venice Charter reaffirmed.

Whilst not rejecting modern techniques of analysis, the value of a careful observation and appraisal for training architects and engineers in the appreciation of the structural behaviour of historic buildings, thus encouraging a qualitative intuitive understanding, was emphasized as the appropriate design technology. After all, it was technique the masons used in the past to build their breathtaking masterpieces.

The members of the workshop were P. Beckman (Denmark), B. M. Feilden (ICCROM), J. Heyman (U.K.), M. Kolaric (Yugoslavia), R. W. Mainstone (U.K.), G. Musumeci (Italy), W. Preiss (D.D.R.), P. Sanpaolesi (Italy), E. Schulze (F.D.R.), G. Tampone (Italy). The summary is by B. M. Feilden with the help of R. Mainstone.

Historic buildings as structures: forms, observation, analysis and diagnosis of weaknesses.

Several broad classifications of the structural forms used in the past and of characteristic responses to wind, weather, earth movements and the ever present action of gravity are possible. They are a helpful, perhaps even a necessary, starting point for appreciating the condition of a particular building. But it must be emphasized that each building is an individual and, like an individual human patient, must be so considered by the 'doctor architect' or 'doctor engineer'. As with the human patient its past history was important, and also its environment. Above all, the historic building, must also be considered as a whole, which might mean paying as much attention to the ground beneath as to the visible superstructure, and in terms of the superstructure it means, for instance, that there was little value in considering the stability of an arch by itself for the stability of its supports or abutments and the firmness of the ground on which they rested would often be the crucial matters.

Detailed measurements and analyses should be guided by the qualitative picture gradually built up from direct visual observation and study of the past history through documents, etc. Perspective or other drawings with overlays, or even simple Perspex models, are a useful means of concretizing this picture. Standard notations for cracks, displacements, etc. are also helpful. Much can in fact be achieved by such observation alone and by the visualization, based upon it, of the possible modes of collapse. This was, after all, virtually the only means available for structural analysis until a century or two ago. Detailed measurements are valuable today to distinguish, for instance between movements that largely occurred long ago and are not stabilized apart from inevitable small seasonal fluctuations about a mean. Detailed calculations are valuable in giving quantitative precision where it would otherwise be lacking and in distinguishing between alternative possibilities.

Measurements of deformations to an accuracy of $\pm$ 3 to 5 mm is considered adequate for most preliminary observation, but much greater accuracy is called for in long-term monitoring of possible increases or of the effects of interventions. A firm datum is required and measurements should be made at frequent and regular intervals. They should be plotted as made and regularly reviewed. Out-of-plumb deformations are not easy to measure. The use of plumb bobs is costly in labour, subject to interference by wind and weather externally, and calls for damping if reasonable accuracy is to be attained. Optical plumb bobs and precision climometers also have practical limitations. The correlation of inclinations from the vertical, particularly if carried out in association with a study of other related deformations including changes in level, is, however, a possible fruitful means of elucidating the structural history of a building where other evidence is lacking or equivocal.

In carrying out analyses of the structural condition the most appropriate technique must be selected for each case individually in the light of all the observations made and the questions posed. The problem as a whole and the inevitable limitations of the analysis must never be lost from sight. Techniques ranging from simple thrust-line graphic analyses of arched systems to computerized finite-element analyses all have their parts to play, though little role was seen for the costly and often unrealistic photoelastic experimental technique. Above all the "Code-of-Practice" approach has been found to be irrelevant, not only because the structures of historic building mostly differ considerably from those envisaged by current codes, but also because historic buildings are structures that have already existed for a long time thereby, demonstrating both their overall stability and their particular weaknesses. For the same reason, though with slightly less force, current design criteria and procedures are unlikely to be directly relevant. The 'moment of decision' is essentially one for the exercise of the responsible engineer's or architect's own judgment, supported, if need be, by that of his peers. A reminder that present overall stability is never a self-sufficient guarantee of future stability was provided by a recent partial collapse of the Ospizio di San Michele, Rome. On 31 March 1977 it was declared unsafe and evacuated as signs of distress were noted, and about 12 hours later it collapsed, probably partly as a result of the thermal shock of a particularly cold night.

BELOW-GROUND INTERVENTIONS

With uniform loading on ground that offers uniform support, a building should settle uniformly even if the loading is excessive by modern standards. It thus forms its own foundations. In the case of a historic building such settlement will usually have taken place long ago and now matters little. Even a linearly varying settlement, as a result, perhaps, of a continuous variation over the length or breadth in the support conditions, matters little if the resulting bodily tilt of the building is not excessive in itself or in relation to its height. Differential settlements of a non-linear kind, such as a greater settlement in the center of a building, are the ones that matter most, since they can be absorbed only by weakening deformations of the superstructure. Observations of comparable structures may help in assessing how much differential settlement a building can accept, though it must be remembered that this tolerance is partly dependent on the original speed and sequence of construction. With a slow building programme in which construction was carried up fairly uniformly over the whole extent of the building, much of the initial settlement was accommodated without structural deformation, by built-in changes of level as occurred with St. Paul's Cathedral, London. In such cases settlement histories can, and should, be constructed, as has been done for the Campanile in Pisa and for York Minster.

Usually conditions below ground remain virtually unchanged through the centuries while the structure above ground suffers a progressive loss of strength due to weathering and decay of materials and the disruptive effects of cyclic temperature changes, etc., interrupted from time to time by human interventions. This situation should not, however, be taken for granted. Water levels in particular may change as a result of drainage, pumping, obstruction of underground flows, or other interventions and conditions may also be changed by adjacent works of other kinds. The effects of a change in the water table may be difficult to predict, but are usually undesirable. Preservation of the water table is therefore usually important. It was, for instance, reported that two thirds of the present increase in the lean of the Campanile in Pisa was due to water abstraction and that the earlier water table was now being reinstated by pumping in water. Local de-watering or pumping constitutes a similar danger, particularly if it leads to the removal of silt, for example, where running water under a building leached sand from beneath it and led to a settlement of 300 mm; stopping the flow stabilized the situation.

Where differential settlement is leading to excessive deformations of the superstructure, the situation should be analyzed in full in both its above-ground and below-ground aspects. The relative merits and costs of strengthening the superstructure, underpinning it (i.e., carrying the foundation down to an existing firmer stratum), and improving the soil conditions should then be weighed against one another to select the best course of action. Possible methods of improving the soil condition (each with the advantage of leaving the historic building untouched) include:

a) Weighting the surroundings to prevent adjacent uplift,
b) Local water extraction to cause local shrinkage and thereby a corrective differential settlement.
c) Drainage or de-watering

Adoption of these methods call, however, for thorough prior investigation and careful skilled control. It is also possible to stabilize the soil through high pressure injection but this requires special technology, an expensive plant and is difficult in built-up areas. In all cases of possible hazard from ground movement, it is desirable to investigate the general geological background in order to locate and identify the particular hazard which may, for instance, be a geological fault line or the presence of fine laminations in a clay soil.

ABOVE-GROUND INTERVENTIONS

Apart from questions of observation, analysis, and diagnosis of weakness, above-ground interventions concentrated chiefly on the choice of materials for consolidation or repair and the treatment of the cracks inevitably found in buildings constructed without pre-formed expansion or other movement joints.

Thermal movement and movements due to changes in moisture content must be reviewed. Severe cracking can occur, also, as a consequence of fire or the introduction of central heating. Because, even in the absence of extreme events such as a serious fire, some cyclic movements must continue to take place, it is useless to attempt to eliminate all cracking from historic buildings. Necessary reinforcement should be designed simply to keep it under control. Materials must be considered both in relation to structural consolidation and weather protection of masonry structures. In relation to the latter, Swedish data emphasize, in particular, the great merits of traditional elastic, relatively absorbent and easily renewed lime mortars for pointing and rendering. Portland cement mortars are, on the other hand, stiffer, almost impermeable and excessively strong so that repairs tend to break away in large sections or weathering destroys the weaker brick or stone rather than the pointing. It must be recognized though, that climatic conditions vary greatly and that the role of an external wall as weather skin and environmental filter likewise varied. The correct choice of materials in any particular case must be made in terms of the local conditions and considering the total function of the wall (which might, for instance, have an important fresco on the other face), the existing construction and materials and the available materials and skills.

In any wall or pier it is desirable that the core should be as strong and stiff as the facings and should be well bonded to them. Except in some solid brick walls, a few walls of pure ashlar masonry, and most Roman concrete walls, this is rarely found to be the case. Short of completely reconstructing walls and piers with weak rubble cores and the like, grouting is the only available technique of consolidation, possibly assisted by the introduction of a limited amount of reinforcement. Stronger mortars were then desirable, though Portland cement mortar again can be criticized on the grounds of excessive hardness, lack of elasticity and impermeability. This topic needs full discussion with the benefit of contractors' experience.

CONCLUSIONS AND RECOMMENDATIONS

Amongst a wide range of experts there is general agreement on the following conclusions and tentative recommendations.

1. Before starting an investigation and certainly before undertaking any major intervention the engineer and architect should have a clear idea of the objective. What are the important characteristics of the buildings? Which buildings is it most desirable to conserve, and for what future use? Continued 'use' in the normal sense of the word is always preferable to mere preservation as a monument, museum, or simply part of the scenery, since it enables the

building to continue to play a full social role and provides the best guarantee of continued attention and proper maintenance care. But there are also buildings or remnants of buildings with an important future use as physical embodiments of past cultures or examples of supreme past achievements without which we should be much poorer and which should be lovingly conserved for the real contribution they make to the fullness of our lives.

2. Whatever the objectives, each historic building presents unique problems. It is an individual structure and its needs should be individually assessed, while keeping a proper sense of proportion about the justifiable depth of investigation.

3. Investigation of the building's needs should take into account all relevant facts including not only the future use but also the environmental conditions, the foundation conditions and its past history. This last could be very important in correctly interpreting apparent signs of distress; usually the present condition of the structure should provide some clues, but documentary sources should also be consulted.

4. A qualitative structural assessment should usually precede and guide quantitative analyses which may otherwise be based on mistaken assumptions or misleadingly concentrate on the more obvious aspects of the problem to the neglect of the real total situation. Analyses should also start from first principles and not attempt to take short cuts by using rules from current "Codes of Practice" or other current design procedures, since these are never truly applicable to historic buildings and if applied may cause damage.

5. Where remedial interventions are considered to be necessary they should respect, as far as possible, the character and integrity of the original structure. They should, as far as possible, use similar materials. Where different materials are substituted, care must be taken not to introduce elements of excessive strength or stiffness into a structure which will usually be less stiff and more accommodating to long-term movements than contemporary structures.

6. The final choice of the approach to be adapted should be made only after a proper appraisal (consistent with the scale of operations and the resources available) of alternatives and with some eye to the future. In general interventions that can be undertaken in stages, that can be controlled by monitoring of their effects, and that can be repeated, reinforced or reversed as necessary are preferable to those that are irreversible, 'once for all', and call for a complete advance commitment to a single course of action. Whatever

is done, it should be fully recorded and the records deposited with a competent authority for future reference.

7. The best further safeguard for the future is to place the building under the continuous care of someone like a Dom Baumeister or a Cathedral Surveyor, preferably assisted by a permanent small staff of skilled craftsmen who learn to know the structure intimately.

8. Because of the very limited relevance of current design procedures to the conservation of historic buildings it was also felt that there should be more training of architects and engineers in an appreciation of the structural behaviour of such buildings. They should at least be given some qualitative intuitive understanding on which to build and a basic vocabulary with which to formulate and communicate their insights. They should also be made fully aware of the need to have an adequate picture of the structural action as a whole before attempting detailed analysis of any part.

Bernard Feilden 4.10.77
Revised Rowland Mainstone 13.11.77
Revised Bernard Feilden 15.5.79

On Earth as It Is: Recent Losses of Historic Structures from Earthquakes and Natural Disasters

W. Brown Morton, III

In Indonesia not very long ago as I was standing in a hotel shop the floor began to heave, the light fixtures swayed on their chains and the objects on the shelves rocked back and forth while some fell over. I had been in my first earthquake.

My initial reaction was incomprehension. Before I could react further it was over, finished. No one was injured; no buildings were damaged; none of the historic monuments in the area collapsed. Others have not been so fortunate.

From time to time, natural disasters of unusual intensity or unexpected location will undo in a few seconds or a few days the work of centuries. Earthquake, flood, drought or volcanic eruption strikes like a thief in the night and the world is the poorer for it. The terrible flood in Florence in 1966 is an excellent example of this. (Figure 1.9)

In the past decade alone we have suffered dramatic losses of our cultural patrimony from natural disasters, especially earthquakes. Recent events in the Friuli and Naples area of Italy, in Montenegro, in Guatemala and in Nicaragua, have been life-taking tragedies as well as occasions of serious loss to our shared heritage. (Figure 1.10) These unfortunate events present those of us who constitute the world's conservation community with a dramatic challenge. Can we learn from the past to provide more effective protection in the future? Fortunately for us in historic preservation, other professions can provide us with a lot of significant data:

The World Data Center A for Solid Earth Geophysics published, in July 1981, a Catalog of Significant Earthquakes from 2000 B.C. to 1979 [Ganse and Nelson, 1984]. The catalog includes events which in most instances meet at least one of three criteria: moderate damage (approximately $1 million or greater in 1979 U.S. dollars), or at least 10 deaths, or magnitude 7.5 or greater. This highly informative catalog identifies 2,484 significant earthquakes; the earliest having taken place in the year 2000 B.C. in Western Turkmenia and the most recent occurring on December 26, 1979 in the United Kingdom.

The World Data Center A for Solid Earth Geophysics and the National Geophysical and Solar Terrestrial Data Center have also published a very informative large map entitled Significant

Figure 1.9. Florence, Italy: River Arno Showing Ponte Vecchio After Flood of
November 4-5, 1966.

Figure 1.10. Montenegro, Yugoslavia:
Frescoed Church After Earthquake of
April 15, 1979.

40

Earthquakes 1900 - 1979 with destructive earthquake information. [Ganse and Nelson, 1980]

This map shows the location and relative importance of 1,277 significant earthquakes from 1900 to 1979. Earthquakes are shown if the number of deaths was 10 or more, or if the amount of damage was "limited" or greater, or if the magnitude was at least 7.5. The Destructive Earthquake Information at the base of the map lists 682 earthquakes where the number of deaths was 10 or more, and the damage was moderate, severe, or extreme, and the magnitude was 7.5 or greater. This list of 682 earthquakes gives the date, time, latitude, longitude, focal depth in kilometers, magnitude, deaths, damage and reference sources. 98 of the most destructive earthquakes are shown in bold faced type. For example, the destructive earthquake of the greatest magnitude listed occurred on January 31, 1906 at 15:36 hours in universal time at 1.0 North Latitude and 81.5 West Longitude; off the west coast of Colombia. 1000 deaths were recorded; damage was moderate. The greatest number of deaths listed occurred on July 21, 1976 at 19:42 hours in universal time at 39.5 North Latitude and 117.9 East Longitude in northeastern China, with a focal depth of 23 k., a magnitude of 7.8; damage was extreme, 240,000 people died.

The United States Geological Survey also publishes a World Seismicity Map showing the location of earthquakes from July 1963 to July 1972.

Of particular interest and usefulness to the historic preservation and art conservation community is a publication issued by the United States Department of Commerce, National Oceanic and Atmospheric Administration, Environmental Data Service. It is titled Catalog of Earthquake Photographs, Key to Geophysical Records Documentation. [Coffman, 1976] It is a catalog of a collection of earthquake damage photographs from 63 different government and private sources. It contains chronologically by date approximately 750 references to earthquake photographs with a description of each photograph and illustrations of examples from the collection. It contains photographs of earthquake damage from the December 16, 1811 earthquake in New Madrid, Missouri to the earthquake of September 6, 1975 in Turkey.

An early photograph shows the courthouse in San Leandro, California wrecked by earthquakes in 1868. (Figure 1.11) This photograph provides invaluable information about both the event and the building. We can see not only the extent of the damage but also the nature of it. We can see where the building failed and where it did not.

Another dramatic view shows the tower of Saint Philip's Church in Charleston, South Carolina following the earthquake of August 1, 1886. (Figure 1.12) Here we see that the fifth stage of the tower partially collapsed. The outer wall fell away altogether leaving only the central spine of the timber framing in place. However, this was enough to keep the upper stages of the tower and the spire in place. Any restoration project for St. Philip's church would be immeasurably aided by the information in this photograph.

Figure 1.11. San Leandro, California: Alameda County Courthouse After Earthquake of October 21, 1868. Univ. of California, Berkeley.

Figure 1.12. Charleston, South Carolina: St. Philip's Church, Joseph Hyde, Arch., 1835–1836, 145 Church Street after Earthquake of August 31, 1886. South Carolina Art Association.

Less happy is the photograph of a row of two story buildings in San Francisco, California taken during the earthquake of April 18, 1906, showing the buildings collapsed backward away from the street where the ground slumped beneath their foundations. (Figure 1.14) This photograph gives us valuable information about the architecture of early San Francisco, its construction and its failure by earthquake. Later the great San Francisco fire destroyed the entire block.

Current data about recent losses from earthquakes are available from the NOAA Environmental Data and Information Service, Boulder, Colorado. [NOAA, 1979, see also World Data Center A, 1981]

In the ten year period from 1970 to 1979 there were 63 earthquakes with damage of $5 million or greater or more than 500 deaths. In this period the earthquakes of the greatest magnitude were the quake of April 21, 1977 in the Solomon Islands and the quake of September 12, 1979 in West Irian, Indonesia. Both had a magnitude of 8.1. The greatest damage in monetary terms followed the May 16, 1976 quake in northeastern Italy around Friuli, where the losses were estimated at $9,900 million. The greatest number of deaths occurred in the July 27, 1976 quake in northeastern China, already mentioned, where 240,000 men, women and children lost their lives.

When we look at the World Seismicity Map (Figure 1.13) or study the other data already referred to it is tragically apparent that the areas of the planet earth most affected by destructive earthquakes are also areas exceptionally rich in cultural resources. This unfortunate affinity between areas of intense seismic activity and high concentration of great historic buildings makes a doleful litany: northern China, Italy, Greece, Turkey, Iraq, Iran, the Soviet Union, Afghanistan, Pakistan, Nepal, Burma, Indonesia, China, Japan, The Philippines, and the entire west coast of the United States, Mexico, Central and South America.

Those of us responsible for the preservation of historic monuments and artistic works have been particularly shocked by the terrible losses of the cultural heritage to earthquakes in Guatemala on February 4, 1976; at Friuli in northeastern Italy, a few weeks later on May 17, 1976 and again in September of the same year; in Montenegro, Yugoslavia on April 15, 1979; and most recently in Campania in central Italy in November, 1980. Three photographs from Campania give poignant testimony to the tragedy there. In the first photo a church facade survives but through the open door it can be seen that the roof collapses. (Figure 1.15) In the second photo a car survives but the garage that was its home collapses. (Figure 1.16) In the last photo of a stricken town nothing survives and even hope collapses. (Figure 1.17)

These are images of recent losses that grieve us all. These are images of natural disaster on earth as it is. These are images that challenge us all.

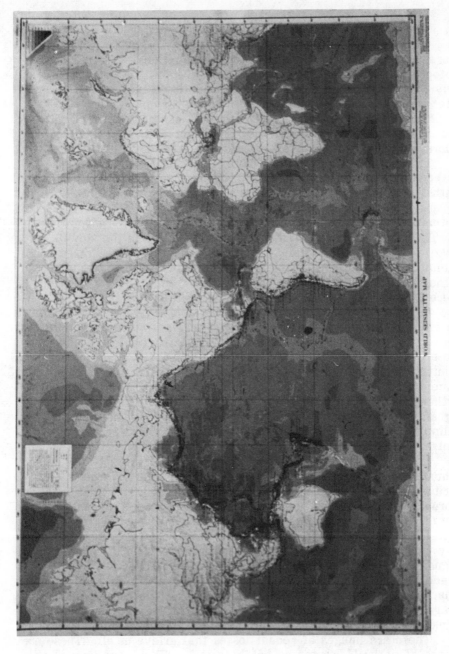

Figure 1.13. World Seismicity Map: July 1963-1972. USGS.

Figure 1.14. San Francisco, California: Buildings Affected by Ground Subsidence in Earthquake of April 18, 1906. NOAA/EDIS.

Figure 1.15. Campania-Basilicata, Italy: Church Facade after Earthquake of November 23, 1980.

Figure 1.16. Campania-Basilicata, Italy: Collapsed Modern Building after Earthquake of November 23, 1980.

Figure 1.17. Campania-Basilicata, Italy: Village Street after Earthquake of November 23, 1980.

REFERENCES

Coffman, Jerry L.   Catalog of Earthquake Photographs, Key to Geophysical Records Documentation No. 7. Boulder, Colorado: National Geophysical and Solar-Terrestrial Data Center, National Oceanic and Atmospheric Administration, December, 1976.

Ganse, Robert A. and John B. Nelson. Map of Significant Earthquakes 1900 - 1979 with Destructive Earthquake Information. Boulder, Colorado: National Geophysical and Solar-Terrestrial Data Center, National Oceanic and Atmospheric Administration, 1980.

Ganse, Robert A. and John B. Nelson.   Catalog of Significant Earthquakes, 200 B.C. - 1979. Report SE-27. Boulder, Colorado: World Data Center A For Solid Earth Geophysics, U.S. Department of Commerce, National Oceanic and Atmospheric Administration, Environmental Data and Information Service, July, 1981.

National Oceanic and Atmospheric Administration. List of Worldwide Earthquakes, 1970 - 1979, with Damage of $5,000,000 or Greater or More than 500 Deaths. Boulder, Colorado: Environmental Data and Information Service, National Geophysical and Solar-Terrestrial Data Center, National Oceanic and Atmospheric Administration, 1979.

World Data Center A for Solid Earth Geophysics. Earthquake Data Services and Publications, Key to Geophysical Records Documentation No. 15. Boulder, Colorado: National Geophysical and Solar-Terrestrial Data Center, National Oceanic and Atmospheric Administration, 1981.

Lessons to be Learned from Friuli

Paul M. Schwartzbaum, Arch. Riccardo Mola, and Constance S. Silver

The region of Friuli Venezia-Giulia constitutes the northeast portion of the Italian peninsula and shares common borders with Austria on the north and Yugoslavia on the east. (Figure 1.18) Geographically and historically, the region's limits were determined by its position between the Adriatic Sea and the Alps. Its landscape consists of plains in the south rising gradually into the foothills of the Alps in the center and terminates in the Alps themselves in the extreme north.

Particularly important is the region's location at a point of interaction between the rigid, crystalline European Alpine system and the neo-sedimentery and plastic Dinaric alpine system. The entire area therefore is subject to intense phenomena of compression with subsequent separation and displacement of large land masses. The degree of seismic activity in certain areas is extremely elevated because of residual activity of the great tertiary mountain building period, which formed the European Alps.

In our century there have been not less than twelve earthquakes which attained at least grade VII on the Mercalli-Sieberg Scale. The history of the region, however, bears witness to many others of which those of 1511, 1899 and 1928 deserve special mention, having been estimated as corresponding to grade IX on the Mercalli Scale.

Between May 6 and September 15, 1976, the Friuli Region of northeastern Italy was devastated by a series of violent earthquakes averaging 6 on the Richter Scale. A total of 4,800 square kilometers were affected; 1,000 individuals were killed; 2,400 were injured and 44,000 were left homeless. More than 150,00 suffered varying degrees of damage to their homes or places of work.

The losses suffered by the artistic patrimony of the region were also disastrous. While the exact figures will never be known, conservative estimates indicate that:

63 churches were destroyed while 247 were seriously damaged,
5 castles were destroyed and 13 seriously damaged, and
14 mural painting cycles were destroyed or very
heavily damaged.

49

AUSTRIA

Hermagor

Ravascletto

Pontebba Tarvisio

Ampezzo Dogna

C A R N I A Tolmezzo Resuitta

Amaro Portis

△ Venzone

Lusevera

Trasaghis Gemona

Osoppo Montenars

Meduno Forgaria Artegna

Tarcento

Buia Attimis

Majano Tricesimo

Maniago Faedis

S. Daniele

Colloredo

Spilimbergo Fagagna Cividale

Udine

F R I U L I

Codroipo Cormons Gorizia

Pordenone Palmanova

S. Vito

Monfalcone

Portogruaro San Giorgio

Marano Trieste

Latisana Grado GULF OF TRIESTE

Lignano

Caorle Bibione

ADRIATIC SEA

Venice

P O R D E N O N E

Y U G O S L A V I A

○ Epicenter (May)
△ Epicenter (September)

0   10 km

Figure 1.18. Map of the Friuli Region, Italy.

14 other murals required intense emergency intervention to ensure their survival.

These statistics define a chaotic situation in which tens of thousands of individuals suddenly found themselves exposed to the elements, with their homes in rubble, without water or electricity. In some areas entire towns were isolated by landslides followed by torrential rains.

The lasting result has been a total transformation of the Friulan landscape caused by the destruction of entire towns, small rural villages, innumerable churches, and the traditional works of art that gave the area its characteristic culture and appearance. (Figures 1.19 and 1.20)

The earthquakes were ruinous for the historic complexes, often of medieval origin, as well as for the more modest vernacular architecture. Built from low quality materials, mostly washed cobbles collected from riverbeds, the Friulan structures offered little resistance to seismic shock. Moreover, inadequate maintenance procedures were a major cause of the structural failure.

Immediately after the first earthquake of May 6, the necessity of providing for the populace and aiding the injured and those still buried under the rubble rendered impossible any efforts towards the conservation of cultural property. Because the artistic patrimony of the Friuli had not been inventoried, it was impossible to implement coordinated conservation efforts in response to the gravity of the situation. Interventions were undertaken in the early stages without any comprehensive plan or even an idea of the true needs of the region as a whole. Decisions were taken following "reports" or "tips" from whomever happened to observe a damaged work of art. The necessity of examining the reality and urgency of these reports impeded rapid interventions when they were required. Some damaged buildings which had considerable local value were demolished before feasibility studies for their preservation could be initiated.

All of these factors hopelessly overloaded the conservation capacity of the Friuli, which was insufficient even in normal times. But more importantly they also contributed to an often dangerous lack of communication. For example, the civic administration of one of the few surviving historic towns in Friuli requested permission to demolish the damaged but recuperable historic center because of an excessive fear of continuing building collapse. Too often the conservation specialists on the scene had to fight not only the enormous technical problems, but also local officials and inhabitants beset with fear.

Therefore, from the beginning, conservation efforts were an immense and difficult undertaking. The first interventions were directed towards recuperating everything that had been spared from destruction. A meticulous search for paintings, sculpture, decorative work and architectural elements was carried out in the rubble of collapsed churches and castles. Larger works such as altars, wooden choir screens, and large frescoes requiring detachment from damaged walls exposed to the elements, presented far more difficult logistical

51

Figure 1.19. Gemona del Friuli, Italy:
Church after Earthquake of May 6, 1976.

Figure 1.20. Venzone, Italy: Conservation
Team from the Instituto Centrale del
Restauro led by Mrs. Laura Mora Inspecting
the Thirteenth Century Church of Saints
Giacomo and Anna.

52

problems. (Figures 1.21 and 1.22) Additional information on specific treatments that were undertaken has been given elsewhere. [Schwartzbaum, Silver and Grissom, 1977]

Conservation efforts were further complicated by the danger of entry into many partially collapsed buildings and the sudden appearance of older, unknown mural paintings which became visible when successively applied layers of whitewash and plaster became detached during tremors.

In almost all phases of the conservation interventions, field workers had to confront conditions of extreme physical and mental stress, danger, and frustratingly few means to meet the immensity and urgency of the situation.

Available human and material resources were always insufficient. Due to the lack of specialized conservation personnel, rescue efforts for cultural property were often entrusted to the many volunteers and soldiers deployed in the overall post earthquake relief. These individuals assisted in the search for damaged works and their transport to specially organized depositories where provisional cataloguing was undertaken in preparation for future conservation treatments. In this way thousands of objects were housed in the Church of San Francesco, Udine; the Civic Museum, Pordenone; and other small storage areas in Venzone, Tolmesso and Gorizia. (Figure 1.23)

Interventions for monuments and buildings consisted first of the construction of temporary roofs and propping up unstable structures at risk of imminent collapse. (Figures 1.24 and 1.25) It was usually possible to intervene effectively for monuments of significant historic and artistic value. However, often the gravity of the structural damage did not permit adequate propping and protection to be realized in time to ensure that the damaged structure would resist subsequent tremors. Thus with the second round of major earthquakes, four months later in September, some monuments which had been well propped, such as the Duomo of Spilimbergo (Figure 1.26) remained standing, while others such as the Duomo of Venzone were reduced to rubble. (Figures 1.27, 1.28, 1.29, 1.30, 1.31)

Also it is important to note that the second series of earthquakes caught everyone by surprise. Although we learned later that one prediction had been made, this warning never reached those of us in the field. Moreover, being already intent upon repairing the damage suffered during the May earthquakes, so violent a repetition of the devastation seemed unimaginable.

Now six years after the earthquakes in the Friuli, it should be possible for conservationists to learn some valuable lessons from this disastrous experience. The caption of Figure 1.32 can be translated as "Epicenters in the Friuli from 365 A.D. to 1976". Earthquakes have been recorded in this area for the last one thousand six hundred and seventeen years. Obviously, here destruction caused by earthquakes is a recurring phenomenon, and, as such, some degree of predictability must be possible, and careful contingency planning can play

Figure 1.21. Villuzza of Ragogna, Italy: Eleventh Century Fresco Fragments Being Removed with their Supporting Masonry, "Stacco a Massello," Church of San Lorenzo. These Frescoes Came to Light as a Result of Earthquake of May 6, 1976.

Figure 1.22. Villuzza of Ragogna, Italy: Removal of Eleventh Century Fresco Fragments, Church of San Lorenzo.

Figure 1.23. Udine, Italy: Depository for Displaced Objects, Church of San Francisco. View of Depository Immediately after Earthquake of May 6, 1976, and before Subsequent Reorganization.

Figure 1.24. Venzone, Italy: Church of Saints Giacomo and Anna after Construction of Temporary Roof and Counterform for Supporting the Frescoes of the Barrel Vault Following Earthquake of May 6, 1976.

Figure 1.25. Villuzza of Ragogna, Italy: Church of San Lorenzo, Propping and Temporary Roofing Constructed to Protect Frescoes on Walls Which Were to Remain in situ.

Figure 1.26. Spilimbergo, Italy: Cathedral Damaged in Earthquake of May 6, 1976 Showing Proppings that Helped it Survive Earthquake of September 15, 1976.

Figure 1.27. Venzone, Italy: Cathedral after its Collapse in Earthquake of September 15, 1976.

Figure 1.28. Venzone, Italy: Cathedral Before Earthquake of May 6, 1976.

Figure 1.29. Venzone, Italy: Cathedral after Earthquake of May 6, 1976.

Figure 1.30. Venzone, Italy: Detail of Late 14th Century Frescoed Vault, Gonfalone Chapel, Before the Earthquake of 1976. These Paintings, Influenced by the School of the Paduan Painters Altichieri, Were Among the Most Beautiful and Important in the Friuli.

Figure 1.31. Venzone, Italy: Cathedral, the Gonfalone Chapel after its Collapse and the Complete Destruction of the Vault Paintings in the Earthquake of September 15, 1976.

59

a significant role in reducing the extent of the damage suffered by the cultural property.

RECOMMENDATIONS

Based on the problems encountered in the Friuli, it appears that the most important steps to be taken to minimize damage caused by natural disasters involve contingency planning and effective coordination. To this end, for areas with a recurring history of natural disasters, one could propose the following recommendations:

1) on a local level, inventories of all monuments and works of art should be completed as soon as possible. These should include at least some historical data and art historical priorities; condition reports, photographic, graphic, or photogrammetric documentation, and information pertaining to the identity of responsible authorities and details of access.

2) a local natural disaster committee should be formed with a cultural property subcommittee. This committee would include representatives of local government, locally based national government, clergy and military leaders, and local or regional experts in relevant disciplines.

This local natural disaster committee should prepare contingency plans and take steps to minimize delays in reacting to future natural disasters. For example, it should apply political pressure to have emergency funds set aside by local and national government agencies or at least obtain approval for emergency administrative procedures that would minimize bureaucratic entanglements.

The local committee should arrange for periodic inspections of monuments and museums, to be undertaken so as to evaluate the potential for damage during future natural disasters due to the structures' location, construction or state of repair. It should help arrange for the enactment of all possible preventive seismic interventions. It should arrange to store, or at least locate materials and equipment that will be needed in the event of a natural disaster, for example, propping materials, materials for constructing temporary roofs, conservation products and fumigation equipment. The local committee should also locate and equip depositories for displaced objects.

3) On a national level, decisions must be taken in advance as to the types and quantity of personnel that will be required if a disaster strikes. Efficacious administrative procedures must be developed to ensure that the needed personnel arrive at the site as soon as possible. In Friuli, after conservation relief funds finally arrived they lay unused for months because the government agency lacked sufficient personnel to administer them and because the transfer and assignment of personnel in Italy is a lengthy procedure.

60

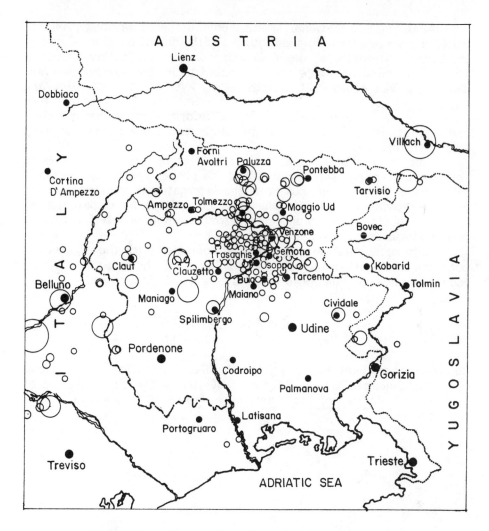

SEISMICITY OF FRIULI-VENEZIA GIULIA REGION

DISTRIBUTION OF EPICENTERS
FROM 365 TO 1976

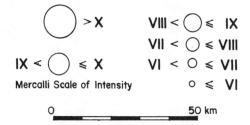

Figure 1.32. Friuli Region, Italy: Epicenters of Earthquakes from 365 A.D. to
1976 A.D.

4) On an international level, a committee or working group on national disasters should be established with the sponsorship of one of the larger international organizations concerned with conservation. The group would be made up of specialists in the various relevant disciplines who could visit disaster sites, evaluate the situation and advise local authorities. However, more importantly the committee should prepare in advance a variety of information–gathering "tools" and booklets which can serve as guidelines to field workers and local administrators.

This committee could act as a clearing house for foreign volunteers offering their services and for proper use of international relief funds. To do this, however, the international committee would have to provide liaison with the local committee by dispatching at least one international volunteer who would remain on site full time to coordinate international relief efforts.

It is hoped that these proposals, combined with the suggestions put forth by the other authors in this volume, will help in the effort to reduce earthquake damage to cultural property in the future.

REFERENCE

Schwartzbaum, Paul M., Constance S. Silver, and Carol A. Grissom. "Earthquake Damage to Works of Art in the Friuli Region of Italy." Journal of the American Institute of Conservation, 1977, pp. 9-16.

Section One References

ACCOUNTS OF NATURAL DISASTERS

Alexander, David. "The Florence Floods—What the Papers Said." Environmental Management. Volume 4, No. 1, January 1980, pp. 27-34.

Algermissen, S. T., et al. A Study of Earthquake Losses in the San Francisco Bay Area: Data and Analysis. Prepared for National Oceanic and Atmospheric Administration, Office of Emergency Preparedness. Washington, D.C.: U.S. Department of Commerce, 1972.

Algermissen, S. T., K. V. Steinbrugge, et al. A Study of Earthquake Losses in the Los Angeles, California Area. Washington, D.C.: U.S. Department of Commerce, 1973.

Ambraseys, Nicholas N. "The Romanian Earthquake of 4 March 1977." Disasters. Volume I, No. 3, 1977, pp. 175-177.

Ambraseys, Nicholas N. "Value of Historical Records of Earthquakes." Nature. Volume 232, 1971.

Ambraseys, Nicholas N. and J. Despeyroux. "The Earthquake of 4 March 1977 and its Principal Effects" (Part I, Ambraseys), "Analyse du Comportement des Constructions" (Part II, Despeyroux), in Le Tremblement de Terre du 4 Mars 1977. UNESCO Report No. FMR/SC/GEO/78/102. Paris: UNESCO, 1978.

Ambraseys, Nicholas N., A. A. Moinfar, and M. Amin. Iran Earthquake 1970. Technical Research and Standard Bureau, Plan and Budget Organization Publication No. 53. Tehran, Iran: Plan and Budget Organization, 1975.

Ambraseys, Nicholas N., A. A. Moinfar, and J. S. Tchalenko. Ghir Earthquake of 10 April 1972. UNESCO Serial No. 2789/RMO.RD/SCE. Paris: UNESCO, 1972.

Ambraseys, Nicholas N., G. Lensen and A. Moinfar. The Pattan Earthquake of 28 December 1974. Technical Report RP/1975/76/2.222.3. Prepared for the Government of Pakistan. Paris: UNESCO, 1975.

American Iron and Steel Institute. Committee of Structural Steel Producers. The Agadir, Morocco Earthquake, February 29, 1960. New York: AISI, 1962.

Anderson, William and Robert Whitman. A Few Preliminary Observations on "Black Tuesday": The 7 February 1967 Fires in Tasmania, Australia. Columbus, Ohio: Disaster Research Center, Ohio State University, 1967.

Barkun, Michael. Disaster and the Millenium. New Haven, Ct.: Yale University Press, 1974.

Barkun, Michael. "Disaster in History." Mass Emergencies. Volume 2, No. 4, 1977.

Barlay, Stephen. Fire: An International Report. Brattleboro, Vt.: Stephen Greene Press, 1969.

Berberian, Manuel. "Tabas-E-Golshan (Iran) Catastrophic Earthquake of 16 September 1978: A Preliminary Field Report." Disasters. Volume 2, No. 4, 1979.

Berberian, Manuel. Tabas-E-Golshan (Iran) Catastrophic Earthquake of 16 September 1978: A Preliminary Field Report. Department of Geodesy and Geophysics, University of Cambridge. London: Pergamon, 1979.

Berg, Glen Virgil. The Skopje, Yugoslavia Earthquake, July 26, 1963. New York: American Iron and Steel Institute, 1964.

Best, Alfred M. Best's Special Report on San Francisco Losses and Settlements of the Two Hundred Forty Three Institutions Involved in the Conflagration of April 18-21, 1906. San Francisco, California: A. M. Best Co., 1907.

Bode, Barbara. Explanation of the 1970 Earthquake in the Peruvian Andes. Ann Arbor, Michigan: Xerox University Microfilms, 1974.

Bourque, Linda Brookover, et al. The Unpredictable Disaster in A Metropolis: Public Response to the Los Angeles Earthquake of February, 1971. Los Angeles, California: UCLA Survey Research Center, 1973.

Brandow, G. E. and D. J. Leeds. Reconnaissance Report: Imperial County, California Earthquake, October 15, 1979. Berkeley, California: Earthquake Engineering Research Institute, 1980.

Bronson, William. The San Francisco Earthquake: The Earth Shook, The Sky Burned. Garden City, N.Y.: Doubleday, 1959.

Butler, John E. Natural Disasters. London: Heinemann, 1977.

Cluff, J. S. "Peru Earthquake of May 31, 1970." Bulletin of the Seismological Society of America. Volume LXI, June 1971, p. 511.

Coffman, Jerry L. and Carl A. VonHake., Eds. Earthquake History of the U.S. Revised Edition (Through 1970). Washington, D.C.: U.S. Government Printing Office, 1973.

Cornell, James. The Great International Disaster Book. New York: Scribner's, 1976.

Division of Water Resources. Report on Physical Effects of Arvin Earthquake of July 21, 1952. Sacramento, California: State of California, 1952.

Dworkin, Judith. Global Trends in Natural Disaster 1947-1973. Natural Hazard Research Working Paper No. 26, 1974. Boulder, Colorado: University of Colorado, Institute of Behavioral Science, 1974.

Earthquake Engineering Research Institute. Miyagi-Ken-Oki, Japan, Earthquake, June 12, 1978. Berkeley, California: Earthquake Engineering Research Institute, 1978.

Earthquake Engineering Research Institute. Philippines Earthquake Committee. Reconnaissance Report, Mindanao, Philippines, Earthquake, August 17, 1976. Berkeley, California: Earthquake Engineering Research Institute, 1977.

Earthquake Engineering Research Institute. Reconnaissance Report: Northern Kentucky Earthquake, July 27, 1980. Berkeley, California: Earthquake Engineering Research Institute, 1980.

Eisenberg, A., R. Husid and J. E. Luco. "The July 8, 1971 Chilean Earthquake: A Preliminary Report." Bulletin of the American Seismological Associatin. Volume 62, 1972, p. 423.

Ergin, K., U. Guclu and V. Hz. A Catalog of Earthquakes for Turkey and Surrounding Areas (11 A.D. to 1964). Istanbul, 1967.

Ericksen, Neil J. "A Tale of Two Cities: Flood History and the Prophetic Past of Rapid City, S.D." Economic Geography. Volume 51, 1975, pp. 305-320.

Frank, N. L. and S. A. Husain. "The Deadliest Cyclone in History." Bulletin of the American Meteorological Society. Volume 52, 1971, pp. 438-44.

Geipel, Robert. Disaster and Reconstruction (Friuli). London: George Allen and Unwin, 1982.

Given, Jeffrey. "Earthquake!" Steel '78. Number 2. American Iron and Steel Institute, 1978.

Gupta, H., B. Rastogi and H. Narain. "The Koyna Earthqauke of December 10, 1967: A Multiple Seismic Event." Bulletin of the Seismological Society of America. Volume LXI, February 1971, p. 167.

Haas, J. Eugene and Robert S. Ayre. The Western Sicily Earthquake Disaster of 1968. Washington, D.C.: National Academy of Engineering, 1970.

Halacy, Daniel Stephen. Earthquakes: A Natural History. Indianapolis: Bobbs-Merrill, 1974.

Hanley, Kathryn T. "Libraries Gone with the Wind." Mississippi Library News. Volume 33, December 1969, pp. 184-5.

Healy, J. H., W. W. Rubey, D. T. Griggs, and C. B. Raleigh. "The Denver Earthquakes." Science. Volume CLXI, 27 September 1968, pp. 13-1-1310.

Heck, H. H. "Japanese Earthquakes." Bulletin of the Seismological Society of America. Volume 34, No. 3, July 1944, pp. 117-136.

Hewitt, Kenneth and Lesley Sheehan. A Pilot Survey of Natural Disasters of the Past Twenty Years. Working Paper No. 11. Boulder, Colorado: University of Colorado Natural Hazards Research and Applications Information Center, 1969.

64

Ives, Ronald L. "Earthquakes in the Denver Area." Geographical Review. Volume LIX, October 1969.

Kawasumi, Hirosi. General Report on the Niigate Earthquake of 1964. Tokyo: Tokyo Electrical Engineering College Press, 1968.

Keightley, Willard Otis. Destructive Earthquakes in Burdur and Bingol, Turkey, May 1971. Washington, D.C.: National Research Council, 1975.

Kendrick, T. D. The Lisbon Earthquake. Philadelphia: Lippincott, 1957.

Kondorskaya, N. V. and N. V. Shebalin. The Catalog of Strong Earthquakes in the Territory of the USSR From Ancient Times to 1975. (In Russian-English Translation Available from National Geophysical and Solar-Terrestrial Data Center). Moscow: USSR Academy of Sciences, 1977.

Lagorio, Henry J. and George G. Mader. Earthquake in Campania Basilicata, Italy, November 23, 1980. Berkeley, California: Earthquake Engineering Research Institute, July 1981.

Latter, J. H. "Natural Disasters." Advancement Sci. Lond. Volume 25, No. 126, 1969, pp. 362-380.

Lee, W. H., F. T. Wu and C. Jacobsen. "Catalog of Historical Earthquakes in China Compiled from Recent Chinese Publications." Bulletin of the Seismological Society of America. Volume 66, No. 6, December 1976, pp. 2003-2016.

Leeds, David J., Ed. Reconnaissance Report: Imperial County, California, Earthquake of October 15, 1979. Berkeley, California: Earthquake Engineering Research Institute, 1980.

Lomnitz, C. "Major Earthquakes and Tsunamis in Chile During the Period 1535-1955." Geologische Rundschau. Bd. 59, Heft 3, 1970, pp. 938-960.

McComb, David. Big Thompson: Profile of a Natural Disaster. Boulder, Colorado: Pruett Publishing Company, 1980.

Marx, W. Acts of God, Acts of Man. New York: Coward, McCann and Geogheghan, 1977.

Mayer-Rosa, D. The Swiss Historical Earthquake File (SHEF): April 4, 1980, Revision. Zurich: Institute of Geophysics, Federal Institute of Technology, 1980.

Mitchell, William and Edward A. Glowatski. "Some Aspects of the Gediz (Turkey) Earthquake." Journal of Geography. Volume 70, 1971, pp. 224-229.

Moore, H. E. Tornadoes over Texas: A Study of the Waco and San Angelo Disaster. Austin, Texas: University of Texas Press, 1958.

Morelli, Ugo. "Triangle of Tragedy (Southern Italy)." Emergency Management. Volume 1, No. 3, Spring 1981, pp. 14-20.

Mussari, Anthony J. Appointment with Disaster. Wilkes-Barre, Penn.: Northeast Publishers, 1972.

Neumann, Charles J. et al. Tropical Cyclones of the North Atlantic Ocean, 1871-1980. Asheville, N.C.: National Climatic Center, July 1981.

Olson, Robert A. "Individual and Organizational Dimensions of the San Fernando Earthquake." San Fernando, California, Earthquake of February 9, 1971. Volume II: Utilities, Transportation and Sociological Aspects. Neil A. Benfer and Jerry L. Coffman, Eds. Washington: U.S. Government Printing Office, 1973.

Penick, James, Jr. The New Madrid Earthquakes of 1811-12. Columbia, Mo.: University of Missouri Press, 1976.

Petrovski, Jakim and Trifun Paskalov, Eds. The Montenegro, Yugoslavia Earthquake of April 15, 1979. Publication No. 65 of the Institute of Earthquake Engineering and Engineering Seismology. Skopje, Yugoslavia: IZIIS, November 1981.

Pichard, Pierre, Nicholas N. Ambraseys, and G. N. Ziogas. "Les Monuments Historiques du Frioul Apres le Seisme du 6 Mai 1976 (Pt. 1, Pichard). "The Gemona di Friuli Earthquake of 6 May 1976." (Pt. 2, Ambraseys). "Educational Facilities in the Area of Friuli Destroyed by the Earthquake of 6 May 1976." (Pt. 3, Ziogas). The Gemona di Friuli Earthquake of 6 May 1976. UNESCO Serial No. FMR/CC/SC/ED/76/169, UNESCO Restricted Technical Report No. RP/1975/2,222,3. Paris: UNESCO, 1976.

Rankin, R. W., Ed. Studies Related to the Charleston, South Carolina Earthquake of 1886. Washington, D.C.: U.S. Government Printing Office, 1977.

Russell, Clifford S. "Losses from Natural Hazards." Land Economics. 1969-70.

Scholl, Roger E., Ed. EERI Delegation to the People's Republic of China (September 19 to October 6, 1980). Berkeley, California: Earthquake Engineering Research Institute, January 1982.

Sozen, Mete Anvi. Structural Damage Caused by the Skopje Earthquake of 1963. Civil Engineering Studies, Structural Series No. 279. Urbana, Illinois: University of Illinois, 1964.

Steinbrugge, Karl V. The Santa Rosa, California, Earthquake of October 1, 1969. Washington, D.C.: U.S. Government Printing Office, 1970.

Stratta, James L. and Loring A. Wyllie Jr. Reconnaissance Report: Friuli, Italy Earthquakes of 1976. Berkeley, California: Earthquake Engineering Research Institute, August 1979.

Stratta, James L., et al. Earthquake in Campania-Basilicata, Italy: November 23, 1980: A Reconnaissance Report. Washington, D.C.: National Academy Press, 1981.

Sugg, Arnold L., et al. Memorable Hurricanes of the United States Since 1873. Technical Memorandum NWS SR-56. Washington, D.C.: National Oceanic and Atmospheric Administration, 1971.

Sutherland, Monica. The Damnedest Finest Ruin. New York: Ballantine Books, 1971.

Suzuki, Z. General Report on the Tokachi Oki Earthquake of 1968. Tokyo: Keigaku Publishing, 1971.

Thompson, Herbert J. "The Black Hills Flood." Weatherwise. Volume 25, 1972, pp. 162-167, 173.

Thompson, J. N., E. W. Kiesling, J. L. Goldman, K. L. Mehta, J. Wittman and F. B. Johnson. The Lubbock Storm of May 11, 1970. Washington, D.C.: National Academy of Sciences, National Academy of Engineering, 1970.

UNESCO. Annual Summary of Information on Natural Disasters. Paris: UNESCO, Annual.

UNESCO. The Caracas Earthquake of 29 July 1967. Paris: UNESCO, 1968.

UNESCO. The Skopje Earthquake of July 26, 1963. Paris: UNESCO, 1968.

U.S. Army Corps of Engineers. Flood Report: Cheyenne River Basin, South Dakota Black Hills Area: Flood of June 9-10, 1972. Omaha, Nebraska: U.S. Army Corps of Engineers, District Office, 1972.

U.S. Department of Commerce. United States Earthquakes. Annual Publication, Prepared by the U.S. Congress and U.S. Geological Survey 1928-68, and by NOAA and USGS 1973-77. Washington, D.C.: U.S. Government Printing Office, annually.

U.S. National Oceanic and Atmospheric Administration. Some Devastating North Atlantic Hurricanes of the 20th Century. Washington, D.C.: U.S. Government Printing Office, 1977.

U.S. National Research Council. Committee on the Alaska Earthquake. The Great Alaska Earthquake of 1964. Washington, D.C.: National Academy of Sciences, 1970.

Walford, Cornelius. "Chronological Sketch of the Destruction of Libraries by Fire in Ancient and Modern Times, and of Other Severe Losses of Books and Mss. by Fire or Water." Appendix V to Transactions and Proceedings of the Second Annual Meeting of the Library Association of the United Kingdom. London, 1880, pp. 149-154.

Wettenhall, R. L. Bushfire Disaster: An Australian Community in Crisis. Sydney: Angus and Robinson, 1975.

White, Gilbert F., Ed. Natural Hazards. New York: Oxford University Press, 1974.

RECENT LOSSES OF ARTIFACTS AND COLLECTIONS

Allentown College Library Suffers $100,000 Flood Loss." Library Journal. Volume 96, November 1, 1971, pp. 3553-54.

Book, D. Joleen. "Two-Year College Learning Resource Center Buildings." Library Journal. Volume 108, Number 21, December 1, 1983, pp. 2219-21.

"Books Came Raining Down." American Libraries. Volume 2, March 1971, p. 227.

Brewer, Norval L. "Fire Destroys Aerospace Museum." Fire Engineering. Volume 131, No. 6, June 1978, pp. 24-5.

Brugger, Walter. "Damage to Other Buildings." The San Fernando Earthquake of February 9, 1971. Geological Survey Professional Paper No. 733. Washington, D.C.: U.S. Government Printing Office, 1971.

Burns, Mildred. "Tornadoes Struck Greenwood Schools." Arkansas Libraries. Volume 25, Summer 1968, pp. 18-19.

Chadwick, H. A. "Burning Down the Data Center." Datamation. Volume 21, No. 10, October 1975, pp. 60-64.

Charlottesville, Virginia, Fire Department. "Report of Fire at Alderman Library." August 7, 1974.

Ciborowski, Adolf. Warsaw: A City Destroyed and Rebuilt. Warsaw: Interpress, 1970.

Ciborowski, Adolf. Warsaw Rebuilt. (trans. Warszawa Odbudowana). Warsaw: Polonia Publishing House, 1962.

Crosby, E. "Cyclone Tracy and the Museum in Darwin." Kalori. The Journal of the Museums Association of Australia. No. 50, June 1975, pp. 28-32.

Darling, Pamela W., et al. "Books in Peril." Library Journal. Volume 101, No. 20, November 15, 1976, pp. 2341-2351.

"Earthquake in L.A.: Damage and a Lesson." Library Journal. Volume 96, March 15, 1971, p. 906.

"Brief Description of the Earthquake Damage at the San Fernando Valley State College Library." A. B. Bookman's Weekly. Volume 47, March 15, 1971, p. 802.

Fischer, David J. "Problems Encountered, Hurricane Agnes Flood, June 23, 1972 at Corning, N.Y. and the Corning Museum of Glass." Conservation Administration. North Andover, Mass.: New England Document Conservation Center, 1975, pp. 170-187.

"The Floods of June 1972". American Libraries. Volume 3, No. 11, December 1972, pp. 1202-1204.

Fyan, Loleta D. "The Michigan State Library—An Account of Water Damage and Salvage Operations." ALA Bulletin. Volume 45, May 1951, pp. 164-66.

Gannett, Fleming, Corddry and Carpenter, Inc. Tropical Storm Agnes: Flood Damage Inventory for the Commonwealth of Pennsylvania. Harrisburg, Penn.: Department of Environmental Resources, State of Pennsylvania, 1974.

Goetz, Arthur H. "Books in Peril: A History of Horrid Catastrophes." Wilson Library Bulletin. Volume 47, No. 5, January 1973, pp. 428-439.

Hamilton, Robert M. "The Library of Parliament Fire." The American Archivist. Volume XVI, April 1953, pp. 141-144.

Hemphill, B. F. "Lessons of a Fire." Library Journal. Number 87, 1962, pp. 1094-5.

Horton, Carolyn. Report and Recommendations on the Rescue of the Water-Damaged Books and Prints at the Corning Glass Center, Corning, New York, June 1972. Mimeographed. Cooperstown, N.Y.: New York State Historical Association Library, 1972.

"Hurricane Celia." American Libraries. Volume 2, February 1971, p. 138.

"Hurricane Loss." ALA Bulletin. Volume 2, December 1969, pp. 1502-4.

Leighton, Phillip. "The Stanford Flood." College and Research Libraries. Volume 40, September 1979, pp. 450-459.

Martin, John H., Ed. The Corning Flood: Museum Under Water. Corning, N.Y.: The Corning Museum of Glass, 1977.

"A Needless Disaster (New York State Library Fire)." Public Libraries. Volume 16, No. 5, May 1911, pp. 200-201.

Ontario Fire Marshal. "Fire of November 12, 1973, St. Clair College of Applied Arts and Technology." January 15, 1974.

Organ, Robert M. and Eleanor McMillan. "Aid to a Hurricane-Damaged Museum (Biloxi)". Bulletin of the American Group—IIC. Volume 10, No. 1, October 1969, pp. 31-39.

Pool, Brady and Roy C. Mabry. "Fire in Unsprinklered Warehouse Destroys Bindery and A Million Books." Fire Engineering. Volume 130, No. 8, August 1976, pp. 71-4.

Rubinstein, Nicolai. "Libraries and Archives of Florence." Times Literary Supplement. December 1, 1966, p. 1133.

Schell, H. B. "Cornell Starts a Fire." Library Journal. Volume 85, No. 17, October 1, 1961, pp. 3398.

Schwartzbaum, Paul M., Constance Silver and Carol A. Grissom. "Earthquake Damage to Works of Art in The Ariculi Region of Italy." Journal of the American Institute for Conservation. Volume 17, No. 1, 1977, pp. 9-16.

Sellers, David Y. and Richard Strassberg. "Anatomy of a Library Emergency." Library Journal. Volume 98, No. 17, October 1973, pp. 2824-2827.

Stender, Walter W. and Evans Walker. "The National Personnel Records Center Fire: A Study in Disaster." The American Archivist. Volume 37, No. 4, October 1974, pp. 521-550.

"The Public Record Office, Kew." Fire Prevention. No. 125. London: Fire Protection Association, June 1978, pp. 16-19.

Toronto, Ontario, Fire Department. "Report of Fire at University of Toronto." February 11, 1977.

Tribolet, Harold W. Florence Rises from the Flood: The Full Picture Story of the November 1966 Flood as Dramatically Reported in National Geographic. Chicago: The Lakeside Press, 1967.

"University of Maryland Flood Hits Library Materials." Library Journal. Volume 95, September 1, 1970, pp. 2757.

"Victim of Camille." Publisher's Weekly. Vol. 196, October 20, 1969, pp. 34-35.

Virden, Kathryn M. "Hurricane Damage to Libraries in South Texas." Texas Library Journal. Volume 43, Winter 1967, p. 164.

"Walker Library Destroyed by Fire." Cass County Independent. Walker, Michigan, April 8, 1976.

"Water Damage in Libraries." Library Journal. Volume 94, June 15, 1969, pp. 2402-3.

SECTION TWO

Policy Issues

Facing Disasters

Barclay G. Jones

Natural disasters, as the preceding section makes clear, exact a heavy toll from our cultural heritage of structures and artifacts. Once one acknowledges that fact, it is necessary to confront it and take a position regarding it. Ignoring the situation or doing nothing is the equivalent of determining not to do anything. One way or another, if only by default, a natural disaster policy is established.

POLICY PARADIGM

Having a policy or making one implies that a decision process has taken place —either an elaborate or complex one or an implicit one that may not have been even entirely conscious. Policy is usually discussed today in terms of the ways in which we make decisions. Herbert A. Simon demonstrates that it is useful to disaggregate decision processes into three distinct phases: intelligence, design and choice. [Simon, 1960] The intelligence phase consists of searching the environment for problems which require decision. That which is taken for granted at one point in time or by one society may be identified as a problem at or by another. Design is the procedure of generating alternative solutions to the problem. This may involve considering existing actions or objects or devising or creating entirely new ones. Choice requires predicting the consequences in light of possible events of selecting one alternative as compared with another with respect to the problem and assessing the relative preferability of these possible outcomes.

Policies are made manifest by planning. Planning, whether individual, organizational or societal, is a decision making process by which policy issues are probed and examined, and alternative resolutions of them are scrutinized. [Dyckman, 1961] Policy analysis and planning are tools for specifying problems, devising ways of dealing with them, and evaluating possible courses of action. They include diagnosis, therapeusis and prognosis. The purpose of these tools is to be sensitive to changing situations by careful monitoring

71

and to call attention to needs for new decisions. Policies cannot be permanent nor plans fixed. Policy analysis and planning are response processes by which we become aware of new circumstances and mobilize resources to meet them.

DISASTER POLICY

Natural disaster policy necessitates that one identify and recognize, that is be aware of, hazards that exist in one's environment; one must also have some basic understanding of the causality of these hazards and other phenomena that are associated with them; and one must also have determined that it is worthwhile and not futile to take precautions that will diminish the impacts of them. [Burton, Kates, and White, 1978]

We deliberately expose ourselves to hazards all the time and often completely rationally. Essentially, we have assessed the risk, estimated the cost or trouble of risk avoidance and determined that it is reasonable to incur it. [Starr, 1968] How we behave with respect to ourselves or our own personal property is one matter, but when others are involved it is quite another. Exposing other individuals to risk involves moral and financial liabilities as does exposing to risk the property of others whether or not we are stewards of it. [Dacy and Kunreuther, 1969] Establishing what we think our reasonable responsibility is in such matters constitutes making a policy determination. These policies within a society, of course, must be part of some broader frame of reference which also encompasses the expectations that we have concerning our responsibility to assist others who have had misfortunes, and what we can expect from them if we, too, are unfortunate. These broader societal images involve not only individual response but organizational and institutional arrangements. The more clearly these societal images are articulated and the more sharply policies are defined, the easier it is for us to resolve crisis situations.

Public policies have been classified into four types: distributive, regulatory, constituent, and redistributive. [Lowi, 1972] The types are obviously interactive. Regarding natural hazards, for example, redistributive policies recognizing responsibility to assist unfortunate victims of disasters lead directly to regulatory policies recognizing responsibility to induce or force behavior reducing the exposure of potential victims to natural hazards. [Petak and Atkisson, 1982] In recent years there has been an accelerating concern on the part of governmental organizations to promote regulatory measures of enormous variety intended to control activities which expose persons and property to natural and other environmental hazards. Enthusiastic public response attests to major transformations in societal attitudes. Making people protect themselves and keeping people from endangering others has assumed the proportions of a preoccupation.

72

Automobile seat belts and uniform seismic building codes are all part of the same social phenomenon.

CULTURAL HERITAGE DISASTER POLICY

The cultural heritage of documents, artifacts, buildings and other structures constitutes a trust, not only for society at large but for generations to come, which is vested in the individuals and organizations who own or have charge of them. Trustees may be private owners or collectors, dealers, curators, archivists, librarians, superintendents, directors, boards, officials or legislative bodies. Until recently social attitudes towards trustees as regards depredations from natural disasters were nebulous. Consequently, responsibilities were ill-defined and policies either non-existent or vague to the point of being of little or no use. Acts of God, as such events were frequently called, were beyond the realm of mortal reckoning, and victims of them were proper objects of sympathy and succor without any implication of negligence or liability. However, with the expansion of our scientific knowledge and the better understanding we have acquired of our natural environment and potentially catastrophic events that it can induce, these attitudes are changing. We have extremely elaborate information gathering, monitoring, reporting and recording systems. We have large accumulations of historical data newly informed by a recently developed knowledge. We have spent vast amounts of effort finding out how man-made objects behave under different conditions of environmental stress in order to diminish the harmful effects of adverse conditions. [White and Haas, 1975] Concepts of what constitute avoidable or preventable loss or destruction are being redefined. In general, when social attitudes change, the designation of victims and culprits are often reversed.

Those who hold the cultural heritage in trust must confront the necessity to develop policies relating to natural hazards. The first step is to acknowledge that such hazards exist, and that there is a responsibility to be aware of them and to take actions to mitigate their impacts. It then follows that one must determine the hazards one is subject to and the levels of risk from them. This requires achieving some degree of understanding of the nature of the hazard and the kinds of damage or destruction it can cause.

TYPOLOGY OF POLICIES

Recognition of hazard and risk must then be transformed into policies in several dimensions. Among these one must consider: 1, policies on the impacts on various kinds of elements comprising the risk situation; 2, policies that relate to different phases of disasters—

pre-event, crisis and post-event periods; and, 3, the relationship of policies of different organizations to each other. Policies allocate resources and are implemented when expenditures of efforts and funds are made. Not everything can be done; it will be necessary to make trade-offs; and hard choices must be confronted.

Elements at Risk

It is necessary to establish clear policies with respect to a variety of items at risk. The first concerns life safety of visitors or staff associated with the location. We need also to have policies regarding the contents of the structure, whether these are non-structural elements of the building, utilities, furnishing and equipment or collections on display or in storage, whether belonging to the institution or on loan. Policies must also exist with respect to the structure and its appurtenances on the site. Nothing can ever be completely safe or invulnerable to absolutely any kind of event. Policies establish thresholds of risk which we consider tolerable and reasonable. Different criteria may apply to different categories. For example, we may wish to exclude visitors and perhaps some staff from certain areas. Climate control equipment may be protected with greater care than office equipment. Objects less easy to replace, of greater merit or value, may be restricted to more secure locations. Chimneys or steeples may be considered expendable while we may choose to make other architectural features as secure as possible.

Disaster Phases

Policies must be established and articulated in plans for various phases of natural disasters. Taking few preventive measures, for example, implies policy emphasis has been given to salvage and recovery. The pre-event phase requires planning for protection and mitigating the effects of a disaster. This may involve inventorying and recording, modifying techniques of displaying and storing, and making structural and non-structural elements stronger and better able to withstand impact. Policies for the emergency phase should be reflected in detailed contingency plans which address safety, security and salvage. Necessary external assistance should be anticipated and appropriate relationships to ensure it established. Post-event policies concern strategies for recovering as rapidly and as completely from the disaster as is feasible. Appropriate kinds and amounts of insurance, other forms of financial aid, and channels of access to experts who can assist in conservation and reconstruction should receive attention.

74

It needs to be recognized at the outset that hierarchies of policies within and among organizations will exist that are in many ways interdependent upon each other and which must be reviewed for conflicts and complementarities. The policies of one level of organization can have the effect of cancelling out those of another. Assumptions about responsibilities may result in lacunae such that important aspects are not covered at all. Policies will exist at the level of a single collection or sub-group of objects. Others will relate to assemblages of collections or museums. Policies for one collection may conflict with or prevent implementing those of another. What seems best for the total museum may be less than optimal for a particular collection. Policies will apply to structures some of which will house museums, collections or objects. Other policies may apply to complexes of buildings or buildings in general. For example, policies intended to reduce the vulnerability of all the buildings in an area may adversely affect particular ones. Various levels of government—municipal, county, state and federal—will have policies for mitigation, emergency, relief and reconstruction. [Petak and Atkisson, 1982] Inconsistencies and conflicts may exist. Important aspects may not be covered at all anywhere in the hierarchy.

The necessity of coordination within organizations to control conflicting policies, decisions and behavior is a clearly recognized problem. Organization Theory and Operations Research have dealt with the subject for forty years. [Simon, 1957] Sometimes called the Executive Decision Problem, it acknowledges that actions which are directed at achieving the objectives of one sub-unit may impede or preclude achieving the objectives of others.

> These problems are a direct consequence of the functional division of labor in an enterprise, a division which results in organized activity. In an organization each functional unit (division, department, or section) has a part of the whole job to perform. Each part is necessary for the accomplishment of the over-all objectives of the organization. A result of this division of labor, however, is that each functional unit develops objectives of its own ... These objectives are not always consistent; in fact, they frequently come into direct conflict with one another. [Churchman, Ackoff, and Arnoff, 1957, p. 4]

When numerous organizations are involved, the problem is compounded. The governmental agencies at federal, state and local levels which deal with some aspect of one or more natural hazards present a bewildering array. Attempting to relate to them is a formidable undertaking.

Attitudes change constantly and evolve over time. Policies reflecting these attitudes must be reviewed and revised periodically for their appropriateness, but first they must be initiated. The lack of recognition of the problem natural hazards pose to the cultural heritage and the consequent absence of policies with respect to them is no longer tolerable. Institutions and public bodies must face the problem and establish policies. The general position is as true today as it was when it was so clearly stated over a generation ago after the April 15, 1958 fire in the New York Museum of Modern Art in which one person died and thirty-three were injured, two paintings lost and seven damaged.

> Society's trust in museum officials for the protection of art and historic objects must be fully accepted by these officials and the hazards that threaten to destroy these objects understood in order that absolute protection be planned, incorporated, and maintained. [Wilson, 1958, p. 77]

Over the last decade or so, de-accessioning has received increasing publicity and attention. Both public and professional controversy have ensued in an atmosphere of often stormy conflict. The recognition of the importance and necessity of clear policy regarding this matter is analogous. Natural disasters can be thought of as a particularly violent and terminal form of de-accessioning. Establishing policies to deal effectively with disasters will require tremendous efforts and raise many troublesome issues.

REFERENCES

Burton, Ian, Robert W. Kates, and Gilbert F. White. The Environment As Hazard. New York: Oxford University Press, 1978.

Churchman, C. West, Russell L. Ackoff, and E. Leonard Arnoff. Introduction to Operations Research. New York: John Wiley & Sons, Inc., 1957.

Dacy, Douglas C. and Howard Kunreuther. The Economics of Natural Disasters: Implications for Federal Policy. New York: The Free Press, 1969.

Dyckman, John W. "Planning and Decision Theory." Journal of the American Institute of Planners, Volume 27, Number 4, November 1961, pp. 335-345.

Lowi, Theodore J. "The Four Systems of Policy, Politics and Choice." Public Administration Review, Volume XXXII, Number 4, July-August, 1972, pp. 298-310.

Petak, William J. and Arthur A. Atkisson. Natural Hazard Risk Assessment and Public Policy. New York: Springer-Verlag, 1982.

Simon, Herbert A. Administrative Behavior. New York: The Free Press, 1957.

Simon, Herbert A. The New Science of Management Decision. New York: Harper and Row, Publishers, 1960.

Starr, Chauncey. "Social Benefit Versus Technological Risk." Proceedings of Symposium on Human Ecology. Public Health Service, Department of Health, Education, and Welfare. Washington, D.C.: U.S. Government Printing Office, 1969, pp. 24-39.

White, Gilbert F. and J. Eugene Haas. Assessment on Research on Natural Hazards. Cambridge, Mass.: The MIT Press, 1975.

Wilson, Rexford. "The New York Museum Fire." Quarterly of the National Fire Protection Association, July 1958, pp. 67-77.

Disaster Preparedness and Response Policy

Robert R. Garvey, Jr. and Peter H. Smith

During the last century there has been a growing awareness of the need to protect cultural resources ranging from archeological sites containing prehistoric data and more recent information to individual historic buildings, to museum collections, to historic districts and even to entire towns. The urge to preserve historic architecture and maintain museum collections is strong. In the United States well over five hundred towns and cities and most States have established legal mechanisms to protect and preserve their historic properties. On the national level, the U.S. Congress recently passed a broad new national historic preservation act. This, along with numerous other pieces of legislation, is designed to provide substantial protection for historic properties. Not only is the nation bent upon protecting historic properties, there is also a great emphasis on making productive use of these resources. Favorable tax treatments for expenses of rehabilitating historic buildings clearly indicate this.

Efforts to protect cultural resources in the United States mirror those around the world. Preservation objectives are an important goal of virtually every national government. On the international level, during the last twenty-five years, UNESCO has been extremely active in the protection of historic and cultural resources and has adopted numerous recommendations including the World Heritage Convention to deal with this subject. UNESCO is not alone in this concern. They are joined by the International Center in Rome, ICOMOS, and ICOM and others. UNESCO also recognized the threat that disasters pose to cultural resources and sponsored the international convention that deals with the treatment of a nation's cultural resources in times of armed conflict. Nevertheless, less attention has been paid to protecting cultural resources in times of natural disaster than to the general responsibility for routine conservation and protection measures.

This fact is reflected in the United States as elsewhere. While there is much emphasis on protecting historic properties from the hand of man, there has not been the same thought and attention given to protecting these resources from disasters such as earthquakes and floods. What has been carefully maintained in an appropriate

79

conservation program for many years can be wiped out in moments by a natural disaster, unless precautions are taken. Because of recent experience and a growing body of scientific data concerning natural disasters, we now have the ability to develop a framework for coherent policies for the protection of cultural resources in event of a natural disaster—policies that if implemented with intelligence and forethought can go a long way toward protecting cultural resources in which we have invested much time, money, and energy.

The papers in this volume deal with natural disasters rather than with manmade disasters or catastrophes like war although the interaction between man and nature frequently make a clear separation difficult. The natural phenomena that should be considered in developing policy on the protection of cultural resources in time of disaster include, obviously, earthquakes, floods, hurricanes or typhoons with accompanying rains and/or tidal action, tornados and volcanic eruption. There are other less obvious types of disasters that should be included in policy formulation as well. They include such events as the action of unstable soil, resulting in earth slides or de-stabilized foundations, an event experienced in recent years during the restoration of the historic Dolly Madison House in Lafayette Square in Washington, D.C.

Subsidence of soil from mining activities is another type of natural disaster. This has threatened buildings in Pennsylvania and in some of the western mining states. Shock waves caused by supersonic aircraft can also be treated as natural disasters that have the potential to damage severely cultural resources. This was the case when sonic booms apparently caused damage to the cliff dwellings at Mesa Verde National Park.

Several other phenomena which can and do affect cultural resources cannot rightly be placed in the category of unexpected disaster, but nevertheless deserve attention. Among these are the effects of pollution on cultural resources. The adverse effects of pollution, especially automobile emissions, on historic stone and masonry buildings can be seen in virtually any major city in the world. Vibration caused by blasting, excavation work, excessive vehicle weight or pedestrian traffic are all capable of causing damage to cultural properties. Finally, rising damp is of increasing concern in many places.

The development of a policy flows from the recognition of a problem that demands attention. Despite the recognition of natural disasters as an enemy of cultural resources, many public and private institutions have not yet adopted firm policies to prepare for or react to the effects of natural disasters on cultural resources. Let us examine who is responsible for setting forth policy concerning disasters and cultural resources, the consequences of failing to articulate a policy and what elements should be considered in developing such a policy.

The proprietor of cultural resources has specific legal responsibilities and liabilities for damage to or loss of cultural resources even in the event that the loss is attributable to a natural disaster. This applies to officials at all levels as well as to the private sector. Specifically, a proprietor may be held liable for damage to cultural resources if he does not exercise reasonable care to protect the resources from foreseeable damage. Generally, a proprietor of cultural resources functions as a trustee for the property in question. The role of the proprietor may be explicit and detailed in a trust instrument. For example, a museum may be established by the gift or bequest of a private donor under a specific trust instrument. In such a case, the board of directors of the museum must manage the property according to the terms of the trust instrument. A governmental proprietor must also adhere to the same general fiduciary standards as a private trustee. A trustee may be held liable to the beneficiaries of the trust for mismanagement, loss or damage to the trust if he violates the standard of care expected of him.

One of the standards of care that may reasonably be expected of a trustee of cultural resources is explicit policy to guide present and future decisions for the property entrusted to him. A policy to deal with actions to be taken in time of disaster undergirds disaster management standards and practices. In developing a policy to deal with the protection of cultural resources in times of natural disaster, among the first questions that should be examined are those dealing with the probability and predictability of the occurrence of a natural disaster. Obviously, policies will be considerably different for cultural resources which are located in known seismic zones or in coastal areas that regularly experience hurricanes than for those which are located in areas which have a low rate of severe natural phenomena having the potential to damage cultural resources. The degree of predictability will, in part, dictate the disaster policy. In areas with a high degree of predictability for natural disaster, the policy should emphasize systemic solutions over specific actions that should be taken at the time of the disaster. While systemic solutions are obviously the best approach to dealing with the possibilities of damage to cultural resources, they may be impractical for institutions located in areas that have a low degree of predictability. The very first policy concerning predictability should relate to searching out and maintaining contact with information sources such as the National Hurricane Center.

Earthquakes can generally be predicted in specific geographical areas. The ability to predict is limited to where an earthquake may occur, but not when. Because of this the major effort in protecting cultural resources in earthquake zones has gone into strengthening basic structures in order to reduce possible seismic damage. Unless strengthened, little can be done to ameliorate the devastating effects of a damaging earthquake on structures, their contents and occupants. To deal with this problem the California Commission on Seismic Safety recognized this and listed as its principal goal:

the methodical reduction of . . . hazards by strengthening, rehabilitating, or replacing such buildings or changing their uses to lower occupancies, thus reducing the risk of life. [Olson, 1980]

To meet this goal, the Commission developed extensive policies:

1. Practical standards for strengthening or rehabilitating hazardous buildings must emphasize life safety. Life safety standards for such buildings should be designed (a) to insure adequate protection against death or injuries during earthquakes, and (b) to be realistic and feasible for hazardous buildings capable of being rehabilitated. Local governments must be encouraged to adopt hazard mitigation policies adapted to the situation and needs of their communities.

2. Local governments must recognize the magnitude of the undertaking, including the social, economic, fiscal, and engineering problems. Local programs should include adequate and equitable processes for notifying and negotiating with building owners in seeking workable ways to reduce hazards.

3. Programs for hazard reduction are more likely to succeed if local officials and the public are well informed of the nature and extent of the hazards they may be exposed to, and what can be done about them.

4. Adequate technical information and expert advice must be provided by the state to local governments wishing to implement programs to reduce earthquake hazards risk in unsafe buildings.

5. Buildings that possess unusual architectural or historical significance should be considered for special treatment under the hazardous buildings program. Owners of these buildings might be allowed to take more time for compliance, to reduce levels of occupancy, or seek rehabilitation measures that achieve desired safety levels without undue damage to architectural or historical values. [Olson, 1980]

A case in point involving a historic building is the Cooper-Molera Adobe, in Monterey, California, one of the historic properties of the National Trust for Historic Preservation. There, the adobe structure has been strengthened and reinforced against earthquake damage. From a life safety point of view, the building is probably as safe as possible at the present time; however, the additional bracing and materials required to strengthen the building have compromised the historical integrity of the property.

The method of protection for cultural resources in flooding disasters is substantially different from the systemic solutions that are currently being used to protect such resources from earthquakes. For most parts of the country a disaster policy dealing with flooding can only be implemented in the sense of responding to the flood, because flooding and water damage, while predictable in certain zones, may occur at any place. The potential for severe damage from flooding is especially great for museum collections. Following the extensive damage to the collections at the Corning Museum of Glass in Corning, New York, as a result of hurricane generated floods, the museum came up with a three part policy to be implemented in time of natural disaster. [Martin, 1977] The policy deals with actions to be taken prior to, during, and after a disaster. All are straightforward, simple actions that require advance preparation and thought. Combined they can minimize damage to museum collections. The policy stresses the importance of developing a working relationship with local governmental authorities, particularly the police and fire departments.

In many areas, such as coastal zones and flood plains in general, the likelihood of flooding can be considered as predictable as it is for earthquakes. There is no question that a flood will occur, the only question is when. In such areas, a systemic policy that attempts to deal with more structural solutions to this type of disaster is possible. The AIA Research Corporation under contract to the Federal Insurance Administration has studied this problem and the end product, Design Guidelines for Flood Damage Reduction, sets forth a number of policy considerations that can be used to deal with the potential for flood damage to cultural resources. [AIA, 1981] Existing buildings in flood-prone areas can be flood-proofed in a number of ways: for example, by elevating the building above the base flood level or by providing mechanisms to close securely building openings that may be below the base flood level. In developing solutions for flood-proofing existing buildings, the authors of the study stress consultation with appropriate local agencies.

In developing a policy for natural disasters preparedness and response, it is important to cooperate closely and extensively with local authorities. During a disaster, governments can be expected to provide protection, assistance and direction. In Tokyo, Japan, for instance, it is established policy that the fire department will have primary responsiblity for coordinating disaster services in the event of an earthquake or flood. [Fire Service in Tokyo, 1980]

The experience of the Corning Museum also demonstrates the importance of working closely with fire and police departments, because their help can be a two edged sword.

> Outside assistance—police, fire, other public service units--can be of tremendous assistance. Unfortunately they can also do great damage inadvertently. Police can keep outsiders away from the problem area and so safeguard collections or important buildings; they can also bar staff from the scene at a time when staff knowledge can be of major importance. Likewise, firemen may need information about the building and its collections so that their efforts do the least damage and the most good. It is important, therefore, that firemen and police have an opportunity to review emergency plans with management and to get to know the affected buildings so that their efforts during emergencies do not become counter-

83

productive. Key staff members should be known to them, and some system of identification or badge should be worked out so that staff are not barred from the scene at the time they can be helpful. [Martin, 1977]

Museum professionals and cultural resources specialists should meet with public safety personnel as disaster preparedness plans are developed. Public safety personnel should be invited to tour museum facilities and professionals should be available to them to assist in planning for a disaster. Consideration should be given to attaching cultural resource specialists to public safety units to offer advice and guidance on the protection and immediate care of cultural resources during times of disaster.

A related area involving public safety personnel that should be given specific policy attention is the question of the physical jurisdiction of responsibility in areas of overlapping political boundaries. Both the trustees of cultural resources and public safety personnel should firmly understand the extent of responsibility. In Washington, D.C., a recent aircraft accident caused considerable confusion regarding the specific authority responsible for carrying out rescue operations. This tragedy caused the Washington Metropolitan Area to highlight the need for effective policies on the jurisdiction and responsibility of public safety personnel in times of a disaster.

A disaster policy to protect cultural resources should contain, at a minimum, elements dealing with the following subjects. (1) In most instances, normal channels of approval for actions will be set aside. For example, the amendments to the National Historic Preservation Act provide that the requirements of the Act may be "waived in whole or in part in the event of a major natural disaster." (Section 110(j)). Disaster planning must take this into account. (2) Priorities should be established regarding what is to be saved first. For example, the Corning Museum has established a priority inventory that begins with the most important objects in the collection, listed by their degree of importance and proceeding in decreasing order of importance all the way down to office supplies. (3) There should be a clear understanding of where necessary supplies are stored or can be obtained to meet the emergency. For example, sources of plywood should be noted for boarding up openings of buildings for security reasons. Likewise, museums should note the locations of freezer plants outside the threatened area that could be used to freeze collections which may be damaged by water. (4) Provision should be made to train personnel in actions necessary to respond to disasters. For example, the location and use of cutoffs for electricity, gas, steam, water, and sewer should be known to specific individuals, and they should be adequately trained in their use. (5) The policy should also take account of the use of volunteers to respond to a disaster. While volunteers may be quite useful in many instances, too many volunteers can result in additional problems. Screening of volunteers is therefore necessary. (6) Finally, provisions should be made for calling in experts following the disaster and for the exchange of personnel and equipment. For example, a museum should be able to call upon conservators to assist in evaluating and repairing damage to collections. For buildings, historical architects and engineers should be involved before decisions are made as to whether to demolish a building as unsalvageable.

In conclusion, those responsible for caring for cultural resources have a responsibility to develop firm policies to protect these resources in times of natural disaster. Much can be done to minimize damage to historic architecture and museum collections resulting from a disaster with planning and prudent actions. To do less is to fail in the responsibilities we have accepted and to treat our heritage with callous disregard.

REFERENCES

AIA Research Corporation. Design Guidelines for Flood Damage Reduction. Washington, D.C.: AIA Research Corporation, 1981.

Fire Service in Tokyo. Tokyo: City of Tokyo, 1980.

Martin, John H., Ed. The Corning Flood: Museum Under Water. Corning, NY: The Corning Museum of Glass, 1977.

Olson, Robert A. "A Policy Approach to Building Rehabilitation for Earthquake Safety" in Cathy Americus, Ed. Building Rehabilitation Research and Techology for the 1980's. Dubuque, Iowa and Toronto, Canada: Kendall/Hunt Publishing Company, 1980.

Section Two References

POLICY ISSUES

Association of Bay Area Governments. A Guide to ABAG's Earthquake Hazard Mapping Capability. Berkeley, California: Association of Bay Area Governments, 1980.

Avgar, Amos. Post-Disaster Development: Implications for Public Policy. Cornell Dissertations in Planning. Ithaca, N.Y.: Graduate Field of City and Regional Planning, Cornell University, 1978.

Brown, J. P., B. Contini and C. B. McGuire. "An Economic Model of Floodplain Land Use and Land Use Policy." Water Resources Research. Volume 8, 1972, pp. 18-32.

Butson, Keith D. and Warren L. Hatch. Selective Guide to Climatic Data Sources. Key to Meteorological Records Documentation No. 4.11. Asheville, N.C.: U.S. Department of Commerce. National Oceanic and Atmospheric Administration, Environmental Data and Information Service, National Climactic Center, 1979.

California Seismic Safety Commission. Assessment of Public Policy Regarding Lifelines and Critical Facilities. 2 volumes. Sacramento, California: California Seismic Safety Commission, 1980.

Council for Science and Society. The Acceptability of Risks. London: Barry Rose, 1977.

Dacy, Douglas C. and Howard Kunreuther. The Economics of Natural Disasters: Implications for Federal Policy. New York: Free Press, 1969.

Davis, Morris and S. T. Seitz. Disasters and Governments: A Theory and Some Data. Urbana-Champaign: University of Illinois, 1980.

Elms, D. G., J. B. Berrill, and D. J. Darwin. "Appropriate Distribution of Resources for Optimum Risk Reduction." Large Earthquakes in New Zealand. Wellington, New Zealand: The Royal Society of New Zealand, 1981, pp. 69-75.

Fischhoff, B., C. Hohenemser, R. E. Kasperson and R. W. Kates. "Handling Hazards." Environment. Volume 20, Number 7, 1978, pp. 16-37.

Haas, J. Eugene and Patricia Bolton Trainer. Issues and Power in Reconstruction Following Disaster. Presented at the Annual Meeting of the Society for the Study of Social Problems, August 27-30, 1976, New York City.

Harbridge House, Inc. An Inquiry into the Long-Term Economic Impact of Natural Disasters in the United States. Prepared for the Office of Technical Assistance, Economic Development Administration, U.S. Department of Commerce. Boston: Harbridge House, 1972.

Kates, Robert W., Ed. Managing Technological Hazard: Research Needs and Opportunities. Boulder, Colorado: University of Colorado, Institute of Behavioral Sciences, 1978.

Kunreuther, Howard. Disaster Insurance Protection: Public Policy Lessons. New York: John Wiley and Sons, 1978.

Kunreuther, Howard. Limited Knowledge and Insurance Protection: Implications for Natural Hazard Policy. Springfield, Va.: National Technical Information Service, 1977.

Kunreuther, Howard and Elissandra S. Fiore. The Alaskan Earthquake: A Case Study in the Economics of Disaster. Arlington, Va.: Institute for Defense Analysis, Economic and Political Studies Division, 1966.

Lowrance, W. W. Of Acceptable Risk. Los Altos, Calif.: William Kaufman, 1976.

National Research Council. Earthquake Reduction and Public Policy. Springfield, Va.: National Technical Information Service, PB-290-355, 1975.

Olson, Robert and Mildred M. Wallace. Geologic Hazards and Public Problems. Washington, D.C.: U.S. Government Printing Office, 1969.

Petak, William J. and Arthur A. Atkisson. Natural Hazard Risk Assessment and Public Policy: Anticipating the Unexpected. New York: Springer-Verlag, 1982.

Roberts, R. Blaine, Jerome W. Milliman and R. W. Ellson. Earthquakes and Earthquake Predictions: Simulating Their Economic Effects. Report to National Science Foundation under Grant PFR 80-198ZG. Columbia, S.C.: University of South Carolina, College of Business Administration, September 1982.

Steinbrugge, Karl V. Earthquake Hazard in the San Francisco Bay Area: A Continuing Problem in Public Policy. Berkeley, Cal.: Institute of Governmental Studies, University of California, 1968.

Tuller, J. The Scope of Hazard Management Expenditures in the U.S. Worcester, Mass.: Clark University, Hazard Assessment Group, 1978.

U.S. General Accounting Office. Report to the Chairman and Ranking Minority Member, Senate Committee on the Budget, U.S. Senate: Federal Disaster Assistance—What Should the Policy Be? Washington, D.C.: U.S. General Accounting Office, 1980.

Wade, Nicholas. "Earthquake Research: A Consequence of the Pluralistic System." Science. Volume 178, Number 4056, October 6, 1972, pp. 39-43.

Wright, James D. and Peter H. Rossi. Eds. Social Science and Natural Hazards. Cambridge, Mass.: ABT Books, 1980.

Wright, James D., Peter H. Rossi, Sonia R. Wright and Eleanor Weber-Burdin. After the Clean-Up: Long Range Effects of Natural Disasters. Beverly Hills, California: Sage Publications, 1979.

SECTION THREE

Assessment of Hazards and Vulnerability

Assessing Dangers

Barclay G. Jones

Once individuals and organizations have confronted the very real possibility of a danger, acknowledged the devastation that it can cause, and decided to take measures to prepare for it, the next step is to determine the kinds of disasters that may occur, establish their likelihood and their probable severity. It is then necessary to estimate the impact they will have on structures and objects and determine the potential loss that one considers an inevitable condition. Since complete safety from every kind of danger is unattainable, the question is how much safety one considers it feasible to achieve. Or conversely the question can be put as to how much danger one is willing to tolerate.

HAZARD, VULNERABILITY AND RISK

Three distinct concepts are involved in assessing dangers: hazard, vulnerability and risk. [UNDRO, 1980] It is useful to be clear about these concepts and their interrelationships. By hazard we mean the probability that a disastrous event of a given magnitude or severity will occur in a particular place. By vulnerability we mean the degree of loss that will be sustained by an element from a disastrous event of a given magnitude. By risk we mean the probable loss from natural disasters of various kinds combining the hazards of a location and the vulnerability of objects there. Risk assessment derives from hazard and vulnerability analysis. It is the basis for defining acceptable levels of risk and making decisions about locations and preventive measures.

Hazards are an attribute of regions or sites. Vulnerability is an attribute of structures and objects. Consequently, human beings, their objects and artifacts and the structures that support and shelter them incur varying levels of risk as a result of their own characteristics and their location in space at different points in time.

Consideration of hazards which are characteristics of regions and sites provides a suitable framework. The question to be addressed is what is the probability that a natural disaster of a particular type in a given degree of severity will occur in a locale. All specific locations or sites within a geographical region may or may not be equally susceptible to a given type of disaster. It is necessary not only to make a hazard assessment of a region but also a very specific and often quite technical hazard assessment of a site.

The possibility of natural disasters of various kinds cannot be established with certainty because their occurrences are apparently the consequence of an enormous number of variables that are not completely clear and among which the interrelationships are not completely understood. The accumulation of experience, the systematic gathering of large quantities of information by sensitive measurement devices and extensive monitoring systems, the results of enormous research efforts and the development of elaborate theories have advanced our understanding considerably. Regions with certain characteristics and sites with specific attributes are clearly more prone to certain kinds of disasters than others. However, such knowledge still does not permit us to state with a high degree of certainty that an event of a given magnitude will or will not occur within a particular period of time. Another important approach to assessing hazards is through the prevalence of events of various kinds. It is a matter of historical record, even though the causes may not be completely understood, that certain regions and certain locations have suffered more or less severe events with greater or lesser fequency than others over time. The assessment of hazards often involves combining a knowledge of relevant attributes with information about prevalence. To use an analogy, we employ an approach that draws upon both etiological and epidemiological methods.

The natural environment confronts us with an enormous array of hazards. [Burton, Kates, and White, 1978] Ultimately, it is the cause of death of all living things and the destruction of all objects. The creation of the natural environment is achieved through the release of awesome forces which transform it by destroying its previous characteristics and replacing them with new ones. All of these forces cannot be considered here. Attention will be limited to a very select group of rather generally defined natural disasters which are ones that most commonly claim our attention. Several of these relate to lack of stability of the earth. As one author put it, terra firma is an inapt term and a concept unrelated to reality. Included in this group are earthquakes, landslides and expansive soils. Other disasters relate to inundations by water. Two major types of such events are included: both riverine and flash flood and sea surges in which the level of the ocean rises substantially and often quite rapidly either as a result of storms or of earthquakes, in which case they are referred to as tsunami. Wind storms are the third major category and these may or may not be accompanied by sea surges and water spouts and heavy downpours of rain resulting in flooding. The first approach to hazard assessment involves enumerating the attributes of areas prone to disasters and briefly reviewing their prevalence.

VULNERABILITY ANALYSIS

The purpose of hazard assessment is to determine the kinds of dangers to which one is exposed and the likelihood of their occurring. Vulnerability analysis concerns assessing the kind and likely extent of damage that can be done by a given hazard. In many instances we may be able to do very little to change our exposure to hazards, but in others we may be able to do a great deal to reduce vulnerability.

The vulnerability of buildings and other structures and objects is of tremendous variety. On the one hand it derives from the characteristics of the natural disaster under consideration and other events that may accompany it. On the other hand it is determined by the characteristics of the buildings and objects that are of concern. However, the kinds of damage that can be inflicted can be generally grouped rather simply under three types of effects: kinetic, chemical and bacteriological.

Kinetic effects imply motion in which some force is brought to bear on an object. Damage results when there is physical deformation of the object. This kind of damage can occur when objects fall onto hard surfaces, overturn violently, are struck by other objects in motion whether airborne or waterborne, and when objects are subjected to the stress of shear, torsion and bending. The motion does not need to be violent to cause damage but may be relatively subtle such as is the case with spalling and eroding and the actions of freezing and thawing. Abrasion and wear are similar.

Chemical effects are ones that result in changes in the chemical composition of the object. Extremes of temperature, the action of fire, long immersion in water, exposure to air, contact with quite foreign chemical substances of various sorts can lead to these kinds of changes. Oxidization of metals is a familiar form of this effect.

Bacteriological effects are ones in which disasters in one way or another precipitate bacteriological action which may have deleterious effects on objects. Mildew, mold, fungus growths and other harmful bacteriological actions are examples. The rotting of wood, mildewing of paper and deterioration of textiles are examples. These effects are often precipitated by drastic changes in wetness and dryness and immersion in water.

Vulnerability analysis consists of anticipating the kinds of effects that can damage or destroy buildings or objects. Measures can then be taken to prevent conditions from occurring that would result in those effects. In many cases it is sufficient to be prepared to reverse the effect quite rapidly after it has occurred.

The surface of the earth is made up of a number of huge tectonic plates which are constantly moving with respect to each other at very slow rates that are undetectable to human senses and can be measured at all only by the most sensitive instruments. [Bolt, 1978; Gere and Shah, 1984] Most earthquakes occur in seismic zones where the great plates come together as a consequence of friction in their differential movements against each other. The geographical distribution of earthquakes, measurements of their magnitudes and their frequency distribution over time defines the seismicity of a region. Tremendous amounts of energy are released by an earthquake, and the origin point of this energy is called the focus, which may be quite shallow near the surface, or quite deep. The point on the earth's surface directly above the focus is known as the epicenter.

The magnitude or amount of energy released by the earthquake is measured and expressed for convenience and comparison in terms of the Richter Scale, first devised by Charles F. Richter in 1935 in California and much refined and modified since then. The release of energy sends waves of vibration through the earth. The first type of seismic wave moves through the body of rock. The primary body wave alternately compresses and dilates. The secondary body wave shears rock sideways to the direction of travel of the wave and results in vertical and horizontal shaking. The second major type of seismic wave is the surface wave restricted to shallow depth. The first kind of surface wave moves the ground horizontally back and forth at right angles to the direction of movement. The second kind of surface wave moves material up and down and back and forth in a vertical plane in the direction of movement. [Bolt, 1978, pp. 27-33]

Seismic waves result in disturbances of the ground surface such as both vertical and horizontal shaking. The vibration at the surface defines the intensity of an earthquake, and this is usually expressed in terms of the Mercalli scale developed in Italy in 1902 by Father Giuseppe Mercalli and since further refined and modified. Intensity is measured at a particular place in terms of the tremors felt and the effects observed there. Obviously, intensity will vary from place to place and with distance from the epicenter, and earthquakes of the same magnitude may have different intensities. The intensity assigned a seismic event is usually the maximum recorded at any point. Vibratory effects are described by acceleration or the rapidity of movement, velocity or the duration of a complete vibration cycle, and displacement or the amplitude of the wave.

Both horizontal and vertical slippage can occur along fault lines. These shear actions result in horizontal disalignments or displacements and vertical changes of slope and the creation of scarps. Slow slippage along fault lines is a common phenomenon which may be imperceptible until its accumulated effects are observed after the passage of years. (Figure 3.1)

The earliest notable earthquake in North America struck Boston on November 18, 1755, only 17 days after the great Lisbon earthquake. Walls and chimneys collapsed, beams cracked and windows broke. No deaths were reported. New Madrid, Missouri, was stricken by the most violent earthquake in the United States history on December 16, 1811. Land levels were changed, the course of the Mississippi was altered, lakes were created, swamps drained and others created and hundreds of thousands of trees felled. Since the area was sparsely populated, little is known of casualties. [Penick, 1976]   The first devastating urban earthquake occurred on August 31, 1886, in Charleston, South Carolina, leveling chimneys and damaging many historic buildings. (Figure 3.2) Severe building damage was caused by the San Francisco earthquake of April 18, 1906, but the greatest destruction of the city resulted from the fires following the rupture of gas and electric lines at the same time that the water supply system was destroyed. (Figures 3.3, 3.4)   The Anchorage, Alaska, earthquake of March 27, 1964, measured 8.3 on the Richter Scale and is the most violent ever recorded in North America. Anchorage suffered the greatest damage though many smaller centers were completely destroyed. The action of the earthquake was compounded by a tsunami, liquefaction of soils and sand boils, and rock and land slides. The most recent earthquake causing substantial destruction in the United States was San Fernando, California, February 9, 1971. The Richter magnitude was 6.6; many buildings were damaged including two hospitals and freeway overpasses collapsed. Sixty-four people died. [Coffman and von Hake, 1973; Cornell, 1976, pp. 117-128]

The vulnerability of objects to seismic shock derives from a number of effects and the response of a particular kind of object to them. In very simple terms there can be strong vertical movement or upthrow in which enormously heavy objects can be literally lifted off of the surface on which they rest. Damage is caused by impact when they strike the surface again or by horizontal displacement when they do not fall back on their original position. Horizontal movement both in the direction of the wave movement and at right angles to it can occur. Through inertia objects may not move at the same rate as the surfaces on which they sit and consequently may be displaced from their foundations and toppled or thrown from tables or shelves or other positions in which they may be located. (Figures 3.5, 3.6)

A somewhat related but substantially different effect occurs from horizontal movement in which the base of an object or structure moves approximately in the same fashion as the surface on which it is resting. However, the top of the structure or object through inertia does not move at the same rate initially and then is brought into original relationship with the base through more violent movement. The result is a whiplash effect in which there is greater horizontal movement at the top than at the bottom creating both bending and shear stress. Objects made of brittle materials can be snapped and the breaking of limbs of marble statues, shear failure of chimneys and towers and the creation of shear cracks in buildings and other structures can occur. Tall objects with high centers of gravity not

95

Figure 3.1. Central California: Drain Offset Along San Andreas Fault at Almaden Winery. Univ. of California, Berkeley.

Figure 3.2. Charleston, South Carolina: Damage to Hibernian Hall, 1840, 105 Meeting Street, from Earthquake of August 31, 1886. USGS.

Figure 3.3. Palo Alto, California: Stanford University Library, Shepley, Rutan and Coolidge, Archs., 1887-1891, Damage from Earthquake of April 18, 1906. USGS.

Figure 3.4. Palo Alto, California: Stanford University Museum, Shepley, Rutan and Coolidge, Archs., 1887-1891, Damage from Earthquake of April 18, 1906. USGS.

Figure 3.5. Fairbanks, Alaska: Fairbanks Library, Books Thrown from Shelves by Earthquake of July 21, 1967. Fairbanks Daily News.

Figure 3.6. Hilo, Hawaii: Kurtistown, Three Hundred Pound Urn Thrown to Ground by Earthquake of November 29, 1975. George Abe.

fastened down can be toppled. The overturning of display cases, shelving, file cabinets, sculpture and other objects are frequently the result of these forces. Chimneys and towers can fall and adjacent buildings can batter each other from these same actions. (Figures 3.7, 3.8) Torsion can occur when horizontal forces are induced both parallel to the line of movement of seismic waves and at right angles to them or when the direction of waves is different from the alignment of axes of the object. Lack of symmetry in foundations, the layout and the structural properties of buildings and objects can result in differential horizontal stresses in different portions inducing torsion also. [Arnold, 1980; Wang, 1981] This twisting motion can result in shear failure.

Different types of soil behave variously. Structures built on different subsoils or with differential foundations can move vertically at different rates producing vertical shear in joints, walls and other members. Similar conditions in response to horizontal forces can result in horizontal shear and displacement. Some soils liquefy and lose their bearing capacity causing objects and buildings to overturn. One of the most dramatic examples of this effect was in the earthquake that struck Niigata, Japan, June 16, 1964, in which reinforced concrete multi-storied structures tilted over to 80 degree angles and further. [Gere and Shah, 1984, pp. 36-38; Cornell, 1976, p. 126] (Figure 3.9)

The vulnerability of objects that are fixed firmly to solid soils or to the structures in which they are housed is potentially great from a variety of effects. However, it is impractical to fix many objects. In such cases secondary effects may be vastly more damaging. Objects can be thrown from their locations to the floor, toppled over violently or struck by other loose objects possibly tumbled in a heap. These kinds of secondary effects are potentially the cause of far greater damage than the primary effects.

LANDSLIDES

The hazard of landslides or lateral movement of the surface of the earth derives from two conditions: the composition of the soil and the slope of the topography. A disastrous event occurs when environmental conditions change causing a once stable situation to become unstable. Some of the most extensive and traumatic landslides have been precipitated by earthquakes which set ground material in motion. (Figure 3.10) The landslide on Mount Huascaran following the earthquake in Peru on May 31, 1970 measured 30 meters high and sped down a long valley at 120 miles per hour burying an estimated 25,000 people. [Gere and Shah, 1984, pp. 29-31] An earthquake on July 9, 1958 caused a huge amount of rock and ice to fall from a glacier into Lituya Bay, Alaska creating a wave 60 meters high. [Bolt, 1978, p. 78; Cornell, 1976, p. 191] (Figure 3.11) Others have been caused by snow avalanches when shocks of one kind or another or

Figure 3.7. Santa Barbara, California: Santa Barbara Mission, 1820, Damage to Bell Towers by Earthquake of June 29, 1925. California Geology.

Figure 3.8. Lice, Turkey: Minaret Damaged by Earthquake of September 6, 1975. URS/John A. Blume & Associates.

Figure 3.9. Niigata, Japan: Apartment Houses Tilted by Failure of Soil from Liquefaction in Earthquake of June 16, 1964. NOAA/EDIS.

Figure 3.10. Anchorage, Alaska: Aerial View Showing Landslide Area after Earthquake of March 27, 1964. NOAA/EDIS.

101

Figure 3.11. Lituya Bay, Alaska: Large Rockslide Induced by Earthquake of July 9, 1958, Plunged into Gilbert Inlet and Generated Wave that Surged 1,720 Feet up Mountainside. NOAA/EDIS.

Figure 3.12. Guatemala City, Guatemala: Foundation Failure Due to Landslide Beneath Structures. USGS.

thaws have caused potentially unstable snow masses to descend slopes. Temperature changes resulting in freezing and thawing of water between strata of rock or expansion or shrinkage of soil layers of differing permeability can also precipitate slides. Saturation of the soil with water from melting snow or excessive rain over long periods of time are a very frequent cause and the one most associated with slides.

The granular material of which soil is composed has varying adhesive qualities which differ considerably with the size of particles of which it is composed and the amount of moisture contained. Different types of soils tend to be relatively stable at different maximum angles of slope (angle of repose) under the climatic conditions that prevail in a region. Creeping is a natural continual process in which the top strata of earth on a slope gradually moves downward. Slumping occurs at the bottom of slopes as a number of strata experience slippage over a period of time. More dramatic rock falls and landslides occur as granular material rapidly moves down hill. Other landslides are in the form of mud flows in which supersaturated soils rapidly descend a slope. Soils with a high clay content composed of extremely fine particles can be extremely hard when dry and very unstable when wet. Formations in which deposits of top soil of varying thickness overlay strata of clay can be particularly treacherous.

All earth is susceptible to some movement. The normal weathering process of climatic conditions is constantly reformulating the topography. Situations susceptible to rapid and potentially damaging landslides are assessed by detailed analysis of the soil and the slope characteristics of the topography. Since climatic conditions play such a major role, historical records of landslides and their prevalence in a region are also used in making hazard assessments.

The hazard assessment of a specific building site is a highly technical undertaking involving soil mechanics and foundation engineering. The characteristics of a specific building site may be dramatically different from the general conditions in an area only a few hundred yards away. This kind of analysis should be carried out not only when designing new structures but also in dealing with older ones which may have existed for many years undamaged because the necessary combination of circumstances that could result in a disaster in a potentially hazardous location never prevailed.

Vulnerability to landslides derives from two effects. On the one hand the earth can slide out beneath a structure or an object carrying it with it or leaving it precariously perched. (Figure 3.12) On the other hand, rock, soil and mud can descend upon a structure from above inundating, burying or crushing it. For the first type of problem carefully designed foundations which penetrate loose layers of soil or massive floating honeycomb foundations where this is not possible provide some protection. For the second kind of problem massive solid walls, deflecting earth works and channelization of potential flows can be helpful.

It is a terrifying situation when a hillside starts to descend bringing with it in addition to millions of tons of earth, buildings,

103

walls, roads, bridges, vehicles and trees piling them helter skelter on structures at the foot of the slope.

EXPANSIVE SOILS

Soil expansion and contraction in areas where the necessary conditions exist is probably the least dramatic of all natural disasters. However, the hazard is extremely prevalent throughout the country, and the damage it causes annually has been estimated to be exceeded only by floods. [Wiggins, 1978] Since the damage is frequently subtle, this estimate is probably conservative when a long span of years is considered.

Soils composed of different sized grains of particulate matter are capable of absorbing different quantities of water when wet and have differing degrees of permeability or the rapidity with which water passes through them. As a consequence some soils expand enormously when wet and shrink again when dry. The volume of certain types of clay can be under certain degrees of wetness ten times or more greater than when dry. The force exerted by a large quantity of soil of this kind when it expands can be enormous. Measured in tens of thousands of pounds per square foot it can heave buildings upwards to drop them again, and it can crush in foundation walls and structures below ground level.

Expansive soil hazards are greatest in regions where the amount of precipitation and moisture in the ground vary substantially at different times of the year. Even within a region certain locations may vary tremendously in their wetness and dryness at different times while others may maintain relatively stable levels of moisture.

Specific sites require highly technical hazard assessment because soil conditions can vary tremendously over short horizontal and vertical distances. Highly technical analysis by soils engineers or engineering geologists is necessary to determine the extent to which problems exist and to predict the effects that may be encountered.

Although they are not classifiable as expansive soil hazards, several other conditions can be mentioned here because they have somewhat similar effects. Subsidence and upheaval generally characterize relatively large areas and refer to the lowering and raising of the surface of the earth. There are many places in which this is a troublesome problem, and it is sometimes cyclic and sometimes permanent in a single direction. In some instances it is related to the movement of the tectonic plates forming the earth's surface in which case it is occasionally referred to as bradyseism. A notable example is the ancient Greek city colony of Sybaris, located at the foot of Italy on the Ionian Sea, famous for its great wealth and luxury, which apparently sank beneath the Mediterranean. Subsidence often results from depletion of underground deposits of water, oil or gas. Perhaps the most famous instance is Mexico City, built over an underground lake, and the most important in terms of its threat to the cultural heritage is Venice. Sink holes are depressions in the earth's surface frequently found in karst formations. They can also occur suddenly and violently after underground deposits of water, oil or gas have been depleted or in other instances by mine cave-ins.

The vulnerability of buildings and large objects to expansive soil conditions derives from the differential movement to which they are subjected and for which they were not designed. Walls can be caused to crack and fissures created. The structural integrity of the building can be lost. No longer weather tight, further damage can be caused by climatic conditions to buildings penetrable by the elements. The problem can be severe enough to lead to abandonment of the building because of the enormous expense involved in maintaining it. It can also lead to the necessity to demolish the building, because it has become so structurally unsound that it is a threat to life safety. In some instances it can cause the collapse of the building itself. Historical research could probably establish that the destruction of a number of architecturally important and ambitious buildings over the centuries has been the result of expansive soils.

When buildings or large objects are located on sites or are to be built or erected where expansive soil conditions exist, measures can be taken to provide them with protection. Soil stabilization procedures including site drainage and reinforced or stronger foundations can reduce the dangers substantially. Great and tragic losses can be avoided.

FLOODS

Floods cause more damage than any other single kind of natural disaster. More than 400,000 buildings are damaged or destroyed in the United States by floods each year. [Wiggins, 1978] Two types of flooding will be considered here: riverine and flash floods. Flooding caused by rising sea levels will be taken up subsequently.

Rainfall and other precipitation is normally disposed of by the environment through percolation or seeping into the ground, through evaporation into the atmosphere, and through runoff over the surface of the land along routes established over long periods of time. Problems arise when these normal methods of disposal are insufficient to carry the load as a consequence of one or another or a combination of two conditions. Either the downpour is so large in volume and so rapid in the time in which it occurs that the slower process of percolation cannot take care of its normal share and an excessive proportion becomes groundwater runoff. This is the standard situation in the case of flash floods. Relatively minor falls of precipitation when condensed in very short periods of time can result in conditions of this sort. The other situation is one in which rainfall has been sustained at more moderate levels over such a long period of time of days or weeks that the earth is supersaturated and further percolation is impossible. Subsequent precipitation then becomes primarily runoff.

Both situations can be exacerbated by temperature conditions. When quantities of rain fall on ground which is still frozen, runoff can be excessive. When heavy rains follow recent thaws and the ground is saturated by melted snow or the frozen accumulation of precipitation through the winter, the same thing occurs. Sudden freezing after a period of heavy rains can create ice jams and back up large and dangerous impoundments of water. The same can occur with rapid thaws in which floating ice can clog channels and prevent the flow of water.

Flash floods occurring suddenly and involving the rapid movement of large quantities of water can be terrifying, dangerous and extremely destructive in sloping topography. They can occur in areas not normally subject to flooding and with no historical record of floods. Other areas have histories of sudden heavy downpours and are known to be subject to flash floods. One of the most disastrous cases of a flash flood damaging a museum occurred at the Houston Contemporary Arts Museum. After a week of heavy rains, a storm on June 15, 1976 dropped 12 inches of water in a few hours. Rising water on adjacent Berthea Street poured down the inclined truck loading ramp flooding the lower level of the four-year old building to a depth of more than nine feet with an estimated 600,000 gallons of water. Galleries, offices, storage, shipping areas, and mechanical equipment were submerged, files, records and works of art were lost and the museum closed for nine months. [Brutvan, 1982]

Riverine floods are defined as situations where streams overflow the normal high water level of their banks and innundate the surrounding countryside. Riverine flooding performs a useful function despite its disastrous consequences. The environment in a region has been confronted with disposing of an unusual burden of millions of cubic feet of water. The quantity is far beyond the normal capacity of the traditional channels to drain it. Overflowing the banks of the streams and distributing vast quantities of water on flood plains in essence stores the excess water until it can be drained through normal channels. Without this capacity to store, speed and volume of the water in the channels would be enormous and the force would be so great as not only to eliminate everything in the channel but substantially transform and alter the channels themselves.

Floods involve a tremendous force. A flash flood resulting from rain over a limited region of a hundred square miles or less amounting to 12 to 15 inches of water falling in less than a 24 hour period can deposit 2.5 billion cubic feet of water weighing 78 million tons. Riverine flooding can result in heights of water 20 to 35 feet above normal levels. Depending upon the topography it can move at very rapid speeds. Rivers which normally flow at a rate of less than half a mile per hour can reach speeds of 5 to 10 miles per hour and even as much as 20 miles per hour under flood conditions.

Since flooding is the result of a set of combinations of complex climatic conditions and topography, specific assessment of the hazard is extremely difficult in general terms. The customary approach is to use empirical data compiled from historical records to assess the possibility of flooding and to assign probabilities that flood conditions will reach certain predicted levels over a given period of time. Such information is frequently readily accessible making the task of assessing flood hazards in a region relatively easy.

The hazard assessment of a site is generally somewhat simpler since the specific location is given and its relationship to surrounding topography is known. Records of flooding of specific sites are frequently very complete. Whether or not a site falls within a 25 year, 50 year or 100 year flood plain is usually easy to determine from locally available maps. However, such information should be used with caution. The destructive floods resulting from the rains produced in the Susquehanna River Basin by Hurricane Agnes in 1972, which have been already referred to, caused enormous damage at the Corning Glass Museum which was theoretically above the hundred year flood plain, and the Wyoming Historical and Geological Society in Wilkes Barre was damaged when flood waters rose above the levees which were at the hundred year flood level mark.

A series of steps have been undertaken to reduce hazards due to flooding. Sensitive measuring and monitoring devices continually provide information about water levels in streams throughout the United States. These provide essential information to permit anticipating flood conditions and issuing warnings. Evacuation resulting from these warning systems has done much to reduce the loss of life from floods. The warnings also permit taking protective measures to move sensitive material out of the way of danger. Emergency structures can also be erected using sandbags, bulldozing channels and creating dikes to meet the situation. Long-run hazard reduction measures include the building of impoundments upstream which can help to regulate the flow of water. In downstream areas channelization projects are intended to divert water and permit it to move more rapidly through an area and preclude flooding. The construction of levees and dikes and other permanent protective measures are intended to remove areas subject to flooding from the flood plain. Relocating objects and activities out of the flood plain is another heavily encouraged activity.

The vulnerability of buildings and objects to flooding derives from a variety of sources. First, water can inundate elements soaking them and causing subsequent deterioration from fungus and bacteria when they dry. Paper, wood and textiles are particularly susceptible to this kind of damage. In addition to damage from wetness itself, the water is frequently flowing at a relatively high velocity. Areas are subjected to this action which are not accustomed to it and abrasion, toppling, overturning and washing away may cause extensive damage. The flowing waters frequently carry debris with which to batter structures and objects. The waters are usually laden with silt and mud which buries, abrades, soils and otherwise damages objects.

Another type of flooding which has special characteristics of its own is the temporary dramatic rising of the sea along the coast line. Sometimes this is very rapid and of short duration, and in other instances the water rises more slowly and remains high for longer periods of time. Such rising levels of the sea are usually classified according to their cause. Those that result from storms are usually referred to as sea surges and those resulting from earthquakes or volcanoes are usually called seismic sea surges or tsunami.

Sea surges are usually associated with violent storms at sea. Most commonly they are thought of in connection with tropical storms such as cyclones, hurricanes and typhoons. However, they can occur in other regions as well. Notable events of this kind have occurred in the North Sea in 1099, December 14, 1287, and January 31, 1953. The East Coast of England and the Netherlands suffered particularly. [Cornell, 1976 p. 143-146]

The high gales of wind accompanying these storms drive large quantities of water ahead of them in the direction of movement of the storm. Water to the depth of 30 to 40 feet can be superimposed upon normal tides. When these surges reach the coast line they can inundate large areas far inland. Coastal regions can be covered by substantial depths of water. In addition the normal drainage of the inland waterways is impeded. Frequently heavy rains accompany the storm with greater than normal runoff requirements. Consequently, substantial inland flooding can compound the situation caused by the sea surge. Further inundations and water damage can result. In addition to the extraordinary height of the water which produces heavy wave action by itself, the driving winds exacerbate the effect creating tremendously powerful waves the repeated pounding of which can transform coastlines, disintegrate structures and ships. Frequently, most of the deaths and much of the damage attributable to tropical storms and hurricanes is a consequence of the accompanying sea surge. (Figures 3.13, 3.14)

Hazard assessment is again arrived at through a combination of topographic and climatic information. Any area not many feet above sea level and not many miles from the coast is potentially subject to such disasters. However, devastating sea surges are substantially more prevalent along some parts of the coastline than others. Historical data are usually taken into consideration in this type of hazard assessment.

Tsunami or seismic sea surges are generally caused by fault rupture along a submerged fault in an earthquake. Submarine landslides which may or may not accompany an earthquake can also result in tsunami. The only other major source is large volcanic eruptions.

The resulting sea surges move rapidly away from the source like ripples in a pond. In the deep water of the open ocean the crests are very low, less than a meter, and may be undetectable to boats and

Figure 3.13. La Libertad, Ecuador: High Wave Breaking Over Pier Wall in Sea Surge of March 6, 1981. Instituto Oceanografico de la Armada, Guayaquil.

Figure 3.14. La Libertad, Ecuador: People Fleeing Wave Breaking Over Pier Wall in Sea Surge of March 6, 1981. Instituto Oceanografico de la Armada, Guayaquil.

ships at sea. The crests may be relatively far apart, 100 kilometers or so, and they move with great speed up to 500 miles per hour. When the waves reach distant coastlines, they slow down in the shallow water and become much higher. The speed may drop to 25 miles per hour and the crest may rise to as much as 100 feet. A wall of water called a bore penetrates estuaries and strikes coastlines. [Bolt, 1978]

Damage is caused by two effects. The first of these is water damage as a consequence of inundation. Obviously, areas and objects quite high and normally not subject to flooding can be immersed. However, the second effect is by far the more disastrous and results from the violent action of the wave itself which can crush and wash away everything in its path. (Figure 3.15)

Tsunami are usually associated with the Pacific Ocean, and coastal areas that rim the Pacific and its islands are considered the most prone to this kind of disaster. However, there are records of such waves almost 2500 years ago in the Mediterranean where they still occur. The Indian and Atlantic Oceans and the Caribbean Sea are also subject to this disaster. The earthquake that did so much damage to Lisbon, Portugal, on November 1, 1755 that was referred to earlier was accompanied by a major tsunami which accounted for much of the devastation and loss of lives. [Cornell, 1978, pp. 188-189] Three waves five to seven meters high swept over the harbor area. A tsunami followed the earthquake that destroyed Port Royal, Jamaica on June 7, 1692. [Cornell, 1978, p. 116] The Alaskan Earthquake of March 28, 1964 was accompanied by a tsunami that not only caused much of the destruction associated with the event in Alaska but caused a major disaster in Crescent City, California, and damage in Hawaii. [Bolt, 1978, pp. 81-83] (Figure 3.16) The worst tsunami in history occurred on August 27, 1883, in Krakatoa Island between Java and Sumatra. [Bolt, 1978; Cornell, 1976, pp. 195-196] The volcano which formed the island was approximately 2,000 meters high. In a series of violent explosions an enormous quantity of ash and pumice was ejected (5 cubic miles), and the mountain vanished leaving a depression in the ocean 250 meters deep. The resulting tsunami is reported to have been over a hundred feet high and was still measurable when it reached the English Channel. Although the volcanic eruption of Mount Tambora on April 10 and 11, 1815 was of greater magnitude, the resulting tsunami was much smaller (4 meters) because the crater was 20 km. from the sea. [Stothers, 1984]

The vulnerability of buildings and objects to sea surges derives both from their becoming soaked with water and with the physical violence that may accompany this. Paper, wood, textiles, paintings and other objects may be damaged by immersion in saline water. The violence of the wave action may wash buildings away entirely, crush them and pound them to pieces, sweep away their foundations or batter them with other structures or debris. Objects in structures may be violently thrown about and smashed or washed away completely. Elevating structures on pilings and fastening them securely down may provide protection in many cases. Securely fastening objects within structures may also reduce their vulnerability.

Figure 3.15. Oahu, Hawaii: Largest Wave Rolls Toward Camp Erdman in Tsunami of April 1, 1946. Univ. of California, Berkeley.

Figure 3.16. Seward, Alaska: Waterfront Looking North After Earthquake Induced Underwater Landslides, Surgewaves, and Tsunamis of March 27, 1964. USGS.

Cyclone is a generic term referring to a specific type of storm. A low pressure area in the center is surrounded by high pressure areas. The body of warm air in the center rises, expands and is replaced by air from the cooler high pressure surrounding areas and is turned by the rotation of the earth in a spiral pattern counterclockwise in the the northern hemisphere and clockwise in the southern. The rising warm air in the center has a high moisture content particularly when traveling over oceans or large bodies of water. Around the center or eye of the storm the moist warm air produces clouds and heavy rains resulting in a release of heat energy increasing the upward motion and accelerating the velocity of the inward spiraling winds. Many storm systems are of this type, and when the pressure and temperature differences are not too great and the diameter very large, a thousand miles or more, cloudiness, precipitation and moderate winds are all that result. Tropical cyclones are known as hurricanes in the Caribbean and the Atlantic Coast of the United States, as typhoons in the Indian Ocean and China Sea, as baquios in the Philippines and as cyclones in Australia and New Zealand. These more intense and violent storms may have an eye from 5 to 50 miles in diameter and the storm itself a diameter of 300 to 600 miles. (Figure 3.17) Tropical storms of this type are usually classified as hurricanes when the winds reach sustained velocities of 74 miles an hour or more and as great hurricanes when the winds exceed velocities of 125 miles per hour. Hurricanes winds have been measured at 150 to 175 miles per hour and more.

During the major season between June and October, 6 to 10 tropical storms will usually become severe enough to be classified as hurricanes in the Caribbean, the Gulf of Mexico and the Atlantic Ocean. The highest prevalence of storms of this type is in the southwestern portion of the north Pacific Ocean where 20 or more such storms will form each year near the Philippines and move northward. While not the most frequent nor the most violent, storms of this type in the Indian Ocean are frequently the most destructive. The single natural disaster causing the greatest loss of life in the 20th century was probably the typhoon which struck Bangladesh, then East Pakistan, on November 13, 1970. The number of people killed are estimated to be as many as 1 million. [Cornell, 1978, pp. 89–90]

The first recorded storm of this kind in the United States was the one that struck Jamestown, Virginia, on August 27, 1667. The event was referred to as a "Hurry Cane." [Cornell, 1976, p. 92] The most deadly Atlantic hurricane was the one that swept the Caribbean Islands October 10–12, 1780, which may have claimed as many as 30,000 lives from Barbados to Puerto Rico. Many of these were lost in the sinking of English, French and Spanish naval fleets. Recent notable hurricanes include the one that completely devastated Galveston, Texas, on September 8, 1900, and another which struck the rebuilt city on August 5, 1915. The first major hurricane to strike New England in

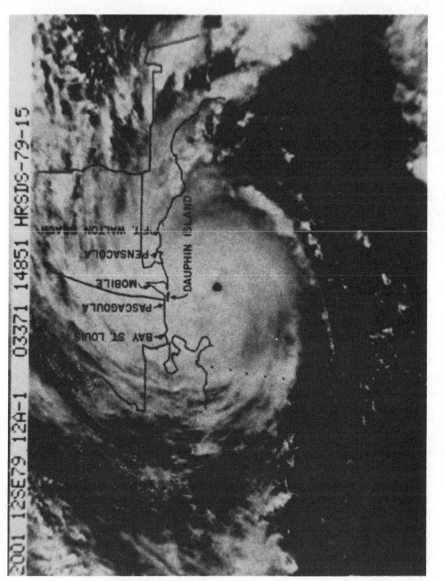

Figure 3.17. Satellite Photograph of Hurricane Frederick, June 12, 1979.

113

modern times occurred on September 21, 1938. It did enormous damage along the New Jersey coast, devastated Long Island and swept through New England to Quebec. The same area was struck again August 25-31, 1954 and August 17-19, 1955. The southeastern portion of the United States was badly battered by a hurricane October 5-18, 1954. Damage from Hurricane Camille on August 14-22, 1969, mentioned earlier, caused substantial damage to libraries as did Hurricane Celia on August 3, 1970. [Goetz, 1973] The devastation caused in the mid-Atlantic states by Hurricane Agnes June 14-23, 1972, which is considered the most costly disaster in the United States, has also been mentioned.

Hazard assessment is extremely difficult on the basis of characteristics of regions. Quite careful records have been kept particularly since the devastation of 1938, and historical data are customarily used for determining probabilities of hurricanes of various magnitudes sweeping a region. Because of the enormously destructive sea surges that accompany hurricanes, the most careful assessment of probabilities of hazards of this type have been tabulated for coastal zones.

The hazard assessment of a site derives from four aspects of the storms: high winds, heavy rains, inland flooding and sea surges. Coastal locations and low elevations are subject to sea surges. Inland sites in flood plains and in low locations can experience inland flooding as described earlier. Damage from high winds and driving rains can occur anywhere in a region where this hazard exists and historical records form the basis for making an assessment.

Vulnerability to the effects of hurricanes derives also from the four aspects of the storms. The first of these is immensely high winds which can rip off roofs and batter structures and objects with uprooted trees and windborne objects of all sorts. Spires, steeples, towers, chimneys are often badly damaged or destroyed. High pressures strike structures in the direction in which the wind is blowing and great vacuums can be created on the opposite side. Because of the spiraling effect of the winds their direction can be quite different from that of the movement of the storm and can change and reverse in the course of the storm. Windows, doors and other wall openings may be penetrated exposing contents of the building to damage.

A second major aspect of hurricanes is the heavy downpours and driving rains that invariably accompany them. These can produce substantial damage in themselves but are even more serious when the structural integrity of a building has been violated. These rains contribute to the third devastating aspect of hurricanes which is inland flooding. Most of the property damage and much of the loss of life attributable to hurricanes is the consequence of the accompanying floods. This problem has already been mentioned. The fourth destructive aspect of hurricanes are the sea surges created in the path of the storm by the intense winds and the violence of the wind driven wave action. The most dramatic devastation from hurricanes results from this aspect which also has been covered earlier.

114

The vulnerability of objects to damage by the various aspects of hurricanes is to a large extent a function of the vulnerability of the structure in which they are housed. If the structure is extremely secure, damage to the contents will be slight. If it is not, they will be subject to wind and rain water damage. Objects outside buildings may be struck by falling trees or flying objects and damaged or destroyed in this fashion. Vulnerability as a consequence of inland flooding or sea surges has been described in an earlier section.

TORNADOS

The term tornado is used to refer to a specific type of cyclonic storm. Such storms usually occur in a low pressure weather system in which they are substantially lower pressure centers. The eye of the storm is much smaller than in the case of hurricanes measuring from 10 feet to 2 miles in diameter with the most common width being one-quarter to three-quarters of a mile. These centers have much lower pressure than areas around them, and high velocity spiraling winds surround them to form funnels which reach from the ground to high clouds. The storm moves at a rate usually between 30 and 70 miles per hour and may touch the ground for only a few hundred feet or as much as 200 miles. The most common distance seems to be between 15 and 20 miles. The usual duration of a tornado at any location, therefore, is between 2 and 5 minutes. The greatest damage is restricted to the area where the wind column touches the ground and the path along which it moves. The causes of damage are: the sudden drop in barometric pressure which may be so rapid and so great as to cause tightly sealed structures to explode quite literally, the extremely high velocity winds up to several hundred miles per hour, and the enormous amount of debris that is carried along with the storm. Accompanying severe hail storms and rain storms may inflict additional damage.

Tornados are the most deadly of all natural disasters in the United States and over a period of years cause the greatest number of casualties. Six hundred to seven hundred tornados usually take place each year resulting in 120 to 150 deaths. [Burton, Kates and White, 1978, p. 30] The greatest number of tornados occur in April and May although the season extends from February to September. These storms are most prevalent in the mid-West and southern Great Plains in a region stretching from Texas to North Dakota but they have been reported in every state in the country. [White and Haas, 1975, pp. 276-277]

Tornados are classified both by their violence and their impact. The Fujita classification system developed by Tetsuya Theodore Fujita in 1970, assigns a numerical value from 0 to 5 to tornados according to their maximum wind velocity in a range from 40 to 318 miles per hour. The Pearson Scale, devised by Allen Day Pearson classifies tornados by the width and length of their path. The FPP classification combines both systems. [Petak and Atkisson, 1982, pp. 41, 157-159]

Governor John Winthrop made the first record of a tornado in the country which struck Newberry, Massachusetts, July 5, 1643. On June 5, 1805, the first mid-western tornado was recorded in southern Illinois, and it was reported that fish were sucked up from the rivers and lakes and scattered over the prairie. Washington, D.C. was struck by a tornado on August 25, 1814, just after the British had captured the city in the War of 1812 and at the time they were burning the White House, the Capitol and the Library of Congress. Some thirty British soldiers were killed which was the largest number of casualties sustained in that battle. [Cornell, 1978, p. 180] More than 300 people were killed in five minutes in a tornado which hit Natchez, Mississippi, 1840 in the greatest natural disaster in the period before the Civil War. In the ten days between February 9 and 19, 1884, a series of tornados in the south-central states inflicted great damage and may have killed as many as 600 people. Louisville, Kentucky was badly damaged by a tornado which never actually touched the ground on March 27, 1890. It demolished the city hall, main hotel and railroad station among hundreds of buildings and killed 106 persons. St. Louis was the first major city to suffer severe devastation from a tornado. The one that hit it on May 27, 1896, killed an estimated 300 to 400 people and destroyed Exposition buildings. The city was struck again on September 29, 1927. The most devastating tornado on record is that of March 18, 1925, which is sometimes referred to as the Murphysboro Tornado. At least 8 severe tornados swept across a path more than 200 miles wide from Missouri to Kentucky inflicting the greatest damage in southern Illinois. The official death toll is 689 although the initial estimate was 950. Thirteen thousand people were injured in the 3 hours the storms took to traverse their paths. [Keylin and Brown, 1976, pp. 72-73]

In recent years there have been a number of devastating tornados causing increasing property damage but fewer deaths. On June 8, 1953, a tornado did a great deal of damage in Flint, Michigan, and the following day another struck Worcester, Massachusetts, with particularly devasting effects. Perhaps as many as 40 separate tornados hit 6 mid-western states on Palm Sunday, April 11, 1965, killing 272 people and injuring 5,000. On April 3 and 4, 1974, a large number of tornados variously reported at 125 to 148 hit 13 states from Georgia to the Canadian border killing over 300 people. The damage to historic buildings in Xenia, Ohio, from this event has already been mentioned. While tornados are particularly prevalent in the United States, they do occur elsewhere, and one in Dacca, Bangladesh, then East Pakistan, on April 14, 1969 killed an estimated 540 people.

Assessing the hazards of tornados is extremely difficult in a general way because of the large number of climatic variables involved and the influence of topographic features not well understood. Assessment within a region is based on historic records, and probabilities are derived from the longest and most complete time series that can be developed. Apparently all sites in a region are

116

equally prone to tornados. Since the area of impact is so small the probability that a specific site will be hit is an extremely small number even in areas where tornados are relatively frequent occurrences.

The vulnerability of structures to tornados derives from three effects. The first, the sudden drop in atmospheric pressure, can cause buildings to explode and windows and doors to be broken. The second effect is the more important one and that derives from the exceptionally high velocity winds spiraling upward. This can carry off heavy objects for great distances and batter structures and objects with debris. Debris from the Worcester tornado in 1953 was carried as far as 40 miles to Boston. The force of the winds is great enough to level buildings completely and reduce frame structures to kindling. Reinforced concrete and other rigid structures designed for great lateral stress suffer less damage.

The vulnerability of objects relates directly to the vulnerability of the structures that house them. Objects outdoors no matter how heavy can be carried off or thrown hundreds of feet unless they are securely fastened to foundations. They are still subject to battering by debris. Vulnerability to the effects of hail and rainstorm is acute because of the strong possibility that roofs will have been damaged and the coverings of wall openings broken.

Much of the problem of protecting against a danger is being prepared for it. Being prepared requires being aware of the danger, conscious of it and its likelihood, and alert to it. It also involves understanding thoroughly the varieties of damage that it can inflict.

REFERENCES

Arnold, Christopher. "In Earthquakes, Failure Can Follow Form." American Institute of Architects Journal. Volume 69, Number 7, June 1980, pp. 33–41.

Bolt, Bruce A. Earthquakes. San Francisco: W. H. Freeman and Company, 1978.

Brutvan, Cheryl A., Compiler, with Marti Mayo and Linda L. Cathcart. In Our Time: Houston's Contemporary Arts Museum, 1948-1982. Houston, Texas: Contemporary Arts Museum, 1982.

Burton, Ian, Robert W. Kates and Gilbert F. White. The Environment as Hazard. New York: Oxford University Press, 1978.

Coffman, Jerry L. and Carl A. von Hake. Earthquake History of the United States. Publication 41-1, U.S. Department of Commerce, National Oceanic and Atmospheric Administration, Environmental Data Service. Washington: U.S. Government Printing Office, 1973.

Cornell, James. The Great International Disaster Book. New York: Charles Scribner's Sons, 1976.

Gere, James M. and Haresh C. Shah. Terra Non Firma: Understanding and Preparing for Earthquakes. New York: W. H. Freeman and Company, 1984.

Goetz, Arthur H. "Books in Peril: A History of Horrid Catastrophes." Wilson Library Bulletin. Volume 47, Number 5, January 1973, pp. 428-439.

Keylin, Arleen and Gene Brown. Disasters: From the Pages of the New York Times. New York: Arno Press, 1976.

Penick, James, Jr. The New Madrid Earthquakes of 1811-1812. Columbia, Missouri; University of Missouri Press, 1976.

Petak, William J. and Arthur A. Atkisson. Natural Hazard Risk Assessment and Public Policy. New York: Springer-Verlag, 1982.

Stothers, Richard B. "The Great Tambora Eruption in 1815 and Its Aftermath." Science, Volume 224, Number 4654, June 15, 1984, pp. 1191-1198.

United Nations. Office of the United Nations Disaster Relief Coordinator. Natural Disasters and Vulnerability Analysis, Report of the Expert Group Meeting 9-12, July 1979. Geneva: Office of the United Nations Disaster Relief Coordinator, 1980.

Wang, Marcy Li. "Stylistic Dogma vs. Seismic Resistance." American Institute of Architects Journal. Volume 70, Number 13, November 1981, pp. 59-63.

White, Gilbert F. and J. Eugene Haas. Assessment of Research on Natural Hazards. Cambridge, Mass.: The MIT Press, 1975.

Wiggins, J. H. Company. Building Losses from Natural Hazards: Yesterday, Today and Tomorrow. Redondo Beach, Calif.: J. H. Wiggins Company, 1978.

Multi-Hazard Assessment of Localities and Sites

L. Neal FitzSimons, FASCE

INTRODUCTION

We have become increasingly sensitive to the fact that structures modify the environment and have an impact on it. We must, however, continually recognize the obverse, which is that the environment is constantly having a variety of effects on the structure through diverse forces and agents. All man-made objects are ephemeral. We cannot prevent their destruction but we can delay it. Those who are responsible for the protection of an existing structure and its contents must define the hazards to which they are exposed in a useful way, and establish an acceptable level of risk which is a function of the resources which can be allocated to ameliorate it.

A building, new or old, must successfully resist all those forces imposed on it during its lifetime and all those agents to which it is exposed so that this lifetime is not unexpectedly shortened. The imposed forces must not induce excessive deformations and the exposed structure must not have excessive deterioration caused by aggressive agents. Thus, it is imperative that the architect/engineer responsible for the original design or the rehabilitation plans thoroughly assess all threatening forces and agents and account for them as economically as possible. Because most architects and engineers are trained to create new buildings rather than evaluate old ones, their tendency is to design structures analytically deriving loading assumptions solely from standards and building codes and generally ignoring hazardous agents. Hazard analysis must concern itself in depth with all the factors acting to deteriorate or destroy a structure. The hazards considered are mainly those impacting on structural strength, stiffness, stability and durability; but they may also affect function (such as the binding of doors and windows) and aesthetics (such as ugly cracks or unsightly stains). Further, these hazards include perhaps the most ubiquitous of all, water penetration of the building envelope.

119

For convenience, forces acting on a building may be classified as vertical, lateral or dilational. (Figures 3.18, 3.19) The principal vertical forces which act on roof surfaces are snow and rain, when ponded. On floors there are forces caused by functional use of the building, the "live loads". The weight of the structure itself, its cladding, finishings and fixed equipment constitute another set of vertical forces, the "dead load". If the equipment rotates or cyclically translates, it can induce dynamic forces or deleterious vibrations. The effects over long periods of time can be quite severe. Compressors, generators, and ventilating and air conditioning equipment can contribute.

Lateral forces, the greatest of which is the wind, principally act on the walls and windows of the building. A special case is wind borne objects which act as missiles. Wind can also act on sloping roof surfaces and on building appurtenances such as marquees, signs, flagstaffs, etc. Lateral forces on the buried portions of basement walls are from adjacent soil and water. Sometimes vehicular traffic near basement walls adds to the lateral earth pressures. In addition, this vehicular traffic can cause deleterious vibrations. Further, freeze/thaw action in the adjacent soil can impose lateral forces. Seismic forces are primarily lateral, and they act through the interfaces of the structure and the surrounding earth. (Figure 3.20) Differential response of different parts of buildings or adjacent structures to seismic forces can lead to battering of one against the other. Buildings in low-lying areas near large streams or other bodies of water may be subject to lateral forces of flood waters, repeated battering by waves, and the pressure and battering of flood borne debris. (Figure 3.21)

Dilational forces associated with expansion and contraction of the building elements are induced by temperature or moisture variations. Particularly hazardous dilational forces can be developed: 1) at the interface of different construction elements such as a brick wall and a concrete frame; 2) at the border between different masses of the same construction material when arranged in an awkward geometry; or 3) within a large mass of the same construction material that permits the development of large temperature or moisture differentials with the mass. Shade tree configurations can result in some portions of a structure receiving more sunlight than others with consequent differential expansion and contraction. Freeze/thaw of water particles within porous construction materials can cause dilational forces resulting in cracking and spalling. Hydration of metallic materials creates similar dilational forces such as those that cause steel reinforcement to rust and burst its concrete matrix.

One other dilational force sometimes overlooked is that of root activity. Plant roots growing from seeds in crevices of building elements can create expansive forces great enough to cause spalling, and large tree roots can also disrupt pavements or crack walls that

Figure 3.18. Ground Surface Failure from Collapse of Subterranean Chamber.

Figure 3.19. Texas City, Texas: Rail Yard Explosion.

Figure 3.20. Sylmar, California: Olive View Hospital after Earthquake of February 9, 1971.

Figure 3.21. Arlington, Virginia: Flood Damage to Bridge Following Hurricane Agnes, June 22, 1972.

retain earth. Also, root systems can create soil moisture conditions adjacent to foundation walls that cause undesirable movements. Once forces are identified, their magnitude must be estimated and translated into loads for the purpose of structural analysis. This is not a trivial task for sporadically violent natural forces such as winds, waves, and flood flows.

HAZARDOUS AGENTS

Hazardous agents are chiefly of two types: chemical and biotic. The chemical agents affect structures and objects primarily through the media of water and air. Biotic agents include plant material of various sizes from bacteria and fungus to trees, and animal life ranging from insects such as ants and beetles to rodents, birds and larger species.

Probably the most hazardous agent of all to buildings is water. Its relationship to dilational forces has already been mentioned. Also, it reacts both chemically and physically with protective coatings such as paint to reduce their effectiveness by peeling; with finishings such as plaster to create unsightly furuncles; and with masonry materials to leach and re-deposit their chemical constituents.

Atmospheric pollutants can have particularly serious consequences. Particulate matter such as soot aesthetically mars exterior walls. Inept cleansing of this grime can result in the removal of a protective patina on some masonry structures, thereby exposing the vulnerable porous substratum and accelerating deterioration. Vapors condensing on exposed and unprotected surfaces of metal or masonry can initiate destructive chemical reactions. Tainted ground water can have similar effects on foundation elements.

Water can also play a major role in relation to biotic agents. Moisture, generally in combination with heat, can have devasting effects on wood elements by abetting the growth of fungi. Allied to this problem is the deterioration of timber pilings or cribs that were originally submerged in ground water but later exposed to unsaturated soil conditions when ground water levels became lower.

Wood is also vulnerable to threats from a variety of insects, especially ants, beetles, and marine worms. Animal nests and droppings can also create conditions which accelerate the deterioration of wood, metal, and even masonry elements.

Examination of buildings themselves near or at the site of interest can be very helpful. High water marks are often found on buildings in flood plain areas. Studying repairs made to damaged portions of a building can give useful clues to past overloads or to damage by biotic agents. Evidence of movement or settlement can indicate geological conditions.

SOURCES

There are three broad sources of data on hazardous forces and agents: governmental organizations, local records and local physical evidence. The Federal government is the principal source for geophysical information such as on wind, snow, rain, flooding, and seismic activity. (Figures 3.22, 3.23, 3.24) There are about 12,000 reporting stations in the National Weather Service, Grammax Building, Silver Spring, Maryland 20910. The National Climatic Center, which maintains the historical records, is located in Asheville, North Carolina 28801 and operates six Regional Centers in New York, Texas, Missouri, Utah, Alaska, and Hawaii. Normally, reports from a given station indicate data on a daily basis for a given period such as a month. Some places can provide records on a finer time scale, and the Asheville Center can also provide historical information on maxima, minima, averages, etc. A special office concerned with high wind (tornados and hurricanes) is located at the National Severe Storm Laboratory, Norman, Oklahoma 73069. Information on hazards from earthquakes, volcanos and landslides is available through the United States Geological Survey, Reston, Virginia 20244.

It should be emphasized that using any of this information about geophysical hazards requires careful interpretation based on an understanding of how the information is collected and processed, as well as the geographical relationships between the reporting station and the actual site of the building. Wind patterns are very sensitive to local topography and, of course, to height above ground. Seismic activity is very dependent on local geology as are landslide hazards.

Information on loads is found in building codes such as the Uniform Building Code, International Conference of Building Officials, Whittier, California 90601; the Basic Building Code, Building Officials Conference of America, Chicago, Illinois 60637; the National Building Code, American Insurance Association, Chicago, Illinois 60603; and the Building Code, Southern Building Code Congress, Birmingham, Alabama 35222. there are also many state, county and city codes that contain information on "live loads". However, in evaluating the past performance of an existing building or in planning for its rehabilitation, it should be realized that codes have varied widely both historically and geographically. For example, in 1912 residential live load was 50 psf in Boston, but 70 psf in Philadelphia; in 1970 it was 40 psf in London, but 30 in Tel Aviv.

Fortunately, dead load weights of structural members, cladding and finishings are more stable in time and space, and all engineering handbooks give similar unit values.

For information on biotic agents, probably the best source is the state or county Cooperative Extension Service. However, the U.S. Forest Products Laboratory, Madison, Wisconsin is an excellent resource for research data on enemies of wood.

Local newspapers, libraries, and historical societies can be valuable sources of information on such hazards as high winds, heavy

Figure 3.22. National Weather Service: Lightning Bolts.

Figure 3.23. National Weather Service, Tornado Funnel.

Figure 3.24. National Weather Service: Hailstones.

snowfalls, hostile floodwaters, and even temperatures. Reports on failures of local buildings and other structures such as water towers may also be found at these places.

RESISTANCE

Three terms useful in hazard analysis are strength, stiffness and stability. How do the hazardous forces and agents affect the strength of the structure and its capacity to withstand future loads? The differential stiffness of adjacent structures or various components of or elements within a structure may cause it to respond destructively to various forces and agents to which it is subject. Stability refers not only to structural stability but also to the materials that have been used. Structural stability relates to the overall geometry of the structure and also to the connections of the elements of the frame. Material stability involves dimensional and volumetric stability of the materials composing the building in relation to each other. Structures are in continual movement in response to changing environmental conditions and various forces and agents. While it is a normal state the effects can sometimes be deleterious. (Figure 3.25)

In the analysis of existing structures it is useful to distinguish between damage caused by an external force and defects inherent in the way the structure was designed and built. Distortion can result from either or can be the consequence of the way the structure has accommodated itself to the loadings to which it is subject. (Figure 3.26) Manifestations of movement or change such as cracks and deformations may or may not be symptomatic of structural deficiences or failures.

A successful structural evaluation of an existing building involves a careful analysis of the forces and agents that will probably act upon it during its expected life. The keyword is "probably". Usually, the term "probability" connotes an a priori relationship between the occurrence of an event and its likelihood; whereas, the term "statistical" connotes an a posteriori relationship.

In dealing with forces and agents affecting buildings, it is customary to combine the two relationships and to use historical statistics for predicting future occurrences. This has some intrinsic dangers. First, unless the record covers a period of 30 years or more, it might well be used with caution. Second, even with relatively long records, there is no guarantee that larger or smaller values could not occur at any time in the future. Further, it must also be noted that the resistance of a given element of a building to the various forces and agents is, itself, subject to variation with time and circumstance. This variation of resistance should also be taken into consideration. (Figure 3.27)

This probabilistic analysis of forces, agents and structural resistance has been developing since World War II. The papers of engineers such as A. Freudenthal, E. Rosenblueth, J. Benjamin, A.

126

Figure 3.25. Coalbrookdale, England: Iron Bridge Across the Severn River Built in 1779. This First Important Structural Use of Cast Iron was Saved from Effects of Gradual Ground Movement by Inserting a Massive Concrete Bed Underground Between the Stone Piers.

Figure 3.26. Philadelphia, Pennsylvania: Frankford Avenue Bridge over Pennypacker Creek Built in 1694 Showing Metal Straps Reinforcing Center Arch.

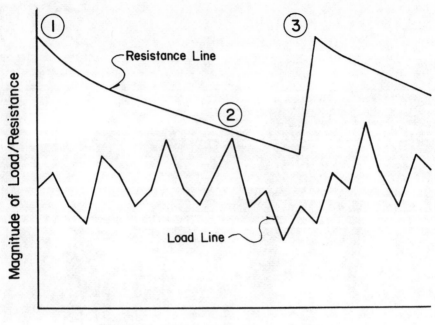

Elapsed Time After Construction

1 Initial strength of member/connection
2 Imposed load almost exceeded available strength/resistance
3 Improvement of strength during rehabilitation

Figure 3.27. Resistance/Load Chronogram Concept.

Ang, et al. should be consulted for the theoretical basis of this type of analysis. Probably the best single work which includes a comprehensive list of references of those just mentioned and many others is Wind, Snow and Temperature Effects on Structures Based on Probability. [Ghiocel, 1975] More recently a symposium was held in October 1981 on this subject at which 25 papers were presented. [Shinozuka and Yao, 1981]

SUMMARY

Architects and engineers involved with projects concerned with monumental or historical structures must take the time to complete a thorough assessment of the hazardous forces and agents to which the building is exposed. Many information sources are available to assist them in this analysis, but these sources must be used with caution.

REFERENCES

Ghiocel, Dan and Dan Lungu. Wind, Snow and Temperature Effects on Structures Based on Probability. Translated by Michaela Blandu. Tunbridge Wells, England: Abacus Press, 1975.

Shinozuka, Masanobu and James T. P. Yao. Proceedings of the Symposium on Probabilistic Methods in Structural Engineering, St. Louis, Missouri, October 26 27, 1981. New York, N.Y.: American Society of Civil Engineers, 1981.

Assessing the Seismic Vulnerability of Museums and Historic Structures

Eric Elsesser

Protection of museums and their collections and historic structures from damaging earthquakes is a special and unique engineering challenge. In contrast to the usual structural engineering goal of providing only for life safety in the design of buildings in seismic regions, the protection of historic buildings and collections requires an unusual awareness of seismic response in order to achieve the goal of complete protection without damage to buildings and artifacts.

The conventional building in a seismic design is designed with protection of life as the primary goal with damage to non-structural components as an acceptable consequence. [Structural Engineers Association of California, 1980] The reasons for this are simple, the structure must respond in the inelastic range to satisfy energy dissipation demands and by so doing large deformations are expected which will damage the usually brittle non-structural elements such as ceilings, partitions, exterior cladding walls, etc. To overcome this type of structure response and be able to protect the contents and non-structural elements requires a structure which does not undergo large lateral deformations or a system which is partially isolated from the ground motion.

In order to assess the vulnerability of museums and historic buildings to earthquakes three things must be known: 1) the goals and criteria by which to measure performance, 2) the earthquake input motion or loads, and 3) the seismic response of the building and its contents.

The generally accepted goal of seismic design for buildings is protection of life, while protection of the building and its contents is generally a secondary goal. The goal for seismic resistance of historic buildings is two-fold: 1) protection of the building with minimum damage, and 2) protection of life. The goal for seismic design of museum structures needs to be three-fold: 1) protection of contents, 2) protection of the building, and 3) life safety. These goals are clearly based on expectations and appear to be quite rational, but the implementation requires careful evaluation and innovative techniques.

Although museums and historic structures are similar in their roles in society, they require completely different approaches to achieve seismic safety. Museums may be either housed in new buildings, in which case new state-of-the-art concepts may be used for seismic protection, or they may occupy old buildings which require both strengthening and attention to details for safety of artifacts. Whereas historic buildings are artifacts themselves, excessive requirements or heavy-handed seismic strengthening may in fact destroy the historic value of the building. In the latter case a fine line must be drawn between seismic safety and historic value, and the goals must be clearly established.

MUSEUMS AND HISTORIC STRUCTURES

Many buildings are used to house collections, which range from paintings and sculptures, to objects of natural history, and those of science and industry. Collections may be large or small and be composed of objects some of which are small, some large, some soft, some heavy, and some very fragile. Some buildings are initially built as museums to house specific collections, while others house collections as a secondary function or in a second life.

Most major museum buildings, designed with the primary function of housing a collection, are large imposing structures. Some are old; a few are recently constructed. Some typical examples from Northern California are: California Palace of the Legion of Honor, San Francisco, cast-in-place concrete construction, 1916's (Figure 3.28); San Francisco Museum of Modern Art, San Francisco located on the 3rd and 4th floors of a monumental building, steel frame and concrete construction, 1932's (Figure 3.29); University of California Museum of Art, Berkeley, dramatic cast-in-place concrete construction, 1972's (Figure 3.30); State of California Railroad Museum, Sacramento, long span timber frame with concrete wall construction, 1970's (Figure 3.31).

Some buildings are in themselves museums, that is their construction and materials are unique, or the building and the contents are special only because they exist together. This type of museum-building varies in size and type. Various examples are: Parthenon, Athens, Greece, an example of a special structure unique because of its history and its design; Cooper-Molera Adobe Complex, Monterey, California, the adobe construction techniques and the building's history make this a special museum building, 1840's (Figure 3.32); Cable-Car Barn, San Francisco, California, this working barn for historic cable cars is another type of old masonry building (Figure 3.33); Wooden Structures, (Sacramento Delta), Locke, California, these old wood buildings are examples of early California construction now also serving as a museum of the times, 1860's (Figure 3.34).

Historic buildings come in all sizes, shapes and ages and represent society's heritage. Some are unique and very old; others are

132

Figure 3.28. San Francisco, California: California Palace of the Legion of Honor, George A. Applegarth, Arch., 1916, Cast-in-Place Concrete Construction.

Figure 3.29. San Francisco, California: San Francisco Museum of Modern Art, Brown and Landsburgh, Archs., 1932, Steel Frame and Concrete Construction.

Figure 3.30. Berkeley, California: University of California Museum of Art, Mario J. Ciampi, Arch., 1972, Cast-in-Place Concrete Construction.

Figure 3.31. Sacramento, California: State of California Railroad Museum, 1970's, Long Span Timber Frame with Concrete Wall Construction.

Figure 3.32. Monterey, California: Cooper-Molera Adobe, 1840's, Historic House
Museum, Adobe Construction.

Figure 3.33. San Francisco, California: Cable Car Barn, Working Barn for
Historic Cable Cars, Masonry Construction.

simply good examples of an era and are, as such, valuable. Some are used as museums, others are being restored for continued commercial or residential use. Typical examples are: Fort Point, at the Golden Gate, San Francisco, a Civil War vintage, masonry walled fort now used as a museum, 1853-1861 (Figure 3.35); State of California Capitol Building, Sacramento, completely rebuilt, restored and seismically strengthened, 1864-1874 and 1980 (Figure 3.36); Academic Quadrangle Stanford University, Palo Alto, seismically strengthened and remodeled masonry construction used for classrooms and offices, 1887-1891 and 1980 (Figure 3.37); Palace of Fine Arts, San Francisco, 1915 Pan Pacific exhibition theme building, originally built with timber, rebuilt with reinforced concrete in 1960's (Figure 3.38); Hallidie Building, San Francisco, architecturally significant early glass curtain-walled building, 1918 (Figure 3.39).

Although all the buildings listed above, with one exception, are located in California, they are representative of many museums and historic buildings elsewhere. They are all vulnerable to earthquake damage. The seismic problems of each and corresponding goals are listed in Table 1. The problems are similar; however, the goals divergent.

SEISMIC EVALUATION CRITERIA

The normal source for seismic performance criteria is our building codes which represent the consensus of experts. Most codes that deal with earthquake protection are primarily concerned with life safety and secondarily with protection of property and then only as a means to protect life. The most commonly referenced code in the United States is the Uniform Building Code (UBC) which is modeled after the SEAOC Recommended Lateral Force Requirements. [International Conference of Building Officials, 1970] Another common reference is the Applied Technology Council proposed seismic provisions (ATC-3). [Applied Technology Council, 1978] Other codes have been developed by several government agencies but generally they follow the same, or similar, concepts and details stated in the UBC or ATC-3 documents. All these codes are focused on new building performance.

Two recent codes in California, the California Historic Building Code (Title 24 Part 8) and the Los Angeles City Earthquake Safety Ordinance have a different purpose and emphasis. Their goal is earthquake safety and preservation of old-non-conforming structures. To achieve these ends, these codes use strength criteria which are reduced from those specified in normal codes. The argument for lower strength is that life safety can be achieved, if preventing building collapse is the only goal, at a lesser seismic design force than normally required for new construction. This is done with the knowledge that the structure will be allowed to crack, and that non-structural elements will be damaged.

Figure 3.34. Locke, California: Historic Town Museum, 1860's, Wooden Structures.

Figure 3.35. San Francisco, California: Fort Point, 1853-1861, Nineteenth
Century Fort Used as Museum, Masonry Construction.

Figure 3.36. Sacramento, California: California State Capitol, Miner Frederick Butler, Arch., 1864–1974, Rebuilt, Restored and Seismically Strengthened, 1980.

Figure 3.37. Palo Alto, California: Stanford University Academic Quadrangle, Shepley, Rutan and Coolidge, Archs., 1887–1891, Masonry Construction Seismically Strengthened and Remodelled, 1980.

Figure 3.38. San Francisco, California: Palace of Fine Arts, Bernard Maybeck, Arch., 1915, Pan Pacific Exposition Theme Building, Originally Lath and Plaster, Rebuilt with Reinforced Concrete, 1960's.

Figure 3.39. San Francisco, California: Hallidie Building, Willis Polk, 139 Arch., 1918, Among First Examples of Glass Curtain Wall Construction.

Table 1

Seismic Vulnerability Issues and Goals for Typical Buildings

TYPE OF BUILDING	SEISMIC VULNERABILITY	GOALS
Museums		
1. California Palace of the Legion of Honor San Francisco, CA	Damage to structure, loss of artifacts	Protect artifacts
2. San Francisco Museum of Modern Art San Francisco, CA	Damage to structure, loss of artifacts	Protect artifacts
3. University of California Museum of Art Berkeley, CA	Loss of artifacts	Protect artifacts
4. California Railroad Museum Sacramento, CA	Damage to trains and objects	Protect objects
Museum–Building		
1. Parthenon Athens, Greece	Collapse of structure, historic loss	Strengthen structure to prevent any damage
2. Cooper Molera Adobe* Monterey, CA	Collapse of structure, loss of objects	Strengthen structure to prevent collapse
3. Cable Car Barn* San Francisco, CA	Collapse of structure, loss of cable cars	Strengthen structure to protect contents
4. Wood Buildings Locke, CA	Collapse of structures, loss of contents	Strengthen structures to prevent collapse
Historic Buildings		
1. Fort Point San Francisco, CA	Minor damage	Maintain facility
2. California State Capital* Sacramento, CA	Damage	Strengthen structure to protect life and maintain function
3. Quad Buildings* Stanford University, CA	Damage and/or collapse	Strengthen structure to protect life
4. Palace of Fine Arts* San Francisco, CA	Damage and/or collapse	Strengthen to protect life and structure
5. Hallidie Building San Francisco, CA	Damage to glass work	Protect life

---

* These buildings have been seismically strengthened in recent years, and the vulnerability listed no longer exists.

The applications and goals of the several codes are summarized in Table 2. These data raise several significant questions about the appropriateness of these codes for seismic resistance of museums and historic structures. Namely, should we classify some museums and historic structures as special, socially significant buildings and require higher levels of protection similar to essential facilities (hospitals, public safety buildings, etc.) to insure their protection? Or, should we allow a lesser level of protection of historic buildings to insure their preservation, at least for the short term? These questions are not easily answered.

In lieu of using building codes as a source for seismic design criteria, specific earthquake data may be generated for a site, and a unique building response developed. If the dynamic characteristics of a structure can be determined, individual floor response spectra can also be developed which will enable the seismic behavior of contents and artifacts to be estimated. This work may be done on an elastic or an inelastic basis. With each increasing step beyond the simple code basis, the process becomes more complex and more costly. These special techniques, however, are probably the only way in which a realistic seismic response and corresponding design for museums can be developed.

STRUCTURAL SYSTEMS

To evaluate properly the seismic response of buildings, it is important to understand the behavior of the primary structural system. For convenience, we have classified structural systems in most contemporary building codes into one of the following categories which progress from least favorable to most favorable: [International Conference of Building Officials, 1970; Applied Technology Council, 1978]

1. Bearing Wall, or Box-Type Systems

   This class includes masonry or concrete bearing walls which share both vertical and lateral loads.

2. Vertical Load Frame with Shear Walls, Braces, or Non-Ductile Moment Frame Lateral Load Systems.

   This class is a catch-all which only requires that there be a complete vertical load carrying frame to insure stability should the lateral load resisting elements be seismically damaged.

Table 2

Applications and Goals of Seismic Codes

CODE	APPLICATION	GOALS
Uniform Building Code, 1982	New construction (rehabilitation criteria is the same as new construction)	Protection of life, some damage control
California State Building Code (Title 24)	New construction (hospitals, schools, buildings) (rehabilitation criteria is similar to new construction)	Protection of life, damage control for protection of property in hospitals, otherwise nominal
Department of Defense, 1981 (Tri-Services)	New construction	Protection of life, Some damage control
Design Guidelines (GSA), 1976	New construction, rehabilitation criteria	Protection of life, some damage control
ATC-3	New construction, rehabilitation criteria (reduced level)	Protection of life, some damage control
Los Angeles Masonry Building Ordinance	Existing masonry buildings	Protection of life
California Historic Building Code (Title 24, Part 8)	Historic buildings	Protection of life, (preservation of buildings)

3. Dual Systems with Ductile Moment Frames and Ductile Shear Walls or Braces.

   This class combines the ductility of moment frames with the drift control of walls or braces.

4. Ductile Moment Frame Systems

   This class resists all lateral loads in frame action with ductile behavior.

The above classifications have been used for about 25 years, and are based on conventional types of construction commonly used in the 1950's and 1960's. It is, however, important to understand the general range of seismic resisting structural systems and when they evolved. These systems are shown in Table 3, which indicates a continual evolution and perfection of ideas. It should be noted that only recently have significant changes evolved.

When building failures are observed in earthquakes, researchers and engineers are motivated to find more satisfactory solutions. The current search is focusing on structural systems which are more like mechanisms, those which dissipate energy without failure. The recent advances in this direction are: with eccentric braced frames [Roeder and Popov, 1979]; dual systems such as with frame and slitted shear walls [Muto, 1969]; and base isolation techniques. [Dynamic Isolation Systems, 1984; Kelley, Eidinger and Derham, 1977] The goal with the above systems is to limit damage as well as to protect life.

To comprehend the relation between successful structural performance and protection of building contents, it is essential to understand that systems such as moment frames dissipate seismic energy with large lateral deformation, forcing the building contents to experience correspondingly large deformations and accelerations. The mounting systems for artifacts in museums must accommodate these conditions. In comparison, shear wall systems such as masonry and concrete construction are not flexible or ductile, and dissipate energy by fracturing and/or rocking. The building contents in these structures may not experience large deformations, but they may experience high accelerations with damaging consequences.

These relationships between building response and content response are complex. We must understand the structural system first. Figure 3.40 shows the expected relative structural system flexibilities generally expected under lateral loads. These are only shown for a monotonic lateral load case; the real seismic performance must take into account cyclic loads, non-linear behavior and degradation of stiffness and strength. A brief summary of observed or projected structural system behavior is presented in Table 4, and it is useful to understand the real performance based on observation and testing, not simply the system performance implied by the building code.

143

Table 3

History of Seismic Resisting Structural Systems

TIME	BEARING WALLS	BUILDING FRAME	MOMENT FRAME	DUAL SYSTEM
1800	Adobe			
	Timber Frame			
	Masonry (Timber Frame)			
1900	Masonry (Steel Frame)	Steel Frame (Masonry Walls)		
1910	Concrete Walls and Framing	Concrete Frames and Walls		
1920		Steel Frame (Concrete Walls)	Steel Frame (Ordinary)	
1930			Concrete Frames (Ordinary)	Steel Frame and Concrete Shear Walls
1940	Concrete Walls (Light Framing)			
1950			Steel (Ductile)	X-Braced and Steel Frame
1960	RGBM or CMU (Light Framing)	X-Braced Steel Frame (Light Walls)	Concrete (Ductile)	
1970	Ductile Shear Walls			Steel Frame and Steel Walls
1980				Eccentric Braces
				*Progressive Resistance System
				*Isolation System

144

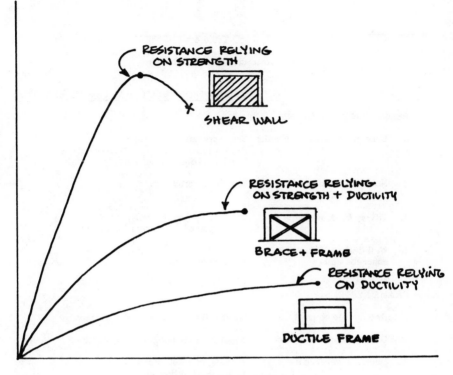

Figure 3.40. Relative Flexibilities of Structural Systems.

Table 4

Structural System Behavior

SYSTEM	PROJECTED STRUCTURAL SEISMIC BEHAVIOR
BEARING WALL SYSTEMS:	
1. Unreinforced masonry walls	Shear cracking of masonry, Separation of walls from floors/roofs, Torsional rotation and warping of walls.
2. Nominally reinforced concrete walls	Significant cracking.
3. Tilt-up concrete walls	Distortion of wall panels, Separation of walls from floors/roofs.
4. Well designed "ductile" concrete walls	Repairable wall cracking, Small deformations.
FRAME SYSTEMS:	
1. Non-ductile concrete frame	Shear failure of columns and girders.
2. Ductile concrete frame	Repairable cracking, large distortions.
3. Ductile steel frame	Yielding of steel, minor distress, Large deformations.
4. Concentric steel brace	Buckling of steel, fracture of connections.
5. Eccentric steel brace	Yielding of steel, large deformations.
COMBINED SYSTEMS:	
Ductile frame and wall	Repairable cracking, small deformations.
BASE ISOLATION:	Minimum effects.

146

By understanding the seismic behavior of primary structural systems, we can decide which systems are most appropriate for life safety as contrasted with those which will also protect property such as museum artifacts. We know that the well designed ductile moment steel frame will insure structural safety and probably life safety, but may cause significant non-structural component damage. We also know that a more rigid shear wall building will limit distortions and may consequently be less damaging to building contents; but verification of this assumption is required.

BUILDING CONFIGURATION

Building configuration can be an intrinsic source of problems in seismic response and can significantly increase the seismic vulnerability of a structure. Configuration is defined as building size, shape and the location and nature of structural elements oriented both vertically and horizontally. Several studies of configurations provide insight to this complex problem. [Arnold and Reitherman, 1982; Arnold, 1979; Kalevras, 1982]

Configuration is significant in two ways: 1) the effect that configuration has on the selection of the structural system, and 2) the effectiveness of the configuration derived structural system. Building configuration can be classified as either regular or irregular from the structural response standpoint. Regular buildings are generally uniform in structural strength and stiffness, without discontinuities, and frequently symmetrical in plan. Irregular buildings do not possess these characteristics, but instead have discontinuities, points of stress concentration, unbalanced capacity, and poor energy dissipation characteristics.

Only in recent years after many observations of earthquake damage and after many studies of that damage in relation to building configuration has a pattern of vulnerability with relation to configuration been established and guidelines been informally developed. [Arnold and Elsesser, 1980]

Configuration has been recognized by knowledgeable structural engineers as an important influence in seismic response, yet only nominal criteria have been included in building codes. The reason is simple: the problem is complex, with many variables, and consequently difficult to codify with a set of simple rules. As a result, the codes are written for conventional, regular buildings. The only provision as stated in the Uniform Building Code (Chapter 23), which is representative of all codes, is that for structures with irregular shapes or framing systems, the distribution of lateral forces must be determined considering the dynamic characteristics of the structure. Unfortunately, this does not completely solve the analysis problem, because current dynamic modeling techniques do not consider all the important issues, such as non-linear behavior and energy dissipation, so that a realistic solution is not readily available.

147

Until structural analysis techniques are developed which adequately represent the real-world condition, some "arbitrary" design rules based on observations of actual earthquake response will have to suffice. Tentative guidelines have been developed which will serve as aids for evaluation and design. [Applied Technology Council, 1978; Arnold and Elsesser, 1980]

Configuration issues can be classified into five basic categories, as follows:

1. Size or Scale Considerations (Figure 3.41):

    When structures do not conform to buildings of "normal" dimension, that is, those which are addressed by code provisions, unanticipated problems may develop. Buildings which are tall and slender, or of large plan dimension, or long and narrow, are examples of buildings which may experience unusual dynamic response in an earthquake.

2. Plan Irregularities (Figure 3.42):

    Buildings which are not regular in plan (asymmetrical) or those with re-entrant corners (L-shaped, T-shaped, U-shaped, etc.) or those with eccentric mass distribution are said to have a plan irregularity. These buildings generally will be subjected to large torsional motions and high stress concentrations. Plan irregularities are very common.

3. Vertical Irregularities (Figure 3.43):

    Buildings with tall first stories, discontinuous frames or shear walls, variations in column stiffness or vertical offsets, have vertical discontinuites of strength or stiffness and are not considered regular in terms of conventional seismic codes. These structural irregularities are serious and may cause collapse because of severe overstress conditions or because of inadequate energy dissipation capacity. Vertical discontinuities are very common with current architectural building forms.

4. Resistance or Strength Irregularities (Figure 3.44)

    This type of problem occurs when an unbalanced lateral strength occurs because of unequal structural capacities which result from architectural or form requirements. If unbalanced plan resistance exists (a short, overstressed wall in conjunction with a long, understressed wall, for example), the structure may experience unanticipated torsion and/or failure. If unanticipated strength or stiffness occurs because non-structural infill walls are added to the structural frame, collapse of the frame may occur.

148

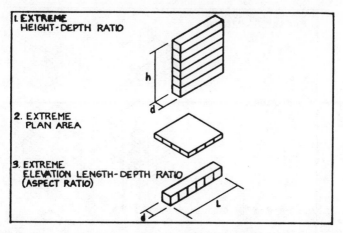

Source: Christopher Arnold and Robert K. Reitherman, **Building Configuration and and Seismic Design** (New York: Wiley Interscience, 1982).

Figure 3.41. Configuration Issues: Size and Scale.

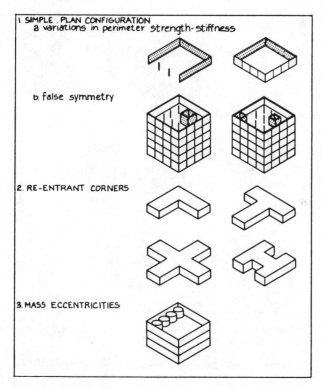

Source: Christopher Arnold and Robert K. Reitherman, <u>Building Configuration and and Seismic Design</u> (New York: Wiley Interscience, 1982).

Figure 3.42. Configuration Issues: Plan Irregularities.

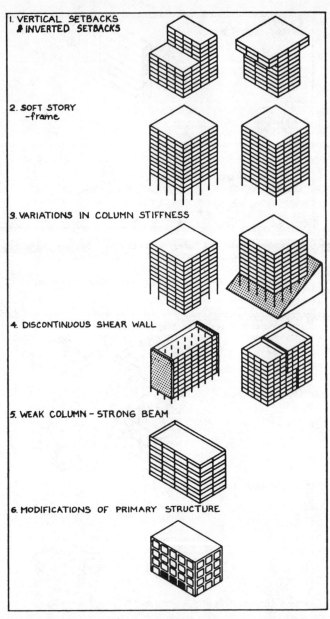

1. VERTICAL SETBACKS
   & INVERTED SETBACKS

2. SOFT STORY
   -frame

3. VARIATIONS IN COLUMN STIFFNESS

4. DISCONTINUOUS SHEAR WALL

5. WEAK COLUMN - STRONG BEAM

6. MODIFICATIONS OF PRIMARY STRUCTURE

Source: Christopher Arnold and Robert K. Reitherman, Building Configuration and and Seismic Design (New York: Wiley Interscience, 1982).

Figure 3.43. Configuration Issues: Vertical Irregularities.

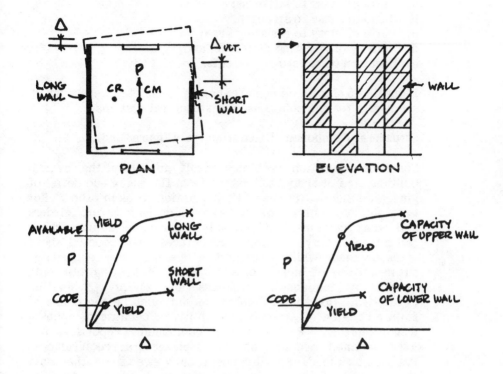

Stress ratios between code level (full stressed) elements
and overcapacity (partially stressed) elements

Figure 3.44. Configuration Issues: Resistance or Strength Irregularities.

151

Significant parameters for the evaluation of seismic performance are:

a. Ratio of mass to stiffness;
b. Ratio of mass to strength;
c. Ratio of mass to resisting area;
d. Density of resisting elements; and,
e. Location of resisting elements.

Figure 3.45 shows the significance of these parameters which are useful for the comparison of structural systems.

5. Structural Component Discontinuities (Figure 3.46):

Some configuration problems result not from the overall building size or shape, but rather from the shape and detail of girders, columns, walls and their relation to each other. For example, moment frame systems which have strong girders and weak columns will probably experience column shear failures and may collapse. Structures with coupled shear walls or shear walls with random openings may experience shear failure of link beams or weak connecting elements caused by inadequate stiffness and energy dissipation capacities. Horizontal diaphragms may also be the cause of failure because of excessive flexibility or because of opening discontinuities. Problems with component proportions are very common because of the architectural requirements imposed on the structural concept, or, viewed in another way, the inappropriateness of the structural system for the problem at hand.

The consequence of a configuration with an inappropriate structural system, or of an incorrect configuration in a region of high seismicity, is illustrated by the classic soft story failure of the Olive View Hospital in the 1971 San Fernando earthquake, Figure 3.47.

CONFIGURATION OF NON-STRUCTURAL ELEMENTS AND DISPLAY SYSTEMS

In addition to seismic ground motions, structural systems and building configuration, the non-structural building components such as ceilings, partitions, equipment and exterior cladding, must also be considered in order to evaluate realistically the seismic behavior of a normal building. With museums and historic structures, the artifact display systems must be added to the above list.

Recent studies of non-structural components have been made to define the problems and establish design criteria. [McCue, Skaff and

Mass to
Stiffness

Mass to
Strength

Mass to
Resisting
Area

Density of
Resisting
Elements

Location of
Resisting
Elements

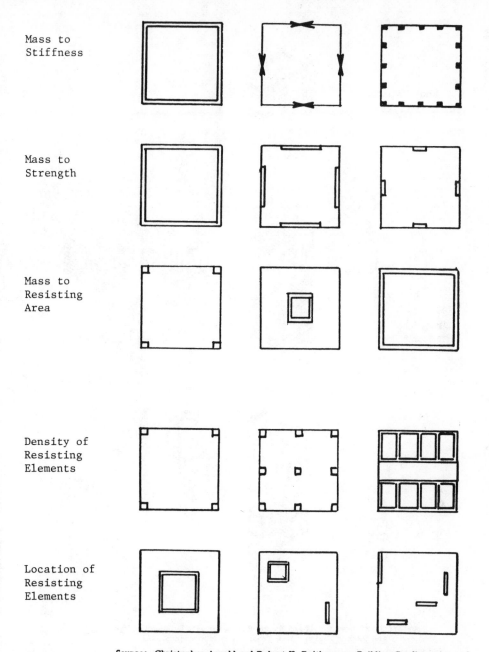

Source: Christopher Arnold and Robert K. Reitherman, Building Configuration and
and Seismic Design (New York: Wiley Interscience, 1982).

Figure 3.45. Structural Response Parameters.

153

Weak Column,
Strong Beam

Shear Walls

Diaphragm

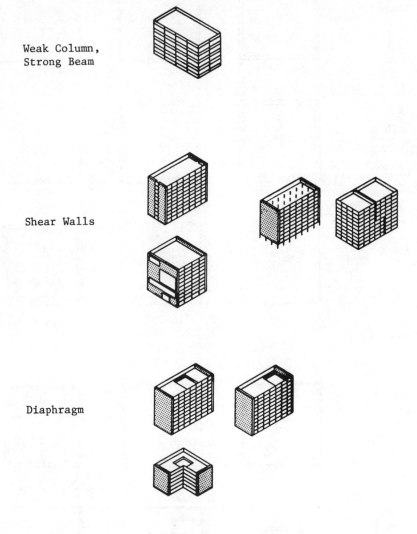

Source: Christopher Arnold and Robert K. Reitherman, Building Configuration and and Seismic Design (New York: Wiley Interscience, 1982).

Figure 3.46. Configuration Issues: Structural Component Discontinuities.

154

Figure 3.47. Sylmar, California: Olive View Hospital Showing Damage from San
Fernando Earthquake of February 9, 1971.

Boyce, 1978; Earthquake Engineering Research Institute, 1984]
Current codes such as the Uniform Building Code simplify the seismic
response problem and cover only "rigidly" attached and "flexibly"
attached objects. [International Conference of Building Officials,
1970] This approach may be sufficient for building components such as
ceilings and partitions, where life safety is the prime consideration,
but protection of artifacts requires more sophistication. An
appropriate dynamic analysis is required with floor response spectra
and mounting details consistent with seismic forces and displacements.

Typical non-structural components within a museum building are
shown in Figure 3.48. The ceilings, walls and floor may all serve as
display surfaces or mounting surfaces. Each must, in turn, be analyzed
and then detailed for separation response and strength. These
elements will require the same care as used for hospital design in
California which requires complete operational capability after a
major earthquake.

The display systems commonly used in a museum are illustrated
in Figure 3.49. Objects may be floor-mounted, pedestal mounted,
mounted in isolation cases, suspended, or wall mounted. Each of these
mountings requires analysis of the non-structural component and of
the primary structural system supporting that component. The
problem is complex.

QUALITY OF CONSTRUCTION

Assessment of structural vulnerability requires knowledge of the
as-built conditions. We need to know both the details of construction
and the quality and strength of the work which constitute the building.

For new museum construction, the design intent, the concept,
and the details of construction are known. If the concept and details
are sound, then that aspect of the vulnerability can be assessed. The
construction, if completely reviewed, inspected, and tested and found
to be in conformance with the design intent and specifications, can
also be trusted for compatibility with the original criteria. If all is
positive, then the building will be satisfactory. It will provide for life
safety and protection of property.

This process of establishing appropriate criteria and details and
then reviewing the quality of construction appears to solve all of our
quality problems: however, the process is complex and only buildings
with simple details and concepts have a good likelihood of being
successfully constructed. A significant jobsite review effort is
required with contemporary construction attitudes to insure
conformance with the original design intent. For example, to insure
success with hospital and public school construction, the State of
California, Office of the State Architect (OSA), requires extensive
design review, full time project inspection, full testing, and maintains
a random inspection of jobs under construction. This level of effort to
insure quality has yielded good quality construction and a high level of

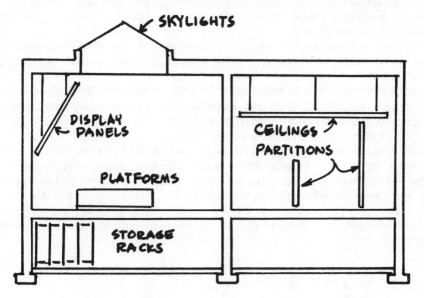

Figure 3.48. Critical Non-Structural Components in a Museum.

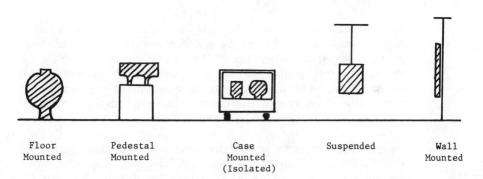

| Floor Mounted | Pedestal Mounted | Case Mounted (Isolated) | Suspended | Wall Mounted |

Figure 3.49. Museum Artifact Mounting Systems.

seismic performance. Vulnerability, therefore, for new construction can be assessed based on the design criteria, the details, and the quality of construction.

The evaluation of seismic response of existing buildings is, however, quite different. Knowledge of all site conditions, construction details and material strengths is required. An investigative process is required to discover the answers to questions about the following: 1) soil capacities; 2) foundation profiles; 3) structural profiles and strengths of all walls, columns, floors and roofs; and 4) continuity and ties between individual elements. To uncover these data, a review of original construction documents, if available, is most helpful: failing that, exposing the construction may be required. Testing of samples or loading the actual construction for strength may be required. This applies to both the primary structure and the non-structural elements as well. With data on the physical characteristics, an analysis can be undertaken and a seismic response predicted.

THE SEISMIC ASSESSMENT PROCESS

Important individual issues to be considered in the assessment process have been discussed; now the entire process will be outlined. There are seven basic steps:

1. Establish Goals and Expections

    The first step is to establish goals for earthquake response: 1) only life-safety, 2) life-safety and protection of the building, or 3) life-safety, protection of the building, and protection of the building's contents. The goals then become the expectations. The next issue to be resolved is the feasibility of the stated goals and the costs related to implementation. The goals and costs must be compatible.

    The goal of property protection leads to the expectation of post-earthquake function. This may, however, require a more restrictive and expensive level of building design than usually expected.

2. Develop Seismic Ground Motion Criteria

    A code level seismic design (Uniform Building Code, 1979) will usually provide a solution without structural damage, but with varying degrees of damage to contents and non-structural elements. Clearly, this level of design is probably not adequate for new museum structures, but may be tolerable for historic buildings where preservation is only feasible with a "realistic" level of reconstruction to achieve seismic strengthening. Consequently, the Uniform Building Code, 1979, or some lesser criteria such as the Los Angeles City Hazardous Building Code might be appropriately selected for rehabilitation or preservation of historic buildings.

3. Survey of Conditions (Existing Buildings)

The assessment of existing buildings requires knowledge of the building configuration, its strength, and its anticipated seismic performance. We can obtain the information about the building by the following means:

a. Physical survey of as-built conditions;
b. Review of original contract drawings;
c. Review of other sources (photographs, historic documents, and discussions with builders and owners);
d. Sampling, measuring and testing of soils and materials;
e. Survey of non-structural component attachments;
f. Previous earthquake exposure and/or damage; and,
g. Load tests and/or model testing.

4. Analysis of Structural Capacity

This applies to both new and existing buildings.

Building configuration issues must first be reviewed. Do regular or irregular forms exist, and if irregular, what are the implications? What is the past earthquake history of the particular building form? Is the structural system compatible with the configuration?

Second is the formal analysis of structural capacity. Conventionally, this is first performed assuming elastic behavior, and material stresses are determined. Next, an ultimate capacity, assuming non-linear behavior, is suggested. The failure modes must be established. These can be based on tests of similar structural systems, or on observed performance in actual earthquakes.

A state-of-the-art analysis requires knowledge of both the dynamic characteristics (frequencies, damping, etc.), and the full range of material behavior and energy dissipation capacity. This information can be obtained by cyclic load testing or shake-table testing.

5. Evaluation of Non-Structural Elements

Types of elements must be defined, and whether they are rigidly or flexibly attached, or seismically separated from the

159

primary structure determined. Their behavior must be evaluated and the design reviewed by either code criteria or by using floor spectra techniques.

6. Review of Artifacts (for Museums)

Establish the nature of the display and the properties of the artifacts displayed (flexible, rigid, hard, soft, heavy, brittle, ductile, etc.). Next, establish the display concept, the type of support, the type of mounting.

The next step is most significant, that of establishing the relationship between the response of the structural system and the artifact mounting. Table 5 indicates a range of systems and the tentative seismic responses. These must be clearly defined and the interaction understood.

Both the artifact and its mounting needs to be reviewed to define whether sliding, overturning, rocking or yielding will occur. It may be necessary to perform dynamic testing to discover the answer.

7. Predicting the Seismic Response

The prediction of what will happen in an earthquake is only as good as the data and analysis effort. And regardless of the technique, there are no earthquake-proof solutions. Nevertheless, it is usually possible to provide these general comments with regard to vulnerability:

New Museum Facilities (subjected to a major earthquake):

Predicted Response	System
Major structural damage	Non-ductile structural systems.
Minor structural damage	Ductile structural systems.
No structural damage, but damage to contents	Dual-ductile systems.
No damage	Base isolated system with sophisticated artifact mounting.

Historic Structures (subjected to a major earthquake)

Predicted Response	System
Major structural damage	Non-ductile structural system (existing or added for strenthening).

160

Table 5

Estimated Interaction of
Artifact Mounting with Structural Systems

ARTIFACT MOUNTING TYPE

STRUCTURAL SYSTEM	Object on Floor	Object on Pedestal	Object on Isolator*	Object Suspended	Object on Wall
SHEAR WALL	Potential problem	Response problem	Minimum problem	Large distortion, minimum problem	Minimum problem
BRACED FRAME	Potential problem	Response problem	Minimum problem	Large distortion, minimum problem	Potential problem
MOMENT FRAME	Large distortion, mimimum problem	Large distortion, problem	Minimum problem	Large distortion, mimimum problem	Large distortion, potential problem
COMBINED WALL AND FRAME	Minimum problem	Response problem	Minimum problem	Large distortion, minimum problem	Minimum problem
ECCENTRIC BRACED FRAME	Potential problem	Response problem	Minimum problem	Large distortion, minimum problem	Minimum problem
BASE ISOLATED STRUCTURE**	Minimum problem	Minimum problem	Dynamic interaction problem	Large distortion, potential problem	Minimum problem

* Objects in dynamically isolated display cases have excellent potential to minimize seismic response.

** Based isolated buildings will minimize the response of most artifacts mounted within the building.

161

| Minor structural damage | Dual-ductile system, added for strengthening. |
| No structural damage, but damage to contents | Base isolated system added to strengthen structure for altered response. |

SOLUTIONS FOR MUSEUMS AND HISTORIC BUILDINGS

A program for assessing the seismic vulnerability of museums and historic buildings should start with a survey of the structures involved, both old buildings and proposed new facilities. The assessment process outlined should be followed for individual structures. The unique aspect in this undertaking is the realization that protection of artifacts is the new goal, and that the normal structural engineering procedures which are life-safety oriented are not appropriate. State-of-the-art analytical techniques and innovative structural and display systems are required.

New museum facilities will require special solutions, some examples of which are illustrated in Figure 3.50. Display and mounting concepts must also be selected to be compatible with the building structure.

Providing seismic protection for historic buildings generally requires extensive review and analysis and the selection of economical and historically appropriate structural strengthening techniques which are generally compromise solutions. Figures 3.51 illustrates several conceptual solutions. The pre-earthquake initiative of strengthening is of course preferred to the post-earthquake response of having to pick up the pieces and reconstruct the historical building which only resembles the old.

REFERENCES

Applied Technology Council. Tentative Provisions for the Development of Seismic Regulations for Buildings (ATC-3). Washington, D.C.: U.S. Department of Commerce, National Bureau of Standard, 1978.

Arnold, Christopher. "Configuration and Seismic Design: A General View," Proceedings of the 2nd U.S National Conference on Earthquake Engineering. Berkeley, California: Earthquake Engineering Research Institute, 1979, pp. 22-36.

Arnold, Christopher and Eric Elsesser. "Building Configuration: Problems and Solutions," Proceedings of the Seventh World Conference on Earthquake Engineering," Volume 4, Istanbul, Turkey: 1980, pp. 153-160.

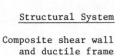

Composite shear wall
and ductile frame

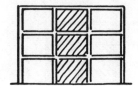

Drift limitation and
strength with resulting
damage control

Eccentric braced
steel frame

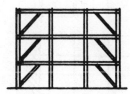

Drift limitation and
energy dissipation with
resulting damage control

Ductile moment frame
with artifact isolation

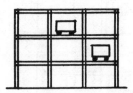

Ductility and structural
safety with artifact
protection

Base isolation of
entire structure

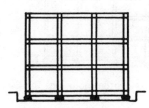

Seismic response
reduction with damage
control and artifact
protection

Figure 3.50. Conceptual Solutions for Museums.

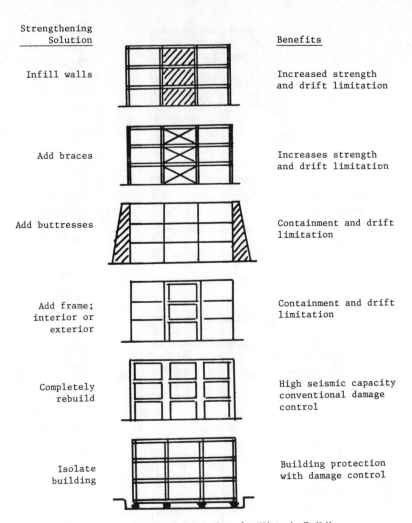

Strengthening Solution		Benefits
Infill walls		Increased strength and drift limitation
Add braces		Increases strength and drift limitation
Add buttresses		Containment and drift limitation
Add frame; interior or exterior		Containment and drift limitation
Completely rebuild		High seismic capacity conventional damage control
Isolate building		Building protection with damage control

Figure 3.51. Conceptual Solutions for Historic Buildings.

Arnold, Christopher and Robert K. Reitherman. Building Configuration and Seismic Design. New York: Wiley Interscience, 1982.

Dynamic Isolation Systems. Base Isolation of Buildings. Berkeley, Calif.: Dynamic Isolation Systems, 1984.

Earthquake Engineering Research Institute. Non-Structural Issues of Seismic Design and Construction, Workshop Proceedings. EERI Publication Number 84-14. Berkeley, California: Earthquake Engineering Research Institute, 1984.

International Conference of Building Officials. Uniform Building Code. Whittier, California: International Conference of Building Officials, 1970.

Kalevras, Vladimir C. "Reducing Overstress Probability in Existing RC Structures," Proceedings of the Seventh European Conference on Earthquake Engineering, Volume 3, Athens, Greece: September 1982.

Kelley, James M., John M. Eidinger, and C. J. Derham. A Practical Soft Story Earthquake Isolation System. EERC Report Number 77-27, November 1977.

McCue, Gerald M., Ann Skaff, and John W. Boyce. Architectural Design of Building Components for Earthquakes. San Francisco, California: MBT Associates, 1978.

Muto, Kiyoshi. "Earthquake Resistant Design of 36-Storied Kasumigaseki Building," Proceedings of the Fourth World Conference on Earthquake Engineering, Volume III, Santiago, Chile, 1969.

Roeder, Charles W. and Egor P. Popov. "Eccentrically Braced Steel Frames for Earthquakes," Journal of the Structural Division, ASCE, Volume 105, Number ST11, Paper 14982, November 1979, pp. 2261-2277.

Structural Engineers Association of California, Seismology Committee. Recommended Lateral Force Requirements and Commentary. San Francisco, California: Structural Engineers Association of California, 1980.

Section Three References

MULTI-HAZARD ASSESSMENT OF A LOCALE AND A SITE

Aki, K. and P. G. Richards. Quantitative Seismology: Theories and Methods. San Francisco: W. H. Freeman, 1980.

Algermissen, S. T. Regional and National Seismic Hazard and Risk. Denver, Colorado: U.S. Geological Survey, Branch of Earthquake Tectonics and Risk, ongoing project.

Algermissen, S. T. and M. D. Perkins. A Probabilistic Estimate of Maximum Acceleration of Rock in the Contiguous United States. U.S. Geological Survey, Open-File Report No. 76-416. Washington, D.C.: U.S. Geological Survey, 1976.

Ambraseys, Nicholas N. "Middle East: A Reappraisal of Seismic Safety." Quarterly Journal of Engineering Geology. Volume II, 1978, pp. 19-32.

Ambraseys, Nicholas N. "Notes on Engineering Seismology." Engineering Seismology and Earthquake Engineering. Julius Solnes, Ed. Leiden: Noordhoff International Publishing Co., 1974, pp. 33-40.

Ambraseys, Nicholas N. "On the Seismicity of Southwest Asia: Data from a XV Century Arabic Manuscript." Revue pour L'Etude des Calamites. No. 37. Union Internationale de Secures, Geneva, Switzerland, 1961.

Ambraseys, Nicholas N. "A Test Case of Historical Seismicity: Isfahan and Chahar Mahal, Iran." The Geographical Journal. The Royal Geographical Society, London. Volume 145, Part 1, March 1979, pp. 56-71.

Atlas on Seismicity and Volcanism. Zurich, Switzerland: Swiss Reinsurance Company, 1978.

Ayre, Robert. Earthquake and Tsunami Hazards in the United States. Boulder Colorado: Program on Technology, Environment and Man, Monograph Series No. NSF-RA-E-75-005, University of Colorado, 975.

Baird, A., P. O'Keefe, K. Westgate and B. Wisner. Towards an Explanation and Reduction of Disaster Proneness. Disaster Research Unit Occasional Paper No. 11. Bradford, England: University of Bradford, Disaster Research Unit, 1975.

Bath, H. Introduction to Seismology. Halsted Press, 1978.

Bauman, Duane D., and Robert W. Kates. "Risk from Nature in the City." Urbanization and Environment. Belmont, California: Duxbury Press, 1972.

Beavers, James E., Ed. Earthquakes and Earthquake Engineering: The Eastern United States. 2 volumes. Proceedings of a Conference held September 14-16, 1981, at Knoxville, Tennessee. Ann Arbor, Michigan: Ann Arbor Science Publishers, 1981.

Blume, John A. "Predicting Natural Hazards—State of the Art." ASCE-ICE-CSCE Joint Conference on Predicting and Designing for Natural and Man-Made Hazards. New York: ASCE, 1978.

Bolt, Bruce A., et. al. Geological Hazards. New York: Springer-Verlag, 1977.

Brabb, E. D., Ed. Progress on Seismic Zonation in the San Francisco Bay Region. Geological Circular No. 807. Washington, D.C.: U.S. Department of the Interior, U.S. Geological Survey, 1979.

167

Brandsma, M., D. Divoky and L. Hwang. Tsunami Atlas for the Coasts of the U.S. Springfield, Va.: National Technical Information Service No. NUREG/CR-1106, 1979.

Brinkmann, Waltraud A. R., et al. Hurricane Hazard in the U.S.: A Research Assessment. Report No. NSF-RA-E-75-007. Boulder, Colorado: University of Colorado, Institute of Behavioral Sciences, Program on Technology, Environment and Man, 1975.

Brune, J. N. "The Physics of Strong Earthquake Motion." Seismic Risk and Engineering Decisions. C. Lomnitz and E. Rosenblueth, Eds. Amsterdam: Elsevier, 1976.

Building Losses From Natural Hazards: Yesterday, Today and Tomorrow. Redondo Beach, California: J. H. Wiggins Company, 1978.

Burton, Ian and Robert W. Kates. The Flood Plain and the Seashore: A Comparative Analysis of Hazard Zone Occupance. New York: American Geographical Society, 1964.

Burton, Ian, Robert W. Kates and Gilbert F. White. The Environment as Hazard. New York: Oxford University Press, 1976.

California Legislature. Joint Committee on the San Fernando Earthquake Study. Earthquake Risk: Conference Proceedings. Sacramento, California: California Legislature, 1971.

Chiu, A. N. Risk Analysis for Natural Hazards Damage Mitigation. Honolulu: University of Hawaii Department of Civil Engineering, to be published.

Cluff, Lloyd S. "Urban Development Within the San Andreas Fault System." Proceedings of the Conference on Geologic Problems of the San Andreas Fault System. San Francisco: Conference on Geologic Problems of the San Andreas Fault System, n.d.

Cornell, C. Allin, et al. "Seismic Risk Analysis of Boston." Proceedings Paper 11617. Journal of the Structural Division, ASCE. Volume 101, No. ST10, 1975.

Donovan, N. C., B. A. Bolt, and R. V. Whitman. "Development of Expectancy Maps and Risk Analysis." Journal of the Structural Division, ASCE. August 1978, pp. 1175-1152.

Earthquake and Windstorm. London: Commercial Union Assurance Company, Ltd., 1975.

Eguchi, Ronald T. and John H. Wiggins. A Bayesian Seismic Risk Study of California, With Loss Estimates. Technical Report No. 79-1328-1. Redondo Beach, California: J. H. Wiggins Co., 979.

Elby, G. A. Earthquakes. New York: Van Nostrand Reinhold, 1981.

Environmental Risk Assessment. Anne V. Whyte and Ian Burton, Eds. SCOPE Report No. 15. Chichester England: J. Wiley, 1980.

Ericksen, N. J. Scenario Methodology in Natural Hazards Research. Boulder, Colorado: University of Colorado Institute of Behavioral Science, Program on Technology, Environment and Man, 1975.

Fleming, Robert W. and Fred A. Taylor. Estimating the Costs of Landslide Damage in the United States. Geological Survey Circular 832. Washington, D.C.: U.S. Geological Survey, 1980.

"Flood Hazards in Pennsylvania." The Pennsylvania Geographer. Volume 16, No. 4, December 1978.

Friedman, Don G. Computer Simulation in Natural Hazard Assessment. Boulder, Colorado: University of Colorado, 1975.

Gasparini, C., G. Iannacone, and R. Scarpa. "On the Focal Mechanisms of Italian Earthquakes." Rock Mechanics. Supplement 9, 1980, pp. 85-91.

Giorgetti, F. and E. Iaccarino. Italian Earthquake Catalog from the Beginning of the Christian Age up to 1968. Trieste, Italy: Osservatorio Geofisico Sperimentale, n.d.

Gutenberg, B. and C. F. Richter. Seismicity of the Earth and Associated Phenomena. New York: Hafner Publishing Company, 1965.

Hammond, E. H. "Classes of Land Surface Form in the Forty Eight States, U.S.A." Annals of the American Association of Geographers. Volume 54, No. 1, Map Supplement No. 4, Scale 1:5,000,000, 1964.

Hart, Gary C. Natural Hazard: Tornado, Hurricane, Severe Wind. Redondo Beach, California: J. H. Wiggins, December 1976.

Hays, Walter W., Ed. Facing Geologic and Hydrologic Hazards: Earth-Science Considerations. Geological Survey Professional Paper 1240-B. Washington, D.C.: U.S. Government Printing Office, 1981.

Hays, Walter W. Program and Plans of the U.S. Geological Survey for Producing Information Needed in National Seismic Hazards and Risk Assessment: Fiscal Years 1980-84. U.S.G.S. Circular 816. Washington, D.C.: U.S. Geological Survey, 1979.

Hebert, Paul J. and Glenn Taylor. Hurricane Experience Levels of Coastal County Populations: Texas to Maine. Coral Gables, Florida: National Hurricane Center, July 1975.

Hewitt, Kenneth and Ian Burton. The Hazardousness of a Place: A Regional Ecology of Damaging Events. University of Toronto, Department of Geography Research Publications. Toronto: University of Toronto Press, 1971.

Hiramatsu, Toshisuke. "Urban Earthquake Hazards and Risk Assessment of Earthquake Prediction." Journal of Physics of the Earth. Volume 28, No. 1, 1980, pp. 59-101.

Ho, Francis, et al. Some Climatological Characteristics of Hurricanes and Tropical Storms: Gulf and East Coasts of the U.S. Report No. NWS-15. Springfield, Va.: National Technical Information Service No. COM-75-110-88, May 1975.

International Association of Volcanology and Chemistry of the Earth's Interior. "List of the World's Active Volcanoes." Bulletin of Volcano Eruptions. Special Issue, 1971.

Jones, Barclay G. "Estimates of Buildings Stocks as a Basis for Determining Risk." Proceedings: Third International Conference: The Social and Economic Aspects of Earthquakes and Planning to Mitigate Their Impacts, Bled, Yugoslavia, June 29-July 2, 1981. Ljubljana, Yugoslavia: Institute for Testing and Research in Materials and Structures, 1982.

Jones, D. E. and W. G. Holtz. "Expansive Soils—The Hidden Disaster." Civil Engineering. Volume 43, No. 8, pp. 45-51, 1973.

Kanamori, H. "Quantification of Earthquakes." Nature. Volume 271, pp. 411-414, 1978.

Kantorovich, L. V., V. L. Keilis-Borok and G. M. Molchan. Seismic Risk and Principles of Seismic Zoning. Translated by Chivvis Shahnazarov. Springfield, Va.: National Technical Information Service, 1974.

Karnik, V. Seismicity of the European Area. Dordrecht, Holland: D. Reidel, 1971.

Kates, Robert W. Risk Analysis of Environmental Hazard. SCOPE Report 8. New York: John Wiley and Sons, 1978.

Krohn, J. P. and J. E. Slosson. "Landslide Potential in the U.S." California Geology. October 1976, pp. 224-231.

Lee, Larry T., John D. Chrostowski, and Ronald T. Eguchi. Natural Hazards: Riverine Flooding, Storm Surge, Tsunami. Redondo Beach, California: J. H. Wiggins Company, June 1976.

Lee, Larry T. and Thomas L. Essex. Urban Headwater Damage Potential. Washington, D.C.: National Science Foundation, Technical Report No. 1282, October 1977.

Lewis, James. The Analysis of Vulnerability to Natural Disaster: Towards a Comparative Methodology. Paper presented to the Center for Development Studies, University of Bath, 10 February 1978. Publication of the International Disaster Institute.

Lewis, James. "Comprehensive Analysis of Vulnerability to Natural Disaster—The Socio-Economic Component" to be published.

Lomnitz, C. Global Tectonics and Earthquake Risk. Developments in Geotectonics Series No. 5. Amsterdam: Elsevier, 1974.

Mississippi-Arkansas-Tennessee Council of Governments. Regional Earthquake Risk Study: Progress Report No. 2. Springfield, Va.: National Technical Information Service No. PB-223-186, 1973.

Munich Reinsurance Company. World Map of Natural Hazards. Munchen: Munchener Ruckversicherungsgesellschaft, 1978.

National Survey on Library Security. Briarcliff Manor, N.Y.: Burns Security Institute, 1973.

Okamoto, Shunzo. Introduction to Earthquake Engineering. New York: John Wiley and Sons, 1973.

Otway, H. J. Risk Assessment. Vienna: The Joint IAEA/IIASA Research Project, 1975.

Perla, R. I. and M. Martinelli, Jr. Avalanche Handbook. Agriculture Handbook 489. Washington, D.C.: U.S. Department of Agriculture, U.S. Forest Service, 1976.

Richter, Charles F. Elementary Seismology. New York: Freeman and Company, 1958.

Rossi, Peter H., et al. The Adequacy of Natural Disaster Data Bases for Location and Damage Estimates. Data Base Workshop. Boulder, Colorado: NHRAIC, n.d.

Scientific American Magazine. Earthquakes and Volcanoes. San Francisco: W. H. Freeman and Company, 1980.

Sorenson, John H., Neil J. Ericksen, and Dennis S. Mileti. Landslide Hazard in the U.S.: A Research Assessment. Program on Technology, Environment and Man Monograph No. NSF-RA-E-75-009. Boulder, Colorado: Institute of Behavioral Sciences, University of Colorado, 1975.

State-of-the-Art for Assessing Earthquake Hazards in the U.S. Series of 15+ reports. Springfield, Va.: National Technical Information Service, various dates.

Tag-Eldeen, Mustafa. Disaster Mitigation Vulnerability Mapping in Disaster-Prone Areas. Stockholm, Sweden: Tekniska Hegskolan, Sektionen for Arkitektur, 1975.

Tubbesing, Susan K., Ed. Natural Hazards Data Resources: Uses and Needs. Springfield, Va.: National Technical Information Service, No. PB-194-912, 1979.

U.S. Geological Survey. Geologic Map of North America. Scale 1:2,500,000. Washington, D.C.: U.S. Geological Survey, 1974.

U.S. Geological Survey. Landslide Overview, Coterminous U.S. Miscellaneous Field Studies Map MF-771. (Radbruch-Hall, et al.). Washington, D.C.: U.S. Geological Survey, 1976.

U.S. National Oceanic and Atmsopheric Administration. Earthquakes. Washington, D.C.: U.S. Government Printing Office, Stock No. 0317-0058, Monthly Catalog No. 5942, April 1972.

Urban Scale Vulnerability: Proceedings of the U.S.-Italy Colloquium on Urban Design and Earthquake Hazard Mitigation, 12-16 October 1981, Rome, Italy. Seattle, Washington: University of Washington, June 1982.

White, Gilbert F. Flood Hazard in the United States. Boulder, Colorado: The University of Colorado, 1975.

Whittow, John. Disasters: The Anatomy of Environmental Hazards. London: Alan Lane/Penguin Books, 1980.

Wiggins, John H., James E. Slosson, and James P. Krohn. Natural Hazards: Earthquake, Landslide, Expansive Soil. Redondo Beach, California: J. H. Wiggins Company, October 1978. CCC.

Witham, K., W. G. Milne, and W.E.T. Smith. "The New Seismic Zoning Map for Canada." June 15, 1970.

World Distribution of Thunderstorm Days. Geneva, Switzerland: World Meteorological Organization, 1969.

Wuorinen, V. A Methodology for Mapping Total Risk in Urban Areas. Unpublished Ph.D. Dissertation, Department of Geography, University of Victoria, British Columbia, 1979.

VULNERABILITY ASSESSMENT OF A STRUCTURE

Abstract Journal in Earthquake Engineering. Berkeley, California: University of California, Earthquake Engineering Research Center, published annually.

Arnold, Christopher. "The Building on Your Board Won't Hurt You—Some Thoughts on the Seismic Hazard of Existing Buildings." Talk presented at Fix 'Em: EERI Seminar on Identification and Correction of Deficiencies in Earthquake Resistance of Existing Buidings. Berkeley, California: Earthquake Engineering Research Institute, February 25, 1982.

Arnold, Christopher. "In Earthquakes, Failure Can Follow Form." American Institute of Architects Journal. June, 1980, pp. 33-41.

Blejwas, T. and B. Bresler. Damageability in Existing Buildings. Report No. UCB/EERC-78-12. Berkeley, California: University of California, Earthquake Engineering Research Center, August 1979.

California Seismic Safety Commission. Evaluating the Seismic Hazard of State-Owned Buildings. Sacramento, California: California Seismic Safety Commission, 1979.

Chopra, Anil K. Dynamics of Structures—A Primer. Berkeley, California: Earthquake Engineering Research Institute, 1981.

Culver, C. G., H. S. Lew, G. C. Hart and C. W. Pinkham. Natural Hazards Evaluation of Existing Buildings. NBS BSS-61, Building Sciences, Series 61. Washington, D.C.: U.S. National Bureau of Standards, January 1975.

Czarnecki, R. M., E. C. Wang and S. A. Freeman. "Procedures for Evaluation of Earthquake Risk to Buildings." Proceedings of the ASCE Annual Convention. Preprint 2804. Philadelphia, Pa.: The Convention, September-October 1976.

Daldy, A. F. Small Buildings in Earthquake Areas. Garston, Watford, Hertfordshire: Building Research Establishment, 1975.

Degenkolb, Henry. "Earthquake Performance of Old Buildings." Talk presented at Fix'Em: EERI Seminar on Identification and Correction of Deficiencies in Earthquake Resistance of Existing Buildings. Berkeley, California: Earthquake Engineering Research Institute, February 25, 1982.

Dowrick, D. J. "Survivability of Structures in Extreme Magnitude Earthquakes." Large Earthquakes in New Zealand. Wellington, New Zealand: The Royal Society of New Zealand, 1981, pp. 77-81.

Earthquake Engineering Research Institute. Notes to Accompany Fix 'Em: EERI Seminar on Identification and Correction of Deficiencies in Earthquake Resistance of Existing Buildings. Berkeley, California: Earthquake Engineering Research Institute, February 25, 1982.

Freeman, S. A. "Evaluation of an Existing Building Complex for Earthquake Response." Preceedings of the ASCE Specialty Conference, Methods of Structural Analysis. Madison, Wisconsin: The Conference, August 1976.

Freeman, S. A. "Rapid Dynamic Analysis." Proceedings, 50th Annual Convention of the Structural Engineers Association of California. Coronado, California: The Conference, October 1981.

Freeman, S. A., J. P. Nicoletti and J. V. Tyrrell. "Evaluation of Existing Buildings for Seismic Risk—A Case Study of Puget Sound Naval Shipyard, Bremerton, Washington." Proceedings of the U.S. National Conference on Earthquake Engineering, 1975. Ann Arbor, Michigan: The Conference, June 1975, pp. 113-122.

Freeman, S. A., F. J. Willsea, and A. T. Merovich. "Evaluating Old Buildings for New Earthquake Criteria." Proceedings of the ASCE National Convention. Preprint 3565. Boston, Mass.: The Convention, April 1979.

Gauchat, U. P. and D. L. Schodek. Housing in Disaster Prone Countries: A Codification and Vulnerability Analysis of Housing Types. Cambridge, Mass.: Harvard University Graduate School of Design, 1977.

Hanson, Robert D., Ed. Proceedings of the United States/People's Republic of China Workshop on Seismic Analysis and Design of Reinforced Concrete Structures. Ann Arbor, Michigan: Department of Civil Engineering, University of Michigan, May 1981.

Ho, Alan Darrell. "Determination of Earthquake Intensity from Chimney Damage Reports." Master of Science Thesis. Cambridge, Mass.: MIT Press, 1979.

Holmes, William T. "Non-Structural Components." Outline of talk given at Fix 'Em: EERI Seminar on Identification and Correction of Deficiencies in Earthquake Resistance of Existing Buildings. Berkeley, California: Earthquake Engineering Research Institute, February 25, 1982.

Housner, George W. "Vibration of Structures Induced by Seismic Waves." Shock and Vibration Handbook. C. M. Harris and C. E. Crede, Eds. New York: McGraw-Hill, 1961.

Japan Society for the Promotion of Science. Seismic Risk Analysis and its Application to Reliability-Based Design of Lifeline Systems. Proceedings of Review meeting. Honolulu, Japan Society for the Promotion of Science, January 1981.

Jephcott, Donald K. and Donald E. Hudson. The Performance of Public School Plants During the San Fernando Earthquake, February 9, 1971: Lessons from a Moderate Earthquake on the Fringe of a Densely Populated Region. Los Angeles: California Institute of Technology, Earthquake Engineering Research Laboratory, 1974.

Krishna, J., B. Chandra and S. Kanungo. "Behavior of Load Bearing Brick Walls During Earthquake." Proceedings, Third Symposium on Earthquake Engineering, Roorkee, India, 1966. Volume II, pp. 19-25.

Latour, H. S. Building Construction and Earthquakes in Guatemala. Individual Studies by Participants in the International Institute of Seismology and Earthquake Engineering, Tokyo, Japan, December 1965.

Lefter, J. and M. Swatta. "A Strategy for Setting Priorities for the Evaluation of Seismic Resistance of Existing Buildings." Proceedings of the 7th World Conference on Earthquake Engineering, Istanbul 1980: Volume 9—Socioeconomic Aspects, Earthquake Reports and Progress Reports. Ankara, Turkey: The Conference, 1981, pp. 293-300.

Lew, T. K. and S. K. Takahashi. Rapid Seismic Analysis Procedure. Technical Memorandum No. Sl-78-02. Port Hueneme, California: U.S. Department of the Navy, Civil Engineering Laboratory, April 1978.

Liu, Ben-Chieh, et al. Earthquake Risk and Damage Function: An Integrated Preparedness and Planning Model Applied to New Madrid. Springfield, Va.: National Technical Information Service PB-80-170-368, 1979.

Mayes, R. L. and Clough, R. W. State-of-the-Art in Seismic Shear Strength of Masonry: An Evaluation and Review. Berkeley, California: University of California, Earthquake Engineering Research Center, Report No. EERC 75-21, 1975.

Mayes, R. L., Y. Omote, S. W. Chen, and R. W. Clough. Expected Performance of Uniform Building Code Designed Masonry Structures. Berkeley, California: University of California, Earthquake Engineering Research Center, Report No. EERC 76-7, 1976.

Page, Robert A., John A. Blume and William B. Joyner. "Earthquake Shaking and Damage to Buildings." Science. Volume 189, Number 4203, August 22, 1975, pp. 601-608.

Parducci, A. and M. Mezzi. "Repeated Horizontal Displacements in Infilled Frames Having Different Stiffness and Connecting Systems: Experimental Analysis." Proceedings of the 7th World Conference on Earthquake Engineering, Istanbul. Ankara, Turkey: The Conference, 1980.

Razani, R. and K. L Leek. The Engineering Aspects of the Qir Earthquake of 10 April 1972 in Southern Iran. Washington, D.C.: National Academy of Sciences, National Academy of Engineering, 1973.

Roeder, C. W., J. Stanton, N. M. Hawkins. "A Preliminary Study of the Seismic Resistance of the Olympic Hotel, Seattle, Washington." Report to the Board of Regents. Unpublished, University of Washington, April 1979.

Schodek, Daniel L. "Assessing the Relative Vulnerability of Urban Housing to Earthquakes." Unpublished ms., 1982.

Schodek, D. L. and U. P. Garchut. "Patterns of Housing Type and Density: A Basis for Analyzing Earthquake Resistance." Cambridge, Mass.: Harvard University, Department of Architecture, 1981.

Simpson, Gumpertz and Heger, Inc. Earthquake Resistance: Old State House, Boston, Massachusetts. Prepared for NSF project on "Deducing Ground Motion Parameters by Analysis of Conteporary Construction with Known Damage: The 1755 Cape Ann Earthquake." Cambridge, Mass.: Simpson, Gumpertz and Heger, Inc., January, 1980.

URS/John A. Blume and Associates, Engineers. Effects Prediction Guidelines for Structures Subjected to Ground Motion. Springfield, VA.: National Technical Information Service, No. JAB-99-115/UC-11, July 1975.

U.S. General Services Administration and Pregnoff, Mathew, Beebe, Inc. Earthquake Resistance of Buildings, Volume II: Evaluation of Existing Structures. Washington, D.C.: U.S. Government Printing Office, 1976.

Whitman, R. V., F. J. Heger, R. W. Luft and F. Krimgold. "Seismic Resistance of Existing Buildings." Journal of the Structural Division, ASCE. Volume 106, No. ST7, Proceedings Paper No. 15564, July 1980, pp. 1573-1592.

Wiggins, J. H., G. C. Hart, and R. W. White. Methodology for Hazard Risk Evaluation of Buildings. Springfield, Va.: National Technical Information Service, December 1973.

SECTION FOUR

Preventive Measures to Mitigate Losses

Preventing Damage

Barclay G. Jones

Vulnerability reduction can be accomplished through conscious planning as a consequence of a policy determination to take action in recognition of hazards that exist. Planning to reduce vulnerability includes but is more comprehensive than emergency preparedness planning. Individuals and organizations have to take deliberate measures to lessen the potential impact of natural hazards. This requires the investment of much time and effort and careful thought. Other tasks, duties and interests may seem more urgent and too demanding, and the required activities may be deferred, postponed or indefinitely delayed. The consequences may be highly unfortunate.

ASSIGNING RESPONSIBILITY

Once a clear, articulate policy has been established, it will be necessary to designate groups and individuals who have primary responsibility for planning. Delegation of authority should be lucid and specific, and deadlines for the development of plans and for periodic review should be definite. Otherwise there is a substantial likelihood policies will never be transformed into plans and plans implemented in courses of action. Within an institution designation of responsibility should start at the highest level. A committee of the Board of Directors or Trustees should be charged with developing and implementing plans. Officers of the organization should be given similar clear responsibility. Specific staff members at different levels in various branches of the organization should have sharply defined tasks and responsibilities. Hierarchical relationships in the ways in which plans are produced from the most specific operating levels to the most general institutional level should be established. For example, a staff member in each department might be designated the responsible individual. Preparation of the original plan by some deadline and periodic review at specified intervals should be an assigned task. An Associate Director of the organization might be given the assignment of receiving and discussing the departmental plans and coordinating them into an overall institutional plan. This individual might meet periodically with and report to a specified committee of the Board of Trustees charged with final approval of a plan and presentation of it to the Board for its adoption and implementation.

The reduction of vulnerability requires incurring real costs, and therefore it must be dealt with at the highest administrative and policy levels. The staff cannot be expected to operate responsibly, if other priorities are continually given precedence at higher policy and administrative levels. The costs will involve not only time and effort that must be reallocated to these planning tasks from other duties but often other very real kinds of expenditures as well. In some instances greater degrees of protection can be achieved at relatively minor costs. For example, it may be decided to store objects damageable by water in attic rather than basement space in a flood prone area. However, such cases are likely to be the exception rather than the rule, and the real costs involved in providing protection will frequently be very high.

Organizations dealing with artifacts are confronted continually with problems of this sort in different ways. Keeping proper inventories, cataloging, conserving or restoring, and making items accessible may be enormously expensive and use scarce resources that could be devoted to acquisitions. Quite often there is a strong temptation to take advantage of opportunities to acquire new items to expand collections and hope that at some time in the future more resources will be available to ingest them properly into the system. Libraries, for example, must continually find a balance between allocating budgets to acquisition and cataloguing and shelving books. They must also allocate resources between these two major aspects of building the collection and servicing it and making it accessible to users. Proper protection of objects will incur expenditures that compete also for funds available for acquisitions. Building a collection and protecting it may be in conflict with each other. The consequences of failing to provide proper protection may be substantial loss or attrition of a collection assembled through patient efforts over many years.

HAZARDS, OBJECTS AND OWNERS

Reducing vulnerability of the cultural resources in an area must be viewed both macrocosmically and microcosmically. A comprehensive plan within a region for reducing vulnerability of the cultural heritage can be viewed as a three dimensional matrix concerned with: classes of objects, sets of organizations or individuals who own or are responsible for those objects, and specific natural hazards to which the region is subject.

Plans will be object specific and different measures will need to be taken regarding different classes of items. Structures, artifacts of different kinds, library materials, and archives and documents will all require different kinds of treatment. Each organization or individual in possession of various objects will have a plan at greater or lesser degrees of elaboration regarding them. Preparations and preventive measures for different kinds of hazards will be institutionalized within organizations and at the communal level in different ways. Some of the linkages and interinstitutional relationships may be formalized in some instances more highly than in others. Hurricane warning, emergency procedures, protective measures and information systems may be drastically different from those concerned with earthquakes. Protective measures, rescue and conservation procedures for documents and other paper materials will be quite different from those for sculpture. Libraries may have more elaborate networks of communication and for sharing information than individual collectors and dealers. [Breuer, 1981] Rescue and recovery operations after a disastrous event will be facilitated or made more difficult by the pervasiveness, quality and comprehensiveness of these plans.

ESTABLISHING THRESHHOLDS OF RISK

A policy issue that must be confronted at a very early stage is that of determining threshholds of tolerable risk. Threshholds will vary again with the elements of the matrix: objects, organizations or individuals, and hazards. Great precautions may be taken to protect against certain types of hazards and little or none against others. The literature indicates that attitudes towards the danger of various hazards often relate to the most recent disastrous event rather than the most likely or the most threatening. Care needs to be taken that an objective evaluation of the probability of damage by various hazards is made in determining threshholds rather than relying upon the experiences of the staff members.

Some organizations and individuals who own or have responsibility for resources may have entirely different attitudes towards risk and set completely different threshholds in similar situations. In some instances taking identical protective measures may be easily affordable while in others it may be prohibitively expensive. The capacity of an organization or an individual to take care of an object is quite unrelated to the fact of possessing it. For example, a church may have acquired extremely valuable stained glass or statuary many years ago as a benefaction and have a very meager budget which permits little maintenance and protection.

Differing classes of objects will be more vulnerable to different kinds of hazards than others. Those who possess the objects may attach greater importance or value to some types of objects than others. Within a single class some objects may be considered more important or more valuable than others. Different threshholds may be set in all instances of this kind. Differing degrees of protection may be accorded the objects.

ADOPTING A STRATEGY

Establishing threshholds of acceptable risk for objects by hazard is a difficult policy matter within each organization. Absolute security is unattainable. Various strategies can be followed but they should be adopted consciously and only after careful deliberation. A frequent strategy is one that is often described as the easy first approach. Here the easiest steps that can be undertaken within the normal operations of the organization to increase the level of protection and reduce risk are the ones that are embarked upon first. The presumption is that further more difficult measures will be undertaken at subsequent stages. Another frequently observed strategy is to give priority attention to the most important or valuable objects. This requires establishing some criteria for importance or value and inventoring and classifying objects accordingly. This strategy is frequently pursued subconsciously and somewhat automatically. To carry it out systematically requires greater effort. Still another kind of strategy is one which attempts to achieve the greatest degree of protection for a given expenditure of resources. This requires surveying natural hazards, determining vulnerabilities and assessing risks and inventorying collections and classifying them by importance and value. Frequently referred to as a cost effective procedure, such a process may be quite costly in itself.

PLANNING TO REDUCE VULNERABILITY

Vulnerability reduction plans must be devised and instituted. Regardless of the type of organization or individual responsible, the kinds of objects involved, or the types of natural hazards that exist, the elements of vulnerability reduction plans are simple, straightforward and stable. They include: inventory; recording and documentation; risk avoidance; protection; emergency procedures; rescue measures; and restorative processes.

Plans pertain to the macrocosmic view of the total sets of cultural resources within a region as well as to the microcosmic view of the possessions of a particular organization or a specific collection. They pertain to buildings and their appurtenances as well as to artifacts and must relate to them whether they are in storage or on display.

Surveying

Any plan must be based upon a sound inventory. The inventory provides the data base which permits perceiving the scope of the problem. Without complete knowledge of what is at risk, coherent protective measures can not be undertaken. In recent years local surveys of historic structures sometimes undertaken in connection with and sometimes independently of state and national registers of historic places have provided initial sets of inventories. In very few instances are these inventories complete and rarely are they systematic and accurate reflections of the resources in an area. In spite of substantial efforts over the last fifteen years much remains to be done. Libraries usually have shelf lists of their books, and major museums catalogues of their holdings. The records of archival collections are often much less complete. Minor museums, local historical societies, historic house museums, dealers, individuals and organizations with other primary purposes such as churches, colleges and universities, and governmental agencies frequently have quite inadequate inventories. Not only are complete and detailed inventories essential, but they must exist at least in duplicate. Obviously the duplicate copy must be in a location that is securely protected from all natural hazards. In the fire that destroyed the Charles Klein Law Library at Temple University July 25, 1972, the public card catalog was saved by an impromptu human chain of faculty, students, staff and passersby and the shelf list was fortuitously located in an area firemen were able to protect. [Willey, 1979]

Documenting

The second stage of a plan is that of recording and documenting the items on the inventory. Beyond some level of risk it will not be possible to protect objects. In many instances, this may be for unavoidable reasons a relatively low threshhold for certain hazards. Careful records and documentation may permit extensive conservation or restoration in situations which would otherwise represent complete loss. For structures themselves, when architectural and engineering drawings exist, they should be duplicated and carefully preserved. Other drawings and visual evidence should be acquired and filed. Measured drawings, photographs, and photogrammetric recordings should be made where possible. [McKee, 1970] After World War II it was possible to reconstruct the market square that forms the historic center of the city of Warsaw because generations of architectural students had been assigned the task of making measured drawings of the structures that composed it. [Ciborowski, 1970] These drawings had been carefully preserved in a very secure location throughout the war. In assembling documentary evidence on the city of Nantucket, an Historic American Buildings Survey Project attempted to inventory all known maps, town views, collections of photographs, bibliographic sources and primary source material including municipal records. [Hugo-Brunt, 1969] Extensive systematic inventories of town views can be helpful. [Reps, 1984]

Risk avoidance measures should be undertaken as a systematic element of any plan. Various natural hazards affect different portions of a location in different ways. Some natural hazards are distributed differently throughout time. Taking care to relocate objects in time and space may provide an important element of protection. Basements and lower stories may be more subject to flooding hazards of various kinds. Attics and upper stories may suffer more in hurricanes, tornados, and subsequent rain storms. Basements may be more secure from earthquake and tornado damage. The tornado which damaged the Wichita Falls, Texas, Museum on April 10, 1979, did no major damage to the main collection. The director of the museum, conscious of the prevalence of tornados in that region in April and May, scheduled exhibits of the work of school children at that time and had the major items of the permanent collection in secure storage. [Francell, 1980] Hurricanes, sea surges, flash floods, windstorms, earthslides are more prevalent in certain places at some times of the year than others. Aftershocks frequently follow earthquakes for weeks or months. Careful scheduling, relocating objects, shuttering openings, bracing and other actions at particular times may avoid risk.

Protecting

Plans for protection will vary with objects, organizations and hazards also. Once careful inventories have been made that define the nature of the problem, recording and documentation have been carried out as a measure against loss, and appropriate steps have been taken to avoid exposure to risk, protective measures must be instituted. Protection is the most complex, technical, involved and potentially costly element of the plan. [Jenkins, 1970, Morris, 1979] It covers the entire range of activities from the decision on a location to the placement of a small object in a display case. Such an enormous topic can only be briefly summarized. The amounts of protection provided will depend upon threshholds of acceptable risk that have been determined. Natural hazards of various kinds have tremendous differences in prevalence from one location to another. Within the general location, proneness to certain types of natural hazards will be site specific. Archaeological and historic sites may be fixed. It may be deemed undesirable to relocate historic structures. Freedom to select sites on the basis of lack of proneness to natural hazards may be constrained by other criteria such as accessibility, availability, amenity, cost, etc.

Buildings must be made as secure against the impacts of natural hazards as possible. The building may have intrinsic value in itself because of historical associations, architectural merit or other attributes, and it may house and provide protective shelter for artifacts and other objects. Securing the structure involves incorporating protective measures in the design, strengthening and retrofitting existing buildings and carrying out programs of maintenance that insure continued performance at top capacity. Building security involves, first, structural integrity and the capacity to withstand various stresses that different kinds of natural hazards are likely to impose. However, arrangement, plan, or layout also matter. This includes the capability of evacuating occupants of the building, easily relocating contents, and possibly removing them in times of danger. Non-structural building elements are also of major importance. Temperature and humidity control systems, plumbing, wiring and other sorts of mechanical systems are critical. Such equipment is frequently large, heavy and may not only be expensive to replace but may cause direct damage to other objects by impacting them or falling on them or indirect damage through operating failure. The failure of heating systems in extremely cold weather may adversely affect objects, for example. Mechanical systems often include conduits of liquids or gases, the spillage of which may constitute a catastrophe in itself. The Stanford Meyer Library Flood on November 4, 1978 was the result of the failure of an eight inch pressurized water main which served the fire sprinkler system. [Buchanan and Leighton, 1981] Other non-structural elements such as surface finishes, ceilings, ornament and decoration may fall under various conditions such as earthquakes causing injuries or damage or blocking access. There are numerous instances in which emergency electrical systems were themselves made inoperable in earthquakes because the equipment was not properly secured and protected. [Schiff, 1980]

Artifacts require protective measures also. Some of these may have little or no intrinsic value such as furnishings, but they may cause damage to others which do, prevent access or impede normal operations. Auxiliary furnishings such as file cabinets, book shelves, storage racks, and display cases can directly affect the security of important or valuable objects they contain. The failure of furnishings of these kinds has frequently been the primary cause of damage to valuable objects and artifacts in many situations involving disasters. Much experience has been accumulated regarding the performance of these types of furnishings, and it is necessary to exercise proper care in selecting, installing and using furnishings of this kind. [Stone, Marraccini and Patterson, 1976; Ayres and Sun, 1973] Valuable artifacts will require various kinds of protection depending upon the type and importance. Pottery, glass, ceramics, stone, metal, fabric, paper, prints, paintings are all subject to different kinds of dangers from different types of hazards. The principles governing display are frequently concerned with the most effective presentation of the object and may be extremely hazardous because protection is not given appropriate consideration. Principles governing storage usually concern ease of access, protection from environmental conditions and security. Protection is seldom taken into consideration, and storage areas are often those in which the greatest damage occurs.

Ethnographic and archaeological collections of pottery or ceramics are especially vulnerable whether on display or in storage. This becomes particularly critical when frequently the overwhelming proportion of the collection is normally in storage. In research collections this may be the total collection. Furniture, of course, often has intrinsic value in itself and is the major object comprising the collection. Providing protection to furniture as artifacts can be a particularly troublesome problem.

Preparing for Emergencies

Plans for reducing vulnerability should also include procedures to be instituted during emergencies. While such actions are properly considered in a later section, they should be mentioned here because they are an aspect of being prepared for disasters which is the essence of protection. Sets of steps to be taken when a natural disaster strikes to provide immediate protection and contain damage should be carefully thought out and developed into a formal plan. Necessary tasks should be drawn up with much deliberation and responsibilities for carrying them out clearly assigned to specific individuals. Necessary protective materials should have been listed, acquired and accessibly stored. For many types of natural hazards, periods of incipient danger are often known preceding the event. In some instances specific warnings can be given hours in advance of the impact. In these kinds of situations, protective actions taken in the space of a few hours immediately preceding events can be extremely effective in reducing the damage that is incurred. Obviously, such actions vary tremendously with the nature of the hazard. They may consist of tying things down, covering windows and other openings and securing breakable objects in wind storms and similar events. In the threat of floods relocating damagable articles to higher positions may be a possibility. Larger scale evacuations are sometimes possible for the most important or valuable objects or much of a collection. In the floods of the Monongahela and Allegheny rivers after Hurricane Agnes in June 1972 the Fort Pitt Museum at the confluence of those rivers in Pittsburgh received advanced warning of the threat. The director, realizing no secure places existed on the site, took the extraordinary measure of acquiring a tractor trailer truck, placing the entire collection in it and driving off to higher ground before the floods came. [Whipkey, 1973] Even during emergencies it is possible to carry out preventive action. As flood waters rise objects can be moved, as winds rise objects can be lashed down, after the first tremor objects can be safely stowed away. Preventive measures can be carried out until the last bit of damage has been done.

Rescuing

Rescue plans immediately after a disastrous event are a separate subject that will be taken up in the next section in greater detail. However, planning operations of this kind before a disaster occurs is properly an aspect of vulnerability reduction planning. The most important aspect of a planning operation that should be mentioned here is that of anticipating specific kinds of damage, devising in advance sets of activities to be carried out, and obtaining and storing in a secure place the necessary supplies and equipment to conduct such operations. Again, what is appropriate will vary with type of object, organizations and the type of hazard. An archive will need to take different steps to prepare against the water damage of paper than a museum will to repair earthquake damage to sculpture.

Recovering

Restoration plans are appropriate subjects for a later section also. However, preparation for restoration, reconstruction and conservation procedures properly constitute an important element of a comprehensive plan to reduce vulnerability. The plan must cover restoring operations, structures and objects. It, too, will obviously vary with the nature of the organization and type of hazard.

Perhaps the best way to approach this element of the plan is to create a number of disaster scenarios involving different types of natural hazards at different levels of severity. Scenarios and simulations should attempt to anticipate as much as possible the types and magnitude of damage that may be suffered. [Foster, 1980, pp. 125-150] Contingency plans for restoring operations as rapidly as possible should be developed. [Lewis, 1977] Making the organization internally operative again is the first priority. Sets of tasks and duties for the personnel composing the organization should be thought out and detailed. Of course, they must be clearly communicated. Getting various elements of the organization back into operation at as high a level as possible is the principle objective. Priorities should be established and the more critical aspects of the operation should take precedence. Restoring access to the facility and the services it provides, probably in phases, should be planned and scheduled. Restoring structures and taking advantage of the situation to make desirable modifications should be thought out in advance. Steps that will reduce vulnerability in subsequent disasters should certainly be taken. Restoring the integrity of the structure includes a number of aspects. Structural stability is obviously a primary concern. The ability of the structure to provide security and protection from the elements is of almost as great consequence. The capacity of the building to support operations requires that heating, ventilating, plumbing and lighting systems be restored as rapidly as possible. Fans, pumps, generators, transformers, elevators and a wide variety of specialized equipment may be involved. Necessary measures to restore artifacts and objects should be considered and planned too. These of course will vary tremendously by type of object and nature of hazard.

Plans for reconstruction will indicate various preparatory measures that need to be taken. In recovering from a disastrous event, rapid and ready access to different kinds of assistance is necessary. First there must be access to the funds required to support extraordinary activities. Obviously appropriate insurance at suitable levels is a principal source. Possibilities for other types of sources should be anticipated and the feasibility of pursuing them when necessary determined. Rapid access to certain kinds of supplies and equipment will be needed also. Stocks of such supplies and equipment may have been destroyed in the region by the disaster, and they are likely in any case to be in short supply because of increased demands on the part of other organizations and individuals. Plans should be made to identify the existence, location, and probable availability of resources of these kinds in disaster situations. A third kind of resource that will be badly needed is expertise in dealing with conservation and restoration. Not only will specialized knowledge be necessary, but additional cadres of individuals who possess the required knowledge and experience to meet the tremendous demands that recovery and reconstruction entail will also be needed. Preparing restoration plans and working through various disaster scenarios may lead to modification of other elements of the plan. The burdens recovery will place on the organization may cause priorities to be shifted, particularly in terms of avoiding exposure and assuring protection.

REVISING PLANS

The whole process of reducing vulnerability must be recognized as iterative rather than sequential. Proceeding through each step may lead to re-evaluations and revisions of previous steps. It must also be conceived as a continuous process which becomes part of the normal operation of the organization. By its nature it will be long-run and will require many years in most instances to institute completely. In the course of time, it should be reviewed, re-evaluated and revised to reflect changing attitudes and conditions. The functions of assuming and delegating responsibility for reducing vulnerability will shift over time as organizations transform and conditions modify. Plans will differ with respect to specific objects, organizations and hazards, and there can be changes in all of these over time. Attitudes toward risk and the definition of acceptable threshholds may change with conditions and individuals. Differing strategies to achieve protection goals and objectives may seem more appropriate at different points in time. The specific elements of a vulnerability reduction plan, because of their great detail, will be extremely sensitive to changing conditions and the transformation of organizations over time. Vulnerability reduction can be satisfactorily achieved only as a constant concern and effort. It cannot be accomplished by simply instituting a number of steps to be carried out over a number of months or years and considering the task finished. Constant awareness of continuing threats is essential for maintaining the attitude of preparedness which will result in higher levels of protection of the cultural heritage embodied in artifacts and structures.

REFERENCES

Ayres, J. Marx, and Tseng-Yao Sun. Criteria for Building Services and Furnishings in Building Practices for Disaster Mitigation. Building Science Series 46. Washington, D.C.: U.S. Department of Commerce, National Bureau of Standards, 1973.

Buchanan, Sally and Philip D. Leighton. "The Stanford Meyer Library Flood Report." Disasters: Prevention and Coping. James N. Myers and Denise D. Bedford, Eds. Stanford, California: Stanford University Libraries, 1981, pp. 70-122.

Breuer, J. Michael. "Regional Cooperation for Disaster Preparedness." Disasters: Prevention and Coping. James N. Myers and Denise D. Bedford, Eds. Stanford, California: Stanford University Libraries, 1981, pp. 41-51.

Ciborowski, Adolph. Warsaw: A City Destroyed and Rebuilt. Warsaw: Interpress, 1970.

Foster, Harold D. Disaster Planning: The Preservation of Life and Property. New York: Springer-Verlag, 1980.

Francell, Lawrence John, Director of Operations, Dallas Museum of Art. Personal Communication. July 7, 1980.

Hugo-Brunt, Michael. A Historical Survey of the Physical Development of Nantucket: A Brief Narrative History and Documentary Source Material. Ithaca, N.Y.: Center for Housing and Environmental Studies, Cornell University, April 1969.

Jenkins, Joseph F. Ed. Protecting Our Heritage: A Discourse on Fire Protection and Prevention in Historic Buildings and Landmarks. Boston: National Fire Protection Association, 1970.

Lewis, James. A Primer of Precautionary Planning for Natural Disaster. Occasional Paper No. 13. Bradford, England: The University of Bradford, Disaster Research Unit, 1977.

McKee, Harley J. Recording Historic Buildings. Washington, D.C.: Historic American Buildings Survey, U.S. Department of Interior, National Park Service, 1970.

Morris, John. Managing the Library Fire Risk. Berkeley, California: Office of Risk Management and Safety, University of California, 1979.

Reps, John W. Views and Viewmakers of Urban America: Lithographs of Towns and Cities in the United States and Canada, Notes on the Artists and Publishers, and a Union Catalog of Their Work, 1825-1925. Columbia, Missouri: University of Missouri Press, 1984.

Schiff, Anshel J. Pictures of Earthquake Damage to Power Systems and Cost-Effective Methods to Reduce Seismic Failures of Electric Power Equipment. West Lafayette, Indiana: Center for Earthquake Engineering and Ground Motion Studies, Institute for Interdisciplinary Engineering Studies and School of Mechanical Engineering, Purdue University, February 1980.

Stone, Marraccini and Patterson, Consulting Engineers. Studies to Establish Seismic Protection Provisions for Furniture, Equipment and Supplies for V.A. Hospitals. Washington, D.C.: Veterans Administration, Office of Construction, February 1980.

Whipkey, Harry E. After Agnes: A Report on Flood Recovery Assistance by the Pennsylvania Historical and Museum Commission. Harrisburg, Pennsylvania: Pennsylvania Historical and Museum Commission, 1973.

Willey, A. Elwood. "The Charles Klein Law Library Fire." In John Morris, Managing the Library Fire Risk. Berkeley, California: Office of Risk Management and Safety, University of California, 1979, pp. 20-26.

Reducing Vulnerability

Melvyn Green, P.E.

I. INTRODUCTION

This paper presents a process to reduce vulnerability of historic structures, museums and collections due to earthquakes and other natural disasters.

The procedure assumes that the possibility of future problems has been identified. This information may have been received through knowledge of the building, past history of earthquakes, wind, etc., an engineer's report or similar sources. The vulnerability of artifacts, too, should be considered an identified problem. One should also consider internal disasters such as fire, explosion or bursting pipes.

The process also assists in selecting the desired level of performance for protection of the structure and the methodology of setting standards with which to evaluate the structure.

The process involves the following steps:

A. Identify Specific Hazards
B. Identify Specific Goals
C. Selecting and Setting Appropriate Standards
D. Evaluation
E. Mitigation of Deficiencies

Each step is discussed in detail in the paper.

The paper identifies several other factors such as non-structural damage and cost factors in the evaluation process. Also suggested are some methods to consider in strengthening buildings constructed with archaic materials and for protecting collections.

II. THE PROCESS

A. The first step is to <u>identify specific hazards</u>. Earlier papers in this series have discussed the process of identifying vulnerability.

This paper will consider the steps one should take to protect particular buildings and property from such hazards as:

Earthquakes
High Winds
Floods
Landslides
Fire

Clearly, risks will vary based on the specific building type. For example, unreinforced masonry buildings are a seismic hazard but not a hazard in high winds; light wood frame buildings may be a problem in high winds but not in earthquake areas.

B. The second step is to <u>identify specific goals</u>. These include:

Protection of Life
Protection of Buildings and Structures
Protection of Collections and Artifacts

1. All buildings should, at a minimum level of performance, protect the life of both public and employees. Concern with protection of life should <u>begin</u> with compliance with codes, not only to reduce liability concerns, but to show responsibility to those visiting a museum. Alternatively, in a few historic structures (such as some of the California missions), the public is warned that the building is unsafe in an earthquake and they choose to enter at their own risk. However, one should consider such a system only as a last resort and with competent legal advice.

Protection of life measures acknowledge that the damage to the structure and contents, resulting from a disaster, will exceed the damage in an equivalent new structure. Two additional factors should be considered, however: first, that in historic structures, the strengthening may cause an unacceptable level of damage to the historic fabric; secondly, that budget constraints may encourage the acceptance of disaster risks and the costs of repair after damage occurs.

2. Protection of Buildings and Structures. Protection of life measures will generally prevent outright destruction of a building but may still allow for an unacceptable level of damage, requiring demolition of the structure in a post disaster situation.

Even design to current building codes may result in significant damage in a major earthquake. The intent of the building code provisions for seismic safety notes that buildings should be able to:

a. Resist minor earthquakes without damage;
b. Resist moderate earthquakes without structural damage, but with some non-structural damage;

c. Resist major earthquakes, of the intensity of severity of the strongest experienced in California, without collapse, but with some structural as well as non-structural damage.

Clearly, limitation of damage in museum buildings requires more strengthening than that necessary only for life safety. However, determination of an acceptable level of property protection is fortunately more flexible than life safety, particularly when one retrofits an existing building. Building codes reflect a consensus on how to provide a new building or structure with the most cost effective amount of protection.

The level of protection may be dictated by other factors such as accreditation requirements, individuals or governments fearful of losing displays, or conditions of removing artifacts from a country.

3. Protection of Collections and Artifacts. One can protect a building without being concerned about contents, but the reverse is not necessarily true; the protection of contents requires that the building at least survive an earthquake. Once one reaches this minimum level, one can then address the protection of the collection or artifacts rather than the building itself. Protection may include an entire collection, or certain parts; it may be limited to areas in storage rather than on display; or it may concentrate on display items. One must realize, however, that only certain features of a collection may be protected. Each decision on protection produces a different problem and requires a unique solution. And each solution, such as the anchoring of an object with glue or metal, must be reversible to protect the object.

C. The third step entails selecting and setting appropriate standards for evaluation. A variety of codes and standards may establish the level of building performance and become the basis for mitigation methods. One should first consider the legal requirements, as reflected in building codes and other regulations. Second, one should consider the standards professional associations set for making an institution accredited and eligible for exhibits. Third, one should consider developing "in-house" standards, either because no criteria exist addressing the specific mitigation problem or because of the value of the collection.

1. Legal Codes and Regulations

Codes and regulations fall into three general groups:

Construction Regulations
 Building Code
 Electrical Code
 Plumbing Code

Mechanical Code
Health Code
Maintenance Regulations
Fire Prevention Code
Health Code
Dangerous Buildings Abatement Code
Property Maintenance Code
Retroactive Regulations
Fire Safety – Stairways, Sprinklers and Smoke Detectors
Seismic – Unreinforced Masonry and Elevators

One should thoroughly study and understand these codes when considering them as a standard for a building. What follows is the explanation of the intent and compass of these codes.

a. Construction Regulations

The Building Code sets the standards for new building construction, alterations, and additions. These requirements may be difficult to implement for existing buildings. However, by careful reading and understanding of code intent, one can make the code a useful tool in setting levels of design.

Plumbing, Electrical and Mechanical Codes each relate to safe construction of those portions of the building. The Mechanical Code regulates heating, ventilating and air conditioning systems, gas piping and similar equipment. Each may be useful in setting standards or identifying safety concerns.

The Health Code generally relates to sanitation and kitchens. Health Departments generally have the standards for areas where food is stored, prepared and served and other maintenance requirements.

b. Maintenance Regulations

Maintenance regulations, which usually involve housekeeping rather than construction, should also be considered in setting standards. The Fire Prevention Code is a maintenance code and relates to the appropriate storage of hazardous materials, the required maintenance of emergency systems and extinguishers, and similar items. It may contain requirements for emergency lighting, exit hardware and other factors useful in disaster pre-planning and mitigation.

One should consider those codes used to abate dangerous or substandard buildings as establishing a bottom line safety level for any building. Thus, they provide important guidance for structural and life safety.

c. Retroactive Codes

Two retroactive codes types are of interest. First, numerous recent retroactive fire safety ordinances have been adopted, some of which relate to assembly buildings and buildings without enclosed stairways. Seismic safety ordinances for unreinforced masonry buildings make up the second retroactive code type. These codes again establish a level of performance usable as a standard, proving a valuable guide if not a city law to ensure minimum performance levels.

2. In addition to legal codes, the standards of professional associations or societies provide an institution with guidance or mandatory minimum levels of compliance. Generally, these standards relate to environmental controls, security and fire protection. Seldom do they contain specific provisions for structural design of buildings, but they may establish a certain level of performance for accreditation or provide guidance in setting levels.

3. While legal codes and professional codes provide directions reflecting particular concerns, many of the hazards we are addressing in this paper do not have developed standards, and in some cases little information is available. Should such a situation occur, one must develop a draft standard or "in-house" guideline that reflects the appropriate design and safety level that one wants for the particular building.

A reasonable procedure for developing a new standard would be to prepare a draft and circulate it, either among staff or other institutions or professionals. This would provide independent input into the process. After the standard has been reviewed and agreed upon, it then becomes the base line for design for that particular building or feature.

The development of a standard need not be excessively complex if one is careful to outline clearly one's goals. Other codes and standards can help form the basis for the new standard. For example, if one is concerned with seismic safety of unreinforced masonry buildings or infill wall, some of the regulations adopted by Los Angeles or the State of California may provide significant guidance.

Life safety from fire relates to the local Building Code, the National Fire Protection Association (NFPA), Standard 101 Life Safety Code, and the Fire Prevention Code. Each of these will provide specific information related to the minimum standards for life safety.

One should also take care to avoid setting a standard that cannot reasonably be met. The standard should reflect the specific building, the value of the structure to the institution and the community and the value of the contents. One may clearly want higher standards than the Building Code for property protection.

Obtaining protection of contents from earthquakes is difficult and potentially complex. The complexity increases based on the size and weight of the objects, the display case or support, and the fastening between the object, case or support and building.

D. Evaluation

Once one establishes the standard (or level of desired performance to be achieved), then one can evaluate the building, or portions thereof, against the standard. This applies to the elements of the collection including storage racks, display cabinets and other pieces. This process thus identifies deficiences, types of failures and possible damage and becomes the basis for mitigation efforts. The evaluation may reveal a building either equal to, above or below the standard. Obviously, features above or equal to standards should be considered acceptable, while those that fall below the standard must be upgraded. This phase must be performed carefully, since accurate prediction of any mode of failure ensures that remedial efforts are targeted at real problems. Because of the significant difference between designing new buildings and retrofitting old, this process will usually involve an engineering analysis, performed by an individual experienced in restoration of historic structures and aware of the criteria for museum collections.

E. Mitigation of Deficiencies

Where the building falls short of the performance level specified in the standard, various mitigation methods may be considered. In most cases, one can easily meet the specific prescriptions of the standard or code through use of conventional design methods. However, with historic buildings or unusual structures, one may have to meet the intent of the standard through an equivalent method, different from the code-stated solution. This alternative will be particularly important when the buildings are constructed of materials such as unreinforced masonry, stone or materials not commonly used today. For example, wood lath and plaster used to brace buildings under seismic loads lack code-stated design values. Older codes or some state-of-the-art information do, however, provide reasonable guidance on values for such materials. For the protection of artifacts, there may be no standards available and one may be working at the state-of-the-art level.

We call the method used in our office for dealing with historic structures a "damage control approach" as opposed to a "code approach". Essentially, we establish a primary goal—safety to life— and then design improvements to reasonably assure that the structure will not collapse catastrophically. We then look at the next several modes of failure and mitigate each until the desired level of property protection is reached. Determining this level usually involves a cost/benefit evaluation (discussed later). Protecting collections, however, is often far more complex than protecting just the building. The building may be compared to a spring, the display case a second spring and the object yet a third spring—all attached in a linear form. Identifying how each of these vibrates and acts on each other determines the design problem. Solutions have been attempted to permit movement at the object's base through "teflon" pads but to resist movement elsewhere by bracing the artifact or case at its side or top. Other methods may involve securing the base of the display to prevent overturning of racks, cases or pieces of the collection.

Specific disasters make specific building types particularly problematic:

Earthquakes
    Unreinforced masonry, brick, clay tile, block
    Split level wood frame
    Tilt up concrete (pre 1973 California code)
    Concrete structures with a "soft" first story (generally constructed between 1950 and 1973)
Winds
    Light wood frame building
    Wood frame roofs
Floods
    Light structures not bolted to foundations
Landslides
    Any type of construction
Fire
    Any type of construction

III. FACTORS TO CONSIDER IN MITIGATION DESIGN

A. Cost Factors

Cost effectiveness of any structural or protective upgrading should be carefully considered once life safety is assured. In some cases, one might more appropriately make repairs after the damage occurs. For instance, partitions between offices may lend themselves simply to being fixed, if necessary, after a disaster, since they may not pose a life threatening situation. In other cases, however, easily addressed weaknesses should be corrected prior to a potential disaster to prevent unnecessary distress should such an event occur. For example, minor or non-structural damage may block exits and stairways sufficiently to cause a panic, particularly among persons not familiar with the building. Furthermore, materials might block elevator shafts or in other ways cause elevators to cease operating. A cost/benefit analysis must therefore be done to weigh preventive costs against potential cost and probability of repair and reparation. Clearly, with many pieces in a collection, the cost effectiveness of improvements will be difficult to determine. In just one of many decisions, one has to weigh methods of protecting exhibits from falling building elements against working to mitigate damage to the entire structure.

B. Non-Structural Damage

While the non-structural elements of the building, such as suspended ceilings, may pose a non-life threatening hazard, non-structural damage may destroy the collection or may place the structure out of service for a sustained time period. Only recently have non-structural elements been regulated by building codes. One might appropriately review the seismic supports for suspended ceilings, interior partition walls as well as the exterior walls if they are of curtain wall construction or glass. In addition to the built-in features, one should attend to the building contents other than collections. This may include desks, filing cabinets and other pieces of furniture which can overturn and cause damage or injury in earthquakes.

C. Operational Controls

In some cases, it may be possible to provide higher levels of safety with other than built-in features, namely operational controls. For example, one could limit the number of groups or individuals in a group that tour a building or collection; one could also have visitors tour with a trained docent or staff person; relocation of collections to other portions of a building or site is another option. In addition, an operational analysis may identify safe areas that could house a collection with minimum or no construction while relocating storage to more potentially hazardous areas.

D. Phasing

The methodology presented in this paper can be used to identify the primary and secondary problems and can be a guide to effective phasing of the required mitigation efforts.

The Mitigation and Prevention of Earthquake Damage to Artifacts

Dr. John A. Blume

Earthquakes have been occurring for millions of years, and they will continue to do so in most parts of the world. Ground motion has been felt and has caused damage in virtually every state in the United States, but the most frequent and violent activity, at least in recent geologic time, has been west of the Rocky Mountains, especially in California, Nevada, Washington, and Alaska. For the protection of valuable artifacts, no area should be considered immune. There can be little doubt that many historical and rare artifacts, known and unknown, have already been destroyed by earthquakes.

In considering earthquakes, it is well to keep in mind that they often lead to secondary disasters, such as flood and fire, which can destroy artifacts even though the ground shaking per se may not. Broken dams or water pipes release unwanted water, and overturned stoves or damaged furnaces and boilers can lead to fire as can damage to electrical systems. History has also shown that fire-fighting systems may be destroyed by earthquake shaking and that routes of access to fires may be blocked. Another hazard is theft during the confused state of events following a major earthquake. This is usually controlled to a certain extent by the military or national guard, who in the past have been ordered to shoot looters on sight.

In spite of these hazards, artifacts can be protected against earthquake damage.

SOME ELEMENTARY CONCEPTS

Every object or system, whether it be a building, a process plant, an artifact, or a machine, can be modeled dynamically so that its natural vibrational characteristics are known or well estimated. With this model, one can then estimate the response of the entity to any dynamic disturbance, such as an earthquake. Knowing the response and whether or not it is in the damaging range, one can take necessary steps to decrease the response and reduce or prevent damage. In addition to this somewhat sophisticated approach, one should also consider historical and empirical evidence and add the necessary ingredient of good judgment; there are valid reasons why some objects have failed and others have not failed in earthquakes. So-called anomalies can be described simply as matters an expert does not yet understand.

Certainly it is not necessary to design a museum as one would design a nuclear power plant. However, most of the same principles apply and can be utilized with a few simple ground rules.

Earthquake motion is three dimensional. What is stable under normal gravity conditions may not be stable during an earthquake. Unless objects are anchored or restrained, they tend to slide or to tip over and may fall from a support or shelf to the floor. However, if objects are anchored (at the base, for example) inertial forces will be induced, causing internal stress and possible failure either in the object per se or at the anchorage points. In addition, the vertical component of the earthquake acceleration may reduce normal resistance to overturning. Ground motion that can derail locomotives can certainly tip over a tall, slender Ming vase.

It is vital to avoid impact because impact multiplies local stress levels and breaks objects. The impact may result from the object's overturning, from its dropping to the floor or ground, or from its contacting some other object. Impact effects are resisted by the storing of elastic energy (if there is resiliency) and by what is called doing work. Work is the integral of force relative to deformation. If the object is brittle, its deformation before reaching the breaking point is quite limited. After breakage occurs, any residual kinetic energy is converted to work in making fragments and perhaps scattering these fragments. If the object is ductile, it can deform (dent, for example) without fracturing, and work is done in causing the deformation. Denting is usually less objectionable than shattering, but neither is desirable. Of course, there are various degrees between brittle and quite ductile.

These catastrophes can be avoided in most cases without complex mathematical analyses. Pitfalls and their avoidance constitute the subject of this paper, which is purposely given without complex equations or rigorous treatment even though some of the problems include many elements from the classical theory of mechanics, dynamics, material properties, energy conservation, and seismology.

THE EARTHQUAKE SHAKING

The ground motion from major, close-by seismic events may vary from a few seconds to a minute or more. In addition to the main shock, aftershocks of lesser intensity may continue at a slowly reducing scale for weeks or months. Earthquake magnitude alone is not a significant indicator of intensity at a given location; its distance from the moving fault or from the epicenter must also be known for magnitude measurements to be meaningful. There are various intensity scales that reflect the degree of local shaking after the fact by judgmental assessment of damage, earth slides (if any), human reaction, etc. The Modified Mercalli Scale is the most popular of the intensity scales currently in use in the United States.

Ground shaking consists of various types of waves, some causing rapid, or high-frequency, motions and others causing long-period swaying, particularly in the case of tall buildings. A local earthquake of moderate magnitude generally lasts only a few seconds and gives the sensation of rapid motion. A major earthquake, especially one at some distance, causes smoother and longer waves to be felt. All of these, and the many intermediate combinations, are generally frightening and can be damaging. Ground motion is three dimensional, although motion in one horizontal direction may tend to dominate.

RESPONSE TO GROUND SHAKING

Response to ground shaking depends not only upon the characteristics and duration of the shaking but also upon the structures or items being shaken. All buildings, statues—in fact all objects—have natural periods of vibration that may "tune in" to the dominant periods of the ground motion. If they do, the response is greatly amplified. Ordering marching soldiers to break step while crossing a bridge is a valid precaution against possible tuning perturbation. It is also possible, theoretically at least, to break glass with a voice or violin tuned to a natural frequency of the glass. All types of objects but one have natural periods of vibration that are constant for all reasonable amplitudes of motion, provided there is no damage. However, the type that is the exception often exists in the world of museums and artifacts—it is a very rigid object situated without bond or connection on a rigid base, as for example, a sculptured bust placed without connection or adhesive on a rigid pedestal. The shaking may be of sufficient intensity to induce rocking. The rocking of a rigid body on a rigid base has natural frequencies that vary with the amplitude of the rocking motion. One can hear this change in frequency by dropping a silver dollar (if indeed one can be found) on a hard table top. This phenomenon undoubtedly saves some artifacts from overturning by preventing resonant amplification, but no reliance should be placed on this.

The size, weight, shape, and material properties of an object are all important in its response as is the question whether it is brittle, ductile, or somewhere in between. Glassware is generally brittle—it is unable to withstand much impact—but a tennis ball is quite ductile and can sustain tremendous impact without damage. Tall or slender objects tend to overturn if not anchored at the base or braced laterally. They also tend to "walk," or change position, or even fall off their supporting bases under continued motion.

199

Buildings. Although the basic subject of this paper is artifacts, not buildings, it is essential to touch briefly on the subject of buildings for the reason that if a building fails most of its contents are usually damaged or destroyed. Artifacts are generally kept in buildings, so the first step to save such artifacts is to put them in good, earthquake-resistant buildings. This can be done and should be done. Moreover, buildings per se may be architectural classics or historical monuments, and they, too, can be retrofitted for preservation. A prime example is the recently renewed California State Capitol. We should not overlook the need for musuem buildings to be as resistant as possible to earthquakes, as well as to theft, water, fire, wind, and deterioration. Protection in all of these areas can be accomplished with expert and careful design.

Building Ornamentations. The original California State Capitol, constructed from 1864 to 1874, had life-size statues of various persons at the roof level around the building periphery. Some of the statues were violently removed by the distant 1906 earthquake, and the rest of them by man shortly thereafter. Figure 4.1 shows the original building before the statues were removed.

Another elevated statue, of the geologist and naturalist J. L. R. Agassiz (1807-1873), was forced to make a perfect dive into a walkway at Stanford University during the 1906 earthquake, as shown in Figure 4.2.

Building ornamentations and appendages, whether representing men, women, birds, flowers, grapes, animals, snakes, trees, or whatever, must either be sculptured into sound walls or be extremely well anchored on a permanent, non-deteriorating basis. Projections respond not to ground motion per se but to greatly amplified motion at some height in the building. The earthquake-generated horizontal forces at these upper levels may well be several times those at the ground level. This is a problem of dynamics, requiring advanced dynamic analysis for a proper solution. The anchorages not only must be strong but also must be able to withstand the elements for decades.

Parapet walls are not always artifacts—in fact many of them are the opposite—but they, too, are very precarious and dangerous in earthquakes unless specifically designed and anchored.

Exterior Artifacts. Such objects as statues of persons, animals, men on horseback, birds, arches, gates, murals, towers, pillars, etc., may be of historical as well as artistic interest; some may have been used for some purpose, now extinct. Most exterior artifacts are at or near ground level although some, like the Dewey Monument in Union Square, San Francisco, are elevated far above the ground. Figure 4.3 shows the Dewey Monument, which survived the 1906 earthquake with some minor damage, not because of a miracle but because of some anchorage and its dynamic behavior. Most exterior artifacts are large, at least life size, and most have a rather substantial base.

The base usually poses little or no earthquake problem if it is on stable ground that will remain stable during the shaking. This should

Figure 4.1. Sacramento, California: California State Capitol Built 1864–1874
Showing Statues on Parapets Some of Which Were Dislodged and Destroyed in
Earthquake of April 18, 1906.

Figure 4.2. Palo Alto, California: Statue of J. L. R. Agassiz (1807-1873) Dislodged From a Building at Stanford University in Earthquake of April 18, 1906.

Figure 4.3. San Francisco, California: Dewey Monument, Union Square, a Tall Column and Statue Which Survived Earthquake of April 18, 1906.

be verified. However, objects mounted on bases are themselves usually quite precarious unless well anchored. Where a tall, slender statuary object touches the base at only one or two points (for example, the feet of persons or the shoes of horses), there will be a strong tendency for contact points to be broken in an earthquake. Should the statue fall over, it will no doubt be broken further by impact with the base or the ground. This is really a problem in dynamics and engineering. The use of metal rods—preferably of stainless steel and often of copper—extending from deep in the base well up into the statue's legs or torso is desirable if not essential. (In fact, sculptors would do well to start with a corrosion-resistant interior frame in addition to strong rods extending full height in the figure.) The anchorage rods must also be well bonded to the figure and to the base or else be mechanically connected. Simple dowels set loosely in holes or sockets invite impact, which multiplies the forces.

In addition to rod or mechanical anchorages, there is a method termed rather optimistically vibration "isolation," in which special materials are used as supporting pads and/or buffers. The objective is to allow some controlled motion at the base connection and, in the process, to do work by compressing the material (which is designed to rebound), thus absorbing at least some of the kinetic energy. Such devices are sometimes used for machinery to prevent or curtail oscillation and/or to avoid transmitting motion away from the machine. Automobile engines, in fact the cars per se, are mounted on various absorbers, springs or buffers. Vibration-absorption devices could be used for large artifacts and could be mostly, if not entirely, concealed. However, because more harm than good could ensue from faulty mounting, this approach should be made with the aid of expert dynamicists.

Slender projections on statues or other artifacts are also subject to violent shaking and the resulting forces. The higher the projection above the base, the greater the potential force. Arms, wings, extended rifles, swords, etc., are examples of dynamic projections that could be snapped off if not reinforced. What happened, for example, to the arms of the Venus de Milo? Sometimes projections can be reinforced with slender, hidden wires that would at least prevent their falling off should breaking occur.

Thus far, discussion of exterior artifacts and their reinforcement against earthquake motion has been limited to concealed methods of strengthening and applies mostly to protection for new creations. What can be done about existing objects? The answer is: not a great deal, if total concealment of bracing is desired. Perhaps the most could be gained by devising concealed connections as the points of contact with the base. This would involve cutting into the existing material; installing rods, vibration pads, and connections; and then replacing or restoring the removed materials. This is not a simple or a completely satisfactory solution.

The alternative is to resort to visible bracing, which might be classified as either barely visible or frankly exposed. Wires can be used as guys to prevent the object from overturning. The wires will show, even if colored black, and birds may fly into them or otherwise use them to the concern of caretakers and perhaps the public. If wires are to be employed, several things are necessary. They must oppose each other in the sense that there will always be wires in tension, no matter in which direction the objects tend to move. The wires must be well anchored at both ends, and they must be tight; a loose wire is worse than none at all. Turnbuckles may be essential to ensure tightness. Vibration-absorbing springs can be injected into the wire system at less visible locations. Above all, the wires must be properly sized and should be of non-corrosive material such as stainless steel.

There may be a few cases where structural brackets or a small bracing system can be placed between the object and its base or the ground. These lateral supports might be honestly visible but could be located strategically so as to leave an unobstructed view of the most essential parts of the object. Unlike guy wires, such installations need not surround the object because they can work in compression as well as in tension. A combination of wires and brackets is also possible.

What about the extreme case of an object that is tall, slender, and extremely fragile, perhaps deteriorated from the elements? Let us presume that such an object could not be supported solely with wires or brackets, and certainly not by simply reinforcing it at its base. What it needs, if it is to be preserved, is gentle but firm support at several locations. One solution is the bold, honest approach of building a suitable framework, appropriately designed in every sense of the word, around the object, probably with a roof and siding to keep out the elements. This framework would be designed to be strong and to resist any earthquake possible in the area. It would be spaced away from the object to permit visibility and could even provide viewer access if desired. The siding could be of glass if external visibility is desired. Wires and/or small struts could be placed between the object and the strong framework so that the object would be well braced. With suitable spacing, the bracing would actually serve to strengthen the object as well as to prevent its toppling over.

There may be those who prefer not to anchor vertical objects on the basis that unanchored objects will slide or "walk" around on their bases and thus relieve the earthquake forces. This has happened rarely. It is a possible phenomenon—but improbable and unreliable. I do not recommend it except for a low, flat object on a large base and not even then if it is fragile because there may be a rocking or pounding.

In the very early days of earthquake engineering (which is still an art as much as a science, and not very old), investigators were impressed by the fact that during an earthquake some of the tombstones in graveyards were overturned and others were not. They reasoned that since they knew the geometry of the various tombstones, and since Newton said force equals mass times acceleration, they could compute the horizontal acceleration on a simple static basis. The force created an overturning moment, and the base dimensions and the mass gave the resistance to tipping over. The answers obtained were unreliable and quite erratic because of several factors that were overlooked, including:

1. The motion of the ground during an earthquake is three-dimensional.
2. Although the tombstone was quite rigid, the soil below it was not. (This would be true almost by definition; one does not locate a graveyard in a spot where digging would have to be done in competent rock.)
3. The tombstone and the soil thus created a dynamic system of three dimensions and six possible degrees of freedom that had generally inelastic properties; i.e., the soil acted as a set of nonlinear springs. This system was shaken by three-dimensional ground motion of an erractic nature.

Their static model thus in no way represented the prototype system, nor did the forces obtained represent the real, dynamic forces or accelerations.

Therefore, if exterior artifacts are to be planted on or in the soil without large bases, do not rely upon the tombstone theory. Even with large bases, there could be trouble should the soil settle, heave, liquefy, or be cracked. Peculiar things happen, and do not happen, in earthquakes. One should not generalize from one location to others. Each case can be prepared for if it is studied properly.

Restoration, repair, or patching is also a means of at least mitigating earthquake damage. For example, an old brick kiln can be made more resistant by restoring damaged or badly weathered bricks and, especially, by replacing very weak or missing mortar. Old bridges of historic interest can be repaired or restored whether or not they are open to traffic. Earthquake shaking seeks out weaknesses—in design, materials, and construction or from deterioration. Thus, if the weaknesses are reduced or eliminated, the chance of survival will be increased. The California missions are good examples of this. When buildings are improved for withstanding earthquakes, they are usually renovated and updated in other ways as well, electrically and mechanically, for example.

Interior Artifacts of Large Size. Museums, galleries, and collections contain all sizes, shapes, and types of artifacts. In general, the objects are much smaller than the external artifacts, although there are some large figures and statues in many museums. If such large objects are on the ground floor of the building, the treatment described for external artifacts would apply in most cases. However, if such items are placed at an elevated floor level, a new factor enters the problem: the filtering and amplifying effect that a building has on ground motion. The elevated object then responds not directly to the ground motion but to the motion of the floor on which it is situated. At the building's natural frequency, elevated-level motion may be amplified as much as several times beyond that of the ground. Should the natural frequency of an object or of any of its projecting parts fall into the same range as that of the building, the compounded dynamic amplification could be disastrous. In such cases, the large objects should be placed on the ground floor unless it is possible to create a special, dynamic building design to accommodate the situation.

Objects in Glass-Covered Cases. Museums as well as jewelry stores commonly enclose valuable or fragile items in glass-covered cases. One is to look at but not touch the displayed items. The cases are usually fairly strong, and their failure during an earthquake is doubtful, especially if they are free to slide without banging into anything. The legs should be strong and well connected, and neighboring cases should be clamped to each other. One must keep in mind, however, that the objects they contain may be fragile. Fragile or not, they should not be scratched. For example, a numismatist would consider it a disaster to have a scratch appear on a rare, proof gold coin. The point here is that each object within each case is also subject to response, sliding, tipping over, and impact with its neighbors; an earthquake shakes everything. The solution seems to be some combination of soft padding as a base, generous space for separation or padded individual receptacles, placement of slender objects in a horizontal position or as near that as possible, and prevention of rolling. Should anything fall from the ceiling of the room (plaster is known to do this), glass covers of cases would be broken, and the glass fragments as well as pieces of the ceiling could damage the contents of the cases. Look to your ceilings and light fixtures.

Objects on Shelves. One of the most common forms of damage in earthquakes occurs in liquor stores, where the vertical bottles on shelves simply crash to the floor. Probably the next most common is found in supermarkets, where not only bottles but also cans and cartons fall to the floor. Drugstores suffer as well, but they frequently have sliding glass doors that prevent many of the floor-crashing events. Anyone who displays or stores things on shelves or in library stacks can expect trouble of four possible types in earthquakes:

1. The shelf or stack falls over, breaking essentially everything breakable that was on it and possibly crashing into another shelf as well.
2. Objects fall off the shelf to the floor and break.
3. Objects remain on the shelf but fall over and break.
4. Objects on the shelf bump into each other and are damaged or broken.

The first rule should be to anchor wall shelves or stacks securely to the wall. Free-standing shelves and stacks must be secured to the floor and also tied to each other and to the walls by struts at their top level. It is imperative that shelving and stacks not fall over, or even lean, under severe shaking and lateral forces.

Recall that the higher the position in the building the greater the horizontal motion. Therefore, massive objects should be placed on lower shelves—at low or ground-floor stories, where feasible, of course. But regardless of where the shelf is, the objects on it are subject to items 2, 3, and 4, above. Thus, extremely fragile or valuable objects should be stored in some other manner unless great precautions are taken.

It is debatable whether sliding is better than tipping over. Frankly, neither is good for fragile objects. If one first covered the shelf with soft padding of considerable friction value, sliding would be mitigated but tipping would be accentuated. The padding would mitigate the effects of tipping, unless tipping caused the object to fall off the shelf onto the floor. An object that drops only 6 feet has a striking velocity of 20 feet per second, or 13 miles per hour. It has kinetic energy of six times its pound weight, in foot-pounds. It takes 0.61 second to fall. Unless it is very ductile (tough and resilient) and/or lands on a soft mattress, it is going to break. One way to minimize falling is to place objects well back on the shelf. With books, one might jam them in so tight that friction between books and arch action could prevent their falling. Of course, that method would lead to damage of books in daily use.

A good program might exclude very fragile or very valuable objects from shelving. The items displayed on a shelf should be well separated and preferably would be placed on the back part of the shelf; the shelf might have a felt cover or some thicker padding. Slender objects should be laid flat; round objects should be checked against rolling. Special pieces should be put in lined boxes. One could also consider the use of modern plastic belting material with tiny plastic hooks of the kind used for internal belting in clothing.

A small edge piece might be installed along the outer edge of the shelf. Even better would be an elastic rope of small diameter, pulled tight and hooded in such a manner as to be a few inches above the shelf and parallel to it. This could prevent almost all kinds of objects from falling to the floor.

Wall Displays. Anything hung on a wall, such as a framed canvas painting, is obviously subject to earthquake motion in three idealized dimensions—horizontally, parallel to the wall surface; normal to the wall; and vertically. Not only the building but the wall as well must survive. A crack or two in the wall might not be catastrophic unless the anchorage to the wall were loosened by the crack. If the wall anchors or hangers are not adequate for the increased loading produced by seismic conditions, the painting or object will fall to the floor and probably will be damaged, perhaps seriously. The type of anchorage that relies entirely on plaster or plasterboard is not very strong, regardless of what the manufacturer claims, and should not be used for heavy objects or large paintings. The anchorage value should be several times the static weight to be placed on it. Multiple anchorages are desirable in that they provide redundancy, a most useful characteristic for earthquake resistance.

Paintings will tend to bang against the wall, and the resulting impact stresses may damage the frame if not the canvas. A simple device to mitigate the effects of any banging is to provide thick elastic pads at each corner of the painting. These not only absorb considerable shock but tend to keep the frames in place at all times because of their friction or adhesive value.

Stored items. Even stored items are subject to damage. The same rules apply with regard to shelving, stacks, large objects, etc., as noted above for exterior and interior displayed objects. There are two basic differences, however. One is that stored goods are often placed with less care and precision. The other is that stored items can be packaged or crated.

Stored items that are not required frequently are often packed together to save space. This can lead to scratches, or worse, during earthquake motion. Here one should take a lesson from good furniture-moving techniques: (a) every piece is surrounded by quilting or soft packing material, (b) all space is used; i.e., no gaps are left for relative motion between the pieces to take place, and (c) ropes or straps are used to restrain the whole mass from moving differentially during transport. Materials so packed should sustain no damage in an earthquake. A carefully designed inventory system will reduce difficulty of retrieval.

If there is need for rather frequent access to the stored items, the foregoing system becomes a nuisance. In such cases, there is a tendency to resort to shelf storage or loose storage on the floor. This is not good unless the objects are crated or boxed, and even then they may fall from elevated shelving unless restrained. Storage shelves, of course, should be as well anchored as display shelves.

It is possible to pack a fragile item so that it can be shipped, dropped, or even go over Niagara Falls without breaking. The principle is energy absorption—a box within a box within a box, etc., with suitable packing material around the object and between boxes and no void spaces. There are all sorts of very efficient packing materials available today, but one should check for fire-resistance capacity before using such materials. Anything extremely rare or valuable should be placed in a strong box on the floor to prevent crushing from falling objects, and the strong box should contain no void spaces.

The principle is straightforward—avoid differential motion and impact of any kind, and separate objects with energy-absorbing materials.

Another procedure for both display and storage is to suspend objects from a roof or ceiling and let them sway without inducing severe stresses during the earthquake. Of course, the anchorage and the rope or chain must be substantial, and objects should not be allowed to sway into each other as they get out of phase; this means that they should have adequate separation or else be tied together.

CONCLUSION

Artifacts of all types can be saved from earthquake damage if the structure in which they are housed is earthquake resistant in all respects, including its ceilings, light fixtures, and walls. Such structures can be designed and built. The artifacts—indoors or outdoors, displayed or stored, large or small, fragile or not—need special attention before the earthquake strikes. It is hoped that some of the principles and ideas presented here will prove useful in saving things worth saving.

Museum Disaster Preparedness Planning

John E. Hunter

Previous papers have given case histories of natural disasters, and have discussed vulnerability assessment and reduction. We will later turn our attention to emergency measures and recovery operations. The body of knowledge derived from past experiences in coping with natural disasters can be useful only if it guides efforts toward the prevention and mitigation of future disasters. Therefore, the lessons of the preceding papers can be applied only by engaging in disaster planning.

Why plan for disasters? Hilda Bohem of the University of California Library System provides the dictum that, "A disaster is what happens only if you are not prepared for it." [Bohem, 1978] Preparing for disasters may not prevent them but will lessen their impact. Preparing and following a disaster response plan can help to avoid costly or fatal damage and can prevent a disaster from becoming a tragedy.

Planning for museum emergencies and disasters is a four-phase process. The first phase requires identification of natural events that might threaten the institution, that is, conducting a multi-hazard vulnerability assessment, and determing what the effects of such hazards could be under varying circumstances. The second phase consists of designing and assessing strategies for coping with the identified events. Strategic goals should include disaster prevention where possible, minimization of damage during a disaster, mitigation of further damage or deterioration afterwards, and recovery and resumption of normal operations. The third phase entails writing a plan to guide the museum staff before, during and after a disaster. The fourth phase calls for regular reviews of the disaster plan to keep it current, training in the plan's execution, periodic drills to test the plan's effectiveness, and evaluation of the plan's performance after any disastrous occurrence.

Developing and implementing a disaster plan does not require a lot of technical knowledge. It does require the attention and dedication of at least one staff member. The planner must have the full managment support and access to all relevant information on the museum's contents and operations. Developing a plan for a large or complex museum may take a year or more. Effective implementation of the plan—the training, testing, and evaluation steps—will usually take longer than the design and production of a written plan.

The examination of the museum necessary to prepare a plan should make the museum's staff aware of the institution's vulnerabilities and may stimulate them to thinking about improvements that can be made in ordinary museum operations. For example, the survey required to identify the institution's most valuable assets can be carried out in conjunction with a conservation needs survey. The preventive actions that can be taken to prepare a museum for surviving an earthquake may also help protect it from burglary and vandalism and can enhance building maintenance and upkeep.

There are at least ten discrete steps or stages in the four-phase development, writing, and evaluation of a disaster plan. The rest of this paper outlines what a disaster plan should contain and how an effective plan can be organized.

The first step in the preparation of a plan is designation of the person responsible for developing and writing the plan and the naming of an advisory committee. In a small institution, it is possible that everyone on the staff will play some role in developing the plan. In a large institution, a senior staff member will usually be in charge, assisted by individuals appointed from each department and perhaps from the museum's board. This planning team eventually may become the museum's Disaster Control Organization; its members would be the persons in charge of disaster mitigation and recovery efforts. Care in their selection is imperative.

Once the planning team has been selected, it should be given authority in writing and should enjoy the full support of management. Full support from the director, senior management, department heads, and the board of trustees is vital to the success of the planning effort. Without enough support, the planning team may not get full cooperation from all departments and may not be able to implement any new policies or administrative changes needed to establish a disaster preparedness program.

Once a team has been appointed and authorized to prepare a disaster plan, the second step is for them to locate sources of planning assistance and information. They should become familiar with disaster planning literature and should review plans developed by other museums. They should obtain as-built architectural drawings of the museum's building and, if possible, talk with the museum's architect and builder about its vulnerability to various disasters. They should find out what kinds of support local fire and building inspection offices can offer, not only in helping when disaster strikes but also in assessing the museum's vulnerability and helping with the planning effort. The team should contact other museums in the region to learn how they plan to deal with disasters and to explore the feasibility of mutual aid agreements. The team also should identify talents and capabilities possessed by the museum's own staff, trustees, and volunteers. One of the museum's trustees or volunteers may have responsibility for corporate disaster planning in his or her business and could be invited to serve on the planning team.

The planning team must also contact state and local police, fire, and public health agencies, state and local civil defense agencies, the Red Cross, and state and regional museum organizations. Such contacts are advisable for two reasons. First, local organizations can provide planning assistance and technical advice and can explain the museum's place in existing community disaster plans. Second, local organizations must know of the museum's plans in order to incorporate disaster support for the museum into their own respective plans.

The third planning step is vulnerability assessment. Neal FitzSimons' and Eric Elsesser's papers have so ably discussed this topic that I don't need to describe this crucial planning step again. I do want to emphasize, however, the importance of thoroughly assessing the total vulnerability of the museum <u>before</u> deciding how to protect it. Failure to consider the possibility of a particular disaster prevents planning for it. Faulty estimation of the damage that might result from a disaster plan will produce a disaster plan that falls short of affording full protection. Finally, inadequate vulnerability assessment may generate a false set of priorities for allocating the museum's resources to disaster prevention and mitigation.

The fourth step in the planning process is a survey to identify assets requring protection against loss or damage from a disaster. This survey will produce an inventory or a summary of the museum's assets listed by importance to the museum and to its continued operation. Among the assets to be surveyed are: the collections and their catalog and registration records; photograph and research files; the library and its card files; lab, shop, and maintenance equipment and supplies; administrative files and records; the building and its operating systems; and sales shop merchandise. In conducting the survey, do not forget people, the museum's most important asset. Protection of visitors and staff must always come first in planning.

Evaluation of the museum's material assets will be based on the broad and somewhat subjective criteria of irreplaceability and value. The specific criteria used by a given museum will depend upon the nature of its assets, particularly the nature of the collections. Original works of art, natural history specimens, archeological collections, and most ethnographic specimens are unique and irreplaceable. Books, prints, copies of sculpture, and taxidermic specimens may be replaceable, but only at great cost. Library materials, tools, equipment, and supplies may also be considered. The building itself may be replaceable or economically reparable. If it is an important historic structure, however, this may not be true.

Criteria for determining the value of assets can include the following considerations:

1. Intrinsic, sentimental, or historic value.
2. Aesthetic or scientific value.
3. Legal and administrative value.

4. Research and documentary value.
5. Monetary value.

Considerations of monetary value may be inapplicable to cultural materials or may be determined by the other considerations. Nonetheless, monetary value has an important bearing on the practicality of replacing damaged or destroyed assets and thus must be included in relative evaluations of the museum's property.

Evaluation will classify the museum's contents into at least three broad categories:

Priority 1: Assets of such importance that their safety must be guaranteed at all costs because their loss would be catastrophic.

Priority 2: Assets of relatively great importance, the loss of which would be serious but not catastrophic.

Priority 3: Assets of relatively little importance, the loss of which would not be a handicap.

In general, assets in the first group will be limited in number and will receive the maximum possible protection. The second group will be somewhat larger and will receive special protection only within the constraints of personnel availability, facilities, reasonable expense, and time. The third group will include the majority of the museum's assets. These assets will initially receive only the protection offered by the museum building. Only after assets in the first two groups have been protected appropriately will resources be devoted to protection of third priority assets.

The importance of prioritizing the museum's assets cannot be over-emphasized. Just as an earthquake vulnerability assessment can result in false assumptions about disaster risks, so too can inadequate setting of priorities result in misapplication of scarce resources during disaster recovery.

After the planning team has identified threats to the museum and established priorities for protecting its assets against those threats, it is ready to determine specific methods of protection. This phase of the planning process contains two steps, protection of assets in advance of disaster and recovery of assets after a disaster. These two steps are among the most difficult, time-consuming, and crucial in the entire planning process. The decisions made during these steps will determine the ultimate success and workability of the plan itself.

Step 5, is the design of protective measures. Selection of protective measures should be based on the following six considerations:

1. The degree of danger to which the museum's assets would be exposed during and after a disaster.
2. The level of protection currently afforded collections and other portable assets by the museum building and by the exhibit and storage cases in which they are kept.

214

3. The physical characteristics of the assets; that is, the fragility of their materials and their susceptibility to various kinds of damage.
4. How the assets are being used and whether such uses might contribute to risk. For example, objects on exhibit or left out for interpretive programs may be at greater risk than objects in storage.
5. The values assigned earlier when assets were being prioritized.
6. The funds, personnel, and other resources available for providing protection.

The sixth step in the planning process is formulation of recovery plans. In this step, the planning team determines how the museum is to recover from the unavoidable effects of disasters. When planning for earthquakes, floods, hurricanes, and other major natural events, there are relatively few true preventive measures that can be taken. Planning aims to minimize the risk of asset losses to lessen the impact of losses that occur.

The kinds of measures selected by the planning team for incorporation into a recovery plan will depend upon the assets to be protected. More diversified collections will need a greater variety and complexity of recovery methods. Planning for recovery should provide for immediate and successful completion of certain tasks in the aftermath of disaster. Briefly, those tasks are:

1. Assessment of damage to determine what has been damaged and the location and extent of damage.
2. Assignment of specific priorities for recovery efforts, based on the general priorities established earlier in the planning process; these priorities will provide a basis for decisions about which assets to treat first.
3. Selection of specific recovery methods from among the methods identified in advance as those the museum must be prepared to execute.
4. Requesting assistance with recovery operations from outside the museum (e.g., other museums, outside conservators, local tradesmen and craftsmen, volunteers, and local governmental authorities.)

If the organization of recovery efforts has been well-planned, recovery will be less difficult, less costly, and more efficient. A critical part of the recovery plan will be providing for the protection of supplies and equipment that will be needed to begin the recovery effort. Such materials are much more valuable and much harder to obtain after a disaster than they might be under normal circumstances. Materials used for two primary purposes should be stockpiled: (1) materials for repair of the museum building, its operating equipment and protection systems and (2) supplies for emergency stabilization of the collections and collection records.

215

Stockpiled emergency materials must be given the same degree of protection from disaster as the collections themselves.

Emergency supplies and equipment can be classified into the following groups:

Materials for removing dirt and debris.
Tools and equipment for demolition, repairs, and rescue.
Construction materials.
Emergency lighting, communications, and protection equipment.
Materials for protecting the health and safety of personnel.
Conservation supplies and equipment.
Miscellaneous supplies and equipment.

A suggested list of supplies and equipment is included at the end of this paper. Most museums probably keep most of these materials on hand routinely. If so, it remains only for the disaster plan to ensure their protection during a disaster so they will be ready for use afterwards. Subsequent papers will address the topic of specific recovery supplies and techniques.

In Step 7 the planning team brings the first two phases of the planning process to their logical conclusion by writing out the plans it has developed. There are many good reasons why the museum's disaster plan must be written. Perhaps the most important reason is that a written plan shortens response time when disaster strikes and will minimize the number of decisions that have to be made. In the absence of a written plan, everyone with responsibility for emergency action would have to confer on the division of recovery tasks.

A written plan will define the museum's emergency command structure and the scope of each person's authority and will identify staff responsibilities. A written plan will include assessment and inventory of the resources needed to support the museum during and after a disaster. Rapid access to emergency supplies, equipment, and personnel will be vital to the success of the plan; the written plan will help locate these resources. Finally, a written plan can and should be used to train all employees in carrying out their disaster recovery responsibilities.

The act of writing a disaster plan will point out gaps in the planning and will ensure that planning objectives have been met. Writing the plan will also suggest needed improvements in the museum's day-to-day operations, such as the need for more extensive fireprotection, a more efficient organizational structure, or better internal communications. The written plan will describe the museum's Disaster Control Organization and will determine if that organization is sufficient to control disaster and to recover from it. Finally, a written plan may be required by the museum's insurers or by persons from whom it has borrowed objects for exhibition. A plan also may be reequired if the museum is part of a larger organization, such as a university or a city or county government. In such a case, the museum's plan will probably be part of the plan for the entire organization and must be compatible with that plan.

The written plan should be characterized by flexibility, simplicity, detail, and adaptability. The plan should be flexible enough to allow for changes in the staff, in the availability of outside help and recovery supplies, or in threats to which the museum may be vulnerable. The plan should also allow for reduced vulnerability assessment following the implementation of disaster preventive measures. The plan should be simple enough to be understood easily and executed quickly. Yet it must be detailed enough to minimize the number of decisions necessary during an emergency. The plan should be adaptable to situations it is not specifically designed to cover. It should be oriented to the effects of disasters, not their causes. For example, instead of including one plan for floods, a second for broken water pipes, and a third for water damage due to fire fighting, it ought to include a single, multi-purpose plan for water damage in general. Similarly, a single plan for dealing with structural damage could be used for recovery from an earthquake, a tornado, or an explosion.

There is no standard format for a museum disaster plan. Some authors have recommended seven to ten sections and I have seen plans with as many as thirty sections. I believe that most museums will find their needs met by a plan with six major sections and a series of appendices. The major sections would be: Introduction and Statement of Purpose, Authority, Scope of the Plan, Disaster Avoidance Procedures, Disaster Mitigation Procedures and Disaster Recovery Procedures.

Section 1, Introduction and Statement of Purpose, states why the plan has been developed and what it is intended to achieve. This is a good place to indicate how and by whom the plan was developed and how it is to be kept current.

Section 2, Authority, has three purposes. First, it documents the authority for preparation and implementation of the plan. Normally, the plan will be prepared under the authority of the museum's board of trustees or its director. Second, this section delegates responsibility for execution of the plan to a staff member designated Emergency Services Officer and placed in charge of the Disaster Control Organization. Third, this section establishes a Disaster Control Organization and indicates by name or title those responsible for coordinating all emergency activities.

Section 3, Scope of the Plan, identifies each of the emergencies and disasters the plan is intended to cover. It first lists and describes each of the events that could occur in the museum; these events will have been identified during the vulnerability assessment step of the planning process. Then this section indicates the probability of occurrence for each event, its expected frequency of occurrence, and the expected effects of the event on museum operations. The most likely events should be listed first. Vulnerability assessment must consider the "trigger effect", wherein one event triggers others that create a more serious situation than that brought about by a single event. For example, in describing the potential impact of an earthquake, the plan should note that the losses may include not only structural damage to the building and its contents, but also death and

217

injury, water damage, fire, contamination by chemicals and fuels, and looting. Planned responses to each of these events, including those "triggered" by others, will be detailed subsequently in Sections 4 and 5.

A museum consisting of several buildings, particularly if they are widely scattered, may have an individual plan for each building or a single plan for the entire institution. If only one plan is written, Section 3 should describe its application to each building. This section should also describe how the disaster plan relates to any other emergency or operating plans that may exist, either within the institution or in the community (a medical emergency plan, a fire reaction plan, or a general security plan). An explanation of how all plans relate to and complement each other and an indication of the circumstances under which they should be executed individually or simultaneously will enable a coordinated disaster response.

Sections 4, 5, and 6 are the heart of the disaster plan because they describe techniques for coping with every possible disaster. These sections will be based on the choices of protection and recovery methods made in Steps 5 and 6 of the planning process. They should assign responsibilities for implementing and executing each part of the overall plan, explain the circumstances dictating partial or complete execution of the plan, and detail necessary response procedures.

Section 4 will outline actions the museum can take to reduce disaster vulnerability such as structural modification to help withstand an earthquake or installation of fire protection systems. The actions outlined in the plan should be implemented as funds and other resources become available, ideally before the events whose effects they are to minimize.

Section 5 will treat disaster mitigation—response to unavoidable disasters normally preceded by a warning. Mitigation emphasizes reducing the impact of the events as they occur. For example, response to a hurricane warning will include weather-proofing buildings, relocating or evacuating artifacts and records to safer quarters, and covering objects that cannot be moved. The plan will also list procedures for recovering from the effects of the hurricane.

Recovery procedures may not have to be fully executed if predisaster mitigation is carried out successfully. Subsections should describe all activities to be carried out in response to each of the disaster events itemized in Section 3. If plans for the individual events share many features, a general subsection followed by a listing of the unique aspects of each event may suffice. The paramount goal is that the plans be accessible, understandable, and workable.

Section 6 will cover disaster events for which there will normally be no warning. Plans in this section will place primary emphasis on recovery. For example, plans for recovering from major earthquake or flash flood damage will probably include: evacuating objects threatened by building collapse or looting; freezing water-soaked paper; drying metals subject to rusting; locating pieces of broken objects; securing the building against vandalism and theft; and, most importantly, evacuating and treating any injured people. The emphasis

218

of this type of plan is not prevention of damage during the disaster event but protection from further damage afterward.

These five sections will be the main part of the disaster plan. But these sections alone are not sufficient. They must be supplemented by appendices containing information necessary for execution of the plan but so subject to change that including it in the major sections of the plan would be impractical. The planning team will have to decide what kinds of information to include in the appendices. In most plans, the following appendices will be useful.

Appendix 1 should include an organization chart of the museum, showing all divisions and at least the key staff positions. If the museum is part of a larger organization, such as a university or a local government, the appendix should include a chart showing the museum's position within the larger organization. Reference to these charts during emergencies will facilitate communications and help to maintain the chain of command. The charts should be simple and clear. It will usually be sufficient to show only division and office names, functions, and the names and titles of their key personnel. Members of the Disaster Control Organization should be indicated on the organizational charts or perhaps on a separate chart. Colored markers can be used to highlight the key personnel or activities.

Appendix 2 can consist of lists of key museum staff needed for execution of the plan. The list should include each person's name and title, home address, and home telephone number. This list may also include a brief resume of each person's responsibilities under the plan. The same appendix might well include a roster of the museum's entire staff in case there is an incident requiring a head count to determine if everyone is safe.

Appendix 3 should list emergency contacts outside the museum. Such contacts would include: police and fire departments; the local Civil Defense organization; local utility companies, hospitals, and ambulance companies; plumbers, electricians, and glass companies; the museum's insurance agents; and any other organizations or persons the museum might have to contact in case of emergency. Both daytime and after-hours telephone numbers should be listed. Specific contacts in the listed agencies should be listed where appropriate.

Outside curators and conservators may be needed for advice and assistance. A list of various experts' addresses and specialties should be appended. If they must travel to the museum, transportation and compensation arrangements should be detailed. Previous arrangements may have been made to borrow personnel from nearby museums or sister organizations for assistance in evacuation or recovery operations. Record such arrangements and the appropriate contacts. List any volunteers you may need to call upon, along with their special skills. If anybody on the staff, including volunteers, has promised to bring certain equipment and supplies with him for personal or museum use, indicate what they are.

It is critical that this and all other call-up lists be kept current. They should be reviewed and revised at least once a month. Using a word processor can speed revisions.

Appendix 4 can be a description of the circumstances requiring a call to various outside agencies or persons and the kinds of services or assistance available from these outside sources. Appendices 3 and 4 might be combined if not too cumbersome.

Appendix 5 might include plans of the museum, its grounds and its immediate neighborhood. Floor plans can indicate vulnerable parts of the museum or those containing the most valuable assets. They should show the locations of emergency exists and evacuation routes, gas and electric cutoffs, telephone closets, fire fighting equipment, burglar and fire alarm devices and controls, emergency supplies and equipment stockpiles, and other such information.

Maps can show sidewalks, streets, driveways, gates, fences, buried and overhead utility lines, fire hydrants, manholes, and other pertinent information. Certain floor plans might be posted at key locations around the non-public parts of the museum to facilitate movement during an emergency and to orient outside maintenance and service crews. Floor plans and maps will prove particularly useful if the museum depends upon volunteers or other non-staff personnel for help after a disaster. The inclusion of sensitive information in this appendix, like plans of the intrusion detection systems, may require restricting distribution of the museum's disaster plan or keeping the appendix in a sealed envelope or safe.

Appendix 6 might be an inventory of all collections, records, and other valuable assets and the priority for their protection. With this record could be a floor plan that shows the location of each asset or group of assets on the inventory. A similar plan can be posted in museum storerooms and conservation labs to speed access to these assets by emergency evacuation personnel unfamiliar with your facility. Caution in including such details on a posted floor plan is prudent. It could become a shopping list for burglars. Some sort of private coding, such as with colors, might eliminate this problem.

Appendix 7 might be a summary of arrangements for evacuating and relocating the collections. This appendix would include packing and crating instructions and the location of available supplies and materials. This appendix would also indicate several possible sites for temporary storage in case the primary site suffers the same disaster that strikes the museum.

Appendix 8 could be instructions for emergency management of the building's utilities and for service and operation of vital building support systems. Such systems might include: burglar and fire alarm systems, fire suppression system, fire fighting equipment, elevators and escalators, emergency lighting, emergency generator, heating and air conditioning equipment, humidifiers, and dehumidifiers. This appendix could either include information from manufacturers' instruction manuals or could refer to the manuals. If the vital information is only referenced the cited manuals must be protected as well as emergency plan itself.

Appendix 9 is one of the most important appendices; it contains an inventory of supplies, equipment, and other local resources useful in time of disaster. Stockpiled emergency supplies and equipment should be described, as to purpose, quantity and location. Arrangements to borrow equipment like portable generators, power tools, fans, and dehumidifiers should be recorded and delegated to certain staff for execution.   Arrangements to procure supplies like plywood, nails, plastic sheeting, tissue paper, cardboard boxes, tape, and disinfectants should be in place and fully described.   See the list of suggested materials at the end of this paper.

Appendix 10 might be a glossary of terms used in the disaster plan.   A glossary will ensure that everyone using the plan will be speaking the same language.

An index would make a highly useful addition to the plan. However, because the plan will change fairly frequently, an index may be difficult to keep current.   Nonetheless, an index should be considered and included if its usefulness would outweigh the effort required to keep it current.

Because the disaster plan will evolve, it can be kept most conveniently in a three-ring binder. The original should be stored in a secure, fire-resistant safe or vault.   Each member of the Disaster Control Organization should have a copy of the plan.   The Emergency Services Officer will be responsible for keeping the plan updated and should have a copy in which to make pen and ink changes.   As he makes changes to his copy, a typist can revise the original. (This is another good application for a word processor.)   If the museum occupies more than one building, at least one copy of the plan should be in each building.   Additional copies should be placed at critical spots around the museum in disaster-resistant containers.   Each copy of the plan should list the locations of all other copies. It is vital that the original and all copies be updated often. Changes should be posted as they occur, changed pages should be retyped including the change's date, and obsolete pages should be removed and destroyed.

At least one copy of the plan kept in the museum should be accompanied by selected publications for reference during emergency stabilization and conservation efforts following a disaster.   For example, if you anticipate having to salvage and preserve wet paper, you would want to have Peter Waters' book Procedures for Salvage of Water-Damaged Library Materials published by the Library of Congress.   If the museum has a staff conservator, he or she may prepare instructions tailored specifically for your collections, instead of using existing published instructions.   If so, these special instructions would be kept with the plan or perhaps even made part of it.

The plan ought to be accompanied by a carefully selected assortment of blank forms, typing supplies, and other materials needed for preparing purchase orders and reports during and after an emergency.

If the museum office is damaged during a disaster, these materials will permit the carrying out of vital administrative duties.

The disaster preparedness process does not end with preparation and distribution of a written disaster plan.   The effectiveness of the plan during a disaster depends upon training all personnel who will

221

execute the plan and upon regular testing of the plan under simulated conditions. The continued usefulness of the plan will depend upon how well it performs during actual emergencies, as determined by post-event evaluations.

The eighth step in the disaster preparedness process is training of the museum staff. Three purposes to training are:

1. To guarantee that every employee will react rapidly in an emergency.
2. To ensure that each person on whom execution of the plan depends will know his or her responsibility.
3. To ensure that each responsible person has acquired the skills and the confidence to do his or her job efficiently and without panic.

Two kinds of training are needed to achieve these purposes. The first is briefing everyone on the museum staff on the disaster plan's goals and on their individual roles and responsibilities in case of disaster. Such training can be held in conjunction with regular museum employee training and skills development programs. New employees should be trained as soon as possible after joining the staff. Retraining should take place every time the plan changes enough to warrant it.

The second kind of training is for members of the Disaster Control Organization. They will need a higher level of training than the rest of the staff. They should probably take courses offered by local and state Civil Defense organizations; these courses are usually free and are excellent training opportunities. Major businesses and industries often have internal disaster preparedness courses and may be willing to train museum staff people. Local public protection agencies, such as the fire department, offer training in such skills as fighting small fires with hand held equipment and controlling crowds during an emergency. Reading as widely as possible on the subjects of emergency planning and disaster preparedness is also good practice. Particularly useful works are cited in the bibliography at the end of this paper.

The ninth step in disaster preparedness takes place after the plan is written and training of the museum's staff has begun. This step calls for testing the plan.

To ensure the plan's effectiveness under actual disaster conditions, the Disaster Control Organization must test it thoroughly under simulated disaster conditions. As Timothy J. Healy warns, the effectiveness (or ineffectiveness) of the disaster plan should not be discovered first during an actual disaster. [Healy, 1969] Testing will reveal the plan's deficiencies and unrealistic features and may expose a need to add or revise procedures. In testing the plan, the Disaster Control Organization will receive valuable training in operation under emergency conditions.

Testing consists of holding periodic exercises covering the full range of expected emergency and disaster situations. The Disaster

Control Organization can write test problems for each potential disaster event and present them for solution. Senior administrative and curatorial personnel should test the plan first, as soon as possible after the Disaster Control Organization itself is fully functioning. After they have participated in a series of exercises helping to improve the plan, the entire staff and the staffs of agencies supporting the museum in disaster can be tested. All exercises should be as realistic as possible and held with as little advance notice and preparation as feasible. Test exercises should be concerned with the full range of possible emergencies, from minor incidents to major disasters. Each exercise should conclude with a critique and suitable modification of the plan.

Constant evaluation of the disaster plan is essential to keeping it always up to date and fully capable of dealing with every event it is intended to. Evaluation is the tenth and last step in the disaster preparedness process. The most effective way to evaluate a plan is to examine how well it functions during actual disasters. For this reason, it is vital that the Disaster Control Organization keep records whenever any part of the plan must be executed. After the crisis has passed, all those involved in executing the plan should meet to discuss any problems they encountered. They should try to improve the plan so that similar problems do not arise in the future.

As part of the evaluation, it is very important to observe and record exactly what damage resulted from the disaster and why it occurred. Such records will enable the plan to be refined to focus on the kinds of damage that actually occur rather than on the kinds of damage predicted to occur. Analyzing the causes of damage might permit the rebuilding or remodeling of the museum for greater resistance to the same kinds of damage in the future. Records of damage sustained may also be required by the museum's insurance carriers. Photographs are particularly useful as part of complete, graphic records. It is important that one or more cameras and accessories and a quantity of film be included in the museum's stockpile of protected emergency supplies.

CONCLUSION

The previous papers have stressed that emergencies are a part of the life of a museum. You may never have been involved personally in a serious emergency, let alone a disaster. If so, count yourself lucky. On the other hand, you may already be prepared. If you are prepared, please keep vigilant and stay prepared. I hope that this handbook and my paper will have demonstrated the need for preparedness planning in every cultural institution.

The primary goal of emergency planning is to avoid or minimize loss of the museum's assets, and preparation is the key to achieving that goal. Reducing the impacts of a disaster and avoiding loss depend upon how well you have planned for meeting all possible emergencies and disasters, how well you and your staff react when a disaster occurs, and how much learning from experiences during actual disasters you apply to revising your plan and preparing for the future.

Some emergencies cannot be prevented. The impact of some disasters cannot be avoided. But, you can plan in advance. You can commit a plan to paper. You can keep the plan up to date. As you can train yourself and your staff to execute the plan. By taking these steps, you will be able to cope with any unavoidable emergency or disaster.

SELECTED REFERENCES

PART I: EMERGENCY AND DISASTER PREPAREDNESS AND PLANNING

American Society of Coporate Secretaries, Inc. Continuity of Corporate management in Event of Major Disaster. Washington, DC: Office of Civil Defense, Department of Defense. December 1970. 56 pp., bibliography.

Association of Records Executives and Administrators. Protection of Vital Records. Washington, DC: Office of Civil Defense, Department of Defense. July 1966. 24 pp., bibliography.

Bahme, Charles W. Fire Officer's Guide to Disaster Control. Boston, MA: National Fire Portection Association. 1978. 404 pp., illustrated, bibliography.

Bahme, Charles W. Fire Officer's Guide to Emergency Action. Boston, MA: National Fire Protection Association. 1976.

Bohem, Hilda. Disaster Prevention and Disaster Preparedness. Berkeley, CA: Office of the Assistant Vice President for Library Plans and Policies, Systemwide Library Administration, University of California. April 1978. 22 pp.

Committee on Conservation of Cultural Resources. The Protection of Cultural Resources Against the Hazards of War. Washington, DC: National Resources Planning Board. February 1942. 50 pp., bibliography.

Cox, David L. "Training for Facility Self-Protection." Security Management, October/November 1972. Reprinted by Defense Civil Preparedness Agency. 2 pp.

Disaster Operations: A Handbook for Local Governments. Publication No. CPG 1-6. Washington, DC: Defense Civil Preparedness Agency. July 1972.

Disaster Planning Guide for Business and Industry. Publication no. CPG-25. Washington, DC: Defense Civil Preparedness Agency. May 1974. 54 pp.

Disaster Response and Recovery Program Guide. Washington, DC: Federal Emergency management Agency. February 1980. 28 pp.

Fennelly, Lawrence J. (Ed.) Museum, Archive, and Library Security. Woburn, MA: Butteworth Publishers. (To be released in the fall of 1982).

Healy, Richard J. Emergency and Disaster Planning. New York: John Wiley and Sons. 1969. 290 pp.

Local Government Emergency Planning. Publication No. CPG 1-8. Washington, DC: Federal Emergency Management Agency. July 1978. 101 pp.

Myers, James N. and Denise D. Bedford. Disasters: Prevention and Coping, Proceedings of the Conference, May 21-22, 1981 organized by Sally Buchanan. Stanford, CA: Stanford University Libraries. 1981. 177 pp., illustrated. Various authors.

Noblecourt, Andre F. Protection of Cultural Property in the Event of Armed Conflict. Museums and Monument Series VIII. Paris: UNESCO, 1958, 346 pp., illustrated, bibliography.

Tillotson, Robert G. and the International Committee on Museum Security. Museum Security/La Securite Dans Les Musees. Paris: International Council of Museums. 1977. 244 pp., illustrated, bibliography.

Upton, M. S. and C. Pearson. Disaster Planning and Emergency Treatments in Museums, Art Galleries, Libraries, Archives, and Allied Institutions.

Belconnen, A.C.T., Australia: Institute for the Conservation of Cultural Materials, Canberra College of Advanced Education. 1978. 54 pp., 4 figures, bibliography.

PART 2: SALVAGE AND RECOVERY

Agricultural Research Service. How to Prevent and Remove Bildew: Home Methods. Home and Garden Bulletin No. 68 (Rev.). Washington, DC: U.S. Department of Agriculture. 1971. 12 pp.

Cohen, William. "Halon 1301: Library Fires and Post-Fire Procedures." Library Security Newsletter, May 1975, pp. 5-7.

First Aid for Flooded Homes and Farms. Agriculture Handbook No. 38. Washington, DC: U.S. Department of Agriculture. 1972. 31 pp., tables, recipes, and checklist.

Fischer, David J. "Problems Encountered, Hurricane Agnes Flood, June 23, 1972 at Corning, NY and the Corning Museum of Glass." Conservation Administration by George M. Cunha. North Andover, MA: New England Document Conservation Center. 1975. pp. 170-187.

Fischer, David J. and Thomas Duncan. "Conservation Research: Flood-Damaged Library Materials." AIC Bulletin, Vol. 15, No. 2 (Summer 1975), pp. 27-48.

Haas, J. Eugene and others (Eds.) Reconstruction Following Disaster. Cambridge, MA: The MIT Press, 1977.

Keck, Caroline K. "On Conservation: Instructions for Emergency Treatment of Water Damage." Museum News, Vol. 50, No. 10 (June 1972), p. 13.

Koesterer, Martin G. and John A. Getting. "Restoring Water-Soaked Papers and Textiles: Applying Freeze-Drying Methods to Books and Art Objects." Technology and Conservation, Fall 1976, pp. 20-22.

McGregor, L. and J. Bruce. "Recovery of Flood Damaged Documents by the Queensland State Archives." Archives and Manuscripts, Vol. 5, No. 8 (August 1974), pp. 193-199.

Martin, John H. "Resuscitating a Waterlogged Library." Wilson Library Bulletin, November 1975, pp. 241-243.

Martin, John H. (Ed.). The Corning Flood: Museum Under Water. Corning: NY, Corning Museum of Glass. 1977. 60 pp., illustrated, bibliography, checklist.

Minoque, Adelaide. "Treatment of Fire and Water Damaged Records." American Archivist, Vol. 9, No. 1 (January 1946), pp. 17-25.

Montuori, Theodore. "Lesson Learned from Agnes." The Journal of Micrographics, Vol. 6, No. 3 (January-February 1973), pp. 133-136.

Morris, John. Managing the Library Fire Risk. Berkeley, CA: Office of Risk Management and Safety, University of California. 1979 (2nd Edition). 147 pp., illustrated, bibliography. (Available only from author at 333 Nutmeg Lane, Walnut Creek, CA 94598.)

Sellers, David Y. and Richard Strassberg. "Anatomy of a Library Emergency." Library Journal, Vol. 98, No. 17 (October 1973), pp. 2824-2827.

Spawn, Wilman. "After the Water Comes." Bulletin of the Pennsylvania Library Association, Vol. 28, No. 6 (November 1973), pp. 243-251.

Surrency, Erwin C. "Guarding Against Disaster." Law Library Journal, Vol. 66, No. 4 (November 1973), pp. 419-428.

Walston, S. "Emergency Conservation Following the Darwin Cyclone." ICCM Bulletin, Vol. 2, No. 1 (March 1976), pp. 21-25.

Waters, Peter. Procedures for Salvage of Water-Damaged Library Materials. Washington, DC: Library of Congress. 1975. 30 pp.

Whipkey, Harold E. After Agnes: A Report on Flood Recovery Assistance by the Pennsylvania Historical and Museum Commission. Harrisburg, PA: Pennsylvania Historical and Museum Commission. 1973. 23 pp., illustrated.

The supplies and equipment listed here include a variety of items that may be needed to cope with emergencies or disasters; some items can be used to prevent or minimize damage and others can be used afterwards to clean up or recover from damage. Few museums will need to use all of these items. Each museum should acquire only those items that will be needed to cope with the range of emergencies and disasters that it can expect. On the other hand, this list is not all inclusive; it is intended only as a guide. Any museum may find that it will require items not listed here.

Items listed here do not necessarily have to be obtained or stockpiled exclusively for use in an emergency. Some of the listed items will be found in all museums as a matter of routine. They can be diverted for use in cleanup and repair operations when they are needed. However, keep in mind that the items you may count on using in an emergency may be damaged or destroyed by the disaster. Therefore, those items that will be critical to the survival or recovery of the museum and that cannot be procured promptly from elsewhere after the disaster should be set aside or stockpiled in a safe place so they will be available if ever they are needed.

Remember, too, that some items—such as dry cell batteries and certain first aid supplies—have a limited shelf life. Plan on replacing such items periodically so that fresh stock is always on hand in your stockpile.

Finally, remember always to include operating manuals or instructions with items of mechanical and electrical equipment in case persons not experienced with their operation are required to use them.

Supplies and Equipment for Debris Removal and Cleanup

Low sudsing detergents
Bleaches
Sanitizers (such as chloride of lime or high-test hypochlorite)
Fungicides
Disinfectants
Ammonia
Scouring powders or other household cleaners
Rubber gloves
Brooms
Dust pans
Mops, mop buckets, and wringers
Scoops and shovels
Scrub brushes
Sponges and rags or cloths
Buckets and tubs
Water hoses and nozzles
Throw-away containers or bags for trash
Wet/dry vacuum cleaner with accessories

Tools and Equipment for Demolition, Repairs, and Rescue

Hammers (both claw and machinists)
Wrenches (pipe, channel lock, and Vise Grips in various sizes)
Pliers (adjustable, lineman's, and needle nose in various sizes)
Screwdrivers (straight blade and Phillips in various sizes)
Wood saws
Hand drill with bits
(Power saws and drills may be selected if a source of electricity can be assured.)
Metal saw with blades
Utility knife with extra blades
Wire cutters with insulated handles
Tin snips
Pipe cutters and possibly pipe threaders
Bolt cutter
Pry bar or crowbar
Axes, including fireman's axe
Rope
Dollies or handcarts
Folding rule or retractable tape measures
3-ton hydraulic jack
Sledgehammer
Block and tackle
Pit cover hood (if applicable)
Hydrant and post indicator valve wrenches (if the museum has a sprinkler or hose and standpipe system)
Staple gun and staples
Ladder(s) and step-stool(s)

Construction Materials

Plywood for covering or replacing windows
Dimensional lumber
Nails, screws, and assorted fasteners
Tapes of various kinds (masking, duct, electrician's, etc.)
Glue
Twine and cord
Plastic sheeting for protection against leaks and splashes
Binding wire

Emergency Equipment

Emergency gasoline powered electrical generator
Portable lights (to be powered from the generator if electricity unavailable)
Emergency lights with extra batteries
Flashlights or lanterns with extra batteries
Fire extinguishers (ABC type recommended)
Battery-operated AM/FM radio(s) with extra batteries

Walkie-talkie radios with extra batteries
CB radio with extra batteries
Portable public address system or bullhorn, electrical or battery-powered
Geiger counter and dosimeters
Gas masks with extra cannisters
Air breathers with extra oxygen tanks
Resuscitation equipment
Gasoline powered water pump (or pump that can be powered from the electrical generator) with hoses
Extension cords, preferably equipped with ground fault interruptors

Personal Equipment and Supplies (some of these items may be provided by the individual employees and volunteers who are to use them)

Necessary protective clothing
Rubber boots or waders
Hard hats
Rubber lab aprons
Protective masks
First aid kits and medical supplies
Food and food preparation equipment
Potable water
Sanitation facilities
Changes of clothing
Sleeping bags and blankets

Conservation Supplies and Equipment

Polyester (Mylar) and Polyethylene film (in rolls)
Newsprint (unprinted)
Polyethylene bags, various sizes (such as Zip-Lock and produce bags)
Plastic garbage bags
Thymol
Ethanol
Acetone
Industrial denatured alcohol
White blotter paper
Weights (such as shot bags)
Various sizes of thick glass or smooth masonite
Japanese tissue
Towels or clean rags
Clothes pins
Scissors
Sharp knives
Water displacement compound (such as WD-40)
Waxes and dressings (determined by nature of collection)
Other preservatives

Miscellaneous Supplies

Boxes for packing and moving artifacts, records, and equipment. (Record transfer boxes are the easiest to use, carry, and store. They come flat for storage and are set up as needed; they may be re-flattened for future use.)

Box sealing and strapping tapes

Tissue paper, clean newsprint, plastic "bubble pack", foam "noodles", and other such materials for packing and padding artifacts for movement.

Marking pens, preferably ones that are not water soluable.

Insecticides and rodenticides.

Miscellaneous Equipment

Fans

Space heaters, either electric or gas operated

Portable dehumidifiers

Hygrometers

Photographic equipment (camera, lenses, flash, light meter, etc.)

Essential office equipment (manual typewriter, pocket calculator, pencil sharpener, stapler, rulers, scissors, etc.)

Essential stationery and blank forms and other such supplies to ensure continuity of minimal administrative operations.

The Use and History of Traditional Recording Techniques for the Documentation of Sites and Monuments in Disaster-Prone Areas

Dr. John C. Poppeliers

The tragic and dramatic loss of life, and the damage to the natural and man-made environment which are caused by earthquakes, volcanic eruptions, floods, typhoons, hurricanes, and tidal waves are frequently parallelled by dramatic attempts to save and rebuild. This in part is achieved by projects to reinforce the structural remains of buildings and to rebuild where necessary. Such efforts can not only be facilitated but in some instances really made possible by recording and documentation prior to the destructive event.

The development of documents which record the built environment has little of the drama which characterizes most activities associated with preventing destruction in disaster areas. On the contrary, the documentation of monuments and sites appears a relatively passive activity. Documentation, however, provides the rational basis of any rebuilding which involves an awareness of the past and its importance for future generations. Such records are often the only evidence we have about the existence or the appearance of a vanished structure. There are innumerable examples of the use of records in repairing damaged structures and restoring demolished ones. No attempt will be made to list such efforts here; instead attention will focus on the historical development of one type of record and this will serve to indicate the kinds of records that may exist that document a particular structure.

Basically there are three main "techniques" or means of recording structures and communities. Though not listed here in order of historic development nor importance, they include written or verbal accounts, record drawings and photographs or allied technology-based imaging techniques. Each of these is important and possesses certain attributes which the others do not have. Each deserves consideration. This paper will deal with only one aspect of documentation—one of the oldest and yet still one of the basic and most useful—record drawings.

Record drawings fall into two groups: those that suggest the unique nature of an existing structure or group of structures and are motivated essentially by artistic perceptions, and those that are motivated by an archaeological or scientific interest. This last group is often referred to as measured drawing.

231

As early as the third millenium B.C. a recorder found reason to illustrate his observations of a building in a form which we would now describe as a floor plan. A schematic representation of a modest dwelling in Nippur is certainly among the earliest efforts to indicate the location of doors, windows and the thickness of walls. [McConn, Haines and Hansen, 1967]

Later, ancient Greek and Roman coins, as well as Roman wall paintings, sought to suggest the appearance of temples, monuments, amphitheaters, city gates, villas and ports. [Donaldson, 1859] Most of these convey the basic information diagrammatically; yet from these coins it would be difficult for the non-specialist to distinguish immediately the portico of the Greek temple of Artemis at Ephesus from that of the Roman temple of Trajan at Rome—except for the differentiation of basic proportions and the emphasis given to salient features. Character, and certainly not accuracy, are the essential qualities of these representations of facts. (Figure 4.4)

Later medieval architectural drawings not only record identifiable structures, but also sometimes indicate the reasons why they were drawn. A thirteenth-century album of thirty-three parchments, which is now in the Bibliotheque Nationale, reveals for the first time an "architect" recording existing buildings. Villard de Honnecourt, a maître d'oeuvre or maître de chantier, who was active in northern France between 1225 and 1250, observed and recorded in his sketchbook the construction of such Gothic monuments as the cathedrals of Rheims and Laon. [Villard de Honnecourt, 1858] Such notes reveal important information about the building arts in the Middle Ages and provide remarkable evidence regarding the dissemination of Gothic architecture throughout Europe. (Figure 4.5)

The development of the techniques of architectural drawing is comparatively modern. Not until the early years of the Italian Renaissance can it be said that architectural drawings as we know them existed. Some fifteenth-century German designs of "geometrical elevations of a Gothic facade" are even drawn to scale. But the basic techniques of graphic architectural representation were not, it appears, fully developed until the late fifteenth or early sixteenth century in the work of Bramante, Giuliano da San Gallo and Peruzzi. [Falb, 1902] The development of this art is integrally related, in fact, to the emergence of the professional architect.

The forms of accurate architectural drawings—perspectives, plans, elevations, sections, and details—which are today still used in design presentations are possibly a product of a need to systematically record, and permanently maintain, the observed data of ancient Roman monuments. The necessity for two-dimensional representation seems not to have been felt by those responsible for the design and execution of structures as long as architecture was primarily a craft-oriented art. When the monuments of antiquity became the basis for architectural design, it became evident that models, rough schemata, and on-site solutions based on craft transmittal of tradition were no longer adequate for either the design or the construction of a more intellectualized architecture. It has been noted that the Emperor

TEMPLE TO TRAJAN ROME

Figure 4.4. Rome, Italy: Temple to Trajan, Numismatic Representation.

Figure 4.5. Laon, France: Sketch of Detail of Cathedral by Villard de Honnecourt, 13th Century.

Hadrian in the second century A.D. "took architects abroad with him to measure ancient buildings" in order to "reproduce them in his famous Villa at Tivoli", but not until Filippo Brunelleschi in the early fifteenth century is there specific evidence that men concerned with buildings purposely recorded old structures.

Generally credited with having developed—along with his later contemporary Leon Battista Alberti (1404-72)—the new Western perspective system of transferring three-dimensional space to a two-dimensional surface, Filippo Brunelleschi (1377-1446) both "excavated" and measured structures in Rome in order to wrest from them the "secrets" which he would use in his innovative early Renaissance buildings in Florence. For him the development of a system of scale drawings which accurately recorded the physical structures of antiquity was a most practical concern, for, according to his quattrocento biographer Antonio di Tuccio Manetti, he did not accept either the construction techniques or the decorative detail system of the late medieval period in Italy. Both Brunelleschi and the Florentine sculptor Donatello resolved to record Roman monuments in situ.

Even the development of geometric perspective, so important and overriding a concern for later quattrocento and cinquecento painters, was essentially a product of Brunelleschi's desire to record the physical structure of classical ruins accurately. Anyone who has been confronted with the behemoth that is in fact an historical and architecturally important building—particularly when analysis, restoration, or the production of a documentary record are involved—recognizes the necessity of a systematized, annotated recording system. The assessment of an historic building is almost impossible without this graphic analysis, and certainly no structural analysis of a disaster-struck building can accurately be made without a graphic record.

In the early 1430s, Alberti proposed measuring the buildings of ancient Rome in order to compile a Descriptio urbis Romae. Alberti approached this Herculean endeavor with "scrupulous diligence by means of instruments which he himself devised". The necessity to devise a system which would adequately record the past obviously was a precondition for Alberti in organizing a coherent system of architectural theory, which he presented to Pope Nicolas V in 1452 in his De re aedificatoria. None of the architectural drawings of Brunelleschi or Alberti exists and only written accounts remain to describe their interest.

In September 1499 Donato Bramante moved to Rome. Already in his fifties, with an architectural career in Milan behind him, he responded to the ancient monuments of Rome in a way that would ultimately leave almost no aspect of the building arts in western Europe unaltered. In anticipation of throngs of pilgrims in the Holy Year, 1500, the improvement of squares and streets—involving the destruction of many buildings—formed a major part of the plans authorized by Alexander VI, and both the Roman Forum and the Colosseum were scheduled to be quarried to support this urban development. Though Bramante recognized the need for measures to rescue Rome from the incrustations of the centuries, he also responded to the finality of the destruction of these monuments. He proposed, therefore, that studies and drawings should be made to record imperial Rome and devoted his first years in the City to this study. This provides an early example of documentation of threatened structures.

Bramante perfected surveying and measuring instruments, such as a type of goniometer to record the angles of buildings. His methods eventually, and permanently, replaced models and the simplistic drawings that had been the basis of professional architectural convention.

Throughout the sixteenth century the recording of structures from antiquity and from the Early and High Renaissance by artists and architects flourished. An artistic tradition, in which representations of extant buildings and cityscapes were used as a basis for composition, developed independently from an emergent architectural tradition which observed and recorded existing buildings as the basis for the design of future buildings, for architectural theory, and for precise information about the achievements of classic antiquity. Rome, in the cinquecento—as portrayed by Raphael and by such vedutisti as Domenico Taselli, Giovanni Dosio, and the northerner Maerten van Heemskerck (1498-1574)—established a dynamic, productive tradition which would inform and inspire other artists from Poussin, Piranesi, and Pannini to Utrillo and Mondrian. (Figure 4.6) These record drawings, varying considerably in the degree of "artistic liberty" they exercised, are a major documentary resource not only for architectural historians but also often for those engaged in reconstruction.

Raphael's preeminence as a painter has overshadowed his career as an architect, antiquarian, and archaeologist. These are important yet neglected aspects of his art. Raphael's appointment as Bramante's successor permanently brought him into contact with Roman antiquities. A papal brief in 1517 appointed him commissioner of antiquities, and he proposed to illustrate the ancient city. A famous letter, attributed at various times to Bramante, Castiglione, and Raphael, outlined the recording methods and techniques to be used in this undertaking. Giorgio Vasari, the sixteenth century architect, painter, and art historian, observed that Raphael even "maintained draftsmen all over Italy, at Pozzuolo, and even in Greece". Some sources also maintain that he had completed the "First Region" by the time of his death in 1520; however, written documents are again the only evidence we have to support Raphael's role as an important innovator and developer of the art of the measured drawing.

Early sixteenth-century developments in the art of printing offered vast new potentials. The first illustrated edition of Vitruvius was published in 1511 [Vitruvius Pollios, 1511]; however, the first architect to realize fully the usefulness of the new printing techniques was Sebastiano Serlio (1475-1554). [Serlio, 1584] A Bolognese, who began his career as a perspective painter, Serlio studied later in Rome with the architect Baldassare Peruzzi whose word on the antiquities of

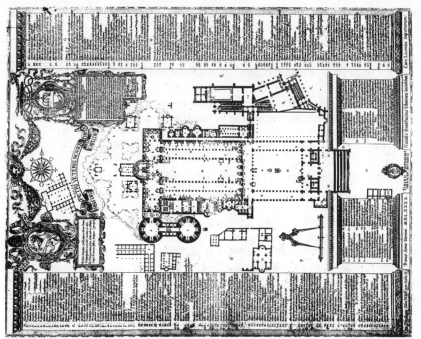

Figure 4.7. Rome, Italy: Old St. Peter's Cathedral, Plan by Tiberio Alfarano, 1590.

Figure 4.6. Rome, Italy: St. Peter's Cathedral, Interior View of the Main Aisle Under Construction, by Maerten van Heemskerck, 16th Century.

236

Rome he later incorporated into his own architectural treatises. A comparison of a plan of the Pantheon by Peruzzi and the woodcut of a plan of the Pantheon by Serlio leaves little doubt about this debt, which Serlio freely acknowledged.

The influence of ancient Roman monuments and of Vitruvian principles is nowhere more powerfully revealed in the cinquecento than in the designs and theory of Andrea Palladio (1508-80). In his thirties, Palladio—a Paduan stonecutter—came under the influence of the humanist poet-mathematician Giangiorgio Trissino and paid several visits to Rome with this wealthy patron. There he devoted himself to measuring, analyzing, and drawing ancient structures, and—like Serlio before him—the buildings of Bramante and Raphael. Returning to the Veneto, Palladio wrote his I Quattro libri dell' architectura, which was published in Venice in 1570. [Palladio, 1742] The fourth volume, the most pertinent to the development of architectural measured drawings, is devoted to antique Roman temples et alcuni altri, che sono in Italia, e fuori d'Italia. Palladio describes, discusses, and illustrates nine Roman temples, other extant structures such as the Pantheon, and a single modern structure, the Tempietto of Bramante.

Although the illustrations of the original 1570 edition of Palladio are considerably more detailed and accurate than those in the 1511 edition of Vitruvius or those in the Serlio volumes that had appeared since the late 1530s, they still are relatively rudimentary and unsophisticated compared to a 1590 engraved plan of the old basilica of St. Peter's by a Vatican cleric, Tiberio Alfarano. (Figure 4.7) It has been proposed that the engraving reproduces a manuscript plan of about 1571. This plan may well be the first architectural presentation that we can regard in the strictest sense as a measured drawing. [Alfarano, 1914]

A precise definition of an architectural measured drawing is necessary. Few authors have written on the subject, and research at this stage has not revealed a scholar who attempted a full and accurate definition prior to 1970. Evidently it was assumed to be self-explanatory. Yet it is curious that the term appears not to have been used until the nineteenth century, and then not frequently. It may first be useful to consider what a measured drawing is not. Certainly it is not a conjectural drawing though on occasions a measured drawing has incorporated conjectures about missing elements of historic structures; nor is it a restoration drawing, though this, too, has been a function which occasionally has been assigned to it; nor is it, assuming the guise of accuracy, mere fantasy. Yet a measured drawing is essentially an ideal—and, as such, it is unattainable.

In varying degrees, all architectural drawings that might be termed measured drawings represent attempts to attain the ideal of a complete and accurate representation of a structure at one precise moment in time—the present. In his 1970 manual for the Historic American Buildings Survey, Professor Harley J. McKee succinctly defined a measured drawing: "Such drawings, made by measuring each part of the subject, are accurate, to scale, show proportions accurately, are measurable, highly informative, and can emphasize or de-emphasize parts according to their historic importance." [McKee, 1970]

Only two concepts, in my opinion, seem to be missing in this definition. They can best be summed up with the words the art of and at this moment in time. The first implies aesthetic awareness and, therefore, a concern for excellence of delineation; the second implies an archaeological concern for the accurate observation and recording of an artifact at the moment it is observed. Our subsequent development of the history of measured drawings will use as a gauge these supplemented criteria.

The Alfarano manuscript of 1571 and the 1590 engraving appear at this time to be the earliest known architectural record drawings that meet these criteria. Each part of the old basilica of St. Peter seems to have been measured, and Professor Turpin Bannister has noted that archaeological investigations of the 1940s at St. Peter's generally confirm the accuracy of the dimensions given in the 1590 engraving.

Although the scale of the Alfarano plan is so small that only approximate readings are possible, it nevertheless remains true that the plan is scaled, that it is based on an attempt to measure accurately, and that the proportions confirm what we know from an archaeological excavation. Add to this the fact that Alfarano did not hesitate to show later accretions such as tombs, monuments, and chapels. In other words, he recognized that he was recording at a specific moment in the development of the basilica, and he was at least partially aware of an obligation not to editorialize. Finally, the plan has a definite aesthetic appeal. These all seem to justify the assertion that Alfarano's plan, therefore, is a measured drawing, and that it is the first to qualify fully as an architectural drawing.

Created, initially developed, and nurtured in Italy, architectural measured drawings nevertheless ultimately received a more complete expression in France and northern Europe. One of the earliest, and perhaps most important, of sixteenth-century French architects to respond to Italian architectural record drawing techniques was Jacques Androuet du Cerceau, who founded a flourishing dynasty of architects. Though he designed a number of important buidings, he is best known for his books on architectural subjects which included his own fine engravings, and for inaugurating the French tradition for the accurate recording of existing buildings. An indefatigable draftsman, Androuet produced an impressive number of architectural publications on a wide variety of subjects from 1549 until his death in 1585. For our purpose the most important are the two folio volumes published in 1576 and 1579, in which, perhaps for the first time—with the notable exception of Palladio's delineation of Bramante's Tempietto—an architect concerned with accurate record drawings included monuments of the more recent past. [Androuet, 1868] His attention was drawn to the medieval and contemporary châteaux of France, and it was his ambition to cover all the great houses of France in these volumes. With our criteria for measured drawings, it is noteworthy that Androuet's scaled plan for the now-destroyed Château de Verneuil, parts of which he supposedly built, specifically stated that it was a drawing made at a precise moment in time to indicate existing conditions: "Le plan du bastiment neuf comme il est de present". (Figure 4.8) This interest in time and his awareness of topography and architectural complexes are milestones which made important contributions in the evolution of measured drawings. The comprehensiveness of Androuet's concerns can be gauged in the drawings of the Château de Montargis. It appears that measured drawings, then as now, are an essential first step taken by an architect to restore or alter an existing structure.

The French tradition initiated by du Cerceau reached its apogee when Antoine Desgodets produced what may still today be regarded technically and artistically as the finest published work based on architectural measured drawings. Desgodets was sent to Rome in 1674 on a special mission to measure ancient structures as they existed. (Figure 4.9) With the official support of Colbert, Desgodets received assistance in the preparation of a publication in 1683 generally known as Les Édifices. [Desgodets, 1682]

Les Édifices had particular influence in England, where a growing general interest in historical inquiry produced a coterie of men of learning who were particularly receptive to the detailed archaeological approach to historic structures which Desgodets's drawings exemplify. In fact, Desgodets was the acknowledged inspiration for a number of the most influential architectural publications based on the accurate observation of antiquity during the mid and late eighteenth century. Stuart and Revett in their 1748 proposals to undertake an ambitious project to document the antiquities of Athens, [Stuart and Revett, 1762-1830] and Robert Wood, who led an even more ambitious expedition resulting in The Ruins of Palmyra in 1753 (Figure 4.10) and The Ruins of Baalbec in 1757, acknowledged their indebtedness to Desgodets. [Wood, 1827]

A plethora of published and unpublished architectural measured drawings is available from the late seventeenth and early eighteen centuries. Many of them, such as Colen Campbell's of Inigo Jones' Queen's House at Greenwich (1616-35) and Banqueting House at Whitehall (1619-22) are masterpieces of this oeuvre. Campbell's drawings were included in his survey of British architecture, the three-volume Vitruvius Britannicus, or the British Architect of 1715, 1717, and 1725, which is a tribute to English Palladianism. [Campbell, 1715-1725] Not until after the discovery of Herculaneum and Pompeii in the 1730s and 1740s, and the subsequent emergence of the science of archaeology, however, are there any developments in architectural measured drawings that proceed beyond the techniques used by Desgodets.

One of the most widely known architectural history studies is the multi-volume series, The Antiquities of Athens, which is basically a collection of measured drawings. The original proposal outlining the scope of this recording project was drawn up by James Stuart (1713-88) late in 1748. The subsequent trip of Stuart and Revett to Greece took place in 1751; the first volume appeared in 1762, and then other

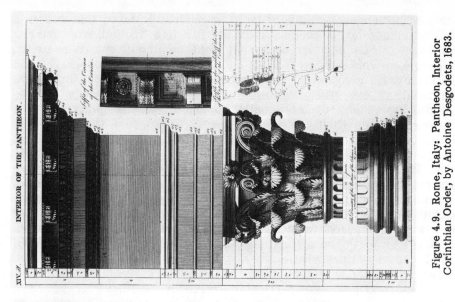

Figure 4.9. Rome, Italy: Pantheon, Interior Corinthian Order, by Antoine Desgodets, 1683.

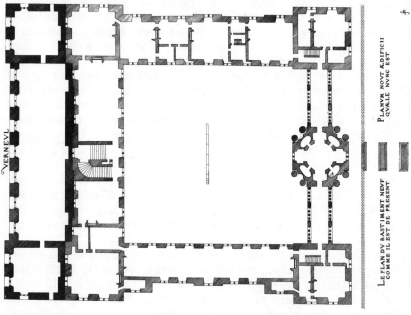

Figure 4.8. Verneuil, France: Chateau, Scaled Plan by Jacques Androuet du Cerceau, 1576.

volumes were published in 1789, 1794, 1816, and 1830 with the support of the Society of Dilettanti. It should be noted that copies of Stuart's proposal were immediately available in Rome, in 1751 in London and in 1753 in Venice, and that other recording projects such as that of the French architect Julien-David LeRoy (1724-1803)—who in effect appropriated Stuart and Revett's initiatory position by publishing his Les Ruines des plus beaux monuments de la Grèce in 1758—may have received their original inspiration from this 1748 project. [LeRoy, 1758]

Until recently there has been a tendency in English-speaking countries to underestimate the accomplishments and importance of LeRoy's Les Ruines. In part this is directly attributable to the denigrating comments made in the first volume of The Antiquities of Athens regarding the accuracy of LeRoy's measurements. It is true that more attention was given to detailed measuring by Stuart and Revett than by LeRoy. A comparison of the durations of their campaigns in Athens itself clearly indicates completely different attitudes; Stuart and Revett—although their work was interrupted by political unrest, the suspicions of local authorities, and the plague—worked for over a year-and-a-half in Athens; LeRoy completed his work in Athens in three months. LeRoy himself stated that his "work was intended to bring to light the first principles of architecture, and not to be a source of specific details or accurate measurements".

Although LeRoy's work does have a claim to being a first, its real importance is perhaps in its relation to architectural theory and the study of architectural history. This dichotomy was new to the age; in fact no one had either clearly perceived or expressed the concept that architectural theory and history were not one and the same. LeRoy did, as is distinctly expressed in the subtitle of Les Ruines: "ouvrage divisé en deux parties, où l'on considere, dans la première, ces monuments du côté de l'histoire; et dans la seconde, du côté de l'architecture". There is, therefore, some justification in attributing the origin of the study of architectural history—as a distinct historical discipline—to Julien-David LeRoy.

All of the fine volumes of the 1750s and 1760s which have been discussed must inevitably, however, stand comparison with The Ruins of Palmyra, otherwise Tedmor in the Desert of 1753 and The Ruins of Baalbec, otherwise Heliopolis in Coelosyria in 1757. Perhaps the greatest and the earliest of all the major mid-eighteenth-century folio publications on the architecture of the ancient world, these volumes of Robert Wood and James Dawkins were the acknowledged yardstick of Stuart and Revett, LeRoy, and Robert Adam.

Robert Adam was the first English-speaking architect to view the ruins of the ancient Mediterranean professionally. Stuart and Revett, at the start of their work in Athens, were both artists; Wood, Dawkins, and Bouverie were dilettantes or antiquaries who hired an Italian draftsman to record their architectural observations. Adam was a trained architect who conducted his entire Italian sojourn, from 1755 to 1757, as a professional Grand Tour. Robert Adam himself did not actively produce measured drawings in these years. For this type

241

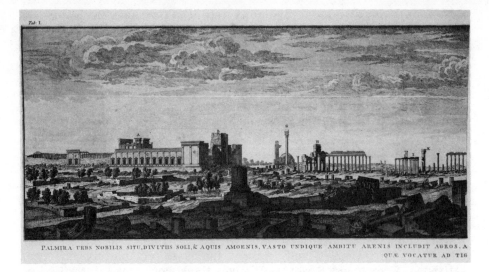

Figure 4.10. Palmyra, Syria: View of the Ruins, by Robert Wood, 1753.

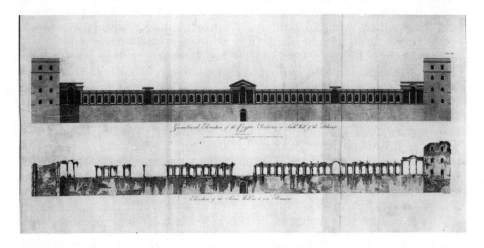

Figure 4.11. Split, Yugoslavia: Palace of Diocletian, Facade by Robert Adam, 1764.

of detailed work he subsidized Clerisseau and hired two draftsmen. Adam organized the recording campaigns; he was a type of entrepreneur and collector, who at the same time intended to refine his drawing and rendering techniques, to establish his credentials and reputation, and to nurture his talents.

Even his selection of the Palace of Diocletian for detailed recording, and then for publication, was based on a professional ambition to establish a reputation as a scholar and architect and to create a reference work which would serve as a tool for design. The large palace complex was a Roman building type which could be adapted to house the British aristocracy; and of course, too, Spalatro had not yet been the subject of either research or publication. (Figure 4.11) In the introduction to the Ruins of the Palace of Emperor Diocletian at Spalatro in Dalmatia, which was published by Robert Adam himself in London in 1764, he emphasized that other publications had concentrated on ancient temples, monuments, or public buildings, but that his was the first to present an example—a most elaborate example—of the domestic architecture of ancient Rome. [Adam, 1764] Also, Herculaneum and Pompeii were as yet largely unexcavated, and he exercised his professional good sense in selecting a site that was relatively intact and accessible, for Spalatro belonged to Venice. The magnitude of the achievements of these men can be assessed by comparing the overall dimensions of the palace–fortress–town (i.e., 700 feet by 580 feet) with the duration of the campaign (July 22, 1757-August 28, 1757—a total of five weeks). A review of even a few of these drawings indicates an almost Herculean effort and determination. In particular, one notes Adam's sharp distinction between what actually exists and what he determines to be the original state—between fact and conjecture.

The art of architectural measured drawings in the eighteenth century in a technical sense did not progress beyond the late seventeenth-century achievements of Desgodets. Gaspard Monge (1746-1818) is generally credited with being the founder of descriptive geometry. Described variously as a mathematician, physicist, or military engineer, he held the professorship of hydrodynamics at the Paris Lyceum prior to the French Revolution. As a result of his work with descriptive geometry, his method of projection became the "common language of engineering and architectural drawing in Europe", and the relationship of architectural plans with side and front elevations was standardized in the form now known as "first angle projection". This work gave access to a whole system of algebraic concepts peculiar to analytic geometry which would affect the traditional approach to perspective, which had always necessitated the development of elaborate and accurate plans and elevations as a first step. [Monge, 1810, 1799]

A further development in methods of graphic presentation was a systematic approach for projection which came to be known as an isometric drawing. Although the concept of an isometric had existed in a rough way for centuries, it appears that Professor William Farish (1759-1837) of Cambridge University was the first to provide rules for its development. A professor of chemistry, Farish developed and used the isometric projection in order to demonstrate the assembly of mechanical apparatus that he was discussing in his university lectures. He first described this form of projection in a paper which he presented in two parts in 1820 to the Cambridge Philosophical Society. It appears that Farish was the first to use the term "isometric project" or "isometric perspective" and that later writers credit him with having invented the system. Olinthus Gregory made this system of projection more widely available, ca. 1833, in his publication Mathematics For Practical Men. [Gregory, 1862] In Chapter VII, entitled "Professor Farish's Isometrical Perspective", Gregory estimates the value of the isometric drawing: it has all the primary assets of perspective drawing, revealing immediately the relationships of parts, and in addition it reveals true dimensions because it is accurately and uniformly scaled in all its parts. (Figure 4.12)

Late eighteenth and nineteenth-century romanticism occasionally exerted certain negative influences on the discipline of measured drawings. The drawings of Viollet-le-Duc, the important architectural restorer of many monuments, for the Château de Pierrefonds are conjectural restoration drawings, that do nothing to dispel the impression that what is being viewed actually existed at that particular moment and parade as measured drawings. Although Pierrefonds was originally constructed between 1390 and 1420, almost the entire fabric was rebuilt in the mid-nineteenth century by Viollet-le-Duc for Napoleon III and his Empress Eugénie.

Illustrative and perhaps archetypal of studies based on architectural drawings in the nineteenth century are the publications of the buildings on the Athenian Acropolis, particularly the Parthenon, by the English architects John Pennethorne and Francis Cranmer Penrose. Before the mid-nineteenth century the structures on the Acropolis were in general no more admired or studied than others built by the Greeks. In large part it was the field work of Thomas Leverton Donaldson (1795-1885) and then of Pennethorne and Penrose, which securely established their legitimacy as supreme achievements. Pennethorne in 1844 was essentially the first to suggest that fifth-century B.C. Athenian architects had developed a comprehensive mathematically regulated program which subtly disavowed strict level-and-plumb-line, trabeated architecture. Based on several trips to the now-independent Greece in the 1830s, and prompted initially by his interest in architectural polychromy, Pennethorne's 1844 volume was regarded by him as an "abridged summary" of these perceived mathematical principles. His observations were possible because of the partial clearing of the rubble which had previously obscured the base of the Parthenon.

For the first time the Parthenon presented to a visually-trained, professional architect the opportunity to disengage himself from the traditional visual bias of post-Renaissance architects, who perceived the art of classic architecture as a static system based entirely on rigid horizontals and verticals locked immutably in a 90° relationship.

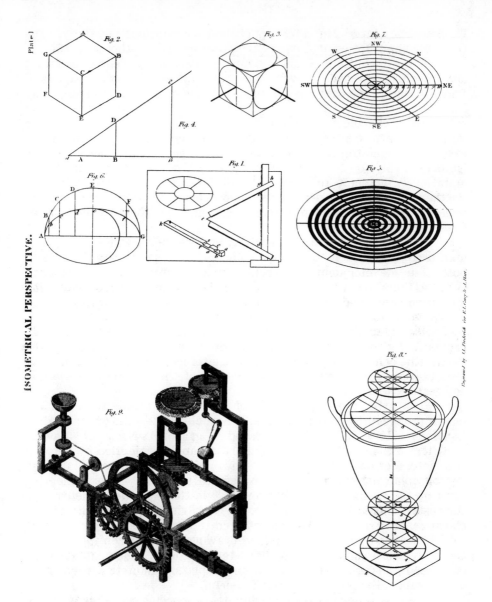

Figure 4.12. Isometrical Perspective: Olinthus Gregory, 1836.

245

Pennethorne later, in 1878, published a substantive study, The Geometry and Optics of Ancient Architecture. [Pennethorne, 1878]

In the meantime, Francis Cranmer Penrose—a fellow architect and Englishman—had proven most of the basic contentions of Pennethorne's 1844 essay in a volume published in 1851. [Penrose, 1851] Plates in Penrose's volume are particularly informative regarding the scientific-archaeological mentality of architectural recording in the mid-nineteenth century. Not only was accuracy in measurement assiduously maintained but a keyed system graphically presented the historic evolution of the Parthenon. Several plates then also ambitiously attempt to record the architectural polychromy of the Parthenon. These two architects corroborated the literary evidence of ancient Greek and Roman authors regarding the theoretical basis of Greek architecture.

The late nineteenth and early twentieth-century proliferation of measured drawings in published volumes is of great significance in both the development of architectural history and of historic preservation; however, most were still developed from laborious hand measurements and utilized graphic methods of representation available almost a century before. In the mid-nineteenth-century, technological developments provided a potential that would not only dramatically alter the production of measured drawings in the twentieth century but would also, therefore, affect the study of architectural history and the effectiveness of the historic preservation and restoration.

Soon after the development of a chemical means to retain the image produced by a camera lens, a French officer and savant, Aimé Laussedat (1819–1907), "demonstrated a graphic system of drawing fortifications and other buildings in orthographic projection by plotting the intersections in space of lines of sight projected through photographic images taken at two camera stations." This pioneering work by the "father of photogrammetry" in the 1850s nevertheless was seriously handicapped by the narrow field and imperfections of the photographic lenses of that period, and it was not until ca. 1867 that fully-developed, accurate measured drawings of a church in Freiburg, Germany were made by Albrecht Meydenbauer. Later, in 1885, he organized the first great collection of photogrammetric records of architecture, the Messbildanstalt in Berlin.

Great advances in photogrammetric recording were made in the 1890s by the Austrian professor, Edward Dolezal. His work with geodetic surveying resulted in stereophotogrammetry which today is the basic technique for all measured drawings developed from photographs. (Figure 4.13) For the layman it is a complex process involving special cameras, photographic stereopairs, and elaborate plotting machines; but because of this advanced technological procedure, vast irregular sites and monumental structures can be fully recorded. (Figure 4.14) Now when we are increasingly aware that the preservation of our manmade environment should be an integral part of our concerns and programs, the expanded potential to record and

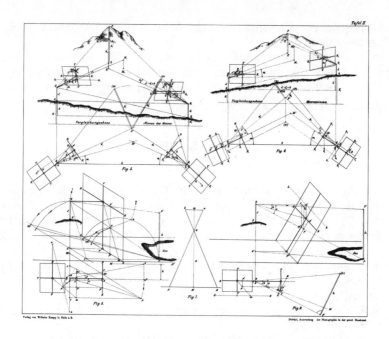

Figure 4.13. Stereophotogrammetry: Edward Dolezal, 1896.

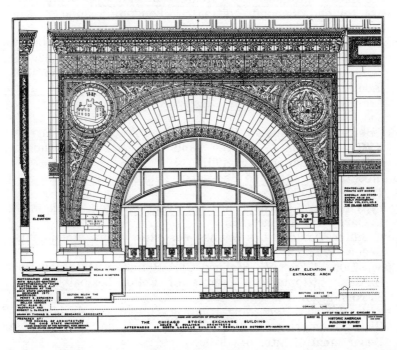

Figure 4.14. Chicago, Illinois: Stock Exchange Building, East Elevation of Entrance Arch, Adler and Sullivan, Architects, 1893, Drawing Produced Photogrammetrically by Perry E. Borchers, 1971.

produce measured drawings by this complicated technical procedure are of enormous utility.

In brief summation, it can be noted that initially, measured drawings formed the basis of designs for structures which were to be built. Next they played a primary role in assessing the past. Now they can help to form the future and preserve the past.

REFERENCES

Adam. Robert. Ruins of the Palace of Emperor Diocletian at Spalatro in Dalmatia. London: Printed for the Author, 1764.

Alfarano, Tiberios or Tiberius Alpharanus. "De basilicae Vaticanae antiquissima et nova structura," Vol. 26 of Studi e testi. Ed. M. Cerrati. Rome: 1914.

Androuet, Jacques (du Cerceau). Les plus excellents bastiments de France, 2 vols., facsimile edition under the direction of H. Destailleur. Paris: A. Levy, 1868.

Campbell, Colen. Vitruvius Britannicus. London: The Author, 1715, 1717, and 1725.

Desgodets, Antoine or Desgodetz . Rome in Its Ancient Grandeur (Édifices antiques de Rome, dessinés et mesures très exactement, Second edition). London: John Weale, and Sherwood, Gilbert and Piper, 1848.

Dolezal, Edward. Die Anwendung der Photographie in der praktischen messkunst. Encycklopadie der Photographie, Heft 22. Halle a Salle, Germany: Druck und Verlag von Wilhelm Knapp, 1896.

Donaldson, Thomas Leverton. Architectura Numismatica, or Architectural Medals of Classic Antiquity. London: Day and Son, 1859.

Egger, Hermann. Romische Veduten: Hand Zeichmungen aus dem XV-XVII Jahrhundert. Erster Band (Vol. 1). Wien und Leipzig: Friedr Woltrum and Co., 1911.

Falb, Rodolfo. Il taccuino Senese de Giuliano da San Gallo. Siena: The Author, 1902.

Gregory, Olinthus. Mathematics for Practical Men. Philadelphia: E. L. Carey and A. Hart, 1836.

LeRoy, Julien-David. Les Ruines des plus beaux monuments de la Grèce. 1758.

McCown, Donald Eugene, Richard Carl Haines, assisted by Donald P. Hansen. Nippur I: Temple of Enlid, Scribal Quarter, and Surroundings. Chicago: 1967.

McKee, Harley J. Recording Historic Buildings. Washington, D.C.: Historic American Buildings Survey, National Park Service, U.S. Department of Interior, 1970.

Monge, Gaspard. Traité élémentaire de statique. Paris: Courcier, 1810.

Monge, Gaspard. Leçons de géométrie descriptive. Paris: Baudouin, 1799.

Palladio. I Quattro libri dell'architectura. (English Leoni edition). 1742.

Pennethorne, John. The Geometry and Optics of Ancient Architecture. London and Edinburgh: Williams and Norgate, 1878.

Penrose, Francis Cranmer. An Investigation of the Principles of Athenian Architecture. London: W. Nicol, 1851.

Serlio, Sebastiano. Tutte l'opera d'architettura de Venetia. Preffo Francesco de' Franceschi Senese. 1584.

Stuart, James and Nicholas Revett. The Antiquities of Athens. 5 vols. London: Printed by John Haberkorn, 1762, 1789, 1794, 1816, 1830.

Villard de Honnecourt. (Rev. Robert Willis, Ed.) Facsimile of the Sketchbook of Wilars de Honecort, an Architect of the Thirteenth Century. London: John Henry and James Parker, 1859.

Vitruvius Pollios. M. Vitruvius per iocundum solito castigatior factus, cum figuris et tabula ut iam legi et intelligi posit, ed., Fra Giovanni Giacondo. Venice: Ioannes de Tridino, 1511.

Wood, Robert. The Ruins of Palmyra, otherwise Tedmor in the Desert. London: Robert Wood, 1753.

Wood, Robert. The Ruins of Baalbec, otherwise Heliopolis in Ceolyosyria. London: Robert Wood, 1757.

Applying Photogrammetry to the Protection of Historic Architecture and Museum Collections from Earthquakes and Other Natural Disasters

Perry E. Borchers

ABSTRACT

Photogrammetry can be applied to the protection of historic architecture and museum collections from earthquakes and other natural disasters as a means of

(1) Documenting historic architecture and major sculptural or structural items of museum collections in undamaged condition for permanent record, and for study and understanding;
(2) Monitoring movements and deformation of historic architecture and other structural elements, such as the bases of monumental sculpture, under continued stress of thermal changes, water penetration, earth movements, and their own structural loads;
(3) Recording and evaluating the damage caused by a natural disaster in order to plan quick and effective means to strengthen structural elements of historic architecture and museums against further damage or collapse; and
(4) Analyzing historic photographs—where no thorough photogrammetric documentation had existed before a disaster—to recover dimensions and details necessary for restoration or reconstruction of damaged or lost cultural resources.

The report discusses the characteristics of this science of measuring by means of photography, and describes the photogrammetric requirements for survey control and for duplication of camera stations and camera axes necessary to satisfy the general purposes listed above.

DEFINITION

Photogrammetry is the science of measuring by means of photography. It is concerned with the measurable geometric relationships between photographic images and the real objects and space recorded upon these images. Photogrammetry employs mathematical, mechanical, graphical and computerized procedures to determine—and to print in digital tabulation or to plot in orthographic projection—the form, the dimensions and the location of objects from perspective views of those objects recorded photographically.

HISTORY

The science of photgrammetry is based on the geometry of central projection. This is the geometry of perspective drawing and of the camera obscura, two methods of graphic recording which preceded by several centuries the development of photography as a photochemical means of recording perspective views within a camera. With allowance for the curvature of the retina, this is the geometry of vision also.

A series of drawings by Albrecht Durer, ca. 1525 A.D., show the artist's devices for drawing and teaching the principles of perspective. His drawing which is reproduced here as Figure 4.15 illustrates major elements of the geometry of central projection in a form applicable to the understanding of photogrammetry.

Durer's drawing establishes the definite and unique geometric relation between a point of central projection—in this example, the eye of the wall screw—and the intersections with an image plane which occur when a tightly stretched cord tied to the tip of a spike is held by the demonstrator to a series of points on a musical instrument. An assistant measures x and y coordinates where the cord passes through a frame representing the image plane. He then records the intersection of these coordinates on the actual image plane, which has been swung to one side.

The eye of the wall screw is a perspective center similar to the human eye or the camera lens. The various positions of the stretched cord can represent either lines of sight from a human eye to the object or rays of light from the object through a camera lens.

The data needed to make this drawing into a photogrammetric diagram include:

(a) Determining and marking the point on the image plane intersected by a perpendicular from the "perspective center". This would be the "principal point of the image plane" which in this drawing seems to lie just within the upper boundary of the frame. The perpendicular line itself would be directionally equivalent to a "camera axis".

Figure 4.15. Principles of Perspective Projection: Albrecht Durer, 1525.

(b) Determining and recording the length of the perpendicular from the eye of the wall screw to the principal point of the image plane. This would be equivalent to the focal length of a camera, also known as the "camera constant".

(c) Determining that the sides of the frame, which form the boundaries of the image plane, are truly vertical and horizontal, or else determining the inclinations of the frame.

Shortly after Renaissance artists grasped the principles of perspective drawing, there came the development of the camera obscura—a dark chamber (camera = room) with a pinhole or lens through which an image of exterior, illuminated space was projected onto an interior surface. The camera obscura could be large enough to house an artist in darkness while he traced an inverted image projected through the pinholde or lens in the opposite wall onto a frame stretched over an interior wall, or it could be an easily transportable tent with a pole-mounted lens and mirror above the hooded drafting board at which the artist sat. The camera obscura could also be a small box in which the image projected through the lens was reflected by a mirror onto the underside of a translucent surface over which the artist could trace.

One panoramic drawing of Stockholm, ca. 1695, when tested photogrammetrically at the Royal Institute of Technology there, revealed such accurate angular perspective to existing church spires and known locations of former castle and defensive towers as to indicate it was produced within a portable camera obscura at a specific site overlooking the city, with the image plane at an angle so that the light rays passed over the shoulder of the artist who was copying them. [Hallert, 1963]

It must be assumed that the camera obscura was widely used by Baroque and Rococo artists in the 17th and 18th centuries to gain accurate perspective in drawings and paintings. Where the camera obscura has been employed, photogrammetric data may be secured from the paintings and drawings produced. Similarly, historic photographic negatives on glass plates may also provide photogrammetric data, although they were taken at a time when photogrammetric use of them was never anticipated.

The modern science of photogrammetry began with Colonel Aimé Laussedat in 1850—shortly after the first daguerreotypes introduced the era of photography—when he demonstrated (Figure 4.16) a system for drawing fortifications and other buildings in orthographic projection by graphically plotting the intersections in object space of corresponding lines of sight recorded in photographic images taken at two or more surveyed camera stations.

Under the direction of the German architect Albrecht Meydenbaer, the Messbildanstalt in Berlin began in 1885 to systematically collect photogrammetric records of architecture consisting of multiple photographs of single structures from widely separated and carefully surveyed camera stations. The strongly convergent intersections of corresponding lines of sight from the

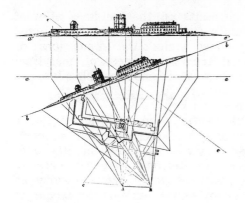

Figure 4.16. Vincennes, France, Chateau, Site Plan Constructed from Photographic Views, Colonel Aime Laussedat, 1850.

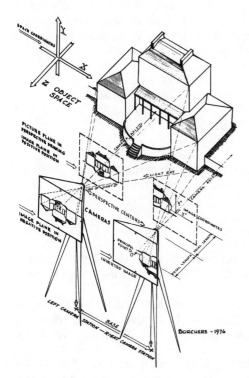

Figure 4.17. Stereophotogrammetric Camera Stations: Perry E. Borchers, 1976.

camera stations to architectural elements on the buildings allowed graphic methods of plotting architectural plans and elevations. Similarly—convergent photography now yields the dimensions of architecture through the much more accurate process of analytical photogrammetry, with precise measurement of photographic plates in photogrammetric comparators resolved by computation into dimensions of the architecture in object space.

At the beginning of the 20th century the Austrian professor Edward Dolezal developed the techniques of stereophotogrammetry, which is now the most widely used system of photogrammetry both from the air and from terrestrial camera stations. With photography along parallel—or near parallel—camera axes, which are perpendicular to—or nearly perpendicular to—the horizontal base of displacement between the two camera stations, this system allows stereoscopic examination of architectural form prior to and during the detailed labor of photogrammetric plotting and drawing. A typical setup for stereophotogrammetry is shown in Figure 4.17.

DOCUMENTING HISTORIC ARCHITECTURE AND MAJOR SCULPTURAL AND STRUCTURAL ITEMS OF MUSEUM COLLECTIONS FOR PERMANENT RECORD

The typical architectural use of photogrammetry has been to document structures in existing historic condition before possible major changes, such as:

(a) Prior to stabilization—i.e., the temple base of Pu'ukohola Heiau, Island of Hawaii, 1976
(b) Before planning adaptive renovation—i.e., the Schermerhorn Block, Lower Manhattan, to become a New York State Maritime Museum, 1977
(c) Prior to renovation and adjacent construction which could cause major accidental damage—i.e., the Villard Houses, Central Manhattan, at the base of the towering Helmsley Palace Hotel, 1977
(d) Prior to possible overrunning and destruction during energy exploration—i.e., Fort La Clede and La Clede Station on the Overland Trail, Wyoming, 1979, 1980
(e) Prior to feared damage in civil disorders—i.e., the dome of the Old State Capitol, Annapolis, Maryland, 1970
(f) Prior to dismantling for rebuilding on a new site—i.e., the Stock Exchange Room of the Old Chicago Stock Exchange Building, rebuilt in new wing of the Chicago Art Institute, 1971
(g) Prior to final demolition—i.e., the ruins of the Pauson House, Phoenix, Arizona, by Frank Lloyd Wright, burnt 1943, demolished 1980.

(h) Prior to further natural deterioration—i.e., the Arroyo del Tajo Pictograph Site, New Mexico, 1981.

To this list should now be added the documentation in existing historic condition of the most significant structures and works of art in areas subject to earthquakes, hurricanes and floods.

Photogrammetric recording is a process of two stages involving (1) photography and survey control upon the site, securing all the data needed later for (2) orientation of the photographs and plotting and drawing in the laboratory. This second stage of photogrammetric recording is one that may be postponed, awaiting available funds or immediate need for detailed drawings.

The various major techniques of photgrammetric recording include:

(a) Monophotogrammetry, with any of the following procedures:
    (1) On site rectified photography of essentially flat surfaces.
    (2) Laboratory rectification of photographs necessarily inclined or angled on site to record essentially flat surfaces.
    (3) Recording by the method of luminous sections.
(b) Analytical photogrammetry, with digitized computer calculation or coordinate dimensions and plotting in various orthographic projections; and
(c) Stereophotogrammetry, employing either photogrammetric stereocameras, adaptable for rapid recording of regular structure at close distance, or phototheodolites, adaptable to recording large complex forms such as very tall buildings, church towers, cliff dwellings and Indian pueblos under more difficult conditions requiring more ingenuity of photographic coverage. The phototheodolite is also well adapted to analytical photogrammetry.

The conditions on site and the required accuracy of photogrammetric plotting and drawing determine the most cost-efficient choice among many types of photogrammetric cameras, varying techniques of photography, and the use of various analog or digital plotting instruments. There is a somewhat more detailed discussion of these techniques— about which there is a considerable technical literature—in Photogrammetric Recording of Cultural Resources, published by the U.S. National Park Service. [Borchers, 1977; See also Borchers, 1965 and Borchers, 1968]

To the discussion of survey control in that publication, there should be added the observation that the camera stations and the targets for survey control used for documentation—as distinguished from those used in monitoring change and deformation—can be set up for the photography on site and removed immediately thereafter.

For documentation, the plotting and drawing of historic structures or major items of museum collections can be in either topographic or planimetric drawing, or in a combination of the two. (Figure 4.18) Smaller items of museum collections can be recorded very effectively in controlled color stereophotography mounted for steroscopic viewing and examination.

MONITORING MOVEMENTS AND DEFORMATION OF HISTORIC ARCHITECTURE AND OTHER STRUCTURAL ELEMENTS OF MUSEUM COLLECTIONS

In principle, the measurement of structural movement requires the use of a phototheodolite or some other precise camera, of fixed interior orientation and flat glass photographic plates, to take successive photographs at appropriate time intervals from a fixed camera station along a fixed camera axis.

It is necessary to photograph from two camera stations, with strongly convergent lines of sight, to measure three-dimensional movement in structure. Movement in two image planes, as measured between successive plates from each of the two stations, is then resolved by projection to intersection in space, into movement of the structure in three coordinate directions in object space.

A project of measurement of structural movements begins with the choice of camera stations and camera axes. Sites chosen for the camera stations must allow photographic coverage of the structure within the viewing angle of the phototheodolite. It is impossible to measure what does not appear in the photographic image. The requirements for accuracy of measurement affect the choice of camera stations, because a relatively constant error of measurement of the image plane grows proportionally with distance of sight lines carried into object space. Also, an acute intersection of lines of sight from two camera stations exaggerates the error in the depth direction of object space.

For recording of long-term movements, the horizontal space coordinates of the camera stations should be precisely marked in metal caps set in concrete bases carried below frost line. Additional permanent control is necessary to repeatedly re-establish the height of the camera and the turn of its axis.

In the object space recorded in the photogrammetric image there must be a series of control points. Ideally, these should be located symmetrically to each side of the camera axis, and above and below the horizon in the photographic image, but this is not always possible. These should be fixed points, or, at least, they should not be subject to the forces which are causing the structural movements which are

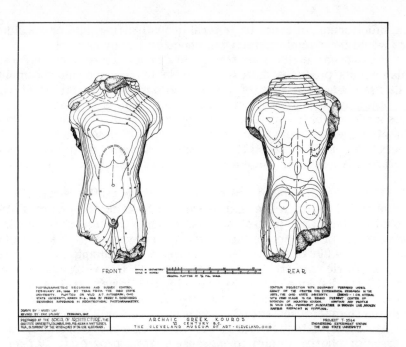

Figure 4.18. Cleveland, Ohio: Torso of Archaic Greek Kouros, 6th Century, B.C. in Cleveland Museum of Art, Drawing Produced Photogrammetrically by Perry E. Borchers.

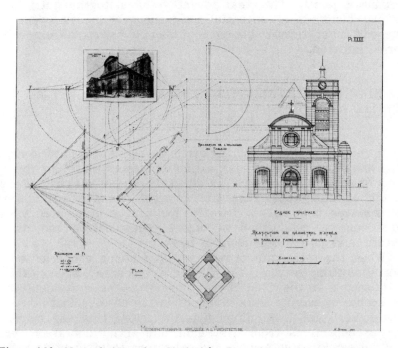

Figure 4.19. Metrophotography: Method for Preparing Architectural Plans and Elevations from Historic Photographs, by Deneux de Montbrun, 1930.

259

being monitored. In areas of general ground tilting, slip or subsidence there would be special difficulty in choosing survey control.

Photogrammetric monitoring or measurement of structural displacements produces data in the form of relative measurements—parallaxes—between pairs of plates photographed at different times with the same camera at the same camera station. The correspondence between successive pairs of plates, measured against each other, effectively eliminates systematic error caused by lens defects and makes possible the measurement of movements of structure with greater accuracy than measurement of the structure itself.

With an adjustment procedure for substantial correction of relative radial error in the plates—caused by lack of perfect flatness of photogrammetric plates and emulsions—the standard error of measurement in the photographic image has varied in practice from 1/9,000 to 1/50,000 of the width of the image, depending upon choice of photgrammetric camera. In a structure 300 ft. wide, photographed from 300 ft. distance, as in Figure 4.16, this lower level of accuracy (1/9,000) would result in a standard error of 3/8", below which dimension the measurement of structural movements may be in doubt.

At closer distances and lesser width of photographic coverage, the error of photogrammetric measurement is progressively reduced; but strain gauges are still the cost-effective means of measuring movement where movement can be definitely localized, as at cracks or expansion joints. The great advantage of photogrammetry is that, recording hundreds of potentially significantly measurements in a moment of time, structural movement may be discovered where it was never anticipated.

RECORDING AND EVALUATING DAMAGE CAUSED BY A
NATURAL DISASTER

In recording and evaluating damage caused by a natural disaster photogrammetric recording is particularly appropriate, in the same manner that it is appropriate for tall buildings and all structures with difficult or dangerous access. Physical contact with unstable structures can be avoided. Scaffolding can be eliminated. Survey control can be established in object space before the damaged structures and quite independent of them.

When the steropairs of a damaged building are oriented in a universal plotting instrument of first order accuracy—such as the Wild A7 Autograph at the Ohio State University—the movement of the stereoscopic measuring mark in any of the three coordinate directions in the optical model will immediately disclose tilts and bulges and slopes as departures from a straight line of horizontal or vertical travel. It would be unfeasible and dangerous to attempt to set up a comparable coordinate system on the site for direct measurement of deformations.

The topographic contour drawings which are regularly used to express ground forms can be used as easily to express deformations, sags and bulges in walls, domes and vaults which disturb the geometry of architectural structures.

There is attached to this report as Appendix No. 1, the conclusions and recommendations of an ICAP colloquium on the photogrammetric recording of historic structures in earthquake zones based on experience of the Friuli earthquake of northern Italy.

ANALYZING HISTORIC PHOTOGRAPHS TO RECOVER DIMENSIONS AND DETAILS NECESSARY FOR RESTORATION OR RECONSTRUCTION

It is possible to recover dimensions and details necessary for restoration or reconstruction of damaged or lost structures by means of photogrammetric analysis of historic photographs. This is especially true when dimensionally-stable glass plate negatives still exist. Then measurements can be taken from the negative plate or from a diapositive glass plate printed in direct contact with the negative.

The methods involve analysis of either single photographs or multiple photographs. An entire book of methods to arrive at measured drawings from reverse perspective analysis of single photographs was published by Deneux de Montbrun in 1930. (Figure 4.19) [Montbrun, 1930]

These methods, involving analysis of perspective vanishing points of horizontal lines of structure and pavement, of mitered edges and diagonals and cast shadows, etc., allowed a determination of three necessary elements of geometry:

a. The location of the camera station in relation to the photograph,
b. The direction of the camera axis and principal point of the photograph,
c. The focal length of the camera at time of photography.

The success of Deneux's methods depends upon the geometric regularity of architectural elements; that is, truly horizontal and vertical architectural surfaces and edges, true circles, rectangular corners and sets of parallel lines. It also depends upon at least one known dimension to establish scale for the drawings.

The analysis of single photographs cannot be successfully carried out for structures or portions of structures which are deliberately deformed for optical illusion, as in Baroque architecture, which are sculptural and irregular, as in primitive mud and adobe architecture, or which have been deformed by structural loads or foundation movement.

261

In these cases the analysis of multiple historic photographs establishes intersecting lines of sight to determine the locations in space of structure which has vanished since the time of photography.

The procedure, as it has been applied to Indian pueblos and farming villages in the Southwestern United States, has usually begun with photogrammetric measurement and drawing of existing villages in good detail. At the time of photogrammetric recording on site an attempt is made to locate the historic camera stations approximately and to take photographs from these stations along the historic camera axes. This allows the inclusion of distant horizons as part of the system of "fixes" by which to determine more precisely the historic camera locations.

A "fix" consists of two points, one in the foreground and one in the background of object space, appearing one above the other in the photographic image, and therefore lying in the same vertical plane projected outwards from the center of the lens into object space. The intersection of two fixes determines the camera station.

When the camera stations have been determined, lines of sight are drawn—in the modern plan prepared by photogrammetry—from the camera stations to points of structure still remaining in place since the time of the historic photographs. Horizontal dimensions of the photographs are fitted to these lines of sight drawn in plan to determine the location of the image planes. A line drawn from the camera station perpendicular to the image plane determines the direction of the camera axis and the principal point of the image plane. The measurement of this line indicates the focal length of the camera at the time of photography.

Then it is only necessary to project other lines of sight from two or more camera stations to intersections in space at the locations of vanished structure.

The photogrammetric analysis of historic photographs allows one to distinguish between original and reconstructed structure. It also has very important applications to the preparation of restoration drawings for structures destroyed by earthquakes or other natural disasters.

REFERENCES

Borchers, Perry E. "Photogrammetric Measurements of Structural Movements," Journal of the Surveying and Mapping Division, American Society of Civil Engineers (January 1968).

Borchers, Perry E. "Photogrammetric Recording of Cultural Resources," Publication Number 186, Washington, D.C.: National Park Service, U.S. Department of Interior, 1977.

Borchers, Perry E. "Trois Types de Mesures Photogrammétriques Utilisées en Architecture," Société Française de Photogrammétrie, Volume 19 (July 1965).

Montbrun, Deneux de.   La Métrophotographie appliquée à l'Architecture, Paris: P. Latin 1930.

Hallert, B.   "Undersökning av Perspektivet hos Panoramamålning" "Fotogrammetri och Kulturhistoria" Svensk Lantmäteritidskrift, 5-6 (1963).

Report of the Colloquium on the Photogrammetry of Historic Centers in Earthquake Zones, Venzone (Frioul), Italy, 24–27 October 1981

The subject of the colloquium organized by the Venzone Commune (Udine Province) and the ICOMOS International Committee on Architectural Photogrammetry (ICAP), was the contribution of photogrammetry to the protection and reconstruction of historic centers damaged by earthquakes.

The colloquium participants, having,

—studied, in situ, the photogrammetric surveys carried out by the Bundesdenkmalant (Vienna) and ICCROM after the Frioul 1976 earthquakes, and

—examined the important operations—of high quality and unique in ICAP records—carried out in Venzone and destined for the reconstruction of the historic center of that town,

make the following recommendations:

1. In the programs for establishing photogrammetric archives for historic monuments and centers, it would be advisable to give priority to earthquake zones and, in general, to those zones which are continually menaced by natural disasters.

2. In such regions, photogrammetric archives should be used in a systematic and effective manner, with the support of all other sources of documentation, in particular for defining the priorities for protecting cultural assets when disasters occur. To this end, it will be necessary for the experts who have to take urgent action on the damaged monuments to have access to accurate information on the existence and the nature of those archives and on the value of the documentation contained in them.

3. After a disaster, it is recommended, as far as it is compatible with the requirements imposed by the rescue aid which must be supplied to the population, that the arrival, as rapidly as possible, of a photogrammetric survey team should be included amongst the urgent actions. That operation should be set in motion and coordinated by the local authorities, who should also attempt to indicate by appropriate marking the most important architectural elements, even if they have already been destroyed, in order to avoid further damage being caused during clearing operations.

4. When an earthquake occurs, top-priority photogrammetric surveys, combined with other measurement methods which might be used, in the first place should make it possible to obtain the data (tilt of remaining pieces of wall, bulging due to internal disturbances, sliding and shearing phenomena, width and orientation of cracks, etc.) required for

strengthening those architectural elements which are still standing, this being both effective and economic in manpower and equipment. The possibility of using photogrammetric surveys must be thoroughly studied by photogrammetrists, architects, building engineers, seismologists and, in particular, by the ICAP and the ICOMOS Seismology Committee. That study should also lead not only to a more precise analysis of the conditions (methods, instruments) for the optimum use of photogrammetry for this particular objective but also to the drafting of directives so enabling photogrammetry experts to take action with a good knowledge of the effects of earthquakes on buildings.

5. At the same time, or as soon as possible after those top-priority operations, it will be necessary, especially if no photogrammetric archives existed before the disaster, to produce by photogrammetric photography the maximum number of documents of all the edifices or those parts which remain standing before other destructions occur or the degradations grow worse. It would be very advisable to double the photography in order to quickly store one set in complete security. The team of photogrammetry experts carrying out those operations should, in addition, be able to count on assistance from the technical staff of the historic center. Finally, it is recommended organizing, when possible, the taking of photographs destined for plotting at the 1:50-scale, such plotting being carried out as soon as possible afterwards in order to serve as a basis for protection studies of the historic center.

6. For those studies, large-scale aerial photographs would also be very useful, both for the photogrammetric archives established beforehand as well as the surveys carried out after a disaster.

7. After the restoration or reconstruction of the edifices, it would be wise to carry out regular photogrammetric examinations in order to detect any signs of new disorders.

8. Special case of Venzone Cathedral: A study of the photogrammetric surveys carried out after the first earthquake in 1976 makes it possible to state that those surveys constitute an essential basis for the reconstruction of the cathedral and that, completed by the numerous documents produced before the earthquake, they will guarantee the "historic" value of that reconstruction. It is very necessary that those surveys should be used effectively by those persons who will be responsible for that operation.

Section Four References

VULNERABILITY REDUCTION OF STRUCTURES

ACI Standard Building Requirements for Reinforced Concrete. Detroit, Michigan: American Concrete Institution, 1977.

AIA Research Corporation. Design Guidelines for Flood Damage Reduction. Washington, D.C.: AIA Research Corporation, 1981.

Americus, Cathy, Ed. Building Rehabilitation, Research and Technology for the 1980's. Dubuque, Iowa and Toronto, Canada: Kendall/Hunt Publishing Co., 1980.

Amrhein, J. E. Reinforced Masonry Engineering Handbook: Brick and Other Structural Clay Units. 1st Edition. Los Angeles: Masonry Institute of America, 1972.

Applied Technology Council. Seismic Regulations for Building. California: National Bureau of Standards, 1978.

Arens, E. "Designing for an Acceptable Wind Environment." Proceedings., ASCE Convention, Atlanta, Georgia, 1979. Preprint No. 3756.

Baker, Earl J. and J. G. McPhee. Land Use Management and Regulation in Hazardous Areas: A Research Assessment. Boulder, Colorado: University of Colorado, Program on Technology, Environment and Man, 1975.

Black, W. C. "Reinforcing Bars in Earthquake-Resistant Concrete Building Construction." Workshop on Earthquake-Resistant Reinforced Concrete Building Construction (ERCBC). Berkeley, California: University of California, 1977, pp. 1242-52.

Blair, Martha L. and Spangle, William E. Seismic Safety and Land Use Planning: Selected Examples for the San Francisco Bay Region, California. Geological Survey Professional Paper 941-B. Washington, D.C.: U.S. Government Printing Office, 1979.

Blume, A., N. W. Newmark, and L. H. Corning. Design of Reinforced Concrete Buildings for Earthquake Motions. Portland Cement Association, 1961.

Botsai, Elmer, et al. Architects and Earthquakes: Research Needs. Washington, D.C.: AIA Research Corporation, 1976.

Ciborowski, Adolf. "Urban Design and Physical Planning as Tools to Make Cities Safer in Earthquake-Prone Areas," Large Earthquakes in New Zealand: Anticipation, Precautions, and Reconstruction. Wellington, New Zealand: The Royal Society of New Zealand, 1981, pp. 55-65.

Clough, R. W., K. L. Benuska, and T. Y. Lin. FHA Study of Seismic Design Criteria for High-Rise Buildings. Washington, D.C.: U.S. Department of Housing and Urban Development, Federal Housing Administration, Report HUD TS-3, August 1966.

Cocconis, Angelos. Aseismic Design of Building Structures. Ithaca, N.Y.: Cornell University, Unpublished Master's Thesis, 1959.

Degenkolb, Henry. "Preliminary Structural Lessons from the Earthquake," The San Fernando, California Earthquake of February 9, 1971. Geological Survey

Professional Paper 733. Washington, D.C.: U.S. Government Printing Office, 1971, pp. 133-34.

Design and Construction Manual for Residential Buildings in Coastal High Hazard Areas. Prepared for U.S. Department of Housing and Urban Development and the Federal Insurance Administration, Federal Emergency Management Agency, 1981.

Dowrick, Donald J. Earthquake Resistant Design. London: J. Wiley and Sons, 1977.

Dowrick, Donald J. "Must Earthquakes Always Win?" New Scientist. December 28, 1972, pp. 735-7.

Erley, Duncan and W. J. Kockelman. Reducing Landslide Hazards: A Guide for Planners. Planning Advisory Service Report No. 359. Chicago: American Planning Association, March 1981.

Feilden, Bernard M. "Earthquakes and Historic Buildings." Proceedings of the Seventh World Congress on Earthquake Engineering, September 8-13, 1980, Istanbul, Turkey. Volume 9: Socio-Economic Aspects, Earthquake Reports, Progress Reports. Ankara, Turkey: Seventh World Congress, 1981, pp. 213-226.

Fleming, Robert W., David J. Varnes and Robert L. Schuster. "Landslide Hazards and Their Reduction." American Planning Association Journal. Volume 44, No. 10, October 1979, pp. 428-439.

Foster, Harold D. "Disaster Mitigation: A Geomorphological Contribution." Emergency Planning Digest, 1975, pp. 2-9.

Galic, Risto. Skopje: Urbanisticki Plan. Skopje, Yugoslavia: Nova Makedonija, 1968.

Gori, Paula L. and Walter W. Hays, Eds. Proceedings of Conference XVIII: A Workshop on "Continuing Actions to Reduce Losses from Earthquakes in the Mississippi Valley Area". Reston, Virginia: U.S. Geological Survey, 1983.

Green, Melvyn and Associates. Survey of Building Code Provisions of Historic Structures. National Bureau of Standards Technical Note 918. Washington, D.C.: U.S. National bureau of Standards, September 1976.

Griggs, Gary B. and John A. Gilchrist. The Earth and Land Use Planning. North Scituate, Mass.: Duxbury Press, 1977.

Hanson, Robert D., Ed. Proceedings of the United States/People's Republic of China Workshop on Seismic Analysis and Design of Reinforced Concrete Structures. Ann Arbor, Michigan: Department of Civil Engineering, University of Michigan, May 1981.

Harris, James R., Steven J. Fenves and Richard N. Wright. Analysis of Technical Seismic Design Provisions for Buildings. National Bureau of Standards Technical Note No. 1100. Washington, D.C.: U.S. Government Printing Office, 1979.

Hays, Walter W. Guidelines for Developing Design Earthquake Response Spectra. Champaign, Illinois: Construction Engineering Research Laboratory, Technical Report M-114, 1975.

Housner, George W. and Paul C. Jennings. Earthquake Design Criteria. Berkeley, California: Earthquake Engineering Research Institute, September 1982.

Howard, Arthur D., Irwin Ramson, et al. Geology in Environmental Planning. New York: McGraw-Hill, 1978.

Isbell, John E. and J. M. Biggs. Seismic Design Decision Analysis: Report No. 12— Inelastic Design of Building Frames to Resist Earthquakes. Springfield, Va.: National Technical Information Service, 1974.

Jaffe, Martin S., Jo Ann C. Butler and Charles Thurow. Reducing Earthquake Risks: A Planner's Guide (September). Chicago, Illinois: American Planning Association, 1981.

Jensen, Rolf, Ed. Fire Protection for the Design Professional. Boston, Cahners Books, 1975. AAC.

Jones, Barclay G. and James H. Mars. Regional Analysis for Development Planning in Disaster Areas. Ithaca, N.Y.: Water Resources and Marine Sciences Center and Department of City and Regional Planning, 1974.

Kantorovich, L. V., V. L. Keilis-Borok and G. M. Molchan. Seismic Risk and Principles of Seismic Zoning. Translated by Chivvis Shahnazarov. Springfield, Va.: National Technical Information Service, 1974.

Keune, Russell. Assessment of Current Building Regulatory Methods as Applied to the Needs of Historic Preservation Projects. Washington, D.C.: National Bureau of Standards, 1978.

Klingner, H. and V. Bertero. Infilled Frames in Earthquake Resistant Constructions. Berkeley, California: Earthquake Engineering Research Center, Report No. EERC W-76-32.

Krimgold, Frederick. Seismic Design Decisions for the Commonwealth of Massachusetts State Building Code. Publication No. R77-27, Seismic Design Decision Analysis Report No. 32. Cambridge, Mass.: Massachusetts Institute of Technology, Department of Civil Engineering, 1977.

Krishna, J. and G. Chandra. "Strengthening of Brick Buildings in Seismic Zones." Proceedings, Fourth World Congress on Earthquake Engineering, Santiago, Chile, 1969. Volume III, pp. B-6-11—B-6-21.

Kuroiwa, J. H. Earthquake Engineering Problems in Peru. Individual Studies by Participants in the International Institute of Seismology and Earthquake Engineering, Tokyo, December 1965.

Kusler, Jon A. and Thomas M. Lee. Regulations for Flood Plains. Chicago: American Society of Planning Officials, 1972.

Kustu, Onder. "A Practical Approach to Damage Mitigation in Existing Structures Exposed to Earthquakes." Proceedings of the 2nd U.S. National Conference on Earthquake Engineering. Berkeley, California: Earthquake Engineering Research Institute, 1979.

Lagorio, Henry J. and Elmer Botsai. "Urban Design and Earthquakes." Proceedings of the Second International Conference on Microzonation for Safer Construction. Volume I. San Francisco: Second International Conference, December 1978.

Latour, H. S. Building Construction and Earthquakes in Guatemala. Individual Studies by Participants in the International Institute of Seismology and Earthquake Engineering, Tokyo, Japan, December 1965.

"The Latest in Design: Student Housing Megastructure, Track Stadium Physical Education Center, and Library Building (Earthquake Proof Library Building at Boston State College)". American School and University. Volume 47, No. 2, p. 44-44L, October 1974.

Los Angeles Earthquake Safety Study Committee. Earthquake Hazard Reduction in Existing Buildings. Division 68, Los Angeles Building Code, Preliminary Draft, 1978.

Lucht, David A. "Basic Considerations: How Safe is Safe?". Specifying Engineer. May 1978, pp. 66-69.

MacCabe, Marilyn P., Ed. Earthquake Hazards Reduction Program Project Summaries— 1979-80. U.S.G.S. Open-File Report No. 81-41. Washington, D.C.: U.S. Geological Survey, 1980.

Mader, George G. "Land Use Planning for Seismic Safety." Summer Seismic Institute for Architectural Faculty: Proceedings. Washington, D.C.: AIA Research Corporation, 1977.

Mader, George G., et al. "Land Use Restrictions Along the San Andreas Fault in Portola Valley, California." Proceedings of the International Conference on Microzonation for Safer Construction. Seattle: The Conference, 1972.

Mader, George G. and Martha L. Blair. "After the Earthquake: A Safer City?" Proceedings of the 2nd U.S. National Conference on Earthquake Engineering. Berkeley, California: Earthquake Engineering Research Institute, 1979.

Mader, George C., et. al. Videorecording: Seismic Design for Architects. Produced by AIA Research Corporation. Berkeley, California: Education Television Office, University of California, 1970.

Magoon, D. T. "Structural Damage by Tsunamis." Proceedings of the ASCE Coastal Engineering Specialty Conference. New York: ASCE, 1966.

Mainstone, Rowland J. Developments in Structural Form. Cambridge, Massachusetts: MIT Press, 1975.

Mainstone, Rowland J. and Edwin H. Gaylord, Eds. Tall Building Criteria and Loading Group Coordinators. New York: ASCE, 1980.

Mattoch, A. H. and W. G. Corley. "Progress Report on Code Clauses for "Limit Design'." ACI Journal. September 1968, pp. 713-715.

May, Gerald W., Ed. International Workshop on Earthen Buildings in Seismic Areas, Albuquerque, New Mexico, May 24-28, 1981. 3 Volumes. Washington, D.C.: National Science Foundation, September 1981.

Mayes, R. L. and Clough, R. W. State-of-the-Art in Seismic Shear Strength of Masonry: An Evaluation and Review. Berkeley, California: University of California, Earthquake Engineering Research Center, Report No. EERC 75-21, 1975.

Mele, M., Ed. Seismic Engineering. 2 Volumes. New York/Berlin: Springer-Verlag, 1976.

Metcalf, Keyes D. Planning Academic and Research Library Buildings. New York: McGraw-Hill, 1965.

Morton, W. Brown III. "The Preservation of Borobudur, Indonesia." Parks. Volume 2, No. 4, January-March, 1978, pp. 1-4.

Mulholland, K. S. "Dealing with the Problme of Earthquake-Risk Buildings: The Wellington City Council Approach." Large Earthquakes in New Zealand. Wellington, New Zealand: The Royal Society of New Zealand, 1981, pp. 83-86.

Newmark, Nathan M. "Earthquake Resistant Building Design." Structural Engineering Handbook. E. H. and C. H. Gaylord, Eds. New York: McGraw-Hill, 1968.

Newmark, Nathan M. and W. J. Hall. Earthquake Spectra and Design. Berkeley, California: Earthquake Engineering Research Institute, 1982.

Nichols, Donald R. Seismic Hazards and Land Use Planning. Geological Circular No. 690. Washington, D.C.: U.S. Geological Survey, 1974.

Nichols, Donald R. and J. M. Buchanan Banks. "Seismic Hazards and Land Use Planning." Geology in the Urban Environment. Russell Utgard, Garry McKenzie, and Duncan Foley, Eds. Minneapolis, Minnesota: Burgess Publishing Co., 1978.

Nyberg, Folke, et al. Strategies for Restoring Older Buildings in Seismic Regions. Seattle: University of Washington, to be published.

O'Donoghue, Daniel. Reduction of Hazardous Structures: Financial and Economic Implications.

Office of Science and Technology Policy. Earthquake Hazards Reduction: Issues for An Implementation Plan. Springfield, Va.: National Technical Information Service, PB-290-467, 1978.

Office of Science and Technology Policy. The National Earthquake Hazards Reduction Program. Springfield, Va.: National Technical Information Service, PB-291-311, 1978.

Oppenheim, Irving J. "Economic Analysis of Earthquake Engineering Investment." Proceedings, 2nd U.S. National Conference on Earthquake Engineering. Stanford University: The Conference, 1979.

Park, R. and T. Paulay. Reinforced Concrete Structures. New York: John Wiley and Sons, 1975.

Paulay, T. Ductility of Reinforced Concrete Shearwalls for Seismic Areas. ACI Publication SP-53, Paper SP 53-7, pp. 127-47. Detroit, Michigan: American Concrete Institute, N.D.

Petak, William J., Arthur A. Atkisson, and P. H. Gleye. Natural Hazards: A Building Loss Mitigation Assessment (Final Report). Redondo Beach, California: J. H. Wiggins Co., 1978.

Recommended Lateral Forces Requirements and Commentary. San Francisco: Structural Engineers Association of California, Seismological Committee, 1975.

Reed, Richard E. Living with Seismic Risk: Strategies for Urban Conservation. Washington, D.C.: American Association for the Advancement of Science, 1977.

Reps, W. F. and E. Simiu, Eds. Design, Siting and Construction of Low-Cost Housing and Community Buildings to Better Withstand Earthquakes and Windstorms. Washington, D.C.: U.S. Agency for International Development, Report No. NBS-BSS-48, 1974.

Rosenblueth, Emilio, Ed. Design of Earthquake Resistant Structures. Halsted Press, 1979.

Sawyer, H. A. "Comments on Model Code Clauses." ACI Journal. September, 1968, pp. 715-719.

270

Selna, Martin I., R. Park and Loring Wyllie. "Strong and Tough Concrete Columns for Seismic Forces." Journal of the Structural Division, ASCE. August 1980, pp. 1717-1734.

Sheaffer, John. Introduction to Flood Proofing. Chicago: University of Chicago, 1967.

Slosson, J. E. The Role of Engineering Geology in Urban Planning. The Governor's Conference on Environmental Geology, Speical Publication No. 1. Denver, Colorado: Colorado Geological Survey, 1969.

Solomon, K. A., D. Okrent, and M. Rubin. Earthquake Ordinances for the City of Los Angeles, California: A Brief Case Study. Los Angeles, California: Chemical, Nuclear and Thermal Engineering Department, University of California, 1977.

Spangle, William E. et. al. Land Use Planning After Earthquakes. Portola Valley, Calif.: William Spangle and Associates, 1980.

Steinbrugge, Karl V. "Earthquake Damage and Structural Performance in the U.S." in Earthquake Engineering, R. L. Wiegel, Ed. Englewood Cliffs, N.J.: Prentice-Hall, 1970.

Steinbrugge, Karl V. "Earthquake Hazard Abatement and Land Use Planning: Directions Toward Solutions." Geologic Hazards and Public Problems. San Francisco: Office of Emergency Preparedness, 1969.

Tag-Eldeen, Mustafa. "Predisaster Physical Planning—Integration of Disaster Risk Analysis into Physical Planning—A Case Study in Tunisia." Disasters. Volume 4, 1980, pp. 211-222.

Trezza, Alphonse F. Library Buildings: Innovation for Changing Needs. Chicago: American Library Association, 1972.

U.S. Army Corps of Engineers. Flood Proofing Regulations. Washington, D.C.: U.S. Government Printing Office, 1972.

U.S. General Services Administration and Pregnoff, Mathew, Beebe, Inc. Earthquake Resistance of Buildings, Volume I: Design Guidelines. Washington, D.C.: U.S. Government Printing Office, 1976.

U.S. General Services Administration and Pregnoff, Mathew, Beebe, Inc. Earthquake Resistance of Buildings, Volume III: Commentary on Design Guidelines. Washington, D.C.: U.S. Government Printing Office, 1976.

U.S. National Bureau of Standards. Building Practices for Disaster Mitigation. Washington, D.C.: National Bureau of Standards, Building Sciences Series No. 46, 1973.

U.S. National Bureau of Standards. Development of Improved Design Criteria to Better Resist the Effects of Extreme Winds for Low-Rise Buildings in Developing Countries. Building Science Series No. 56. Washington, D.C.: National Bureau of Standards, 1974.

U.S. National Bureau of Standards. Building to Resist the Effect of Wind. Building Science Series No. 100. Washington, D.C.: National Bureau of Standards, 1977.

U.S. Water Resources Council. Regulation of Flood Hazard Areas to Reduce Flood Losses. Washington, D.C.: U.S. Water Resources Council, 1972.

Waananen, A. O., J. T. Limerinos, W. J. Kockelman, W. E. Spangle, and M. L. Blair. Flood Prone Areas and Land Use Planning. Washington, D.C.: U.S. Geological Survey, 1977.

Wang, Marcy L. "Stylistic Dogma vs. Seismic Resistance." AIA Journal. November 1981, pp. 59-63.

Whitman, Robert V. Damage Probability Matrices for Prototype Buildings. Seismic Design Decision Analysis Report Number 8, Structures Publication Number 380. Cambridge: MIT Press, 1973.

VULNERABILITY REDUCTION OF NON-STRUCTURAL ELEMENTS

Alsford, Dennis B. An Approach to Museum Security. Ottawa: Canadian Museums Association, 1975.

Association of Records Executives and Administrators, Inc. Protection of Vital Records. Washington, D.C.: Office of Civil Defense, July 1966.

Banks, Paul H. "Environmental Standards for Storage of Books and Manuscripts." Library Journal. Volume 99, No. 3, February 1, 1974, pp. 339-343.

Beeman, Robert. "Records Protection Equipment." Office Management. No. 17, May 1956, pp. 49-62.

Blume, John A. Seismic Study of Industrial Steel Storage Racks. Prepared for the National Science Foundation and the Rack Manufacturers' Institute. San Francisco, California: URS/John A. Blume and Associates, April 1980.

Bopp, Hans Peter. "Orientation and Calibration Method for Non-topographic Applications." Photogrammetric Engineering and Remote Sensing. Volume 44, No. 9, September 1978, pp. 1191-96.

Borchers, Perry E. "Photogrammetric Measurement of Structural Movements." ASCE. Volume 94, No. SU1, Proceedings Paper 5747, January 1968, pp. 67-80.

Borchers, Perry E. Photogrammetric Recording of Cultural Resources. Washington, D.C.: U.S. Department of the Interior, National Park Service, Office of Archeaology and Historic Preservation Division of Technical Preservation Services, 1977.

Chapman, Joseph. "Stepping Up Security." Museum News. Volume 44, No. 3, November 1965, pp. 18-21.

Cole, Richard B. The Application of Security Systems and Hardware. Springfield,, Illinois: Charles C. Thomas Publishers, 1970.

Cosher, Howard. "Elevators 'React and Prevent' in Building's Security System." Security World. Volume 16, No. 3, March 1979, pp. 23-4.

Darling, Pamela W. "Preservation: A National Plan at Last?' Library Journal. Volume 102, No. 4, February 15, 1977, pp. 447-449.

Devich, R. N. and F. M. Weinhaus. "Image Perspective Transformations: Urban Scenes." Optical Engineering. Volume 20, November/December 1981, pp. 912-21.

Fall, Frieda Kay. "New Industrial Packing Materials: Their Possible Uses for Museums." Museum News. Volume 44, No. 4, December 1965.

Foramitti, Hans. Mesures de Securite et d'Urgence pour la Protection des biens culturels. Rome: ICCROM, 1972.

Gadde, Rem P. R. "Disaster Planning." Patamation, January 1980, pp. 112-118.

Hamlin, Arthur T. "First Consideration for the Flood Season." Wilson Library Bulletin. Volume 48, April 1974, pp. 660-663.

272

Holmes, William T. "Non-Structural Components." Outline of talk given at Fix 'Em: EERI Seminar on Identification and Correction of Deficiencies in Earthquake Resistance of Existing Buildings. Berkeley, California: Earthquake Engineering Research Institute, February 25, 1982.

Hyzer, W. G. "Instant Photogrammetry with a Grid." Optical Engineering. Volume 17, November 1978, pp. SR-124.

James, L. D. "Non-Structural Measures for Flood Control." Water Resources Research. Volume 1, 1965, pp. 9-24.

Keck, Caroline K., et al. A Primer on Museum Security. Cooperstown, N.Y.: New York State Historical Association, 1966.

Keck, Caroline K. "Security Depends on People." Curator. Volume 10, No. 1, 1967, pp. 54-59.

Kingsbury, Arthur A. Introduction to Security and Crime Prevention Surveys. Springfield, Illinois: Charles C. Thomas Publishers, 1973.

Library Technology Project. Protecting the Library and Its Resources: A Guide to Physical Protection and Insurance. Chicago: American Library Association, 1963.

McCue, Gerald M., Ann Skaff and J. W. Boyce. Architectural Design of Building Components for Earthquakes. San Francisco, California: MBT Associates, 1978.

McQuarie, Robert J. "Security." Museum News. Volume 49, No. 7, March 1971, pp. 25-7.

Metcalf, Keyes D. "The Design of Bookstacks and the Preservation of Books." Restaurator. Volume 1, No. 2, 1969, pp. 115-25.

Montgomery and Roberts, Consulting Engineers. Design of Restraints for Flexibly Mounted Equipment to Resist Earthquake Forces. Los Angeles, Calif.: Montgomery and Roberts, January 15, 1974.

Reeves, Robert G., Abraham Anson and David Lamden, Eds. Manual of Remote Sensing. Falls Church, Va.: American Society of Photogrammetry, 1975.

Schiff, Anshel J. Cost-Effective Methods to Reduce Seismic Failures of Electric Power Equipment. West Lafayette, Indiana: Purdue Research Foundation, 1980.

Stone, Marraccini and Patterson. Study to Establish Protection Provisions for Furniture, Equipment and Supplies for Veterans Administration Hospitals. Washington, D.C.: Veterans Administration, Office of Construction, January 1976.

"Surveying and Photogrammetry Research Needs." Civil Engineering. Volume 52, February 1982, pp. 62-66.

Tillotson, Robert G. Museum Security. Paris: International Council of Museums and American Museums Association, 1977.

UNESCO. Final Report on the Seminar-Cum-Training Course on the Protection of Monuments in Seismic Areas. Paris: UNESCO, May 1980.

DISASTER PREPAREDNESS PLANNING: GENERAL

Advisory Committee on the Protection of Archives and Record Centers. Protecting Federal Records Centers and Archives from Fire. Washington, D.C.: General Services Administration, April 1977.

Amoroso, Louis J. "Where is Your Company in a Fire Emergency?" Security World. Volume 12, No. 3, March 1975, pp. 20-21, 46-48, 51.

Ayre, Robert. Technological Adjustments to Natural Hazards. Boulder, Colorado: Program on Technology, Environment and Man, University of Colorado, 1975.

Bahme, Charles W. Fire Officer's Guide to Extinguishing Systems. Boston: National Fire Protection Association, 1977.

Bohem, Hilda. Disaster Prevention and Disaster Preparedness. Berkeley, California: Office of the Assistant Vice President, Library Plans and Policies, Systemwide Administration, 1978.

Bostick, William A. "What is the State of Museum Security?" Museum News. Volume 46, No. 5, January 1968, pp. 13-19.

Committee on Conservation of Cultural Resources. The Protection of Cultural Resources Against the Hazards of War. Washington, D.C.: National Resources Planning Board, February 1942.

Coremans, Paul. La Protection Scientifique des Oeuvres d'Art en Temps de Guerre: L'Experience Europeene pendant Les Annees 1939 a 1945. Bruxelles: Laboratoire Central des Musees de Belgique, 1946.

Couch, Virgil L. "Blueprint for Industrial Disaster Readiness." Environmental Control and Safety Management. February 1971, pp. 33-36.

Cresswell, M. M., Compiler. Large Earthquakes in New Zealand: Anticipation, Precaution, Reconstruction. Wellington, New Zealand: The Royal Society of New Zealand, 1981.

"Disaster." Journal of Architectural Education. Volume 33, No. 4, Summer 1980.

Disaster Planning Guide for Business and Industry. Washington, D.C.: Defense Civil Preparedness Agency, May 1974.

"Disaster Prevention/Disaster Recovery Roundup: Guide to Manufacturers and Suppliers of Products and Services for Fire Flood and Water Damage Control." Technology and Conservation, Volume 8, Number 2, Summer 1983, p. 37.

Dynes, Russell R. Organized Behavior in Disaster. Lexington, Mass.: D.C. Heath, 1970.

Dynes, Russell R., Enrico L. Quarantelli and Gary A. Kreps. A Perspective on Disaster Planning. Disaster Research Center Report Series No. 11. Columbus, Ohio: Disaster Research Center, Ohio State University, 1972.

"Ekistics Learning From Disasters." Ekistics. Volume 44, Number 260, July 1977.

"Emergency Preparedness." Special issue of Public Management. Volume 66, No. 3, March 1984.

Emergency Preparedness and Security Measures: Guidelines, Policies and Procedures for Financial Institutions. Prepared for the Bank Administration Institute's Security Commission, 1978.

FitzSimons, Neal. "Emergency Measures and Museums." Museum News. Volume 43, No. 6, February 1965, pp. 23-4.

Foramitti, Hans. Mesures de Securite et d'Urgence pour la Protection des biens culturels. Rome: ICCROM, 1972.

Foster, Harold D. Disaster Planning: The Preservation of Life and Property. New York/Berlin: Springer-Verlag, 1980.

Fournier D'Albe, E. M. "The Prevention of Natural Disasters." Unpublished paper, presented at the London Technology Group's Seminar on Disaster Technology, September 1971.

Fritz, Charles E. "Disaster." Contemporary Social Problems. R. Merton and R. Nisbet, Eds. New York: Harcourt, Brace and World, 1961.

Gervasio, Louis. "Emergency Planning: Getting Down to Basics." Security Industry and Product News. Volume 7, No. 1, January 1978, pp. 24-26.

Graphic Arts Research Center. Rochester Institute of Technology. "Disaster Plans Needed." PhotographiConservation. March 1979.

Guldbeck, Per E. "Security." The Care of Historical Collections: A Conservation Handbook for the Non-Specialist. Nashville, Tennessee: American Association for State and Local History, 1972, pp. 7-11.

Healy, Richard J. Emergency and Disaster Planning. New York: John Wiley and Sons, 1969.

Healy, Richard J. and Timothy J. Walsh. Industrial Security Management: A Cost-Effective Approach. New York: American Management Association, 1971.

Hewitt, Kenneth, Ed. Interpretations of Calamity. Boston, Mass.: Allen and Unwin, Inc., 1983.

Honeywell Fire and Security Planning Guide. Minneaplis, Minnesota: Honeywell, 1977.

Howard, Richard Foster. Museum Security. AAM Publications, New Series No. 18. Washington, D.C.: American Association of Museums, 1958.

Hunter, John E. Emergency Planning for Museums. Presented to National Park Service Curators' Conference, Harper's Ferry, West Virginia, September 1978.

Johnson, Edward M., Ed. Protecting the Library and Its Resources: A Guide to Physical Protection and Insurance. Chicago: American Library Association, 1963.

Jones, Barclay G. "The Eclecticism of Regional Science--Expanding the Choices of Scientific Method: With an Application." Northeast Regional Science Review. Volume 8, 1978, pp. 1-19.

Jones, Barclay G., Donald M. Manson, John E. Mulford and Mark A. Chain. The Estimation of Building Stocks and Their Characteristics in Urban Areas: An Investigation of Emprical Regularities. Ithaca, N.Y.: Program in Urban and Regional Studies, Cornell University, 1976.

Joseph, James. "Shelter Against Holocaust[" Security World. Volume 15, No. 3, March 1978, pp. 10-17.

Lewis, James. A Primer of Precautionary Planning for Natural Disaster. Occasional Paper No. 13. Bradford, England: University of Bradford, Disaster Research Unit, 1977.

Lewis, James. A Study in Pre-Disaster Planning. Occasional Paper No. 10, University of Bradford Disaster Research Unit. Geneva, Switzerland: League of Red Cross Societies, 1975.

Lewis, James. Philip O'Keefe, and Kenneth Westgate. "A Philosophy of Precautionary Planning." Mass Emergencies. Volume 2, No. 2, June 1977, pp. 95-104.

Lewis, Ralph H. Manual for Museums. Washington, D.C.: National Park Service, U.S. Department of the Interior, 1976.

Mannings, J. "Security of Museums and Art Galleries." Museums Journal. Volume 70, June 1970, pp. 7-9.

Marke, J. J., C. Morrow, M. Cohen, J. Vincent, and D. Daviss. "Preservation of Law Library Materials and Disaster Planning." Law Library Journal. Volume 73, No. 4, 1980.

Marx, W. Acts of God, Acts of Man. New York: Coward, McCann and Geogheghan, 1977.

Michael, Douglas O. Disaster Preparedness Manual. Auburn, N.Y.: Cayuga County Community College, April 1981.

Michaels, A. J. "Security and the Museum." Museum News. Volume 43, November 1964, pp. 11-16.

Mitigation in Emergency Management Plans: An Overview. Durham, N.H.: New England Municipal Center, no date.

Model Disaster Preparedness Program. Chicago, Illinois: Building Officials and Code Administrators International, Inc., 1975.

Noblecourt, Andre. Protection of Cultural Property in the Event of Armed Conflict. Museums and Monuments VIII. Paris: UNESCO, 1958.

Office of Civil Defense. In Time of Emergency. Washington, D.C.: Department of Defense, 1968.

Ohta, Hideaki. The Methods of Survival in a Major Earthquake. Tokyo: Tokyo Sports Newspaper Co., 1977.

O'Connell, Mildred. "Disaster Planning: Writing and Implementing Plans for Collections-Holding Institutions." Technology and Conservation, Volume 8, Number 2, Summer 1983, pp. 18-24.

O'Keefe, P. and K. Westgate. "Preventive Planning for Natural Disasters." Long Range Planning. Volume 10, No. 3, 1977, pp. 25-29.

O'Riordan, Timothy. Perspectives in Resource Management. London: Pion, 1971.

Parr, A. R. "A Brief on Disaster Plans." EMO Digest. Volume 9, Number 4, 1969, pp. 13-15.

Plenderleith, Harold James. "Preservation of Museum Objects in War-Time." Nature. Volume 152, 1943, pp. 94-97.

Post, Richard S., Arthur A. Kingsbury and Charles L. Buckley, Jr. Security Administration. Springfield, Illinois: Charles C. Thomas Publishers, 1975.

Protection of Museums and Museum Collections. NFPA 911. Boston: National Fire Protection Association, 1980.

Quarantelli, Enrico L. Studies in Disaster Response and Planning. Springfield, Virginia: National Technical Information Service No. AD-A065523, 1979.

Quarantelli, Enrico L. and Kathleen J. Tierney. Disaster Preparation Planning. Columbus, Ohio: Ohio State University, Disaster Research Center, 1979.

Report of the American Commission for the Protection and Salvage of Artistic and Historic Monuments in War Areas. Washington, D.C.: U.S. Government Printing Office, 1946.

Rorimer, James J. Survival: The Salvage and Protection of Art in War. New York: Abelard Press, Inc., 1950.

Rubin, Claire B. "Disaster Mitigation: Challenge to Managers." Public Administration Times. Volume 2, No. 1, 1979.

"The Schroder Report." ICOM News. Volume 28, No. 4, 1975, pp. 141-144.

Scott, Stanley. Learning from San Fernando: Summary Report on the UCLA Earthquake Conference. Joint Committee on Seismic Safety, California State Legislature. Berkeley, California: Institute of Governmental Studies, University of California, 1971.

Stratta, J. L., et al. Learning from Earthquakes: 1977 Planning and Field Guides. Oakland, California: Earthquake Engineering Research Institute, 1977.

Strobl, Walter M. Security. New York: Industrial Press, 1972.

Surrency, Erwin C. "Guarding Against Disaster," Law Library Journal. Volume 66, No. 4, November 1973, pp. 4109-4128.

Sutherland, S. "'Exercise London': A Community Disaster Plan." Emergency Planning Digest. Number 3, 1975, pp. 11-12.

Symposium on Natural Hazards in Australia. Canberra: Australian Academy of Science, 1976.

Tierney, Kathleen J. and Barbara Buisden. Crisis Intervention Programs for Disaster Victims: A Source Book and Manual for Smaller Communities. Rockville, Maryland: National Institute of Mental Health, 1979.

University of Toronto. Disaster Contingency Planning: Assignment of Responsibility for Salvage and Other Operations. Unpublished chart, 1976.

University of Toronto. Disaster Contingency Planning: Goods and Services for Salvage Operations. Unpublished chart, 1976.

Trelles, Oscar M. "Protection of Libraries." Law Library Journal. Volume 66, No. 3, August 1973, pp. 241-258.

Underwriters' Laboratories. Standards on Safety. Brochure series, various titles and dates.

United Nations. Office of the Disaster Relief Coordinator. Disaster Prevention and Mitigation: A Compendium of Current Knowledge. 5+ volumes. Geneva, Switzerland: UNDRO, 1977.

United Nations Disaster Relief Office. Guidelines for Disaster Prevention. 3 volumes. Geneva: UNDRO, 1976.

Universal Teleprograms Company and Universal Training Systems Company. "In Preparation for a Terrorist Attack." Security Industry and Product News. Volume 7, No. 8, August 1978, pp. 28, 30.

Upton, M. S. and C. Pearson. Disaster Planning and Emergency Treatments in Museums, Art Galleries, Libraries, Archives and Allied Institutions. Canberra, Australia: Institute for the Conservation of Cultural Materials, Canberra College of Advanced Education, 1978.

U.S. Federal Emergency Management Agency. "Museum Collections Involve Unique Emergency Problems." Disaster Information. (FEMA Newsletter), March 1980.

Walsh, Timothy J. and Richard J. Healy. Protection of Assets Manual. Santa Monica, California: The Merritt Company, 1974.

Walsh, Timothy. Archives and Manuscripts: Security. Chicago: Society of American Archivists, 1977.

Weldon, Stephen. "Winterthur: Security in a Decorative Arts Museum." Museum News. Volume 50, No. 5, January 1972, pp. 36-7.

Wright, Gordon. "When Disaster Strikes: Protecting Our Libraries and Their Valued Resources." Emergency Planning Digest. Volume 7, No. 2, April-June, 1980, pp. 5-10.

DISASTER PREPAREDNESS PLANNING: EARTHQUAKES

Alfors, John T. et al. Urban Geology Master Plan for California: Phase I—A Method for Setting Priorities. Sacramento, California: Division of Mines and Geology, Open-File Report No. 72-2, 1971.

Ambraseys, Nicholas N. "Earthquake Hazards and Emergency Planning." Build International. 1972.

Anderson, Cay W. "Regional Community Planning for Mitigation of Earthquake Effects." Proceedings of the 2nd Conference on Designing to Survive Severe Hazards. Chicago, Illinois, 1977.

Berlin, G. Lennis. Earthquakes and the Urban Environment. 3 volumes. Boca Raton, Fla.: CRC Press, 1980.

Bertero, V. "Earthquakes: Prevention and Reconstruction." Proceedings. Rotary International Study Convention, Terni, Italy, May 9, 1981.

Blundell, D. J. "Living With Earthquakes." Disasters. Volume 1, No. 1, 1977.

"Conference Reports: The Guatemala Earthquake: Lessons and Priorities for Earthquake Planning and Relief." Papers from a Symposium held at the Royal Society, London, June 14, 1976, by the London Technical Group. Disasters. Volume 1, No. 2, 1976.

Daddy, A. F. "Precautions by Government in Earthquake Areas." Proceedings of the CENTO Conference Ankara, Turkey: U.S. Economic Coordinator for CENTO Affairs, 1968.

Duke, Martin and Donald F. Moran. Learning From Earthquakes: Project Report 1973-79. Berkeley, California: Earthquake Engineering Research Institute, 1978.

Earthquake Engineering Research Institute. Learning from Earthquakes: 1977 Planning and Field Gudies. Oakland, California: Earthquake Engineering Research Institute, 1977.

Fournier D'Albe, E.M. "Earthquakes—Avoidable Disasters." Impact Sci. Soc. Volume 16, No. 3, pp. 189-202.

Kockelman, William J. Examples of the Use of Earth-Science Information by Decisionmakers in the San Francisco Bay Region, California. Open-File Report No. 80-124. Menlo Park, California: U.S. Department of the Interior, U.S. Geological Survey, Office of Land Information and Analysis, 1980.

May, Gerald W., Ed. International Workshop on Earthen Buildings in Seismic Areas, Albuquerque, New Mexico, May 24-28, 1981. 3 Volumes. Washington, D.C.: National Science Foundation, September 1981.

Olson, Robert A. "An Evaluation of the Seismic Safety Element Requirement in California." Communicating Earthquake Hazards Reduction Information. Walter W. Hays, Ed. Open File Report 78-933. Washington, D.C.: U.S. Geological Survey, 1978, pp. 68-93.

Pavicevic, Bozidar. "Review of Some Activities and Results Concerning Effects and Required Technical, Design and Town Planning Aspects Undertaken for the Purpose of Elimination of the Direct Damages Caused by the Disastrous Montenegro Earthquakes." Proceedings of the International Research Conference on Earthquake Engineering, Skopje, Yugoslavia, June 30–July 3, 1980. Skopje, Yugoslavia: IZIIS, 1982, pp. 489–502.

Petrovski, Jakim and Jack G. Bouwkamp, Eds. Proceedings of the International Research Conference on Earthquake Engineering, Skopje, Yugoslavia, June 30–July 3, 1980. Skopje, Yugoslavia: IZIIS, 1982.

Thiel, Charles C., Jr. and Ugo Morelli. "Enhancing Seismic Safety in the Central United States" prepared for Workshop on Preparing for and Responding to a Damaging Earthquake in the Eastern United States. Knoxville, Tennessee: The Workshop, September 16–18, 1981.

UNESCO. Intergovernmental Conference on the Assessment and Mitigation of Earthquake Risks. New York: UniPub, 1978.

U.S. Federal Emergency Management Agency. An Assessment of the Consequences and Preparations for a Catastrophic California Earthquake: Findings and Actions Taken. Washington, D.C.: U.S. Government Printing Office, 1980.

U.S. National Academy of Sciences. Toward Reduction of Losses from Earthquakes: Conclusions from the Great Alaska Earthquake of 1964. Washington, D.C.: National Academy of Sciences, 1969.

Wiggins, John H. Development of An Exposure Model for the U.S. Building Wealth and Annual Economic Loss from Consequences of the Various Seismic Risk Maps. Redondo Beach, California: J. H. Wiggins and Co., n.d. given.

DISASTER PREPAREDNESS PLANNING: FLOODS

Baur, E. Jackson and Jack M. Weller. Flood Plain Management: Administrative Problems and Public Responses. Manhattan, Kansas: Water Resources Research Institute, Kansas State University, 1979.

Boisvert, Richard N. Impact of Floods and Flood Plain Management Policy on Economic Development and Recovery. A 'Project Agnes' Report prepared for the U.S. Department of Commerce. Economic Development Administration. Ithaca, N.Y.: Cornell University, Department of Agricultural Economics, June 1975.

Dzurik, Andrew A. "Flood Plain Management Trends." Water Spectrum. Volume 12, No. 3, Summer 1980, pp. 36-42.

Federal Register. Flood Plain Management Guidelines. Washington, D.C.: U.S. Water Resources Council, 1978.

James, L. D. "Economic Analysis of Alternative Flood Control Measures." Water Resources Research. Volume 3, 1967, pp. 333-343.

James, L. D. "Role of Economics in Planning Flood Plain Land Use." US Journal of the Hydraulics Division, Proceedings of the American Society of Civil Engineers. Volume 98 (HY 6, No. 8935), 1972, pp. 981-992.

Kusler, Jon. Regulation of Flood Hazard Areas to Reduce Flood Losses. Volume 3. Update of Volumes 1 and 2 Published by the U.S. Water Resources Council in 1968 and 1971. Boulder, Colorado: Natural Hazards Research and Applications Information Center, University of Colorado, 1982.

Lee, Larry T., John D. Chrostowski, and Ronald T. Eguchi. Natural Hazards: Riverine Flooding, Storm Surge, Tsunami. Redondo Beach, California: J. H. Wiggins Company, June 1976.

Montuori, Theordore. "Lessons Learned from Agnes." The Journal of Micrographics. Volume 6, No. 3, January-February 1973, pp. 133-136.

New England River Basins Commission. The River's Reach: A Unified Program for Flood Plain Management in the Connecticut River Basin. Springfield, Va.: National Technical Information Service, 1976.

Office of State Planning and Economic Development. Disaster Recovery Planning Report. Harrisburg: State of Pennsylvania, 1975.

Owen, H. James. Guide for Flood and Flash Flood Preparedness Planning. Silver Spring, Md.: National Weather Service, Disaster Preparedness Staff, 1977.

Owen, H. James. Information for Local Officials on Flood Warnings Systems. Silver Spring, Md.: National Weather Service, 1979.

Parker, Dennis J. and Donald M. Harding. "Planning for Urban Floods." Disasters. Volume 2, No. 1, 1978.

Parr, Richard Arnold. "Flood Preparation—1969 Observations Concerning the Southern Manitoba Spring Flood Preparations." EMO National Digest. Volume 9, 1969.

Penning-Rowsell, E. C. and J. B. Chatterton. The Benefits of Flood Alleviation: Manual of Assessment Techniques. Farnborough, England: Saxon House, 1977.

U.S. Department of Commerce. National Oceanic and Atmospheric Administration. Equipment for Flood and Flash Flood Warning Systems. Silver Spring, Md.: National Weather Service, 1981.

White, Gilbert F. Choice of Adjustment to Floods. Department of Geography Research Paper No. 93. Chicago: University of Chicago, 1964.

Williams, Stan. "Mitigating Flood Losses." Emergency Management. Volume 1, No. 3, Spring 1981, pp. 21-2.

Wright, Stewart K. Planning Guide: Self-help Forecast and Warning System, Swatara Creek Watershed, Pennsylvania. Mechanicsburg, Pa.: Susquehanna River Basin Commission, Publication No. 42, 1976.

Wright, Stewart K. and SRBC Staff. Neighborhood Flash Flood Warning System Manual. Mechanicsburg, Pa.: Susquehanna River Basin Commission, Publication No. 45, 1976.

Baker, Earl J., Ed. Hurricanes and Coastal Storms. Florida Sea Grant College Report No. 33. Gainesville, Fla.: Florida State University, 1980.

Brinkmann, Waltraud A. R., et al. Hurricane Hazard in the U.S.: A Research Assessment. Report No. NSF-RA-E-75-007. Boulder, Colorado: University of Colorado, Institute of Behavioral Sciences, Program on Technology, Environment and Man, 1975.

Building Research Station. Tropical Building Legislation: Model Regulations for Small Buildings. Garston, Watford, Hertfordshire: Building Research Station, 1963.

Earthquake and Windstorm. London: Commercial Union Assurance Company, Ltd., 1975.

Economic and Social Commission for Asia and the Pacific, World Meterological Organization, and League of Red Cross Societies (With the help of the Typhoon Committee Secretariat). Guidelines for Disaster Prevention and Preparedness in Tropical Cyclone Areas. Geneva, Switzerland: World Meteorological Organization, 1977.

Frank, N. L. and S. A. Husain. "The Deadliest Cyclone in History." Bulletin of the American Meteorological Society. Volume 52, 1971, pp. 438–44.

Fujita, T. Theodore. "Tornadoes Around the World." Weatherwise. Volume 26, No. 2, April 1973, pp. 56–83.

Kessler E. "Tornadoes." Bulletin of the American Meteorological Association. Volume 51, 1970, pp. 926–936.

Mathieson, David F. "Hurricane Preparedness: Establishing Workable Policies for Dealing with Storm Threats." Technology and Conservation, Volume 8, Number 2, Summer 1983, pp. 28–29.

Miller, Christopher and Geraldine Bachman. "Planning for Hurricanes and Other Coastal Disasters." Urban Land, January 1984, pp. 18–23.

Simpson, Robert H. and M. B. Lawrence. Atlantic Hurricane Frequencies Along the U.S. Coastline. NOAA Technical Memorandum NWS SR-58. Washington, D.C.: U.S. Department of Commerce, 1971.

Simpson, Robert H. and Herbert Riehl. The Hurricane and Its Impact. Baton Rouge, Louisiana: Louisiana State University Press, 1981.

Sohl, Stanley D. "Tornado in My Museum." Papers, 64th Annual Meeting of the American Association of Museums, San Francisco, 1969, pp. 56–9.

Sugg, Arnold L. "Economic Aspects of Hurricanes." Monthly Weather Review. Volume 95, March 1967, pp. 143–146.

Tornado Protection: Selecting and Designing Safe Areas in Buildings. Washington, D.C.: Civil Defense Preparedness Agency, 1976.

U.S. National Bureau of Standards. Development of Improved Design Criteria to Better Resist the Effects of Extreme Winds for Low-Rise Buildings in Developing Countries. Building Science Series No. 56. Washington, D.C.: National Bureau of Standards, 1974.

282

Commonwealth of Virginia. Office of Emergency and Energy Services. Disaster Preparedness Handbook: Hurricane Hazard Mitigation for Coastal Virginia. Richmond, Va.: Commonwealth of Virginia, 1980.

SECTION FIVE

Emergency and Rescue Measures for Structures and Artifacts

Confronting Emergencies

Barclay G. Jones

In spite of the very best care and precautions, disasters can and will occur and will cause damage to the cultural heritage. No region is entirely safe over a very long period of years from absolutely all kinds of natural disasters. The safest site may suffer some kind of disaster in the long run. That no disastrous event has taken place for decades or even centuries may simply indicate a very long periodicity. We are told of "a wise man, which built his house upon a rock . . . and a foolish man, which built his house upon the sand." [Matthew, 8:24-27] This stricture must be understood as a means of avoiding danger but not as a guarantee of absolute safety.

We can reduce vulnerability by recognizing hazards and the threats they pose and selecting appropriate locations and sites. But site selection manages and controls vulnerability rather than eliminates it. We can mitigate losses by taking suitable preventive measures and developing appropriate plans. We can in this manner lower the probability of loss but not to zero. We can reduce the magnitude of the loss from an event of a particular type and severity, but we can not assure that there will be none. Measures to provide ultimate levels of protection may be self-defeating. After all, the purpose of protecting the heritage is so that we and future generations can learn about the past and thereby gain insights about ourselves from observing, experiencing and studying objects that were the products of cultures and civilizations that have been replaced by the present. Objects immersed in water, buried in mud or soil have survived for thousands of years. However, in most cases of this kind, they are hidden from view, removed from daily experience and consequently have lost their ability to educate, enlighten, and enrich the lives of thousands who could have observed them.

The possibility of disaster must be confronted straightforwardly. This will vary with locations and objects. Structures in broad, fertile valleys may be more susceptible to more frequent occurrences of different kinds of events than those in remote, rocky strongholds. Under most circumstances marble is more durable than textiles and bronze less fragile than glass. Precautions will vary from situation to situation.

287

Once the possibility of disaster is acknowledged it follows that steps must be taken to insure preparedness. Mitigation customarily is used to refer to actions taken prior to or in anticipation of an event, but it is possible to mitigate the effects of a disastrous event through actions that are taken during and immediately after the emergency. Readiness to undertake appropriate rescue measures and to implement plans for rapid recovery can reduce the potential loss from a given type and severity of natural disaster. Such steps will be more efficacious the more carefully the emergency has been anticipated and more thoroughly plans have been worked out. The question that must be addressed is what to do when disaster strikes? [Bohem, 1978; Waters, 1981; Buchanan, 1981; Upton and Pearson, 1978]

RESPONDING RAPIDLY

Perhaps the most important single attribute of emergency plans is to be prepared for rapid response when a disaster occurs. Quick action has two primary objectives. The first of these is to protect objects and structures from further damage. Further damage can be inflicted both directly and indirectly. Examples of protection from further direct damage would be to remove objects that have not yet been inundated out of the path of rising flood waters or to get objects out of swift currents that might batter or sweep them away. [Whipkey, 1973] In the case of earthquakes, objects which did not fall or shatter in the first tremor might be removed to safer locations or positioned so that they would not be damaged by aftershocks. Examples of providing protection from indirect damage would be removing to places of shelter objects that were exposed to rain and the elements when wind storms blew away roofs and the protective covering of wall openings. In the case of earthquakes, while objects and building elements may be secure in themselves, they could be damaged by falling objects from other structures in aftershocks or the battering effects of adjacent buildings. Secondary disasters such as fires, explosions and flooding from broken pipes may follow the primary one. Other kinds of indirect damage can be caused by decay, mildew and mold.

The second purpose of rapid response is to improve prospects for salvage of objects and structures which may have been damaged. Immediate attention to water soaked paper may immensely improve the possibilities for restoring it. Immediately collecting the pieces of a shattered object may make its reconstruction more feasible. It is essential to have contingency plans for disasters so that response is both rapid and efficacious. Roles should be assigned to various staff members of organizations and responsibilities clearly spelled out. Lines of authority should be sharply drawn, and the capacity to manage and control immediate response in the most effective way determined. After the Meyer Library Flood at Stanford approximately 50,000 soaked volumes were stabilized within 43 hours of the first alarm. Rapid response kept the damage no greater than it was. [Buchanan and Leighton, 1981]

SEARCHING

A number of salient response measures should be thought out, planned and prepared for. The first task is that of searching the impacted region for cultural objects and structures that may have suffered damage. In many instances there may be little in the way of clear information as to what cultural resources existed in a region struck by a disaster and precisely where they were located. Inventories of various kinds, guidebooks and research materials may be immensely helpful in this regard. However they may be partial, fragmentary and incomplete even when they exist and are readily available at all. Even under the best of circumstances it will be necessary to go beyond existing lists and inventories.

Two approaches may be particularly useful in the search process. The first of these consists of surveying key informants both outside and within the region. Types of outside experts who should be consulted include: those who are intimately familiar with the region; those who specialize in the kinds of objects and structures that existed within the region; and specialists in the periods that represent the region's major phases of accumulation of significant objects and structures. The types of informants within the region who should be consulted include not only experts in various structures and objects there but also individuals who are simply thoroughly familiar with the region or parts of it.

The second approach involves field survey by knowledgeable or expert individuals. When possible aerial survey can be immensely helpful in providing direction that may make ground survey more efficient and effective. As much of the region should be traversed on the ground as possible. Objects and structures may be found that were not known to exist or were hidden and are now exposed. Structures and objects in private ownership in particular may not be listed on inventories or be part of the public record. There are numerous instances in which lost or forgotten cultural elements were revealed by disasters. After the Center for International Affairs and the office of its former associate director, Dr. Henry A. Kissinger, housed in the Harvard Semitic Museum were bombed by protestors at midnight October 14, 1970, damage search procedures led to the discovery of dozens of forgotten crates under the eaves in the fourth-floor attic. They contained 28,000 negatives, lantern slides and prints, including 800 by the Bonfils family, which constitutes the largest collection in the world of nineteenth century views of the Middle East, an enormously valuable historic record. [Gavin, 1982; Tassel, 1982] The World War II bombing of the Italian-held port city of Zadar on the Dalmatian coast revealed extensive remains of the buildings comprising the ancient Roman Forum which had been completely hidden by overbuilding with later structures through the ages and opened the center of the city to archaeological research and restoration.

DETERMINING STATUS

The purpose of the search process is not merely to inventory and locate significant structures and artifacts but also to determine their status. Some will be undamaged and intact. Others may be damaged or not but threatened with damage or destruction. Others may be slightly damaged and in need of minor repair or conservation while some may need immediate attention and extensive work. Some may be extensively damaged and in need of complete reconstruction. Others may be totally destroyed and their loss in need of recording. The status of the structure or object will not necessarily be related to its importance or significance, and both aspects need to be noted. Together the inventory and the status report produced by the survey indicate the dimensions of the loss incurred, the rescue, conservation, rehabilitation and reconstruction effort that needs to be undertaken. This is a fundamental step in developing a recovery plan and in assembling the resources and types of expertise and activities needed to carry out the plan.

RECORDING DAMAGE

A third very important emergency period activity is that of recording the present situation as completely and carefully as possible. This can be carried out as part of the search process or as supplementary to it. Field notes and other written statements must be made and should be supplemented as extensively as possible by photographs. Photographs of shattered objects as they lie strewn about may prove invaluable clues to reassembling and reconstructing not only artifacts but structures. [Martin, 1977] Clearing away debris to permit the resumption of essential community activities as rapidly as possible will cause much important evidence to be lost. Careful documentation and recording can substantially reduce the ultimate effect of the disaster. Of course, such records also provide invaluable evidence as to the way in which and the reasons things failed and suffered damage in disasters and give important clues as to appropriate preventive measures that can be taken elsewhere in the future. [Schiff, 1980] It will be possible to make the complete kinds of records that are desirable and most useful only if necessary preparations have been made and appropriate equipment, supplies and personnel have been made available.

290

STABILIZING

The fourth most urgent activity is stabilizing the situation to the greatest extent possible. The primary purpose is to protect structures and objects from further damage either by relief operations or continued effects of the disaster: continuing winds, further inundation, scouring and washing way, and the effects of aftershocks on already weakened structures. Buildings must be shored and braced. Openings must be covered. Exposed objects must be protected from the elements. Objects must be protected from falling and floating debris. Further disturbance and damage by natural or human actions must be prevented. Items intended for salvage must be clearly identified and protected from demolition and clean-up operations.

All of the potential damage and loss from the disaster will not have occurred immediately after the event. In subsequent days and weeks after the disaster damage can be inflicted which can transform a recoverable situation into a total loss. In other words, a second period of enormous danger follows in the wake of a catastrophic event. Stabilization procedures can be extremely important in mitigating the effects and reducing the losses of this second order catastrophe. [Spawn, 1973] Wet objects must be dried. Textiles and paper must be removed from water and the damp and dried out. Furniture and wooden objects must be dried slowly and carefully. [Martin, 1977] Bacteriological and fungus deterioration must be arrested. Flaking of paints, spalling of masonry, and rotting of wood must be deterred. [Upton and Pearson, 1978]

SECURING

In addition to stabilization, attention must be given to security. It is entirely likely that the integrity of structures housing valuable objects will have been breached. Walls may have been broken, roofs removed, windows and doors smashed. Such damage may have been a consequence of the disaster itself or may have occurred in the course of rescue and relief operations. The protection afforded by the structure may be substantially diminished. In addition elaborately devised security systems may no longer be operative or functioning as they are intended to under normal circumstances.

Objects, fragments of objects, portions of structures may be picked up and carried away. In some instances this may be done with regard only for the usefulness of the object in the emergency situation. Timbers taken for shoring, masonry for infill, stones to build barriers or fill crevices, and doors or shutters to cover openings are items commonly appropriated in this way. In other instances objects may be stolen for their intrinsic value. Normally after a natural disaster the population in a stricken region experiences high levels of altruism, and individuals actively search the surroundings for other people they can help and to whom they can provide one kind of assistance or another. Usually theft and looting are not characteristic behavior of stricken populations. However, such actions are not unknown and should be anticipated. Far more threatening are outsiders who soon arrive in the stricken area. Some of these have come to see the devastation and others to try to be of assistance. Theft and looting on the part of outsiders is not uncommon. Since the arrival of such individuals is to be anticipated, security measures need to be undertaken as rapidly as possible.

Conflicts may arise with various officials in attempting to institute security measures. Inspectors will be assigned to determine the integrity of structures and their safety for continued occupancy and use. They will want to inspect buildings carefully from top to bottom. Others will be assigned rescue missions and will be searching for disaster victims. Still others will be engaged in making damage estimates and will want to make detailed inspections. Organizations which have security officers will want to have them immediately on hand carrying out contingency plans to restore the security of the collection. Less elaborate organizations will need to have staff members assigned the task of concerning themselves with security. In planning for emergency periods it is useful to identify building sections, rooms, storage areas that can be made secure and safe even when much of the building has become vulnerable. Particularly valuable objects should then be removed to such areas as rapidly as possible. It must also be anticipated that the damage may be so extensive that no area can be made sufficiently secure. In such situations plans should be made in advance to identify other sites and locations to which valuable objects can be removed. Contingency arrangements should have been made before the disaster, and plans for the logistics of removal prepared.

MOBILIZING RESOURCES

Effective emergency measures will require mobilizing a wide variety of resources rapidly. The ability to do this efficiently will depend upon how carefully the activity has been planned. The resources that will be needed include supplies, material, equipment, personnel and funds of money. Obviously these will vary tremendously by the nature of the object or structure and the type of disaster. Supplies to dry things out, prevent them from becoming wet, put shattered pieces back together and prevent them from being broken should be thought out, listed and acquired in anticipation of an emergency.

Since natural disasters usually cover fairly sizable regions and many similar objects from a number of collections are likely to be involved, one of the first tasks is often that of identifying specialized treatment centers where damaged objects can be removed to receive expert conservatorial care. Even large institutions which are relatively self-sufficient may find it desirable to make access to off-premise facilities of various kinds. For example, large facilities for the freeze drying of library or archival material in substantial quantity may be unreasonable to attempt to arrange on the premises. [Waters, 1975; Buchanan and Leighton, 1981] Removal requires packing, crating and transporting. Supplies and equipment for these purposes will be needed just at the time that many inventories of them within the region will have been destroyed. Anticipatory planning of appropriate supplies and materials for packing and crating may prove extremely useful. Both unskilled and skilled personnel will be needed. People will be needed to clear debris, clean off residue, dry, move objects from one place to another, pack, crate, transport, make carpentry and masonry repairs, fix plumbing, ventilating and electrical systems. The more people that can be mobilized, the more rapidly the emergency response activities can be carried out.

While it involves a limited disaster to only a part of a single facility rather than a regional disaster affecting many institutions, the fire on July 12, 1973 at the National Personnel Records Center in Overland, Missouri, demonstrates the magnitude of the logistical operations that can arise. Perhaps the most extensive archival fire in history, it was confined to the sixth and top floor of the Center, an area of more than two hundred thousand square feet, but substantial quantities of water flooded each of the other floors. Two million personnel jackets, four hundred thousand cubic feet of records, were destroyed by fire, and ninety thousand cubic feet of records had to be dried. Thirty thousand plastic milk carton baskets were used to transport and dry the records by open-shelf drying, and vacuum-drying processes in facilities as far away as Ohio. Arrangements to place refrigerated freight cars on a nearby siding were cancelled when the vacuum process proved to be as satisfactory as freeze-drying. Removing all water soaked material took more than two weeks. The resources of the federal government and the facilities of a major metropolitan area greatly simplified the task of coping with the emergency. [Stender and Walker, 1974]

ESTABLISHING PRIORITIES

The assigning of priorities to objects and scheduling activities is a vital emergency activity. In the confusion and the trauma that follow a disastrous event, rescue, stabilization and salvage activities are frequently carried out in a somewhat irrational manner. Consideration should be given immediately to the life safety of staff and visitors. The rescue and salvage of objects and structures must then follow. Objects can be classified as having various degrees of value. They will also have suffered varying degrees of damage or threat. Limited resources of time, energy and materials must be allocated in ways that will do the most good. It will not be possible to give attention to all objects, and difficult choices will have to be made. Immediate attention can be given to only a very few objects, and others may have to wait for long periods of time.

ENLISTING EXPERT AID

It is necessary to obtain expert assistance as rapidly as possible and emergency plans should anticipate this requirement. Obviously, what is necessary will vary with type of object and the nature of the disaster. In developing an emergency plan an organization should identify the kind of technical assistance it is likely to need and the kinds of disasters to which it is subject. A directory of individuals who can offer different kinds of assistance to certain types of objects or certain types of damage should be developed and kept up to date. Conservation centers that can provide different kinds of assistance should also be listed. Specialized facilities and personnel not directly related to conservation specifically but more general in nature should also be listed. These might include large facilities for drying, fumigating, sterilizing, freezing, transporting, providing emergency shelters, making temporary repairs to structures and other similar activities. Again, what is appropriate to be included will vary with the type of object involved and of disaster anticipated. [Breuer, 1981]

Fortunately it is characteristic of human behavior to respond actively to emergency situations. Individuals become energized and prove to be capable of extraordinary efforts. The effectiveness and efficiency of these efforts can be substantially enhanced by careful planning for possible emergencies of various kinds. The potential usefulness of such plans is enormous. The actions that are carried out during a disaster and the first few hours and days afterwards can have a great deal to do with determining its ultimate effect. Preventive planning can reduce the losses that are likely to occur when a disaster strikes. However, extensive further losses can be incurred in the period immediately following the event. Carefully prepared emergency plans can mitigate these losses.

REFERENCES

Bohem, Hilda. Disaster Prevention and Disaster Preparedness. Berkeley, California: Office of the Assistant Vice President-Library Plans and Policies, University of California, April 1978.

Breuer, J. Michael. "Regional Cooperation for Disaster Preparedness." Disasters: Prevention and Coping. James N. Myers and Denise D. Bedford, Eds. Stanford, California: Stanford University Libraries, 1981.

Buchanan, Sally. "Disaster Planning." Disasters: Prevention and Coping. James N. Myers and Denise D. Bedford, Eds. Stanford, California: Stanford University Libraries, 1981.

Buchanan, Sally, and Philip D. Leighton. "The Stanford Meyer Library Flood Report." Disasters: Prevention and Coping. James N. Myers and Denise D. Bedford, Eds. Stanford, California: Stanford University Libraries, 1981.

Gavin, Carney E. S. The Image of the East. Chicago: University of Chicago Press, 1982.

Martin, Mervin. Emergency Procedures for Furniture After a Flood. 46(A) Winterthur, Delaware: H. F. du Pont Winterthur Museum, 1977.

Schiff, Anshel J. Pictures of Earthquake Damage to Power Systems and Cost-Effective Methods to Reduce Seismic Failures of Electric Power Equipment. West Lafayette, Indiana: Center for Earthquake Engineering and Ground Motion Studies, Institute for Interdisciplinary Engineering Studies and School of Mechanical Engineering, Purdue University, February 1980.

Spawn, Willman. "After the Water Comes." PLA Bulletin of the Pennsylvania Library Association, Volume 28, Number 6, November 1973, pp. 243-251.

Stender, Walter W. and Evans Walker. "The National Personnel Records Center Fire: A Study in Disaster." The American Archivist, October 1974, pp. 521-549.

Tassel, Janet. "The Semitic Museum Rises Again." Harvard Magazine, March-April 1982, pp. 40-46.

Upton, M. S. and C. Pearson. Disaster Planning and Emergency Treatments in Museums, Art Galleries, Libraries, Archives and Allied Institutions. Canberra: The Institute for the Conservation of Cultural Material, Inc., 1978.

Waters, Peter. Procedures for Salvage of Water-Damaged Library Materials. Washington, D.C.: Library of Congress, 1975.

Waters, Peter C. "Disasters Revisited." Disasters: Prevention and Coping. James N. Myers and Denise D. Bedford, Eds. Stanford, California: Stanford University Libraries, 1981, pp. 6-12.

Whipkey, Harry E. After Agnes: A Report on Flood Recovery Assistance by the Pennsylvania Historical and Museum Commission. Harrisburg, Pennsylvania: Pennsylvania Historical and Museum Commission, 1973.

Emergency Protection to Damaged Structures

Donald del Cid

When an observer first enters upon one of these earthquake shaken towns, he finds himself in the midst of utter confusion. The eye is bewildered by a city become a heap. He wanders over masses of dislocated stone and mortar. Houses seem to have precipitated to the ground in every direction of the azimuth. There seems no governing law, nor any indication of a prevailing direction of overturning force. [Mallet, 1862]

INTRODUCTION

In any region of the world stricken by an earthquake, the period of time between the occurrence of a major earthquake and restoration of the damaged structures is the most vital, dangerous and important phase affecting the survival of the region's architectural heritage.

It is during this period that the future of a building, a group of buildings, cities, and even territories is decided. The character of squares, neighborhoods, towns, cities and countrysides can be preserved or lost forever in this short stretch of time, depending upon the decisions and consideration made. Many valuable and irreplaceable historic buildings and cities throughout the world have been affected, altered, destroyed or lost forever in this brief emergency response period.

In order to try to save as many damaged historical buildings as possible from the hands of the demolition team and the tremors of the aftermath, buildings have to be protected in every imaginable way in a very short length of time. They may simply be marked, shored, labeled, fenced, or covered so that when the demolition team arrives, they will see that "somebody" has already done "something" and will spare the damaged.

In this report, I will concentrate on protection procedures for damaged structures during the emergency period immediately following the earthquake and ending with the restoration phase.

VERNACULAR ARCHITECTURE AND PROPORTIONS IN TRADITIONAL STRUCTURAL SYSTEMS

Any person in work related to the construction world who eventually might be involved in the safeguarding of historical buildings and their contents under threat of natural disasters, <u>should be very knowledgeable</u> about vernacular architecture and structural systems. Without a clear understanding of local traditional construction, those in charge of emergency measures are bound to make serious mistakes resulting in losses either of human life or historical elements.

The <u>New Comprehensive International Dictionary of the English Language,</u> Funk and Wagnalls, 1978 defines:

Vernacular: "Originating in or belonging to one's native land; indigenous. Vernacular arts: characteristic of a specific locality or country, local. Rare, peculiar to a particular region."

Tradition: "The transmission of knowledge, opinions, customs, practices, etc., from generation to generation originally by word of mouth and by example. A custom so long continued that it has almost the force of law."

Structure: "That which is constructed; a combination of related parts."

System: "Orderly combination or arrangement of parts, elements, etc., into a whole; especially such combination according to some rational principle; any methodological arrangements of parts."

From the previous definitions, we can understand that a traditional structural system will be that 'orderly combination of related parts according to rational principles transmitted by example from generation to generation, in a way that almost had the force of a law'.

Proportions

Since the industrial era started, man has known the resistance limit of the building materials he has been using. Modern technology made man aware of when steel would snap, mortar would disintegrate or brick break. He therefore learned to design structures based on knowledge of structural limitations. Adding a safety margin to these known limitations assured that the structure would work safely.

Before the industrial era, the master builders had other measures and methods of design for structural systems. Centuries of experience had given them a series of principles which constituted a workable and rather sophisticated technology: <u>Proportions</u>. Funk and Wagnalls defines proportion as: "Relative magnitude, number or degree, as existing between parts, a part and a whole, or different things. Fitness and harmony, to form with harmonious relation of parts."

The master builder was aware that in order to put a building together, other components were required besides the construction materials. Other factors included sources of materials and the means of their extraction, transportation and handling. Construction methods depended upon available building technologies and upon the size, weight, height, bearing capability and performance of the materials employed. The pyramids, cathedrals and ordinary houses were all built with materials that were easily accessible physically and economically. For instance, there are no oversized stones in the pyramids because the worker could not move, raise and set them in place. Those which were oversized for the existing technology and systems of proportion still rest in their place of origin or were cut to smaller sizes. The sizes of bearing architectural elements, the clearances of arches, architraves and beams, the geometry of the floor plans and the arrangement of the facades were established by a clear knowledge of proportions.

The protectors of traditional structures must thoroughly understand the historic buildings' structural systems, construction methods and limitations. They must also be aware of the risk of various natural disasters occurring at the locations of historic buildings under their care in order to perform their duty in a fully responsible way.

THE CRITICAL EARTHQUAKE

Areas where seismic activity takes place have been charted already and are known today. In a historic building the original construction campaign, the damage it has suffered during its lifetime, and maintenance and repairs by the persons who have occupied and added to it are all visible in the organization of constructive materials. For the trained eye reading the bare walls is like reading the chapters of a history book which has recorded the struggles of the building and its occupants against earthquakes.

A historic building damaged by seismic action may have been damaged by one critical earthquake or by a series of them. A <u>critical earthquake</u> is that one in a series, period or season of earthquakes which causes the most damages. A building may be lightly, severely, critically damaged, or destroyed by the last critical earthquake that affects it. A building which has undergone one or a series of critical earthquakes but has not yet been destroyed by them will show in its scars their frequency and intensity as well as the "Achilles' Heel" of its structure.

The Greek God Achilles was protected against all manly dangers except in one vulnerable place: his heel. Buildings hide within their structures one or a series of weak points that eventually may destroy them. The task of the architect and/or structuralist who works with historic buildings threatened by seismic movements is to find those weak points before the earthquake does.

Studying series of damaged and destroyed buildings in different parts of the world has helped identify some patterns of structural behavior. Depending upon the kind of movements to which the structure is exposed during seismic activity, the building will behave in a specific manner. Many times it will survive the motion or will be damaged or destroyed in a way that can be predicted or expected.

This applies only to those structures which are located away from the epicenters and away from where the ground fractures and distorts the geometry of foundations.

As a general rule, the earthquake will always damage the structure in its weakest points; the sound and well-proportioned parts of a building will either survive or will be damaged by the failure of the weak parts. To find the "Achilles Heel" of a determined structure may require a long and meticulous structural analysis, yet an earthquake will find it in a matter of seconds.

The weakest points of a traditional building are usually:

a) Those places where large structural loads rest on small areas of weight transmission.
   e.g.: Large volumes of bearing walls resting on arches supported by thin columns.
   Vaults resting on thin walls, or walls without buttresses.
   An architrave which supports a heavy roof bearing on column capitals.

b) Perforations in bearing walls, especially in multi-storied buildings where alignment of the perforations forms a geometrical or repetitive pattern.
   e.g.: The vertical alignment of doors and windows which breaks a continuous bearing wall into piers.
   Openings too close to the end or corner of a building, or too close to the bearing level of the roof on a wall.
   An arch resting on columns with a bearing wall resting on them.

c) The ties between the structural elements of a roof and the bearing walls, which change the direction of transmission of thrust and transfer the thrust from one material to another.
   e.g.: Where domes rest on arches.
   Where vaults rest on walls
   Where wooden roof structure sits on walls.

d) Where tension stresses are incorporated to a structure which was designed and built for compression stresses only.

300

e.g.: The upper portions of masonry arches.

The upper portion of a bearing wall.

e) The end corners of a block of buldings that are all in a row.

BEHAVIOR OF THE STRUCTURE

In order to talk about this subject, we have to establish some parameters:

a) We shall not talk about structures whose foundation geometry has been highly deformed by large ground movements. These will suffer total collapse or a high level of destruction.
b) Existing structures that have survived previous seismic activity with light or heavy damage should and will be analyzed as completely different structures from those originally planned and built.
c) Existing structures damaged and repaired in earlier earthquakes and restoration or repair campaigns should be considered as two buildings—the original structural system and the effects that later structural repairs and additions have created in the original structure.
d) The behavior of a structure will vary radically depending upon whether it is:
   1. A self–standing building.
   2. Part of a group of aligned buildings.
   3. Part of an area of buildings, (group).
   4. Part of a conglomerate of buildings situated within the area of a city and flanking one of the streets.

PARAMETERS OF DESIGN IN A TRADITIONAL STRUCTURE

As stated above, modern structural design is based on knowledge of the limitations of structural materials. Traditionally, proportions were the basis of this structural design. With theories highly tested by centuries of design, construction, success and failure, the master builders of earlier periods were able to produce an incredible number of structures that have survived to become the legacy of those epochs.

Applying mathematical computations to the work which was done by traditional proportions, we can establish some fundamental concepts of vernacular buildings:

$$\Sigma = \frac{P}{A}$$

Σ = the stress which a material can take or is taking in an existing structure.

P = the load which is being created by the weight of the material itself, plus what rests or acts on top of it.

A = the area of the structural element through which the load is transmitted to the ground or to another section of the structure.

This mathematical relation tells us that generally:

The stress to which a structural material is being exposed is directly proportional to the load it supports and inversely proportional to the area upon which the weight rests.

This means:

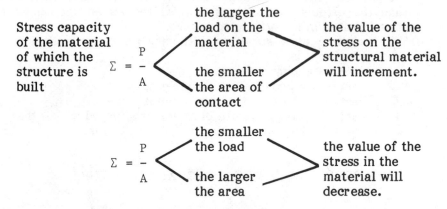

Stress capacity of the material of which the structure is built
$\Sigma = \frac{P}{A}$
the larger the load on the material
the smaller the area of contact
the value of the stress on the structural material will increment.

$\Sigma = \frac{P}{A}$
the smaller the load
the larger the area
the value of the stress in the material will decrease.

In traditional or vernacular buildings, the value of Σ is usually very low, because design by proportions builds in extensive areas of support for large masses of construction.

The masses of an existing building will oscillate and accelerate with seismic movement. In a stable structure, the area of transmission of loads will not change. When an earthquake hits the structure, the existing stresses in the structure will change with the addition of the new inertia values generated by the earthquake. This new extra load and changes in the geometry of the structure's elements will damage or destroy the structure, since it depends on a determined geometrical configuration, and on the stability of the acting loads.

The accelerations created by the seismic movement upon an existing structure are two: <u>tension</u> and <u>compression</u>.

Torsion will also be present in a structure during the seismic movement, but torsion will act as shear, which in turn translates into tension stresses.

Tension

The natural materials that man used in traditional structures to absorb tension stresses included: natural veins, ropes made out of natural fibers, animal hides and wood. It was not until the Iron Age that man was able to manipulate and produce metallic items to absorb tension: plates of limited sizes, rods and chains.

Because production of metal required a highly developed technology and an availability of certain natural resources, metallic structural members were not used extensively in traditional and vernacular architecture. As a consequence, many traditional buildings located in areas threatened by seismic movements are ill-prepared to withstand telluric movements.

Compression

The types of construction materials used for both tension and compression loads through the centuries varied with local availability. Traditional construction methods and systems use mostly materials able to withstand compression. These materials, wood, stone, mud, adobe and brick, were used in their natural condition or altered by man with the available resources.

Compression is very seldom a critical stress in seismic motion. Buildings usually contain large masses of masonry, which means they have large areas for load transmission (A in the formula of proportions) and large amounts of load to direct to the foundations (P in the formula).

STUDY CASES

After analyzing some basic structural concepts, understanding the roots of vernacular architecture and examining the principles that rule traditional structural systems, we can use these principles to analyze the following study cases. The study cases are within the parameters established and described in the section related to Behavior of the Structure. They are in different parts of the world and reflect local conditions existing when protective measures were taken.

The projects described are:

1. Main Street, Gemona del Friuli, Italy
2. Palazzo Comunale, Gemona del Friuli, Italy
3. Osoppo Cathedral, Osoppo, Friuli, Italy
4. Church of San Martino, Artegna, Friuli, Italy
5. Cathedral of Antigua, Antigua Guatemala, Guatemala
6. Compania De Jesus', Antigua Guatemala, Guatemala
7. XVI Century San Francisco, Antigua Guatemala, Guatemala
8. Psychological Shoring, Santo Tomas Chichicastenango, Quiche, Guatemala.

1 - Main Street, Gemona del Friuli, Italy

Before being damaged during the May 6, 1976, earthquake, the main street in Gemona was a narrow, twisting street set between the cathedral or Duomo at one end and the Palazzo Comunale at the other end.

The street was flanked by a covered arcade on both sides, which was also the ground floor of the four-storied dwellings. Along one side of the street, the buildings were aligned in one plane facing the street with a continuous elevation. There were gaps in the block of structures at two points: one flanking the Palazzo Comunale and the other between two private houses.

As would be expected, the two end buildings suffered considerable damage from the earthquake of May 6, and since the upper stories rested on arches, the condition in which they remained was alarming. The earthquake provoked the collapse of a good portion of the street elevation and the displacement of the end column. (Figure 5.1) Demolition was considered. After convincing the local authorities that there was a way to protect the street, using salvaged wood beams with the aid of a battalion of German mountain engineers, we shored the displaced end corner, saving the building from demolition.

If we go back to the formula $\Sigma = \dfrac{P}{A}$ and apply the principle to this study case, we can see how after the earthquake the value of Σ was increased considerably, since the upper portion of the building remained (P in the formula) while some of the arches and their supporting columns had collapsed. The gap in the wall formed a natural arch in the masonry and one end of this arch rested on the end column which was displaced about 60 centimeters. The total area of transmission of load was reduced to about 40 x 40 centimeters. (A in the formula.) As alarming as it was, the structure was still working and transmitting the loads to the ground since it was still standing up.

Emergency measures aimed first to reduce the value of Σ by filling the gaps in the wall and the supporting arches with brick masonry. Closing the openings in the bearing wall increased the value of A in the formula by increasing the area of load transmission. A second measure was to improve and enlarge the preliminary wood shoring at the end of the displaced corner. Finally, bracing between

Figure 5.1. Gemona del Friuli, Italy: Ground Story of Dwellings on the Main Street after Earthquake of May 6, 1976.

Figure 5.2. Gemona del Friuli, Italy: Brick Infill and Wood Bracing Reinforcement Installed in Buildings on the Main Street after the Earthquake of May 6, 1976 Which Protected Structures from Aftershock on September 15, 1976.

the damaged structure and the buildings across the street created continuity of support between the city blocks and reduced the number of 'end buildings' or gaps within the fabric of the city. (Figure 5.2)

The street was left in this condition until on September 15, 1976, four months afterwards, a major aftershock hit the area, causing large amounts of damage and destruction. Figure 5.2 shows the arches and the bricked-up gaps in the wall as well as the bracing across the street after the second earthquake of that year. The system protected the damaged structure from the second seismic shock.

2 - Palazzo Comunale, Gemona Del Friuli, Italy

The building situated at the other end of the alignment of buildings facing Main Street in Gemona was the Palazzo Comunale. The arches of this 1502 building [Italian Tarry Club, 1949] were also braced with salvaged wood beams erected with the aid of the German Battalion of Mountain Engineers after the May 6, 1976, earthquake (Figure 5.3)

Recommendations to brick up the arches were left behind as the recovery team moved to the next town. This was another case where the loads of the second floor were transmitted to the ground through thin stone columns. Before the 1976 earthquake, and probably after the last time that the building was damaged by another quake, tension rods had been installed between the columns to prevent lateral displacement.

Flanking the Palazzo Comunale was another building incorporated into the municipal offices. This was the end building opposite the four-storied dwelling previously described.

During the second phase of the emergency protection campaign, when the carpenters and the bricklayers were filling up the arches along the arcade in Main Street, Gemona, they failed to fill the arches of the Palazzo Comunale or to shore the end corner of the neighboring building. On September 15, 1976, when the second major earthquake hit the area, the corner building gave way and the Palazzo Comunale lost half of its flanking arch. (Figure 5.4)

3 - Osoppo Cathedral, Osoppo, Friuli, Italy

Osoppo was hit severely by the May 6, 1976, earthquake. Some days later, another more destructive catastrophe hit Osoppo: the arrival of the mechanized demolition squadron. During a very short length of time, Osoppo disappeared in front of tractors and on top of heavy dump trucks. Once the operation was completed, Osoppo was a grey, dusty, empty space, where once there had stood a medieval town. Only the street pattern survived, along with the remains of a small chapel and transept of the cathedral. Demolition had been

Figure 5.3. Gemona del Friuli, Italy: Palazzo Comunale, Built in 1502, Showing Bracing Erected After Earthquake of May 6, 1976.

Figure 5.4. Gemona del Friuli, Italy: Palazzo Comunale, Built in 1502, Showing Destruction Following Earthquake of September 15, 1976.

offered free of charge as part of the international rescue aid. Local authorities, affected by the 'demolition fever' characteristic of the aftermath of any major earthquake, decided to proceed with the demolition, thinking that the central government was going to rebuild everything. The central government, however, did not have the financial capability to do so.

During this systematic demolition period, it was established that the only valuable items to be preserved were the altar piece in the cathedral and a fresco still attached to a portion of the lateral surviving cathedral wall. With a force of five firemen and with no more tools than hammers and nails, the emergency team set out to protect such items.

The only surviving structure was the vaulted transept and its tiled roof. The altar piece was a 16th Century marble ensemble holding a marble sculpture of a recumbent saint. The materials and tools available, such as salvaged timbers, were used to build a pyramidal wooden structure over the altar. The vault above was of wood lattice and plaster decorated with colored geometrical patterns. (Figure 5.5) It took half a day's work to complete the protective framework together with the surveying and recording of other damaged structures in the town before their demolition.

After the September 15, 1976, earthquakes, I returned to inspect the damage to the remaining transept. It was satisfying to find that the wood latticed vault had fallen on top of the pyramid built over the altar and that the altar remained intact under it. (Figure 5.6) The same kind of protection saved the fresco situated to one side of the altar on the wall surviving from the first quake. Using salvaged beams and boards and plastic sheets, an inclined structure had been installed over the fresco to protect it from the rain, environmental elements, the transept vault, and the lateral collapse of the wall itself. This protective structure was also demolished by the collapse of the transept vault, but the wall and fresco survived. After the second earthquake, it took a short time to rebuild the same structure over the existing bearing timbers of the pyramid, and install some more plastic sheets. Both the altar piece and the fresco were saved.

Such protection lasted months until a team of qualified workers and restorers came to remove the fresco from the wall and to protect, in a far better way, the only surviving element of what once had been the Cathedral of Osoppo.

4 - Church of San Martino, Artegna, Friuli, Italy

A church situated on top of a hill in Artegna has a marble tablet located above the keystone of its entrance arch inscribed in Latin to read:

built in 1034, destroyed in 1303, rebuilt in 1519

Figure 5.6. Osoppo, Italy: Cathedral, Transept Showing Surviving Altar after Earthquake of September 15, 1976.

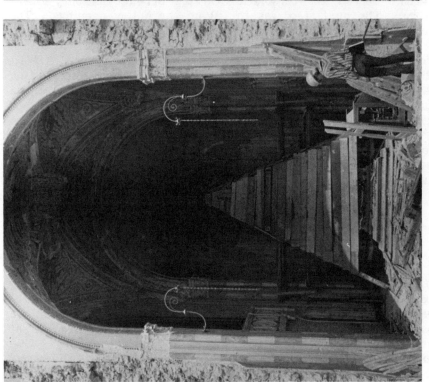

Figure 5.5. Osoppo, Italy: Cathedral, Transept Showing Pyramidal Protective Cover Erected Over 16th Century Marble Altar after Earthquake of May 6, 1976.

and someone came and inscribed once more:

and destroyed once more by another earthquake in 1976.

A team of four bricklayers, a light truck, five cubic feet of cement and some metal scaffolding had been donated by a Sister City in Italy to help with five days of recovery work. Upon arrival, I encountered the team of masons already at work, dismounting the corner stones of the church in order to relocate them in place. After a structural analysis and consideration of the resources available, it was decided to work on the "Achilles' Heel," which was the upper portion of the bell tower, now leaning over the frescoed transept vault. The key stone of one of the four openings of the belfry was also missing and had caused a large deformity of the stone columns supporting the upper portion of the tower. On top of the upper tower, a later addition, a dome covered with a lead roof and bronze statue of an angel topped the derelict structure.

With the small amount of scaffolding available, the team built a tower at one side of the masonry tower in order to reach the openings of the belfry. The inner staircase of the tower was still filled with debris from the earthquake. Through the scaffolding tower, bricks and mortar were raised to the top of the inclined tower and the bells were dismounted and left on the floor of the upper level. Scaffolding pipes installed around the base and around the cornice at the springing of the arches served as tensors to tie the derelict masonry tower together. The next step was to fill up the belfry openings. The purpose of the operation was: 1) Try to keep the tower standing up in order to prevent destruction of the transept and apse. 2) Install tension belts around the weakest points of the stone tower. 3) Wait for the aftershock tremors to enlarge the gaps between the existing stones, thus increasing the tension stresses in the scaffolding pipes. (Figure 5.7) This strategy worked as expected. When we returned to inspect the condition of the church after the second earthquake of that year, we discovered that the protection system had worked. Although the tower was even more distorted and had rotated, the entire system, as well as the tower and church, were still standing up. (Figure 5.8)

5 – Cathedral of Antigua, Antigua Guatemala, Guatemala

This cathedral, as well as the rest of the baroque city of Antiqua, was destroyed on June 10, 1773, by an earthquake. During almost two hundred years, the city was left without any kind of protection, and the large religious complexes and churches remained exposed to the elements, to numerous earthquakes and a series of tremors. In 1948, some repairs were done in different buildings. One series of repairs, in particular, was made in the cathedral. The barrel vault over the central nave fell in 1773. One of the elliptical vaults of

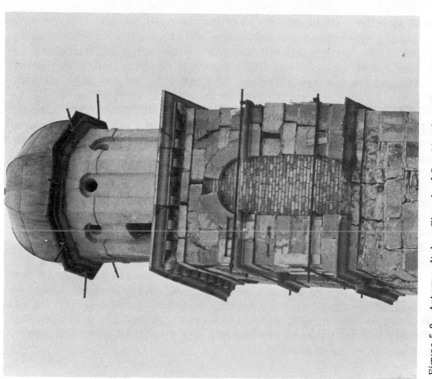

Figure 5.8. Artegna, Italy: Church of San Martino, Tower Showing Survival After Earthquake of September 15, 1976.

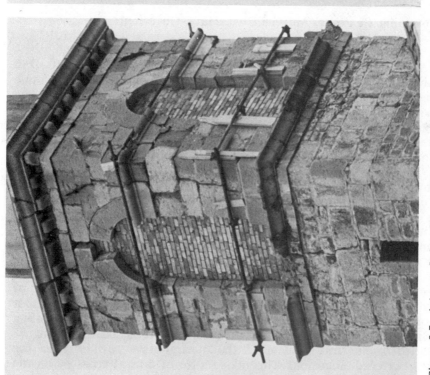

Figure 5.7. Artegna, Italy: Church of San Martino, Tower Showing Reinforcement Erected after Earthquake of May 6, 1976.

the side aisle lost about one-third of its masonry, leaving a large hole in it. During the protection campaign of 1948, instead of completing the brick vault with material similar to the original, two ribs of reinforced concrete had been built between the remaining portion of the vault and the surviving arches. (Figure 5.9) During the February 4, 1976 earthquake, these two concrete members, being so small in area and very rigid in structure, hammered the supporting arches, breaking them and the remaining portions of the vault. The columns and one-third of the outgoing arches remained standing but threatened to collapse under the continuous seismic motion of the aftershocks. (Figure 5.10)

With sawed timbers, some supports were built and attached on the columns, as well as to steel cables anchored in the ground. A series of metal structural members were installed between the portions of the arches still attached to the columns in order to re-establish the structural support provided by the series of arches. (Figure 5.11)

In this condition these columns survived the 1500 shocks of the aftermath which lasted six months; they also survived the average of two thousand tremors per year typical of the site since 1976. Today, six years after the critical earthquake, the columns are still standing up. Slowly but surely each column is being consolidated and anchored independently to the ground.

6 - Compania De Jesus, Antigua Guatemala, Guatemala

This church had been destroyed by an earthquake on June 10, 1773 and abandoned with the rest of the city. When Antigua Guatemala was hit once more on February 4, 1976, by another major earthquake, the central market of the city was located inside of the ruins of this church and convent. Once the loose debris and the portable structures of the market stands had been removed, some emergency protection had to be given to the surviving wall of the church.

The main facade lost the end wall of its side aisle and its belltower. A rectangular window located above the main entrance arch changed in width, and its architrave was fractured at the corners. Since the parapet had been lost 200 hundred years earlier, the window's lintel became a wedge tending to fall through the window opening. With the loss of the end wall of the lateral nave, a great crack appeared running diagonally across the elevation, and the whole upper portion of the wall threatened to fall. (Figure 5.12) As a protective measure, a wood frame was installed inside the opening of the window. A steel cable was also installed around the whole upper part of the elevation in order to prevent the upper portion from failing and sliding down over the diagonal fracture. Behind the elevation, we encountered the first column of the central nave leaning over the already battered elevation. This added a lot of lateral pressure on the self-standing elevation. During the 1948 protection campaign, two

Figure 5.10. Antigua Guatemala, Guatemala: Cathedral, Side Aisle Elliptical Vault Showing Destruction Caused by Battering of Concrete Ribs in Earthquake of February 4, 1976.

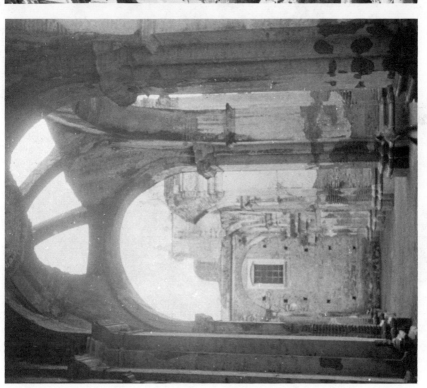

Figure 5.9. Antigua Guatemala, Guatemala: Cathedral, Side Aisle Elliptical Vault Showing Concrete Reinforcing Ribs Installed in 1948.

Figure 5.11. Antigua Guatemala, Guatemala: Cathedral, Reinforcing Timber, Cable and Girder System Installed after Earthquake of February 4, 1976.

Figure 5.12. Antigua Guatemala, Guatemala: Compania de Jesus, Main Facade after Earthquake of February 4, 1976.

314

concrete connectors had been installed between the elevation and the leaning column behind it. (Figure 5.13) Having seen the battering that concrete reinforcement had caused in the cathedral in Antigua, the recovery team suggested to use the stone and brick debris as construction material and build a supportive structure underneath the inclined column. This was done two years after the earthquake, and column and main facade were made independent by removing part of the concrete connectors. (Figure 5.14) With the rest of the debris, the end wall of the lateral aisle was rebuilt in order to become a buttress for the rest of the elevation, as well as for the lateral wall which also lost contact with the elevation. By these measures not only was the future of the elevation assured, but the proportions of the complete elevation were restored up to the second level.

7 - XVI Century San Francisco, Antigua Guatemala, Guatemala

The only remaining parts of this XVI Century church were the main facade, which over time had been incorporated into another building, and three of the four arches from the transept. During the February 4, 1976, earthquake, the central portion of one of the surviving arches rotated out of place and wedged itself between the remaining parts of the arch. (Figure 5.15) As soon as possible, a substructure of wood was built underneath a platform designed to support the rotated masonry hanging wedged in the center of the arch. If this key did fall, the entire structural system of the remaining arches and columns would fail because of the interruption of the system's continuity. The reason for building the platform halfway between the dislodged keystone and the ground was so that the workers, in the event of another strong tremor, could jump down to the ground and protect themselves. (Figure 5.16)

Four years after the earthquake, the rotated portion was removed and the arch was made whole again with the same type of bricks and mortar and with some metallic reinforcement. Today, it stands by itself once more, waiting for restoration.

8 - Psychological Shoring, Santo Thomas Chichicastenango, Quiche, Guatemala

This XVII Century church is one of the most valuable temples in Guatemala, not only as a religious center but also as a tourist attraction where natives perform ritual activities twice a week. The church had been built with mud on top of a pyramid. It was damaged only slightly but the people were afraid to go near it to perform their religious rituals. The priest wanted to demolish it. In order to show the people that something was being done for their church, a series of steel pipes topped with a wooden bracket were placed around the

315

Figure 5.14. Antigua Guatemala, Guatemala: Compania de Jesus, Main Facade Showing Removal of Concrete Connectors and Separate Buttressing of Rear of Facade and Leaning Pillar of Nave.

Figure 5.13. Antigua Guatemala, Guatemala: Compania de Jesus, Main Facade Showing Concrete Connectors Installed in 1948 Between Rear of Facade and Leaning Pillar of Nave.

316

Figure 5.15. Antigua Guatemala, Guatemala: Church of San Francisco, Transept Arch Showing Dislodged Central Portion after Earthquake of February 4, 1976.

Figure 5.16. Antigua Guatemala, Guatemala: Church of San Francisco, Transept Arch Showing Platform Designed to Support Central Portion.

church. The window openings were filled in with adobe and a warning sign was posted. (Figure 5.17)

Many people laughed at the installation of this type of protection. The natives, however, felt secure that their building was not going to be demolished and that somebody with power from the government was involved in the protection of it. When a demolition team came to the town, the fact that some work was being done on the church was enough to prevent its demolition, despite the local priest's continued interest in demolishing it.

The same principle has been applied successfully in other disaster locations, not only in Guatemala, but also in Italy, Nicaragua and Mexico. It has served its purpose—to buy time so that various levels of protection can be carried out later.

CONCLUSION

The only goal of protecting structures during the emergency period should be that of buying time. Restoration must be banned from this emergency protection period. The motto should be: Protect as many buildings as possible with the elements of protection available at the site and at the moment. Instead of restoring three buildings in the emergency period, protect fifty with the same amount of effort and money. If the damaged structures have been given the emergency protection necessary to withstand aftershocks and have been ranked according to the priorities of a long-term consolidation program, there will always be time later to come back and restore them.

REFERENCES

Calder, Nigel. The Restless Earth. Middelsex, England: Penguin Books Ltd. 1978.

CNPAG. Memoria de Labores 1979. Guatemala: Consejo Nacional para la Proteccion de la Antigua Guatemala, Impresos Industriales, 1980.

del Cid, Donald. Conservation and Architecture in Guatemala. York, England: University of York, 1974.

del Cid, Donald. Conservation of Cultural Property: Its definition, its surveying, its recording. Unpublished.

del Cid, Donald. Report of the ICCROM Missions to Friuli. Rome: ICCROM, 1976, 1977.

Feilden, Bernard. Techniques of Repair of Historic Buildings. Photocopies, 1974.

Francia, Peter. Volcanoes. Middlesex, England: Penguin Books Ltd., 1976.

Frick, Otto. Stone and Brick Masonry Construction. Argentina: Editorial Labor, 1953.

Figure 5.17. Quiche, Guatemala: Church of Santo Thomas Chichicastenango, 17th Century, Facade Showing Bracing Installed After Earthquake of February 4, 1976 to Prevent Unnecessary Destruction.

Giedion, Sigfried. Space, Time and Architecture. Cambridge: Harvard University Press, 1962.

Hibbitts, J. Estado de Conservacion de las Iglesias de Antigua Guatemala. Guatemala: Universidad de San Carlos, 1958.

Italian Tarry Club. Italy In One Volume. Paris: Nagel Publishers, 1949. p. 147.

Mallet, R. Great Neapolitan Earthquake of 1857, London, 1862.

Palladio, Andrea. The Four Books of Architecture. New York: Dover Publications, Inc., 1965.

Peragalli, C. Monumenti e metodi di Valorizzazione. Milano: Libreria editrice politecnica, 1954.

Walker, Bryce. Earthquake. Virginia: Time-Life Books, 1982.

Personal field notes, drawings and photographs recollected during the different events witnessed.

Wind and Water Damage to Historic Structures

Nicholas H. Holmes, Jr., FAIA, SOPA

I arose early in the morning of September 12, 1979, to attend a meeting in Montgomery, 180 miles northeast of my home in Mobile intending to return by mid-afternoon. Since August 30 we had followed the sixth hurricane of the season—"Frederic" by name—from its genesis as a tropical depression in the South Atlantic, a thousand miles southeast of Puerto Rico. It followed the traditional westward path—Puerto Rico, the Dominican Republic, Cuba, and into the Gulf of Mexico. Then it turned northwest and headed straight for Mobile. By the evening of September 11, it appeared certain that it would not veer off course and that we had best prepare for a pretty good blow. (Figure 5.18)

The older son, who practices architecture with me, was instructed to first secure the office—put all drawings "in progress" into drawers, place the sets of prints and small items in the closets, and move the furniture back from the windows. Then he was to go to my residence and perform certain chores that I will detail later. Finally, he was to return to his own home and prepare it. My wife was to tend to all food needs, check flashlights, and purchase spare batteries and candles. The younger son was to drive to our beach house facing the Gulf of Mexico, some 5 miles east of Fort Morgan at the foot of Mobile Bay. His instructions were explicit: stow the lamps, pictures and other small items in the closets, move all furniture away from the windows and, by all means, leave before the water began to rise.

As I drove south in the early afternoon, I was practically alone—but the opposite lane was clogged with traffic as residents of low lying areas and coastal zones moved north to safety. The lessons taught by hurricane "Camille" in 1969 had been remembered. "Camille" hit Biloxi and Pass Christian, Mississippi, while hundreds of people ignored the pleadings of civil defense workers and staged "hurricane parties" in beach front hotels, apartments and residences and perished.

I arrived home in mid-afternoon, checked with the boys by phone and then my wife and I started our final preparations—furniture away from exterior walls, pillows handy to stuff into broken glass lights, portable coolers, normally used for fishing and hunting trips filled with

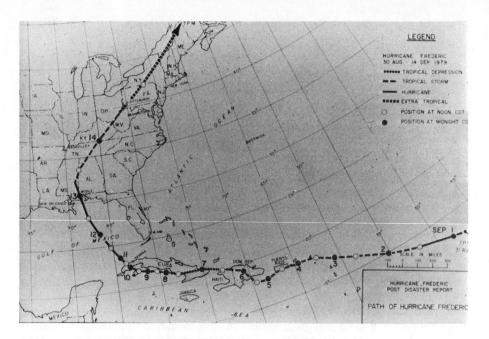

Figure 5.18. Path of Hurricane Frederick, September 12-13, 1979.

Figure 5.19. Map of Damage Caused by Hurricane Frederick,
September 12-13, 1979.

322

ice, battery operated radios checked and plastic jugs filled with potable water.

By 4:30 p.m. power failed and the wind began to pick up. At 9:00 p.m. "Frederic" came ashore on the west end of Dauphin Island—some 25 miles west of our beach house. During the next few hours the barometer fell to 27.8 inches. Gusts of wind were recorded on Dauphin Island at 145 miles per hours, in Mobile at slightly over 100 and in Pascagoula, Mississippi, at nearly 130. The surge of the sea, with a fine fetch reaching all the way to Cuba, rose to somewhere around 20 feet. The rain gage in Mobile recorded 8.5 inches before it was blown away. In Pascagoula it overflowed at 11 inches. By 11:00 p.m. our wood frame house, constructed in 1867, was rocking, rolling, groaning and creaking like a sailing vessel laboring under too much canvas. (Figure 5.19)

We could see trees falling by lightning flashes, but could hear nothing over the howl of the wind and the drumming of the rain. During the early hours of the morning, hurricane force winds were recorded one hundred fifty miles inland and wind and water damage occurred from Ft. Walton Beach, Florida, to Pass Christian, Mississippi. By 6 a.m. the sun was shining, a small breeze was blowing, and residents of three states went outside to have a look at what turned out to be a record setting two and one-half billion dollar property loss. It would have been worse had we not then enjoyed six weeks of beautiful, dry, Indian summer.

The fact that wind and water will periodically affect the daily lives of Mobilians should surprise none of us. In June 1559—26 years before Roanoke, 48 years before Jamestown, 80 years before Plymouth—a fleet of 13 vessels left Vera Cruz, Mexico carrying 1500 European colonists. The expedition was commanded by Don Tristan de Luna, a veteran officer of Phillip II of Spain. These were true colonists—not explorers—and the party consisted of men, women, children, soldiers, and priests. The fleet entered Mobile Bay in early August, then moved slightly eastward and anchored in Pensacola Bay on August 14. The colonists disembarked, but the precious supplies of food, seed, and tools for clearing and farming remained aboard ship until suitable warehouses could be built. Five days later on August 19 our first recorded hurricane struck. Ten of the thirteen vessels sank with great loss of life. The supplies that were to sustain the colony lay at the bottom of the bay. After two years of extreme privation the attempt was abandoned and the survivors withdrawn.

In 1701 the French established a military post 27 miles up river from the head of Mobile Bay. By 1711 frequent flooding had forced them to abandon this site and move down river to the present site of our city. During our French period, 1711 to 1763, four hurricanes were recorded. During our British period, 1763 to 1780, seven occurred. Nature was kinder to our Spanish overlords. There was only one hurricane from 1780 to 1813, when we finally became a part of the United States. Since then we have endured 32 tropical disturbances of which 14 have inflicted moderate to heavy damage. During our roughly 275 years of existence, we have also suffered from frequent flooding.

Sometimes it was caused by our river system that drains most of Alabama and parts of Georgia and Mississippi. Sometimes it was caused by hurricane induced sea surges. During these periods 8 to 10 foot tides are not uncommon at the head of our bay.

Recently a third factor has come into play. Just west of our city a belt of wet lands extended some 25 miles from north to south. It was crossed by only a few roads that led to a hilly area a bit farther west. It was called Wragg Swamp and was the home of bears, water moccasins, and alligators.

Then the Highway Department decided that this was the cheapest, and hence the best, place to build an Interstate, and the Developers latched onto this opportunity. The end result was the relocation of the retail district from the river-front to "West Mobile." Wragg Swamp was paved and renamed "Bel Air" and downtown Mobile, abandoned by the merchants, was dead as a stump.

But you do not re-arrange the ecology of a huge area such as this without side effects. Last May we enjoyed a little spring freshet. Seventeen inches of rain fell on West Mobile in four hours. The Spirit of high, dry, downtown Mobile must have felt some secret pleasure when it learned that Montgomery Ward was four foot deep in water. Unfortunately, the local merchants who had followed the major tenants suffered as well, and many residences, previously secure, were inundated.

What should we do in view of the fact that natural disasters have always occurred in our area and will continue to occur? First, as property owners, we should obtain the right kinds of insurance in the right amounts and adjust our coverage yearly to reflect changing physical and financial conditions. Second, as design professionals, we should avail ourselves of every opportunity to correct any deficiencies in our historic structures, whether they be due to original design inadequacies, bad workmanship, or the effects of age, deterioration, and poor maintenance. A major hurricane has an uncanny ability to discover and exploit any weakness.

With regard to the problem of insurance coverage, I will recount a personal experience that was shared by many others. During the night of September 12, I wondered about my beach house. It had been built in 1940 and had withstood several near misses before I purchased it in 1970. I had made additions and installed heavy timber X-bracings, fixed to the corner piling with galvanized bolts. My neighbor's house had no X-bracing, and I feared the scouring action of the surf would undermine the lee side of his piling and cause the wind force on his house to rotate the piling around the ground line. I did not believe that my X-bracing would allow this. I was right on both counts. His piling are still in place leaning to the west—pointing in the direction his house left. Not so with mine—they are simply snapped off at grade. Only the bottom of my septic tank remained in situ.

Almost immediately the argument started. Did the wind destroy my house and the waves clear the site of debris--or did my house gallantly withstand the wind only to be engulfed by a tidal wave? Each insuror hired Engineers and Testing Laboratories; reports were

324

written, and the sky was darkened by the advent of soaring flocks of legal vultures. Only one thing was certain—there were no witnesses! Just before it drizzled blood, the insurors decided to compromise. I prepared a detailed estimate of my loss—the wind insuror took it from the roof down; the flood insuror took it from the ground up, and they met halfway. I had the right kinds of insurance in the right amounts.

Few of the merchants damaged in the flash flooding of last May were fortunate enough to have flood insurance, and most suffered accordingly. Since this flood, many of us, whose residences and businesses have never before been threatened by high water, have taken out flood insurance. Such is the price we individuals must pay for forty years of over-development and disregard of our wet lands.

Let us review the nature of the hurricane and the types of forces it produces. The hurricane is a cyclonic storm, which means that in the Northern hemisphere winds rotate about a low pressure area, or eye, counter clockwise. The eye of "Frederic" came from the south and passed to the west of us. Therefore, the winds we encountered were from the northeast and east, so direct forces were felt on north and east facades and reverse or suction forces were felt on south and west facades. (Figure 5.19)

In early 1979 my firm was retained by the Vestry of Trinity Episcopal Church to perform certain studies regarding the condition of their structure. The building was designed in 1853 by Henry Dudley and Frank Wills, English trained architects who were anointed, so to speak, after their immigration by the New York Ecclesiological Society. In Trinity, they produced a building faithful to Ecclesiological doctrines with a steeple that is embarrassingly similar to the steeple on St. Oswald's in Liverpool, the building designed by Augustus Pugin that started the whole business.

Our investigation disclosed all three of the deficiencies mentioned earlier. The scissors trusses that spanned the nave rested on wood columns at the top of the clerestory. There were no exterior buttresses or interior tension rods. Therefore, these trusses were delivering both vertical and horizontal forces to the columns which, in turn, were placed into both bending and direct stress. A string line pulled on each side showed that the upper ends of the columns in the middle of the nave had deflected outward 2 to 3 inches. This in turn, created rotation of the joints of both upper and lower truss chords—joints made entirely of wood—which, in turn, allowed the ridge to settle. None of the roof members was fastened against uplift with anything but toe nailing. These were all technical mistakes in the original design.

The steeple had iron tie rods to anchor it to the masonry tower below but none of the tie rods had turnbuckles, and all were very loose. Obviously the steeple would have to move before the tie rods went into tension. This was a mistake in both the original design and an evidence of bad workmanship. The wood framed steeple contained numerous members that had been damaged by rot and termites—all the effects of poor maintenance and time.

325

Figure 5.20. Mobile, Alabama: Trinity Episcopal Church, Henry Dudley and Frank Wills, Archs., 1853, Damage from Hurricane Frederick, September 12, 1979.

Figure 5.21. Mobile, Alabama: Trinity Episcopal Church, Henry Dudley and Frank Wills, Archs., 1853, Damage to Roof of Nave from Hurricane Frederick, September 12, 1979.

Our report warned the vestry that the nave was in serious trouble and that a hurricane would probably destroy the steeple. The cost of remedial work would be enormous and the vestry, understandably, deferred action.

The damage Trinity suffered was awesome. (Figures 5.20, 5.21) A large section of the roof on the west or lee side failed through uplift. The ridge opened the entire length at the nave, the roof deck on both sides was lifted from rafters, rafters from purlins, and purlins from trusses. Additional joint rotation occurred to the trusses and the spread of the nave increased. One of the tie rods on the steeple broke—the others held but only after the steeple had been blown off its base. In moving and then being brought up suddenly, its structural integrity was destroyed. The south wall of the Parish House had been built 20 years ago of concrete block with a brick veneer. It failed through suction and fell outward. (Figure 5.22) The nave was too damaged to be used so services were conducted in the Parish Hall.

Repairs started on September 14, two days after the storm. First temporary framing and canvas tarpaulins were draped over the roof ridge and the section of missing roof. As the areas involved were fairly small, this proved to be effective and further damage to the interior was largely avoided, though some leaking did occur until permanent repairs were made. The removal of the steeple was quite hazardous but was accomplished by lifting it in two sections. (Figure 5.23) Once on the ground, it was carefully measured and photographed.

Repair work to the nave was slow. First the entire area was scaffolded. Then tension rods with turnbuckles were installed to relieve the thrust on the columns. They are barely visible. No attempt was made to bring the columns back into line; we feared this would cause additional damage. We tightened the turnbuckles until the rods were in tension but no more. Steel splice plates were designed and bolted on the truss joints. All roof decks were removed and replaced after repairs to rafters and purlins were accomplished. All members were firmly anchored to their supports and new shingles applied.

After much soul searching, the architects and the Vestry agreed that it would not be wise to rebuild the steeple with wood and slate. The expense of proper maintenance would be prohibitive and the problem of getting good timber today simply cannot be solved. We contracted with a Kentucky firm to build a replica with a frame built of riveted aluminum angles designed to withstand a wind load of 120 miles per hours. The exterior was clad with a combination of anodized aluminum members and shingles made of micro-zinc. As the new steeple was considerably lighter than the old one, a new tie-down system was required so that the weight of much of the masonry tower was used to anchor the steeple. This time the rods had turnbuckles and were tensioned. (Figure 5.24)

The steeple arrived by truck and was reinstalled by crane, almost two years after the damage was done. (Figure 5.25) The cross on top was set by two riggers working from boatswains chairs. The final work

Figure 5.22. Mobile, Alabama: Trinity Episcopal Church Parish House, 1960's, Showing South Wall which Fell Outward Through Suction during Hurricane Frederick, September 12, 1979.

Figure 5.23. Mobile, Alabama: Trinity Episcopal Church, Henry Dudley and Frank Wills, Archs., 1853, Removal by Sections of Steeple Damaged by Hurricane Frederick, September 12, 1979.

Figure 5.24. Mobile, Alabama: Trinity Episcopal Church, Henry Dudley and Frank Wills, Archs., 1853, Metal Replica of Steeple Destroyed by Hurricane Frederick, September 12, 1979.

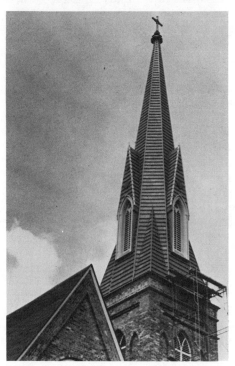

Figure 5.25. Mobile, Alabama: Trinity Episcopal Church, Henry Dudley and Frank Wills, Archs., 1853, Replaced Metal Replica of Steeple Destroyed by Hurricane Frederick, September 12, 1979.

329

has just been completed and consisted of organ repairs—clamping and reglueing of water damaged pews—refinishing of interior woodwork and recarpeting. The total cost—approximately $500,000. Happily for Trinity, it had the right kind of insurance in the right amount.

At my home, protective chores before the storm consisted of closing all window blinds. Most nineteenth century buildings were equipped with these wonderful devices. They provide light and rain control during normal weather and protection to old muntins and thin cylinder glass during storms. The problem is that none of the nineteenth century window frames were designed for insect screening, as it did not then exist. When screening became available, the screens were mounted in the rebates that had accommodated the blinds when they were in a closed position. This means that to close the blinds, one must first remove all screens and store them elsewhere—in my case, in the garage. It is time consuming and tedious, but well worthwhile. We did not have a single broken light.

The City of Mobile was not so fortunate with its museum in the Bernstein House which was originally built as a residence in 1872. Later it became a mortuary, and a coffin display room and a hearse garage were added. In 1972 it was acquired by the City, and we were asked to adapt it for re-use as a city museum. The double parlors became display spaces. (Figure 5.26) The roof of the garage was strengthened, and it was converted into a carriage display area. The coffin room was redesigned for the display of the gowns worn by our Mardi Gras Queens. We originally called for new blinds on all windows but, in an effort to cut costs, these were not installed. (Figure 5.27)

Just east of the Museum lies a circular multi-story stucco and aluminum Sheraton Hotel. During the night of September 12, great chunks of the Sheraton parted company and traveled west. Some were driven through the Museum's cast iron work and some through its unguarded windows. (Figure 5.28) Paintings were damaged by both water and wind-driven glass fragments. The roof membrane was blown off the old coffin room and the Mardi Gras Queens suffered the indignity of having to be undressed and dried out. Attempts at temporary waterproofing were made using polyethylene sheets. These were not nearly as effective as Trinity's use of canvas—partly because of the area involved and partly because plastic is much lighter than canvas, and hence, more subject to movement by even light air.

We were retained to handle the repairs but work was slow getting under way because Alabama has a law that requires competitive bidding on all public works. This meant documents had to be prepared, advertised, bid, and so forth. But the work was accomplished, and this time the Museum Board found the money to install operable blinds. (Figure 5.29)

The problem of protecting glass is most serious in church buildings. Leaded glass is extremely valuable and lead cames simply do not have the strength to withstand hurricane forces. (Figure 5.30) Exterior coverings of plastic materials such as "Lexan" may offend the eye of the purist, but I know of no window so protected that suffered damage. (Figure 5.31)

330

Figure 5.26. Mobile, Alabama: Bernstein House, 1872, Double Parlor Display Area.

Figure 5.27. Mobile, Alabama: Bernstein House, 1872, Without Window Shutters Before Hurricane Frederick, September 12, 1979.

Figure 5.28. Mobile, Alabama: Bernstein House, 1872, Damage to Cast Iron by Hurricane Frederick, September 12, 1979.

Figure 5.29. Mobile, Alabama: Bernstein House, 1872, Restored With Window Shutters after Hurricane Frederick, September 12, 1979.

332

Figure 5.30. Mobile, Alabama: Trinity Episcopal Church, Henry Dudley and Frank Wills, Archs., 1853, Damage to Leaded Glass from Hurricane Frederick, September 12-13, 1979.

Figure 5.31. Mobile, Alabama: Trinity Episcopal Church, Henry Dudley and Frank Wills, Archs., 1853, Leaded Glass Protected by Lexan after Hurricane Frederick, September 12-13, 1979.

Eaves are particularly vulnerable. Some buildings suffered eave damage due to falling trees; others to wind alone. (Figure 5.32) The Gillis House was built in Biloxi in 1839, though it would look more at home in eighteenth century Louisiana. It lost its eaves during "Camille" in 1969. During its rehabilitation, we were particularly concerned with providing additional strength at the corners. Double steel angles were concealed within the corner eave boxings. Steel plates were bolted on the sides of other lookouts—prominent before painting but hardly noticeable after painting. The steel members were rigidly anchored to the main roof framing and these long elegant eaves withstood "Frederic". (Figure 5.33)

Any element that projects vertically above a roof line catches the wind. Numerous modern buildings suffered grievously when roof mounted air conditioning equipment was blown from supports. It is common knowledge in our area that Christ Episcopal Church lost its steeple in the storm of 1906 and it was never rebuilt.

In 1967 we were asked to rehabilitate Barton Academy, the first public school in Alabama. It was designed by James Gallier and Charles Dakin in 1835. (Figure 5.34) Of particular concern to us was its dome—carried on wood trusses supported by both masonry walls and wood columns. We ran interior levels and found that the column foundations had settled 6 inches. This settlement increased the deflection of the trusses and caused the dome to lean. We designed a four-legged steel structure to relieve the older members and the dome suffered no damage in 1979. (Figure 5.35)

The Capitol of the State of Alabama in Montgomery was built in 1850. The original columns on the promenade around the dome had wood shafts and carved wood capitals. (Figure 5.36) In 1906, four of the 12 wood capitals were replaced with terra cotta reproductions. (Figure 5.37) By 1977 all were in advanced states of deterioration and one column collapsed during a windstorm and fell to the roof below. During the exterior rehabilitation of the building we took various parts of the eight remaining wood capitals and made one complete model. Using the original wood members for patterns we had twelve replacements cast in aluminum. Because of the intricacy of the shapes, each capital was made up of sixty different castings, screwed or heliarced to an aluminum drum. The results were delightful—the original chisel marks, knot holes and graining transferred from wood, to sand, to aluminum. (Figure 5.38)

During our work on the dome we found that, because of its shape, it acts much like an airplane wing and leans into the wind. Therefore, we anchored it to the deck below with steel members. It made for a strange sequence of erection—certainly not historical. Steel columns made into sections were threaded through bases and capitals. Then the steel columns were joined with weldments, and finally the original wood shafts were wrapped around the steel columns, then banded, and glued into position. (Figure 5.39)

Nineteenth century masonry buildings in our area were built with lime mortar —a mixture of lime made from burned oyster shells and sand. New lime mortar is weak and prohibited by the Standard

Figure 5.32. Mobile, Alabama: Damage to Eaves of Houses by Hurricane Frederick, September 12, 1979.

Figure 5.33. Biloxi, Mississippi: Gillis House, 1839, Eaves Lost in Hurricane Camille, August 18, 1969, Restored and Strengthened Which Survived Hurricane Frederick, September 12, 1979.

Figure 5.34. Mobile, Alabama: Barton Academy, James Gallier, Sr. and Charles B. Dakin, Archs., 1835.

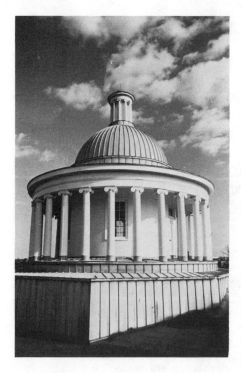

Figure 5.35. Mobile, Alabama: Barton Academy, James Gallier, Sr. and Charles B. Dakin, Archs., 1835, Restored and Strengthened Dome Which Survived Hurricane Frederick, September 12, 1979.

Figure 5.36. Montgomery, Alabama: Alabama State Capitol, 1850, Deteriorated Wooden Capital.

Figure 5.37. Montgomery, Alabama: Alabama State Capitol, 1850, Terra Cotta Replacement Capitals Made in 1906.

337

Figure 5.38. Montgomery, Alabama: Alabama State Capitol, 1850, Cast Aluminum Replacement Capitals Made in 1977.

Figure 5.39. Montgomery, Alabama: Alabama State Capitol, 1850, Sectional Steel Columns Threaded Through Base and Capital Being Wrapped by Wood Shafts.

338

Building Code in hurricane zones. Old lime mortar, and lime stucco, is worse as moisture moving through the walls leaches out the lime and leaves only the sand. Many of our masonry structures suffered wall failures due to the direct force of wind on their north and east facades. Our office is in an 1850 slave wing and was no exception. At first we thought we had survived with little damage but eighteen days later, when we finally regained electric power, we found that the east wall had moved westwardly one and one-half inches, where it came into contact with heavy casework that saved it from total collapse. It was taken down and rebuilt.

The masonry failure at City Hall was more spectacular. (Figure 5.40) Our City Hall was built in 1854 with administrative offices on the second floor and the municipal market on the ground level. It is one of the few of its kind left and is now a National Historic Landmark. The walls in the pedimented east facade of the South Annex and the south wing of the main building were both blown into the attic spaces. (Figure 5.41) The wind then blew into the attics and first blew down the ceilings of the second floors. The entire volume of the second floors was then pressurized until huge sections of the the roof literally exploded. Temporary efforts to secure the building failed—the damaged areas were too great. The City rented temporary offices elsewhere, vacated the building and retained us to do not just storm repairs but a much needed total rehabilitation.

Our first bid package consisted of temporary repairs to get the buildings dry and protect them from further damage. Help arrived from a strange quarter. City Hall had been documented with measured drawings prepared by the Historic American Buildings Survey. We obtained copies, and they enabled us to produce the bid documents and secure the buildings much faster than if we had been required to measure them. It was rather spooky—son Nicholas the third and I, busy using HABS drawings made in 1935 by N. H. Holmes, my father. We installed new framing, a temporary roof and secured all damaged openings with plywood.

The rehabilitation is now under way. Among other items of work, all floors will be raised above the high water mark. All king post trusses will receive relieving steel angles and all structural members will be securely anchored. (Figure 5.42)

And what of the masonry walls whose failure caused all the damage? Barton Academy is twenty years older and had no masonry problems. Nor did the Government Street Presbyterian Church, also designed by Gallier and Dakin in 1835. (Figure 5.43) In my opinion, the difference is that City Hall still had its lime stucco, by now weak and friable. The church had its stucco replaced 20 years ago and Barton received new stucco during our work in 1967. In both cases, lime stucco was not reused and there is no apparent ill effects caused by the change.

I am aware that this is at odds with the thinking of our friends in Technical Preservation Services who have recommended to me reapplying lime stucco and viewing it as a "sacrificial coating".

Figure 5.40. Mobile, Alabama: Mobile City Hall, 1854, Damaged by
Hurricane Frederick, September 12, 1979.

Figure 5.41. Mobile, Alabama: Mobile City
Hall, 1854, Gable Wall Blown into Attic
by Hurricane Frederick, September 12, 1979.

Figure 5.42. Mobile, Alabama: Mobile City Hall, 1854, Restored After
Damage by Hurricane Frederick, September 12, 1979.

Figure 5.43. Mobile, Alabama: Government Street Presbyterian Church,
James Gallier, Sr. and Charles B. Dakin, Archs., 1835, Which
Survived Hurricane Frederick, September 12, 1979.

341

We believe that in our hazardous area we must give our old buildings every help we can. We recommend first the removal of all lime stucco, the application of galvanized self-furring key mesh lath, and then 1 to 1 and 1/4 inches of stucco consisting of a mixture of sand, portland cement, masons mix, and a small quantity of lime for plasticity. In some cases, where the mortar is extremely friable on both exterior and interior, we stucco both sides of the walls.

By now I daresay that many of you wonder why anyone would choose to live in such a place with the sword of Damocles tenuously tethered above, and with the tread constantly subjected to the eroding forces of wind and water. Possibly I have exaggerated. I have lived there for over 55 years—and actually—we've only had one day of bad weather.

Preparedness for Natural Disasters for Monuments and Artifacts

Lawrence J. Majewski

During the Summer of 1953 I was loaned out by the Metropolitan Museum to the Byzantine Institute of America in Istanbul to work on the restoration of the 14th century Byzantine frescoes in the Kariye Djami in Istanbul, Turkey, where I encountered damages to many cultural monuments caused by earthquakes. The destruction that had taken place many decades before my sojourn there was very much in evidence and conservation to prevent additional loss of structures and artifacts became a part of my work activities.

Supporting arches and pendentives for the dome of the Kariye Paraecclesion were cracked and in danger of collapsing. A dome vault in front of the apse of the mortuary chapel had split and the crack caused by the earthquake had separated about four inches, two smaller domes in other parts of the church had cracked and shifted, one was held up with wooden struts. Walls were weakened and drainage gutters were filled with debris and the brick dome of the central church had been lost in a late 19th century earthquake and had been replaced with a wooden structure.

For the first time I became aware of the tremendous destructive force of earthquakes and that the earth is not a solid mass but is in a state of flux. The upper mantle wells up along certain geographical ridges causing movements of large areas of the earth's surface in what is known as "plates". These plates may spread, or subside, and one plate may plunge under another.

The energy released by an earthquake of a magnitude of 8.5 on the Richter scale is equivalent to 12,000 times the energy released by the Hiroshima nuclear bomb. [Office of Emergency Preparedness, 1972] The foci of these cataclysms may be well below the earth's surface and in a few seconds thousands of lives may be lost and whole cities destroyed. Earthquakes are the most difficult disaster phenomena to prepare for as they may occur without warning at any time of day or night. And not only are there damages from earth shaking and surface faulting, earthquakes may trigger other disasters such as floods, fires, landslides and tidal waves.

Since warning of an oncoming earthquake cannot be given, preparedness measures must take into account the vulnerability of

343

certain areas where there is seismic risk. Earthquake-prone areas include some of the most densely populated regions of the world such as Japan, the Western United States, shores of the Mediterranean Sea and Central and South America as well as more remote regions such as Alaska and the Aleutian Islands.

Proper engineering considerations in the construction of shelters, museums and monuments can do much to reduce the loss of life and property during an earthquake. Proper action taken during and immediately after an earthquake will also lessen the vulnerability of those living in an earthquake area.

Earthquake destruction to cultural artifacts may be total in many instances or it may be of such a nature as to allow recovery of a major part of damaged objects through conservation and repair. The restoration process may take years to treat even a fraction of the collapsed, cracked or broken objects.

In any natural disaster, reconstruction priorities must be determined. Of first priority is the rescue of human life and establishment of a security procedure to prevent looting and thefts. Plans for disasters should be established on local, state and national levels, perhaps through the organization of a type of Red Cross for salvaging our cultural heritage in times of destructive natural phenomena. Such an organization for rescuing art may well be put in operation also during times of armed conflict when bombings, air attacks and military ground forces lay waste our historic past.

When flood waters inundated the cities of Florence and Venice on the night of November 4, 1966, the world was shocked to learn of the destruction that flood caused to so many great masterpieces in two centers of the greatest concentration of superb monuments of creative geniuses. In Florence, a city plagued by several recorded floods from that of 1333 through the 19th century, the flood of 1966 proved to be the most severe that had ever occurred. Many great paintings, sculptures and artifacts were destroyed or severely damaged. However, much that might have completely deteriorated after the flood waters receded was saved thanks to almost reflex reactions of first the Italian conservators, students and volunteers and then of International teams such as the United States group known as the Committee to Rescue Italian Art (CRIA).

Art historians including Fred Hart and Bates Lowry responded almost immediately to found CRIA and within a few days I was recruited to organize a group of American art conservators to fly to Italy to do whatever we could to help. Our former first lady, Mrs. John F. Kennedy, accepted the honorary chairmanship of CRIA and a drive was begun to raise funds in America to help pay for materials and skills to save the art of Florence and Venice.

Within a period of ten days I had gathered together 17 from among our nation's best qualified art conservators and we were on our way by Alitalia to Rome arriving on November 15, 1966. By train we travelled to Florence where we were met by the Director of I Tatti and assigned to living quarters from which we could emerge each day to go to assigned museums, churches, or libraries to help in any way possible.

Untrained students from Italian Universities and groups of volunteers under supervision of Italian conservators, curators and other professionals had already performed miracles in administering first aid to critically injured paintings, sculptures, and artifacts of all types as well as inundated library and archival collections. Paintings had been faced with protective tissue papers using whatever was on hand - sometimes even colored facial tissues served this purpose. Broken fragile objects were sorted and collected into plastic bags and suitable containers for later reassembly including such varied artifacts as musical instruments, ceramics and glass, sculpture and artifacts made of metal, leather, wood, stone and other materials.

Our committee met each day with Italian authorities to decide where our next day's efforts could prove most useful. In a relatively short time, thanks to an atmosphere of international cooperation, much was rescued and centers were established for long-term treatment that would follow through the years - some of which still continue now 16 years after that natural disaster.

Both Florence and Venice are unique cities that could inspire such rapid organization of conservation forces. Earthquake and disaster damages in many other parts of the world have never aroused quite as great an activity. And even in Florence perhaps more could have been saved if a Disaster Rescue Mission had existed to be called upon when the cataclysm struck.

We need today and for the future an active International Natural Disaster Committee organized on National, State and Local levels to plan and carry out emergency rescue activities immediately following an earthquake, flood, fire or other sudden destruction. Headquarters for these Rescue Missions may be located within National Laboratories, Regional Conservation Centers, large museums, conservation training centers and universities with fine arts departments.

In order to organize a Natural Disaster Committee for art objects, a feasibility study must first be made, perhaps with a group of no more than eight to ten participants. On the planning committee there should be representatives from government, museum directors and/or curators, conservators, conservation scientists and communications experts. Such subjects as membership, location of centers, objectives and procedures should be discussed and perhaps some kind of constitution and by-laws for a Natural Disaster Committee could be proposed.

After a Natural Disaster Committee is organized, existing laboratories in museums or elsewhere may function as headquarters where personnal are located and materials and supplies are stockpiled for a possible emergency. With proper preparation and organization the emergency squad could be dispatched to the site of disaster and begin to function.

REFERENCES

U.S. Office of Emergency Preparedness. <u>Disaster Preparedness</u>. Washington, D.C.: U.S. Government Printing Office, January 1972, Volume 3, p. 72.

Emergency Conservation of Earthquake-Damaged Objects of Polychromed Wood in Friuli, Italy

Bernard Rabin and Constance S. Silver

INTRODUCTION

The series of earthquakes that struck Friuli, Italy, in 1976 were disastrous both for the inhabitants and cultural resources of this region. 1000 people were killed and hundreds were injured and left homeless. Several historic towns were levelled, hundreds of churches were destroyed or seriously affected, and almost 1000 polychromed wooden objects were damaged, often severely.

Emergency relief for the inhabitants began immediately, and rescue of the art and architecture within a few days after the first earthquakes. Through the assistance of American institutions and foundations, and with the generous support of the Italian authorities, American conservators were given the opportunity to participate in the post–earthquake program to conserve Friuli's damaged art. Specifically, the authors were able to examine 428 damaged objects of polychromed wood, establish a small laboratory for emergency treatments, and treat 21 objects with the assistance of a team of American and Italian conservation students.

This work, and its lessons and ramifications for polychromed wood in the United States' seismic zones, is the basis of this paper. However, in addition to the actual conservation work in Friuli, the authors were also given the opportunity to live for six months in an area that had been devastated by earthquakes, an experience that has shown us the practical constraints and human dimensions that accompany the salvage of art after a disaster. It must be noted, however, that our experience in Friuli does not permit us to construct an airtight "model" that can be applied to polychromed wood in all earthquakes: regions and their art differ too greatly. Rather, we believe that our work in Friuli allows us to make several general observations about the conditions and conservation problems that Americans might expect after an earthquake, and the measures they can take before and after to protect polychromed wood and mitigate damage. Three general points will be discussed in this paper:

1. Types of Damage. Objects are damaged directly from falling rubble during an earthquake or upon impact if the object is dislodged from its support. Indirect, but often serious, damage can occur if the object is subjected to exposure from the elements, shock during transport away from the damaged structure, and poor storage facilities after the earthquake.
2. Materials and Techniques of Emergency Conservation Measures. Although long-term treatments are often required, relatively simple measures can and should be taken to stabilize the object and arrest active deterioration.
3. Preparedness. Damage to objects can be mitigated if preparatory measures are taken before earthquakes occur.

THE FRIULI: CULTURAL PATRIMONY AND THE EARTHQUAKES OF 1976

The province of Friuli is located in the northeastern corner of Italy. It is bordered on the east by Yugoslavia and the north by Austria. Overshadowed by such spectacular near-neighbors as Venice, to the south, Friuli has remained a somewhat isolated and little-known area of Italy where the inhabitants have maintained their own Romance language and distinctive culture.

Geographically, Friuli encompasses the Carnic Alps on the north, while the south is characterized by rolling plains. This topography, coupled with proximity to the Adriatic Sea, give Friuli the highest level of rainfall in Italy, a condition which exacerbated the rescue of both the inhabitants and art after the 1976 earthquakes. The major cities of Friuli, Udine and Pordenone, are located on the plains, but both the plains and mountains boast hundreds of small churches, many of medieval origin. These churches are embellished with the polychromed wooden sculpture that is perhaps the most characteristic art form of Friuli.

Unfortunately, Friuli's sculpture was little-known before the 1976 earthquakes. With the exception of one book, it has been neglected in art history literature. [Marchetti and Nicoletti, 1956] Italian authorities were in the process of making an inventory when the earthquakes struck. Consequently, this aspect of the region's art was not well understood, nor were its large numbers appreciated. The often isolated locations of the scupture had not been noted, nor had the generally poor state of conservation of wood and polychromy.

These conditions combined to exacerbate conservation problems after the earthquakes. For example, wood already weakened by woodworm activity fractured easily from impact of falling rubble. Loose polychromy was detached from the wood during transport away from damaged structures. Due to the isolated sites of churches, some objects remained under rain-soaked rubble for several weeks, until they could be removed by any vehicle that could navigate damaged and often dangerous roads. Rescue personnel were generally ill-equipped

348

because of shortages of supplies. Nevertheless, Italian authorities were able to establish five depositories for displaced and damaged art. The largest of these was located in the deconsecrated medieval church of San Francesco, Udine. 1500 objects were stored in this depository, which was the site of the first stage of the authors' work in Friuli.

THE CONSERVATION OF POLYCHROMED WOODEN SCULPTURE IN FRIULI

From January to September, 1977, the authors carried out conservation measures in three major stages: condition survey of objects in the depository of San Francesco, establishment of a small conservation laboratory in the Chapter Room of the church of San Francesco, Cividale, and treatment of 21 objects. These stages are described.

Condition Survey of Polychromed Sculpture

In the first quarter of 1977, the authors had the opportunity to survey the condition of objects in the most important of the regional depositories, San Francesco, Udine. The depository opened on 10 May 1976, four days after the first earthquake of May 6. It boasted considerable floor space, enlarged by the construction of a temporary first floor in July, 1976. The stone building was unheated, and its relative humidity averaged 85 percent.

At the time the survey was conducted the disposition of over 1500 objects was generally as follows: polychromed wooden sculptures were placed on low wooden platforms in order to prevent direct contact with the damp floor; stone objects, assorted church furniture, altarpieces, and objects of lesser value were stored directly on the brick floor; canvas paintings without stretchers were stacked or rolled on large cylinders on the first floor after facings had been adhered with animal glue; canvas paintings on stretchers and a few panel paintings were scattered throughout the church. Cabinets and tables were set up on the first floor to provide a temporary restoration facility.

Some general observations can be made about the depository of San Francesco. First, by luck this large, empty and unused building was available in an area that had remained relatively undamaged by the earthquakes. Its size allowed both deposition of objects and administrative duties associated with them to be carried in the same building. A very good alarm system was installed in the depository. Finally, the interior climate proved generally conducive to the conservation of the objects, which had previously been housed in cool and damp churches. However, as the temperature of the church rose, mold growth developed on some previously unaffected objects. It is also possible that some objects became infested with woodworms from close proximity to already-infested objects.

Some photographic documentation and emergency treatments were carried out in San Francesco in the first months following the earthquakes of May, 1976. However, no comprehensive survey of the objects had been made. Therefore, FRIAM (Friuli Arts and Monuments) supported a survey to identify objects actively deteriorating and classify them on the basis of urgency of treatment and transportability to another laboratory for treatment. On the basis of the survey, it was possible to select objects which could most benefit by treatment by conservators the following summer. (Figure 5.44)

Because of time limitations, individual examinations were restricted to the most severely damaged category of object, the polychromed wooden sculptures. Four categories, designating different urgency of treatment, proved convenient for classification of the 428 objects examined. Brief examination forms were filled out, accompanied by photographs, for the objects requiring major intervention (174); brief notes were made for minimally damaged sculptures (254). Forms completed in English were deposited with FRIAM, while Italian forms containing the same information were given to the appropriate regional and national authorities.

Many objects suffered direct damage from the earthquake, manifested in support fragmentation, surface abuse, imbedded rubble, and loss of decorative and structural elements. Others suffered damage from exposure to the elements after the earthquake, aggravated by the heavy precipitation in the Summer of 1976. This produced luxuriant mold growth, wood distortion as a result of alternating wet/dry cycles, and dismemberment caused by the dissolution of structural adhesives. Changes in the ambience of the objects generally decreased paint/ground adhesion. Finally, transport to Udine often occurred in old trucks or army jeeps, and associated shock may well have compounded losses. Clearly, the generally poor pre-earthquake condition of the objects exacerbated damage. In particular, marked woodworm tunnelling contributed to the easy breakage of the statues.

Laboratory in the Church of San Francesco, Cividale

The small medieval town of Cividale is located 17 km from Udine. Because there was insufficient space in San Francesco, Udine, it was decided to establish a small conservation laboratory in the Chapter Room of the Church of San Francesco, Cividale. (Figure 5.45) This room measured about 30 feet by 25 feet, had superb natural light from large windows, and a small raised annex that was well adapted to use as a secure and controllable storage area for the objects to be treated.

Figure 5.44. Udine, Italy: Church of San Francesco, Depository for Displaced Objects after Survey and Reorganization of Items Following Earthquake of May 6, 1976.

Figure 5.45. Cividale del Friuli, Italy: Church of San Francesco where Conservation Laboratory was Established in Chapter Room after Earthquake of May 6, 1976.

It should be noted that the actual conservation treatments to stabilize the objects—to be described in the following section—were often complex and required experienced conservators. However, it is also significant to note that relatively few alterations to the room and fairly simple equipment were required to create a functioning laboratory. A sink was installed and nearby plumbing brought in. A steel security door was installed on the storage annex. A hydrothermograph was placed in the annex to monitor ambient conditions, which were found to be extremely stable. A security system of double locks was placed on the two doors of the laboratory. No alarm system was installed.

Sturdy, smooth and inexpensive second-hand school tables and chairs were purchased for use as work tables. New screw-top lamps were purchased. A hydrothermograph was also installed in the work area. Readings commenced on May 10, 1977 and concluded on September 11, 1977. In this four-month period, the temperature ranged from 15° - 21° centigrade, relative humidity from about 85 percent to 65 percent.

The inventory of the laboratory given in Table I is indicative of the materials required for conservation treatments directed at the stabilization of seriously damaged objects.

Treatments of Earthquake-Damaged Objects

21 objects were treated over a four-month period, after selection by Italian authorities. Laboratory personnel generally numbered between 8 - 10 individuals, made up of Italian and American conservation students supervised by a senior American conservator. Throughout, the laboratory remained in contact with Italian conservation authorities in Friuli.

Objects were selected for treatment on the basis of their need for stabilization, to prevent further deterioration from, for example, abrasion or distortion of broken joints, or loss of polychromy and small detached pieces of support. All 21 objects were suffering, in varying degrees, from poorly attached polychromy and supports damaged and weakened by insects, a condition which had contributed to the breakage and dismemberment. Eight samples of wood were analyzed by the Forest Products Lab, Madison, Wisconsin. Six of the eight were identified as basswood or linden (Tilia sp.). The applied drapery on one statue was identified as poplar (Populus sp.). A cross from one scene of the Crucifixion was identified as spruce (Picea so.), indicating that it is almost certainly a modern addition.

The general conservation measures entailed: removal of surface dirt and rubble; attachment of loose paint; consolidation of the wood; and assembly of separated sections. No attempt was made to treat aesthetic problems, such as overpaint or surface lacunae. Fumigation was recommended and ultimately carried out by Italian authorities

352

Table I
Inventory of Materials: Laboratory in Church of San Francesco, Cividale

Electrical Instruments

1 drill
1 saw attachment for drill
1 grinding wheel for drill
3 hot spatulas
1 hair dryer

Clamps

6 German wooden clamps
3 home-made wooden clamps
1 large home-made wooden clamp
5 metal bar clamps
2 large metal bar clamps
2 red "C" clamps
4 10cm metal screw clamps
2 8cm metal screw clamps
2 12cm sliding metal bar clamps
2 10cm sliding metal bar clamps
2 7cm sliding bar clamps

Miscellaneous Instruments

1 tripod
1 flashlight
1 sharpening stone
1 small strainer
1 funnel
1 aluminum pail, 27cm deep

Furniture

6 desks
1 large table
1 temporary table on saw horses
10 chairs
5 screwtop lamps
    fluorescent lamp
1 large storage cupboard with drawers
1 large cupboard with shelves
1 bookshelf
1 foot stool
1 coatrack

Chemicals and Analytical Substances

Concentrated Ammonium
Concentrated Hydrochloric Acid
Saturated Solution of Tin Chloride
$K_2Fe(CN)_6$

KI H_2O distilled
Box of cover slips
Box of pipettes

Hand Tools

1 hand saw
1 hack saw
1 coping saw
1 large claw hammer
1 rubber mallet
2 tack hammers
1 large screwdriver
2 small screwdrivers
1 straight chisel
1 curved chisel
1 pliers
1 scissors
1 paint scraper
1 file (fine)
1 file (medium)
1 file (course)
1 round sureform rasp
1 level
2 folding rulers
1 large awl
1 small awl
5 scalpels
1 tweezers
1 plastic triangle
1 hand drill
8 wood bits
2 palette knives
1 block plane

Conservation Materials

Acryloid B72 ("Paraloid")
Polyvinyl Alcohol
Polyvinyl Acetate Resin
Polyvinyl Acetate Emulsion
Sodium Lauryl Sulphate Detergent (Orvus 1
    WA Paste)
Urea Formaldehyde Resin ("WeldWood")
Liquid Fungicide (made by Mildy Co., Milan)
Surface Active Agent (Foto Flow)
Diluente Nitro (an Italian lacquer thinner)

Diluted Ammonium
Ethanol
Dilute Nitric Acid
$K_2(Hg(CN)_4)$

Box of microscope slides
Micro-pipette
Rubber nipples

when a facility was installed in a new conservation laboratory constructed at Passariano, Friuli.

The conservation problems and treatments of 5 of the 21 objects are described:

Statue of Madonna and Child

From the Chiesa di S. Giovanni, Gemona, 16th century, gilded and polychromed poplar wood. Madonna's torso 87 x 45 x 33 cm. Child's torso 36 x 17 x 12 cm. The back of the sculpture from the shoulder down was concave, but hollow in a U shape.

Condition Before Treatment. The figure of the Madonna was broken in four main sections. Both hands were broken and there were multiple fractures, especially in the base segments. The top half of the Madonna was broken at the waist. (Figure 5.46) The right forearm which holds the Child was also separated. The left knee of the Madonna was the most notable missing piece. Other pieces lost were from the right and left shoulder, left side below chest, and numerous small places at the base. There were multiple fractures of the wood scattered throughout, as well as imbedded rubble. In some areas the paint layer had been washed away by water, exposing raw wood, and in other parts the gesso ground remained. The paint layer on the face and hands had wrinkled from excessive moisture. The area from above the chest and in the forehead and crown appeared dark brown, as if subjected to fire. The right base segment had been crushed by fallen objects during the earthquake. (Figure 5.47) There was also evidence that some of the pieces had been lying in water. These contained dimensional differences, throwing the upper portion of the wood out of plane. All edges of the broken pieces were altered by exposure and subsequent handling, thereby creating difficulties in making close joins. There were many paint losses, abrasions and scratches scattered throughout.

The figure of the Child was broken at both ankles and the left thigh was separated from the torso. The rear of the Child's decorative robe had been lying in water, with the result that it remained without shape. The right hand was missing. The left hand was broken and the head of the Child was broken at the base of the neck.

Treatment. Mud and rubble were brushed off. The wrinkling of the paint in the Madonna's face and hands was brought into plane by the application of rabbit-skin glue. Paint cleavage in other areas was treated by the same means. Cleavage in the gold leaf areas was treated with a solution of PVA-AYAA in "diluente nitro." Because of the weight of the various segments, a pulley system was devised to facilitate joinings. The upper torso of the Madonna was harnessed to it. The two base segments were attached with Vinavil and dowelled for further support. The third bottom segment has been crushed and distorted. It was treated with steam vapor and reset into its proper

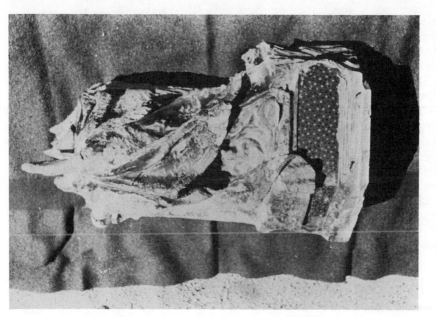

Figure 5.47. Gemona del Friuli, Italy: Chiesa di San Giovanni, 17th Century, Statue of Madonna and Child, Base Segment after Earthquake of May 6, 1976.

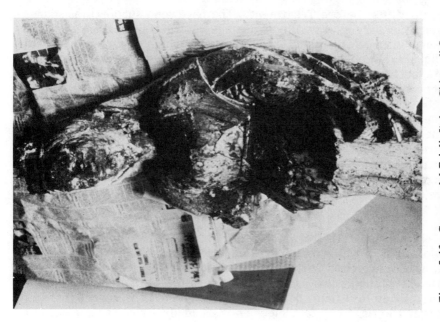

Figure 5.46. Gemona del Friuli, Italy: Chiesa di San Giovanni, 17th Century, Statue of Madonna and Child, Top Half after Earthquake of May 6, 1976.

position and it was also secured with Vinavil and dowelled to the torso. At the reverse side a 7.62 x 2.54 x 1.27 cm dowel was inserted into the two largest base pieces for additional security. The left hand holding the staff was reattached with Weldwood glue and a 1 cm dowel insert. The figure of the Child was positioned at the right knee of the Madonna and her broken hand was adhered to the Child's waist with Vinavil. The Child's head was attached to its neck, the left hand holding the orb was fitted with a 1 cm dowel and the left thigh was attached to the lower torso, all with the adhesive Vinavil. Open areas formed by missing pieces were filled with a putty of fine sawdust and Vinavil to prevent these areas from accumulating dirt and grime. The entire sculpture was given a protective coating of 5% solution of Paraloid B72 in "diluente nitro." (Figures 5.48, 5.49)

Statue of S. Rocco

By S. Urbano, Altarpiece of S. Rocco, Church of the Madonna del Giglio, Aprato di Tarcento, Height 80.5 cm; width 35 cm; depth 16 cm.

Condition Before Treatment. The hardwood support was sponge-like and powdery as a result of damage by wood-boring insects. This weakness apparently exacerbated breakage which occurred during the earthquake. The instability of the sculpture caused by the irregularity of its bottom surface and the statue's top-heaviness led to a fall before we came to the scene. Forty-five fragments were found shortly after the earthquake. The nose, right knee, neck and back of the head were notably missing. (The saint's right hand was lost prior to the disaster according to a pre-earthquake photograph.) Many of the fragments had been abraded, partly because of handling following the earthquake. Checks occurred throughout the sculpture. A second layer of ground had been applied over earlier remaining polychromy. There were scattered areas of poor adhesion between the earlier and later strata.

Treatment. All fragments were immersed in a dilute solution of Paraloid B72 in "diluente nitro" for periods of 48 to 72 hours. Loose paint was reattached with a heated spatula using a dilute solution of Vinavil. Fragments were joined under pressure with Vinavil. Prior to joining, three 6-8 mm dowels were inserted in prepared holes to reinforce the right and left knees and left ankle. A putty composed of Weldwood resin and fine sawdust was used to fill the cavity of the left shin and give leg support lacking in the right knee. A wood-filled putty was applied over the Weldwood putty bringing the lacunae to approximately the level of the original wood surface. Checks were stabilized with Vinavil. Although the neck was missing, it was possible to determine the proper position for reattachment of the head from a pre-earthquake photograph. In order to hold the head with a vertical dowel centered over the body, a balsa wood addition was carved to fit

Figure 5.48. Gemona del Friuli, Italy:
Chiesa di San Giovanni, 17th Century,
Statue of Madonna and Child Before
Earthquake of May 6, 1976, Showing Many
Coats of Repainting.

Figure 5.49. Gemona del Friuli, Italy:
Chiesa di San Giovanni, 17th Century,
Statue of Madonna and Child Reassembled
with much Original Color and Gold Leaf
Uncovered.

on the back center of the head. This was adhered under pressure with Vinavil. A 1 cm dowel was then adhered with Vinavil to holes drilled in the balsa wood and the body of the sculpture so that the head was correctly positioned. The area around the base of the dowel was reinforced with a putty of Vinavil, calcium carbonate and course sawdust.

Crucifixion

From Chiesa di Madonna del Giglio, Aprato di Tarcento, by G. A. Agostini (1604). Estimated dimensions before assembly: 70 x 66 x 15 cm.

Condition Before Treatment. Wood-boring insects had destroyed the support to such a degree that only the ground and paint held the sculpture together. It was impossible to find a single exposed area of wood from which a small sample could be taken for analysis. There were fresh breaks as a result of the earthquake which separated the figure into eight pieces: torso, two shoulders, head, two arms and two legs; the latter, however, were joined together by a nail which originally fastened them to the cross. (Figure 5.50) The left hand and part of the lower arm were carved from a new piece of wood dowelled to the original upper arm which itself showed an old repair. Parts of all the fingers of the left hand were missing and two fingers of the right hand. The right arm and hand were preserved, but so seriously worm-eaten that a small section joining the arm to the right shoulder was missing. The statue had been repainted and regilded at least once. There appeared to be modern gold on the loin cloth, overlaying a thick layer of light blue paint. Where the original flesh paint had been damaged, as in the large loss of Christ's left cheek, it had been covered by subsequent strata of ground and paint. The original flesh paint was yellowish in color, whereas the top layer was of a rosier tint applied with a coarse bristle brush. Cleavage occurred between the original and subsequent paint layers.

Treatment. The many areas of loose paint were fixed with animal glue. Where the loose paint was especially thick at the edges of breaks and could not be fixed successfully by this method, Vinavil in dilute form was applied by pipette and fixed the next day by hot spatula. When the paint surface was secure, grime and dirt were brushed off. Ingrained dirt was resistant to "diluente nitro" and other organic solvents, as well as to detergents. The paint surface, where it was intact, was tough and insoluable, and it was possible to remove much of the grime by rubbing with swabs in an enzyme medium. Cleaning disclosed that the original brown crown of thorns had been overpainted in green. The wood was consolidated with Paraloid B72, first by application of a 5% solution in "diluente nitro," applied with a pipette. The process was repeated each day for seven days; the concentration of Paraloid was gradually increased with each

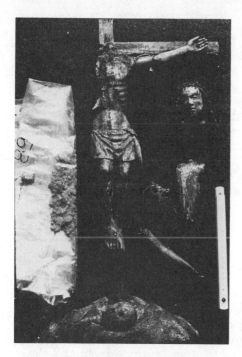

Figure 5.50. Aprato di Tarcento, Italy: Chiesa di Madonna Giglio, Crucifixion by G. A. Agostini, 1604, Damaged Pieces after Earthquake of May 6, 1976.

Figure 5.51. Aprato di Tarcento, Italy: Chiesa di Madonna Giglio, Crucifixion by G. A. Agostino, 1604, As Reassembled after Earthquake of May 6, 1976.

application until it reached about 20%. Between applications the sections were wrapped in aluminum foil to prevent evaporation and to aid penetration. The torso weighted 950 g before treatment, 1050 g after four days, thus absorbing 100 g of Paraloid B72 solution. Each separate section of the statue was consolidated in this way. Christ's right shoulder weighed 350 g before treatment, 400 g after. Shoulders and head were joined to the torso with Vinavil; elastic bands were used to exert the necessary pressure where clamps were not feasible. The joins were not close because so much of the worm-eaten wood had crumbled away. Arms and legs could not be joined to the torso because of the missing intermediate sections. Also, because the lower vertical member of the cross was missing and there was not time to make a new one, there was nothing to support the feet of Christ. (Figure 5.51)

Sixteenth Century Painted Wooden Tabernacle

From Chiesa di S. Giovanni Battista, Maiano. The tabernacle consists of a painted wooden framework with hinged doors painted on the interior (Annunciation) and exterior (beheading of John the Baptist); interior pediment (God the Father with Seraphim). The framework has carved moulding painted in imitation of marble.

The interior central panel is missing. The paint appears to be a "tempera grasso" (mixed oil and tempera medium) applied with low-brush-marking over a thin preparation of gesso. There is no apparent varnish layer. The support is estimated to be softwood, probably pine. Iron nails and hinges, now rusted, have been used to assemble the various panels and mouldings. Certain sections of moulding around the doors appear to be modern replacments as is the lower right section of the proper right door.

	Height (cm)	Width (cm)	Thickness (cm)
Framework	164.5	116.5	14.5
Doors	139	43	1.5
Pediment	40.5	93	

Condition. The tabernacle was in markedly poor and fragmentary condition, covered with a layer of filth and rubble. The support was fractured in numerous places totalling 30 fragments, 13 of which had very little extant design. (Figure 5.52) Each door exhibited a longitudinal split down the entire length which cut the panel in half. The wood was moderately worm-tunnelled but generally was sound and not in need of consolidation. The soft, water-soluble gesso ground was lost or appeared abraded in many areas. Scattered lifting ridges of cleaved gesso were evident, particularly at the bottom of the left door (exterior). In numerous areas the gesso-and-paint film was actively flaking from the support, particularly on the left center of the proper

Figure 5.52. Maiano, Italy: Chiesa di San Giovanni Battista, Tabernacle, 17th Century, Broken Pieces after Earthquake of May 6, 1976.

Figure 5.53. Maiano, Italy: Chiesa di San Giovanni Battista, Tabernacle, 17th Century, Rejoining Segments of Door after Earthquake of May 6, 1976.

right door (exterior) and around the iron hinges. There were numerous losses, abrasions and scratches, some of which were obviously old, such as the large losses of green paint (and underlying gesso) and graffiti at bottom of left door (interior), while others appeared to be the result of the earthquake. The paint was generally quite powdery and required consolidation. The fragments of the left door had suffered a great deal of damage to the paint film as well as the support. The exterior surface of these pieces had been extremely abraded, suffering roughly a 50% loss of paint, thus exposing a large portion of gesso preparation.

Treatment. After mechanically removing accretions of dirt and rubble from the altarpiece, areas of cleaving paint were fixed with dilute rabbit-skin glue. The entire painted surface, which was extremely friable, was then consolidated by brushing on a 5% solution of Gelvatol 40-20, in equal amounts of water and denatured alcohol. Japanese tissue was laid over the Gelvatol-treated area which was then ironed through several layers of facial tissue with a hot spatula to draw out excess moisture. This treatment was found to consolidate the paint while not staining or creating an undesired surface sheen. Stains and a disfiguring layer of grime were removed by lightly cleaning with a dilute solution of Orvus WA Paste.

The long process of reassembly began by eliminating the distortions in the many fragments. This was accomplished by moistening the individual fragments with hot water and clamping or weighting to coax the distortions back into plane. (Figure 5.53) The pieces were joined by glueing with Vinavil, and dowelling where necessary--5 dowels in the proper left door, 12 in the right. Cavities which were created by insect activity leaving an unsupported design layer were filled with a putty composed of sawdust, calcium carbonate and Vinavil. Three lacunae in the right door, through which daylight was visible, were filled with thin balsa wood inserts, toned to match the surrounding wood, and glued in place with Vinavil. In order further to consolidate the paint and to impregnate the pigments on the fragmentary half of the right door, a dilute solution of Paraloid B72, approximately 5% in "diluente nitro," was brushed on, thus rendering much of the "lost" design visible. A final coating of 5% Paraloid B72 was then applied. Successive procedural steps were necessary to correct the insecurity of the overall structure. Loose member planks were secured with brass mending straps and screws. These were also used to secure the pediment and its moulding and to mount it in place. The severely corroded iron nails which had held the hinges were removed, the holes left in their place were plugged with dowels, and the doors rehung by fastening the hinges with brass screws. Two horizontal wooden battens were attached to the reverse of the tabernacle with brass screws in elliptical slots to provide security to the framework yet allow slight movement of the wood. Finally, temporary battens were mounted to the reverse to facilitate handling. (Figures 5.54, 5.55)

Figure 5.54. Maiano, Italy: Chiesa di San Giovanni Battista, Tabernacle, 17th Century, Rejoined, Closed after Earthquake of May 6, 1976.

Figure 5.55. Maiano, Italy: Chiesa di San Giovanni Battista, Tabernacle, 17th Century, Rejoined, Opened, after Earthquake of May 6, 1976.

16th century. From the Chiesa Matrice di S. Lorenzo, Buia. Size 140 x 40 x 38 cm. The entire sculpture was in pieces. The major segments were torso, base and feet, legs (four pieces), head in multiple pieces with parts missing, and many other fragments. In many areas, paint was all that held pieces together. The wooden support was severely worm-tunnelled, spongy, and mostly powder.

Treatment. The dirt and discolored varnish were removed with 50:50 "diluente nitro" and alcohol. This was not only to clean with sculpture, but also to aid in better penetration during consolidation. Each piece was immersed in a solution of 10% Paraloid B72 in "diluente nitro" for 24 hours. The torso was immersed for 48 hours, increasing the concentration of B72 after the first day. The pieces were air-dried for three weeks, and loose paint was set down with dilute Vinavil, pressure and heat. The segments were assembled with Vinavil and reinforced with Weldwood resin and sawdust. It was not possible to use dowels because there was not enough solid wood at the join areas to drill into.

Most of the wood from inside the head had been eaten away by insects. Once the face and hair segments were assembled, the head was a hollow cavity and it was necessary to fill it with small balsa wood blocks for structural support. The hair section was only paint and linen. This was reinforced with Japanese tissue and Vinavil before setting in place. A 52 cm section of the tree supporting St. Sebastian was missing. A balsa wood insert was constructed to fill the gap. In order for the figure to stand, it was necessary to secure a strip of hardwood to the back of the tree with brass screws. This was attached at the top of the tree, at the balsa strip and tree stump and at the base. It was hoped this support would carry the weight of the figure because the legs were so badly damaged that they could not support the weight. The original base was not level, causing the figure to tip forward. A new base of hardwood was constructed. Wedges were placed between the original and new base, levelling the piece and making it appear to stand properly.

FRIULI AND ITS LESSONS FOR DISASTER PREPAREDNESS IN THE UNITED STATES

From this description of our work in Friuli, it is evident that there are many differences between Friuli and the United States. First, the United States does not have a great number of polychromed wooden objects scattered throughout isolated and almost inaccessible areas. Second, polychromed wood in the United States will most probably be in generally good condition because it is under some form of curatorial care, rather than dispersed throughout hundreds of churches.   Finally, post-earthquake rescue efforts will probably be simpler in the United States.

However, there are several useful lessons that Americans can learn from Friuli's experiences. First, it should be noted that Friuli, like most seismic areas of the world, had not developed a contingency plan for individual buildings, their objects, or for the province in general. Therefore, those in charge of historic buildings and their collections in a given area of known seismic activity should meet to discuss both the risks and ways to alleviate damage before an earthquake strikes.

Those individuals in charge of collections must first consider the structure in which the objects are housed: will it survive an earthquake? what parts of it are liable to collapse? can water and gas pipes be controlled in case they are broken during an earthquake? These questions can only be answered by structural engineers and architects.   When building vulnerability is identified, appropriate structural interventions should be undertaken, including ways to avoid water damage from broken pipes.

If objects must remain in vulnerable buildings, contingency plans should be considered in the advent of an earthquake. As Friuli has shown, damage will be primarily due to falling rubble or impact if the object is dislodged from its stand. Secondary damage occurs from water and vibrations during transport. Finally, objects may be harmed further if they are placed in uncontrollable conditions in emergency storage facilities.

Consequently, it is first essential that objects be in good condition before an earthquake: the generally poor condition of the objects in Friuli exacerbated other types of damage. Next, while on display or in storage, objects should be as securely protected as possible. Particular importance should be given to stands and storage shelves, to ensure that they do not fall or collapse during tremors. With the realization that the worst can occur, measures should be taken to locate and "reserve" a safe depository for displaced objects in a building that has been built to withstand seismic shock. By luck, the Church of San Francesco, Udine, was available after the May 6, 1976, earthquakes.   Although not altered to withstand seismic shock, this medieval church was located in a low-risk area, Udine, that remained relatively unaffected by the May 6 earthquakes and the September 11 and 15, 1976 earthquakes: in Friuli, as in many seismic zones, massive aftershocks often follow the first major earthquake.   Thus, it is important that displaced objects be moved to a building that will survive further earthquakes in good condition.

If damaged objects must be moved from affected structures to a safe depository, trained conservation personnel may not be available to supervise transport and deposition.   However, there are simple measures that can be taken to mitigate damage from water and movement. Curatorial staff should be aware of the steps to be taken and make certain that requisite materials are on hand:

365

1. Make certain to keep all tags and identifying material with the object. If at all possible, photograph the object with a Polaroid camera or a 35 mm camera before you move it: a record of its condition before transport could prove invaluable for a conservator faced with the assembly of pieces and fragments.
2. During transport, the object requires protection from shock and vibrations. The object should be laid carefully in a box lined with bubble wrap or a similar museum padding. Do not wrap objects in cotton or any other fibrous material which can leave a residue of lint and may also pull away or abrade polychromy. Again check to be sure that the object is tagged or its identification is written on the box.
3. Do not wrap objects in newspaper: the ink can rub off.
4. If wood has suffered water damage in conjunction with structural and surface damage from falling rubble, emergency treatment differs somewhat for painted or unpainted objects. The following instructions have been prepared by Mrs. Caroline Keck at the request of Mr. Isar, Editor, Museum, UNESCO:

For unpainted wood and furniture, dry very slowly under polyethylene (or similar plastic) tent or bag. DO NOT use tar paper or any paper with a tar content—this can have disastrous results. Place a tray or pan containing "moth crystals" within the tent or bag to inhibit mold or fungi.

Paintings on panels (and other polychromed wood) are treated as extra-special "furniture" and dried gradually under a plastic tent. Never let the plastic touch the face of the paint. Keep face-up and if the panel (or object) is in a frame, keep it there. Once secured under the plastic tent, move as little as possible. Get conservation help before the drying is complete. Loss or weakening of water-soluble glues in combination with dimensional changes may leave the paint simply resting on the wood, as if it were pieces in a picture puzzle. If you must move this as it dries, move it as cautiously as possible, as though it were a plate of cream soup and not a drop should be spilled. A conservator must undertake the reattachment of separated layers as soon as possible. This is a major operation. Polyethelene and other plastic sheeting may be purchased from hardware stores and from mail order houses. Stored under average environmental conditions (no extremes of heat or cold) these last well and may be purchased in economically ample quantities. The material is reusable if properly cared for and undamaged.

Fungicides are TOXIC. Limit human contact, ventilate while working with these and keep containers SEALED or tightly CLOSED except as needed. These provide exact services as required, but use as directed and with proper caution. Available in hardware stores, department stores and some drug stores. If purchased in advance, make certain that containers are tightly sealed against evaporation. Moth crystals are usually naphthalene or paradichlorobenzene. Thymol and orthophenyl phenol are also used to inhibit mold and fungi growth.

5. The depository must remain under the supervision of an individual who understands the needs of the objects. Ambient conditions must be monitored to ensure stable conditions. Thermohydrographs are ideally to be used, but they are expensive and require calibration. Inexpensive thermometers and relative humidity gages positioned around a depository and read at regular intervals—making some provisions for night readings—can also be used.

6. Wet objects should not be placed with dry objects. All objects should be examined for signs of mold growth or insect activity. Woodworms are evidenced by small round holes in the wood, active woodworms by particles of "saw dust" at the entrance of the holes. Examination with a normal magnifying glass should reveal evidence of mold growth. Infested objects must be isolated from healthy ones.

7. Leave all conservation work on the object for trained conservators. As the descriptions of treatments in Friuli reveal, stabilization of damaged objects can be a complex procedure, even though relatively simple instruments and materials can be employed.

8. Finally, in the face of earthquakes comparable to those in Friuli in 1976, problems of fine arts conservation pale before the suffering of the inhabitants. Throughout the six months of work in Friuli, the authors were constantly impressed by the enthusiasm for the conservation of their art and architecture of the hard-pressed populace—hundreds of whom had lost everything, including loved ones. This is the same spirit that brought the Tuscans through the disastrous 1966 flood that devastated Florence and western Tuscany. However, cultural attitudes differ from country to country. It is thus possible that conservators may find themselves objects of resentment for lavishing attention on art when individuals are in need. Conservators and curators must be prepared to deal not only with art, but also with people.

ACKNOWLEDGEMENTS

The authors wish to acknowledge gratefully the assistance of many individuals and institutions. Particular thanks are expressed to the Italian authorities, Soprintendente Riccardo Mola, Arciprete

Gianpaolo D'Agosto, and Gian Carlo Menis, Director, and Luciana Marioni Bros, Assistant Director, Regional Conservation Center, Passariano, Friuli. Institutional support was provided by FRIAM; the American Academy in Rome; the International Centre for Conservation, Rome (ICCROM); Cooperstown Graduate Conservation Program; and the New York University Conservation Centre. Project administrators included Dr. Henry Millon, Paul Schwartzbaum and John and Maria Train. Further assistance was received from Mrs. Caroline Keck and Mr. Lawrence Majewski.

Ms. Carol Grissom carried out the survey of objects in San Francesco, Udine, and organization of the laboratory in Cividale. Bernard Rabin and Elisabeth Packard directed the conservation laboratory. Assistant directors were Carol Grissom and Constance Silver, with assistant conservators Lawrence Keck and Dorothy Rabin. Participating conservation students at that time included Faye Wrubel, Stephen Bonadies, Terry and Dorothy Mahom, Benita Dumpis, Abigail Quandt, Mario R. Rizzi, and Giuseppina and Teresa Perusini.

REFERENCES

Marchetti, G. and G. Nicoletti. La Scultura Lignea nel Friuli, Rome: 'Silvana' Editoriale d'Arte, 1956.
Friuli Arts and Monuments (FRIAM) Report on Activities of the Conservation Laboratory, Cividale del Friuli. Unpublished report. Rome: American Academy in Rome, 1979.

A Regional Approach to Disaster Coping

Anne Russell and Mildred O'Connell

Every year about one hundred institutions in the northeast region will experience disasters resulting in damage to library or archival materials in their collections. Only a few of these will be major emergencies. Most will be small disasters: a broken water pipe, a leaky roof or a small fire.

Through its free disaster assistance program, the Northeast Document Conservation Center (NEDCC) offers help to any non-profit institution in its region that experiences damage as a result of a disaster. Located in Andover, Massachusetts, NEDCC is a non-profit, cooperative conservation center serving libraries, archives, historical societies and museums.

NEDCC was founded in 1973 with start-up funds from the New England Library Board and the Council on Library Resources. Its original purpose was to serve as a conservation treatment facility, serving the many repository institutions that do not have in-house facilities.

Soon after NEDCC opened its doors, the staff and Board recognized that one of the most valuable services the Center could provide to its constituency would be disaster assistance, and that this service should be free. It was essential that the Center be able to set aside monetary considerations at the height of an emergency.

For many years, NEDCC's disaster assistance service, along with its non-cost-recovering educational functions have been supported by grants from the state library agencies in the states served by the Center. These agencies constitute the governing authority of NEDCC. More recently, the disaster assistance function has been consolidated into the Center's Field Service office, which is supported in part by a grant from National Endowment for the Humanities.

Disaster assistance to an institution which has been hit by a fire or flood typically involves telephone consultation with NEDCC's Field Service Director and with other specialists on the Center's conservation staff as needed. The most immediate danger following a disaster is the growth of mold on water-damaged documents and books. (Figure 5.56) If not treated promptly, micro-organic growth may damage the materials permanently. Furthermore, soaked books

369

Figure 5.56. Growth of Mold on Water Damaged Books not Air Dried nor Frozen Quickly Enough.

Figure 5.57. Leather Bound Volume Distorted by Water Damage.

will swell in width as they absorb water, bursting their bindings unless they are quickly dried or frozen. (Figure 5.57)

In the case of a fire, often the most serious damage to the books is caused by the fireman's hose. (Figure 5.58) Materials that are charred but dry are not in any immediate danger and can be dealt with at leisure. A prime example is material partially burned during the great fire at New York State Library in 1911 that NEDCC is now treating, seventy years later. (Figure 5.59)

The Field Service Director advises staff members of the stricken institution how to assess the damage and how to air dry wet books. If it is not possible to air dry all of the materials immediately, institutions are counseled to freeze the materials until they can be dried. If there are relatively few books, it may be possible to air dry them in-house or at a conservation facility such as NEDCC. For larger quantities of material, freeze-drying may be the most practical technique.

In the aftermath of the disaster, custodians of collections need to determine which materials should be discarded, which replaced and which restored. (Figures 5.60 and 5.61) Members of NEDCC's staff will examine individual items in the collection and make recommendations for their salvage, if appropriate.

In the case of a major disaster, NEDCC is prepared to send a staff member to the scene to help assess damage, supervise recovery operations and organize salvage procedures. Some general suggestions for disaster coping follow, based on our own experiences with many institutions in the Northeast:

DISASTER RESPONSE CHECKLIST

1. Call a conservator immediately. It is essential to act quickly.
2. Have a disaster plan written listing resource people, volunteers, sources of needed supplies, etc.
3. If there is standing water in the building, have an electrician inspect the building before attempting to re-enter.
4. If power is out, provide an alternate power source to operate air conditioners, fans and lights.
5. Restore climate control conditions as soon as possible. Maintain temperature and humidity at low levels to inhibit the mold growth.
6. If there are no air conditioners, open windows and set up fans to create a flow of air. The warmer and more humid it is outdoors, the greater the danger of mold growth.
7. If materials have fallen on the floor, remove these first, preferably to air conditioned space, in order to clear a path for further salvage operations
8. Next, remove the most important or valuable materials in order of priority. Save the shelf list first. Per cubic inch, it

Figure 5.58. Water Stained Drawing.

Figure 5.59. Partially Burned Material from New York State Library Fire of 1911 Currently Being Treated by Northeast Document Conservation Center.

Figure 5.60. Corning, New York: Corning Museum of Glass, Collections Submerged by Flood Following Hurricane Agnes, June 22-23, 1972.

Figure 5.61. Library Collections Shaken from Shelves by Earthquake.

probably has the highest replacement cost of any artifact in the library.

9. Determine which materials can be air dried immediately and which must be frozen. (Figures 5.62 and 5.63)
10. Keep a list of all materials removed from their shelves for air drying or freezing.
11. Separate books from each other with freezer wrap before freezing so that they will not stick together. Pack them in plastic milk crates or in heavy cardboard boxes of about the same size. Wrap wet documents in small packets about the size of a document box. (Figures 5.64 and 5.65)
12. Identify materials wrapped and boxed for freezing on the outside of their packages.
13. Contact insurance company to see if coverage applies.
14. Publicize the disaster in order to mobilize goodwill, services and volunteer help from the community.

After a disaster, NEDCC sometimes plays a role in the fumigation or restoration of damaged materials. Fumigation is performed at NEDCC in the Center's vacuum fumigation chamber. It may be necessary to fumigate material that has gotten wet, or even only slightly damp, especially if the growth of mold is suspected. A common problem is that institutions do not call the Center when the damage occurs, but only weeks or months later when the mold growth is detected. In a large research libary, staff may not even be aware that damage has occurred.

NEDCC's staff of professional book and paper conservators are able to salvage most damaged books and documents, with the exception of books printed on coated stock. (Figure 5.66) Coated pages tend to stick together when wet and can usually be salvaged only by freeze-drying. (Figure 5.67) This requires equipment not available at NEDCC. Salvage of a water-damaged volume might involve simply flattening it, or it might require elaborate restoration, including washing of every page and rebinding of the volume. Restoration is extremely expensive—except for the most valuable books in a collection, it is usually less expensive to replace the book than to restore it.

NEDCC is concerned not only with disaster recovery, but also with disaster prevention and preparedness. In performing basic conservation surveys of libraries and other repositories, the Center places emphasis on minimizing the risk of damage by fire and water. It recommends that institutions make provision for adequate fire and flood detection systems as well as fire extinguishing systems. The Center advises its constituent institutions to develop written disaster preparedness plans and will review written plans drafted by libraries or archives.

In the future, as part of the NEH-funded Field Service project, NEDCC will attempt to organize state-wide disaster recovery teams in states which it serves. The purposes are to identify or train local resource people who can participate in disaster recovery operations; to

Figure 5.62. Corning, New York: Corning Museum of Glass, Wet Pamphlets Hung to Dry after Flood Following Hurricane Agnes, June 22-23, 1972.

Figure 5.63. Pleasant Valley, New York: Arlington High School Library, Air Drying Books That Had Been Frozen for Stabilization for a Week.

375

Figure 5.64. Corning, New York: Corning
Museum of Glass, Wet Books and Documents
Wrapped and Frozen for Stabilization after
Flood Following Hurricane Agnes,
June 22-23, 1972.

Figure 5.65. Vacuum Freeze Drying Large
Masses of Wet Material in Lockheed
Corporation Aerospace Chambers.

Figure 5.66. Charred Books Which Survived Library Fire.

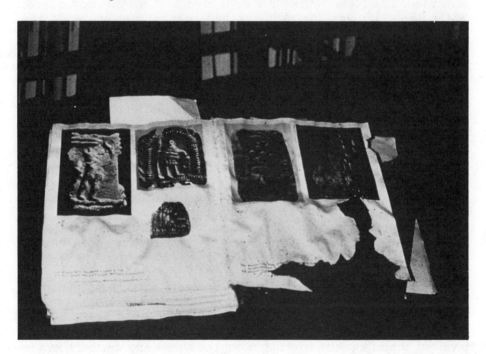

Figure 5.67. Damage to Book Printed on Coated Stock Caused by Fusing of Pages on Drying.

377

identify sources of services which may be needed in a time of emergency, such as cold storage facilities or freeze–drying equipment; and to develop centralized sources of supplies. A pilot project is planned in Rhode Island, to be co–sponsored by the Rhode Island Department of Library Services and the Rhode Island Archivists.

The following case study is a report by NEDCC's Field Service Director, Mildred O'Connell, on disaster assistance provided by NEDCC to the Oliver Wendell Holmes Library, Phillips Academy, Andover, Massachusetts, following the collapse of a temporary roof and extensive water damage to books and archival materials in September, 1981. The Library is located only two blocks from NEDCC in Andover, and for this reason, the possibilities for cooperation between NEDCC's staff and the Library staff were ideal.

REPORT OF A DISASTER AT THE OLIVER WENDELL HOLMES LIBRARY, PHILLIPS ACADEMY, ANDOVER, MASSACHUSETTS

On Tuesday, August 25, 1981, at 9 a.m., Lynne Robbins, Librarian at the Oliver Wendell Holmes Library at Phillips Academy, Andover, MA, called the Northeast Document Conservation Center to ask for assistance in handling a major disaster. The Library was undergoing construction to replace the glass skylighted roof with a copper roof. Water leaks through the skylights had been a problem since the building's construction in the 1920's. On Monday night, the roofers had covered an opening in the roof with tar paper and tarpaulin secured by wooden beams. During the course of a storm and heavy downpour on Monday evening, the covering was blown away and water poured into the Library. Night security guards noticed the damage, started to clean up the water and covered the stacks with plastic sheets.

The most valuable collections in the Library were fortunately not water damaged. Very special rare books kept in a safe on the first floor were not affected at all. The valuable Vergil Collection is kept in a room on the second floor which was inundated with water, that soaked the carpet. The books themselves, however, locked in glass-enclosed bookcases, were not damaged, nor was water found on top of the cases. This room was aired by opening windows (fortunately the day was cool and breezy). The wet carpet was removed and cases were opened for examination and airing. Cases were then closed, locked and covered with polyethylene sheeting in order to prevent future damage since the ceiling continued to drip water in places.

Water damage was unfortunately sporadic, affecting some books on the shelves but not others. There are four levels of stacks open from roof to basement, with no separation between levels except walkways. Water entering from the roof could therefore penetrate all levels of the Library by trickling down the stacks and wetting books in its course, down to and including old and rare books kept in a wire cage in the basement. It was therefore necessary to examine every volume in the collection to identify damp and wet books.

The first priority was to remove all damp and wet books from the Library and begin to dry them. Staff members began to comb the stacks for damaged books, which were removed from the shelves, taken to a first floor sorting area and sorted into several categories: general books (to be air dried or to be frozen) and old and rare books (to be air dried or to be frozen). Staff was instructed to isolate books with coated paper so that they could be placed in the freezer to prevent sticking. Very wet books were also separated out for the freezer. Most of the books were fortunately minimally damaged with wet tops or bottoms. Some mold damage from previous wettings was noted on individual books.

A call went out to Hood dairy for plastic milk crates which were promised for delivery in the afternoon. Cardboard cartons, available at the Academy, were used to transport books until the milk crates arrived. Arrangements were made to use the Commons (the student dining halls) for air-drying books. (Figure 5.68) Trucks and manpower were available from the Academy; electric fans were obtained and set up to circulate air in the drying areas. A call was made to a cold storage warehouse inquiring about space for freezing wet books if needed, but it was then found that the Academy cafeteria's freezer could be used for this purpose. Windows were opened throughout the Library and the Commons to facilitate drying. None of the spaces are air conditioned.

The Library staff proceeded in their efforts to locate, remove, sort and pack wet books, while the janitorial staff worked to clean up water. Removal of materials to the cafeteria building began after noon and continued into the evening. By mid-afternoon all old and rare books had been removed and set up to dry. (Figure 5.69)

It was soon realized that the sorting job was too big to be handled by staff members, and a call was put out to faculty members for assistance. They were set to work in the general stacks and in the archives and asked to remove wet and damp materials. This accelerated the salvage effort to the point where materials were packed faster than they could be removed. The advantages of the assistance, however, outweighed whatever confusion ensued.

Art books on coated paper and very wet books were placed in cartons and separated with sheets of freezer wrap to prevent them from sticking to each other in the freezer. The archivist selected the most important boxes of archival materials to be frozen as well; others were stood up in the drying areas. Documents were not removed from boxes on the day of the accident (unless the box was completely soaked) in order to prevent the chaos of unidentified loose sheets. For the most part only the document storage boxes and the edges of documents were wet.

By Tuesday evening all water-damaged old and rare books were air drying in the Commons, as were all wet books from the general stacks and wet boxes from the archives. Only the foreign language collection remained to be gone through on Wednesday morning. Very wet materials, important archives boxes, and most art books on coated paper were in the freezer.

Figure 5.68. Andover, Massachusetts: Phillips Academy, Oliver Wendell Holmes Library, Air Drying Books in Dining Hall That Were Wet in Storm, August 25, 1981.

Figure 5.69. Air Drying in Cool, Dry Room with Good Air Circulation.

On Wednesday morning the staff examined the foreign language collection for damage, which was minimal. The old and rare stacks and the general stacks were combed once again for wet materials which might have been overlooked. The archives was also reexamined during the course of the day.

Sherelyn Ogden, Book Conservator at NEDCC, and Mildred O'Connell examined the drying books on Wednesday morning and found that they were drying nicely. They recommended the removal of archival materials from their storage boxes. Documents were subsequently removed from boxes to air dry in piles, since only edges were wet. They were placed between trays on cafeteria racks; storage boxes (with identifying labels) were placed close by. Documents which were wet all over were frozen.

They also instructed the Librarian in the eventual drying of frozen materials, which may be done at any convenient time in the future. It was recommended that books set up for air-drying be left to dry until at least Monday or Tuesday of the next week (August 31/September 1). At that time they were to be carefully examined and dry books boxed. They should not be returned to the Library, however, but left in a secure dry place. Removal of dry books from the drying areas at that point will enable staff to focus their attention on getting problem books to dry. Windows in the Commons should be left open if the air outside is dry, and fans should continue to be used to dispel humid air. These conditions must exist on weekends as well.

The Vergil Room and the safe were checked once again and found to be secure. Removal of the valuable Vergil Collection to a safer location was suggested to prevent any possible future damage during the roof construction.

It will be very important to monitor collections carefully for mold over the coming year. The Library building has no climate controls and is hot and very humid in summer. These conditions, exacerbated by the leaky skylight, have resulted in the growth of mold in the past. The collections must be examined carefully and systematically for mold into the Summer of 1982. The effect of water damage to the structure itself should be evaluated by a structural engineer. There is evidence of weakening of floors in the stacks area, and of ceilings, especially in the Vergil Room.

During the entire rescue effort the staff was extremely cooperative, hard-working and cheerful. There was no panic. The Librarian, her staff, maintenance workers and volunteers all deserve commendation for their heroic effort and stamina. The result was a smooth salvage operation, resulting in minimal damage to collections.

Section Five References

EMERGENCY AND RECOVERY MEASURES: GENERAL

Approval Guide: Equipment, Materials, Services for the Conservation of Property. Norwood, Mass.: Factory Mutual System, published annually.

ARTIC Seminar Report: Problems of and Lessons from the Andhra Pradesh Cyclone, 12-14 August 1978. Vijayawada, India: Appropriate Reconstruction Training Information Center (ARTIC), 1978.

Aktkinson, G. A. "Reconstruction after Disaster—Planning Problems Posed." Proceedings of the Town and Country Planning Summer School. London: Royal Town Planning Institute, 1962, pp. 108-115.

Bahme, Charles W. Fire Officer's Guide to Disaster Control. Boston: National Fire Protection Association, 1978.

Brictson, R. C., Ed. Symposium on Emergency Operations. Santa Monica, California: System Development Corporation, 1966.

Cornell University Libraries. Emergency Manual. Ithaca, N.Y.: Committee on Safety and Emergencies, Olin Library, Cornell University, April 1976.

Cuny, Frederick C. Relief Operations Guidebook. 6 volumes. Dallas, Texas: Intertect, Inc., 1975.

Friesma, H. P., J. Caporaso, C. Goldstein, R. Lineberry and R. McCleary. Aftermath: Communities After Natural Disasters. Beverly Hills, California: Sage Publications, 1979.

Graphic Arts Research Center. Rochester Institute of Technology. "A Look at Disaster Recovery." Photographic conservation. May 1979.

Haas, J. Eugene, Robert W. Kates and Martyn J. Bowden, Eds. Reconstruction Following Disaster. Cambridge, Mass.: MIT Press, 1977.

Hinojosa, Jesus and William Gelman. "After the Earthquake." Practicing Planner. Volume 7, 1977, pp. 34-9.

Hirschberg, J., P. Gordon, and W. J. Petak. Natural Hazards Socioeconomic Impact Assessment Model. Redondo Beach, California: J. H. Wiggins Company, 1978.

Jones, Barclay G. "Planning for the Reconstruction of Earthquake Stricken Communities." Proceedings of the P.R.C.-U.S.A. Joint Workshop on Earthquake Disaster Mitigation Through Architecture, Urban Planning and Engineering. Beijing, China: Office of Earthquake Resistance, State Capital Construction Committee, 1981.

Krutilla, John V. "An Economic Approach to Coping with Flood Damage." Water Resources Research. Volume 2, 1966, pp. 183-90.

Lev, Ovadia E. "A System for Evaluation and Mitigation of Regional Earthquake Damage." Proceedings of the 7th World Congress on Earthquake Engineering, Istanbul 1980: Volume 9—Socioeconomic Aspects, Earthquake Reports, Progress Reports. Ankara, Turkey: The Congress, 1981, pp. 256-262.

Mitchell, William. "Reconstruction After Disaster: The Gediz Earthquake of 1970." Geographical Review. Volume 66, 1976, pp. 296-313.

Mitchell, William. Turkish Villages After an Earthquake: Analysis of Disaster Related Modernization. Unpublished Ph.D. Dissertation. Champaign: University of Illinois, 1974.

Pararas-Carayannis, George. A Guide for a Post-Tsunami Survey. Honolulu, Hawaii: International Tsunami Information Center, 1980.

Platt, Rutherford H. and George M. McMullen. Post-Flood Recovery and Hazard Mitigation: Lessons from the Massachusetts Coast. Amherst, Mass.: Water Resources Research Center, University of Massachusetts, February 1978.

Saraoff, Jerome R. and E. Jack Schoop. "Planning in Anchorage After the Earthquake." Journal of the American Institute of Planners. August 1964, pp. 231-233.

Selkregg, Lydia, Edwin B. Crittenden and Norman Williams, Jr. "Urban Planning in the Reconstruction." The Great Alaska Earthquake of 1964: Human Ecology. Washington, D.C.: National Academy of Sciences, Committee on the Alaska Earthquake, 1970, pp. 186-239.

Skeet, Muriel. Manual for Disaster Relief Work. Edinburgh, New York: Churchill Livingstone, 1977.

Spangle, William and Associates, et al. Land Use Planning After Earthquakes. Portola Valley, California: William Spangle and Associates, 1980.

Taylor, Alan J. The Intertect Disaster Management Training Package, No. 1. Dallas, Texas: Intertect, Inc., 1977.

EMERGENCY AND RECOVERY MEASURES: STRUCTURES

Ayarza, Hernan, S. Rojas, and L. Crisosto. Repair of Buildings Damaged by Earthquakes. New York: United Nations, 1977.

Bahme, Charles W. Fire Officer's Guide to Emergency Action. Boston: National Fire Protection Association, 1976.

Bates, Frederick L., et al. A Longitudinal and Cross-Cultural Study of the Post-Impact Phases of a Major Natural Disaster: The February 6, 1976 Guatemalan Earthquake. Washington, D.C.: National Research Council, National Academy of Sciences, 1977.

Ciborowski, Adolf. "Some Aspects of Town Reconstruction: Warsaw and Skopje." Impact. Volume 17, 1965, pp. 31-48.

Conti, M. "Analysis of Repair Methods for Masonry Buildings with Regard to Damages Caused by Earthquakes in Friuli, Italy, 1976." Proceedings of the International Research Conference on Earthquake Engineering, June 30-July 3, 1980, Skopje, Yugoslavia. Skopje, Yugoslavia: Institute for Earthquake Engineering and Engineering Seismology, 1982, pp. 183-198.

Davis, Ian. "Disaster Housing: A Case Study of Managua." Architectural Design. 1975, pp. 42-47.

Davis, Ian, Ed. Disasters and the Small Dwelling. Oxford: Pergamon Press, ltd., 1981.

Davis, Ian. "Housing and Shelter Provision Following the Guatemalan Earthquakes of February 4 and 6, 1976." Disasters. Volume 1, 1977, pp. 82-90.

Davis, Ian. Managua December 23, 1972: The Provision of Shelter in the Aftermath of Natural Disasters. Report on Housing Strategy December 1972-September 1973. Oxford: Department of Architecture, Oxford Polytechnic, 1974.

Davis, Ian. Shelter After Disaster. Oxford: Oxford Polytechnic Press, 1978.

Davis, Ian. "Skopje Rebuilt: Reconstruction Following the 1963 Earthquake." Architectural Design. Volume XLV, No. 11, November 1975, pp. 660-663.

Davis, Ian, Frederick Cuny and Frederick Krimgold, Eds. Studies on the Provision of Shelter Following Disasters. Geneva, Switzerland: United Nations Disaster Relief Office, 1977.

"Disaster Area Housing Conference, Istanbul September 1977: Conference Report." Disasters. Volume 2, 1978, pp. 29-30.

Germen, A. "The Gediz Earthquake: Reconstruction Between 1970 and 1977." Disasters. Volume 2, No. 1, 1978, pp. 69-77.

Gersony, R., T. Jackson, and J. Froman. Analysis of Alternative Reconstruction Models After the February 1976 Guatemalan Earthquake. Washington, D.C.: Agency for International Development, n.d.

Haas, J. Eugene, Robert W. Kates and Martyn J. Bowden, Eds. Reconstruction Following Disaster. Cambridge, Mass.: MIT Press, 1977.

Hackman, R. J. "Photointerpretation of Post-Earthquake Photographs, Alaska." Photogrammetric Engineering. Volume XXXI, April 1964, pp. 604-610.

Harriss, R. C., C. Hohenemser and R. W. Kates. "Our Hazardous Environment." Environment, Volume 20, Number 7, 1978, pp. 6-41.

Hinojosa, Jesus and William Gelman. "After the Earthquake: Managia Replans." Practicing Planner, March 1977, pp. 34-40.

Hogg, Sarah Jane. "Recontruction Following Seismic Disaster in Venzone, Friuli." Disasters. Volume 4, No. 2, 1980.

Kreimer, Alcira. "Post-Disaster Reconstruction Planning: The Cases of Nicaragua and Guatemala." Mass Emergencies. Volume 3, No. 1, 1978.

Lorentz, Stanislaw. "Reconstruction of the Old Town Centers of Poland." Historic Preservation Today. Charlottesville, Va.: University of Virginia Press, 1966, pp. 43-72.

The Oxfam/World Neighbors Housing Reconstruction Programme, Guatemala. Boston: Oxfam/America, 1977.

Parry, J. P. M. "Intermediate Technology Building." Appropriate Technology. Volume 2, 1975.

"Reconstruction Following Catastrophe: The Laissez-Faire Rebuilding of Downtown San Francisco After the Earthquake and Fire of 1906." Proceedings of the Association of American Geographers. Volume 2, 1970, pp. 22-26.

Thompson, C. and P. Preliminary Report on Post-Disaster Housing in Chile. Dallas, Texas: Intertect, Inc., 1976.

Thompson, C. and P. Preliminary Report on Post-Disaster Housing in Peru. Dallas, Texas: Intertect, Inc., 1976.

Thompson, C. and P. Reconstruction of Housing in Guatemala. Dallas, Texas: Intertect, Inc., 1976.

Thompson, C. and P. Survey of Reconstruction Housing in Honduras ... After Hurricane Fifi. Dallas, Texas: Intertect, Inc., May 1976.

United Nations Disaster Relief Organization. "Research Project on Emergency Shelter." UNDRO Bulletin. No. 1, 1976, p. 6.

Warburton, Ralph. "Recertification of Private Sector Buildings: The Dade County Experience." Proceedings of the Second U.S. National Conference on Earthquake Engineering, Stanford University, 1979.

EMERGENCY AND RECOVERY MEASURES:
ARTIFACTS AND COLLECTIONS

"A Look at Disaster Recovery." PhotographiConservation. Rochester, N.Y.: Graphic Arts Research Center, Rochester Institute of Technology, May 1979.

Agricultural Research Service. How to Prevent and Remove Mildew: Home Methods. Home and Garden Bulletin No. 68, revised. Washington, D.C.: U.S. Department of Agriculture, 1971.

Amber, George H. Water Damaged Files, Papers and Records: What to Do About Them. Royal Oak, Michigan: Document Reclamation Service, Inc., 1963.

Beers, R. J. "High Expansion Foam Fire Control for Records Storage." Fire Technology. May 1966.

Burns, Robert. "Space Age Drying Method Saves Library Books." Fire Engineering. Volume 126, No. 12, December 1973, p. 52.

The Care of Records in a National Emergency. Bulletin No. 3. Washington, D.C.: The National Archives, U.S. Government Printing Office, n.d.

Cohen, William. "Halon 1301, Library Fires and Post-Fire Procedures," Library Security Newsletter. May 1975, pp. 5-7.

Coley, Betty A. Planning and Development of a Conservation Facility. Washington, D.C.: ERIC No. ED200239, August 1981.

Cunha, George Martin. Conservation of Library Materials: A Manual and Bibliography on the Care, Repair and Restoration of Library Materials. 2nd Edition. Metuchen, N.J.: Scarecrow Press, 1971-72.

Cunha, George Martin, et al., Eds. Conservation Administration: The 1973 Seminar on the Theoretical Aspects of the Conservation of Library and Archival Materials and the Establishment of Conservation Programs. North Andover, Mass.: The New England Document Conservation Center, 1975.

Cunha, George Martin and Norman Paul Tucker, Eds. Library and Archives Conservation. Boston: The Library of the Boston Atheneum, 1972.

Cunha, George Martin. Conserving Local Archival Materials on a Limited Budget. Technical Leaflet No. 88. Nashville, Tennessee: American Association for State and Local History, November 1975.

Davies, Martin and Ian Rawlins. "The War-time Storage in Wales of Pictures from the National Gallery." London: The National Gallery, 1946.

Directory of Public Refrigerated Warehouses. Washington, D.C.: International Association of Refrigerated Warehouses, periodic.

Duckett, Kenneth W. Modern Manuscripts: A Practical Manual for Their Management, Care and Use. Nashville, Tennessee: American Association for State and Local History, 1975.

Federal Emergency Management Agency. "Museum Collections Involve Unique Emergency Problems." Disaster Information. Washington, D.C., March 1980.

Federal Fire Council. Salvaging and Restoring Records Damaged by Fire and Water. Recommended Practices Number 2. Washington, D.C.: Defense Support Agency, 1963.

387

Fikioris, Margaret. First Steps to be Taken for Emergency Treatment of Textiles. Mimeographed. Cooperstown, N.Y.: New York State Historical Association Library, 1972.

Fischer, David J. and Thomas W. Duncan. "Conservation Research: Flood Damaged Library Materials." Bulletin of the AIC. Volume 15, No. 2, Summer 1975, p. 27-48.

Gallo, Fausta. "Recent Experiments in the Field of Disinfection of Book Materials." ICOM Committee for Conservation, 4th Triennial Meeting. Paris: International Council of Museums, 1975.

Griffith, J. W. "After the Disaster: Restoring Library Service." Wilson Library Bulletin. Volume 58, Number 4, December 1983, pp. 258-65.

Hamblin, Dora Jane. "Science Finds Way to Restore the Art Damage in Florence." Smithsonian. Volume 4, No. 11, February 1974, pp. 26-35.

Horton, Carolyn. "Saving the Libraries of Florence." Wilson Library Bulletin. Volume 41, June 1967, pp. 1034-1043.

"Hurricane Recovery Efforts." Texas Library Journal. Winter 1979, p. 210.

International Council on Archives. Microfilm Committee. Bulletin 1.

Jordan, Mel. "Hurricane Recovery Efforts—University of Corpus Christi Library." Texas Library Journal. Volume 46, Winter 1970, pp. 210-13.

Keck, Caroline K. "On Conservation: Instructions for Emergency Treatment of Water Damages." Museum News. Volume 50, No. 10, June 1972, p. 13.

Keck, Sheldon. "Emergency Care of Museum Artifacts and Library Materials Affected by the Flood." Mimeographed. Cooperstown: New York State Historical Association Library, 1972.

King, Richard G., Jr. A Guide to the Literature on Deterioration, Conservation and Preservation of Library Material. Berkeley, California: University of California, August 1981.

Koesterer, Martin G. and John A. Getting. "Application and Utilization of a Space Chamber for the Drying of Books, Documents and Other Materials and Their Decontamination to Prevent Biodeterioration." Journal of Environmental Sciences. Volume 19, September 1976, pp. 29-33.

Koesterer, Martin G. and John A. Getting. "Restoring Water-Soaked Papers and Textiles: Applying Freeze-Drying Methods to Books and Art Objects." Technology and Conservation. Volume 1, No. 2, Fall 1976, pp. 20-22.

Koplowitz, Brad. et. al. Disaster Manual: Emergency, Evacuation Recovery. Oklahoma City: Oklahoma Department of Libraries, 1982.

McGregor, L. and J. Bruce. "Recovery of Flood Damaged Documents by the Queensland State Archives." Archives and Manuscripts. Volume 5, No. 8, August 1974, pp. 193-199.

Martin, John H., Ed. The Corning Flood: Museum Under Water. Corning, N.Y.: The Corning Museum of Glass, 1977.

Martin, John H. "Resuscitating A Water-Logged Library." Wilson Library Bulletin. November 1975, pp. 241-3.

Martin, Mervin. "Emergency Procedures for Furniture." Mimeographed. Cooperstown, N.Y.: New York State Historical Association Library, 1972.

Minoque, Adelaide. "Treatment of Fire and Water-Damaged Records." The American Archivist. Volume 9, No. 1, January 1946, pp. 17-25.

Morrison, Robert C., Jr. "An Experience in Restoration." Library Scene. June 1976.

Rabin, Bernard. "Emergency Procedures for Musical Instruments." Mimeographed. Cooperstown, N.Y.: New York State Historical Association Library, 1966.

Regan, E. "Damaged Papers Restored by Freeze Drying Techniques." St. Louis, Mo.: McDonnell-Douglas Corporation, 1974.

Schappert, Alice D. "What Did Marion do After Agnes Left." Wilson Library Bulletin. Volume 48, No. 8, pp. 664-5, April 1974.

Schmelzer, Menahem. "Fire and Water: Book Salvage in New York and in Florence." Special Libraries. Volume 59, No. 8, October 1968, pp. 620-625.

Scriven, Margaret. "Preservation and Restoration of Library Materials." Special Libraries. Volume 47, December 1956, pp. 439-448.

Spawn, Willman. "After the Water Comes." PLA Bulletin. November 1973, pp. 243-351.

Still, J. S. "Library Fires and Salvage Methods." The American Archivist. Volume 16, No. 2, 1953, pp. 145-153.

Surrency, Erwin C., Jr. "Freeze-Dried Books." Library Journal. Volume 99, No. 16, September 15, 1974, pp. 2108-9.

Upton, M. S. and C. Pearson. Disaster Planning and Emergency Treatments in Museums, Art Galleries, Libraries, Archives and Allied Institutions. Canberra, Australia: Institute for the Conservation of Cultural Materials, Canbera College of Advanced Education, 1978.

Walston, S. "Emergency Conservation Following the Darwin Cyclone." ICCM Bulletin. Volume 2, No. 1, March 1976, pp. 21-25.

"Water Damage in Libraries." Library Journal. Volume 94, June 15, 1969, pp. 2402-3.

Waters, Peter. Procedures for Salvage of Water-Damaged Library Materials. Washington, D.C.: The Library of Congress, 1975.

Waters, Peter, et al. "Does Freeze Drying Save Water-Soaked Books or Doesn't It? Salvaging a Few 'Facts' from a Flood of (Alleged) Misinformation." American Libraries. No. 6, July-August 1975, pp. 422-423.

Waters, Peter and the Royal College of Art. The Restoration of Books, Florence 1968. (Film). Washington, D.C.: Library of Congress, 1968.

Weidner, Marilyn Kemp. "Instructions on How to Unframe Wet Prints." Mimeographed. Cooperstown, N.Y.: New York State Historical Association Library, 1973.

"Western States Materials Conservation Project: Preliminary Report." Conservation Administration News. April, 1980.

Williams, Howard D. "Records Salvage After the Fire at Colgate University." The American Archivist. Volume 27, July 1964, pp. 375-379.

Williams, John C., Ed. Preservation of Papers and Textiles of Historic Artistic Value. Washington, D.C.: American Chemical Society, 1977.

Wringer, Howard W. and Richard D. Smith, Eds. Deterioration and Preservation of Library Materials. Chicago: The University of Chicago Press, 1969.

SECTION SIX

Public and Private Response Measures

Seeking Assistance

Barclay G. Jones

It is abundantly clear that natural disasters cause tremendous losses to our heritage of historic buildings and artifacts. Protective actions can reduce the vulnerability of sites and objects to this form of destruction. Prompt and appropriate emergency measures can help immensely. However, in spite of the best preparations and precautions, damage is inevitable and relief, recovery and reconstruction efforts will be necessary. Recovery from disaster can be described as consisting of four phases: the emergency period during which coping with the devastation occurs; the restoration period of resuming relatively normal operations; the reconstruction period in which damage is repaired and losses replaced; and the development period in which improvements on the pre–disaster state are accomplished. The pace at which these phases will proceed will vary with degree of organization, level of preparedness and amount of resources that can be mobilized. [Kates and Pijawka, 1977] What kinds of response measures exist and are needed to deal with the impacts of disasters, permit the recovery from them to be more rapid, and lessen the severity of the losses?

In reviewing the kinds of response to recent disasters, three aspects of them seem fundamental: the nature or the type of response, mechanisms for response, and the appropriate magnitude of the response. The nature of the response is basically passive. For the most part, it is the responsibility of the victim of the disaster to evoke the response through a request. In some instances, victims may be queried as to whether or not they wish assistance, but a positive reply is usually required for response to occur. Sometimes the question is in the form of whether or not the victim wants a specific type of assistance that the responder is prepared to supply. What is desperately needed and what is offered may not match very well. The mechanisms for response consist of a large number of organizations, institutions, agencies and individuals with expertise. Finding out in the midst of an emergency what organizations exist and what kinds of assistance they can provide may be an extremely complex and confusing undertaking. The appropriate magnitude of the response is often extremely hard to determine. Assessing the needs for different kinds of assistance in a disaster stricken area may be a very difficult task.

THE NATURE OF DISASTER RESPONSE

In many ways the key individuals in disaster situations are those who own, are responsible for, or manage historic and cultural sites, buildings and artifacts. As described in the previous section, they must do three things immediately: prevent further destruction and deterioration, prevent further loss through demolition and clean-up operations, and obtain the necessary assistance in human and other resources and expertise to stabilize the situation until restoration and reconstruction measures can be undertaken. For these things to occur requires making heroic assumptions about a very large number of people.

The principal characteristic of structures and artifacts in a disaster stricken region will be dispersion. The objects of concern will be in the hands of a multitude of different owners and administrators, will be housed in many different structures and will be spatially dispersed at a large number of different sites. The vast bulk of historic buildings and structures and cultural artifacts in any region will not be under the jurisdiction of historical agencies or collections. For example, while the New York Historical Society owns the Dyckman House, the New York Port Authority owns the Brooklyn Bridge, the National Park Service owns the Statue of Liberty, and the Episcopal Diocese owns Trinity Church.

Many historical buildings will be owned by private individuals, partnerships or corporations, and the accumulated number of objects in the hands of private collectors in the region can easily be vastly greater than the collections in museums. Another large quantity of important objects will be in the hands of intermediaries. Furniture, paintings, artifacts of various kinds will be in storage warehouses or bank vaults. Objects in transition from one collection to another will be in the warehouses or showrooms of dealers, stores, galleries and auction houses. Among the major victims of the London Fire of 1666 mentioned earlier were the hundreds of booksellers around St. Paul's. They packed their inventories of thousands of books in the masonry St. Faith's Church and sealed the openings. The contents of the Church ignited probably by spontaneous combustion and burned for a week scattering charred pages as far as Windsor Forest. Many rare books were lost including nearly all copies of the Third Folio of Shakespeare. [Weber, 1981; Cornell, 1976] The contents of artists' studios are very important also and notable losses throughout history have occurred when disasters destroyed the work places of artists. Arshile Gorky, mentioned earlier, lost twenty-seven paintings in a fire in his studio in January 1946. [Seitz, 1962]

Dispersion has both negative and positive aspects. On the negative side, one must assume that the owner knows what the object is, has some idea of its value, and knows how to care for it and protect it. This is not always the case. It also means that experts who know the importance of objects and how to care for them in emergency situations will be faced with the very difficult task of determining who has what and where it is located. The positive aspect to dispersion is that it probably constitutes a vulnerability reduction measure in itself. Since all sections of a region will not be subject to the same degree of damage in a disaster, dispersion is a way of insuring that many things survive. Too large a single concentration means that a disaster striking that specific location would result in tremendous loss. While the museum in Bucharest, shaken by the earthquake of March 4, 1977 mentioned earlier, contains the largest single collection of the works of Constantin Brancusi, it represents only part of the total work of this sculptor. Most of the eighty paintings composing a retrospective exhibit of the Uruguayan Constructivist Joaquin Torres-Garcia, which constituted a major portion of his life's work, were destroyed in the fire that gutted the Museum of Modern Art of Rio de Janeiro on July 8, 1978. One of the worst museum fires, this disaster destroyed more than a thousand paintings, sculptures and prints including works by Picasso, Miro, Klee, Dali, Magritte, Ernst and Dubuffet. [Fire . . . , 1978]

RESPONSE MECHANISMS

An enormous number of institutions and programs exist to provide various kinds of general relief from human suffering and property destruction resulting from natural disasters. Many of them were created to cope with the emergency caused by a particular event or consequent recovery and reconstruction operations. Many are designed to deal with specific hazards or specific effects of disasters. They are prepared to spring into action immediately upon learning they are needed.

In contrast, the chief characteristic of the various mechanisms for response to disasters which damage structures and artifacts is that they are ad hoc. For the most part they exist for some other purpose and have as one of their functions the capability to respond to disaster situations. Plans for response, organizations drafted and in place and ready to be mobilized, and cadres of various kinds of experts who have been enlisted and who are prepared to take action on short notice almost do not exist. As a consequence much precious time must be lost in mobilization, and response efforts, while heroic, are less effective than they could be.

At the international level response to general relief needs can be made by numerous multilateral, bilateral and private organizations. The primary intergovernmental organization is the United Nations. The United Nations Disaster Relief Coordinator (UNDRO) plays a central role, but various kinds of relief, preparedness, prevention and mitigation programs are carried out by specialized United Nations organizations and agencies. UNDRO and other United Nations agencies cannot initiate any relief activity without a request from the government of the affected country, and this communication may be directed to the field office of an agency in the country or to international headquarters. United Nations Development Programme (UNDP) represents UNDRO at the field level. Whatever agency is approached, UNDRO is to be informed. United Nations Educational, Scientific and Cultural Organization (UNESCO) is increasingly active regarding protection of cultural property and the International Center for the Study of the Preservation and the Restoration of Cultural Property (ICCROM) can provide assistance. [Brown, 1979]

Other intergovernmental organizations, for example, NATO (North Atlantic Treaty Organization) and PAHO (Pan-American Health Organization), are prepared to supply disaster relief needs of various kinds. The most prominent in relation to protecting cultural resources are the International Council of Museums (ICOM) and the International Council on Monuments and Sites (ICOMOS).

Offers of bilateral assistance by the foreign ministries of national governments to stricken regions usually include such items as medical supplies, food, clothing, blankets, temporary shelters, demolition teams and equipment, engineering and technical personnel, and financial aid, but only very rarely assistance to salvage and restore the historic and cultural patrimony.

Federal

Within the United States at the federal level, disaster assistance is coordinated by the Federal Emergency Management Agency. Requests from a locality must go first to the governor of the state, who must then request federal assistance. The President then may declare a disaster or a state of emergency in a specified area. In addition to restoring facilities built or operated by itself, the federal government provides transfers to state and local governments.

Federal assistance is usually directed primarily to governments. The Office of Disaster Response and Recovery is the principal unit within FEMA. However, the resources of a wide array of agencies can be mobilized through access to an extremely diffused set of disaster response progams. Depending on the type of disaster and nature of the destruction, assistance can be provided by agencies and programs within the following Departments: Agriculture, Commerce, Defense (Army), Education, Interior, Health and Human Services, Housing and Urban Development, and Transportation. In addition, a number of independent Administrations, Agencies, Authorities and Commissions also have programs for disaster assistance of specialized kinds within their jurisdictions. [Petak and Atkisson, 1982, pp. 61-63, 74-77] Damage to public buildings under the jurisdiction of local governments, transportation facilities, water and sewer systems and other public infrastructure are eligible for assistance. A destroyed municipal museum can be reconstructed. One belonging to a private, non-profit organization may or may not be eligible for some kinds of assistance.

Other federal programs are intended as temporary relief during the emergency recovery period. They are directed at health, housing, income maintenance through supplemental unemployment benefits, and the restoration of the private sector of the economy, particularly small businesses. A large corporation, the major employer in a community, might be wiped out and yet be ineligible for assistance.

Other federal agencies might be able to provide direct support independently for recovery from damage to cultural property. These could include the National Endowment for the Humanities, the National Institute for Museum Services, the Museums Program of the Smithsonian, the National Park Service, and the Library of Congress. No federal agency has oversight responsibility, and the initiative rests entirely with those in the affected area.

State

At the state level under the present national organization for dealing with emergencies, there is a Comprehensive Emergency Management Director appointed by the Governor and directly answerable to him. A State Emergency Office should exist within the Office of the Governor also. Local officials direct their requests for assistance to the comprehensive emergency manager who forwards it to the Governor. If the needs of the locality appear to exceed its resources for dealing with them, the Governor may act by issuing emergency declarations and providing various forms of state assistance to the localities. If the magnitude of the situation is sufficiently great, the Governor may seek federal assistance. The major functions of state emergency offices are assessing the situation, mobilizing state resources and coordinating them, and channeling requests for various kinds of disaster assistance to the federal level. Again, the primary target of state assistance, in addition to its own facilities, is units of local government including counties, townships, school districts, other special districts and authorities, and municipalities. State agencies which can provide assistance to local museums and historical sites and structures include state historical commissions or associations, state archives, state museums, state park departments, state historic preservation offices and similar agencies which will be organized differently in various states. Assistance can be made readily available to public structures and collections while private ones may or may not be eligible for various kinds of aid.

Local

Emergency organizations at the local level vary tremendously from place to place from rural counties with small populations to major metropolitan centers. The functions are similar to those at higher levels of government. The first task is that of assessing the situation, the second that of mobilizing local resources to deal with it, and the third is directing requests for external assistance if the situation warrants it. Restoring public systems to operating order as rapidly as possible is the major focus of concern. Assisting private individuals and organizations in demolition and clean-up operations, maintaining levels of safety and health, and relieving distress and human suffering are primary concerns. County and municipal libraries, historical societies, museums, and local landmark and art commissions can mobilize resources to support efforts to recover from damage to structures and artifacts of historic or cultural importance within their jurisdictions.

Private

Private organizations provide enormous amounts of disaster assistance. A notable example at the international level is the League of Red Cross Societies which acts only on the request of a national society. (The national Red Cross in the United States acts only in response to requests from local chapters—usually at the county level.) The activities of five major international relief agencies are coordinated by a Steering Committee based in Geneva since 1972. Hundreds of private groups are involved in disaster relief, many exclusively and many in addition to other concerns. [Green, 1977] Private organizations with national, regional or local scope are active in similar ways in the United States.

Private response mechanisms are often the most important source of assistance so far as historic structures and collections of artifacts are concerned. Unfortunately, these are largely without an organizational framework before disasters and develop on an ad hoc basis. This is the case at the international as well as the national, regional and local scale. The International Fund for Monuments does not have a broad base of support or formal structure comparable to the general relief groups mentioned above. Organizations of major foundations, donors and patrons can be assembled if the event seems to warrant such response. In many cases the most effective response comes from within the community itself. Local foundations and local patrons and individuals can see the magnitude of the situation at first-hand and can assess its significance easily. They often provide the most effective resource.

The assistance obtained by the Contemporary Art Museum in Houston after the inundation by the flash flood on June 15, 1976 referred to earlier provides an excellent example. The total assistance from the federal government was a grant of $17,500, the maximum possible amount under the circumstances, from the National Endowment for the Arts. The City of Houston appropriated $25,000. The 38 member Board of Trustees gave $162,000 among themselves. The local Cullen Foundation donated $100,000 towards restoring the physical facility, a Benefit Art Auction raised almost $250,000, and other donors gave more than $130,000 in the first six months. [Brutvan, 1982]

The most important single private resource is insurance. In hazard assessment procedures necessary kinds of coverage should have been identified and acquired at adequate levels. Restoring buildings as well as contents should be included. When objects are loaned for travelling, temporary, or permanent exhibit, care should be taken that coverage against natural disasters is included. Both contents and building were completely covered by insurance in the fire mentioned earlier at the New York Museum of Modern Art on April 15, 1958 in which Monet's 18 foot "Water Lilies" was destroyed as was Portimari's "Festival St. John's Eve," and seven other paintings were damaged. Fortunately, a special Seurat exhibit consisting of more than 150 works assembled from more than 90 museums and collectors was rescued and not affected. [Wilson, 1958]

Professional organizations with varying degrees of institutionalization and organization provide important resources also. The Earthquake Engineering Research Institute has emerged over the last 25 years as a model organization of this kind. Specialized regional organizations such as the Northeast Document Conservation Center are organized and prepared to provide emergency services. [Cunha, 1967, pp. 165–177; Breuer, 1981] The Conservation Center at New York University functions in a similar capacity. [Schur, 1983] State historical societies such as the Pennsylvania Historical and Museum Commission and the New York State Historical Society can provide similar sorts of assistance. The American Institute for Conservation of Historic and Artistic Works provides another avenue for obtaining expert assistance. With respect to structures, the potential role that can be played by such organizations as the Committee on Historic Resources of the AIA, the Committee on History and Heritage of American Civil Engineering of the American Society of Civil Engineers, the Society of Architectural Historians, and the National Trust for Historic Preservation is still developing.

There are clear gaps in the existing response mechanisms that urgently need to be filled. Since the burden of seeking assistance rests largely on those who have suffered the catastrophe, there needs to be greater clarity and simplicity to the response structure so that what to do, where to go, and who to ask can be more rapidly perceived and attrition diminished.

DETERMINING THE NECESSARY MAGNITUDE OF RESPONSE

Determining what was lost and knowing precisely the magnitude of the destruction caused by a major natural disaster can never be very precise. Teams of technical experts will come into the stricken region, make counts and tally them, and eventually publish figures. These will convey an illusion of accuracy. If the destruction was severe, stating how many buildings were demolished requires knowing how many buildings were there before the event, and this information is seldom available. In a similar fashion, it is even more difficult to know precisely how many dwelling units were contained in demolished structures and how many households and individuals they housed. The number of fatalities is usually the most accurate single piece of information. For a recent earthquake (Tang'shan, China, July 27, 1976) published estimates of the number of those who died ranged from 148,000 to 670,000—a considerable spread.

The essential requirement for determining losses from a natural disaster to historic structures and cultural objects and artifacts is that of knowing what was in the impacted area before the event. In other words, it is an inventory problem. Such inventories are conceptually impossible, and we can never know with any precision what was lost. However, we do have some means of making estimates, and our inventories are improving all the time. As a class of institutions, libraries are probably the most advanced in the field. Library union registries provide a basic source of information. However, they are designed to answer the question in which library can one find a specific book, rather than to answer the question what books a particular library contains. Archival materials and collections are reported but of course their detailed contents are not specified. Computer search procedures are expanding these capabilities.

The National Archives Registry of Paintings and Works of Art is a great step forward in determining where significant works of art are. However, again it is not designed to search for the holdings in a locality. The state and national registers of historic places are organized by locality. However, they list only a fraction of the significant buildings in the community. A city with the historic character of Charleston certainly contains more than 60 significant buildings, the National Register listings in 1976. Local surveys and records may be more complete and more help. Local sources may in all regards be the best available record. However, this requires that the local inventories survive. If the shelf list of a library is destroyed in the catastrophe, it may be impossible to determine what the losses were.

Frequently in disaster situations, experts go into the area seeking salvagable objects and works of art and paying little attention

400

to the things that are completely lost or irretrievable. The record of what was saved then becomes the statistic rather than the record of the losses. This is one of the reasons that we have so little information about the seriousness of the threat of natural disasters to our cultural heritage. Perhaps one of the reasons that historic structures and cultural objects are accorded such a low priority in the consideration of things to be dealt with after disasters is because we have so little information about the magnitude of the depredations. Individuals who own or are responsible for important objects usually want to forget about the losses they have suffered and certainly do not tend to call undue attention to what was lost. It is not only extremely difficult to find public records of museum losses through natural disasters, it is often impossible to extract them from the records of the museum itself. Private losses are at least an order of magnitude more difficult to assess.

THE DESIGN AND ORGANIZATION OF RESPONSE MEASURES

The preceding generalized description of disaster response situations was intended to identify salient characteristics that can be useful in devising more effective forms of response measures. Against this background it is now possible to delineate the response process.

Organizational

The key individual that emerges from the preceding description is the individual owner, proprietor, curator, director or administrator of an historic property or collection. The success of the response process depends to a very large extent on these individuals. A major pre-condition for effective response will be the extensiveness and detailed nature of inventory and documentation of the cultural property involved. Protective actions in anticipation of disasters will mitigate their impacts and reduce the need for aid. Another critical element will be the emergency preparedness and immediate emergency measures that are undertaken. These include removing items from danger, recording destruction, protecting from further damage including that resulting from demolition and clean-up operations.

The first step in the response process is that of determining the exact nature and the total magnitude of the loss and specifying the assistance that is needed. The resources that are required must be established, and whether or not they are within the means of the organization itself must be determined. Whether assistance is needed or not, the information about damage then should be communicated outside of the organization to the next level of concern. This action will result in the pooling of information from diverse sources to determine what the total impact of the disaster has been on the cultural resources of the locality.

Local

The second level of response is within the locality. This may be at the level of a municipality, a county or a metropolitan area. Three steps are again involved. The first of these is determining the magnitude of the loss and the nature and amount of assistance needed. Since this involves inter-organizational relations, it is a more complex step. The initiative should be taken by a lead organization such as a local public historical society or museum or some other agency which should be identified in the emergency planning process. A list of potential victims of the disaster must be assembled. Of course, it would be immensely helpful if such lists had been prepared in advance of the disaster. They should include all of the museums, book, manuscript and archive collections, and historic sites and structures whether public or private in the locality. The lists should include antique stores, galleries and rare book and other dealers as well as collections. Dealers may be very helpful in identifying significant private collections which may not be generally known. Contacts should be made by telephone as soon as possible. Use of the radio and other media can inform individuals to make contact with the central organization.

Information must be gathered concerning the specific nature and magnitude of losses that have been incurred, whether or not coping with the situation is within the capability of the responsible individuals and organizations, as well as information about the amount and nature of the assistance that is needed. This process can also help to identify resources available within the community that can be mobilized to aid those who need external assistance. Information must be conveyed to those who have suffered damages about appropriate emergency and recovery measures to be undertaken. This can be accomplished through information sheets or bulletins dealing with specific topics. The availability of expertise of various kinds both within and outside the community should also be communicated to victims. Means of acquiring necessary resources to carry out recovery processes should be part of the information conveyed.

The third step of the process is that of communicating to a larger community. This will again involve the pooling of information with other similar areas nearby which have been subject to the same disaster and making needs known to a larger community about the nature of the assistance needed. There must be communication with the local emergency management organization. Ideally, relationships with this organization should have been established before the emergency, and concerns for cultural properties should have been incorporated in local emergency management plans. Requests for appropriate kinds of assistance should be channeled through this agency.

State

Similar steps occur at the state level. Appropriate state agencies should immediately begin the task of identifying potential victims in the region stricken by the disaster. These would include local historical societies, properties on the state register of historic places, state and other public historic properties, museums, libraries and archival collections. Contacts should be established immediately to acquire information about the kinds of losses that have been incurred and whether or not external assistance is needed. State agencies can play major roles in mobilizing assistance. First, information bulletins and brochures concerning appropriate emergency and recovery measures to undertake should be available or easily acquired and readily supplied to the stricken area. The mobilization of external assistance, locating specialized facilities, dealing with the logistics of deploying experts and removing damaged items to facilities and conservation centers can be immensely helpful services that are most appropriately carried out at the state level. Communicating the resources needed to deal with the disaster is again a very appropriate state function.

Mobilizing state aid and forwarding requests for federal assistance are necessary functions at this level. Generating private support may also be most effectively coordinated at this level. There are innumerable local foundations of varying size which can be approached to deal with the needs. Again at this stage, it will be necessary to coordinate with the State Comprehensive Emergency Management Director. Awareness of potential threats to cultural resources should have been communicated prior to emergencies and consideration of them built into the state emergency management plan. Relationships between appropriate state cultural officers, such as the Archivist, Historical Commissioners, Historic Preservation Officers, State Museum Directors, and State Park Directors with the Comprehensive Emergency Management Director should already have been established.

Federal

At the federal level, two kinds of response mechanisms exist. The first of these is through the emergency management organization and the other is through direct access to sources of technical assistance. If a disaster is sufficiently extensive in its effects to transcend the available resources at the state and local level, a region may be declared eligible for federal assistance. The Federal

Emergency Management Agency coordinates response by federal agencies. This is the organization that will allocate resources in response to requests from governors. In the case of disasters involving more than a single state, the agency will determine the magnitude of the total losses and the types of assistance needed. It will then coordinate and mobilize assistance on the part of various federal agencies and provide funds and other resources for emergency relief and recovery operations. The second kind of response can occur whether or not the situation is designated a federal disaster. Various federal agencies may be contacted directly by disaster victims for specific kinds of technical assistance. These have already been referred to but include the Museum Program of the Smithsonian, the National Park Service, the National Archives, the Library of Congress, and others. Direct requests for financial assistance may be made to the National Endowment for the Humanities, the National Institute for Museum Services, and others.

The Federal Emergency Management Agency and appropriate other federal organizations should have established relationships before the disaster. These may have been informal or in the nature of an inter-agency committee. Included in this exchange of information about potential threats to the national cultural heritage should have been such organizations as the President's Advisory Council on Historic Preservation, the National Register of Historic Places, the National Park Service, the National Archives, the Library of Congress, the Smithsonian Institution, the National Gallery of Art, and other appropriate organizations. Liaison should have been established with private organizations such as the American Association for State and Local History, the American Association of Museums, the National Trust for Historic Preservation, the American Institute for Conservation of Historic and Artistic Works, and other possible resources.

Private

The individuals involved in this kind of inter-agency communication would provide an optimal resource for the identification of members to form a small expert group that would be available to mobilize private philanthropy to assist in major disasters. The group should have some formal structure and limited support. it could be operated under the aegis of some existing organization or independently with modest foundation support. By being in existence in advance of the disaster, it would be able to take maximum advantage of the critical time element to mobilize and channel private support in those situations in which it is needed. Since such a large percentage of the cultural heritage that is of concern is in private hands and not eligible for various forms of public assistance, such an organization would be extremely useful.

The response process must operate from the bottom up. It must be initiated in the first instance by those who have directly suffered the impact of a natural disaster. Resources for assistance to victims exist and are available in many situations when requested. Since this is the case, for response measures to be more effective potential victims must be better informed about and know how to initiate them. Organization for response to natural disasters has been highly elaborated and institutionalized. However, it has not taken explicit consideration of possible depredation to cultural properties or accorded historic structures and museum collections an appropriate priority. Modifications need to be made in our response mechanisms to see that these considerations receive proper attention. By better articulation of the potential loss to our national heritage through natural disasters, the possibility of devising more adequate response measures and the capability of mobilizing more appropriate levels of resources will be easier to realize. Recovery of irreplaceable elements of our heritage from natural disasters can start to claim the higher priority it deserves.

REFERENCES

Breuer, J. Michael. "Regional Cooperation for Disaster Preparedness." Disasters: Prevention and Coping. James N. Myers and Denise D. Bedford, Eds. Stanford, California: Stanford University Libraries, 1981, pp. 41-51.

Brown, Barbara J. Disaster Preparedness and the United Nations. New York: Pergamon Press, 1979.

Brutvan, Cheryl A. In Our Time: Houston's Contemporary Art Museum, 1948-1982. Houston, Texas: Contemporary Art Museum, 1982.

Cornell, James. The Great International Disaster Book. New York: Charles Scribners' Sons, 1976.

Cunha, George Daniel Martin. Conservation of Library Materials. Metuchen, N.J.: The Scarecrow Press, Inc., 1967.

"Fire Devastates Rio Museum." Americas. September 1978, p. 54.

Green, Stephen. International Disaster Relief. New York: McGraw-Hill Book Company, 1977.

Kates, Robert W. and David Pijawka. "Chapter I; From Rubble to Monument--The Pace of Reconstruction." Reconstruction Following Disaster. J. Eugene Haas, Robert W. Kates, Martyn J. Bowden, Eds. Cambridge, Mass.: The MIT Press, 1977, pp. 1-23.

Petak, William J. and Arthur A. Atkisson. Natural Hazard Risk Assessment and Public Policy. New York: Springer-Verlag, 1982.

Schur, Susan E. "Laboratory/Training Profile: The Conservation Center of New York Univerity." Technology and Conservation, Volume 8, Number 2, Summer 1983, pp. 30-36.

Seitz, William C. <u>Arshile Gorky</u>. New York: The Museum of Modern
    Art, 1962.

Weber, David C. "The Vulnerability of Graphic Artifacts." <u>Disasters:</u>
    <u>Prevention and Coping</u>. James N. Myers and Denise D. Bedford,
    Eds. Stanford, California: Stanford University Libraries, 1981,
    pp. 2-5.

Wilson, Rexford. "The New York Museum Fire." <u>Quarterly of the</u>
    <u>National Fire Protection Association</u>, July 1958, pp. 67-77.

International Programs for the Rescue of Cultural Property

Dr. Hiroshi Daifuku

INTRODUCTION

International cooperation preserving the cultural heritage of mankind is an old ideal. Provisions in The Hague Conventions of 1899 and 1907 called for the protection of monuments, works of art, historical documents and other forms of cultural property. Similar provisions were also included in the Roerich Pact signed at Washington, D.C. in 1935. During the period between the two World Wars the League of Nations established the International Institute of Intellectual Cooperation in Paris, France which set up in turn the International Museums Office. Among the latter's publications was the bulletin <u>Mouseion</u>, the two volume work <u>Museographie</u> and the Athens Charter.

On the basis of this experience, albeit abortive, the allies not only proposed the creation of the United Nations, but also decided to establish an Agency of the UN to succeed I I I C to be called the United Nations Educational, Scientific and Cultural Organization or UNESCO. UNESCO began in 1945 with forty-four Member States. Its statutes state, <u>inter alia</u>, that it would be responsible for programs concerned with the preservation of works of art and of history. Its statutes also indicate that it will not interfere in the internal activities of its Member States.

In carrying out this mandate, within the restriction noted above, UNESCO has taken part in a number of projects to preserve cultural property at the request of the government concerned. Its program can be divided into three principal categories:

a) <u>international standards:</u> the preparation and application of international conventions such as the Hague Convention of 1954 on the Protection of Cultural Property in the Event of Armed Conflict, and that on the Protection of the World Cultural and Natural Heritage, adopted in 1972. Recommendations are also prepared as standards for Member States to follow on such problems as the preservation of cultural property endangered by public and private works or the conservation of historic quarters.

b) research and publication: a quarterly, Museum, is published as well as a news bulletin and several series of technical handbooks. Research in conservation and meetings of experts are encouraged in cooperation with other international and national organizations and institutions.

c) operational programs: consultants, experts and fellowships as well as grants of equipment and funds are provided at the request of Member States. This program is financed by UNESCO's regular budget and from extra-budgetary sources including the United Nations Development Program (UNDP), the World Bank, the Inter-American Development Bank, and the World Heritage Fund. Voluntary contributions from both public and private sources for the conservation of monuments and the development of museums also help support UNESCO's operational programs.

During the first few years of its existence, UNESCO concentrated on re-establishing contacts among conservation specialists that had been disrupted by war. It was the first of the UN Agencies to accept Italy, the Federal Republic of Germany and Japan as Member States. UNESCO membership has grown rapidly with the acquisition of independence by former colonies. By 1982 it had over 150 Member States. The programs of the United Nations and its agencies have been affected by this change. The needs of the developing countries have stimulated projects through which technical, scientific and administrative techniques could be transmitted to these States under international auspices. While the interchange of information is still important in UNESCO's program, one of the ways UNESCO has met this need is by establishing other organizations able to work more closely with national institutions and individual specialists.

The International Council of Museums (ICOM) was one of several international non-governmental organizations which existed before UNESCO and soon became identified with it. In the absence of a comparable non-governmental organization for monuments and sites, UNESCO formed an advisory committee, "The International Committee on Monuments, Artistic and Historical Sites and Archeological Excavations" to help establish the main lines of the UNESCO program during its formative years. The Committee recommended the establishment of an international governmental organization to develop programs, coordinate research and participate in the training of specialists in the conservation of cultural property. In 1959, UNESCO accepted the invitation of the Government of Italy to establish The International Center for the Study of the Preservation and Restoration of Cultural Property in Rome (ICCROM), with Dr. Harold J. Plenderleith as its first director.

Also on the recommendation of the Committee, a non-governmental organization, The International Council of Monuments and Sites (ICOMOS) was established with its headquarters in Paris in 1965. ICOMOS provides a forum for professionals and specialists in the preservation of monuments and sites. Its international committees, working closely with the other organizations mentioned above, have held meetings on the preservation of stone, wood, and other building materials. Both ICOM and ICOMOS run international documentation centers under contract to UNESCO and receive subventions from UNESCO and other sources.

In addition to the international assistance provided by UNESCO, UNDP and the organizations mentioned above, support has also been received from other governments, national and private institutions and individuals. The existence of UNESCO, ICCROM, ICOMOS and other organizations have facilitated contributions from national and private sources. A review follows mentioning several disasters in which States were aided in the preservation of their heritage.

PROGRAMS FOR THE RESCUE OF CULTURAL PROPERTY DAMAGED BY SEISMISM

Cuzco, Peru

The first request UNESCO received from a government to aid it in the preservation of monuments and sites following a natural disaster was in 1952 following the earthquake of May 21, 1950, which had severely damaged the city of Cuzco. Over 3,000 dwellings were destroyed and many monuments severely damaged. (Figure 6.1) Cuzco had been the capital of the Inca empire and many traces of Inca construction survive including the megalithic fortress of Sacsahuaman located near the city. After the Spanish conquest it had become the colonial capital, and many monuments built in the Spanish tradition date from this period.

The Peruvian government gave high priority to the reconstruction of Cuzco. While the loss of lives was low (much of the population was outside the city at a soccer game when the quake took place) the extent of the damage was great. In one act of serendipity, the shocks caused much of the stucco to flake off construction dating from the Colonial period exposing their foundations of Inca masonry whose existence had been long forgotten. A special tobacco tax was levied to finance repairs in Cuzco and plans prepared for the restoration and renovation of the city. Prior to the final approval of the plans, however, the government asked UNESCO to send a team to review the problems and prepare recommendations on the proposed solutions. [Kubler et al., 1952]

Many of Cuzco's dwellings made of adobe—unbaked clay bricks strengthened with chopped straw and formed in molds—were completely destroyed. This was caused not only by the comparative lack of resistance of the material, but also by poor construction or

409

Figure 6.1. Cuzco, Peru: Church after Earthquake of May 21, 1950.

lack of maintenance. Some of the buildings used relatively good masonry but some monuments were composite, mixing adobe with fired brick or cut stone which also offered little resistance to the shock. One of the problems in the historic quarter was that many of the buildings were originally built to house well-to-do families and their servants, but during the intervening years such families had left. These buildings became multiple family units, often housing four or five individuals in each room. The crowding resulted in inadequate or absent hygienic facilities, kitchens and other amenities and little or no maintenance of the buildings. In spite of this, their handsome doors and facades made them well worth preserving. In some cases Inca ashlar masonry was used as their foundations, adding to their historic value. The team suggested that several blocks containing the best examples of dwellings from this period be zoned as a historic quarter and renovation take place.

The pattern of Inca construction in squares linked by narrow lanes—their widths due to the lack of wheeled vehicles and the traffic of porters and llamas—formed the basis of Spanish Colonial Cuzco. Well cut and fitted Inca masonry formed the foundations for homes of the Spanish period, but prior to the earthquake plans were being considered to demolish the foundations and buildings in a number of areas to widen the lanes into streets for the use of motor traffic. The team recommended retaining the existing pattern of lanes and building a ring road beginning at the airport which would use existing terraced land, outside of the city, freeing the historic center from motor traffic. This recommendation was accepted. It was also recommended that the Inca masonry revealed by the quake should be left exposed. This suggestion was also adopted.

The growth of air transportation and the importance of international tourism to the economy since the fifties has caused the government to develop Cuzco and its surroundings. In 1973 a UNESCO/UNDP/IDB (Inter-American Development Bank) project began with a total projected budget of $70 million, including a loan of $20 million from IDB. $12 million was allotted for restoration. The UNESCO/UNDP component provided experts, fellowships and equipment. [Agurto-Calvo, 1979] In addition to the preservation and restoration of historic monuments and sites, the plan included the expansion of the airport, improvement of hotels, highways and other infrastructure required for tourism. Because of the large number of international experts required for the project, UNESCO/UNDP began a regional training project for students coming from other Andean countries to gain practical and theoretical experience in conservation and restoration.

Pagan, Burma

Pagan, located on the east bank of the Irrawaddy River in central Burma, not far from Mandalay, was the capital of the Burmese people from the 11th to the 13th centuries. The city was the focus of a network of roads commanding the fertile plain which during the two centuries of its hey-day had more than 5,000 monuments raised in honor of Buddha. Of these monuments, 2,000 have been identified by the Burmese archeological service while many of the remainder were destroyed by the meandering Irrawaddy and other factors. Most domestic architecture is built of wood, thatch and other perishable materials, but the surviving monuments were built with fired brick, bonded together with mud mortar strengthened with vegetable glue. Many monuments are also coated with a stucco of lime plaster which, while protecting the monument, also obscures the details which were carved in brick. Pagan's role came to an end with the Mongol conquest of 1287 A.D. The site, however, was never completely abandoned as many of the shrines, temples and monasteries are still in use and visited by pilgrims. They owed their survival also to their massive construction, characterized by brick walls up to 12 feet in thickness. Two major types of buildings have been found in Pagan:

a) the stupa: a solid bell shaped structure set upon super-imposed terraces crowned by a finial or spire. The stupa usually housed relics and is circular in cross-section although some polygonal examples exist;

b) temples and monasteries: usually a terraced plinth which may have external stairs leading to terraces, gateways and pinnacles with a central square tower (sikara) or a small central stupa with a finial above. Three variants are found:

   i)   a central room forming a sanctuary usually housing a statue of Buddha with the sikara resting on the roof without a support below.
   ii) a central room surrounding a pillar supporting the roof and the sikara above;
   iii) a central room surrounding the supporting pillar which in turn is surrounded by other concentric rooms.

On July 8, 1975 an earthquake (5.6 on the Richter scale) caused considerable damage to many of the monuments in Pagan. One of them, the 11th century stupa known as Bupaya collapsed completely. The government services as well as religious groups immediately began shoring up weakened structures and rebuilding the most seriously damaged ones. At the request of the government, while the work was underway using traditional materials and techniques, UNESCO sent a consultant to review the damage, assess the work and possibly recommend alternative methods. [Pichard, 1976]

In an assessment of the damage, it was found that taller, rigid structures had suffered the most and that many of the finials were damaged or had collapsed completely. On the other hand, the stupas, with the exception of Bupaya, seemed to have survived with little damage. In the case of the latter, Pichard, the consultant, noted that the collapse of Bupaya may have been due to other factors aggravated by the quake. The roof and superstructure of the temple structures which did not have a supporting pillar (Figure 6.2) usually collapsed into the central chamber. Many of the structures which survived had had stone, wood or metal reinforcements set at the summits, cornices, lintels and other areas of weaknesses before the quakes occurred.

The presence of prior repairs also affected the survival of the temples and monasteries. In some a portland cement/lime mortar had been used to replace the old mud mortar. In these buildings, instead of individual bricks shaking loose and falling the bonded bricks fell in masses of up to a ton and caused considerable damage to the lower parts of the structure. The use of a softer mortar was considered, but this would have the disadvantage of lessening resistance to the effects of weathering and vegetation growth. The solution proposed by the UNESCO consultant was to insert belts of cast reinforced concrete at vulnerable points of the building (Figure 6.3), such as for one of the best known of the Pagan monuments, the Shwezigon Pagoda.

Because of the isolationist policy practiced by the Ne Win government, equipment and supplies required for technical work had been unavailable for a number of years. At the request of the government, UNESCO sent drawing tables, drafting equipment, cameras, drawing paper, etc., to the Department of Antiquities. Bullock carts had been used to bring water from the Irrawaddy to the site for the workmen and to mix mortar and cement. In negotiation with the Government it was possible to have the Japanese contribute dump trucks, stake bodied trucks, water tank trailers, etc., for the Pagan project under the Japanese/Burmese bilateral aid program.

Trujillo, Peru

On May 31, 1970, a severe earthquake (7.8 on the Richter scale) occurred about twelve miles southwest of Chimbote in the north central coast of Peru. Besides heavy loss of life due to the collapse of dwellings made of adobe a number of Spanish Colonial monuments were badly damaged as well as such pre-Columbian structures as the pyramids of the Sun and of the Moon at Sechine. UNESCO furnished an expert to conduct a survey of the damaged monuments, prepare preliminary plans for the restoration of momuments and aid in reconstruction and restoration work. [de Mesa, 1972] The survey found that buildings of adobe were the least resistant to shocks.

One of the problems encountered at Trujillo was the lack of documentation on previous repairs and modifications to the buildings. At times 5 to 6 phases of change could be identified without any records as to time or circumstance. Hence careful analysis was required to determine the original form of a monument before its restoration. Many older monuments resisted the quake better than later construction because two methods were used to add to the strength of adobe construction: 1) a sort of half timbered system in

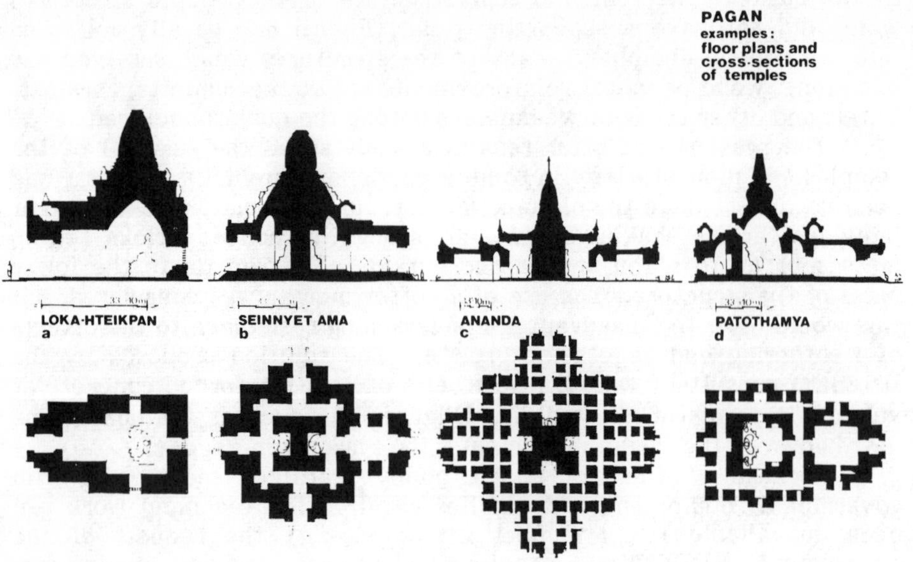

PAGAN
examples:
floor plans and
cross-sections
of temples

LOKA-HTEIKPAN
a

SEINNYET AMA
b

ANANDA
c

PATOTHAMYA
d

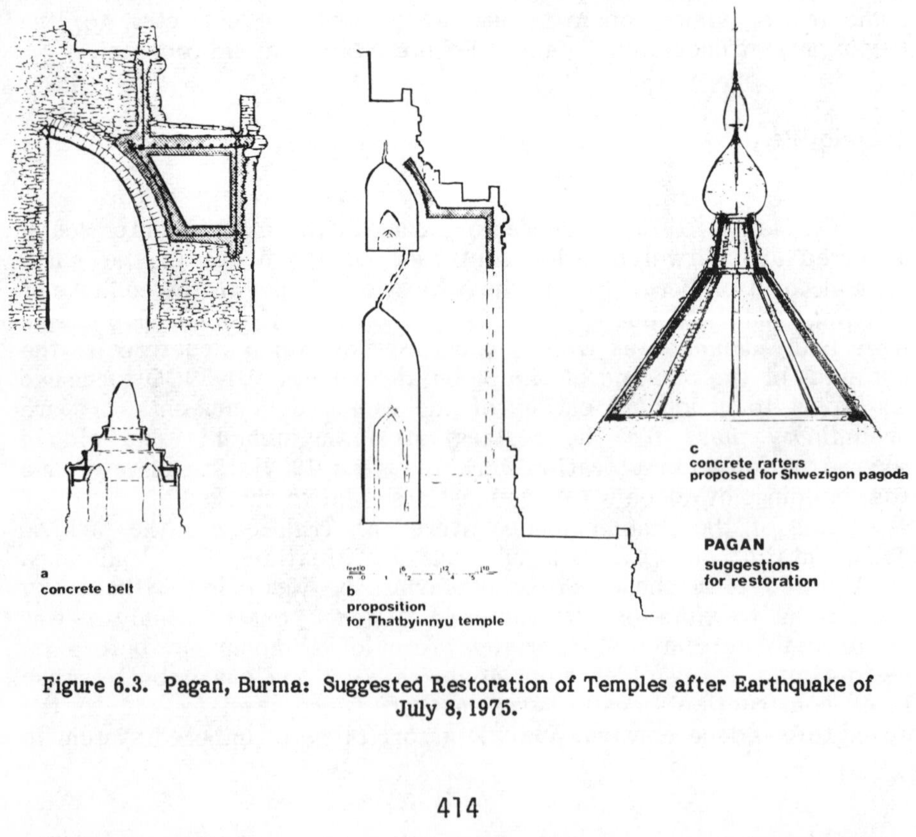

a
concrete belt

b
proposition
for Thatbyinnyu temple

c
concrete rafters
proposed for Shwezigon pagoda

PAGAN
suggestions
for restoration

Figure 6.3. Pagan, Burma: Suggested Restoration of Temples after Earthquake of
July 8, 1975.

414

which wooden beams gave stability to the structure while the spaces were filled with adobe and covered with mud plaster; and 2) the use of adobe buttresses. In addition to the restoration work, a central monumental zone, historic quarters, and regulations were established to ensure the continued protection of the monuments.

Antigua, Guatemala

On February 4, 1976, an earthquake took place in the highlands of Guatemala which measured 7.5 on the Richter scale. It was followed by a number of after shocks resulting in extensive damage to monuments and dwellings. (Figure 6.4) An estimated 23,000 people were killed and 75,000 injured. The scale of the disaster was such that the Government requested UNESCO to launch a campaign to aid it in the preservation of its cultural heritage.

The most important center of historic monuments in the affected area is found in the former capital city of Antigua which was known as "Santiago de los Caballeros de Guatemala" when it was founded in 1527. It was the headquarters of the Captaincy General, the most important administrative center of the Spanish Colonial period located between Mexico City to the north and Lima, Peru to the south. The city was destroyed by an eruption in 1542, rebuilt and then destroyed again by an earthquake in 1773. Following the second cataclysm the capital was moved to what 's now known as Guatemala City. The earlier capital was then known as "La Antigua Capital" and eventually as "Antigua". Ruins of the period preceding the 1773 quake had been preserved or rebuilt in many cases. The 1976 quake damaged many of the ruins and surviving monuments and many of the surrounding dwellings, particularly those made of adobe, collapsed trapping their inhabitants within them.

In response to the government's request and in view of the scale of damage UNESCO established an office in Guatemala City to aid in coordinating the work to be done. Urgently needed equipment was furnished and consultants sent to establish inventories, to assess damage and repair costs, and to aid in preparing plans for reconstruction. The aim of the project was to carry out a program analogous to the Venice campaign, in which UNESCO prepared a list of damaged cultural property with a summary of the conditions of each monument, the work to be carried out and an estimated budget. The availability of such a list would permit States, institutions or individuals to take over one or more projects to aid in the work of restoration.

A seminar-cum-training course on the protection of monuments in seismic areas was held in Antigua during 4 - 11 November organized jointly by UNESCO, ICOMOS and the UN Disaster Relief Coordinator (UNDRO). ICCROM was also represented. The seminar profited from a review of conditions in Guatemala, the work underway, and the problems affecting historic buildings in seismic areas. Among the

Figure 6.4. Chimaltenango, Guatemala: Destruction of Vernacular Buildings in
Earthquake of February 4, 1976.

recommendations adopted was the necessity to develop analyses of dynamic stress factors and vibratory processes; the need for models to establish seismic codes applicable to historic buildings; and the advisability of having an expert on cultural property attached to emergency services or advisory bodies. [UNESCO, 1980] While the Seminar reviewed plans for restoration in Guatemala and the work continued, it has not been possible to carry out the project as planned because of the current political unrest which prevails in the country.

Gemona di Friuli, Italy

On May 6, 1976, an earthquake occurred in the Upper Tagliamento Valley in northeastern Italy, a region noted for its strong tectonic deformation where a number of quakes have been recorded historically. The Gemona quake was classified as 6.5 on the Richter scale with a foreshock registerd at 4.5 and a series of aftershocks. At the request of the government UNESCO sent a team of experts to work with the authorities concerned during July-August that year. [Ambraseys, Pichard, and Ziogas, 1976]

More than three-quarters of the houses in the affected area were old, their walls made up of badly. laid rubble masonry, sometimes mixed with bricks and thickly laid clay or lime plaster mortar. Many were two to three stories high with heavy floors and roofs supported by joists of timber which were inserted a few inches into the masonry but which were otherwise unsupported. Some of them had tie rods placed to give greater support to floor beams and such buildings had a better survival rate. Without such reinforcement a slight outward movement of the walls caused the joists to pull free and roofs or floors to collapse. (Figure 6.5 and 6.6) Many of the old houses had been abandoned for several years or had deteriorated badly through lack of maintenance. Such buildings offered little resistance to the earthquakes. Ambraseys added that:

> Both old and new houses which had recently been renovated suffered the most. Some of them had a second or third story added, supported partly by old walls and partly by new reinforced concrete columns. Masonry houses had also been tampered with at different times. A common cause of unintentional weakening is the installation of new electricity and water conduits, the relocation of bathrooms and sewer and drainage pipes in old walls. Improper repairs that have weakened the walls and the cumulative effects of such interference with the stability of the structure, have produced buildings each with its own problems; almost none of these damaged are capable of being strengthened economically. [Ambraseys, Pichard and Ziogas, 1976, Part II, p. 10]

417

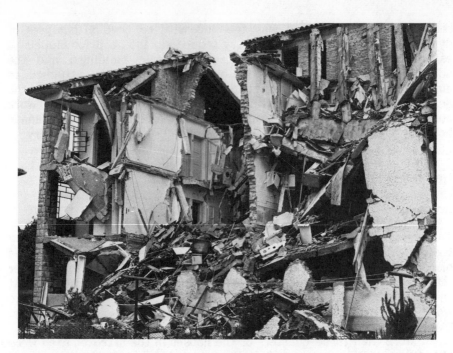

Figure 6.5. Gemona del Friuli, Italy: View of Damaged Buildings after Earthquake of May 6, 1976.

Figure 6.6. Gemona del Friuli, Italy: View of Pancaked Modern Reinforced Concrete Structure after Earthquake of May 6, 1976.

Of the historic monuments, about 600 churches were destroyed or damaged beyond repair. Many were poorly built as the mortar used in this region was poorly made with a high proportion of sand to lime. It would be difficult to make up for the poor quality of mortar used as the systems of injecting grout or even a synthetic plastic would not work. In one case, part of a historic church which had been reinforced survived but in another section of the same edifice the reinforced area fell causing considerable damage because of its mass and weight. In another case the City Hall (Palazzo Comunale) of Venzone suffered minor damage such as cracks and movement of the masonry while it was surrounded by the ruins of others. The City Hall had suffered severe damage from aerial bombs during World War II and had been rebuilt. The measures taken in this particular case should be studied and applied widely in restoration programs of the area.

Montenegro, Yugoslavia

On April 15, 1979, the Adriatic coast of Yugoslavia was rocked by a quake which registered 7.0 on the Richter scale, preceded by a shock of 5.1 and followed by numerous aftershocks. At the request of the Government of Montenegro, UNESCO sent a team to aid the authorities in assessing damage and to recommend a plan for the most rapid and permanent recovery of the affected area. [Ambraseys, Ciborowski and Despeyroux, 1979]

The team found that the most severely affected buildings were old houses—usually built of stone, one to three stories in height—many of which had artistic or historic value. The most important historic complex was the walled town of Opstina Kotor, in which the majority of buildings were weakened or damaged. The second group of importance included the Palace of the Sea Captains in Dobrota and a number of small rural and town churches dating from the 12th to 14th century. Of 454 churches about a fourth (134) were totally destroyed and about the same number (138) heavily damaged. (Figure 6.7 and 6.8)

Coincidentally, a UNDP/South Adriatic Project for the development of cultural tourism was underway in the coastal area. The Master Plan for the project had been adopted in 1968/1969. While much of the work was on the infrastructure required, such as improved highways and accommodations, attention had also been given to the problem of the development and presentation of historic monuments and sites. The Master Plan was revised to take into account the damage caused by the quakes and the work of reconstruction required.

In addition to consultants UNESCO also furnished equipment, which was in short supply because of the severity of the quakes. The area is rich in sites dating from Classic Greek and Roman times; Latin, Mediterranean, Islamic and Byzantine examples of architecture as well as Early Christian, Medieval, Renaissance and Baroque period buildings. There are also historic towns and fishing villages, as well as rural settlements containing expressions of local folk art. They

419

Figure 6.7. Montenegro, Yugoslavia: Destruction in Historic Town Center after Earthquake of April 15, 1979.

Figure 6.8. Montenegro, Yugoslavia: Church, Showing Destruction Caused by Earthquake of April 15, 1979.

constitute one of the chief attractions of the area for international tourism and their preservation is important, not only for their value as cultural heritage, but also for economic development.

The reconstruction and rehabilitation of the historic towns of Kotor, Budva and Ulcinj and the restoration of important monuments and sites in other towns and villages will be expensive and require time. In addition to the work foreseen for the three towns mentioned above partial reconstruction is being planned in Herceg Novi and Risan. The cost is estimated at $150 million.

MAJOR INTERNATIONAL CAMPAIGNS

Borobudur (Java), Indonesia—Anticipating Seismism

The projects summarized above represent examples of international participation in restoration activities after quakes have occurred. In principle, however, a much more fruitful approach would be to anticipate the possibility of earthquakes in the design of monuments. An example of such a project is the design adopted for the restoration of Borobudur, located in central Java, Indonesia, not far from the city of Yogyakarta. Borobudur was built on a natural hill in a fertile valley system surrounded by verdant rice fields. One of the mountains rimming the valley is Gunung Merapi, an active volcano usually marked by a plume of smoke. Its eruptions in the past have buried, for example, temples which were in use built at the same time as Borobudur (8th - 9th centuries A.D.). It is not surprising that earthquakes also occur in Java although, to date, Borobudur has been spared the effects of a major quake.

Borobudur was built during the Sailendra dynasty and is a mandala in stone depicting Buddhist cosmology. The monument is built in the form of a stepped pyramid. The base is square, each side being approximately 123 meters in length. The four lower terraces are rimmed with balustrades, and on the sides of the terrace and the balustrades are carved panels illustrating the life of Buddha, the lives of the people, illustrations of "jakata" tales or parables, followed by the lives of Boddhisatvas who also attained Buddhahood. The carved panels are 2.5 k.m. or 1.3 miles in length. Above are three consecutive circular terraces, devoid of carvings, but having statues of Buddha covered with stone trellises and in the center a hollow stupa. [Marzuki and Awuy, 1978]

The cut stones of andesite seem to have been made from boulders found in the nearby river, for their color varies and they are not of good quality. It is estimated that 55,000 m^3 of stone was used in building Borobudur, and the enormous mass must have caused settling in the subsoil. The stones were laid dry (i.e., without mortar), which meant that heavy monsoon rains could penetrate the interior readily. At the same time, its flexibility probably contributed to the monument's survival from its abandonment at the end of the Sailendra dynasty until its rediscovery during the colonial period.

After Borobudur was cleared, some reconstruction took place. Lack of maintenance during the second World War and Occupation contributed to the deterioration of the monument. Lichens and mosses weathered the cut and carved stones. Many of the lower terraces were out of plumb and in some cases the tilt was so alarming that the Antiquities Service dismantled the Balustrades and part of the terraces. Consultants who examined the monument recommended dismantling and strengthening the foundations as even a slight quake might have caused tons of cut stone to descend in a slide ruining one of the world's most important monuments south of the equator.

The services of consultant engineers engaged by UNESCO were subsequently extended by the Netherlands under their bilateral aid program. Soil mechanics studies were carried out as well as experiments on cleaning and consolidating the carved stones. In reviewing the proposed solutions the international consultative committee recommended that the design take into account the possibility of seismism (up to 5.6 on the Richter scale). The design of the supports for the four lower terraces was modified to take this factor into account. Massive concrete slabs are to be placed beneath the four square terraces (Figure 6.9)—two lower slabs approximately 66 c.m. (26.4 inches) thick and two upper slabs 44 c.m. (17.6 inches) thick. Other features of the design called for the placement of water tight barriers to prevent rain water from seeping into the monument and to protect against capillary action. [NEDECO/Netherlands Technical Assistance, 1972]

American contributions for the project included the gift of equipment from the John D. Rockefeller 3rd Fund (now the Asian Cultural Council) of New York, a contribution of about $1.2 million raised by a private committee, and computer time and services from IBM to keep tracks of the thousands of carved stones as they were dismounted, cleaned, consolidated, and replaced in the monument. Many other countries have also contributed to Borobudur, the total amount in cash and in kind being well over $5 million. Work on the reconstruction was begun in 1972 and is scheduled to end in 1982.

Florence and Venice, Italy

The General Conference of UNESCO was in session during 3 - 4 November 1966 when the news arrived of unprecedented floods in northern Italy. The Arno River had flooded the central part of the city of Florence destroying or damaging many art treasures and historic monuments. In Venice the level of rivers flowing into the lagoon rose not only because of torrential rains but also because of unusually high tides brought about by a violent scirocco which had driven the waters of the Mediterranean up the shallow Adriatic. The waters rose so rapidly that attempts to save works of art or private

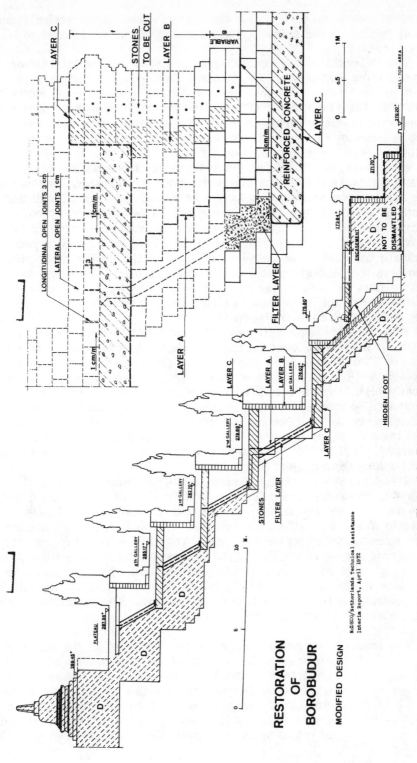

Figure 6.9. Borobudur, Indonesia: Restoration Plan.

possessions were hindered. As the waters receded oil stains from heating systems, dead animals, furniture and other debris marked the flooded areas.

The Delegate of Italy called upon UNESCO and the international community for assistance. The General Conference voted at once to launch an international campaign for the safeguarding of cultural property in the two cities. Offers for assistance poured in, and art restorers from many parts of Europe made their way to Florence where emergency measures to save paintings and other works of art and history were urgently required. UNESCO sent two large hospital type autoclaves, modified for ethylene oxide impregnation of books and documents, to prevent mold growth and insect attacks. Handmade paper from Japan was shipped by air to be pasted over oil paintings preventing flaking paint from dropping off its backing. Many college students went to Florence to help rescue the vast collections of the Archives. ICCROM also participated in the emergency and helped to coordinate the work of volunteers with that of the Italian authorities. A conservation laboratory and workshop was built in the Fortezza da Basso as part of a long term conservation project in which many paintings were kept in storage in high humidity to prevent premature drying before they could be treated.

While Venice also suffered from the flood or unusual "Aqua Alta", most mobile works of art had already been located in the second floors of buildings, since high water was all too common a phenomenon. The city had been in a long period of decline, and the unusually high flood accelerated the deterioration caused by lack of maintenance, demographic changes, and declining cultural importance. The disaster caused the decision to arrest this long term decline and to ensure the survival of the city. The measures called for required time and money, so that the safeguarding of the city and its surroundings became a long term project.

The problems affecting Venice had been known for some time. Unhappily, however, scientific and technical studies to define the parameters of the problems had never been carried out. Between the two world Wars, in an effort to improve the economy, a petrochemical plant was constructed on the mainland. Together with this a new city, Mestre, rose nearby at the end of the causeway linking the mainland to the island. This contributed to the abandonment of Venice as homes were modern, comfortable and dry in the Mestre—while the chemical plant contributed to the pollution of the lagoon. The problems which beset Venice can be summarized as follows:

Physical: long term changes in the sea level of the Adriatic; changes in the ecology of the lagoon (fishing is still important in the Venetian economy); sinking of the island due, in part to the use of artesian wells; sinking of the piles which form the foundations of the buildings; salt water contributing to the erosion of bricks and stone; atmospheric pollution; etc.

Social and Loss of population, economy dependent upon summer
tourism; economic:
> unhealthy living conditions—high humidity, run-down
> public buildings; lack of social amenities for
> permanent population; inadequate public services,
> etc.

Cultural: lack of activities and cultural life during the off
season; absence of education and cultural activities
which would attract visitors or scholars during the
off season.

In an unprecedented move, the Parliament of Italy adopted a
Special Law to safeguard Venice on April 13, 1973, with a budget of
approximately $500 million. It specifically takes into account
UNESCO's presence in the execution of this project. In order to carry
out the responsibilities foreseen UNESCO established a Liaison Office
in Venice and has played an important catalytic role. It sponsored and
bore much of the expense (particularly before the enabling act was
passed) of a series of studies on atmospheric pollution, oceanography,
social studies, and an inventory of historic buildings. One of the early
publications which resulted from the preparatory stage of work was
"Venice Restored", which listed historically interesting buildings,
monuments, and works of art in need of restoration. Each was
accompanied by a summary of its history and importance, the work
required and an estimate of costs. They provided a ready reference to
governments, institutions, special committees or individuals on work
which could be undertaken. [UNESCO, 1971; UNESCO, 1978; Rinaldo,
1975; Davis, 1973]
Despite delays, a number of results have been achieved. New
legislation controls industrial discharge into the lagoon and imposes
strict limits on atmospheric pollution. On the historic island,
institutional and domestic heating have been modified by replacing
coal and oil furnaces with gas to lessen atmospheric pollution. The
banks of many of the canals have been repaired and modern sewage
disposal systems introduced on most of the islands except for Venice,
which will have its waste water piped to the mainland. Aqueducts
have been built, permitting the closing off of all industrial artesian
wells and most of the private wells, so that the island is no longer
sinking.
The Municipality of Venice has been working on a program to
upgrade housing in the poorer residential quarters, and has built an
indoor swimming pool and gymnasium for the use of the people.
Among the projects to keep the city "alive" during the winter months
has been the organization of an international course on the preservation of stone as a building material by UNESCO with the cooperation
of Italian authorities. ICCROM is the executing Agency under
contract to UNESCO. A course given by the Council of Europe on the
training of artisans in the skills required for the restoration of historic
buidings is underway.

One of the most successful aspects of the Campaign has been the support received from private committees and institutions in Australia, Belgium, Federal Republic of Germany, France, Iran, Italy, Netherlands, United Kingdom, United States, Sweden and Switzerland. Contributions in cash and in kind have come from a number of Member States and organizations (e.g., special exhibition and concert in favor of Venice organized by the Asahi Newspaper of Japan and a department store). Six of the private committees were from the U.S., notably the Committee to Rescue Italian Art (CRIA), the Venice Committee of the International Fund for Monuments, Save Venice, Inc., etc.

Besides its normal role of initiation and coordination of international assistance, UNESCO has been represented on ad hoc committees organized by the Italian government to implement the program foreseen. The Italian Government has also permitted private committees to carry out work, exempt from local taxes provided that the contracts are processed through UNESCO. The project has been an outstanding example of the cooperative effort of governmental authorities, international organizations, contributions of Member States, private institutions and individuals.

SUMMARY AND CONCLUSIONS

UNESCO, while not neglecting its regular program to raise standards in conservation and encouraging member States to cooperate in the preservation of man's cultural heritage, has seen the greatest growth of its program in operational projects. During 1954/1955, for example, the budget for the preservation of the cultural heritage under its Program of Participation (provision of consultants, scholarships, equipment, etc.) amounted to $50,000. No extra-budgetary projects existed. During 1979/1980 UNESCO spent over $1 million for Participation projects and the extra-budgetary projects amounted to approximately $6 million. While budget expansion is a crude measure of growth it does indicate the support and interest of Member States as well as of people in conservation.

In surveying the effects of seismism it is clear that a general pattern can be discerned. Soundly built buidings, as might be expected, tend to survive particularly if they have been strengthened in advance to resist unusual shocks. Unfortunately many historic buildings, while having a superficial impression of solidity, are quite fragile. Adobe or rubble cemented by mortar, when covered with stucco or painted mud plaster, may appear to be quite strong although it is actually incapable of resisting any shock of importance. Many historic quarters are also run down. Frequently the families which had built the homes in such quarters have left for newer and more comfortable dwellings elsewhere and have been succeeded by the poor. Under this circumstance overcrowding is common and maintenance non-existent or barely adequate. On the other hand, modernization of buildings may improve living conditions but weaken the fabric of the buiding.

There is a need for technical analyses of the effect of quakes on old buildings using traditional materials, such as adobe, in earthquake zones. Tests should be carried out on the means—preferably not too expensive—that might be employed to strengthen such buildings and the test results should be widely disseminated.

In summary, international assistance has become an important factor in the preservation of the cultural heritage of all peoples. At a time of rapid social and cultural change, preservation enhances a feeling of identity and, for contributors, reinforces appreciation of the traditions of others, thereby contributing to international understanding.

REFERENCES

Agurto-Calvo, S. Cuzco la Traza Urbana de La Cuidad Inca. Project PER/39. Paris: UNESCO and the Instituto Nacional de Cultura del Peru, 1979.

Ambraseys, Nicholas N., Adolf Ciborowski and J. Despeyroux. Socialist Republic of Yugoslavia: The Earthquake of 15 April 1979 in Montenegro. Paris: UNESCO, 1979.

Ambraseys, Nicholas N., Pierre Pichard and G. N. Ziogas. Italy: The Gemona de Friuli Earthquake of 6 May 1976. Paris: UNESCO, 1976.

Davis, J. H. Venice. New York: Newsweek Book Division, 1973.

de Mesa, M. J. Peru: La Restauracion de Los Monumentos de la Zona Affectada por el Sismo del 31 de Mayo de 1971. Paris: UNESCO, 1972.

Kubler, G. et al. "Cuzco: Reconstruction of the Town and Restoration of its Monuments." Museums and Monuments Series, UNESCO, Volume 3, 1952.

Marzuki, Y. and F. Awuy. Namo Buddhaya. Amsterdam: Indonesia Overseas Bank, 1978.

NEDECO/Netherlands Technical Assistance. The Restoration of Borobudur, Interim Report. Indonesia: UNESCO, April 1972.

Pichard, Pierre. Burma: The Restoration of Pagan. Paris: UNESCO, 1976.

Rinaldo, M. "The Other Venice" in The Conservation of Cities. London and Paris: Croom, Helm and the UNESCO Press, 1975.

UNESCO. Final Report on the Seminar-cum-Training Course on the Protection of Monuments in Seismic Areas. Paris: UNESCO, 1980.

UNESCO. Sauver Venise. Paris: Robert Laffont, 1971.

UNESCO. Venice Restored. Paris: UNESCO, 1978.

Federal Response Measures to Natural Disasters

Richard W. Krimm

INTRODUCTION

The Federal Emergency Management Agency (FEMA) is developing a coordinated national plan for response, recovery, mitigation and preparedness with respect to natural disasters. The program features a partnership between potential impact victims and various levels of government. Cooperation between FEMA and managers of museums and historic properties may be expected to occur as part of the program's operation.

The FEMA program provides for the mobilization of a broad spectrum of Federal resources following a major disaster. Before the event and in the hours after a disaster, however, building owners must take steps to minimize losses. The Southern California Earthquake Preparedness Project (SCEPP), in which a partnership between national response activities and local predisaster preparation is the cornerstone, is one example of such a step.

This paper describes the FEMA concept, a national coordinated plan for response to manmade and natural disasters, giving an outline of the principal FEMA programs in the area of natural disasters. An explanation of the national disaster assistance system will show how local, State and Federal officials work together in time of a major natural disaster.

THE FEDERAL EMERGENCY MANAGEMENT AGENCY (FEMA)

1. Formation

In June of 1978 emergency-related federal agencies and programs were brought together into a new independent agency called the Federal Emergency Management Agency (FEMA). They included, by statute, the Federal Insurance Administration (FIA) from the

Department of Housing and Urban Development (HUD), the National Fire Prevention and Control Administration (NFCPA) from the Department of Commerce, and the Federal Emergency Broadcast System oversight responsibility from the Executive Office of the President.

Other programs and agencies later transferred by Executive Order include: the Defense Civil Preparedness Agency (DCPA) from the Department of Defense, the Federal Disaster Assistance Administration (FDAA) from HUD, the Federal Preparedness Agency (FPA) from the General Services Administration, the National Weather Service Community Preparedness Program (NWSCPP) from the Department of Commerce, the Earthquake Hazard Reduction Office and the Dam Safety Coordination Program from the Executive Office of the President, and two emergency functions not assigned to any agency: Federal Response to Consequences of Terroristic Incidents and Coordination of Emergency Warning.

2. A National Plan for Comprehensive Emergency Management (CEM) for Natural Hazards

The formation of FEMA was an attempt to develop a coordinated, comprehensive national emergency management plan to deal with natural hazards, man-made emergencies and nuclear attack. The approach proposed was a partnership between Federal, State and local governments with aid from private organizations, business and industry. FEMA would coordinate activities on the Federal level and, through regional and state offices, help to mitigate, prepare for, respond to and recover from a range of major hazards. The diagram in Figure 6.10 shows the components of the National CEM program for the Federal, State and local levels of government.

Similar hazard situations affect areas differently. Because the same amount of damage in dollars will have different effects upon different localities, FEMA does not set a dollar figure above which assistance is offered. Rather, a flexible system of evaluation is used on a case-by-case basis. Requests to the President for help may be made only by the governor, and such requests must be made through the appropriate FEMA regional office.

3. Comprehensive Emergency Management (CEM) for Natural Hazards

Comprehensive Emergency Management (CEM) means more than the FEMA coordination role in time of a natural disaster. The four phases of a comprehensive emergency management approach are mitigation, preparedness (planning and warning), response, and recovery (short and long term). (Figure 6.11)

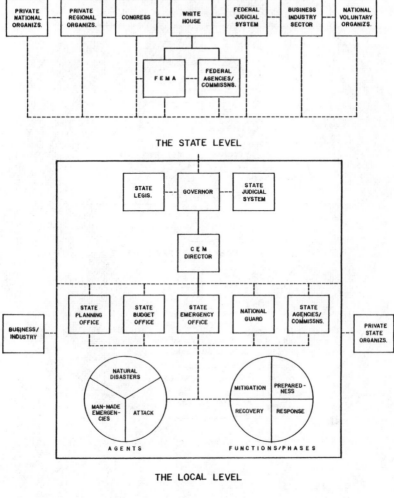

THE FEDERAL LEVEL

THE STATE LEVEL

THE LOCAL LEVEL

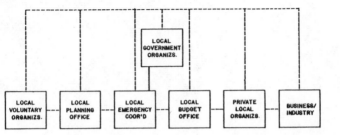

* SOURCE: NATIONAL GOVERNORS ASSOCIATION

Figure 6.10. National Comprehensive Emergency Management.

431

C E M for
NATURAL DISASTER

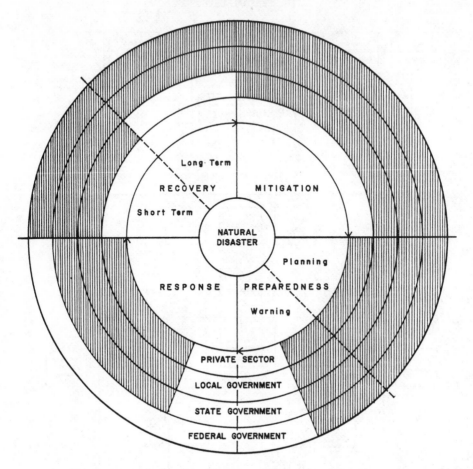

Figure 6.11. Comprehensive Emergency Management for Disasters.

Natural hazards provide the greatest opportunity for coordinated interaction of all levels of government. Impact may be limited to small areas or may be dispersed. An example of a small area of impact is a tornado that hits one town. Multi-state winter storms are an example of a dispersed impact. Natural disasters require Federal agencies to provide recovery assistance for major disasters. State emergency offices prepare for, and coordinate response to state-wide disasters. Local governments maintain warning systems and respond to all disasters in their areas.

Specific activities of various phases of CEM are:

Preparedness
> Technical Information
> Public Education
> Vulnerability Analysis
> Training
> Exercises
> Contingency Planning
> Forecasts and Warnings

Mitigation
> Legislation
> Inspection
> Risk Mapping
> Building Codes
> Financial Incentives
> Land Use Management
> Zoning Ordinances
> Structural Changes
> Research

Response
> Volunteers
> News Media
> Security
> Damage Assessment
> Mobile Communication
> Individual Assistance
> Temporary Housing
> Disaster Declaration
> Search and Rescue
> Emergency Center

Recovery
> Medical Services
> Incident Reporting
> Unemployment Assistance

Tax Information
Intergovernmental Relations
Loans, Grants
Insurance

The key to the CEM concept is for Federal, State and local governments to act in a preplanned, systematic fashion to supply the needed services to the affected population.

4. FEMA Programs in Natural Hazards

A. The National Flood Insurance Program. For decades, the national response to flood disasters was largely limited to building flood control works (dams, levees, seawalls, etc.) and providing relief to flood victims. To compound the problem, the public could not buy flood coverage from insurance companies, and building techniques to reduce flood damage to new construction were often overlooked. In the face of mounting flood losses, Congress created the National Flood Insurance Program in order to reduce annual flood losses through more careful planning and to provide owners with reasonable flood insurance protection.

The program enables property owners to buy flood insurance at a reasonable cost. In return, communities are required to adopt and enforce local flood plain management measures to protect lives, homes and businesses from future flooding. In short, people owning or buying property in flood plains can now insure against flood losses. With more careful local management of the flood plains, the new construction permitted there by local governments will better withstand flooding. As a result, taxpayers will be called upon fewer times to provide costly relief for flood disasters.

The program is graduated in two separate phases—the Emergency and Regular programs. Under the initial Emergency phase, limited amounts of flood insurance are available to local property owners. A community's efforts to reduce flood losses are generally guided only by preliminary flood data. The map FEMA provides the community at this stage is a Flood Hazard Boundary Map that outlines the flood-prone areas within the community. Subsidized rates are available for all structures regardless of their flood risk.

Under the Regular program, the full limits of flood insurance coverage become available locally. The premiums charged for new construction vary according to its exposure to flood damage. As the community's flood plain management efforts become more comprehensive, new structures must be elevated or flood proofed above certain flood levels. These levels are derived from FEMA's detailed on-site engineering survey in the community. A detailed Flood Insurance Rate Map that shows flood elevations and outlines risk zones is based on these engineering surveys.

B. **Hurricane Preparedness Program.** Twenty-two highly vulnerable hurricane areas have been identified in those regions which require contingency plans to respond to hurricane disasters. The hurricane preparedness program provides technical and financial assistance to States for the preparation of preparedness plans to enhance capabilities at the local level. Long-range policy goals are to relieve the extensive property damage and loss of life as well as the socio-economic disruption.

The specific objectives of the program are to foster planning for the extraordinary problems of severe hurricanes in high risk, populated areas, with emphasis on evacuation measures. Through grants, FEMA finances (1) vulnerability analyses of the most densely populated areas susceptible to hurricanes to determine most probable hurricane effects and resulting damage, and (2) State/local "contingency planning" to address the anticipated extraordinary needs in such disasters. Federal/Regional Planning for the same contingencies is carried out with other agencies in conjunction with State and local efforts. Federal/Regional planning is coordinated by FEMA to ensure that technological hazards, risks, and countermeasures are identified, assessed and made known to State/local governments and to provide information and guidance needed for State/local response.

Future activities will include continued guidance and technical assistance to complete vulnerability analyses and to develop State and local contingency plans in hurricane risk areas. Hurricane vulnerability analyses and contingency planning activities are as follows:

1. Initiate vulnerability analyses of Beaumont/Port Arthur, Texas; Hawaii; and the New Jersey coast.
2. Complete contingency plans for Galveston-Houston, Texas; New Orleans, Louisiana; Miami, Florida and the Florida Keys

Activities for the years 1984 through 1987 are planned to include continued vulnerability analysis and contingency planning for population at high risk with emphasis upon the use of methods, procedures and technology developed in the prior years' efforts to effect Federal, State and local coordination and plans. Funding is projected at a level of $800,000 per year for these years.

C. **Earthquake Preparedness Program.** FEMA is mandated by Executive Order 12148 to lead and coordinate Federal agencies' activities for earthquake hazard reduction and preparedness. Because of the potential for catastrophic or moderate earthquakes in approximately 10 high-risk, high-population areas, it is necessary to develop preparedness plans at the State and local level. Specific recommendations and actions affecting FEMA are set forth in a 1980 assessment of the consequences and preparations for a catastrophic California earthquake. Long range policy goals are to assist the earthquake-prone areas in developing preparedness plans, to coordinate activities at the Federal level and to enforce seismic-safety standards in building construction.

The general objective of the program is to provide leadership and coordination for the Federal component of the National Earthquake Hazards Reduction Program, whose specific objective is to reduce risks to life and property from future U.S. earthquakes through the establishment and maintenance of an effective earthquake hazards reduction program. Steps in this process include:

1. preparing a National Plan for the Earthquake Hazards Reduction Program. The National Plan provides the basis for integrating activities of Federal departments and agencies as they pursue programmatic activities which may increase or reduce earthquake safety. It entails the full range of management and programmatic assignments including the establishment of research objectives, mitigation programs, and resource allocations to achieve both overall Federal goals and secondary objectives. In addition, the Plan suggests appropriate roles for Federal agencies, State and local governments, voluntary agencies, business and the public. The Plan addresses specific procedures for incorporation of earthquake hazards reduction activities into the ongoing programs of Federal agencies. It will be reviewed periodically by all interested parties to assure that it incorporates current public needs and the latest developments in research and implementation plans and activities. Review groups are to include representatives of State and local governments, the public, private business, design professions and the research communty.

2. fostering planning for the extraordinary problems of severe earthquakes in high-risk, high-population areas, including response to predicted earthquakes. Through grants, contracts, and cooperative agreement FEMA finances vulnerability analyses of the most densely populated areas susceptible to earthquakes to determine most probable earthquake effects and resulting damage, and State/local contingency planning to address the anticipated extraordinary needs in such disasters. Specific Federal/Regional planning for the same contingencies is carried out with other agencies in conjunction with State and local efforts, and

3. leading the Interagency Committee on Seismic Safety in Construction (ICSSC), which is developing improved seismic building practices, standards, and procedures for eventual adoption by all Federal agencies.

Efforts proposed will provide guidance, technical assistance and funding for the following programs and activities:

— Update San Francisco vulnerability analysis and loss study to identify secondary earthquake effects (e.g., technological hazards);
— Initiate application of lessons learned from Southern California Earthquake Preparedness Project (SCEPP) to San Francisco Bay Area;
— Continue vulnerability analysis and damage assessment in central United States;
— Continue hazard awareness activities and development of outreach programs for policy influentials in central United States;
— Initiate contingency planning for selected high-risk technological hazards in Boston Metropolitan Area;
— Continue contingency planning in Southern California and Puget Sound;
— Complete contingency planning in Alaska and Hawaii;
— Continue development of prototype prediction preparedness program for local government in Los Angeles Metropolitan Area by SCEPP;
— Continue to lead the Interagency Committee on Seismic Safety in Construction (ICSSC);
— Begin development of improved Federal seismic provisions for non-building type structures;
— Provide support of specific state-of-the-art studies of utility distribution systems and of mechanical components of structures;
— Develop guidelines and procedures to ensure servicability after an earthquake of vital facilities constructed or financed by the Federal Government;
— Develop methodology to identify existing hazardous Federal structures;
— Develop safety assessment procedures for use by Federal agencies and departments to review their building inventories and identify high-hazard structures;
— continue the conduct of trial designs initiated in FY 1982 by the Building Seismic Safety Council (BSSC) to test the economic and safety implications of the improved seismic safety provisions developed recently;
— Provide for Federal technical advice and management oversight of the BSSC activities;
— Identify linkages to encourage the public, public officials, voluntary agencies and industry to disseminate information on seismic safety improvements and incorporate them in their activities;
— Design, develop, test and evaluate public education and training approaches and materials.

437

5. The National Disaster Assistance System

The national disaster assistance system operates from the local to the state government, and from the state to the federal level.

When a local area is affected by a natural disaster <u>local officials</u> respond immediately and begin to survey damage. Their initial notification to state emergency officials can come either after or coincident to their survey, depending on the magnitude of the situation. Sometimes local people can handle the situation without further assistance, but often the state is asked to supplement local resources.

If it becomes apparent that local resources are not adequate to deal with the problems caused by the emergency, the mayor(s) or county executive(s) requests state assistance based on an assessment of what is actually needed. Some federal and private assistance is also available upon direct application by local jurisdictions. Elected local and state officials need to know the management considerations, and bureaucrats at each level should be aware of resources and what is necessary to activate them. In several states, state emergency offices hold seminars for local officials to make them aware of what state and federal agencies do what under which circumstances.

<u>State response</u> to a disaster can range in scale from helping with debris clearance to coordinating a request for federal help. The area requesting help usually must demonstrate that local resources are not sufficient to do the necessary work. After the state emergency officer receives the request from the local level, it will be forwarded to the governor along with a recommendation concerning state aid.

Each state's laws, executive orders and regulations specify the governor's power to issue emergency declarations when activating state assistance to localities. Sometimes approval by a state board or the legislature is necessary, and those cases may vary according to the type of emergency. The governor's emergency staff aid and/or the comprehensive emergency manager works with the state attorney general to determine in advance what powers and systems exist to ensure that effective state assistance goes quickly to localities.

This is where the system can break down. All of these steps happen quickly, and because local and state governments do not operate in a vacuum, they sometimes make unnecessary requests. This is especially true for requests to the federal level. Under ideal circumstances, the governor will not request federal assistance until it is determined that local and state resources are insufficient to help with the recovery. The final step is for the state governor to request to the President that the region hit by the disaster be declared a disaster area. Once the area is Presidentially declared a disaster area, the resources of the Federal government can be used to aid disaster victims.

Traditionally, national and State emergency managers have prepared disaster plans for the use of local officials. Often these plans are not tailored to the needs of the local population and are not used. The failure of the traditional approach stems from lack of input at the grass roots level.

It is doubtful that any emergency manager would be specifically oriented to the needs and techniques for protecting works of art. Only curators and other trained professionals could design the protective response to reduce the exposure of museum pieces to the ravages of wind and rain. The "self-help" preparedness planning that is being tried in Southern California may be taken as a model for museum disaster planning.

Experts have predicted that a major earthquake will probably occur in Southern California in the next 30 years. To mitigate this threat, the Southern California Earthquake Preparedness Project (SCEPP) was initiated. This planning approach has great merit and is worthy of consideration, even at a lesser scale, for application to the unique problem of museums and historic structures.

SCEPP is the most comprehensive earthquake planning activity in an urban area now underway in the nation. Supported by a cooperative agreement between FEMA and the California Seismic Safety Commission, SCEPP receives funds from the State of California that are matched by the Federal government, instead of the usual Federal funds matched by State funds. The project is scheduled to complete its work program by June 1983.

SCEPP's planning area includes five counties of the Los Angeles metropolitan area: San Bernardino, Riverside, Orange, Ventura, and Los Angeles counties. This is the area where scientists estimate that there is over 50 percent probability of a catastrophic (8+ Richter Scale magnitude) earthquake within 30 years. SCEPP's goal is to stimulate preparedness for predicted or unpredicted catastrophic earthquakes within this five-county area.

SCEPP's objectives in accomplishing the goal are: (1) to develop a prototypical planning process for earthquake hazard reduction; (2) a prediction warning/communications system; (3) a model comprehensive regional management system; (4) a uniform terminology for expressing earthquake potential; and (5) model education/information approaches and materials. Plans and processes developed by SCEPP will be transferred to other high-risk regions throughout the nation to the extent possible.

Several other aspects of SCEPP are unique. Through "planning partner" arrangements negotiated with selected public and private jurisdictions within the five-county area, SCEPP's prototype plans are being developed from the local level up, involving officials in many agencies. The process and plans thus respond to local needs. SCEPP's approach represents a major departure from earlier preparedness planning approaches and concepts. SCEPP, for example, operates under the executive authority of the California Seismic Safety Commission and a 21-member Policy Advisory Board. The Board is composed of representatives of public and private agencies within the Los Angeles metropolitan area who oversee activities. SCEPP also emphasizes coordination with ongoing agencies such as the California Office of Emergency Services, the USGS, the American Red Cross, the California Division of Mines and Geology, the State Task Force on Earthquake Preparedness, FEMA, regional government associations, private industry, and the schools. Further, SCEPP is developing comprehensive prototype plans for how an earthquake prediction would be validated and communicated to public and private officials, how the region would respond to such a prediction, and how to minimize negative impacts of an earthquake warning.

SCEPP's Work Program calls for development of prototype plans, regional management systems, and model education/information materials. Transferability of SCEPP's processes and plans to other selected high-risk areas and to other hazards will require careful development of appropriate strategies built on the lessons learned in SCEPPs' planning activities and adapted to local conditions in other areas.

7. Concluding Remarks

Specific guidelines concerning assistance to those affected by a natural disaster are contained in the FEMA publication "Eligibility Handbook Pursuant to Public Law 93-288" (DR&R-2, 1981).

In general, historic properties and collections of artifacts that are owned by State or local governments are eligible for assistance under PL 93-288. Under Public Law 93-288 grants to eligible applicants are discretionary and are based on FEMA grant approval of the proposed work, subject to any conditions upon which that grant approval was based. A private non-profit organization or institution owning and operating educational, utility, medical care, and emergency facilities may also be eligible for assistance.

Existing public buildings and related equipment maintained in active use by an eligible applicant and damaged or destroyed by a disaster, are eligible for assistance. For example, replacement of library books and publications in a publicly owned library is based on an inventory of quantities of various categories of books or publications damaged or destroyed. Grants shall be based on used replacements when available. Clearly, good records of the contents of such facilities will facilitate the recovery process.

FEMA is continually updating and improving the disaster assistance programs to make them more uniform. A grass roots approach like that of the SCEPP is probably a fruitful path to take in times of lower federal budgets. We assure you that, where applicable, FEMA programs will aid historic architecture and museum collections in time of disaster.

440

Roles of State and Local Governments in Applying Earthquake Safety Measures and Providing Post Event Assistance to Historic Architecture and to Museums

Delbert B. Ward

INTRODUCTION

The preservation of historic architecture and the safeguarding of museum collections against loss are believed by many of us to be important to our society. For purposes of this paper we accept this point of view without further discussion. Other writers have set forth arguments that validate this point of beginning, including contributors of other papers in this collection, and we see no need here for more discussion of the same arguments.

In the course of this paper, however, the degree of importance to be placed upon preservation of buildings and upon safeguards for museum collections will be examined relative to the safety and general welfare of users of such facilities. It is this relationship which forms one of the most evident reasons for governmental involvement in the matter. Moreover, this relationship occasionally creates conflicts between strict preservationists and governmental agencies which must, of necessity, be treated here.

Our discussion focuses particularly upon earthquake safety aspects of historic architecture and museum collections. In using the term "earthquake safety" we mean to include consideration of preserving the buildings and their valuable contents against loss (property loss) as well as securing the safety of occupants of the buildings plus any other persons who may be nearby from injury or death (life loss).

Government units traditionally have participated in efforts both to safeguard life and to reduce, or at least control the extent of, property losses. Such efforts have included historic buildings and museums along with most other elements of the man-made environment in which we live. Such efforts also have dealt with most of the identified hazards to life and property, including earthquakes, which are associated with buildings. However, as the public policy under which governments are authorized to act has varied, so too have the nature and extent of government involvement varied as hazards of all sorts have been addressed.

441

In many ways, past governmental involvements in matters dealing with earthquake safety have been less extensive and less consistent than have been their involvements in mitigating the effects of other more common hazards—e.g., fire and flood. One consequence of this uneven sort of attention given to earthquake hazards is that the roles of government in applying earthquake safety measures to the special cases of historic architecture and museums, although occasionally to be found, are largely undefined and, except in rare instances, uncodified.

Given this absence of codified roles for governments, one goal of this paper is to identify the types of possible roles available to government in applying earthquake safety measures to historic architecture and museums. In the course of this role definition, we discuss various factors that affect the roles—e.g., standards for upgrading of older buildings, types of assistance that would help to mitigate against loss to museum collections, and the nature of any post-earthquake assistance that might be rendered to these special classes of facilities.

Theoretically speaking, governmental roles in earthquake safety can be classified into two basic types—regulatory measures and assistance measures. Regulatory measures are a high-profile type in the sense that compliance with the regulations is mandatory. The role typically requires some sort of governmental oversight of the activity that is regulated. On the other hand, assistance measures are a low-profile type wherein the governmental role is intended primarily as that of a helpful partner.

Both types of governmental roles have their place in our society. Regulatory measures are applied to situations where certain standards of performance or behavior are deemed necessary for the general safety, health, and welfare of society. Assistance measures are applied where the resources of government can be brought beneficially to aid some particular part of the social system. As will be discussed later in this paper, both types of governmental roles are appropriate in applying earthquake safety measures to historic buildings and museums.

DEFINING SOME TERMS

Earthquake experts, like experts in most other disciplines, have developed over time a special vocabulary of terms that help to speed communication of concepts while retaining the necessary precision needed for communicating. It is helpful to highlight the broader meaning of some of these terms as they might be used in reference to historic buildings and museums.

The distinction between "mitigation" and "post-event assistance" is one of the more important concepts to be acknowledged in all earthquake safety discussions. Both terms will appear repeatedly throughout the paper.

In the most general sense, mitigation is an action taken to reduce the hazardous effects of an earthquake. Reduced risk to life safety and/or reduced losses to property are consequences of a mitigation action. Clearly, there are numerous, almost limitless, possible earthquake mitigation actions. Examples applicable to historic building preservation and museums include structural upgrading of building components known to be vulnerable to damage from earthquakes, limiting the number of occupants or type of occupancy allowed in facilities which might fail (in whole or in part) during an earthquake event, and installing some sort of restraints on shelving and museum artifacts that could be displaced by earthquake forces.

It is important to observe for the examples cited that a particular mitigation action might affect only life safety, only property loss, or both. This observation leads to the conclusion that there are hierarchical levels of mitigation actions based upon the relative importance, or loss-reduction value, of one action as compared to the consequences of another action. Analyzing the problem in this way, one inevitably finds that mitigation actions are weighed subjectively in terms of goals, benefits, and costs. We shall return to this hierarchical concept and its place in role definition for government in earthquake safety matters.

"Post-event assistance," in general and in particular in this paper, comprises actions intended to restore a facility, an economic system, or a social system that has been affected by an earthquake to its pre-event status insofar as is possible. We include pre-event planning for such activities in this category of governmental roles. In one sense, this sort of activity amounts to "picking up the pieces" after an earthquake. However, this simplistic view of post-event assistance should not lead the reader to conclude that recovery assistance is unimportant. Indeed, governments historically have had a more visible role in disaster assistance than they have had in mitigation efforts. Such activities have included providing mass feeding, housing, and health care assistance immediately after an earthquake, longer term economic assistance in the form of grants and low-interest loans, and, especially, planning assistance so that both government units and the private sector are better prepared to cope with problems that might be caused by future disasters.

It is also helpful to note the distinction between another pair of terms—"hazard" and "risk". In earthquake safety jargon, the term "hazard" normally refers to the physical event of an earthquake and its effects, whereas the term "risk" usually applies to the potential loss, either through death, injury, or destruction of property. Accordingly, we often speak about ground vibration as one aspect of the earthquake hazard, and we refer to the possibility of building collapse due to the earthquake vibration in terms of risk to people and property.

Even though the distinction between hazard and risk is somewhat fuzzy in actual use, and even though the terms are frequently interchanged, even among earthquake experts, there is one reason pertinent to this paper for calling attention to them. In particular, it

443

is that earthquake events, i.e., the hazard, cannot be controlled insofar as the scientific community knows to-day, whereas the risk can be controlled, i.e., mitigated. In other words, we may not be able to stop an earthquake from happening today or tomorrow, but we certainly know how to lower the chances for loss of life, injury, or loss of property.

Finally, there is one other group of terms pertinent to any discussion of earthquake safety—namely, those terms we use to describe the various earthquake effects: fault, ground-shaking, liquefaction, ground subsidence, etc. Why distinguish among these earthquake effects? Quite simply, we do so because the choice of mitigation (risk-reduction) actions will vary in accordance with which of the effects is likely to be more hazardous for a particular facility location. Each of the effects named above may not impact every building location. In fact, any one building is not likely to experience all of the effects caused by any single earthquake. Moreover, the sorts of possible risks as a result of each of these earthquake effects likely will be different and so must be treated differently.

As a consequence of the above facts, governmental roles in earthquake safety typically are found to be tailored to answer specific types of problems associated with the earthquakes. Even more important to note is that governmental roles, if they are to be effective, must be quite specific both with respect to the earthquake problem being addressed and with respect to the expected outcome from the action associated with the role. A governmental regulation stating simply that "historic buildings shall be upgraded such that they are safe from earthquakes" is much too general and helps neither the owner, the architect or engineer, nor the overseeing governmental agency. What or who, for example, is to be made safe? Occupants of the building? Passersby? Structural elements of the building? And what degree of risk reduction is considered to be safe? Unless these and other parallel questions are treated in the regulation, no one will know for sure what action is to be taken. Fortunately, regulatory standards established by most governmental agencies are more specific than the example given. When they are not, beware, lest we see unbridled government or unreliable results.

THE PROBLEMS—IN GENERAL TERMS

Before outlining possible roles of government in applying earthquake safety measures to historic buildings and museums, we first examine briefly the types of problems that might be encountered in such facilities. In this context we then consider the possible remedies for problems, noting in particular those situations that can (should?) be remedied by owners or operators of the facilities and those where governmental involvement may be appropriate or even necessary.

In keeping with our earlier observation that earthquake risk may be either risk to life safety or risk to property, the problem analysis which follows treats these cases separately. We note, however, that any situation involving risk to life safety likely also involves property losses, although the reverse is not so.

Risks to Life Safety

Any risk to life safety that might be caused by earthquake effects upon historic buildings and museums likely will be from falling building components and/or falling building contents. One possible exception is that risk to life resulting from fire which might occur as a consequence of earthquake damage to the building. Risk to life safety, of course, ranges in a scale from minor injury to possible death.

A number of types of earthquake-induced building failures can endanger life. The most obvious type of failure is collapse of the building, likely caused by failure of some essential structural component which leads to total or partial collapse of some principal part of the building. Failures of this sort are likely to cause the death of some occupants and to injure most others. However, collapse-type failures are less likely for most buildings, except in rare instances of a strong earthquake, than are localized failures of isolated components. Injury and death occur more often as a consequence of these localized failures—from falling materials such as bricks, stones, ceilings, chandeliers or other lighting fixtures, and other overhead components.

Readers should note that falling components can occur both inside and outside the building, creating risks both for occupants and passersby. Indeed, data from past moderate earthquakes suggest that injury and life loss resulting from falling debris outside a building are at least as likely as that occurring within damaged buildings. One frequently occurring situation is the occupant who is struck by falling debris while running from the building when the shaking begins. Within a building, even the contents sometimes can pose life-safety risks. Shelving and the goods stored on the shelves pose one type of such risk; upright filing cabinets, which tend to be top-heavy, pose another; and in the case of museums, display cases and statuary could be overturned upon viewers inadvertently in the way.

Risks to Property

Earthquake damage to property invariably has an associated loss in dollars. The monetary loss may be in the repairs that are necessary or in the lost use of the facility. In the case of historic buildings and museum collections, the damaged item may be non-replacable or non-

445

reparable, and so the loss is even more severe in that the objective of preservation has been irrevocably lost.

Property loss due to earthquakes can occur in a variety of ways. Some ways are obvious; some may be less apparent; all no doubt will be given serious consideration by dedicated preservationists—whether of buildings or of collections within the buildings.

Building losses consist of structural collapses, displacement of building elements, and cracking or fracturing of elements. For an historic building, the loss might be a cracked stone wall (which may or may not be reparable), a fallen stone frieze (which may or may not be reparable), a fallen brick parapet (which probably is replacable), cracks in plaster walls, a fallen and shattered chandelier, or a broken stained-glass window (which may not be reparable). For a museum collection, the loss might be overturned display cases (which may damage the items displayed), fallen pictures and other exhibits secured to walls or ceilings, overturned statuary, or papers (unbreakable) and glasswares (breakable) knocked from shelves. Secondary sorts of damage to collections also are possible. For example, the collection might be damaged by building elements which fall, or water damage might be caused by broken pipes in the cases when building elements collapse.

The Degree of Risk

The overview of risks to life safety and to property given in the preceding paragraphs begins to look very much like the sort of risk analysis that a safety analyst might perform for a client. In fact, this type of analysis is pertinent as well to understanding government roles in applying earthquake safety measures not only to historic architecture and museum collections but also to other parts of man's built environment. By identifying the kinds of losses and the sorts of situations that can cause these losses, we have set forth one of three essential parts of a risk analysis methodology. The other two parts are, first, determining the degree of risk and, second, suggesting mitigation measures to reduce or prevent the risk.

To determine the degree of risk associated with each of the life-safety and property risks that one can identify requires more complex analytical methods than we can discuss adequately here. We can only allude to some of the considerations.

The degree of risk is derived from the combined consideration of the likelihood of earthquake occurrences and the expected performance of the building elements when they are subjected to particular earthquake forces. In brief, these are engineering problems—both geotechnical and structural. All earthquakes are different—in strength, ground vibration characteristics, regional distribution of effects, etc. Even earthquake experts can only speculate about these for future earthquakes. The pertinent characteristics must be estimated, and these estimates are set forth in

446

probabilistic terms. Given the imprecise data about the characteristics of future earthquakes, structural engineers make assumptions about the forces and carry out their analyses of expected component performance based upon these assumptions.

The point here is that earthquake technology today is still an art as well as a science. Judgment is very much a factor, and consequently one can find different answers to the same problem. This absence of precise scientific knowledge leads to different opinions about the degree of risk in many situations, to different views regarding appropriate governmental roles in earthquake safety matters, and, as well, to different views as to appropriate standards for earthquake safety.

One need not be completely dismayed with the technical community, however, for some reasonably good indicators of risk have been identified by those who have studied earthquakes and earthquake damage. Geotechnical engineers are able to map zones of earthquake occurrences and to suggest where earthquake hazards are geographically more prevalent. Structural engineers also pretty well understand how earthquakes affect buildings. An experienced architect or engineer can identify those building components most vulnerable to damage by earthquakes. Accordingly, guidance can be given for selecting mitigation actions and for placing priorities upon the actions that will most effectively reduce earthquake losses.

"Degree of risk" is a way of describing the chance (probability) that a particular type of loss may occur. Sometimes it is enough simply to know that the possibility of loss exists so that the possibility can be eliminated. However, many risks cannot be completely eliminated, and all that one can do is reduce the odds that the loss will occur. Most building design considers risk in the latter fashion. This approach, although not always explicitly stated, is taken in most building codes. So it is with earthquake safety. Accordingly, most decisions about safety are made based upon the likelihood of an event that will, or could, produce a loss.

Often there are no absolute limits placed upon the degree of risk that makes it acceptable. This is largely because there is no standard definition of what level may be acceptable. What is acceptable for one person may not be acceptable for another. To the extent that the public (and, hence, government) might participate in making policies for safety and thereby participate in defining acceptable risk for a particular situation, it is worthy of note that risks to life safety traditionally have been deemed more serious than risks to property.

Mitigation Measures to Reduce or Prevent Earthquake Losses

Since one can identify buildings and building components which are vulnerable to earthquake damage and categorize them in terms of relative degree of risk, and one can determine which sorts of failures can endanger life safety or cause unacceptable damage to property, one can select corrective measures best suited to mitigate the possible failures. This general methodology for mitigation of earthquake losses is applicable to all types of facilities, including historic buidings and museum collections. What will be different for each particular facility is the nature of the component vulnerability (an engineering problem) and the degree of acceptable risk (a policy question). We shall examine some of the factors that influence policies regarding acceptable risk in the context of historic buildings and museum collections after first indicating a few kinds of mitigation measures that can be applied to different types of problems one might expect to find for historic buildings and museum collections.

Historic buildings, almost by definition, are older buildings that were constructed prior to development of modern earthquake safety codes. Almost without exception, these older buildings were constructed without consideration of lateral forces caused by earthquakes. While this does not necessarily imply that all historic buildings are unable to withstand earthquake forces, many construction materials and construction practices of earlier times are particularly vulnerable to damage or failure due to lateral forces. Unreinforced brick masonry bearing-wall construction and stone veneers are among the more significant of these. Much of the decoration on older buildings—in many cases that decoration which makes buildings culturally significant—is vulnerable to displacement by earthquake lateral forces, especially if the decoration is plaster, carved stone, tile, or other masonry-type materials. Inside finishes of most historic buildings are plaster, sometimes on wood framing, often on masonry. Carved stone, terracotta, and tile work—finishes which add to the magnificence of historic buildings—are commonplace. Unfortunately, these features usually are the first to be damaged by earthquake forces.

Damage to primary structural elements of masonry buildings can be reduced, sometimes even prevented, but to do so often requires that rather major modifications be made. Such modifications, when necessary, usually must be made to parts of the building assembly that are hidden by finish surfaces. It is the removal of these finishes and their subsequent restoration that makes major structural modifications of historic buildings such a problem; for it entails not only high cost but also possible damage to materials which probably have intrinsic cultural value.

Non-structural components posing risk to life safety or to museum collections sometimes can be suitably modified without any apparent visible effect upon the historic qualities of the building. Sometimes they cannot. More secure anchorage of a suspended chandelier, for example, probably can be accomplished quite readily. On the other hand, more secure anchorage of a stone frieze likely entails removal of the material and replacement of the mounting anchors—a tedious, labor-intensive task, but one which probably can be completed without any significant change in the appearance of the building.

One of the most difficult types of high-risk conditions to correct in historic buildings is the overhanging cornice, frieze, turret, or other appendage that is often of stone or other masonry material. In many cases, there is no structural system to which these appendages can be suitably anchored, yet they pose considerable risk to life safety which should not be ignored. Building ordinances and codes often will require that this kind of risk be alleviated—either by improved anchorage or by removal of the appendage—and this is where conflict can arise between the governmental regulatory authority and the historic preservationist.

Mitigation of loss to collections in museums or historic buildings is, perhaps, the easiest to accomplish—both in terms of cost and in terms of the effect on the object—if we consider separately damage that might be caused by failure of building components. To mitigate losses to collections requires only a careful analysis of the damage-causing condition followed by a corrective action to remove the risk condition. For example, display cases vulnerable to overturning usually can be secured in place quite easily. Valuable artifacts can be positioned so that they are away from building elements that might fall. Statuary can be mounted to prevent overturning, and pictures can be hung more securely. It is even possible to place display items on shelves so that they will not be knocked off.

The challenge in mitigating loss to museum collections is to consider all of the possible ways that loss might occur as a result of an earthquake. Such an effort would be easier if a detailed guide were available in which possible loss mechanisms are listed along with an indication of possible mitigation actions. Unfortunately, this writer knows of no such check list in existence that is applicable to museum collections. A similar type of guide has been prepared for hospital earthquake safety in which hospital contents essential to health care are identified and loss prevention techniques are suggested. That document provides a good model which someday may be emulated for museum collections. [Stone, Marraccini and Patterson, 1976]

POLICIES REGARDING ACCEPTABLE EARTHQUAKE RISK

Most of the foregoing discussion has aimed at establishing a framework in which governmental roles may be examined for applying earthquake safety measures to historic architecture and museums. We have described briefly the kinds of risks, the sorts of possible earthquake losses, mitigation techniques, and considerations pertinent to safeguarding historic buildings and museum collections. What we have yet to discuss is how one decides what degree of risk is to be accepted. These conclusions we call simply "policies".

Policies for earthquake safety can be divided into two classes—public policies and private-sector policies. Public policies are those made at a governmental level and, when established, are applied more or less uniformly to all populations and situations within the jurisdiction of the governmental unit. Private-sector policies are those established by a uniquely identifiable entity within the private sector—a business or an institution, for example—and are applicable only within the limits of authority of that private-sector entity. We observe here that earthquake safety policies for historic buildings and museum collections can be of both public and private-sector types.

One of the interesting aspects of public policies is that they derive from public consensus—that is, the policies are developed through interaction of constituent interest groups and take their final form as a result of compromise or as a result of one constituent interest being more persuasive or more powerful than other constituency interests. This is a two-edged sword for owners of historic buildings. On the one side, concern for public safety may be deemed more critical than some kinds of preservation, in which case the owners of historic buildings may find no choice but to comply with safety regulations which have usually been adopted long after the buildings were erected. On the other side, preservationists also have opportunities to influence public policies for earthquake safety so as to obtain special assistance in earthquake risk management or even to obtain certain exemptions from regulatory policies for historic buildings. They may also be able to suggest compromises or alternative strategies to make the impacts of safety regulations upon historic buildings more palatable.

Public policies for earthquake safety take many forms that divide broadly into the two general types identified earlier—regulatory policies and assistance policies. Regulatory policies typically are established to address problems that extend beyond the special case of historic buildings to encompass problems common in a variety of building types. Assistance policies usually are more precisely focused to address specific needs, such as those of historic buildings and museums, for example.

Regulatory Policies of Government

Building regulations which establish safety requirements and construction standards are a particular type of regulatory public policy. Their purpose, established under authority of police powers granted to state and local governments, is to safeguard life and health and to protect the general public welfare. Identifiable risks to life and health typically are addressed in building codes, and building construction is regulated to minimize (not necessarily eliminate) life loss and injury. Protection of the public welfare is a more ambiguous concept viewed differently by groups of citizens. Hence, there is less consistency in public policies of this type from region to region in the nation and from governmental entity to governmental entity.

Modern-day building regulations in seismically active regions address earthquake safety aspects of structural soundness and assembly requirements for building elements in a reasonably consistent fashion. However, because earthquake risk is seen differently among groups of citizens, there is little uniformity in other types of regulatory public policies adopted to deal with the problem. Note also that some governmental jurisdictions require that certain construction standards for earthquake safety be met, and that other governmental entities do not even consider the problem. Also, some governmental jurisdictions adopt regulations requiring only that new buildings be constructed to resist earthquake forces; other governmental jurisdictions adopt regulations requiring also that existing buildings be upgraded to certain standards of earthquake safety. Most building regulations of this sort are limited in scope to matters affecting life safety, but there still are widely different policies and practices, even in such matters as establishing which construction materials and practices affect life safety.

It is, of course, those regulations that retroactively apply to existing buildings which create obligations—and conflicts—for owners of historic buildings. Conflicts arise in two ways. Variances may be sought by owners to alleviate the high cost of modifications, or exemption from the regulations may be sought for historic buildings as a general exception in the policy. In either case, the conflict often reduces to a question of whether or not historic buildings have a cultural value of such importance that higher risk to life safety is warranted. These efforts to obtain special treatment are likely to be resisted by the building department and/or other special-interest groups.

It is useful to note that other strategies than construction modifications can be used to reduce risk to life safety. Sometimes one of these other strategies can be followed to remove the conflicts suggested above. One alternative strategy to reduce risk to life safety is to reduce the occupancy of a building on the basis that the fewer the people in a building, the less chance someone will be injured or killed. A similar strategy is to reduce the hours a building is occupied. Still another strategy is to limit the space that is to be occupied in the building on the basis that most buildings have some areas safer than others. Typically, these strategies also are regulatory in nature.

Governmental Assistance Policies

Because potential and actual losses due to earthquake events can be so extensive and so costly to prevent or restore, it is only natural to look to government to cope with the problems that may arise. Government is a source of assistance for both real resources—money and manpower—and indirect aid that is intended to be helpful. Government is capable of marshalling resources on a scale not possible for most other segments of our social system.

As it pertains to the special case of earthquake risk reduction for historic architecture and museums, the term "governmental assistance" needs some elaboration—not only because the assistance

451

can take so many forms, but also because the term is somewhat ambiguous and so is viewed differently by most of us. Additionally, "assistance" tends to be defined relatively broadly today insofar as governmental involvement is concerned, the general trend being to engage government in a multitude of assistance functions. Some clarification of these assistance roles seems appropriate here.

Another aspect of governmental assistance for earthquake risk reduction is its temporal relationship to damaging earthquake events. Accordingly, we speak of pre-event assistance, post-event emergency assistance, and post-event reconstruction assistance. Governmental assistance traditionally has been available for each of the phases and, accordingly, has taken a variety of forms.

A common misconception of governmental assistance by those in the private sector who seek that assistance after any sort of disaster is that public funds can be obtained to correct the damage or replace the losses. While direct financial assistance is sometimes available to governmental units—usually a flow of funds from a higher level of government to a lower level of government—governmental assistance to the private sector is rarely direct financial aid and instead almost always takes the form of intangible aid, such as information, guidance for actions, and suggestions for solutions to problems. Indirect financial assistance may also include low-interest loans and tax benefits when the losses are substantial and widespread throughout the community or region. Such assistance is mostly from the federal government, although some states also provide disaster relief as a supplement to federal assistance.

Of course, any type of assistance from government has a cost—for personnel, for equipment, and for materials, or for direct or indirect payments. It is because of this cost, and because the limited resources of government are sought competitively by numerous groups, that assistance programs are examined carefully by policymakers before being adopted. As has been noted, assistance programs usually are specifically targeted—that is, specific problems and program actions are identified in the particular policy—and they typically are not open-ended as to the extent or type of assistance.

The implication for obtaining governmental assistance to reduce earthquake risk to historic buildings and museums is that specific kinds of assistance programs need to be identified by the historic architecture and museum constituency groups, procedures for managing the programs established, and, most importantly, policymakers persuaded to adopt the programs. Without the last of these three steps, there is not likely to be any effective governmental assistance for the special case of historic architecture and museums.

Any form of financial assistance that might be obtained from governments as a result of these types of public policies will come only as a result of intense lobbying by preservationist groups and persuasive support from constituents. Competition for public funds, which always are limited, is great, and successful efforts to achieve policies of this sort take political skill.

452

One final observation about earthquake safety policy deals in particular with private policy. So far, little has been said about this. The private sector also is a resource for assistance—both self-help and philanthropic—that ought not be overlooked. Although this type of assistance is not a subject of the paper, we would be remiss in failing to acknowledge it.

While there are almost limitless policies on earthquake safety that might be made by a private sector owner or operator of historic buildings, there is one type of action that will need to occur almost exclusively in the private domain. This is the safeguarding of private collections from earthquake damage and loss. In this writer's view, it is not likely, although not precluded, that governmental units will establish policies that require private collections be safeguarded against loss or that provide financial assistance for securing collections against loss. The private institutions, I believe, will need to provide the leadership in any such activities.

A LISTING OF POSSIBLE GOVERNMENTAL ROLES

We have by now indicated to the reader many of the directions that governments might take in promulgating earthquake safety for historic architecture and museums. In this final section we attempt to state the roles more precisely and at the same time provide a logical ordering of them. The roles are deliberately stated in general terms rather than in terms of specific actions so as to emphasize the role rather than the type of actions that might be entailed. We also have chosen an outline form for the list.

One can identify numerous roles for government to assist owners and operators of historic buildings and museums to reduce potential or real earthquake losses. A more intriguing problem arises besides the one of preparing a shopping list of government roles, however. That problem is to place priorities upon the type of assistance that is needed. Federal, state, and local governments are not likely to adopt an assistance policy for each and every earthquake risk problem that owners and operators of historic buildings and museums might identify. In most cases, the impetus for any assistance policies will derive from initiatives among owners and operators or their supporting constituencies. This means that these groups will need to decide upon the most needed assistance and then persuade the policymakers to adopt the programs.

Possible roles of government are stated below without intending to indicate preference or likely effectiveness, except that one bias of the author merits acknowledgement. That bias is the importance of life safety. Situations where life safety is at risk and where the objectives of preservationists must be compromised to correct the life safety problem create most of the conflicts which arise in applying earthquake safety measures to historic buildings. For this author, life safety is far too important to compromise in order to preserve material things. Accordingly, such issues should not be decided just by preservationists. Governmental involvement in these situations is appropriate, even essential, and should prevail.

There appear to be several ways to organize the listing of governmental roles for applying earthquake safety measures to historic architecture and museums—e.g., by type of risk (to life safety or to property), by type of governmental action (regulatory or assistance), or by type of problem (building collapse, component failure, loss of beneficial use, etc.). In this paper we have chosen to list the roles by type of governmental action in the categories of regulatory roles and assistance roles. This organization is selected not because it is any better than the others but because it helps to highlight an important idea developed in the paper—namely that governmental participation in earthquake safety occurs for a variety of reasons and takes a variety of forms. The selected organization also illuminates the basis for any implied or explicit governmental action consequential to the particular role, yet provides a simplification not present in the other forms of presentation.

Regulatory Roles

Restrictions on the use of land in known earthquake fault zones to prohibit high-occupancy facilities, such as museums and assembly halls.

—Applicable more to construction of new buildings (museums) than to existing buildings (historic buildings).
—Likely a role of local government; possibly a role of state government.

Requirements that new buildings or certain modifications to older buildings comply with current earthquake safety standards and codes.

—Roles available both to state and local governments.

Establishment of new standards of safety for existing buildings that better accommodate conditions unique to such buildings.

—Roles available both to state and local governments.

Providing pre-event assistance intended to encourage and facilitate actions that will preserve historic architecture and museum collections, in the form of:

(a) Information about the types of risks posed by earthquakes.
(b) Financing research on and disseminating information about mitigation measures that are applicable to historic architecture and museums.
(c) Guidelines for immediate post-event risk management.
(d) Information describing risk-reduction actions taken by other owners or operators of historic buildings or museums.

—Possible roles for both federal and state governments.

Providing immediate post-event assistance in the form of:

(a) Handbooks describing the type, scope, and limits of governmental aid—federal, state, and local governments—available under disaster declarations, and procedures under which such programs are administered.
(b) Information on sources of immediate aid for securing damaged premises, for clean-up assistance, and for engineering evaluation of damaged (possibly unsafe) structures.
(c) Information on sources for specialty services that might be needed for historic buildings and museums, e.g., restoration services for building components, art objects, and valuable documents.

—Appropriately a state role, possibly a federal role also.

Providing longer term post-event assistance for restoration and reconstruction of damaged facilities or collections, in the form of:

(a) Financial assistance—grants, low-interest loans, property tax exemptions, etc.—to assist owners and operators of historic buildings and museums in reconstruction.
(b) Financing research on and disseminating information about possible ways to achieve safer buildings and collections against future earthquake losses that is applicable to facilities which may require reconstruction following an earthquake.

—Most likely a federal role, possibly a state role.

Providing geotechnical data on earthquake hazards in a form specific enough to aid owners and operators of historic buildings and museums to make earthquake safety decisions.

—Appropriately a state role.

Providing technical assistance in interpretation of earthquake hazards data and in preparing risk analysis studies.

—Appropriately a state role.

Providing suggested construction and operating standards for historic buildings and museums that deal with occupant safety and safety of valuable collections.

—Possibly a state role; more likely a federal role; perhaps not a role for government at all.

Preparing post-earthquake action plans that specifically deal with historic buildings and museums so that post-disaster losses, disruption, and inconvenience are kept to a minimum.

—Likely a state role; possibly supplemented by local government.

Fleshing Out the Roles

The roles listed above are stated deliberately in general terms so as to preserve the essential nature of the governmental involvement. Specific policies and specific actions within each of the roles will be necessary for any effective governmental involvement. This fleshing out of the roles will need to be done to fit the needs and aspirations of each particular governmental unit and each historic architecture or museum group. We have suggested in other portions of this paper some possible specific actions, but there are many more, far more than can be presented here.

We conclude the paper with a rather obvious, but so far unstated, comment. There are, indeed, appropriate and sometimes essential roles for government in applying earthquake safety measures to the particular cases of historic architecture and museums. Although all of the roles outlined above may not be assumed, or even necessary, by any single unit of government, it is the author's view that progress toward improved earthquake safety for these special classes of buildings will not take place without the participation of the government—both as a partner and a participant.

REFERENCES

Stone, Marraccini and Patterson. Study to Establish Protection Provisions for Furniture, Equipment and Supplies for Veterans Administration Hospitals. Washington, D.C.: Veterans Administration. Office of Construction, January 1976.

Mobilization of Private Philanthropy in Responding to Damages Resulting from Earthquakes and Other Natural Disasters

Harold L. Oram

This paper deals with the enlistment of the private sector (i.e., personal, institutional and corporate philanthropy) in dealing with catastrophes rising out of earthquake, fire, flood and other natural disasters. Throughout history, as the ruins of preceding civilizations attest, succeeding generations have responded to such disasters in accordance with their assessment of the human hurt and of the damage to structures and/or works of art, always limited by the resources available. Philanthropy is the tool developed by modern societies to heal the hurt. Sometimes it is institutionalized in great or lesser foundations, sometimes utilized by corporate managers for their own reasons, but it always involves individuals, whether few or many.

The United States of America has developed a tradition of philanthropy that dwarfs the rest of the world's in terms of contributions, both internally and externally. We need not here explain why this is so—how and why American philanthropy developed over the decades. Private philanthropy in these United States during 1980 consisted of almost $48 billion in gifts, of which more than 85% were given in support of religion, education and health. Of the remaining 15%, just under $3 billion (about 6%) was dedicated to the support of the arts.

Among the arts, performing arts receive the greatest philanthropic support. While there are no separate figures for architecture and museums, it is reasonable to assume that in an ordinary year their share of this outpouring of private philanthropy is relatively small—probably less than $500 million. There are, of course, exceptions, like the magnificent J. Paul Getty bequest for the establishment of the West Coast art museum.

Even within this philanthropic quotient, the bulk goes to museums and art galleries and architectural prizes that are long established. What we are considering here is the flow of philanthropic funds in response to catastrophic happenings, borne of earthquake, fire and/or flood. Virtually no money exists for disaster response before an event. No one has yet dealt systematically with catastrophes in this special field. The traditional and consistently ineffective approach to planning philanthropic campaigns for the relief of disaster impacts has been not to plan.

All of us have observed the difficulty attending fund-raising drives for material or spiritual objectives following a natural catastrophe, whether earthquake, fire or flood. The incidence of human suffering overwhelms the loss of material resources, whether Architecture or Art, in subsequent reportage. Although two aspects of the tragedy, human suffering and material or spiritual loss, compete for printed space and/or broadcast time, media interest is invariably focused on the human suffering. Over time what is featured in the media is solely that concern. By the day following a disaster, the International Red Cross and a host of private philanthropic organizations have dispatched their agents to estimate and report on the human suffering. Lost in the reportage is any estimate of the aesthetic and/or spiritual damage occasioned by the disaster.

In the late 1960's the writer was invited by the Government of Iran to inspect a devastated area in Northeast Iran leveled by an earthquake which caused substantial loss of life. Army bulldozers were already at work when he arrived, some ten days after the event. Amid the ruins of a village, the dozers were systematically reducing to rubble what remained. Among the remains was part of a small temple. It was in the path of the machines and was soon obliterated. Only by accident did the writer learn that the temple—a pride of the village—had been considered one of the prizes of antiquity and was to be celebrated in a forthcoming bimillennial celebration of the Persian Empire. Not one word reflected its loss in the English language press, which devoted major attention to the human tragedy.

This is not to say that the human cost should be disregarded in any such disaster. It merely reports what all of us know—that there are different categories of values and one such category is being routinely neglected. This neglect is an abrogation of responsibility on the part of the few who care—not only for humanity but also for the great and lesser works man has wrought throughout history.

The National Oceanic and Atmospheric Administration (NOAA) has recorded some 83 earthquakes of a magnitude on the Richter scale of above 5.0 during the four-year period 1976-1979. All involve severe damage, the greatest being the February 4, 1976, earthquake in Guatemala which occasioned 23,000 deaths and the May 6, 1976, earthquake in northeastern Italy with 929 deaths and 8 billion dollars damage. Other natural disasters, such as floods and fires, occasioned further human losses and material damage on every continent. A number involved historic structures, museums and art collections, the subject of this conference.

How best to mobilize philanthropic resources to repair the damage to architecture or art, occasioned by such natural calamities, is the subject of this paper. Because of the limited time in which to act effectively following the news of a catastrophic happening, success demands quick action. What is essential is the creation of an ad hoc "watchdog" group with a concern for cultural property, experience in emergency fund drives, and access to philanthropic resources. It should be available from the time the catastrophe occurs. The media story fastest to disappear from public view is a catastrophic happening, and the success of any philanthropic drive depends upon the public's knowledge of the facts to sustain its support.

Two examples of this phenomenon can be seen in well-known foreign disasters. The major earthquake at Friuli, Italy, on May 6, 1976, caused approximately 8 billion dollars in damage including harm to historic structures and art treasures. The news gave birth to a number of ad hoc committees in the United States, as well as a generous infusion of U.S. government aid. But U.S. private contributions were minor in relation to the need and to available philanthropic resources. By the time fund-raising leadership had been recruited, months after the event, very little attention was still being paid by the media to this great tragedy. Moreover, much of the media attention was of a negative nature, focused on inept or dishonest distribution of philanthropic funds. Within the philanthropic spectrum, it is estimated that one hundred dollars went for the relief of human suffering to every dollar provided for the recoupment of architectural or art treasures.

In contrast to the philanthropic failures in the Friuli is the 1964 response to the impending submergence of the 13th century B.C. temple of Abu Simbel in upper Egypt. Construction of the great high dam at Aswan in the early 1960's threatened the temple. An estimated 50 million dollars (equivalent to about $200 million dollars today), of which approximately 25% was to come from private sources, was required to remove the temple and related historic buildings high above the dammed waters. A UNESCO committee, formed well in advance to provide direction and stimulate support, sought government and private contributions. Within a period of five years, the temple had been moved, the task completed and an historic tragedy had been averted.

It is clear that the crisis of Abu Simbel is not analogous to that of a threat by earthquake or flood whose time cannot be anticipated. Yet, what can be anticipated from the philanthropic point of view is the essential experience and judgment which make it possible to mobilize philanthropic leadership to seek resources at the earliest possible time. They can be in place before the event. In Rene Dubos' words: "Modern man has learned to anticipate." We need to learn and act on that dictum. Herewith a modest but practical proposal.

This paper proposes the establishment of a small but expert group suitably supported by limited foundation funds which will be on hand in the event of any catastrophe, U.S. or foreign. In effect they would take the place of UNESCO (in the case of Abu Simbel) in helping to mobilize private philanthropy. This is especially important in a field where the availability of big ticket philanthropy is always a possibility.

Board leadership should be drawn from the architectural, foundation, museum and art communities, not excluding persons of influence and means. Staff personnel should consist primarily of architectural, art and museum experts. Their role would be to designate the objectives of concern. Fund raising experts would advise on methods and open avenues to the major sources of private funds—foundations, corporations and the like. Such a group must be limited with respect to the catastrophes in which it would intervene. Thus, in the United States, it would be bound by a generally accepted register of historic structures, monuments and art treasures, such as that provided by the National Register of Historic Places, U.S. Department of the Interior.

Throughout the world the committee would take cognizance of major disasters and help by supplying correct information, assisting in the recruitment of leadership and keeping open the avenues to major sources of philanthropic funds. It could become a conduit for funds to a respected operating agency in the field. It should not assist save when called upon by those immediately concerned who seek help. The great majority of localized disasters would be dealt with solely by local agencies.

Such a representative agency would be crucial in enabling effective utilization of the critical time between the first notice of a catastrophe and its precipitous disappearance from media sight and public memory. Time is of the essence.

Section Six References

RESPONSE MEASURES: GENERAL

Bolin, R. Research on Reconstruction Following Disaster: Working Paper No. 1. Presented at 2nd Annual Invitational Conference on Natural Hazards, Boulder, Colorado, 1978.

Disasters and the Mass Media. Committee on Disasters and the Mass Media, Commission on Socio-Technical Systems. Washington, D.C.: National Academy of Sciences, National Research Council, n.d.

Fournier D'Albe, E. M. "Natural Disaster: Their Study and Prevention." UNESCO Chronicle. Volume 16, 1970, pp. 195-208.

Jones, Barclay G. "Disasters and Urban Systems." Journal of Architectural Education. Volume 33, No. 4, 1980.

Krimgold, Frederick. Overview in the Priority Subject Area: Natural Disaster. United Nations Environment Programme, 1976.

McLuckie, Benjamin F. Italy, Japan and the United States: Effects of Centralization on Disaster Responses, 1964-9. The Disaster Research Center Historical and Comparative Disasters Series. Columbus, Ohio: Disaster Research Center, Ohio State University, 1977.

Mileti, Dennis S. Disaster Relief and Rehabilitation in the U.S.: A Research Assessment. Springfield, Va.: National Technical Information Service, No. PB-242-976, 1977.

Mileti, Dennis S. Natural Hazard Warning Systems in the U.S.: A Research Assessment. Boulder, Colorado: University of Colorado, Technology Environment and Man Monograph Series No. 13, 1975.

Petak, William, Arthur A. Atkisson, and P. H. Gleye. Natural Hazards: A Public Policy Assessment. Springfield, Va.: National Technical Information Service, PB-297-361, 1978.

Rossi, Peter, James D. Wright, Sonia R. Wright, et al. The Politics of Natural Disasters, to be published.

Scott, Stanley. "Learning to Live with Earthquakes: Research and Policy for Seismic Safety in California." Public Affairs Report. Volume 17, No. 5. Berkeley, California: Institute of Governmental Studies, University of California, 1976, pp. 1-5.

Scott, Stanley, Ed. What Decisionmakers Need to Know: Policy and Social Science Research on Seismic Safety. Berkeley, Cal.: Institute of Governmental Studies, University of California, Research Report No. 79-5, 1979.

Weller, J. M. Organizational Innovation in Anticipation of Crisis. Disaster Research Center Report Series No. 14. Columbus, Ohio: Disaster Research Center, Ohio State University, 1973.

Wiggins, John H. "The Risk Imbalance in Current Public Policies." <u>Proceedings of Symposium on Risk Acceptance and Public Policy.</u> Denver, Colorado: International System Safety Society, 1973, pp. 1-35.

Arnold, Christopher. Earthquake Disaster Prevention Planning in Japan. Report to the National Science Foundation. San Mateo, California: Building Systems Development, Inc., November 1982.

Berkol, F. N. "Natural Disaster—A Neglected Variable in National Development Strategies." International Social Scientist. Volume 28, 1976, pp. 730-35.

Brown, Barbara J. Disaster Preparedness and the United Nations: Advance Planning for Disaster Relief. New York: Pergamon Press, Ltd., 1979.

Charlton, E. "India's Earthquake: Indira Gandhi and the Politics of Emergency." The Round Table. 1976.

Comptroller General of the United States. Observations on the Guatemalan Earthquake Relief Effort, Agency for International Development, Department of Defense, Department of State: Report to the Congress. Washington, D.C.: U.S. General Accounting Office, 1976.

Davis, Ian. "The Intervenors." New Internationalist. No. 53, 977, pp. 21-23.

Earthquake Resistant Regulations: A World List. Tokyo: International Association for Earthquake Engineering, 1973.

Fordham, J. H. "Earthquake Disaster at Agodir." NATO Civil Defense Bulletin. Volume 6, No. 2, July 1960, p. 13.

Gange, John. "NATO's Approach to Natural Disaster Relief." Mass Emergencies. Volume 1, No. 1, 1975.

Green, Stephen. International Disaster Relief: Toward A Response System. New York: McGraw-Hill, 1977.

Hanning, Hugh. "NATO and Disaster Relief." Disasters. Volume 2, Nos. 2/3, 1978.

Harris, W. R. U.S. Participation in the Relief of International Disasters: Issues for a Proposed Task Force. The RAND Paper Series No. P-5662. Santa Monica, California: The Rand Corporation, 1976.

Hingson, Luke L. "The Guatemalan Earthquake of 4 February 1976: Case Study of a Disaster Relief Agency's Operation." Mass Emergencies. Volume 2, No. 2, 1977.

Intergovernmental Conference on the Protection of Cultural Property in the Event of Armed Conflict. Records of the Conference Convened by the United Nations Educational, Scientific and Cultural Organization Held at the Hague from 21 April to 14 May 1954. The Hague: Government of the Netherlands, 1961.

Intergovernmental Conference on the Protection of Cultural Property in the Event of Armed Conflict. Final Act, Convention and Protocol Adopted by the United Nations Conference on the Protection of Cultural Property in the Event of Armed Conflict, Together with Regulations for the Execution of the Convention and Resolutions attached to the Final Act. London: Her Majesty's Stationery Office, 1954.

International Meeting on Earthquakes. Disaster Assistance: Earthquake Hazard Reduction. NATO Committee on the Challenges of Modern Society, CCMS Report No. 9. Brussels, Belgium: North Atlantic Treaty Organization, 1971.

Krimgold, Frederick. Pre-Disaster Planning: The Role of International Aid for Pre-Disaster Planning in Developing Countries. Stockholm, Sweden: Avdelningen for Arkitektur Kth., 1974.

Lewis, James. A Report to Establish Guidelines for the Management of a Regional Fund to Provide Insurance for Natural Disaster. London: Commonwealth Secretariat, 1976.

"Making Disaster Relief More Effective." Nature. Volume 274, 6 July 1978.

McLin, J. Disaster Relief in the United Nations. West Europe Series Vol. 11, No. 5. Hanover, N.H.: American Universities Field Staff, Inc., 1976.

Morison, Robin F. "International Disaster Action: Advancing Slowly, But How Surely?" Disasters. Volume 4, No. 1, 1980, pp. 93-99.

Mosgaard, Christian. International Planning in Disaster Situations. Licentiafhandlinger ved IMSOR Nr. 23. Lyngby, Denmark: Institute of Mathematics, Statistics and Operations Research (IMSOR), 1975.

Mosgaard, Christian. Logistic Planning of Disaster Relief. Copenhagen: Institute of Mathematical Statistics and Operational Analysis, 1973.

NATO Committee on the Challenges of Modern Society. Disaster Assistance: Earthquake Hazard Reduction. CCMS Report No. 9. Brussels, Belgium: Committee on the Challenges of Modern Society, NATO, also NTIS PB 250-155, 157.

Raggio, I. "International Response to Disaster in Guatemala." Disasters. Volume 1, 1977, pp. 80-82.

Rivers, John. "Disaster Relief Needs More Research." Nature, Volume 271, No. 5641, 12 January 1978, p. 100.

"The Schroder Report." ICOM News. Volume 28, No. 4, 1975, pp. 141-144.

Seminar on Post-Disaster Reconstruction at Royal Institute of Technology, Stockholm. Swedish Aid to Post-Disaster Reconstruction: Case Studies from Peru, Turkey, and the Democratic Republic of Vietnam. Stockholm, Sweden: Swedish Council for Building Research. (Also NTIS PB-251-335), 1975.

Stephens, Lynn H. and Stephen J. Green, Eds. Disaster Assistance: Appraisal, Reform and New Approaches. U.N. Association of the United States of America, Policy Studies Book Series. New York: New York University Press, 1979.

Stephens, Thomas. The United Nations Disaster Relief Office: The Politics and Administration of International Relief Assistance. Thesis No. 303, Institute de Hautes Etudes Internationales, Universitie de Geneve. Washington, D.C.: University Press of America, 1978.

Taylor, Alan J. "Disaster Housing Aid: A Program Planning Model from Guatemala." Disasters. Volume 2, No. 1, 1978.

Taylor, Alan J. A Survey and Analysis of Administrative, Technical and Organizational Experience Accruing to Oxfam and to Other Voluntary Agencies Arising Out of the Bangladesh Refugee Relief Operations, April 1971-February 1972. Calcutta: Oxfam, 1972.

UNA-USA Policy Studies Panel on International Disaster Relief. Acts of Nature, Acts of Man: The Global Response to Natural Disasters. New York: The Panel, 1977.

U.S. National Research Council. Committee on International Disaster Assistance. The Role of Technology in International Disaster Assistance. Washington, D.C.: National Academy of Sciences, 1978.

U.S. National Research Council. Committee on International Disaster Assistance. The U.S. Government Foreign Disaster Assistance Program. Washington, D.C.: National Academy of Sciences, 1978.

Wallace, Robert E. "NATO and Quakes." Geotimes. Volume XVI, October 1971, p. 25.

Williams, Sharon Anne. The International and National Protection of Movable Cultural Property: A Comparative Study. Dobbs Ferry, N.Y.: Oceana Publications, Inc., 1978.

World Weather Watch. Consolidated Report on the Voluntary Assistance Programme
Including Projects Approved for Circulation in 1976. Geneva, Switzerland: World
Meteorological Organization, 1977.

RESPONSE MEASURES: FEDERAL

Anderson, William A. Military-Civilian Relations in Disaster Operations. Prepared for U.S. Office of Civil Defense, Office of the Secretary of the Army, as Disaster Research Center Report Series No. 5. Washington, D.C.: U.S. Government Printing Office, 1966.

Anderson, William A. Seismic Sea-Wave Warning in Crescent City, California and Hilo, Hawaii. Disaster Research Center Research Report No. 13. Columbus, Ohio: Disaster Research Center, Ohio State University, 1967.

Arizona Warning Point Operations Guide for Use of National Warning System (NAWAS). Phoenix, Arizona: State of Arizona, Division of Emergency Services, n.d.

Cheatham, Leo R. An Analysis of the Effectiveness of Land Use Regulations Required for Flood Insurance Eligibility. Mississippi State, Mississippi: Water Resources Research Institute, Mississippi State University, 1977.

Conference on Earthquake Warning and Response, San Francisco, 1975. Earthquake Prediction: Opportunity to Avoid Disaster. Washington, D.C.: U.S. Department of Commerce, U.S. Geological Survey, 1976.

Disaster Research Center. "A Prime Time for Disaster: Warning Systems Must Consider a Community's Many Rhythms." Civil Defense Reporter. Volume 1, Number 11, October 1968.

Earthquake Reduction and Hazards Mitigation: Options for USGS and NSF Programs. Washington: U.S. Government Printing Office, 1976.

Federal Emergency Management Agency. Digest of Federal Disaster Assistance Programs. Washington, D.C.: Federal Emergency Management Agency, June 1982.

Federal Emergency Management Agency. Disaster Response and Recovery Program Guide. FEMA Publication MP-91. Washington, D.C.: Federal Emergency Management Agency, 1980.

Federal Register. National Flood Insurance Program. Washington, D.C.: Department of Housing and Urban Development, 1976.

Gillette, R. and J. Welsh. "San Fernando Earthquake Study: NRC Panel Sees Premonitory Lessons." Science. Volume CLXXII, 9 April 1971, pp. 140–143.

Holmes, Beatrice Hort. "Federal Participation in Land Use Decisionmaking at The Water's Edge—Floodplains and Wetlands." Natural Resources Lawyer. Volume 13, No. 2, 1980, pp. 351–410.

Kunreuther, Howard. Recovery from Disasters: Insurance or Federal Aid? Washington, D.C.: American Enterprise Institute, Evaluative Studies Series No. 12, December 1973.

Lazzeri, Denise, Ed. Code of Federal Regulations: Emergency Management and Assistance—Title 44 (Revised as of October 1, 1980). Washington, D.C.: U.S. General Services Administration, National Archives and Record Service, Office of the Federal Register, 1980.

Liddy, John C. "Civil Defense Scheme for Art Galleries and Museums." Kalori. Journal of the Museums Association of Australia. October 1968, pp. 31–34.

Meta Systems, Inc. The NOAA Flood Warning Systems: A Case Study of Tropical Storm Agnes. Report prepared for the National Oceanic and Atmospheric Administration, U.S. Department of Commerce. Cambridge, Mass.: Meta Systems, Inc., 1972.

Disaster Preparedness: A Report to the Congress. Washington, D.C.: U.S. Government Printing Office, 1972.

Oliver, John. Natural Hazard Response and Planning in Tropical Queensland. Natural Hazards Research Working Paper Series No. 33. Boulder, Colorado: University of Colorado, Natural Hazards Research and Applications Information Center, 1978.

O'Riordan, Timothy. The New Zealand Earthquake and War Damage Commission: A Study of a Natural Hazards Insurance Scheme. Natural Hazard Working paper No. 20. Toronto, Canada: Department of Geography, University of Toronto, 1971.

Pickup, Geoffrey and Joseph E. Minor. Assessment of Research and Practice in Australian Natural Hazards Management. Winnellie, Australia: North Australia Research Unit, Bulletin No. 6, 1980.

Power, J. M. and R. L. Wettenhall. "Bureaucracy and Disaster 11: Response to the 1967 Tasmanian Bushfires." Public Administration. Volume XXIX, 1970, pp. 168–188.

Quinn, V. E. and J. Spaulding. Digest of Federal Disaster Assistance Programs. Washington, D.C.: Disaster Response and Recovery Office, 1979.

Sorenson, John H. and Philip J. Gersmehl. "Volcanic Hazard Warning System: Persistence and Transferability." Environmental Management. Volume 4, No. 2, March 1980, pp. 125–136.

Steinbrugge, Karl V. Earthquake Hazard Reduction: Issues for an Implementation Plan. Washington, D.C.: Working Groups on Earthquake Hazard Reduction, Office of Science and Technology, Executive Office of the President, 1978.

U.S. Congress, Senate. Committee on Public Works. Governmental Response to the California Earthquake Disaster of February 1971. Washington, D.C.: U.S. Government Printing Office, 1971.

U.S. Department of Agriculture. First Aid for Flooded Homes and Farms. Agriculture Handbook No. 38. Washington, D.C.: U.S. Government Printing Office, 1972.

U.S. Department of Commerce. National Oceanic and Atmospheric Administration. A Federal Plan for Natural Disaster Warning and Preparedness. Washington, D.C.: U.S. Government Printing Office, 1973.

U.S. Department of Commerce. National Oceanic and Atmospheric Administration. A Federal Plan for Natural Disaster Warning and Preparedness. First Supplement: Fiscal Years 1976–80. Washington, D.C.: U.S. Government Printing Office, 1975.

U.S. Earthquake Observatories: Recommendations for a New National Network. Washington, D.C.: National Academy Press, 1980.

U.S. National Advisory Committee on Oceans and Atmosphere. The Agnes Floods: A Post Audit of the Effectiveness of the Storm and Flood Warning System of the National Oceanic and Atmospheric Administration. Washington, D.C.: U.S. Government Printing Office, 1972.

U.S. National Ocean Survey. Program Development Plan: Coastal Hazards Program. Washington, D.C.: U.S. Department of Commerce, National Oceanic and Atmospheric Administration, 1980.

U.S. National Science Foundation. A Report on Flood Hazard Mitigation. Washington, D.C.: National Science Foundation, 1980.

U.S. Water Resources Council. Unified National Program for Flood Plain Management. Washington, D.C.: U.S.W.R.C., 1980.

Visvader, H. and Ian Burton. "Natural Hazards and Hazard Policy in Canada and the United States." Natural Hazards. Gilbert F. White, Ed. London: Oxford University Press, 1974, pp. 219–30.

Adams, David S. Emergency Actions and Disaster Reactions: An Analysis of the Anchorage Public Works Department During the 1964 Alaskan Earthquake. Prepared for the Office of Civil Defense, Office of the Secretary of the Army, as Disaster Research Center Monograph No.5. Columbus, Ohio: Ohio State University, Disaster Research Center, 1969.

Anderson, William A. Local Civil Defense in Natural Disaster: From Office to Organization. Prepared for U.S. Office of Civil Defense, Office of the Secretary of the Army, as Disaster Research Center Report Series No. 7. Washington, D.C.: U.S. Government Printing Office, 1969.

Baker, George W. and Dwight W. Chapman, Eds. "Disaster Community Organization and Administrative Process." Man and Society in Disaster. New York: Basic Books, 1962, pp. 268-302.

Bartol, John. Role of California Community Colleges in Disseminating Earthquake Hazard Mitigation Information. Springfield, Va.: National Technical Information Service No. PB 299 421, 1979.

Bloomgren, Patricia A. "Strengthening State Floodplain Management." Regulation of Flood Hazard Areas to Reduce Flood Losses. Jon Kusler, Ed. Boulder, Colorado: Natural Hazards Research and Applications Information Center, University of Colorado, Special Publication No. 2, 1982.

Borkan, Bradley and Howard Kunreuther. "Towards a Community Disaster Model for Policy Analysis." Mass Emergencies. Volume 3, No. 1, 1978.

Bourque, Linda Brookover, Andrew Cherlin and Leo G. Reeder. "Agencies and the Los Angeles Earthquake." Mass Emergencies. Volume 1, No. 3, 1976.

California Disaster Office. Guidance for the Development of a County Emergency Plan. Sacramento: California Community Emergency Planning Program, 1969.

Corning Glass Works. The Flood and the Community. Corning, N.Y.: Corning Glass Works, 1976.

Council of State Governments. Comprehensive Emergency Preparedness Planning in State Governments. Lexington, KY: Council of State Governments, 1976.

Council of State Governments. The States and Natural Hazards. Lexington, KY: Council of State Governments, 1979.

Davis, Ron. Coping with Natural Disasters on the Local Level. Washington, D.C.: International Center for Emergency Preparedness, 1977.

Disaster Operations: A Handbook for Local Governments. Washington, D.C.: Defense Civil Preparedness Agency, July 1972 with change 1, June 1974.

Dynes, Russell R. and E. L. Quarantelli. The Role of Local Civil Defense in Disaster Planning. Disaster Research Center Report Series No. 16. Columbus, Ohio: Disaster Research Center, Ohio State University, 1975.

470

Hanson, John. Getting the Disaster Facts: A Guide for Governors' Assistants. Washington, D.C.: National Governors' Association, 1980.

Heffren, Edward. "Interagency Relationships and Conflict in Disaster: The Wilkes-Barre Experience." Mass Emergencies. Volume 2, No. 2, 1977.

Jahns, Richard H. "Seventeen Years of Response by the City of Los Angeles to Geologic Hazards." Geologic Hazards and Public Problems. Edited by R. A. Olson and M. M. Wallace. Washington, D.C.: U.S. Government Printing Office, 1969.

James, Douglas. Flood Damage Mitigation in Utah. Publication UW RL/P/80/0. Logan, Utah: Utah Water Research Laboratory, Utah State University, 1980.

Johnson, G. Wesley and Ronald L. Nye, Eds. Environmental Hazards and Community Response: The Santa Barbara Experience. Public Historical Studies Monograph N. 2. Santa Barbara, California: University of California, 1979.

Kusler, Jon. "Innovation in Local Floodplain Management." Appendix B to Regulation of Flood Hazard Areas to Reduce Flood Losses. Jon Kusler, Ed. Boulder, Colorado: Natural Hazards Research and Applications Information Center, University of Colorado, 1982.

Lardner, John P., James L. Alexander and Michael L. Terstriep. Floodplain Services Available from the Illinois State Water Survey. Springfield, Illinois: State of Illinois, 1979.

Margerum, Terry. Earthquake Hazards and Local Government Liability: Final Report. Springfield, Va.: National Technical Information Service, PB-80-116-924, 1979.

Margerum, Terry. We're Not Ready for the Big Quake: What Local Governments Can Do. Oakland, California: Association of Bay Area Governments, 1980.

Margerum, Terry. Will Local Governments Be Liable for Earthquake Losses? What Cities and Counties Should Know About Earthquake Hazards and Local Government Liability. Oakland, California: Association of Bay Area Governments, January 1979.

Mitchell, G., K. J. Gardner, R. Cook and B. Veale. Physical Adjustments and Institutional Arrangements for the Urban Flood Hazard: Grand River Watershed. Department of Geography, Publication Series No. 13. Waterloo, Ontario: University of Waterloo, 1978.

Pennsylvania Office of State Planning Economic Development. Tropical Storm Agnes: Long-Range Flood Recovery. McLean, Va.: MITRE, 1973.

Platt, Rutherford H. Intergovernmental Management of Floodplains. Boulder, Colorado: University of Colorado, Natural Hazards Research and Applications Information Center, 1980.

Rose, Adam. "Mandating Local Government Emergency Services." The Urban Interest. Volume 2, No. 1, Spring 1980, pp. 65-73.

Rubin, Claire B. Natural Disaster Recovery Planning for Local Public Officials. Columbus, Ohio: Academy for Contemporary Problems, 1979.

Scott, Stanley. Policies for Seismic Safety: Elements of a State Governmental Program. Berkeley, California: Institute of Governmental Studies, University of California, 1979.

"Securing Historic Sites: Atlanta's Protection Plan." History News. Volume 31, September 1976, pp. 166-68.

Stallings, Robert. Preliminary Analysis of Gubernatorial Emergency Declarations in California 1960-1975. Working Paper No. 30. Los Angeles, California: University of Southern California School of Public Administration, 1979.

Taylor, Donald F., William F. Karl, and Hope R. Emerich. The Development of the Emergency Management Coordinator's Handbook. Harrisburg, Pa.: Pennsylvania Emergency Management Agency, 1980 (NTIS AD-A082-454/0).

Taylor, James B., Louis Zurcher, and William H. Key. Tornado: A Community Responds to Disaster. Seattle and London: University of Washington Press, 1970.

University of Southern California. College of Continuing Education and School of Public Administration. Office of Program Development. Emergency Disaster Planning in Los Angeles County: A Multi-Jurisdictional Dilemma. Prepared for the Federal Emergency Management Agency. Springfield, Va.: National Technical Information Service, No. AD-A08-1440, 1979.

Vartez, J. and W. Kelly. Emergency Planning and the Adaptive Local Response to the Mt. St. Helens' Eruption. Final Report to the National Science Foundation, Grant No., PFR 8020876, November 1980.

Whipkey, Harry E. After Agnes: A Report on Flood Recovery Assistance by the Pennsylvania Historical and Museum Commission. Harrisburg, Pa.: Pennsylvania Historical and Museum Commission, 1973.

Wiley, Christopher J. Report on State Agency Programs for Seismic Safety. Sacramento, California: California Seismic Safety Commission, 1979.

Wurtele, Zivia S. A Case Study of Corpus Christi After Hurricane Celia and a Methodology for Evaluating Economic Impacts of Disasters and Disaster Assistance Programs, Volume I. Report No. TM-4907/001/00. Santa Monica, California: System Development Corporation, May 1972.

You are Never Completely Safe . . . . Durham, N.H.: New England Municipal Center, n.d.

Abe, Kitao. At That Moment[You Are the Leader—For Appropriate Action in a Disaster. Tokyo, Japan: Japan Damage Insurance Association, 1976.

Baker, Lawrence C., Jr. "Availability and Desirability of Earthquakes Insurance." Earthquake Risk: Report of the Special Subcommittee to the Joint Committee on the San Fernando Earthquake Study. Sacramento, California: California State Legislature, 1971.

Best's Loss Control and Underwriting Manual. Morristown, J.J.: A.M. Best Co., 1968.

Buffinton, P. G. "Earthquake Insurance in the U.S.—A Reappraisal." Bulletin of the Seismological Society of America. Volume 51, 1961, pp. 315-329.

Earthquakes and Insurance: Papers from the Earthquake Research Affiliates Conference, 2-3 April 1972. Pasadena, California: Center for Research on the Prevention of Natural Disasters, Division of Engineering and Applied Science, California Institute of Technology, 1973.

Evans, Deane, Ed. The Role of Architects and Planners in Post-Earthquake Studies. Berkeley, California: Earthquake Engineering Research Institute, August 1982.

Freeman, John Ripley. Earthquake Damage and Earthquake Insurance. New York: McGraw, 1932.

Kunreuther, Howard. "The Case for Comprehensive Disaster Insurance." Journal of Law and Economics. Volume 11, 1968, pp. 133-163.

Kunreuther, Howard. "Disaster Insurance: A Tool for Hazard Mitigation." The Journal of Risk and Insurance. Volume 41, 1974, pp. 287-303.

Kunreuther, Howard. Recovery from Disasters: Insurance or Federal Aid? Washington, D.C.: American Enterprise Institute, Evaluative Studies Series No. 12, December 1973.

Lewis, James. A Report to Establish Guidelines for the Management of a Regional Fund to Provide Insurance for Natural Disaster. London: Commonwealth Secretariat, 1976.

"Libraries." American Insurance Association Occupancy Bulletin. New York: American Insurance Association, 1971.

Mills, Paul Chadbourne. "Insurance: Are Fine Arts Premiums Out of Line?" Museum News. Volume 57, No. 5, May/June 1979, pp. 54-55.

Piez, Gladys T. "Insurance and the Protection of Library Resources." ALA Bulletin. May 1962, pp. 421-424.

Reitherman, Robert. Insurance Implications of Multi-Hazard Reduction. Washington, D.C.: AIA Research Corporation, 1980.

Syfert, Robert K. "The Unwilling Market for Earthquake Insurance." Best's Review. November 1972, pp. 14-18.

473

Vaughn, Christopher. Natural Hazards Research. Working Paper No. 21, "Notes on Insurance Against Loss from Natural Hazards." Toronto: Department of Geography, University of Toronto, 1971.

Wiggins, John H. and Co. Problems and Issues Associated with Use of Insurance Systems to Mitigate the Impact of Future Earthquake Losses Within the United States. Technical Report No. 80-1388-1. Washington, D.C.: Federal Insurance Administration, 1980.

APPENDIX A

Multi-Hazard Ratings of Counties by States for the United States

Multi-Hazard Ratings of Counties by States for the United States

Ralph W. Rose and David G. Westendorff

INTRODUCTION

An abundant literature exists on natural disasters. Much of it is narrative or technical records of specific disastrous events. These descriptions provide us with most of the information that we have about the extensiveness of events of various kinds in the past and their impacts upon people and the natural and built environment. There is additionally a voluminous scientific and engineering literature on the incidence of hazards of various kinds and the proneness of different regions to hazards. Some of this literature is based upon painstakingly kept records of incidents which have occurred. Some of it is based upon analytical studies of susceptibility although no record exists of events in the past.

The first type of study is very informative as case study material. It provides us with notions of what to expect in certain contingencies. The second type of study is conceived in macro-behavioral terms. It gives us information about what can be expected to occur from a public policy point of view. Such studies help policymakers and responsible public agencies to determine the kinds of precautions and preparatory steps that need to be taken to reduce vulnerability, to provide emergency assistance, and to assess potential needs for recovery and reconstruction programs. Some of these studies explicitly attempt to estimate the losses and extent of damage that are likely to result from natural disasters in future periods. [J. H. Wiggins Company, 1978] This is highly appropriate since these elaborate and expensive studies have usually been undertaken for the purpose of government officials and public agencies.

However, very little information has been made available that is appropriate from a micro–behavioral perspective. Given the fact that one is situated at a specific location, to what hazards is one prone and to what extent? Conversely if one chooses to locate at a given point in space, what risks will one incur? From the point of view of an individual occupying a location or choosing a place to locate, there is little readily available material to indicate what the person should be

477

prepared to expect. For some hazards and for some locations, the potential consequences are self-evident, particularly to experienced individuals. This is especially the case where hazardous events frequently occur in specific types of locations. For other hazards and locations the periodicity of incidents is so long that it transcends the memory span of organizations, administrations and even social systems.

The micro-behavioral decision maker is a critical actor in determining the ultimate impact of a natural disaster. Such an individual needs site specific information. The individual can either locate to minimize proneness or take necessary precautions appropriate to a location to reduce vulnerability. Appropriate individual behavior can have a major effect on minimizing or maximizing the impact of a given event. It can determine whether losses are heavy or light, major or relatively unimportant.

The following tables have been developed specifically for the purpose of assisting in micro-behavioral decisions. Compiled from various sources, they show risk ratings for seven different types of natural hazards for each county in the United States. They can provide only a first point of reference: an index of whether or not and what type of further investigation is necessary. For the tables to be manageable at all, it has been necessary to distill a great deal of information into gross summary measures. While much information is lost in the process, it makes it possible to look up rapidly and easily the general area of a location of concern and obtain some idea of the types of hazards and the degree of proneness that exist. Nevertheless, these gross measures provide an indication to further steps that should be taken. More specific information about hazards and more information about particular sites will need to be obtained in many instances. References are provided to facilitate further investigation. The tables are not intended to give definitive information but only as a point of departure. The summary measures rate only the relative probability of occurrence of a particular hazard somewhere in the county and do not inform about probable level of damage or the locus of highest risk within the county.

The summary measures presented in the tables are based upon variable types and quality of data. Micro-geographical risk analysis of geological hazards, such as earthquakes, landslides and expansive soils, derives from fairly developed disciplines and does not need to rely to a very large extent on past experience to arrive at estimates of proneness to catastrophes. Extensive surveys have been made and presented in cartographic form which have been summarized in the following tables. Ambiguities are introduced because subareas of various counties will have several different hazard levels. The choice of a rating for the county may or may not be very representative of most of the area in the county.

Analyzing risk from climatological hazards such as hurricanes, tornados, floods and storm surges presents different kinds of difficulties. A great deal of the climatological disaster data that are available are based upon records that have been kept of past events.

478

Proneness to a hazard is defined not in terms of characteristics of the area but previous incidence. Some of the data series that are most readily available and easiest to translate into a county basis are far from ideal.

The choice of counties as the units of risk analysis is appropriate to a summary table of the kind presented here. The number of subareas is not so voluminous as to be unmanageable and yet relatively specific subareas can be referenced. However, they are of variable usefulness with respect to different kinds of disasters. This is particularly the case with weather phenomena. Hurricanes, which wreak destruction over a wide area and cause more damage per event than any other kind of natural disaster, clearly endanger the entire area of a county in which their occurrence is regular. [Wright, et al. 1979] Tornados, on the other hand, cut rather narrow swaths of destruction and may pass through a county but endanger only a small portion.

Climatological disasters are frequently recorded in terms of the amount of damage that they produce. A moderate event in a county in which there is a large population and much property may receive a higher rating than a much more severe event in a sparsely populated area. The hurricane and flood data that have been used to prepare these tables are particularly prone to this type of distortion.

Of all climatological disasters, floods are the most susceptible to mapping risk levels for small subareas. The Flood Insurance Administration's hundred year hazard boundary maps enable delineation of flood plains at a detailed micro-geographical level (such data are usually available from local governments). However, floods will be specific to a particular portion of a region as large as a county and not the county as a whole. The ratings will apply to the portions that are flood prone. Unfortunately, it has not been possible to use detailed topographical information to produce the county summary measure for floods. Again, an index derived from damage has been used. For macro-behavioral administrative purposes, damage estimates and the provision of relief and assistance from previous events is a highly relevant measure. For micro-behavioral purposes, tabulations of the frequency and severity of the events themselves would be preferable. It was not possible to obtain this kind of information within the scope of this study.

The tables presented here were undertaken as part of the background preparation for the Seminar on the Protection of Historic Architecture and Museum Collections from Earthquakes and Other Natural Disasters that is reported in preceding sections. It was supported in part by the National Science Foundation through Grant No. PFR 8007116 and by Cornell University. Ralph W. Rose developed the format, carried out the original research, and identified and obtained the basic data sources. Final acquisition of data and the laborious task of assigning values for each of the hazards to each county was done by David G. Westendorff. Jonathan Gitlin edited and prepared the material for publication. Professor Barclay G. Jones supervised the process.

METHODS USED IN DEVISING RATINGS

In the section that follows the ratings developed for each of the seven natural hazards will be defined and the scales used explained. It was not possible to apply a consistent set of ratings to all hazards. Information about some hazards is provided in a larger number of intervals than others. However, the scaling system is consistent in that low numbers represent the least severe and high numbers the most severe conditions. The data sources used in the preparation of the tables are identified for each hazard and the methodology employed in transforming them to tabular form is described. As noted above some of the data series are clearly more appropriate than others. At the end of this section the sources that have been used in compiling the tables are listed with full citation. Other useful references for further investigation into specific hazards are provided also. In addition, various agencies that can be useful sources of information for specific situations are listed. The type of data series and records that they keep and make available is described briefly. Following that a key to the symbols and their definitions and the values assigned in the tables is presented followed by the county tables themselves.

EARTHQUAKE

Each county has two single digit ratings which reflect the intensity of ground shaking caused by an earthquake. The ratings are based on scientifically determined parameters known as Effective Peak Acceleration (Aa) and Effective Peak Velocity-Related Acceleration (Av). In the table counties with the most severe earthquake hazard are rated 7, which corresponds to Aa and Av values of 0.40 seconds. In order of descending severity, ratings of 6 to 1 correspond to respective Aa and Av values as follows: 0.30, 0.20, 0.15, 0.10, 0.05, and less than 0.05. Large counties may have more than one Aa or Av value, thus they receive the rating corresponding to the highest Aa and Av values in the county. Source: Seismic Design Project, Center for Building Technology, U.S. National Bureau of Standards. Tentative Provisions for the Development of Seismic Regulations for Buildings. Washington, D.C.: Center for Building Technology, Seismic Design Project, 1978, pp. 29, 298-299.

LANDSLIDE

Landslide ratings are composed of two pairs of digits. The first pair indicates the highest level of incidence of landslide and the extent to which its occurrence has been distributed over the county. The second pair of digits indicates the highest degree of susceptibility to landslide in the county as determined through investigation of local soil and slope conditions. As with incidence of landslide, the extent to which this phenomenon is distributed over the county is included in the rating. The first digit of each pair is the measure of either incidence or susceptibility. Low, medium, and high incidence (or susceptibility) are assigned values of 1, 2, and 3 respectively. The second digit in each pair indicates the extent to which the given incidence/susceptibility is found in the county. A rating of 1 corresponds to an area not greater than 1/4 of the county; a rating of 2 corresponds to an area approximately between 1/4 and 3/5 of the county; and a rating of 3 corresponds to areas over 3/5 of the county. For example, a county with a rating of 23 33 has a medium incidence of landslide over an area not less than 3/5 of the total area of the county. It is also rated as having a high susceptibility to landslide over the same area. A county with a rating of 21 31 has a medium incidence and high susceptibility over not more than a 1/4 of its total area. In both examples the highest level of incidence of landslide in the county is medium (first digit, first pair = 2). Landslide data for Alaska and Hawaii are not included. Source: U.S. Geological Survey, 1976 Landslide Overview, Coterminous United States, Miscellaneous Field Studies Map MF-771.

EXPANSIVE SOIL

Counties are assigned a two digit rating indicating the highest degree of expansive soil found in the county and the extent to which it covers the county. The first digit measures the degree of soil expansiveness. High, moderate and low degrees of expansiveness are rated 3, 2, and 1 respectively. The second digit refers to the extent of the county's surface area covered by soil type with the given degree of expansiveness. A second digit rating of 1 refers to an area not more than 1/4 of the county's surface area, a 2 refers to between 1/4 and 3/5 of the total surface area, and a 3 refers to more than 3/5 of the county's total surface area. Although a given severity rating has been assigned to each county, it is possible that smaller portions of the county have soils that are more expansive than those indicated. The rating may not apply to the most hazardous conditions to be found in the county in some cases. Data for Alaska and Hawaii are not included in this survey. Source: Expansive Soils Map, prepared by Slosson and Associates, Engineering Geologists, 1978.

FLOOD

Flood ratings range from 1 to 5 with 5 representing the severest hazard. Ratings are based on the number of instances in which the

National Red Cross provided assistance to victims of flood in a given county over the period from 1945 to 1976. Counties receiving Red Cross aid more than ten times during this period are rated 5; those receiving aid from 7 to 9 times are rated 4, etc. Counties where the Red Cross did not provide assistance to flood victims during the period are rated 1. These data do not necessarily represent the actual number of floods occurring in counties during the survey period. Source: U.S. National Weather Service, Office of Hydrology. Flood and Flash Flood Events Map, Silver Springs, MD: U.S National Weather Service, 1976.

STORM SURGE/TSUNAMI

Storm Surge. Coastal and lowland counties of the Gulf and East Coasts are assigned ratings of 1 to 3 based on their susceptibility to property damage by flooding induced by tropical storms/hurricanes. The basis of this rating system is a damage curve which estimates the percent of structural damage at given heights of water above a structure's first floor. There are three damage curves, each representing a different level of wave action that structures are subject to during storm surge flooding. "Stillwater" damage has a rating of 1. In counties where structures are subject to "light to moderate wave action", a greater degree of structural damage results. These are rated 2. The greatest degree of structural damage occurs in counties where rising waters are accompanied by moderate to heavy wave action. These counties are rated 3.

Tsunami. Coastal counties of Alaska, California, Oregon, Washington and the Hawaiian Islands are subject to damage by Tsunami. Damage curves have not been calculated for tsunamis. Counties that may be affected by Tsunamis in the above states are noted with the rating of 4. Counties not subject to storm surge or tsunami damage are noted with 0. Source: Lee, L. T., Chrostowski, J. D., and Eguchi, E. T. Natural Hazards: Storm Surge, Riverine Flooding, Tsunami Loss Models. Redondo Beach, CA: J. H. Wiggins Company, 1978.

HURRICANE

County ratings for hurricanes range from 0 to 6 based on the average incidence of property damage in contiguous counties by tropical storms between 1901 and 1955. Counties where tropical storm damage occurred more than 20 times during the survey period are rated 6. Counties with 15-19 instances of damage are rated 5, those with 10-14 instances of damage are rated 4, those with 5-9 instances of damage are rated 3, and counties with 1-4 instances of damage are rated 2. Counties where there were no recorded instances of damage during the survey period but were traversed by tropical storms are rated 1. Counties not subject to tropical weather systems are noted with 0. Source: U.S. Department of Interior, The National Atlas of the United States of America, Washington, D.C., 1970, p. 1152. Also: A. L. Suss, L. G. Pardue, and R. L. Arrodus, Memorable Hurricanes of the United States Since 1873. NOAA Technical Memorandum NWS SR-56, 1971.

TORNADO

Tornado ratings are based on data from a contour map which displays the average ratio of the area damaged by tornados in a hundred year period to the total area within the contour. Ratings range from a low of 1 to a high of 6. Counties with a rating of 6 are either partially or completely located within a contour which demarks an area where one square mile out of every fifteen is damaged by tornados over a hundred year period. Ratings of 5, 4, 3, 2, and 1 are correlated with regions where one square mile of damage occurs for every 25, 50, 75, 150 and greater than 150 square miles within the contour. Counties crossed by more than one contour receive the rating associated with the highest degree of damage. Alaska and Hawaii are not included in this survey. Source: Staff Members of National Severe Storms Forecast Center, "Tornadoes: When, Where, How Often?", Weatherwise Magazine, April 1980, p. 59.

SOURCES USED

Lee, Larry T., J. D. Chrostowski and E. T. Eguchi. Natural Hazards: Storm Surge, Riverine Flooding, Tsunami. Redondo Beach, California: J. H. Wiggins Company, 1978.

Slosson and Associates. "Expansive Soils Map". Map prepared by Slosson and Associates, Engineering Geologists, 1978.

U.S. Department of the Interior. The National Atlas of the United States of America. Washington, D.C. U.S. Government Printing Office, 1970.

U.S. Geological Survey. Landslide Overview, Coterminous United States. Miscellaneous Field Studies Map MF-771. (Radbruch-Hall, et al.) Washington, D.C.: U.S. Geological Survey, 1976.

U.S. National Bureau of Standards. Tentative Provisions for the Development of Seismic Regulations for Buildings. Washington, D.C.: Center for Building Technology, Seismic Design Project, 1978, pp. 29, 298-299.

U.S. National Weather Service. National Severe Storms Forecast Center. Staff. "Tornadoes: When, Where, How Often?". Weatherwise Magazine, April 1980, p. 59.

U.S. National Weather Service. Office of Hydrology. Flood and Flash Flood Events Map. Silver Spring, Maryland: U.S. National Weather Service, 1976.

Algermissen, S. T. Regional and National Seismic Hazard and Risk. Denver, Colorado: U.S. Geological Survey, Branch of Earthquake Tectonics and Risk, ongoing project.

Ayre, Robert. Earthquake and Tsunami Hazards in the United States. Boulder, Colorado: Program on Technology, Environment and Man, Monograph Series No. NSF-RA-E-75-005, University of Colorado, 1975.

Beavers, James E., Ed. Earthquakes and Earthquake Engineering: The Eastern United States. 2 volumes. Proceedings of a Conference held September 14-16, 1981 at Knoxville, Tennessee. Ann Arbor, Michigan: Ann Arbor Science Publishers, 1981.

Brandsma, M., D. Divoky and L. Hwang. Tsunami Atlas for the Coasts of the U.S. Springfield, Virginia: National Technical Information Service No. NUREG/CR-1106/1979.

Brinkmann, Waltraud A. R., et al. Hurricane Hazard in the U.S.: A Research Assessment. Report Number NSF-RA-E-75-007. Boulder, Colorado: University of Colorado, Institute of Behavioral Science: Program on Technology, Environment and Man, 1975.

Coffman, Jerry L. and C. A. Von Hake, Eds. Earthquake History of the United States. Revised Edition (Through 1970). Washington, DC: USGPO, 1973.

Hart, Gary C. Natural Hazard: Tornado, Hurricane, Severe Wind. Redondo Beach, California: J. H. Wiggins Company, December 1976.

Hewitt, Kenneth and Lesley Sheehan. A Pilot Survey of Natural Disasters of the Past Twenty Years. Working Paper No. 11. Boulder, Colorado: Natural Hazards Research and Applications Information Center, 1969.

Ho, Francis, et al. Some Climatological Characteristics of Hurricanes and Tropical Storms: Gulf and East Coasts of the United States. Report No. NWS-15. Springfield, Va.: National Technical Information Service, No. COM-75-110-88, May 1975.

International Association of Volcanology and Chemistry of the Earth's Interior. "List of the World's Active Volcanoes". Bulletin of Volcano Eruptions, Special Issue, 1971.

Krohn, J. P. and J. E. Slosson. "Landslide Potential in the U.S.". California Geology. October 1976, pp. 224-231.

Munich Reinsurance Company. World Map of Natural Hazards. Munchen: Munchener Ruckversicherungsgesellschaft, 1978.

Rossi, Peter H., et al. The Adequacy of Natural Disaster Data Bases for Location and Damage Estimates. Data Base Workshop. Boulder, Colorado: Natural Hazards Research Applications and Information Center, n.d.

Sugg, Arnold, et al. Memorable Hurricanes of the United States Since 1873. Technical Memorandum NWS SR-56. Washington, D.C.: National Oceanic and Atmospheric Administration, 1971.

484

Tubbesing, Susan K., Ed. Natural Hazards Data Resources: Uses and Needs. Springfield, Va.: National Technical Information Service, No. PB-194-912, 1979.

UNESCO. Annual Summary of Information on Natural Disasters. Paris: United Nations Economic, Social and Cultural Organization, Annual.

U.S. Department of Commerce. United States Earthquakes. Annual Publication prepared by U.S. Congress and the U.S. Geological Survey 1928-68 and by National Oceanic and Atmospheric Administration and U.S.G.S. 1973-present. Washington, D.C.: U.S. Government Printing Office, annual.

U.S. Geological Survey. Geologic Map of North America. Scale 1:2,500,000. Washington, D.C.: U.S. Geological Survey, 1974.

U.S. National Oceanic and Atmospheric Administration. Earthquakes. Washington, D.C.: U.S. Government Printing Office, Annual.

U.S. National Oceanic and Atmospheric Administration. Some Devastating North Atlantic Hurricanes of the Twentieth Century. Washington, D.C.: U.S. Government Printing Office, 1977.

White, Gilbert F. Flood Hazard in the United States. Boulder, Colorado: The University of Colorado, 1975.

Wiggins, J. H. Company. Building Losses From Natural Hazards: Yesterday, Today, and Tomorrow. Redondo Beach, California: J. H. Wiggins Company, 1978.

Wiggins, J. H., James E. Slosson and James P. Krohn. Natural Hazards: Earthquake, Landslide, Expansive Soil. Redondo Beach, California: J. H. Wiggins Company, October 1978.

Wright, James D. and Peter H. Rossi, Eds. Social Science and Natural Hazards. Cambridge, Massachusetts: ABT Books, 1980.

Wright, James D., Peter H. Rossi, Sonia R. Wright and Eleanor Weber-Burdin. After the Clean-Up: Long Range Effects of Natural Disasters. Beverly Hills, California: Sage Publications, 1979.

USEFUL AGENCIES AND DATA BASES

American National Red Cross, Washington, D.C.: Keeps full records on floods, tornados and hurricanes affecting 6 or more families, for which it provides Red Cross assistance.

University of Colorado. Natural Hazards Research Applications and Information Center. Numerous Publications.

U.S. Department of Commerce. National Oceanic and Atmospheric Administration. Climatological Data monthly publication. Boulder, Colorado: National Solar-Terrestrial and Geophysical Data Center, maintains worldwide records of earthquakes. Asheville, North Carolina: National Hurricane Center.

U.S. Department of Commerce. Small Business Administration. Files of SBA Disaster Loan recipients.

U.S. Federal Emergency Management Agency. Federal Insurance Administration. Maintains 1000-year flood boundary maps for over 14,000 U.S. communities covered by federal flood insurance.

U.S. Geological Survey. "Water Supply Papers", a monthly publication with yearly summaries, listing flood events.

U.S. National Weather Service. National Hurricane Center, Miami, Florida. Maintains computer files on U.S. Hurricanes 1886—present. National Severe Storms Forecast Center, Kansas City, Missouri. Maintains computer files on U.S. Tornados 1945—present.

HAZARD	SYMBOL	DEFINITION	RANGE AND UNITS
EARTHQUAKE	Aa	effective peak acceleration	7 = 0.4 seconds
			6 = 0.3
	Av	effective peak velocity	5 = 0.2
			4 = 0.15
			3 = 0.10
			2 = 0.05
			1 = ????
LANDSLIDE	I	incidence of landslide	3 = high
	S	susceptibility to landslide	2 = medium
			1 = low
	E	extent of given incidence or susceptibility	3 = more than 3/5 of county
			2 = 1/4 to 3/5 of county
			1 = less than 1/4 of county
EXPANSIVE SOIL	D	degree of expansiveness	3 = highly expansive
			2 = moderately expansive
			1 = minimally expansive
	E	extent of given expansivity over surface area	3 = more than 3/5 of surface
			2 = 1/4 to 3/5 of surface
			1 = less than 1/4 of surface
FLOOD	Ia	incidence of floods requiring Red Cross Aid (1945-1976)	5 = aided over 10 times
			4 = aided 7-9 times
			3 = aided 4-6 times
			2 = aided 1-3 times
			1 = no floods requiring aid
STORM SURGE	S	susceptibility to damage from --tropical storm and/or hurricane flooding on Gulf and East Coast --tsunami in coastal Alaska, Oregon, Washington and Hawaiian islands	4 = susceptible to tsunami in relevant states
			3 = susceptible to rising water and moderate to heavy wave damage
			2 = susceptible to light to moderate wave action
			1 = susceptible to still water damage
			0 = not susceptible to storm surge or tsunami damage
HURRICANE	Id	incidence of tropical storms causing property damage (1900-1956)	6 = more than 20 instances
			5 = 15-19 instances
			4 = 10-14 instances
			3 = 5-9 instances
			2 = 1-4 instances
			1 = no recorded instance of tropical storm damage
			0 = not susceptible to tropical storms
TORNADO	Er	extent of area damaged by tornadoes in a 100 year period in ratio to total area in incidence contour	6 = 1:15 square miles
			5 = 1:25
			4 = 1:50
			3 = 1:75
			2 = 1:150
			1 = 1:more than 150

ALABAMA

	County	EARTHQUAKE Aa	EARTHQUAKE Av	LANDSLIDE IE	LANDSLIDE SE	EXPANSIVE SOIL DE	FLOOD Ia	STORM SURGE S	HURRICANE Id	TORNADO Er
01 001	AUTAUGA COUNTY	1	1	23	13	13	2	0	3	4
01 003	BALDWIN COUNTY	1	1	13	13	13	3	3	6	2
01 005	BARBOUR COUNTY	1	1	13	21	22	2	0	4	2
01 007	BIBB COUNTY	2	2	13	32	22	1	0	3	5
01 009	BLOUNT COUNTY	2	2	13	13	13	1	0	2	3
01 011	BULLOCK COUNTY	1	1	13	13	32	1	0	3	4
01 013	BUTLER COUNTY	1	1	13	23	31	2	0	4	5
01 015	CALHOUN COUNTY	2	2	13	13	31	1	0	2	2
01 017	CHAMBERS COUNTY	2	2	13	23	31	2	0	2	3
01 019	CHEROKEE COUNTY	2	2	21	13	21	2	0	2	4
01 021	CHILTON COUNTY	2	2	13	21	31	2	0	3	4
01 023	CHOCTAW COUNTY	1	1	13	13	13	2	0	4	3
01 025	CLARKE COUNTY	1	1	13	13	13	3	0	4	5
01 027	CLAY COUNTY	2	2	13	13	23	2	0	2	2
01 029	CLEBURNE COUNTY	2	2	21	13	31	1	0	2	3
01 031	COFFEE COUNTY	1	1	13	13	13	2	0	5	3
01 033	COLBERT COUNTY	2	2	13	31	23	2	0	2	5
01 035	CONECUH COUNTY	1	1	13	13	13	2	0	4	4
01 037	COOSA COUNTY	2	2	13	13	31	2	0	3	5
01 039	COVINGTON COUNTY	1	1	13	33	13	2	0	4	2
01 041	CRENSHAW COUNTY	1	1	13	13	21	2	0	4	5
01 043	CULLMAN COUNTY	2	2	13	13	13	2	0	2	4
01 045	DALE COUNTY	1	1	13	33	13	3	0	5	5
01 047	DALLAS COUNTY	1	1	13	21	31	3	0	3	2
01 049	DE KALB COUNTY	2	2	13	32	21	2	0	2	5
01 051	ELMORE COUNTY	1	1	13	31	31	2	0	2	3
01 053	ESCAMBIA COUNTY	2	2	21	13	13	4	0	5	3
01 055	ETOWAH COUNTY	2	2	13	13	31	1	0	2	3
01 057	FAYETTE COUNTY	2	2	13	31	32	1	0	2	5
01 059	FRANKLIN COUNTY	2	2	13	13	13	2	0	2	5
01 061	GENEVA COUNTY	1	1	13	13	13	2	0	5	5
01 063	GREENE COUNTY	1	1	22	32	31	1	0	2	5
01 065	HALE COUNTY	1	1	13	13	13	2	0	3	5
01 067	HENRY COUNTY	1	1	13	13	13	1	0	3	4
01 069	HOUSTON COUNTY	1	1	22	13	31	5	0	4	4
01 071	JACKSON COUNTY	2	2	23	32	13	1	0	2	3
01 073	JEFFERSON COUNTY	2	2	13	13	31	2	0	2	5
01 075	LAMAR COUNTY	2	2	13	33	31	2	0	2	5
01 077	LAUDERDALE COUNTY	2	2	13	13	13	2	0	2	5
01 079	LAWRENCE COUNTY	2	2	13	13	13	1	0	2	5
01 081	LEE COUNTY	2	2	21	21	31	2	0	3	5
01 083	LIMESTONE COUNTY	1	1	21	21	13	4	0	2	4
01 085	LOWNDES COUNTY	1	1	13	13	31	2	0	2	5
01 087	MACON COUNTY	1	1	21	21	33	3	0	2	5
01 089	MADISON COUNTY	2	2	13	13	13	2	0	2	5
01 091	MARENGO COUNTY	2	2	13	13	13	1	0	2	5
01 093	MARION COUNTY	2	2	21	32	32	1	0	2	5
01 095	MARSHALL COUNTY	2	2	13	13	13	3	0	2	2
01 097	MOBILE COUNTY	1	1	13	13	13	2	3	5	3
01 099	MONROE COUNTY	1	1	13	13	13	1	0	2	4
01 101	MONTGOMERY COUNTY	1	1	21	31	33	3	0	2	4

	County	EARTHQUAKE Aa	EARTHQUAKE Av	LANDSLIDE IE	LANDSLIDE SE	EXPANSIVE SOIL DE	FLOOD Ia	STORM SURGE S	HURRICANE Id	TORNADO Er
01 103	MORGAN COUNTY	1	2	22	22	32	3	0	2	5
01 105	PERRY COUNTY	1	2	22	22	32	2	0	3	5
01 107	PICKENS COUNTY	1	2	23	33	31	2	0	3	5
01 109	PIKE COUNTY	1	2	13	13	23	1	0	4	5
01 111	RANDOLPH COUNTY	2	2	13	31	31	2	0	3	5
01 113	RUSSELL COUNTY	1	1	13	23	31	1	0	3	5
01 115	ST. CLAIR COUNTY	2	2	13	23	33	2	0	4	5
01 117	SHELBY COUNTY	1	2	13	13	31	3	0	2	5
01 119	SUMTER COUNTY	2	2	13	13	22	3	0	3	5
01 121	TALLADEGA COUNTY	2	2	21	31	33	3	0	3	5
01 123	TALLAPOOSA COUNTY	1	1	13	33	23	3	0	3	5
01 125	TUSCALOOSA COUNTY	1	1	13	33	31	3	0	2	5
01 127	WALKER COUNTY	1	1	21	31	31	1	0	3	5
01 129	WASHINGTON COUNTY	1	1	13	13	31	3	0	4	3
01 131	WILCOX COUNTY	1	1	13	13	31	1	0	4	3
01 133	WINSTON COUNTY	2	2	13	33	23	1	0	2	5

ALASKA

		EARTHQUAKE		LANDSLIDE		EXPANSIVE SOIL	FLOOD	STORM SURGE	HURRICANE	TORNADO
		Aa	Av	IE	SE	DE	Ia	s	Id	Er
02 010	ALEUTIAN ISLANDS C.A.	7	7	00	00	00	1	=	0	0
02 020	ANCHORAGE BOROUGH	7	7	00	00	00	1	=	0	0
02 050	BETHEL C.A.	3	3	00	00	00	1	=	0	0
02 060	BRISTOL BAY BOROUGH	7	7	00	00	00	1	0	0	0
02 070	DILLINGHAM C.A.	7	0	00	00	00	1	=	0	0
02 090	FAIRBANKS NORTH STAR BOROUGH	7	7	00	00	00	1	=	0	0
02 100	HAINES BOROUGH	6	6	00	00	00	1	=	0	0
02 110	JUNEAU BOROUGH	7	7	00	00	00	1	=	0	0
02 122	KENAI PENINSULA BOROUGH	7	7	00	00	00	1	0	0	0
02 130	KETCHIKAN GATEWAY BOROUGH	7	7	00	00	00	1	=	0	0
02 140	KOBUK C.A.	1	1	00	00	00	1	=	0	0
02 150	KODIAK ISLAND BOROUGH	7	7	00	00	00	1	=	0	0
02 170	MATANUSKA-SUSITNA BOROUGH	7	7	00	00	00	1	0	0	0
02 180	NOME C.A.	1	1	00	00	00	1	=	0	0
02 185	NORTH SLOPE BOROUGH	1	1	00	00	00	1	=	0	0
02 201	PR OF WALES-OUTER KETCHIKAN	7	7	00	00	00	1	0	0	0
02 220	SITKA BOROUGH	7	7	00	00	00	1	=	0	0
02 231	SKAGWAY-YAKUTAT-ANGOON	7	7	00	00	00	1	=	0	0
02 240	SOUTHEAST FAIRBANKS	7	7	00	00	00	1	=	0	0
02 261	VALDEZ-CORDOVA C.S.	7	=	00	00	00	=	0	0	0
02 270	WADE HAMPTON C.S.	=	4	00	00	00	1	=	0	0
02 280	WRANGELL-PETERSBURG C.S.	7	7	00	00	00	1	=	0	0
02 290	YUKON-KOYUKUK C.S.	7	7	00	00	00	1	0	0	0

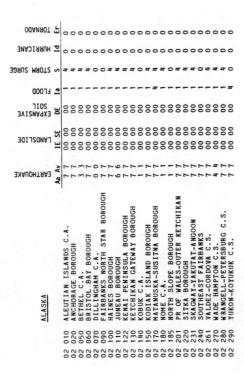

ARIZONA

		EARTHQUAKE		LANDSLIDE		EXPANSIVE SOIL	FLOOD	STORM SURGE	HURRICANE	TORNADO
		Aa	Av	IE	SE	DE	Ia	s	Id	Er
04 001	APACHE COUNTY	1	2	31	31	31	2	0	0	1
04 003	COCHISE COUNTY	3	3	31	31	31	2	0	0	1
04 005	COCONINO COUNTY	2	2	21	21	31	1	0	0	1
04 007	GILA COUNTY	1	2	13	13	32	2	0	0	1
04 009	GRAHAM COUNTY	3	3	13	13	13	2	0	0	1
04 011	GREENLEE COUNTY	3	3	13	13	32	5	0	0	1
04 013	MARICOPA COUNTY	=	4	31	31	13	3	0	0	1
04 015	MOHAVE COUNTY	2	2	31	31	31	1	0	0	1
04 017	NAVAJO COUNTY	2	2	13	13	13	=	0	0	1
04 019	PIMA COUNTY	1	1	31	31	31	4	0	0	1
04 021	PINAL COUNTY	1	2	13	13	13	2	0	0	1
04 023	SANTA CRUZ COUNTY	1	3	21	21	32	2	0	0	1
04 025	YAVAPAI COUNTY	1	5	13	13	13	1	0	0	1
04 027	YUMA COUNTY	5	5	13	13	13		0	0	1

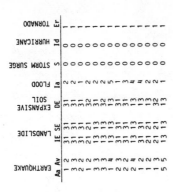

ARKANSAS

Code	County	EARTHQUAKE Aa	EARTHQUAKE Av	LANDSLIDE IE	LANDSLIDE SE	EXPANSIVE SOIL DE	FLOOD Ia	STORM SURGE s	HURRICANE Id	TORNADO Er
05 103	OUACHITA COUNTY	1	2	13	13	31	3	0	1	=
05 105	PERRY COUNTY	2	5	13	23	13	—	0	2	=
05 107	PHILLIPS COUNTY	3	5	13	22	13	2	0	2	=
05 109	PIKE COUNTY	2	5	13	13	32	3	0	1	5
05 111	POINSETT COUNTY	5	5	13	13	13	—	0	2	=
05 113	POLK COUNTY	3	#	13	23	31	—	0	1	=
05 115	POPE COUNTY	2	2	13	13	31	3	0	1	5
05 117	PRAIRIE COUNTY	#	5	13	31	32	5	0	1	=
05 119	PULASKI COUNTY	5	5	13	13	31	3	0	1	=
05 121	RANDOLPH COUNTY	5	5	13	21	13	2	0	2	=
05 123	ST. FRANCIS COUNTY	2	5	31	31	13	2	0	1	5
05 125	SALINE COUNTY	2	2	13	31	31	2	0	1	=
05 127	SCOTT COUNTY	2	2	21	31	31	6	0	1	=
05 129	SEARCY COUNTY	2	#	13	31	31	—	0	2	5
05 131	SEBASTIAN COUNTY	#	#	13	13	31	—	0	2	5
05 133	SEVIER COUNTY	3	#	13	13	31	1	0	1	=
05 135	SHARP COUNTY	3	2	13	31	13	1	0	1	=
05 137	STONE COUNTY	1	2	13	13	13	3	0	2	5
05 139	UNION COUNTY	2	#	13	13	31	2	0	1	5
05 141	VAN BUREN COUNTY	2	2	13	23	13	3	0	1	5
05 143	WASHINGTON COUNTY	#	5	13	22	31	3	0	2	5
05 145	WHITE COUNTY	5	5	13	13	31	2	0	1	=
05 147	WOODRUFF COUNTY	1	2	13	23	32	3	0	1	5
05 149	YELL COUNTY	—	—	13	—	13	2	0	1	5

Code	County	EARTHQUAKE Aa	EARTHQUAKE Av	LANDSLIDE IE	LANDSLIDE SE	EXPANSIVE SOIL DE	FLOOD Ia	STORM SURGE s	HURRICANE Id	TORNADO Er
05 001	ARKANSAS COUNTY	3	3	13	13	33	2	0	2	=
05 003	ASHLEY COUNTY	3	2	13	13	32	2	0	2	=
05 005	BAXTER COUNTY	1	2	13	13	13	—	0	1	=
05 007	BENTON COUNTY	2	2	13	21	13	2	0	1	=
05 009	BOONE COUNTY	2	2	13	13	13	2	0	2	=
05 011	BRADLEY COUNTY	2	2	13	13	13	—	0	2	=
05 013	CALHOUN COUNTY	1	1	13	13	31	2	0	1	=
05 015	CARROLL COUNTY	1	2	13	22	32	2	0	1	=
05 017	CHICOT COUNTY	2	2	13	21	32	—	0	2	=
05 019	CLARK COUNTY	2	2	13	13	13	2	0	1	5
05 021	CLAY COUNTY	5	5	13	13	13	—	0	1	=
05 023	CLEBURNE COUNTY	3	1	13	23	13	2	0	2	=
05 025	CLEVELAND COUNTY	2	2	13	13	32	#	0	1	5
05 027	COLUMBIA COUNTY	2	2	13	13	13	2	0	1	=
05 029	CONWAY COUNTY	2	2	13	23	31	2	0	2	=
05 031	CRAIGHEAD COUNTY	5	5	13	22	32	2	0	1	5
05 033	CRAWFORD COUNTY	2	2	13	13	31	2	0	2	=
05 035	CRITTENDEN COUNTY	5	5	13	13	13	—	0	2	5
05 037	CROSS COUNTY	5	5	13	23	32	3	0	1	5
05 039	DALLAS COUNTY	2	2	13	13	33	2	0	1	=
05 041	DESHA COUNTY	2	2	13	13	32	#	0	2	5
05 043	DREW COUNTY	2	2	13	13	13	3	0	2	=
05 045	FAULKNER COUNTY	3	1	13	23	13	2	0	2	=
05 047	FRANKLIN COUNTY	2	2	13	22	31	2	0	1	5
05 049	FULTON COUNTY	3	#	13	13	13	—	0	1	=
05 051	GARLAND COUNTY	2	2	13	13	13	2	0	2	5
05 053	GRANT COUNTY	2	2	13	13	31	2	0	1	5
05 055	GREENE COUNTY	5	5	13	13	32	2	0	1	=
05 057	HEMPSTEAD COUNTY	2	2	13	13	13	2	0	1	=
05 059	HOT SPRING COUNTY	2	2	13	13	13	#	0	1	5
05 061	HOWARD COUNTY	2	2	13	13	31	3	0	1	5
05 063	INDEPENDENCE COUNTY	#	#	13	31	31	3	0	2	=
05 065	IZARD COUNTY	3	#	13	13	31	2	0	1	=
05 067	JACKSON COUNTY	5	5	13	13	32	2	0	2	=
05 069	JEFFERSON COUNTY	2	2	13	13	32	2	0	1	5
05 071	JOHNSON COUNTY	2	2	13	13	32	2	0	1	=
05 073	LAFAYETTE COUNTY	2	2	13	13	33	3	0	2	=
05 075	LAWRENCE COUNTY	5	5	13	21	32	2	0	1	5
05 077	LEE COUNTY	5	5	13	13	32	2	0	2	5
05 079	LINCOLN COUNTY	2	2	13	13	32	3	0	1	=
05 081	LITTLE RIVER COUNTY	2	2	13	13	13	2	0	2	5
05 083	LOGAN COUNTY	2	3	21	31	31	2	0	1	5
05 085	LONOKE COUNTY	2	2	13	13	32	—	0	1	=
05 087	MADISON COUNTY	1	2	13	23	13	2	0	2	5
05 089	MARION COUNTY	1	2	13	13	13	2	0	2	=
05 091	MILLER COUNTY	5	#	13	13	32	2	0	2	=
05 093	MISSISSIPPI COUNTY	5	5	13	22	31	3	0	2	5
05 095	MONROE COUNTY	2	2	13	13	32	3	0	2	=
05 097	MONTGOMERY COUNTY	2	2	13	21	31	1	0	1	=
05 099	NEVADA COUNTY	2	2	13	13	32	—	0	2	=
05 101	NEWTON COUNTY	2	2	13	13	13	2	0	1	=

CALIFORNIA

	EARTHQUAKE		LANDSLIDE		EXPANSIVE SOIL	FLOOD	STORM SURGE	HURRICANE	TORNADO
	Aa	Av	IE	SE	DE	la	s	Id	Er
06 001 ALAMEDA COUNTY	7	5	31	31	13	3	4	0	1
06 003 ALPINE COUNTY	5	5	13	13	21	1	0	0	1
06 005 AMADOR COUNTY	4	4	31	31	31	1	0	0	1
06 007 BUTTE COUNTY	4	4	31	31	22	2	0	0	1
06 009 CALAVERAS COUNTY	4	4	21	21	33	3	0	0	1
06 011 COLUSA COUNTY	7	3	32	32	31	3	4	0	1
06 013 CONTRA COSTA COUNTY	7	5	13	13	22	2	4	0	1
06 015 DEL NORTE COUNTY	4	4	21	21	31	3	0	0	1
06 017 EL DORADO COUNTY	7	5	21	21	33	5	0	0	1
06 019 FRESNO COUNTY	7	5	32	32	31	1	0	0	1
06 021 GLENN COUNTY	5	6	13	13	31	2	0	0	1
06 023 HUMBOLDT COUNTY	7	7	31	31	31	1	4	0	1
06 025 IMPERIAL COUNTY	7	7	31	31	31	5	0	0	1
06 027 INYO COUNTY	7	7	31	31	32	3	0	0	1
06 029 KERN COUNTY	6	5	32	32	31	3	0	0	1
06 031 KINGS COUNTY	5	7	13	13	23	1	4	0	1
06 033 LAKE COUNTY	7	6	31	31	22	2	0	0	1
06 035 LASSEN COUNTY	5	7	31	31	23	3	4	0	1
06 037 LOS ANGELES COUNTY	7	7	31	31	31	3	4	0	1
06 039 MADERA COUNTY	7	7	32	32	31	3	0	0	1
06 041 MARIN COUNTY	7	7	31	31	13	2	0	0	1
06 043 MARIPOSA COUNTY	3	3	13	13	21	3	0	0	1
06 045 MENDOCINO COUNTY	7	7	31	31	31	1	0	0	1
06 047 MERCED COUNTY	7	7	31	31	31	2	4	0	1
06 049 MODOC COUNTY	5	5	23	23	32	3	0	0	1
06 051 MONO COUNTY	5	5	21	21	32	2	0	0	1
06 053 MONTEREY COUNTY	7	7	13	13	22	2	4	0	1
06 055 NAPA COUNTY	7	6	31	31	31	5	0	0	1
06 057 NEVADA COUNTY	7	7	31	31	23	2	0	0	1
06 059 ORANGE COUNTY	7	7	31	31	31	2	4	0	1
06 061 PLACER COUNTY	6	6	31	31	31	3	0	0	1
06 063 PLUMAS COUNTY	7	7	32	32	31	3	0	0	1
06 065 RIVERSIDE COUNTY	7	7	13	13	31	3	4	0	1
06 067 SACRAMENTO COUNTY	7	7	31	31	23	4	0	0	1
06 069 SAN BENITO COUNTY	7	7	31	31	31	4	0	0	1
06 071 SAN BERNARDINO COUNTY	7	7	31	31	32	2	4	0	1
06 073 SAN DIEGO COUNTY	7	7	31	31	31	3	0	0	1
06 075 SAN FRANCISCO COUNTY	6	6	32	32	31	3	4	0	1
06 077 SAN JOAQUIN COUNTY	7	7	32	32	31	3	0	0	1
06 079 SAN LUIS OBISPO COUNTY	7	7	31	31	31	3	4	0	1
06 081 SAN MATEO COUNTY	7	7	32	32	23	3	0	0	1
06 083 SANTA BARBARA COUNTY	7	7	32	32	31	2	4	0	1
06 085 SANTA CLARA COUNTY	7	7	22	22	31	2	0	0	1
06 087 SANTA CRUZ COUNTY	5	5	21	21	23	3	4	0	1
06 089 SHASTA COUNTY	5	5	13	13	31	2	0	0	1
06 091 SIERRA COUNTY	4	4	23	23	33	2	0	0	1
06 093 SISKIYOU COUNTY	3	3	33	33	33	3	4	0	1
06 095 SOLANO COUNTY	7	7	32	32	32	4	0	0	1
06 097 SONOMA COUNTY	7	7	31	31	31	3	4	0	1
06 099 STANISLAUS COUNTY	7	7	31	31	31	2	0	0	1
06 101 SUTTER COUNTY	3	5	13	13	32	3	0	0	1

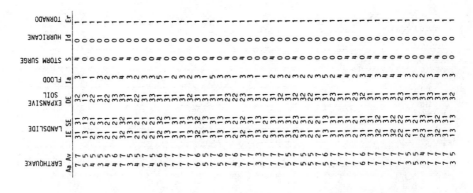

	EARTHQUAKE		LANDSLIDE		EXPANSIVE SOIL	FLOOD	STORM SURGE	HURRICANE	TORNADO
	Aa	Av	IE	SE	DE	la	s	Id	Er
06 103 TEHAMA COUNTY	4	5	21	31	32	3	0	0	1
06 105 TRINITY COUNTY	5	6	31	32	31	2	0	0	1
06 107 TULARE COUNTY	5	7	31	31	31	1	4	0	1
06 109 TUOLUMNE COUNTY	4	7	21	21	22	4	0	0	1
06 111 VENTURA COUNTY	7	7	31	31	11	1	0	0	1
06 113 YOLO COUNTY	5	6	21	21	31	3	0	0	1
06 115 YUBA COUNTY	3	5	13	13	22	3	0	0	1

491

COLORADO

FIPS	County	EARTHQUAKE Aa	Av	LANDSLIDE IE	SE	EXPANSIVE SOIL DE	FLOOD Ia	STORM SURGE S	HURRICANE Id	TORNADO Er
08 001	ADAMS COUNTY	2	2	13	31	33	3	0	0	1
08 003	ALAMOSA COUNTY	2	3	21	31	22	1	0	0	1
08 005	ARAPAHOE COUNTY	3	3	32	32	31	2	0	0	2
08 007	ARCHULETA COUNTY	1	2	13	31	32	2	0	0	1
08 009	BACA COUNTY	2	2	13	31	21	1	0	0	1
08 011	BENT COUNTY	2	1	22	21	21	1	0	0	1
08 013	BOULDER COUNTY	2	2	31	31	31	4	0	0	2
08 015	CHAFFEE COUNTY	2	2	32	31	32	2	0	0	1
08 017	CHEYENNE COUNTY	2	1	23	21	13	1	0	0	1
08 019	CLEAR CREEK COUNTY	2	3	31	31	21	3	0	0	1
08 021	CONEJOS COUNTY	3	3	23	31	21	1	0	0	1
08 023	COSTILLA COUNTY	3	2	21	21	31	2	0	0	1
08 025	CROWLEY COUNTY	1	1	13	31	21	4	0	0	1
08 027	CUSTER COUNTY	2	2	31	32	31	2	0	0	1
08 029	DELTA COUNTY	2	2	13	13	33	2	0	0	1
08 031	DENVER COUNTY	2	2	31	31	32	3	0	0	2
08 033	DOLORES COUNTY	2	2	13	32	31	2	0	0	1
08 035	DOUGLAS COUNTY	2	2	31	31	31	1	0	0	1
08 037	EAGLE COUNTY	2	2	31	31	31	3	0	0	1
08 039	ELBERT COUNTY	2	2	31	31	31	1	0	0	1
08 041	EL PASO COUNTY	2	2	22	31	13	2	0	0	1
08 043	FREMONT COUNTY	2	2	31	31	31	3	0	0	1
08 045	GARFIELD COUNTY	2	2	21	31	31	3	0	0	1
08 047	GILPIN COUNTY	3	3	31	31	13	1	0	0	1
08 049	GRAND COUNTY	2	2	31	31	31	3	0	0	2
08 051	GUNNISON COUNTY	2	2	23	31	31	1	0	0	2
08 053	HINSDALE COUNTY	3	3	31	31	32	3	0	0	1
08 055	HUERFANO COUNTY	2	2	23	32	31	1	0	0	1
08 057	JACKSON COUNTY	2	2	21	31	32	2	0	0	2
08 059	JEFFERSON COUNTY	2	2	31	31	31	3	0	0	1
08 061	KIOWA COUNTY	1	1	13	13	13	1	0	0	1
08 063	KIT CARSON COUNTY	2	1	32	31	31	1	0	0	2
08 065	LAKE COUNTY	3	3	23	32	32	3	0	0	1
08 067	LA PLATA COUNTY	2	2	31	31	31	2	0	0	1
08 069	LARIMER COUNTY	2	2	31	31	31	3	0	0	2
08 071	LAS ANIMAS COUNTY	2	2	13	31	32	1	0	0	1
08 073	LINCOLN COUNTY	1	1	13	13	13	1	0	0	1
08 075	LOGAN COUNTY	1	2	32	31	32	3	0	0	2
08 077	MESA COUNTY	3	3	32	32	32	3	0	0	1
08 079	MINERAL COUNTY	2	2	31	32	32	2	0	0	1
08 081	MOFFAT COUNTY	2	2	23	31	32	1	0	0	1
08 083	MONTEZUMA COUNTY	2	2	13	13	13	1	0	0	2
08 085	MONTROSE COUNTY	1	1	32	32	32	3	0	0	1
08 087	MORGAN COUNTY	2	2	31	31	31	2	0	0	1
08 089	OTERO COUNTY	1	1	13	13	13	1	0	0	1
08 091	OURAY COUNTY	2	2	32	32	22	1	0	0	2
08 093	PARK COUNTY	2	2	13	13	13	1	0	0	1
08 095	PHILLIPS COUNTY	1	1	31	31	22	1	0	0	1
08 097	PITKIN COUNTY	2	2	31	31	31	3	0	0	2
08 099	PROWERS COUNTY	2	1	31	31	31	2	0	0	1
08 101	PUEBLO COUNTY	1	2	31	31	32	3	0	0	2

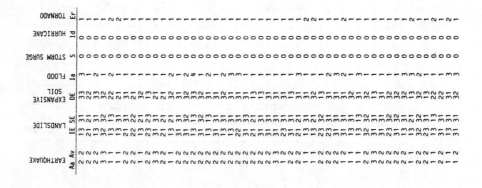

COLORADO (continued)

FIPS	County	EARTHQUAKE Aa	Av	LANDSLIDE IE	SE	EXPANSIVE SOIL DE	FLOOD Ia	STORM SURGE S	HURRICANE Id	TORNADO Er
08 103	RIO BLANCO COUNTY	2	3	32	33	31	2	0	0	1
08 105	RIO GRANDE COUNTY	3	3	31	31	21	1	0	0	1
08 107	ROUTT COUNTY	2	3	32	33	31	2	0	0	1
08 109	SAGUACHE COUNTY	3	3	23	23	31	1	0	0	1
08 111	SAN JUAN COUNTY	2	2	23	31	13	2	0	0	2
08 113	SAN MIGUEL COUNTY	2	1	13	31	32	2	0	0	1
08 115	SEDGWICK COUNTY	1	2	23	13	22	2	0	0	1
08 117	SUMMIT COUNTY	2	2	13	31	13	1	0	0	2
08 119	TELLER COUNTY	1	1	13	32	13	1	0	0	1
08 121	WASHINGTON COUNTY	1	2	13	31	32	4	0	0	2
08 123	WELD COUNTY	2	1	13	31	31	1	0	0	2
08 125	YUMA COUNTY	1	1	13	21	21	1	0	0	2

CONNECTICUT

FIPS	County	EARTHQUAKE Aa	Av	LANDSLIDE IE	SE	EXPANSIVE SOIL DE	FLOOD Ia	STORM SURGE S	HURRICANE Id	TORNADO Er
09 001	FAIRFIELD COUNTY	3	3	21	31	13	3	2	11	2
09 003	HARTFORD COUNTY	3	3	22	32	21	3	0	11	2
09 005	LITCHFIELD COUNTY	3	3	13	13	21	2	0	11	2
09 007	MIDDLESEX COUNTY	3	3	13	13	13	4	2	31	2
09 009	NEW HAVEN COUNTY	3	3	21	21	13	4	2	31	2
09 011	NEW LONDON COUNTY	3	3	13	13	13	2	2	51	2
09 013	TOLLAND COUNTY	3	3	13	13	13	2	0	11	2
09 015	WINDHAM COUNTY	3	3	13	13	13	2	0	11	2

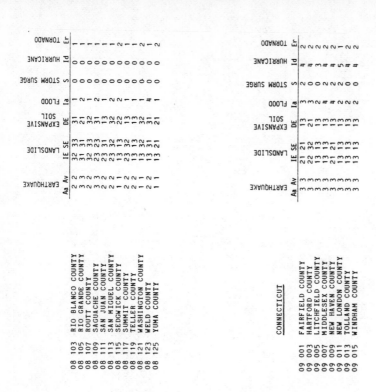

	EARTHQUAKE		LANDSLIDE		EXPANSIVE SOIL	FLOOD	STORM SURGE	HURRICANE		TORNADO
	Aa	Av	IE	SE	DE	Ia	S	Id	Pl	Er
12 001 ALACHUA COUNTY	1	1	13	13	21	1	0		4	2
12 003 BAKER COUNTY	1	1	13	13	13	1	0		4	2
12 005 BAY COUNTY	1	1	13	13	13	2	3		6	1
12 007 BRADFORD COUNTY	1	1	13	13	13	1	0		4	1
12 009 BREVARD COUNTY	1	1	13	13	13	3	2		4	1
12 011 BROWARD COUNTY	1	1	13	13	13	2	2		5	2
12 013 CALHOUN COUNTY	1	1	13	13	21	2	0		6	2
12 015 CHARLOTTE COUNTY	1	1	13	13	13	1	2		5	1
12 017 CITRUS COUNTY	1	1	13	13	13	2	3		4	1
12 019 CLAY COUNTY	1	1	13	13	13	1	0		4	1
12 021 COLLIER COUNTY	1	1	13	13	13	2	2		5	2
12 023 COLUMBIA COUNTY	1	1	13	13	13	2	0		4	1
12 025 DADE COUNTY	1	1	13	13	13	3	3		5	2
12 027 DE SOTO COUNTY	1	1	13	13	13	1	0		5	1
12 029 DIXIE COUNTY	1	1	13	13	13	1	2		4	1
12 031 DUVAL COUNTY	1	1	13	13	13	3	2		4	2
12 033 ESCAMBIA COUNTY	1	1	13	13	21	1	3		6	1
12 035 FLAGLER COUNTY	1	1	13	13	13	1	2		4	2
12 037 FRANKLIN COUNTY	1	1	13	13	13	1	3		5	1
12 039 GADSDEN COUNTY	1	1	13	13	13	3	0		5	2
12 041 GILCHRIST COUNTY	1	1	21	31	13	1	0		4	1
12 043 GLADES COUNTY	1	1	13	13	13	1	0		5	2
12 045 GULF COUNTY	1	1	13	13	13	2	3		5	1
12 047 HAMILTON COUNTY	1	1	13	13	13	2	0		4	2
12 049 HARDEE COUNTY	1	1	13	13	13	1	0		5	2
12 051 HENDRY COUNTY	1	1	13	13	13	2	0		5	2
12 053 HERNANDO COUNTY	1	1	13	13	13	2	2		4	2
12 055 HIGHLANDS COUNTY	1	1	13	13	13	1	0		5	3
12 057 HILLSBOROUGH COUNTY	1	1	13	13	13	3	3		5	1
12 059 HOLMES COUNTY	1	1	13	13	21	1	0		6	3
12 061 INDIAN RIVER COUNTY	1	1	13	13	13	2	2		4	2
12 063 JACKSON COUNTY	1	1	13	13	13	2	0		5	2
12 065 JEFFERSON COUNTY	1	1	13	31	13	1	2		5	2
12 067 LAFAYETTE COUNTY	1	1	13	13	13	1	0		4	1
12 069 LAKE COUNTY	1	1	13	13	13	2	0		4	2
12 071 LEE COUNTY	1	1	13	13	13	1	2		5	2
12 073 LEON COUNTY	1	1	13	13	13	2	0		5	1
12 075 LEVY COUNTY	1	1	31	31	13	2	2		4	1
12 077 LIBERTY COUNTY	1	1	13	13	21	1	0		5	2
12 079 MADISON COUNTY	1	1	13	13	13	1	0		4	2
12 081 MANATEE COUNTY	1	1	13	13	13	2	3		5	2
12 083 MARION COUNTY	1	1	13	13	13	2	0		4	1
12 085 MARTIN COUNTY	1	1	13	13	13	1	2		5	1
12 087 MONROE COUNTY	1	1	13	13	13	3	3		5	1
12 089 NASSAU COUNTY	1	1	13	13	13	2	2		3	2
12 091 OKALOOSA COUNTY	1	1	13	13	13	1	3		6	2
12 093 OKEECHOBEE COUNTY	1	1	13	13	13	1	0		5	2
12 095 ORANGE COUNTY	1	1	13	13	13	3	0		4	1
12 097 OSCEOLA COUNTY	1	1	13	13	13	2	0		5	1
12 099 PALM BEACH COUNTY	1	1	13	13	13	3	3		5	2
12 101 PASCO COUNTY	1	1	13	13	21	2	3		5	2

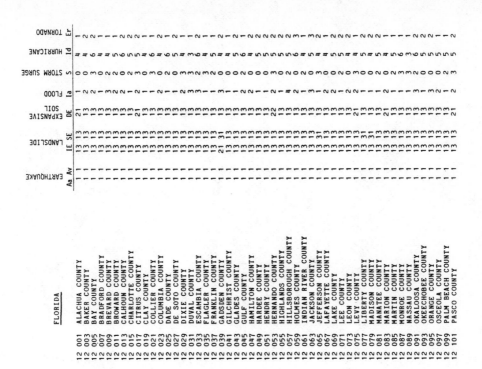

DELAWARE

	EARTHQUAKE		LANDSLIDE		EXPANSIVE SOIL	FLOOD	STORM SURGE	HURRICANE		TORNADO
	Aa	Av	IE	SE	DE	Ia	S	Id	Pl	Er
10 001 KENT COUNTY	2	2	13	13	13	2	2		4	2
10 003 NEW CASTLE COUNTY	2	2	13	23	31	2	2		4	2
10 005 SUSSEX COUNTY	1	2	13	13	13	2	3		4	2

DISTRICT OF COLUMBIA

	EARTHQUAKE		LANDSLIDE		EXPANSIVE SOIL	FLOOD	STORM SURGE	HURRICANE		TORNADO
	Aa	Av	IE	SE	DE	Ia	S	Id	Pl	Er
11 001 DISTRICT OF COLUMBIA	1	2	32	32	13	1	0		3	1

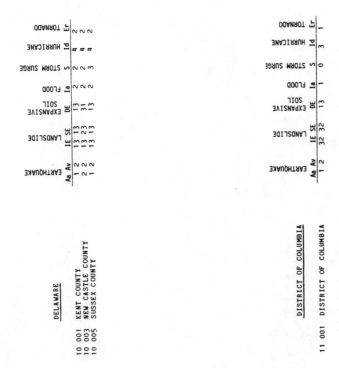

GEORGIA

	Aa	Av	IE	SE	DE	Ia	S	Id	Er
			EARTHQUAKE		LANDSLIDE	EXPANSIVE SOIL	FLOOD	STORM SURGE	HURRICANE	TORNADO

		EARTHQUAKE		LANDSLIDE		EXPANSIVE SOIL	FLOOD	STORM SURGE	HURRICANE	TORNADO
	Aa	Av	IE	SE	DE	Ia	S	Id	Er
13 001 APPLING COUNTY	2	1	13	13	21	1	0	3	2
13 003 ATKINSON COUNTY	1	1	13	13	13	1	0	3	3
13 005 BACON COUNTY	1	1	13	13	13	1	0	4	2
13 007 BAKER COUNTY	2	1	13	13	22	2	0	3	2
13 009 BALDWIN COUNTY	3	3	13	13	31	1	0	2	2
13 011 BANKS COUNTY	3	3	21	13	23	1	0	2	2
13 013 BARROW COUNTY	3	3	22	33	21	1	0	2	3
13 015 BARTOW COUNTY	3	3	13	13	21	1	0	2	3
13 017 BEN HILL COUNTY	1	1	13	13	13	1	0	3	3
13 019 BERRIEN COUNTY	2	2	13	13	31	1	0	3	2
13 021 BIBB COUNTY	2	2	13	13	13	2	0	2	1
13 023 BLECKLEY COUNTY	2	1	13	13	22	1	0	2	1
13 025 BRANTLEY COUNTY	1	1	13	13	13	1	3	3	3
13 027 BROOKS COUNTY	3	3	13	13	21	2	0	3	1
13 029 BRYAN COUNTY	2	1	13	13	21	1	0	4	1
13 031 BULLOCH COUNTY	1	1	13	13	23	2	0	3	3
13 033 BURKE COUNTY	3	3	13	13	22	1	0	2	1
13 035 BUTTS COUNTY	3	3	21	21	21	1	0	2	1
13 037 CALHOUN COUNTY	2	2	13	13	21	1	0	3	3
13 039 CAMDEN COUNTY	1	1	13	13	32	1	3	4	2
13 041 CANDLER COUNTY	1	1	13	13	22	1	0	3	1
13 043 CARROLL COUNTY	3	3	13	13	23	1	0	2	3
13 045 CATOOSA COUNTY	3	3	32	33	13	2	0	2	3
13 047 CATOOSA COUNTY	3	3	23	23	23	2	3	2	3
13 049 CHARLTON COUNTY	1	1	13	13	21	1	0	3	1
13 051 CHATHAM COUNTY	1	1	13	13	21	2	3	4	1
13 053 CHATTAHOOCHEE COUNTY	3	3	13	13	32	1	0	2	1
13 055 CHATTOOGA COUNTY	3	3	13	13	22	2	0	2	3
13 057 CHEROKEE COUNTY	3	3	13	13	23	1	0	2	3
13 059 CLARKE COUNTY	3	3	13	13	21	2	0	3	3
13 061 CLAY COUNTY	1	1	13	13	21	1	0	3	3
13 063 CLAYTON COUNTY	2	2	13	13	22	1	0	2	1
13 065 CLINCH COUNTY	1	1	13	13	23	1	0	3	1
13 067 COBB COUNTY	3	3	13	13	31	2	0	2	3
13 069 COFFEE COUNTY	1	1	13	13	21	1	0	3	1
13 071 COLQUITT COUNTY	3	2	13	13	22	1	0	3	2
13 073 COLUMBIA COUNTY	3	3	13	13	23	2	0	2	2
13 075 COOK COUNTY	2	2	13	13	31	1	0	3	2
13 077 COWETA COUNTY	2	1	13	13	21	2	0	2	2
13 079 CRAWFORD COUNTY	3	3	23	22	22	2	0	2	3
13 081 CRISP COUNTY	3	3	13	13	31	2	0	2	3
13 083 DADE COUNTY	2	2	21	31	21	1	0	2	3
13 085 DAWSON COUNTY	3	3	21	31	32	1	0	2	3
13 087 DECATUR COUNTY	2	2	13	13	32	1	0	3	3
13 089 DE KALB COUNTY	3	3	13	13	31	2	0	2	3
13 091 DODGE COUNTY	1	1	13	13	23	1	0	3	3
13 093 DOOLY COUNTY	2	2	22	32	21	2	0	2	3
13 095 DOUGHERTY COUNTY	2	2	13	13	32	2	0	3	3
13 097 DOUGLAS COUNTY	1	1	21	31	21	1	0	2	2
13 099 EARLY COUNTY	1	1	13	13	13	2	0	3	2
13 101 ECHOLS COUNTY	1	1	13	13	13	1	0	4	1
13 103 EFFINGHAM COUNTY	3	3	13	13	21	1	0	4	1

		EARTHQUAKE		LANDSLIDE		EXPANSIVE SOIL	FLOOD	STORM SURGE	HURRICANE	TORNADO
	Aa	Av	IE	SE	DE	Ia	S	Id	Er
12 103 PINELLAS COUNTY	1	1	13	13	13	2	2	5	1
12 105 POLK COUNTY	1	1	13	13	13	2	0	5	1
12 107 PUTNAM COUNTY	1	1	13	13	13	1	0	3	1
12 109 ST. JOHNS COUNTY	1	1	13	13	13	1	2	6	2
12 111 ST. LUCIE COUNTY	1	1	13	13	13	3	2	5	2
12 113 SANTA ROSA COUNTY	1	1	13	13	13	1	3	4	2
12 115 SARASOTA COUNTY	1	1	13	13	13	1	0	4	2
12 117 SEMINOLE COUNTY	1	1	13	13	13	2	0	4	2
12 119 SUMTER COUNTY	1	1	13	13	21	2	0	4	1
12 121 SUWANNEE COUNTY	1	1	13	13	13	1	3	4	1
12 123 TAYLOR COUNTY	1	1	13	13	13	2	2	5	2
12 125 UNION COUNTY	1	1	13	13	13	3	0	6	2
12 127 VOLUSIA COUNTY	1	1	13	13	13	3	3	6	2
12 129 WAKULLA COUNTY	1	1	13	13	13	2	2	6	2
12 131 WALTON COUNTY	1	1	13	13	13	3	3	6	2
12 133 WASHINGTON COUNTY	1	1	13	13	13	3	0	6	2

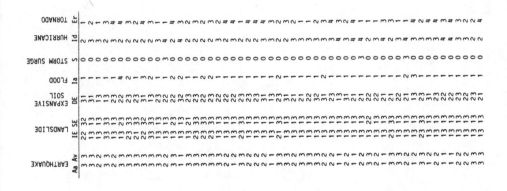

			EARTHQUAKE		LANDSLIDE		EXPANSIVE SOIL	FLOOD	STORM SURGE	HURRICANE	TORNADO
			Aa	Av	IE	SE	DE	Ia	S	Id	Er
13	105	ELBERT COUNTY	3	3	22	32	31	1	0	2	1
13	107	EMANUEL COUNTY	3	3	13	13	31	1	0	3	2
13	109	EVANS COUNTY	2	2	13	13	13	1	0	3	1
13	111	FANNIN COUNTY	3	3	33	33	13	1	0	2	3
13	113	FAYETTE COUNTY	2	2	13	13	23	1	0	3	4
13	115	FLOYD COUNTY	3	3	13	23	22	4	0	2	4
13	117	FORSYTH COUNTY	3	3	23	33	23	2	0	2	3
13	119	FRANKLIN COUNTY	3	3	21	33	23	1	0	2	2
13	121	FULTON COUNTY	3	3	22	32	31	3	0	2	4
13	123	GILMER COUNTY	3	3	33	33	13	2	0	2	3
13	125	GLASCOCK COUNTY	3	3	13	13	23	1	0	3	1
13	127	GLYNN COUNTY	2	2	13	13	22	1	3	4	1
13	129	GORDON COUNTY	3	3	13	23	22	2	0	2	4
13	131	GRADY COUNTY	1	1	13	13	32	2	0	4	3
13	133	GREENE COUNTY	3	3	13	21	23	1	0	2	2
13	135	GWINNETT COUNTY	3	3	23	33	23	1	0	2	3
13	137	HABERSHAM COUNTY	3	3	23	33	22	2	0	2	2
13	139	HALL COUNTY	3	3	23	33	23	2	0	2	3
13	141	HANCOCK COUNTY	3	3	13	13	22	1	0	3	2
13	143	HARALSON COUNTY	2	2	13	13	22	1	0	2	4
13	145	HARRIS COUNTY	1	2	13	13	22	1	0	3	4
13	147	HART COUNTY	3	3	23	33	23	1	0	2	1
13	149	HEARD COUNTY	2	2	13	13	23	1	0	2	4
13	151	HENRY COUNTY	2	2	13	13	23	1	0	2	4
13	153	HOUSTON COUNTY	2	2	13	13	31	1	0	3	4
13	155	IRWIN COUNTY	1	1	13	13	13	1	0	3	3
13	157	JACKSON COUNTY	3	3	21	33	23	2	0	2	2
13	159	JASPER COUNTY	3	3	13	13	31	1	0	2	3
13	161	JEFF DAVIS COUNTY	2	2	13	13	21	1	0	3	2
13	163	JEFFERSON COUNTY	3	3	13	13	21	1	0	3	1
13	165	JENKINS COUNTY	3	3	13	13	22	1	0	3	1
13	167	JOHNSON COUNTY	3	3	13	13	32	1	0	3	2
13	169	JONES COUNTY	2	2	13	13	31	2	0	3	3
13	171	LAMAR COUNTY	2	2	13	13	23	1	0	3	4
13	173	LANIER COUNTY	1	1	13	13	13	1	0	4	3
13	175	LAURENS COUNTY	2	2	13	13	31	1	0	3	2
13	177	LEE COUNTY	1	1	13	13	21	1	0	4	4
13	179	LIBERTY COUNTY	2	2	13	13	21	1	3	4	1
13	181	LINCOLN COUNTY	3	3	13	22	22	1	0	2	1
13	183	LONG COUNTY	2	2	13	13	22	1	0	3	1
13	185	LOWNDES COUNTY	1	1	13	13	21	1	0	4	3
13	187	LUMPKIN COUNTY	3	3	23	33	21	1	0	2	3
13	189	MCDUFFIE COUNTY	3	3	13	13	22	1	0	3	1
13	191	MCINTOSH COUNTY	2	2	13	13	21	2	3	4	1
13	193	MACON COUNTY	1	2	13	13	13	3	0	3	4
13	195	MADISON COUNTY	3	3	23	33	23	1	0	3	2
13	197	MARION COUNTY	1	2	13	13	31	1	0	3	4
13	199	MERIWETHER COUNTY	2	2	13	13	23	1	0	3	4
13	201	MILLER COUNTY	1	1	13	13	22	1	0	4	3
13	205	MITCHELL COUNTY	1	1	13	13	22	1	0	4	4
13	207	MONROE COUNTY	2	2	13	13	23	1	0	3	3
13	209	MONTGOMERY COUNTY	2	2	13	13	22	1	0	3	2
13	211	MORGAN COUNTY	3	3	13	13	23	1	0	2	2
13	213	MURRAY COUNTY	3	3	13	13	21	1	0	2	4

			EARTHQUAKE		LANDSLIDE		EXPANSIVE SOIL	FLOOD	STORM SURGE	HURRICANE	TORNADO
			Aa	Av	IE	SE	DE	Ia	S	Id	Er
13	215	MUSCOGEE COUNTY	1	2	13	13	13	1	0	3	4
13	217	NEWTON COUNTY	3	3	13	13	23	1	0	2	3
13	219	OCONEE COUNTY	3	3	23	33	23	1	0	2	2
13	221	OGLETHORPE COUNTY	3	3	22	32	23	1	0	3	2
13	223	PAULDING COUNTY	2	2	23	33	22	1	0	2	4
13	225	PEACH COUNTY	2	2	13	13	31	1	0	3	4
13	227	PICKENS COUNTY	3	3	33	33	13	1	0	2	3
13	229	PIERCE COUNTY	1	2	13	13	13	1	0	3	2
13	231	PIKE COUNTY	2	2	13	13	22	1	0	3	4
13	233	POLK COUNTY	2	2	13	23	22	3	0	3	4
13	235	PULASKI COUNTY	2	2	13	13	31	1	0	3	3
13	237	PUTNAM COUNTY	3	3	13	13	31	1	0	2	2
13	239	QUITMAN COUNTY	1	1	13	13	32	1	0	4	4
13	241	RABUN COUNTY	3	3	23	33	13	3	0	2	2
13	243	RANDOLPH COUNTY	1	1	13	13	21	1	0	4	4
13	245	RICHMOND COUNTY	3	3	13	13	21	2	0	3	1
13	247	ROCKDALE COUNTY	3	3	21	31	23	1	0	2	3
13	249	SCHLEY COUNTY	1	2	13	13	13	1	0	3	4
13	251	SCREVEN COUNTY	3	3	13	13	21	1	0	3	1
13	253	SEMINOLE COUNTY	1	1	13	13	21	1	0	4	3
13	255	SPALDING COUNTY	2	2	13	13	23	1	0	2	4
13	257	STEPHENS COUNTY	3	3	21	33	23	1	0	2	2
13	259	STEWART COUNTY	1	1	13	13	32	1	0	4	4
13	261	SUMTER COUNTY	1	1	13	13	21	1	0	3	4
13	263	TALBOT COUNTY	2	2	13	13	21	1	0	3	4
13	265	TALIAFERRO COUNTY	3	3	13	13	22	1	0	2	2
13	267	TATTNALL COUNTY	2	2	13	13	22	1	0	3	1
13	269	TAYLOR COUNTY	2	2	13	13	13	1	0	3	4
13	271	TELFAIR COUNTY	2	2	13	13	22	1	0	2	3
13	273	TERRELL COUNTY	1	1	13	13	21	1	0	4	4
13	275	THOMAS COUNTY	1	1	13	13	31	1	0	4	3
13	277	TIFT COUNTY	1	1	13	13	22	1	0	4	3
13	279	TOOMBS COUNTY	2	2	13	13	21	1	0	3	2
13	281	TOWNS COUNTY	3	3	23	33	13	1	0	2	2
13	283	TREUTLEN COUNTY	3	3	13	13	31	1	0	3	2
13	285	TROUP COUNTY	2	2	13	13	23	1	0	3	4
13	287	TURNER COUNTY	1	1	13	13	21	1	0	3	4
13	289	TWIGGS COUNTY	2	2	13	13	33	1	0	3	3
13	291	UNION COUNTY	3	3	13	13	13	1	0	2	2
13	293	UPSON COUNTY	2	2	13	13	23	1	0	3	4
13	295	WALKER COUNTY	3	3	21	23	22	2	0	2	4
13	297	WALTON COUNTY	3	3	22	32	23	1	0	2	3
13	299	WARE COUNTY	1	1	13	13	13	1	0	3	2
13	301	WARREN COUNTY	3	3	13	13	22	1	0	3	1
13	303	WASHINGTON COUNTY	3	3	13	13	31	1	0	3	2
13	305	WAYNE COUNTY	2	2	13	13	21	1	0	3	1
13	307	WEBSTER COUNTY	1	1	13	13	31	1	0	4	4
13	309	WHEELER COUNTY	2	2	13	13	22	1	0	3	2
13	311	WHITE COUNTY	3	3	23	33	22	1	0	2	2
13	313	WHITFIELD COUNTY	3	3	13	23	23	1	0	2	4
13	315	WILCOX COUNTY	2	2	13	13	31	1	0	3	3
13	317	WILKES COUNTY	3	3	13	22	23	1	0	2	1
13	319	WILKINSON COUNTY	2	2	13	13	32	1	0	3	2
13	321	WORTH COUNTY	1	1	13	13	31	1	0	4	4

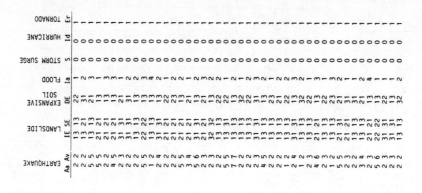

HAWAII

Code	County	EARTHQUAKE Aa	Av	LANDSLIDE IE	SE	EXPANSIVE SOIL DE	FLOOD Ia	STORM SURGE S	HURRICANE Id	TORNADO Er
15 001	HAWAII COUNTY	6	6	00	00	00	5	#	0	1
15 003	HONOLULU COUNTY	3	3	00	00	00	2	#	0	1
15 005	KALAWAO COUNTY	0	2	00	00	00	0	#	0	1
15 007	KAUAI COUNTY	2	2	00	00	00	2	#	0	1
15 009	MAUI COUNTY	4	#	00	00	00	1	#	0	1

IDAHO

Code	County	EARTHQUAKE Aa	Av	LANDSLIDE IE	SE	EXPANSIVE SOIL DE	FLOOD Ia	STORM SURGE S	HURRICANE Id	TORNADO Er
16 001	ADA COUNTY	2	2	13	13	22	2	0	0	1
16 003	ADAMS COUNTY	2	2	13	21	31	3	0	0	1
16 005	BANNOCK COUNTY	5	5	13	13	21	3	0	0	1
16 007	BEAR LAKE COUNTY	5	5	21	21	13	1	0	0	1
16 009	BENEWAH COUNTY	2	2	21	21	13	2	0	0	1
16 011	BINGHAM COUNTY	4	3	31	31	21	2	0	0	1
16 013	BLAINE COUNTY	2	2	31	31	31	4	0	0	1
16 015	BOISE COUNTY	2	2	13	13	13	2	0	0	1
16 017	BONNER COUNTY	2	2	22	22	13	1	0	0	1
16 019	BONNEVILLE COUNTY	5	5	31	31	13	2	0	0	1
16 021	BOUNDARY COUNTY	1	2	31	31	23	2	0	0	1
16 023	BUTTE COUNTY	2	2	21	21	21	1	0	0	1
16 025	CAMAS COUNTY	2	2	21	21	21	3	0	0	1
16 027	CANYON COUNTY	5	5	31	31	31	2	0	0	1
16 029	CARIBOU COUNTY	3	3	31	31	13	1	0	0	1
16 031	CASSIA COUNTY	2	3	31	31	21	2	0	0	1
16 033	CLARK COUNTY	5	7	32	32	13	1	0	0	1
16 035	CLEARWATER COUNTY	7	7	13	13	22	2	0	0	1
16 037	CUSTER COUNTY	2	2	13	13	13	2	0	0	1
16 039	ELMORE COUNTY	2	2	13	13	13	3	0	0	1
16 041	FRANKLIN COUNTY	2	3	31	31	32	2	0	0	1
16 043	FREMONT COUNTY	4	5	13	13	31	1	0	0	1
16 045	GEM COUNTY	2	2	13	13	13	2	0	0	1
16 047	GOODING COUNTY	2	2	31	31	31	2	0	0	1
16 049	IDAHO COUNTY	2	2	13	13	31	1	0	0	1
16 051	JEFFERSON COUNTY	1	2	13	13	13	2	0	0	1
16 053	JEROME COUNTY	1	2	31	31	23	2	0	0	1
16 055	KOOTENAI COUNTY	4	4	13	13	22	1	0	0	1
16 057	LATAH COUNTY	2	1	13	13	13	3	0	0	1
16 059	LEMHI COUNTY	2	2	21	21	32	1	0	0	1
16 061	LEWIS COUNTY	5	5	13	13	13	3	0	0	1
16 063	LINCOLN COUNTY	2	3	31	31	22	2	0	0	1
16 065	MADISON COUNTY	2	3	13	13	13	1	0	0	1
16 067	MINIDOKA COUNTY	5	5	21	21	22	1	0	0	1
16 069	NEZ PERCE COUNTY	3	3	13	13	13	2	0	0	1
16 071	ONEIDA COUNTY	6	6	21	21	23	4	0	0	1
16 073	OWYHEE COUNTY	3	3	13	13	31	1	0	0	1
16 075	PAYETTE COUNTY	2	3	13	13	21	1	0	0	1
16 077	POWER COUNTY	2	2	22	22	31	1	0	0	1
16 079	SHOSHONE COUNTY	5	5	31	31	13	2	0	0	1
16 081	TETON COUNTY	3	3	31	31	22	4	0	0	1
16 083	TWIN FALLS COUNTY	2	3	13	13	13	1	0	0	1
16 085	VALLEY COUNTY	2	2	13	13	13	2	0	0	1
16 087	WASHINGTON COUNTY	2	2	13	13	32	2	0	0	1

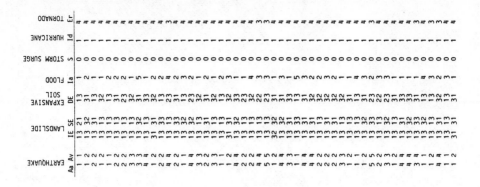

STATE	FIPS	COUNTY	EARTHQUAKE Aa	Av	LANDSLIDE IE	SE	EXPANSIVE SOIL DE	FLOOD Ia	STORM SURGE s	HURRICANE Id	TORNADO Er
17	103	LEE COUNTY	2	2	13	21	13	2	0	1	=
17	105	LIVINGSTON COUNTY	2	2	13	31	31	2	0	1	=
17	107	LOGAN COUNTY	1	1	13	31	13	1	0	1	=
17	109	MCDONOUGH COUNTY	2	1	13	13	13	1	0	1	=
17	111	MCHENRY COUNTY	2	2	13	13	23	2	0	1	=
17	113	MCLEAN COUNTY	2	2	13	32	32	1	0	1	=
17	115	MACON COUNTY	3	3	13	13	31	5	0	1	3
17	117	MACOUPIN COUNTY	3	3	13	32	33	1	0	1	3
17	119	MADISON COUNTY	=	=	31	31	32	=	0	1	=
17	121	MARION COUNTY	=	=	13	13	13	=	0	1	=
17	123	MARSHALL COUNTY	2	2	13	33	31	3	0	1	=
17	125	MASON COUNTY	2	2	13	13	23	1	0	1	=
17	127	MASSAC COUNTY	3	3	13	31	31	3	0	1	3
17	129	MENARD COUNTY	2	2	13	31	32	1	0	1	=
17	131	MERCER COUNTY	1	1	13	31	13	1	0	1	=
17	133	MONROE COUNTY	=	=	31	31	33	=	0	1	5
17	135	MONTGOMERY COUNTY	3	3	13	13	32	3	0	1	3
17	137	MORGAN COUNTY	2	2	13	31	33	2	0	1	=
17	139	MOULTRIE COUNTY	1	1	13	13	23	1	0	1	=
17	141	OGLE COUNTY	=	=	13	31	22	1	0	1	3
17	143	PEORIA COUNTY	2	2	13	31	33	2	0	1	=
17	145	PERRY COUNTY	3	3	13	13	32	3	0	1	3
17	147	PIATT COUNTY	2	2	13	13	13	1	0	1	=
17	149	PIKE COUNTY	2	2	13	13	32	3	0	1	=
17	151	POPE COUNTY	5	5	31	31	23	1	0	1	=
17	153	PULASKI COUNTY	2	2	13	13	22	3	0	1	3
17	155	PUTNAM COUNTY	1	1	32	32	31	=	0	1	=
17	157	RANDOLPH COUNTY	3	3	13	31	33	3	0	1	3
17	159	RICHLAND COUNTY	=	=	13	31	33	1	0	1	=
17	161	ROCK ISLAND COUNTY	1	1	13	31	31	3	0	1	=
17	163	ST. CLAIR COUNTY	=	=	13	31	32	=	0	1	=
17	165	SALINE COUNTY	2	2	13	13	31	2	0	1	3
17	167	SANGAMON COUNTY	2	2	13	31	32	3	0	1	=
17	169	SCHUYLER COUNTY	2	2	13	13	33	2	0	1	=
17	171	SCOTT COUNTY	3	3	13	13	32	3	0	1	=
17	173	SHELBY COUNTY	1	1	13	13	13	1	0	1	=
17	175	STARK COUNTY	1	1	13	31	32	=	0	1	=
17	177	STEPHENSON COUNTY	5	5	13	13	13	2	0	1	3
17	179	TAZEWELL COUNTY	2	2	13	32	22	3	0	1	=
17	181	UNION COUNTY	3	3	13	13	23	2	0	1	3
17	183	VERMILION COUNTY	2	2	13	32	23	2	0	1	=
17	185	WABASH COUNTY	3	3	13	13	33	3	0	1	3
17	187	WARREN COUNTY	1	1	13	13	31	1	0	1	=
17	189	WASHINGTON COUNTY	=	=	13	31	32	=	0	1	3
17	191	WAYNE COUNTY	3	3	13	13	13	3	0	1	=
17	193	WHITE COUNTY	1	1	13	32	31	2	0	1	3
17	195	WHITESIDE COUNTY	2	2	13	32	13	3	0	1	=
17	197	WILL COUNTY	1	1	13	13	13	2	0	1	=
17	199	WILLIAMSON COUNTY	3	3	13	13	32	3	0	1	3
17	201	WINNEBAGO COUN,Y	1	1	13	13	31	2	0	1	=
17	203	WOODFORD COUNTY	2	2	31	31	31	1	0	1	=

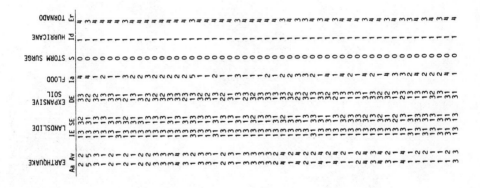

ILLINOIS

STATE	FIPS	COUNTY	EARTHQUAKE Aa	Av	LANDSLIDE IE	SE	EXPANSIVE SOIL DE	FLOOD Ia	STORM SURGE s	HURRICANE Id	TORNADO Er
17	001	ADAMS COUNTY	2	2	13	32	33	=	0	1	=
17	003	ALEXANDER COUNTY	5	5	32	31	31	3	0	1	3
17	005	BOND COUNTY	3	3	13	13	32	3	0	1	3
17	007	BOONE COUNTY	1	1	13	13	13	2	0	1	=
17	009	BROWN COUNTY	2	2	31	31	33	1	0	1	=
17	011	BUREAU COUNTY	1	1	13	31	31	2	0	1	=
17	013	CALHOUN COUNTY	2	2	31	32	23	3	0	1	=
17	015	CARROLL COUNTY	2	2	13	31	13	3	0	1	=
17	017	CASS COUNTY	2	2	13	13	33	1	0	1	=
17	019	CHAMPAIGN COUNTY	2	2	13	13	13	2	0	1	=
17	021	CHRISTIAN COUNTY	3	3	13	31	23	3	0	1	3
17	023	CLARK COUNTY	3	3	13	13	13	2	0	1	3
17	025	CLAY COUNTY	3	3	13	31	31	5	0	1	3
17	027	CLINTON COUNTY	=	=	13	31	33	=	0	1	=
17	029	COLES COUNTY	1	1	13	13	13	1	0	1	=
17	031	COOK COUNTY	1	1	33	33	13	3	0	1	3
17	033	CRAWFORD COUNTY	3	3	13	31	32	3	0	1	3
17	035	CUMBERLAND COUNTY	1	1	13	31	31	2	0	1	=
17	037	DE KALB COUNTY	2	2	31	31	22	5	0	1	=
17	039	DE WITT COUNTY	1	1	13	13	13	1	0	1	=
17	041	DOUGLAS COUNTY	2	2	13	13	23	1	0	1	=
17	043	DU PAGE COUNTY	1	1	31	31	13	2	0	1	=
17	045	EDGAR COUNTY	3	3	13	13	13	3	0	1	3
17	047	EDWARDS COUNTY	3	3	13	32	33	3	0	1	3
17	049	EFFINGHAM COUNTY	3	3	13	13	32	3	0	1	3
17	051	FAYETTE COUNTY	=	=	13	31	33	=	0	1	=
17	053	FORD COUNTY	2	2	13	32	13	1	0	1	=
17	055	FRANKLIN COUNTY	3	3	13	31	32	3	0	1	3
17	057	FULTON COUNTY	2	2	13	13	32	2	0	1	=
17	059	GALLATIN COUNTY	=	=	31	31	32	=	0	1	=
17	061	GREENE COUNTY	3	3	13	13	33	2	0	1	3
17	063	GRUNDY COUNTY	1	1	13	13	13	2	0	1	=
17	065	HAMILTON COUNTY	3	3	13	31	31	3	0	1	3
17	067	HANCOCK COUNTY	2	2	13	13	22	3	0	1	=
17	069	HARDIN COUNTY	3	3	31	31	23	1	0	1	3
17	071	HENDERSON COUNTY	1	1	13	13	13	2	0	1	=
17	073	HENRY COUNTY	1	1	13	13	31	2	0	1	=
17	075	IROQUOIS COUNTY	2	2	13	13	13	2	0	1	=
17	077	JACKSON COUNTY	3	3	13	32	33	3	0	1	3
17	079	JASPER COUNTY	3	3	13	13	13	2	0	1	3
17	081	JEFFERSON COUNTY	3	3	13	31	32	2	0	1	3
17	083	JERSEY COUNTY	=	=	31	31	32	2	0	1	=
17	085	JO DAVIESS COUNTY	2	2	13	13	23	2	0	1	=
17	087	JOHNSON COUNTY	3	3	31	31	13	1	0	1	3
17	089	KANE COUNTY	1	1	31	31	32	2	0	1	=
17	091	KANKAKEE COUNTY	1	1	31	31	13	2	0	1	=
17	093	KENDALL COUNTY	1	1	13	13	13	2	0	1	=
17	095	KNOX COUNTY	1	1	13	13	32	2	0	1	=
17	097	LAKE COUNTY	1	1	31	31	31	3	0	1	=
17	099	LA SALLE COUNTY	2	2	13	13	31	2	0	1	=
17	101	LAWRENCE COUNTY	3	3	13	13	31	3	0	1	3

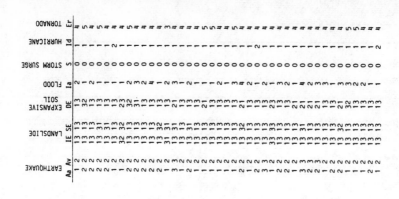

Column headers (both tables): EARTHQUAKE (Aa, Av) | LANDSLIDE (IE, SE) | EXPANSIVE SOIL (DE) | FLOOD (Ia) | STORM SURGE (S) | HURRICANE (Id) | TORNADO (Er)

INDIANA

Code	County	Aa	Av	IE	SE	DE	Ia	S	Id	Er
18 001	ADAMS COUNTY	2	2	13	13	13	1	0		4
18 003	ALLEN COUNTY	2	2	13	31	13	3	0	2	4
18 005	BARTHOLOMEW COUNTY	2	2	13	13	13	1	0	1	5
18 007	BENTON COUNTY	1	1	13	13	13	2	0	1	4
18 009	BLACKFORD COUNTY	2	2	13	13	13	1	0	1	4
18 011	BOONE COUNTY	2	2	13	13	13	2	0		5
18 013	BROWN COUNTY	2	2	13	13	13	3	0		4
18 015	CARROLL COUNTY	2	2	13	13	13	3	0		4
18 017	CASS COUNTY	2	2	13	13	13	2	0		4
18 019	CLARK COUNTY	1	1	13	13	13	3	0	1	4
18 021	CLAY COUNTY	2	2	13	13	13	1	0	1	5
18 023	CLINTON COUNTY	2	2	13	13	13	2	0		4
18 025	CRAWFORD COUNTY	2	2	13	13	21	2	0	1	4
18 027	DAVIESS COUNTY	2	2	31	31	31	3	0		4
18 029	DEARBORN COUNTY	1	2	13	13	13	2	0		4
18 031	DECATUR COUNTY	2	2	13	13	13	1	0	2	4
18 033	DE KALB COUNTY	2	2	13	13	13	3	0	1	4
18 035	DELAWARE COUNTY	2	2	13	13	13	3	0		4
18 037	DUBOIS COUNTY	2	2	13	13	13	1	0	1	5
18 039	ELKHART COUNTY	2	2	13	13	13	3	0	1	5
18 041	FAYETTE COUNTY	2	2	13	13	13	2	0	1	4
18 043	FLOYD COUNTY	1	1	13	13	21	3	0	1	4
18 045	FOUNTAIN COUNTY	2	2	13	13	13	2	0	1	5
18 047	FRANKLIN COUNTY	2	2	13	13	13	2	0		4
18 049	FULTON COUNTY	2	2	13	13	13	2	0		4
18 051	GIBSON COUNTY	3	3	13	13	13	4	0	1	5
18 053	GRANT COUNTY	2	2	13	13	13	2	0		4
18 055	GREENE COUNTY	2	2	13	13	13	2	0	1	4
18 057	HAMILTON COUNTY	2	2	13	13	13	2	0		4
18 059	HANCOCK COUNTY	2	2	13	13	13	2	0		4
18 061	HARRISON COUNTY	1	1	13	13	13	3	0		5
18 063	HENDRICKS COUNTY	2	2	21	21	21	2	0		4
18 065	HENRY COUNTY	2	2	31	31	13	2	0		4
18 067	HOWARD COUNTY	2	2	13	13	13	4	0		4
18 069	HUNTINGTON COUNTY	2	2	13	13	13	2	0		4
18 071	JACKSON COUNTY	2	2	13	13	13	3	0	1	5
18 073	JASPER COUNTY	1	1	13	13	13	3	0		5
18 075	JAY COUNTY	2	2	13	13	22	2	0		4
18 077	JEFFERSON COUNTY	2	2	13	13	13	3	0		4
18 079	JENNINGS COUNTY	2	2	13	13	31	2	0		4
18 081	JOHNSON COUNTY	2	2	13	13	21	1	0	1	4
18 083	KNOX COUNTY	3	3	32	32	13	3	0	1	4
18 085	KOSCIUSKO COUNTY	2	2	21	21	13	2	0	1	3
18 087	LAGRANGE COUNTY	2	2	13	13	13	2	0	1	5
18 089	LAKE COUNTY	1	1	13	13	33	3	0	1	5
18 091	LA PORTE COUNTY	1	1	13	13	13	2	0	1	5
18 093	LAWRENCE COUNTY	2	2	13	13	13	1	0		4
18 095	MADISON COUNTY	2	2	13	13	13	2	0		3
18 097	MARION COUNTY	2	2	32	32	13	3	0		5
18 099	MARSHALL COUNTY	2	2	13	13	13	2	0	1	5
18 101	MARTIN COUNTY	2	2	13	13	31	3	0	1	5

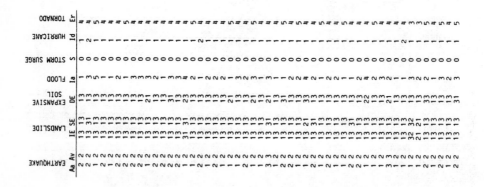

Code	County	Aa	Av	IE	SE	DE	Ia	S	Id	Er
18 103	MIAMI COUNTY	2	2	13	13	13	2	0	1	4
18 105	MONROE COUNTY	2	2	13	13	32	1	0	1	5
18 107	MONTGOMERY COUNTY	2	2	13	13	13	1	0	1	4
18 109	MORGAN COUNTY	2	2	31	31	13	3	0	1	4
18 111	NEWTON COUNTY	1	1	13	31	21	2	0	2	4
18 113	NOBLE COUNTY	2	2	13	13	13	2	0	1	4
18 115	OHIO COUNTY	2	2	13	13	13	2	0		4
18 117	ORANGE COUNTY	2	2	13	13	13	1	0	2	5
18 119	OWEN COUNTY	2	2	13	13	13	1	0		4
18 121	PARKE COUNTY	2	2	13	13	13	3	0		4
18 123	PERRY COUNTY	2	1	13	13	13	2	0	1	5
18 125	PIKE COUNTY	3	2	13	13	13	3	0	2	5
18 127	PORTER COUNTY	1	1	13	13	21	3	0	1	5
18 129	POSEY COUNTY	3	2	13	13	13	4	0	2	5
18 131	PULASKI COUNTY	1	1	13	31	13	1	0	1	4
18 133	PUTNAM COUNTY	2	2	13	13	13	1	0	1	4
18 135	RANDOLPH COUNTY	2	2	13	13	13	2	0		4
18 137	RIPLEY COUNTY	2	2	13	13	13	2	0		4
18 139	RUSH COUNTY	2	2	13	13	13	2	0		4
18 141	ST. JOSEPH COUNTY	1	1	13	13	13	3	0	1	5
18 143	SCOTT COUNTY	2	2	13	13	13	1	0		5
18 145	SHELBY COUNTY	2	2	32	32	13	1	0		5
18 147	SPENCER COUNTY	2	2	13	13	13	3	0	2	5
18 149	STARKE COUNTY	1	1	13	13	13	1	0	1	5
18 151	STEUBEN COUNTY	2	2	13	13	13	2	0	1	4
18 153	SULLIVAN COUNTY	3	3	13	13	23	3	0	1	4
18 155	SWITZERLAND COUNTY	2	2	13	13	13	2	0		4
18 157	TIPPECANOE COUNTY	2	2	13	13	21	3	0	1	4
18 159	TIPTON COUNTY	2	2	13	13	21	1	0		4
18 161	UNION COUNTY	2	2	13	13	21	2	0		4
18 163	VANDERBURGH COUNTY	3	3	13	13	13	3	0	2	5
18 165	VERMILLION COUNTY	3	3	13	13	13	4	0	1	4
18 167	VIGO COUNTY	3	3	13	13	13	3	0	1	5
18 169	WABASH COUNTY	2	2	13	13	13	2	0	1	4
18 171	WARREN COUNTY	2	2	13	13	13	2	0	1	4
18 173	WARRICK COUNTY	3	2	13	32	21	4	0	2	5
18 175	WASHINGTON COUNTY	1	1	13	13	13	2	0	1	5
18 177	WAYNE COUNTY	2	2	31	31	32	3	0		4
18 179	WELLS COUNTY	2	2	13	13	13	2	0		4
18 181	WHITE COUNTY	2	2	13	13	13	2	0	1	5
18 183	WHITLEY COUNTY	2	2	13	13	13	3	0	1	5

498

IOWA

Code		County	EARTHQUAKE Aa	Av	LANDSLIDE IE	SE	EXPANSIVE SOIL DE	FLOOD Ia	STORM SURGE S	HURRICANE Pl	TORNADO Er
19	001	ADAIR COUNTY	2	1	13	13	33	1	0	0	=
19	003	ADAMS COUNTY	2	1	13	13	33	1	0	0	=
19	005	ALLAMAKEE COUNTY	1	1	13	21	23	2	0	0	=
19	007	APPANOOSE COUNTY	2	1	13	13	23	2	0	0	5
19	009	AUDUBON COUNTY	1	1	13	21	31	2	0	0	=
19	011	BENTON COUNTY	1	1	13	13	23	3	0	0	=
19	013	BLACK HAWK COUNTY	1	1	13	13	23	5	0	0	=
19	015	BOONE COUNTY	1	1	13	13	31	2	0	0	5
19	017	BREMER COUNTY	1	1	13	13	23	3	0	0	=
19	019	BUCHANAN COUNTY	1	1	13	13	23	3	0	0	=
19	021	BUENA VISTA COUNTY	1	1	13	13	31	2	0	0	=
19	023	BUTLER COUNTY	1	1	13	22	23	1	0	0	5
19	025	CALHOUN COUNTY	1	1	13	22	23	2	0	0	=
19	027	CARROLL COUNTY	2	1	13	13	32	3	0	0	=
19	029	CASS COUNTY	2	1	13	13	23	3	0	0	=
19	031	CEDAR COUNTY	1	1	13	13	23	1	0	0	=
19	033	CERRO GORDO COUNTY	1	1	13	13	31	3	0	0	5
19	035	CHEROKEE COUNTY	2	1	13	13	23	2	0	0	=
19	037	CHICKASAW COUNTY	1	1	13	13	23	3	0	0	=
19	039	CLARKE COUNTY	1	1	13	13	32	2	0	0	=
19	041	CLAY COUNTY	1	1	13	13	31	3	0	0	=
19	043	CLAYTON COUNTY	1	1	13	21	23	1	0	0	=
19	045	CLINTON COUNTY	2	1	21	22	33	2	0	0	5
19	047	CRAWFORD COUNTY	1	1	13	23	32	3	0	0	=
19	049	DALLAS COUNTY	1	1	13	13	31	1	0	0	=
19	051	DAVIS COUNTY	1	1	13	13	32	2	0	0	=
19	053	DECATUR COUNTY	1	2	13	21	33	2	0	0	=
19	055	DELAWARE COUNTY	1	1	13	13	33	1	0	0	=
19	057	DES MOINES COUNTY	2	1	13	13	32	3	0	0	5
19	059	DICKINSON COUNTY	1	1	13	13	23	1	0	0	=
19	061	DUBUQUE COUNTY	1	1	13	13	23	2	0	0	=
19	063	EMMET COUNTY	1	1	21	21	23	2	0	0	=
19	065	FAYETTE COUNTY	1	1	21	21	23	2	0	0	5
19	067	FLOYD COUNTY	1	1	13	23	23	2	0	0	=
19	069	FRANKLIN COUNTY	3	1	13	13	32	1	0	0	=
19	071	FREMONT COUNTY	1	1	13	13	23	2	0	0	=
19	073	GREENE COUNTY	1	1	13	21	23	2	0	0	=
19	075	GRUNDY COUNTY	1	1	13	13	32	1	0	0	5
19	077	GUTHRIE COUNTY	2	1	13	13	23	2	0	0	=
19	079	HAMILTON COUNTY	1	1	13	13	32	3	0	0	=
19	081	HANCOCK COUNTY	1	1	13	13	32	2	0	0	=
19	083	HARDIN COUNTY	1	1	13	13	22	3	0	0	=
19	085	HARRISON COUNTY	1	1	21	23	32	1	0	0	5
19	087	HENRY COUNTY	2	1	13	13	22	2	0	0	=
19	089	HOWARD COUNTY	1	1	13	13	33	3	0	0	=
19	091	HUMBOLDT COUNTY	2	1	21	21	31	2	0	0	=
19	093	IDA COUNTY	1	1	13	23	31	1	0	0	5
19	095	IOWA COUNTY	1	1	13	22	32	3	0	0	=
19	097	JACKSON COUNTY	1	1					0	0	=
19	099	JASPER COUNTY							0	0	
19	101	JEFFERSON COUNTY							0	0	5
19	103	JOHNSON COUNTY	1	1	13	13	32	2	0	0	=
19	105	JONES COUNTY	1	1	13	13	23	2	0	0	=
19	107	KEOKUK COUNTY	1	1	13	21	33	1	0	0	=
19	109	KOSSUTH COUNTY	1	1	13	13	33	2	0	0	=
19	111	LEE COUNTY	1	2	13	13	33	3	0	0	5
19	113	LINN COUNTY	1	1	13	21	32	4	0	0	=
19	115	LOUISA COUNTY	1	1	13	13	32	4	0	0	=
19	117	LUCAS COUNTY	1	1	13	13	23	2	0	0	=
19	119	LYON COUNTY	1	1	13	13	23	2	0	0	=
19	121	MADISON COUNTY	3	1	13	21	33	2	0	0	5
19	123	MAHASKA COUNTY	1	1	13	23	33	3	0	0	=
19	125	MARION COUNTY	3	1	13	22	33	2	0	0	=
19	127	MARSHALL COUNTY	1	1	21	13	31	1	0	0	=
19	129	MILLS COUNTY	1	1	13	13	23	3	0	0	5
19	131	MITCHELL COUNTY	2	1	13	13	23	2	0	0	=
19	133	MONONA COUNTY	1	1	13	13	33	1	0	0	=
19	135	MONROE COUNTY	1	1	13	13	32	2	0	0	=
19	137	MONTGOMERY COUNTY	3	1	13	13	23	1	0	0	5
19	139	MUSCATINE COUNTY	2	1	13	21	31	2	0	0	=
19	141	O'BRIEN COUNTY	2	1	13	13	31	2	0	0	=
19	143	OSCEOLA COUNTY	1	1	13	33	31	3	0	0	=
19	145	PAGE COUNTY	3	1	13	13	32	1	0	0	5
19	147	PALO ALTO COUNTY	1	1	13	21	31	1	0	0	=
19	149	PLYMOUTH COUNTY	2	1	13	13	23	2	0	0	=
19	151	POCAHONTAS COUNTY	1	1	13	13	23	2	0	0	=
19	153	POLK COUNTY	1	1	13	13	31	3	0	0	=
19	155	POTTAWATTAMIE COUNTY	2	1	21	33	32	3	0	0	5
19	157	POWESHIEK COUNTY	1	1	13	21	23	1	0	0	=
19	159	RINGGOLD COUNTY	1	2	13	21	33	2	0	0	=
19	161	SAC COUNTY	1	1	13	13	23	3	0	0	=
19	163	SCOTT COUNTY	2	1	21	21	23	1	0	0	5
19	165	SHELBY COUNTY	1	1	21	21	23	3	0	0	=
19	167	SIOUX COUNTY	1	1	13	23	23	2	0	0	=
19	169	STORY COUNTY	1	1	13	13	31	3	0	0	=
19	171	TAMA COUNTY	2	1	13	13	31	1	0	0	5
19	173	TAYLOR COUNTY	2	1	13	22	33	2	0	0	=
19	175	UNION COUNTY	1	1	13	23	33	2	0	0	=
19	177	VAN BUREN COUNTY	2	1	13	23	33	1	0	0	=
19	179	WAPELLO COUNTY	1	1	13	13	33	1	0	0	5
19	181	WARREN COUNTY	1	1	13	21	33	3	0	0	=
19	183	WASHINGTON COUNTY	2	1	21	23	33	1	0	0	=
19	185	WAYNE COUNTY	1	2	13	21	33	3	0	0	=
19	187	WEBSTER COUNTY	1	1	13	13	32	3	0	0	5
19	189	WINNEBAGO COUNTY	1	1	13	13	22	1	0	0	=
19	191	WINNESHIEK COUNTY	2	1	13	22	23	1	0	0	=
19	193	WOODBURY COUNTY	2	1	21	23	23	1	0	0	=
19	195	WORTH COUNTY	1	1	13	13	32	3	0	0	5
19	197	WRIGHT COUNTY	1	1	13	13	23	2	0	0	=

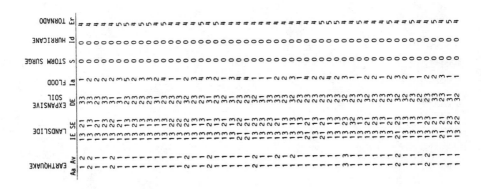

KANSAS

FIPS	County	EARTHQUAKE Aa	EARTHQUAKE Av	LANDSLIDE IE	LANDSLIDE SE	EXPANSIVE SOIL DE	FLOOD Ia	STORM SURGE s	HURRICANE Id	TORNADO Er
20 001	ALLEN COUNTY	2	2	13	13	33	3	0	1	5
20 003	ANDERSON COUNTY	3	3	13	13	33	3	0	1	5
20 005	ATCHISON COUNTY	2	3	13	13	32	2	0	1	5
20 007	BARBER COUNTY	2	2	13	22	23	2	0	1	4
20 009	BARTON COUNTY	1	2	13	13	33	4	0	1	4
20 011	BOURBON COUNTY	3	3	13	13	33	2	0	1	5
20 013	BROWN COUNTY	2	2	13	13	33	1	0	1	5
20 015	BUTLER COUNTY	2	2	13	13	32	3	0	1	5
20 017	CHASE COUNTY	2	2	13	13	23	3	0	1	5
20 019	CHAUTAUQUA COUNTY	2	2	13	13	23	1	0	1	5
20 021	CHEROKEE COUNTY	3	3	13	13	32	3	0	1	5
20 023	CHEYENNE COUNTY	1	1	13	13	31	1	0	1	3
20 025	CLARK COUNTY	2	2	13	13	31	2	0	1	4
20 027	CLAY COUNTY	2	2	13	13	32	1	0	1	4
20 029	CLOUD COUNTY	2	2	13	13	32	2	0	1	4
20 031	COFFEY COUNTY	3	3	13	13	33	3	0	1	5
20 033	COMANCHE COUNTY	2	2	13	13	31	1	0	1	4
20 035	COWLEY COUNTY	2	2	13	13	32	2	0	1	5
20 037	CRAWFORD COUNTY	3	3	13	13	33	3	0	1	5
20 039	DECATUR COUNTY	1	1	13	13	31	1	0	1	3
20 041	DICKINSON COUNTY	2	2	13	13	32	2	0	1	4
20 043	DONIPHAN COUNTY	3	3	13	23	32	3	0	1	5
20 045	DOUGLAS COUNTY	3	3	13	13	33	3	0	1	5
20 047	EDWARDS COUNTY	1	1	13	13	31	2	0	1	3
20 049	ELK COUNTY	2	2	13	13	23	1	0	1	5
20 051	ELLIS COUNTY	1	1	13	13	31	1	0	1	4
20 053	ELLSWORTH COUNTY	2	2	13	13	32	2	0	1	5
20 055	FINNEY COUNTY	1	1	13	13	23	2	0	1	4
20 057	FORD COUNTY	2	2	13	13	32	2	0	1	2
20 059	FRANKLIN COUNTY	3	3	13	13	33	3	0	1	5
20 061	GEARY COUNTY	3	3	13	13	33	3	0	1	5
20 063	GOVE COUNTY	1	1	13	13	23	1	0	1	4
20 065	GRAHAM COUNTY	1	1	13	13	31	1	0	1	4
20 067	GRANT COUNTY	1	1	13	13	23	1	0	1	4
20 069	GRAY COUNTY	1	1	13	13	23	2	0	1	4
20 071	GREELEY COUNTY	1	1	13	13	23	1	0	1	1
20 073	GREENWOOD COUNTY	3	3	13	13	33	2	0	1	5
20 075	HAMILTON COUNTY	1	1	13	13	23	2	0	1	1
20 077	HARPER COUNTY	2	2	13	13	32	2	0	1	5
20 079	HARVEY COUNTY	2	2	13	13	33	2	0	1	5
20 081	HASKELL COUNTY	1	1	13	13	23	1	0	1	1
20 083	HODGEMAN COUNTY	1	1	13	13	31	2	0	1	5
20 085	JACKSON COUNTY	3	3	13	13	33	3	0	1	5
20 087	JEFFERSON COUNTY	3	3	13	13	33	3	0	1	5
20 089	JEWELL COUNTY	1	1	13	13	31	1	0	1	1
20 091	JOHNSON COUNTY	3	3	13	13	33	3	0	1	5
20 093	KEARNY COUNTY	1	1	13	13	23	2	0	1	5
20 095	KINGMAN COUNTY	2	2	13	13	32	2	0	1	5
20 097	KIOWA COUNTY	2	2	13	13	31	2	0	1	5
20 099	LABETTE COUNTY	3	3	13	13	33	2	0	1	5
20 101	LANE COUNTY	1	1	13	13	23	1	0	1	3
20 103	LEAVENWORTH COUNTY	3	3	13	13	33	3	0	1	5
20 105	LINCOLN COUNTY	2	2	13	32	32	2	0	1	4
20 107	LINN COUNTY	3	3	13	13	33	2	0	1	5
20 109	LOGAN COUNTY	1	1	13	13	23	1	0	1	3
20 111	LYON COUNTY	3	3	13	21	33	3	0	1	4
20 113	MCPHERSON COUNTY	2	2	13	13	32	2	0	1	5
20 115	MARION COUNTY	2	2	13	13	33	3	0	1	1
20 117	MARSHALL COUNTY	2	2	13	13	33	2	0	1	5
20 119	MEADE COUNTY	1	1	13	13	23	1	0	1	5
20 121	MIAMI COUNTY	3	3	13	13	33	3	0	1	5
20 123	MITCHELL COUNTY	1	1	13	13	31	1	0	1	1
20 125	MONTGOMERY COUNTY	3	3	13	13	33	3	0	1	4
20 127	MORRIS COUNTY	2	2	13	13	33	2	0	1	5
20 129	MORTON COUNTY	1	1	13	13	23	1	0	1	4
20 131	NEMAHA COUNTY	2	2	13	13	33	2	0	1	4
20 133	NEOSHO COUNTY	3	3	13	13	33	3	0	1	5
20 135	NESS COUNTY	1	1	13	13	31	1	0	1	5
20 137	NORTON COUNTY	1	1	13	13	31	1	0	1	5
20 139	OSAGE COUNTY	3	3	13	13	33	3	0	1	5
20 141	OSBORNE COUNTY	1	1	13	13	31	1	0	1	4
20 143	OTTAWA COUNTY	2	2	13	13	32	2	0	1	5
20 145	PAWNEE COUNTY	1	1	13	13	31	2	0	1	4
20 147	PHILLIPS COUNTY	1	1	13	13	31	1	0	1	4
20 149	POTTAWATOMIE COUNTY	3	3	13	13	33	3	0	1	3
20 151	PRATT COUNTY	2	2	13	13	31	2	0	1	4
20 153	RAWLINS COUNTY	1	1	13	13	31	1	0	1	5
20 155	RENO COUNTY	2	2	13	13	32	2	0	1	4
20 157	REPUBLIC COUNTY	1	1	13	13	32	1	0	1	5
20 159	RICE COUNTY	2	2	13	13	32	2	0	1	5
20 161	RILEY COUNTY	3	3	13	31	33	3	0	1	4
20 163	ROOKS COUNTY	1	1	13	13	31	1	0	1	4
20 165	RUSH COUNTY	1	1	13	13	31	1	0	1	3
20 167	RUSSELL COUNTY	2	2	13	33	32	2	0	1	4
20 169	SALINE COUNTY	2	2	13	22	32	2	0	1	5
20 171	SCOTT COUNTY	1	1	13	13	23	1	0	1	4
20 173	SEDGWICK COUNTY	2	2	13	13	33	3	0	1	5
20 175	SEWARD COUNTY	1	1	13	13	23	2	0	1	4
20 177	SHAWNEE COUNTY	3	3	13	13	33	3	0	1	5
20 179	SHERIDAN COUNTY	1	1	13	13	31	1	0	1	3
20 181	SHERMAN COUNTY	1	1	13	13	23	1	0	1	5
20 183	SMITH COUNTY	1	1	13	13	31	1	0	1	1
20 185	STAFFORD COUNTY	2	2	13	32	32	2	0	1	5
20 187	STANTON COUNTY	1	1	13	13	23	1	0	1	2
20 189	STEVENS COUNTY	1	1	13	13	23	1	0	1	5
20 191	SUMNER COUNTY	2	2	13	13	33	2	0	1	3
20 193	THOMAS COUNTY	1	1	13	13	23	1	0	1	5
20 195	TREGO COUNTY	1	1	13	13	31	1	0	1	1
20 197	WABAUNSEE COUNTY	3	3	13	13	33	3	0	1	1
20 199	WALLACE COUNTY	1	1	13	13	23	1	0	1	5
20 201	WASHINGTON COUNTY	2	2	13	13	32	2	0	1	3
20 203	WICHITA COUNTY	1	1	13	13	23	1	0	1	5
20 205	WILSON COUNTY	3	3	13	13	33	2	0	1	5
20 207	WOODSON COUNTY	2	2	13	13	33	1	0	1	2
20 209	WYANDOTTE COUNTY	3	3	13	23	23	4	0	1	5

KENTUCKY

			EARTHQUAKE		LANDSLIDE		EXPANSIVE SOIL	FLOOD	STORM SURGE	HURRICANE	TORNADO
			Aa	Av	IE	SE	DE	Ia	S	Id	Er
21	001	ADAIR COUNTY	1	2	13	13	23	1	0	2	3
21	003	ALLEN COUNTY	2	2	13	13	23	2	0	2	4
21	005	ANDERSON COUNTY	1	2	13	13	22	2	0	1	2
21	007	BALLARD COUNTY	5	5	22	32	21	3	0	1	3
21	009	BARREN COUNTY	1	2	13	13	23	2	0	2	3
21	011	BATH COUNTY	1	2	13	21	22	2	0	1	2
21	013	BELL COUNTY	3	3	33	33	13	5	0	2	1
21	015	BOONE COUNTY	1	2	32	32	23	2	0	1	3
21	017	BOURBON COUNTY	1	2	13	13	22	2	0	1	2
21	019	BOYD COUNTY	1	2	23	33	13	5	0	1	1
21	021	BOYLE COUNTY	1	2	13	23	22	1	0	1	2
21	023	BRACKEN COUNTY	1	2	31	31	23	4	0	1	3
21	025	BREATHITT COUNTY	1	2	33	33	13	5	0	2	1
21	027	BRECKINRIDGE COUNTY	1	2	13	13	13	2	0	1	4
21	029	BULLITT COUNTY	1	2	13	22	22	3	0	1	3
21	031	BUTLER COUNTY	2	2	13	13	13	2	0	1	4
21	033	CALDWELL COUNTY	3	3	13	13	21	1	0	1	4
21	035	CALLOWAY COUNTY	3	3	13	13	13	2	0	1	4
21	037	CAMPBELL COUNTY	1	2	32	32	23	4	0	1	3
21	039	CARLISLE COUNTY	5	5	22	32	13	2	0	1	4
21	041	CARROLL COUNTY	1	2	13	13	23	4	0	1	3
21	043	CARTER COUNTY	1	2	31	33	13	3	0	1	1
21	045	CASEY COUNTY	1	2	13	22	23	1	0	2	2
21	047	CHRISTIAN COUNTY	2	2	13	13	22	3	0	1	4
21	049	CLARK COUNTY	1	2	13	13	22	2	0	1	2
21	051	CLAY COUNTY	2	2	33	33	13	4	0	2	1
21	053	CLINTON COUNTY	2	2	23	23	23	2	0	2	3
21	055	CRITTENDEN COUNTY	3	3	13	13	21	2	0	1	4
21	057	CUMBERLAND COUNTY	2	2	23	23	23	3	0	2	3
21	059	DAVIESS COUNTY	2	2	13	32	13	3	0	1	4
21	061	EDMONSON COUNTY	1	2	13	13	21	1	0	1	3
21	063	ELLIOTT COUNTY	1	2	32	33	13	2	0	1	1
21	065	ESTILL COUNTY	1	2	32	32	13	3	0	2	1
21	067	FAYETTE COUNTY	1	2	13	13	21	2	0	1	2
21	069	FLEMING COUNTY	1	2	13	13	23	2	0	1	2
21	071	FLOYD COUNTY	2	2	33	33	13	4	0	2	1
21	073	FRANKLIN COUNTY	1	2	13	13	22	4	0	1	3
21	075	FULTON COUNTY	5	5	22	32	21	3	0	1	4
21	077	GALLATIN COUNTY	1	2	31	31	23	3	0	1	3
21	079	GARRARD COUNTY	1	2	31	31	23	2	0	1	2
21	081	GRANT COUNTY	1	2	13	13	23	1	0	1	3
21	083	GRAVES COUNTY	4	4	13	13	13	1	0	1	4
21	085	GRAYSON COUNTY	1	2	13	13	13	2	0	1	4
21	087	GREEN COUNTY	1	2	13	13	23	2	0	1	3
21	089	GREENUP COUNTY	1	2	32	33	13	3	0	1	1
21	091	HANCOCK COUNTY	2	2	13	13	13	3	0	1	4
21	093	HARDIN COUNTY	1	2	13	31	13	4	0	1	3
21	095	HARLAN COUNTY	3	3	33	33	13	4	0	2	1
21	097	HARRISON COUNTY	1	2	13	13	23	3	0	1	2
21	099	HART COUNTY	1	2	13	13	22	2	0	1	3
21	101	HENDERSON COUNTY	3	3	13	32	13	1	0	1	4
21	103	HENRY COUNTY	1	2	13	13	23	3	0	1	3
21	105	HICKMAN COUNTY	5	5	22	32	13	5	0	1	4
21	107	HOPKINS COUNTY	2	3	13	13	13	4	0	1	4
21	109	JACKSON COUNTY	1	2	33	33	13	3	0	2	1
21	111	JEFFERSON COUNTY	1	2	13	13	23	5	0	1	3
21	113	JESSAMINE COUNTY	1	2	13	13	22	2	0	1	2
21	115	JOHNSON COUNTY	1	2	33	33	13	5	0	2	1
21	117	KENTON COUNTY	1	2	31	31	23	3	0	1	3
21	119	KNOTT COUNTY	2	2	33	33	13	3	0	2	1
21	121	KNOX COUNTY	2	2	33	33	13	5	0	2	1
21	123	LARUE COUNTY	1	2	13	13	13	1	0	1	3
21	125	LAUREL COUNTY	2	2	33	33	13	3	0	2	2
21	127	LAWRENCE COUNTY	1	2	13	13	13	3	0	2	1
21	129	LEE COUNTY	1	2	33	33	13	3	0	2	1
21	131	LESLIE COUNTY	2	2	33	33	13	3	0	2	1
21	133	LETCHER COUNTY	3	3	33	33	13	2	0	2	1
21	135	LEWIS COUNTY	1	2	31	31	22	3	0	1	2
21	137	LINCOLN COUNTY	1	2	13	22	23	2	0	2	2
21	139	LIVINGSTON COUNTY	4	4	13	13	22	3	0	1	4
21	141	LOGAN COUNTY	2	2	13	13	22	2	0	1	4
21	143	LYON COUNTY	3	3	13	13	23	2	0	1	4
21	145	MCCRACKEN COUNTY	4	4	13	13	13	3	0	1	3
21	147	MCCREARY COUNTY	2	2	31	33	13	2	0	2	2
21	149	MCLEAN COUNTY	2	2	13	33	13	4	0	1	4
21	151	MADISON COUNTY	1	2	31	31	22	2	0	1	2
21	153	MAGOFFIN COUNTY	1	2	33	33	13	3	0	2	1
21	155	MARION COUNTY	1	2	13	23	22	2	0	1	3
21	157	MARSHALL COUNTY	4	4	13	13	13	2	0	1	4
21	159	MARTIN COUNTY	1	2	33	33	13	4	0	2	1
21	161	MASON COUNTY	1	2	31	33	23	4	0	1	2
21	163	MEADE COUNTY	1	2	13	13	13	2	0	1	4
21	165	MENIFEE COUNTY	1	2	33	33	13	1	0	1	1
21	167	MERCER COUNTY	1	2	13	13	22	2	0	1	2
21	169	METCALFE COUNTY	1	2	13	13	23	1	0	2	3
21	171	MONROE COUNTY	2	2	21	21	23	1	0	2	3
21	173	MONTGOMERY COUNTY	1	2	13	22	22	2	0	1	2
21	175	MORGAN COUNTY	1	2	32	32	13	3	0	2	1
21	177	MUHLENBERG COUNTY	2	2	13	31	13	1	0	1	4
21	179	NELSON COUNTY	1	2	13	22	22	2	0	1	3
21	181	NICHOLAS COUNTY	1	2	13	13	23	2	0	1	2
21	183	OHIO COUNTY	2	2	13	13	13	2	0	1	4
21	185	OLDHAM COUNTY	1	2	13	13	23	2	0	1	3
21	187	OWEN COUNTY	1	2	13	13	23	3	0	1	3
21	189	OWSLEY COUNTY	1	2	33	33	13	2	0	2	1
21	191	PENDLETON COUNTY	1	2	31	31	23	3	0	1	3
21	193	PERRY COUNTY	2	2	33	33	13	5	0	2	1
21	195	PIKE COUNTY	2	2	33	33	13	5	0	2	1
21	197	POWELL COUNTY	1	2	13	23	13	2	0	1	1
21	199	PULASKI COUNTY	2	2	22	32	23	2	0	2	2
21	201	ROBERTSON COUNTY	1	2	13	13	23	1	0	1	2
21	203	ROCKCASTLE COUNTY	1	2	33	33	22	3	0	2	2
21	205	ROWAN COUNTY	1	2	32	32	13	3	0	1	2
21	207	RUSSELL COUNTY	2	2	23	23	23	2	0	2	2
21	209	SCOTT COUNTY	1	2	13	13	22	2	0	1	2

LOUISIANA

FIPS	County	Aa	Av	IE	SE	DE	la	S	Pd	Er
22 001	ACADIA PARISH	1	1	13	13	21	2	2	=	3
22 003	ALLEN PARISH	1	1	13	13	21	3	0	=	=
22 005	ASCENSION PARISH	1	1	31	31	33	2	1	=	3
22 007	ASSUMPTION PARISH	1	1	13	13	32	2	0	=	=
22 009	AVOYELLES PARISH	1	2	13	13	13	1	0	2	=
22 011	BEAUREGARD PARISH	1	2	13	13	21	1	0	2	=
22 013	BIENVILLE PARISH	1	2	13	13	31	2	0	3	3
22 015	BOSSIER PARISH	1	1	13	13	31	3	0	=	2
22 017	CADDO PARISH	1	2	13	13	33	3	2	3	=
22 019	CALCASIEU PARISH	1	2	13	13	23	3	0	3	=
22 021	CALDWELL PARISH	1	1	21	21	21	2	3	=	=
22 023	CAMERON PARISH	1	1	13	13	33	1	0	4	=
22 025	CATAHOULA PARISH	1	2	13	13	31	2	0	3	=
22 027	CLAIBORNE PARISH	1	1	31	33	31	2	0	2	2
22 029	CONCORDIA PARISH	1	1	13	13	33	2	2	=	=
22 031	DE SOTO PARISH	1	1	13	13	32	2	0	=	=
22 033	EAST BATON ROUGE PARISH	1	2	31	31	32	2	0	=	3
22 035	EAST CARROLL PARISH	1	2	33	33	32	1	0	3	3
22 037	EAST FELICIANA PARISH	1	1	13	13	31	2	1	2	3
22 039	EVANGELINE PARISH	1	1	13	13	31	2	0	=	=
22 041	FRANKLIN PARISH	1	1	13	13	31	2	0	3	3
22 043	GRANT PARISH	1	2	13	13	32	2	0	2	3
22 045	IBERIA PARISH	1	1	13	13	32	2	3	5	=
22 047	IBERVILLE PARISH	1	2	22	22	33	2	1	=	3
22 049	JACKSON PARISH	1	1	33	33	23	2	0	2	3
22 051	JEFFERSON PARISH	1	1	13	13	32	1	2	5	=
22 053	JEFFERSON DAVIS PARISH	1	1	13	13	23	1	0	4	=
22 055	LAFAYETTE PARISH	1	1	13	13	31	3	0	=	2
22 057	LAFOURCHE PARISH	1	2	13	13	13	3	2	2	=
22 059	LA SALLE PARISH	1	2	13	13	33	3	0	3	=
22 061	LINCOLN PARISH	1	1	21	21	31	2	0	2	2
22 063	LIVINGSTON PARISH	1	2	13	13	31	2	0	2	=
22 065	MADISON PARISH	1	1	32	32	32	2	0	3	=
22 067	MOREHOUSE PARISH	1	2	13	13	31	2	0	2	=
22 069	NATCHITOCHES PARISH	1	1	23	23	33	3	0	2	=
22 071	ORLEANS PARISH	1	2	13	13	31	1	2	5	=
22 073	OUACHITA PARISH	1	1	13	13	31	2	0	2	3
22 075	PLAQUEMINES PARISH	1	2	13	13	31	1	2	5	3
22 077	POINTE COUPEE PARISH	1	1	33	33	32	2	3	=	4
22 079	RAPIDES PARISH	1	2	13	13	31	2	0	2	=
22 081	RED RIVER PARISH	1	1	13	13	22	2	0	2	2
22 083	RICHLAND PARISH	1	1	21	21	32	2	0	3	=
22 085	SABINE PARISH	1	2	13	13	31	1	0	2	=
22 087	ST. BERNARD PARISH	1	1	13	13	33	1	3	5	2
22 089	ST. CHARLES PARISH	1	1	23	23	33	1	3	5	=
22 091	ST. HELENA PARISH	1	2	13	13	13	2	0	2	2
22 093	ST. JAMES PARISH	1	1	23	23	33	2	0	3	=
22 095	ST. JOHN THE BAPTIST PARISH	1	1	33	33	33	1	3	5	=
22 097	ST. LANDRY PARISH	1	1	31	31	32	1	0	2	3
22 099	ST. MARTIN PARISH	1	1	13	22	33	2	2	=	3
22 101	ST. MARY PARISH	1	1	13	13	31	2	3	=	3

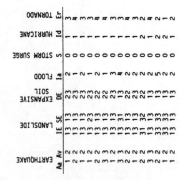

FIPS	County	Aa	Av	IE	SE	DE	la	S	Pd	Er
21 211	SHELBY COUNTY	1	2	13	13	23	2	0	1	3
21 213	SIMPSON COUNTY	2	2	13	13	23	=	0	1	=
21 215	SPENCER COUNTY	2	2	13	13	23	2	0	1	3
21 217	TAYLOR COUNTY	2	2	13	13	22	1	0	1	3
21 219	TODD COUNTY	2	3	11	13	22	3	0	1	=
21 221	TRIGG COUNTY	3	3	13	13	13	=	0	1	3
21 223	TRIMBLE COUNTY	3	2	13	13	23	2	0	1	=
21 225	UNION COUNTY	2	2	31	31	13	2	0	2	3
21 227	WARREN COUNTY	1	2	13	13	22	2	0	1	=
21 229	WASHINGTON COUNTY	2	2	13	13	23	2	0	1	2
21 231	WAYNE COUNTY	3	3	32	32	13	2	0	1	=
21 233	WEBSTER COUNTY	3	3	33	33	13	5	0	2	2
21 235	WHITLEY COUNTY	3	3	33	33	13	2	0	2	=
21 237	WOLFE COUNTY	2	2	13	13	13	2	0	1	2
21 239	WOODFORD COUNTY	1	2	13	13	13	2	0	1	2

MARYLAND

Code	County	Aa	Av	IE	SE	DE	Ia	S	Id	Er
24 001	ALLEGANY COUNTY	1	1	23	33	13	1	0	2	1
24 003	ANNE ARUNDEL COUNTY	1	1	32	32	13	1	2	4	2
24 005	BALTIMORE COUNTY	1	2	13	21	21	1	2	3	1
24 009	CALVERT COUNTY	1	1	13	13	13	1	2	4	2
24 011	CAROLINE COUNTY	1	1	13	13	13	1	0	4	2
24 013	CARROLL COUNTY	1	2	13	13	13	1	0	3	1
24 015	CECIL COUNTY	1	2	13	13	13	1	2	4	2
24 017	CHARLES COUNTY	1	1	31	31	22	1	0	4	2
24 019	DORCHESTER COUNTY	1	1	13	13	13	2	2	4	2
24 021	FREDERICK COUNTY	1	2	13	13	13	1	0	3	1
24 023	GARRETT COUNTY	1	1	22	32	22	1	0	2	1
24 025	HARFORD COUNTY	1	2	13	13	13	1	2	3	1
24 027	HOWARD COUNTY	1	2	13	21	13	1	0	4	2
24 029	KENT COUNTY	1	1	21	21	21	1	0	4	1
24 031	MONTGOMERY COUNTY	1	2	32	32	13	2	2	3	2
24 033	PRINCE GEORGE'S COUNTY	1	2	13	13	13	2	0	3	2
24 035	QUEEN ANNE'S COUNTY	1	1	13	13	13	1	0	4	2
24 037	ST. MARY'S COUNTY	2	1	13	21	21	1	2	4	2
24 039	SOMERSET COUNTY	2	1	31	31	31	3	2	4	2
24 041	TALBOT COUNTY	2	1	21	21	21	1	2	4	2
24 043	WASHINGTON COUNTY	2	1	13	13	32	1	2	2	1
24 045	WICOMICO COUNTY	2	1	13	13	13	2	2	4	1
24 047	WORCESTER COUNTY	1	1	13	13	13	1	2	4	2
24 510	BALTIMORE CITY	1	2	31	31	31	1	2	3	2

MASSACHUSSETTS

Code	County	Aa	Av	IE	SE	DE	Ia	S	Id	Er
25 001	BARNSTABLE COUNTY	3	3	13	13	13	1	3	5	1
25 003	BERKSHIRE COUNTY	3	3	21	21	13	3	0	5	2
25 005	BRISTOL COUNTY	3	3	13	13	13	1	2	5	1
25 007	DUKES COUNTY	3	3	13	13	13	3	0	5	2
25 009	ESSEX COUNTY	3	3	13	13	13	1	3	3	2
25 011	FRANKLIN COUNTY	3	3	21	21	13	2	0	3	2
25 013	HAMPDEN COUNTY	3	3	13	13	13	2	0	3	2
25 015	HAMPSHIRE COUNTY	3	3	13	13	13	2	0	3	2
25 017	MIDDLESEX COUNTY	3	3	21	32	13	2	0	4	2
25 019	NANTUCKET COUNTY	3	3	13	13	13	5	3	5	1
25 021	NORFOLK COUNTY	3	3	13	13	13	1	2	4	1
25 023	PLYMOUTH COUNTY	3	3	13	21	13	2	3	5	2
25 025	SUFFOLK COUNTY	3	3	13	21	13	1	3	4	1
25 027	WORCESTER COUNTY	3	3	13	31	13	2	0	3	2

(LOUISIANA, continued)

Code	Parish	Aa	Av	IE	SE	DE	Ia	S	Id	Er
22 103	ST. TAMMANY PARISH	1	1	13	21	13	1	2	4	4
22 105	TANGIPAHOA PARISH	1	1	13	21	13	1	2	4	4
22 107	TENSAS PARISH	1	2	13	33	31	2	0	3	4
22 109	TERREBONNE PARISH	1	1	13	13	31	3	3	5	2
22 111	UNION PARISH	1	2	13	13	13	2	0	2	3
22 113	VERMILION PARISH	1	1	13	13	31	2	3	4	4
22 115	VERNON PARISH	1	1	13	13	13	1	0	3	4
22 117	WASHINGTON PARISH	1	1	13	13	13	3	0	4	4
22 119	WEBSTER PARISH	1	2	13	13	31	1	0	2	4
22 121	WEST BATON ROUGE PARISH	1	1	22	22	31	2	1	4	4
22 123	WEST CARROLL PARISH	1	2	13	13	31	1	0	2	4
22 125	WEST FELICIANA PARISH	1	1	13	13	31	2	0	3	4
22 127	WINN PARISH	1	2	13	13	32	2	0	3	4

MAINE

Code	County	Aa	Av	IE	SE	DE	Ia	S	Id	Er
23 001	ANDROSCOGGIN COUNTY	3	3	13	13	21	3	0	2	1
23 003	AROOSTOOK COUNTY	3	3	13	13	13	2	0	2	1
23 005	CUMBERLAND COUNTY	3	3	21	32	22	3	3	2	1
23 007	FRANKLIN COUNTY	3	3	31	32	21	2	0	2	1
23 009	HANCOCK COUNTY	3	3	13	13	21	1	3	2	1
23 011	KENNEBEC COUNTY	3	3	13	21	22	2	0	2	1
23 013	KNOX COUNTY	3	3	21	31	23	1	3	2	1
23 015	LINCOLN COUNTY	3	3	31	31	13	2	3	2	1
23 017	OXFORD COUNTY	3	3	21	22	21	1	0	2	1
23 019	PENOBSCOT COUNTY	3	3	31	22	21	1	0	2	1
23 021	PISCATAQUIS COUNTY	3	3	21	21	13	2	0	2	1
23 023	SAGADAHOC COUNTY	3	3	13	21	21	2	3	2	1
23 025	SOMERSET COUNTY	3	3	21	31	21	1	0	2	1
23 027	WALDO COUNTY	3	3	13	13	21	2	0	2	1
23 029	WASHINGTON COUNTY	3	3	31	13	21	2	3	2	1
23 031	YORK COUNTY	3	3	31	32	21	2	3	3	1

MICHIGAN

Right-hand county list:

Code	County
26 103	MARQUETTE COUNTY
26 105	MASON COUNTY
26 107	MECOSTA COUNTY
26 109	MENOMINEE COUNTY
26 111	MIDLAND COUNTY
26 113	MISSAUKEE COUNTY
26 115	MONROE COUNTY
26 117	MONTCALM COUNTY
26 119	MONTMORENCY COUNTY
26 121	MUSKEGON COUNTY
26 123	NEWAYGO COUNTY
26 125	OAKLAND COUNTY
26 127	OCEANA COUNTY
26 129	OGEMAW COUNTY
26 131	ONTONAGON COUNTY
26 133	OSCEOLA COUNTY
26 135	OSCODA COUNTY
26 137	OTSEGO COUNTY
26 139	OTTAWA COUNTY
26 141	PRESQUE ISLE COUNTY
26 143	ROSCOMMON COUNTY
26 145	SAGINAW COUNTY
26 147	ST. CLAIR COUNTY
26 149	ST. JOSEPH COUNTY
26 151	SANILAC COUNTY
26 153	SCHOOLCRAFT COUNTY
26 155	SHIAWASSEE COUNTY
26 157	TUSCOLA COUNTY
26 159	VAN BUREN COUNTY
26 161	WASHTENAW COUNTY
26 163	WAYNE COUNTY
26 165	WEXFORD COUNTY

Left-hand county list:

Code	County
26 001	ALCONA COUNTY
26 003	ALGER COUNTY
26 005	ALLEGAN COUNTY
26 007	ALPENA COUNTY
26 009	ANTRIM COUNTY
26 011	ARENAC COUNTY
26 013	BARAGA COUNTY
26 015	BARRY COUNTY
26 017	BAY COUNTY
26 019	BENZIE COUNTY
26 021	BERRIEN COUNTY
26 023	BRANCH COUNTY
26 025	CALHOUN COUNTY
26 027	CASS COUNTY
26 029	CHARLEVOIX COUNTY
26 031	CHEBOYGAN COUNTY
26 033	CHIPPEWA COUNTY
26 035	CLARE COUNTY
26 037	CLINTON COUNTY
26 039	CRAWFORD COUNTY
26 041	DELTA COUNTY
26 043	DICKINSON COUNTY
26 045	EATON COUNTY
26 047	EMMET COUNTY
26 049	GENESEE COUNTY
26 051	GLADWIN COUNTY
26 053	GOGEBIC COUNTY
26 055	GRAND TRAVERSE COUNTY
26 057	GRATIOT COUNTY
26 059	HILLSDALE COUNTY
26 061	HOUGHTON COUNTY
26 063	HURON COUNTY
26 065	INGHAM COUNTY
26 067	IONIA COUNTY
26 069	IOSCO COUNTY
26 071	IRON COUNTY
26 073	ISABELLA COUNTY
26 075	JACKSON COUNTY
26 077	KALAMAZOO COUNTY
26 079	KALKASKA COUNTY
26 081	KENT COUNTY
26 083	KEWEENAW COUNTY
26 085	LAKE COUNTY
26 087	LAPEER COUNTY
26 089	LEELANAU COUNTY
26 091	LENAWEE COUNTY
26 093	LIVINGSTON COUNTY
26 095	LUCE COUNTY
26 097	MACKINAC COUNTY
26 099	MACOMB COUNTY
26 101	MANISTEE COUNTY

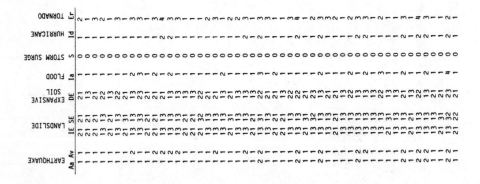

MINNESOTA

FIPS	County	EARTHQUAKE Aa	EARTHQUAKE Av	LANDSLIDE IE	LANDSLIDE SE	EXPANSIVE SOIL DE	FLOOD la	STORM SURGE S	HURRICANE Id	TORNADO Er
27 001	AITKIN COUNTY	1	1	13	13	13	3	0	0	4
27 003	ANOKA COUNTY	1	1	13	13	13	2	0	0	4
27 005	BECKER COUNTY	1	1	13	13	13	1	0	0	1
27 007	BELTRAMI COUNTY	1	1	13	13	31	1	0	0	2
27 009	BENTON COUNTY	1	1	13	13	13	2	0	0	3
27 011	BIG STONE COUNTY	1	1	13	13	22	1	0	0	4
27 013	BLUE EARTH COUNTY	1	1	13	13	13	2	0	0	4
27 015	BROWN COUNTY	1	1	13	13	13	1	0	0	3
27 017	CARLTON COUNTY	1	1	31	31	21	1	0	0	4
27 019	CARVER COUNTY	1	1	13	13	13	2	0	0	3
27 021	CASS COUNTY	1	1	13	13	13	3	0	0	3
27 023	CHIPPEWA COUNTY	1	1	13	13	13	1	0	0	2
27 025	CHISAGO COUNTY	1	1	13	13	13	2	0	0	4
27 027	CLAY COUNTY	1	1	13	13	31	3	0	0	1
27 029	CLEARWATER COUNTY	1	1	13	13	13	1	0	0	1
27 031	COOK COUNTY	1	1	13	13	13	1	0	0	1
27 033	COTTONWOOD COUNTY	1	1	13	13	22	1	0	0	3
27 035	CROW WING COUNTY	1	1	13	13	13	3	0	0	3
27 037	DAKOTA COUNTY	1	1	13	13	13	2	0	0	4
27 039	DODGE COUNTY	1	1	13	13	13	1	0	0	2
27 041	DOUGLAS COUNTY	1	1	13	13	13	2	0	0	4
27 043	FARIBAULT COUNTY	1	1	13	21	21	1	0	0	4
27 045	FILLMORE COUNTY	1	1	13	13	13	3	0	0	4
27 047	FREEBORN COUNTY	1	1	13	13	21	2	0	0	4
27 049	GOODHUE COUNTY	1	1	13	13	13	3	0	0	4
27 051	GRANT COUNTY	1	1	13	13	13	1	0	0	1
27 053	HENNEPIN COUNTY	1	1	13	13	13	3	0	0	3
27 055	HOUSTON COUNTY	1	1	13	13	13	3	0	0	4
27 057	HUBBARD COUNTY	1	1	13	13	13	2	0	0	2
27 059	ISANTI COUNTY	1	1	13	13	21	2	0	0	3
27 061	ITASCA COUNTY	1	1	13	13	31	2	0	0	4
27 063	JACKSON COUNTY	1	1	13	13	13	1	0	0	3
27 065	KANABEC COUNTY	1	1	13	13	21	2	0	0	3
27 067	KANDIYOHI COUNTY	1	1	13	13	13	2	0	0	3
27 069	KITTSON COUNTY	1	1	13	13	32	2	0	0	1
27 071	KOOCHICHING COUNTY	1	1	13	13	21	1	0	0	2
27 073	LAC QUI PARLE COUNTY	1	1	13	13	13	1	0	0	3
27 075	LAKE COUNTY	1	1	13	13	32	1	0	0	2
27 077	LAKE OF THE WOODS COUNTY	1	1	13	13	21	2	0	0	1
27 079	LE SUEUR COUNTY	1	1	13	13	13	2	0	0	3
27 081	LINCOLN COUNTY	1	1	13	13	13	1	0	0	3
27 083	LYON COUNTY	1	1	13	13	13	1	0	0	3
27 085	MCLEOD COUNTY	1	1	13	13	13	2	0	0	1
27 087	MAHNOMEN COUNTY	1	1	13	13	31	1	0	0	1
27 089	MARSHALL COUNTY	1	1	13	13	21	3	0	0	4
27 091	MARTIN COUNTY	1	1	13	13	13	1	0	0	3
27 093	MEEKER COUNTY	1	1	13	13	13	2	0	0	3
27 095	MILLE LACS COUNTY	1	1	13	13	21	2	0	0	3
27 097	MORRISON COUNTY	1	1	13	13	13	2	0	0	3
27 099	MOWER COUNTY	1	1	13	13	13	2	0	0	2
27 101	MURRAY COUNTY	1	1	13	13	13	2	0	0	3
27 103	NICOLLET COUNTY	1	1	13	13	13	3	0	0	3
27 105	NOBLES COUNTY	1	1	13	13	13	1	0	0	1
27 107	NORMAN COUNTY	1	1	13	13	31	1	0	0	1
27 109	OLMSTED COUNTY	1	1	13	13	22	2	0	0	2
27 111	OTTER TAIL COUNTY	1	1	13	13	13	1	0	0	3
27 113	PENNINGTON COUNTY	1	1	13	13	21	2	0	0	1
27 115	PINE COUNTY	1	1	13	13	13	2	0	0	3
27 117	PIPESTONE COUNTY	1	1	13	13	13	1	0	0	3
27 119	POLK COUNTY	1	1	13	13	13	2	0	0	2
27 121	POPE COUNTY	1	1	13	13	13	1	0	0	2
27 123	RAMSEY COUNTY	1	1	13	13	13	2	0	0	4
27 125	RED LAKE COUNTY	1	1	13	13	22	1	0	0	1
27 127	REDWOOD COUNTY	1	1	13	13	13	1	0	0	3
27 129	RENVILLE COUNTY	1	1	13	13	13	1	0	0	3
27 131	RICE COUNTY	1	1	13	13	13	2	0	0	3
27 133	ROCK COUNTY	1	1	13	13	13	1	0	0	3
27 135	ROSEAU COUNTY	1	1	13	13	31	2	0	0	1
27 137	ST. LOUIS COUNTY	1	1	13	13	21	2	0	0	4
27 139	SCOTT COUNTY	1	1	13	13	13	2	0	0	2
27 141	SHERBURNE COUNTY	1	1	13	13	13	2	0	0	3
27 143	SIBLEY COUNTY	1	1	13	13	13	1	0	0	3
27 145	STEARNS COUNTY	1	1	13	13	13	2	0	0	3
27 147	STEELE COUNTY	1	1	13	13	13	1	0	0	3
27 149	STEVENS COUNTY	1	1	13	13	13	1	0	0	1
27 151	SWIFT COUNTY	1	1	13	13	13	1	0	0	2
27 153	TODD COUNTY	1	1	13	13	13	2	0	0	2
27 155	TRAVERSE COUNTY	1	1	13	13	13	1	0	0	1
27 157	WABASHA COUNTY	1	1	13	13	13	2	0	0	4
27 159	WADENA COUNTY	1	1	13	13	13	1	0	0	2
27 161	WASECA COUNTY	1	1	13	13	21	1	0	0	2
27 163	WASHINGTON COUNTY	1	1	13	13	13	2	0	0	2
27 165	WATONWAN COUNTY	1	1	13	13	13	1	0	0	1
27 167	WILKIN COUNTY	1	1	13	21	21	3	0	0	1
27 169	WINONA COUNTY	1	1	13	13	13	2	0	0	3
27 171	WRIGHT COUNTY	1	1	13	13	13	2	0	0	3
27 173	YELLOW MEDICINE COUNTY	1	1	13	13	13	3	0	0	3

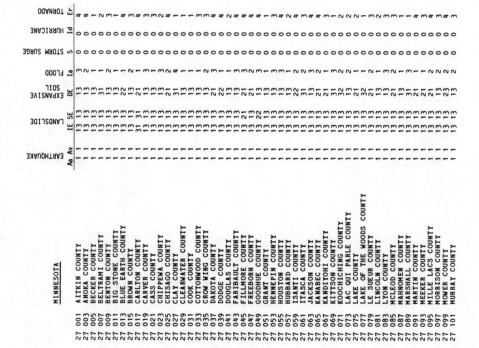

MISSISSIPPI (counties 001–101)

FIPS	County	EARTHQUAKE Aa	Av	LANDSLIDE IE	SE	EXPANSIVE SOIL DE	FLOOD Ia	STORM SURGE S	HURRICANE Id	TORNADO Er
28 001	ADAMS COUNTY	2	2	22	33	31	3	0	3	5
28 003	ALCORN COUNTY	2	2	13	13	13	1	0	2	5
28 005	AMITE COUNTY	1	1	13	13	31	1	0	2	5
28 007	ATTALA COUNTY	1	2	13	13	13	1	0	2	5
28 009	BENTON COUNTY	2	2	13	13	31	1	0	2	5
28 011	BOLIVAR COUNTY	2	2	13	32	32	3	0	2	5
28 013	CALHOUN COUNTY	2	2	13	13	31	1	0	2	5
28 015	CARROLL COUNTY	2	2	22	32	31	2	0	2	5
28 017	CHICKASAW COUNTY	2	2	13	13	31	1	0	2	3
28 019	CHOCTAW COUNTY	1	1	13	13	31	1	0	3	3
28 021	CLAIBORNE COUNTY	2	2	23	32	32	3	0	3	=
28 023	CLARKE COUNTY	2	2	21	31	31	1	0	2	=
28 025	CLAY COUNTY	2	2	13	13	31	1	0	2	=
28 027	COAHOMA COUNTY	3	3	13	32	32	3	0	2	5
28 029	COPIAH COUNTY	1	1	13	13	31	1	0	2	3
28 031	COVINGTON COUNTY	1	=	22	32	32	1	0	2	=
28 033	DE SOTO COUNTY	1	1	13	13	31	1	0	2	=
28 035	FORREST COUNTY	1	1	13	13	31	=	0	5	=
28 037	FRANKLIN COUNTY	2	1	21	31	31	1	0	2	=
28 039	GEORGE COUNTY	1	2	13	13	13	2	0	2	5
28 041	GREENE COUNTY	2	2	13	13	31	2	3	2	=
28 043	GRENADA COUNTY	2	2	22	32	31	2	0	2	3
28 045	HANCOCK COUNTY	1	2	13	13	13	1	3	5	=
28 047	HARRISON COUNTY	1	1	31	33	33	1	3	5	=
28 049	HINDS COUNTY	2	2	22	32	31	2	0	3	=
28 051	HOLMES COUNTY	2	2	13	13	31	2	0	2	=
28 053	HUMPHREYS COUNTY	2	2	13	13	31	2	0	2	=
28 055	ISSAQUENA COUNTY	2	2	13	13	31	3	0	2	5
28 057	ITAWAMBA COUNTY	2	2	13	13	31	1	0	2	=
28 059	JACKSON COUNTY	1	1	13	13	13	1	3	5	=
28 061	JASPER COUNTY	2	2	22	32	31	1	0	2	=
28 063	JEFFERSON COUNTY	2	2	22	32	31	1	0	3	=
28 065	JEFFERSON DAVIS COUNTY	1	=	13	13	32	1	0	2	=
28 067	JONES COUNTY	2	1	13	13	31	2	0	2	=
28 069	KEMPER COUNTY	2	2	22	32	31	1	0	2	=
28 071	LAFAYETTE COUNTY	1	1	13	13	31	1	0	2	=
28 073	LAMAR COUNTY	1	2	13	13	31	1	0	5	=
28 075	LAUDERDALE COUNTY	2	2	13	13	32	1	0	2	=
28 077	LAWRENCE COUNTY	1	1	13	13	31	2	0	2	=
28 079	LEAKE COUNTY	1	1	13	13	31	1	0	2	=
28 081	LEE COUNTY	2	2	13	13	13	1	0	2	=
28 083	LEFLORE COUNTY	2	2	22	32	31	2	0	2	=
28 085	LINCOLN COUNTY	1	1	13	13	31	1	0	2	=
28 087	LOWNDES COUNTY	2	2	22	32	32	1	0	2	5
28 089	MADISON COUNTY	2	2	13	13	31	2	0	3	=
28 091	MARION COUNTY	1	1	13	13	32	1	0	2	=
28 093	MARSHALL COUNTY	3	3	13	13	13	1	0	2	5
28 095	MONROE COUNTY	2	2	23	33	31	2	0	2	5
28 097	MONTGOMERY COUNTY	1	1	13	13	31	1	0	2	=
28 099	NESHOBA COUNTY	1	2	13	13	31	1	0	2	=
28 101	NEWTON COUNTY	1	2	21	31	31	2	0	3	=

MISSISSIPPI (counties 103–163)

FIPS	County	EARTHQUAKE Aa	Av	LANDSLIDE IE	SE	EXPANSIVE SOIL DE	FLOOD Ia	STORM SURGE S	HURRICANE Id	TORNADO Er
28 103	NOXUBEE COUNTY	1	1	13	13	33	2	0	3	=
28 105	OKTIBBEHA COUNTY	2	2	13	13	32	1	0	2	5
28 107	PANOLA COUNTY	3	1	22	32	31	1	0	2	5
28 109	PEARL RIVER COUNTY	1	1	13	13	31	1	0	2	5
28 111	PERRY COUNTY	1	1	13	13	31	2	0	2	3
28 113	PIKE COUNTY	2	2	13	13	31	1	0	2	=
28 115	PONTOTOC COUNTY	2	2	13	13	31	1	0	2	=
28 117	PRENTISS COUNTY	2	2	13	13	31	2	0	2	=
28 119	QUITMAN COUNTY	3	3	22	32	32	1	0	3	=
28 121	RANKIN COUNTY	1	2	22	32	32	2	0	3	=
28 123	SCOTT COUNTY	1	1	13	13	31	1	0	2	3
28 125	SHARKEY COUNTY	2	2	13	13	31	3	0	2	=
28 127	SIMPSON COUNTY	1	1	13	13	31	1	0	2	=
28 129	SMITH COUNTY	2	2	13	13	31	1	0	2	=
28 131	STONE COUNTY	1	1	13	13	31	1	0	2	=
28 133	SUNFLOWER COUNTY	2	2	22	32	31	2	0	2	5
28 135	TALLAHATCHIE COUNTY	3	3	13	32	32	2	0	2	5
28 137	TATE COUNTY	2	2	23	33	32	1	0	2	=
28 139	TIPPAH COUNTY	2	2	13	13	13	1	0	2	=
28 141	TISHOMINGO COUNTY	=	=	31	33	31	1	0	2	5
28 143	TUNICA COUNTY	3	3	13	13	13	1	0	2	=
28 145	UNION COUNTY	2	2	13	13	31	1	0	2	=
28 147	WALTHALL COUNTY	1	1	13	13	32	=	0	2	=
28 149	WARREN COUNTY	1	2	21	31	31	2	0	3	=
28 151	WASHINGTON COUNTY	2	2	13	13	33	2	0	2	=
28 153	WAYNE COUNTY	1	1	13	13	31	2	0	2	=
28 155	WEBSTER COUNTY	1	1	13	13	31	1	0	2	=
28 157	WILKINSON COUNTY	2	2	22	32	31	3	0	2	5
28 159	WINSTON COUNTY	1	1	13	13	31	1	0	2	5
28 161	YALOBUSHA COUNTY	2	2	21	13	13	1	0	2	=
28 163	YAZOO COUNTY	1	2	22	32	31	2	0	2	=

Hazard risk data by county — column headers:

- EARTHQUAKE: Aa, Av
- LANDSLIDE: IE, SE
- EXPANSIVE SOIL: DE
- FLOOD: Ia
- STORM SURGE: S
- HURRICANE: Id
- TORNADO: Er

MISSOURI

FIPS	County	Aa	Av	IE	SE	DE	Ia	S	Id	Er
29 001	ADAIR COUNTY	1	2	13	13	33	1	0	1	4
29 003	ANDREW COUNTY	3	3	13	23	33	3	0	1	5
29 005	ATCHISON COUNTY	3	3	13	21	31	3	0	1	3
29 007	AUDRAIN COUNTY	1	2	13	13	13	2	0	1	4
29 009	BARRY COUNTY	2	2	13	13	13	1	0	1	3
29 011	BARTON COUNTY	2	2	13	13	31	2	0	1	3
29 013	BATES COUNTY	2	2	13	13	31	2	0	1	3
29 015	BENTON COUNTY	5	5	13	13	13	1	0	1	3
29 017	BOLLINGER COUNTY	2	2	13	13	21	5	0	1	5
29 019	BOONE COUNTY	3	3	13	23	32	5	0	1	4
29 021	BUCHANAN COUNTY	5	5	13	13	32	5	0	1	4
29 023	BUTLER COUNTY	2	2	13	13	33	2	0	1	3
29 025	CALDWELL COUNTY	2	2	13	23	33	2	0	1	3
29 027	CALLAWAY COUNTY	2	2	13	13	32	2	0	1	3
29 029	CAMDEN COUNTY	5	5	13	13	13	2	0	1	4
29 031	CAPE GIRARDEAU COUNTY	2	2	13	23	23	5	0	1	4
29 033	CARROLL COUNTY	2	2	13	13	33	5	0	1	3
29 035	CARTER COUNTY	2	2	13	13	13	2	0	1	3
29 037	CASS COUNTY	2	2	13	13	13	2	0	1	3
29 039	CEDAR COUNTY	2	2	13	13	13	1	0	1	3
29 041	CHARITON COUNTY	3	1	13	23	33	2	0	1	4
29 043	CHRISTIAN COUNTY	2	2	13	13	32	1	0	1	5
29 045	CLARK COUNTY	1	2	13	31	13	2	0	1	3
29 047	CLAY COUNTY	3	3	13	13	32	3	0	1	4
29 049	CLINTON COUNTY	3	3	13	13	31	5	0	1	3
29 051	COLE COUNTY	2	2	13	13	13	1	0	1	3
29 053	COOPER COUNTY	2	2	13	22	23	2	0	1	3
29 055	CRAWFORD COUNTY	3	3	13	13	32	2	0	1	3
29 057	DADE COUNTY	2	2	13	13	13	1	0	1	3
29 059	DALLAS COUNTY	2	2	13	13	13	1	0	1	3
29 061	DAVIESS COUNTY	2	2	13	23	33	2	0	1	4
29 063	DE KALB COUNTY	3	3	13	13	33	5	0	1	3
29 065	DENT COUNTY	2	2	13	13	13	1	0	1	3
29 067	DOUGLAS COUNTY	5	2	13	13	21	1	0	1	5
29 069	DUNKLIN COUNTY	5	5	13	31	31	5	0	1	3
29 071	FRANKLIN COUNTY	2	2	13	31	32	3	0	1	3
29 073	GASCONADE COUNTY	2	2	13	13	33	1	0	1	3
29 075	GENTRY COUNTY	2	2	13	23	33	2	0	1	4
29 077	GREENE COUNTY	2	2	13	13	13	1	0	1	5
29 079	GRUNDY COUNTY	2	2	13	23	33	2	0	1	5
29 081	HARRISON COUNTY	3	3	13	21	13	5	0	1	3
29 083	HENRY COUNTY	2	2	13	13	32	1	0	1	3
29 085	HICKORY COUNTY	2	2	13	13	13	1	0	1	3
29 087	HOLT COUNTY	3	3	13	23	33	3	0	1	3
29 089	HOWARD COUNTY	3	1	13	13	32	2	0	1	3
29 091	HOWELL COUNTY	2	2	13	13	13	1	0	1	5
29 093	IRON COUNTY	3	3	13	23	23	2	0	1	5
29 095	JACKSON COUNTY	4	3	13	31	32	5	0	1	5
29 097	JASPER COUNTY	2	2	13	21	31	2	0	1	4
29 099	JEFFERSON COUNTY	4	2	13	13	22	3	0	1	3
29 101	JOHNSON COUNTY	2	2	13	13	31	2	0	1	3
29 103	KNOX COUNTY	2	2	13	13	32	1	0	1	4
29 105	LACLEDE COUNTY	2	2	13	13	13	1	0	1	5
29 107	LAFAYETTE COUNTY	2	2	13	23	31	3	0	1	4
29 109	LAWRENCE COUNTY	2	2	13	13	31	1	0	1	4
29 111	LEWIS COUNTY	1	2	13	21	31	2	0	1	3
29 113	LINCOLN COUNTY	2	2	13	31	32	3	0	1	3
29 115	LINN COUNTY	2	2	13	13	13	1	0	1	4
29 117	LIVINGSTON COUNTY	2	2	13	13	13	3	0	1	3
29 119	McDONALD COUNTY	1	2	13	13	13	2	0	1	3
29 121	MACON COUNTY	5	2	13	13	33	2	0	1	5
29 123	MADISON COUNTY	5	5	13	13	13	2	0	1	5
29 125	MARIES COUNTY	2	2	13	23	13	2	0	1	3
29 127	MARION COUNTY	2	2	13	23	31	2	0	1	3
29 129	MERCER COUNTY	2	2	13	13	13	5	0	1	3
29 131	MILLER COUNTY	2	5	13	33	13	1	0	1	3
29 133	MISSISSIPPI COUNTY	5	5	13	31	33	5	0	1	5
29 135	MONITEAU COUNTY	2	2	13	21	13	1	0	1	3
29 137	MONROE COUNTY	2	2	13	23	32	2	0	1	3
29 139	MONTGOMERY COUNTY	2	2	13	13	32	3	0	1	3
29 141	MORGAN COUNTY	3	2	13	13	13	2	0	1	3
29 143	NEW MADRID COUNTY	5	5	13	31	22	2	0	1	5
29 145	NEWTON COUNTY	1	2	13	13	13	2	0	1	3
29 147	NODAWAY COUNTY	2	2	13	13	33	2	0	1	4
29 149	OREGON COUNTY	2	2	13	23	32	1	0	1	3
29 151	OSAGE COUNTY	2	2	13	13	31	1	0	1	3
29 153	OZARK COUNTY	3	2	13	13	31	1	0	1	3
29 155	PEMISCOT COUNTY	5	5	13	32	32	3	0	1	5
29 157	PERRY COUNTY	5	5	13	13	22	2	0	1	3
29 159	PETTIS COUNTY	2	2	13	13	22	1	0	1	3
29 161	PHELPS COUNTY	1	2	13	13	13	2	0	1	3
29 163	PIKE COUNTY	2	2	13	32	32	3	0	1	3
29 165	PLATTE COUNTY	3	3	13	13	13	2	0	1	5
29 167	POLK COUNTY	2	2	13	13	13	1	0	1	3
29 169	PULASKI COUNTY	1	2	13	13	13	1	0	1	3
29 171	PUTNAM COUNTY	2	2	13	13	13	2	0	1	4
29 173	RALLS COUNTY	2	2	13	31	31	3	0	1	3
29 175	RANDOLPH COUNTY	2	2	13	23	32	2	0	1	5
29 177	RAY COUNTY	2	2	13	23	33	5	0	1	3
29 179	REYNOLDS COUNTY	4	4	13	13	13	1	0	1	3
29 181	RIPLEY COUNTY	5	5	13	13	33	2	0	1	5
29 183	ST. CHARLES COUNTY	4	4	13	13	13	3	0	1	3
29 185	ST. CLAIR COUNTY	2	2	13	13	22	1	0	1	3
29 186	STE. GENEVIEVE COUNTY	4	2	13	13	13	2	0	1	3
29 187	ST. FRANCOIS COUNTY	4	4	13	23	13	1	0	1	3
29 189	ST. LOUIS COUNTY	4	3	13	13	32	5	0	1	5
29 195	SALINE COUNTY	3	1	13	23	33	5	0	1	5
29 197	SCHUYLER COUNTY	1	2	13	13	33	1	0	1	4
29 199	SCOTLAND COUNTY	1	2	13	13	33	1	0	1	3
29 201	SCOTT COUNTY	5	5	13	31	33	2	0	1	3
29 203	SHANNON COUNTY	3	3	13	13	13	1	0	1	3
29 205	SHELBY COUNTY	5	2	13	32	32	2	0	1	4
29 207	STODDARD COUNTY	5	5	13	13	22	5	0	1	4
29 209	STONE COUNTY	1	2	13	13	13	1	0	1	3
29 211	SULLIVAN COUNTY	1	2	13	13	31	1	0	1	4

MONTANA

FIPS	County	EARTHQUAKE Aa	EARTHQUAKE Av	LANDSLIDE IE	LANDSLIDE SE	EXPANSIVE SOIL DE	FLOOD Ia	STORM SURGE s	HURRICANE Id	TORNADO Er
30 001	BEAVERHEAD COUNTY	7	7	31	31	22	2	0	0	1
30 003	BIG HORN COUNTY	1	3	31	32	32	3	0	0	1
30 005	BLAINE COUNTY	1	2	31	31	31	1	0	0	1
30 007	BROADWATER COUNTY	5	5	31	33	31	1	0	0	1
30 009	CARBON COUNTY	1	1	31	32	32	4	0	0	1
30 011	CARTER COUNTY	3	3	21	21	23	2	0	0	2
30 013	CASCADE COUNTY	1	1	31	33	22	2	0	0	2
30 015	CHOUTEAU COUNTY	1	1	13	13	22	1	0	0	1
30 017	CUSTER COUNTY	1	1	13	13	13	2	0	0	1
30 019	DANIELS COUNTY	1	1	13	13	31	1	0	0	1
30 021	DAWSON COUNTY	1	1	31	31	22	2	0	0	1
30 023	DEER LODGE COUNTY	3	3	31	31	31	1	0	0	1
30 025	FALLON COUNTY	1	1	13	13	32	2	0	0	1
30 027	FERGUS COUNTY	3	3	13	33	33	2	0	0	1
30 029	FLATHEAD COUNTY	7	7	21	31	31	2	0	0	1
30 031	GALLATIN COUNTY	3	3	31	31	31	1	0	0	1
30 033	GARFIELD COUNTY	2	2	21	21	21	2	0	0	2
30 035	GLACIER COUNTY	2	3	31	31	21	1	0	0	1
30 037	GOLDEN VALLEY COUNTY	3	3	21	21	31	2	0	0	1
30 039	GRANITE COUNTY	5	5	31	31	13	1	0	0	1
30 041	HILL COUNTY	3	3	31	31	31	1	0	0	1
30 043	JEFFERSON COUNTY	3	3	31	31	32	2	0	0	1
30 045	JUDITH BASIN COUNTY	1	1	13	13	23	2	0	0	1
30 047	LAKE COUNTY	2	2	31	31	13	1	0	0	1
30 049	LEWIS AND CLARK COUNTY	7	7	31	31	31	1	0	0	2
30 051	LIBERTY COUNTY	3	3	13	13	31	2	0	0	1
30 053	LINCOLN COUNTY	2	2	31	31	13	1	0	0	1
30 055	MCCONE COUNTY	3	3	13	13	21	1	0	0	1
30 057	MADISON COUNTY	7	7	21	21	31	2	0	0	2
30 059	MEAGHER COUNTY	7	7	31	31	13	2	0	0	1
30 061	MINERAL COUNTY	2	3	13	13	21	1	0	0	1
30 063	MISSOULA COUNTY	3	3	21	21	31	2	0	0	1
30 065	MUSSELSHELL COUNTY	3	3	13	13	32	2	0	0	1
30 067	PARK COUNTY	7	7	31	31	32	1	0	0	2
30 069	PETROLEUM COUNTY	1	1	21	21	33	2	0	0	1
30 071	PHILLIPS COUNTY	2	2	13	13	31	1	0	0	1
30 073	PONDERA COUNTY	2	3	31	31	13	2	0	0	1
30 075	POWDER RIVER COUNTY	1	1	21	21	21	1	0	0	2
30 077	POWELL COUNTY	3	3	13	13	31	1	0	0	1
30 079	PRAIRIE COUNTY	1	1	31	31	31	1	0	0	2
30 081	RAVALLI COUNTY	4	4	31	31	31	2	0	0	1
30 083	RICHLAND COUNTY	1	1	13	13	21	1	0	0	2
30 085	ROOSEVELT COUNTY	1	1	31	31	31	1	0	0	2
30 087	ROSEBUD COUNTY	1	1	31	31	21	2	0	0	2
30 089	SANDERS COUNTY	1	1	13	13	32	1	0	0	1
30 091	SHERIDAN COUNTY	3	3	13	13	33	2	0	0	1
30 093	SILVER BOW COUNTY	5	5	21	22	13	2	0	0	1
30 095	STILLWATER COUNTY	5	5	31	31	21	1	0	0	1
30 097	SWEET GRASS COUNTY	3	3	31	31	32	2	0	0	1
30 099	TETON COUNTY	3	3	21	21	31	1	0	0	1
30 101	TOOLE COUNTY	1	2	13	13	22	2	0	0	1

FIPS	County	EARTHQUAKE Aa	EARTHQUAKE Av	LANDSLIDE IE	LANDSLIDE SE	EXPANSIVE SOIL DE	FLOOD Ia	STORM SURGE s	HURRICANE Id	TORNADO Er
29 213	TANEY COUNTY	2	2	13	13	13	2	0	1	4
29 215	TEXAS COUNTY	3	3	13	13	13	1	0	1	4
29 217	VERNON COUNTY	2	2	13	13	13	2	0	1	3
29 219	WARREN COUNTY	2	3	13	23	32	2	0	1	3
29 221	WASHINGTON COUNTY	3	5	13	13	22	1	0	1	3
29 223	WAYNE COUNTY	5	5	13	13	21	2	0	—	4
29 225	WEBSTER COUNTY	2	2	13	13	13	1	0	1	4
29 227	WORTH COUNTY	2	2	13	13	33	1	0	—	4
29 229	WRIGHT COUNTY	2	2	13	13	33	2	0	1	4
29 510	ST. LOUIS CITY	3	3	23	23	33	1	0	—	4

MONTANA (continued)

		County	EARTHQUAKE		LANDSLIDE		EXPANSIVE SOIL	FLOOD	STORM SURGE	HURRICANE	TORNADO
			Aa	Av	IE	SE	DE	Ia	s	Id	Er
30	103	TREASURE COUNTY	2	1	13	32	31	1	0	0	1
30	105	VALLEY COUNTY	1	1	33	33	32	2	0	0	2
30	107	WHEATLAND COUNTY	3	4	13	31	31	2	0	0	1
30	109	WIBAUX COUNTY	1	1	13	31	31	1	0	0	1
30	111	YELLOWSTONE COUNTY	1	3	13	32	31	1	0	0	1
30	113	YELLOWSTONE NATIONAL PARK	7	7	21	31	31	1	0	0	1

NEBRASKA

		County	EARTHQUAKE		LANDSLIDE		EXPANSIVE SOIL	FLOOD	STORM SURGE	HURRICANE	TORNADO
			Aa	Av	IE	SE	DE	Ia	s	Id	Er
31	001	ADAMS COUNTY	1	2	13	13	33	2	0	0	5
31	003	ANTELOPE COUNTY	2	1	13	13	21	1	0	0	4
31	005	ARTHUR COUNTY	1	1	13	13	13	2	0	0	2
31	007	BANNER COUNTY	1	1	13	13	21	1	0	0	1
31	009	BLAINE COUNTY	1	1	13	13	13	2	0	0	1
31	011	BOONE COUNTY	1	1	13	13	22	1	0	0	1
31	013	BOX BUTTE COUNTY	2	1	13	13	23	2	0	0	3
31	015	BOYD COUNTY	1	1	13	13	13	2	0	0	1
31	017	BROWN COUNTY	2	2	21	31	23	2	0	0	2
31	019	BUFFALO COUNTY	2	2	13	13	33	2	0	0	3
31	021	BURT COUNTY	1	1	13	13	32	1	0	0	4
31	023	BUTLER COUNTY	2	2	13	13	22	1	0	0	4
31	025	CASS COUNTY	3	2	21	32	22	2	0	0	5
31	027	CEDAR COUNTY	1	1	13	31	13	1	0	0	4
31	029	CHASE COUNTY	2	1	13	13	23	1	0	0	4
31	031	CHERRY COUNTY	2	2	13	13	32	2	0	0	3
31	033	CHEYENNE COUNTY	2	1	13	13	22	2	0	0	2
31	035	CLAY COUNTY	2	2	13	13	23	2	0	0	2
31	037	COLFAX COUNTY	1	1	13	13	21	1	0	0	5
31	039	CUMING COUNTY	2	2	13	13	23	2	0	0	4
31	041	CUSTER COUNTY	1	1	13	13	31	1	0	0	3
31	043	DAKOTA COUNTY	1	1	13	13	23	5	0	0	1
31	045	DAWES COUNTY	2	1	13	13	32	1	0	0	3
31	047	DAWSON COUNTY	2	2	13	13	31	1	0	0	2
31	049	DEUEL COUNTY	1	1	13	13	23	2	0	0	4
31	051	DIXON COUNTY	1	1	21	31	32	4	0	0	4
31	053	DODGE COUNTY	2	2	13	13	31	2	0	0	4
31	055	DOUGLAS COUNTY	3	3	13	13	31	4	0	0	5
31	057	DUNDY COUNTY	1	1	13	13	31	2	0	0	3
31	059	FILLMORE COUNTY	1	1	13	13	23	2	0	0	5
31	061	FRANKLIN COUNTY	1	1	13	13	31	1	0	0	5
31	063	FRONTIER COUNTY	1	1	13	13	31	1	0	0	3
31	065	FURNAS COUNTY	3	3	21	13	33	2	0	0	4
31	067	GAGE COUNTY	1	1	13	13	21	2	0	0	2
31	069	GARDEN COUNTY	1	1	13	13	23	1	0	0	3
31	071	GARFIELD COUNTY	1	1	13	13	23	1	0	0	3
31	073	GOSPER COUNTY	1	1	13	13	31	1	0	0	1
31	075	GRANT COUNTY	1	1	13	13	31	1	0	0	1
31	077	GREELEY COUNTY	1	1	13	13	33	2	0	0	4
31	079	HALL COUNTY	1	1	13	13	21	1	0	0	4
31	081	HAMILTON COUNTY	1	1	13	13	23	1	0	0	4
31	083	HARLAN COUNTY	1	1	13	13	31	2	0	0	5
31	085	HAYES COUNTY	3	3	13	21	23	2	0	0	3
31	087	HITCHCOCK COUNTY	3	3	21	31	13	2	0	0	3
31	089	HOLT COUNTY	1	1	13	13	21	1	0	0	3
31	091	HOOKER COUNTY	1	1	13	13	31	1	0	0	1
31	093	HOWARD COUNTY	1	1	21	31	23	1	0	0	1
31	095	JEFFERSON COUNTY	3	3	13	13	23	2	0	0	4
31	097	JOHNSON COUNTY	3	3	13	13	33	2	0	0	4
31	099	KEARNEY COUNTY	1	1	13	13	32	1	0	0	4
31	101	KEITH COUNTY	1	1	13	13	22	1	0	0	2

509

NEVADA

	EARTHQUAKE		LANDSLIDE		EXPANSIVE SOIL	FLOOD	STORM SURGE	HURRICANE	TORNADO
	Aa	Av	IE	SE	DE	Ia	S	Id	Er
32 001 CHURCHILL COUNTY	7	7	13	13	31	1	0	0	1
32 003 CLARK COUNTY	5	6	13	13	22	3	0	0	1
32 005 DOUGLAS COUNTY	5	5	13	21	23	1	0	0	1
32 007 ELKO COUNTY	7	7	31	31	22	2	0	0	1
32 009 ESMERALDA COUNTY	4	5	31	31	23	1	0	0	1
32 011 EUREKA COUNTY	5	5	31	31	22	2	0	0	1
32 013 HUMBOLDT COUNTY	7	7	31	31	22	1	0	0	1
32 015 LANDER COUNTY	7	4	13	21	22	1	0	0	1
32 017 LINCOLN COUNTY	7	7	13	13	21	1	0	0	1
32 019 LYON COUNTY	7	7	31	31	31	1	0	0	1
32 021 MINERAL COUNTY	7	7	31	31	22	1	0	0	1
32 023 NYE COUNTY	7	7	31	31	22	1	0	0	1
32 027 PERSHING COUNTY	6	6	13	13	22	1	0	0	1
32 029 STOREY COUNTY	7	7	31	31	22	3	0	0	1
32 031 WASHOE COUNTY	7	7	31	31	22	1	0	0	1
32 033 WHITE PINE COUNTY	3	4	32	32	23	1	0	0	1
32 510 CARSON CITY	6	6							

NEW HAMPSHIRE

	EARTHQUAKE		LANDSLIDE		EXPANSIVE SOIL	FLOOD	STORM SURGE	HURRICANE	TORNADO
	Aa	Av	IE	SE	DE	Ia	S	Id	Er
33 001 BELKNAP COUNTY	3	3	13	13	13	1	0	2	2
33 003 CARROLL COUNTY	3	3	32	32	13	2	0	2	2
33 005 CHESHIRE COUNTY	3	3	13	31	13	1	0	3	2
33 007 COOS COUNTY	3	3	31	31	13	3	0	2	1
33 009 GRAFTON COUNTY	3	3	32	32	13	3	0	3	2
33 011 HILLSBOROUGH COUNTY	3	3	13	13	13	2	0	3	2
33 013 MERRIMACK COUNTY	3	3	13	21	13	2	0	3	2
33 015 ROCKINGHAM COUNTY	3	3	21	31	21	2	3	3	2
33 017 STRAFFORD COUNTY	3	3	13	31	21	1	0	3	2
33 019 SULLIVAN COUNTY	3	3	13	31	13	2	0	2	2

(NEBRASKA, continued)

	EARTHQUAKE		LANDSLIDE		EXPANSIVE SOIL	FLOOD	STORM SURGE	HURRICANE	TORNADO
	Aa	Av	IE	SE	DE	Ia	S	Id	Er
31 103 KEYA PAHA COUNTY	1	1	13	32	31	1	0	0	3
31 105 KIMBALL COUNTY	2	2	13	13	32	1	0	0	1
31 107 KNOX COUNTY	3	3	21	13	32	2	0	0	5
31 109 LANCASTER COUNTY	1	1	13	13	33	2	0	0	3
31 111 LINCOLN COUNTY	1	1	13	13	22	1	0	0	2
31 113 LOGAN COUNTY	1	1	13	13	21	1	0	0	2
31 115 LOUP COUNTY	2	2	13	13	13	2	0	0	2
31 117 MCPHERSON COUNTY	2	2	13	13	22	1	0	0	2
31 119 MADISON COUNTY	2	2	13	13	31	2	0	0	1
31 121 MERRICK COUNTY	1	1	13	13	13	2	0	0	5
31 123 MORRILL COUNTY	3	3	13	13	33	1	0	0	2
31 125 NANCE COUNTY	2	2	13	13	33	1	0	0	2
31 127 NEMAHA COUNTY	2	2	13	13	23	2	0	0	2
31 129 NUCKOLLS COUNTY	3	3	13	13	33	1	0	0	2
31 131 OTOE COUNTY	3	3	13	13	31	2	0	0	5
31 133 PAWNEE COUNTY	3	3	13	13	33	1	0	0	2
31 135 PERKINS COUNTY	1	1	13	13	23	2	0	0	2
31 137 PHELPS COUNTY	2	2	13	13	22	2	0	0	2
31 139 PIERCE COUNTY	2	2	13	13	33	1	0	0	2
31 141 PLATTE COUNTY	1	1	13	13	33	2	0	0	3
31 143 POLK COUNTY	1	1	13	13	13	1	0	0	5
31 145 RED WILLOW COUNTY	3	3	13	13	23	1	0	0	5
31 147 RICHARDSON COUNTY	1	1	31	21	33	2	0	0	1
31 149 ROCK COUNTY	2	2	13	13	13	1	0	0	5
31 151 SALINE COUNTY	2	2	13	13	23	2	0	0	2
31 153 SARPY COUNTY	3	3	13	13	23	2	0	0	3
31 155 SAUNDERS COUNTY	2	2	13	13	33	1	0	0	1
31 157 SCOTTS BLUFF COUNTY	2	2	13	13	13	2	0	0	5
31 159 SEWARD COUNTY	2	2	13	13	33	2	0	0	2
31 161 SHERIDAN COUNTY	2	2	13	13	13	1	0	0	2
31 163 SHERMAN COUNTY	2	2	13	13	23	1	0	0	3
31 165 SIOUX COUNTY	2	2	13	13	31	2	0	0	3
31 167 STANTON COUNTY	2	2	13	13	31	2	0	0	5
31 169 THAYER COUNTY	2	2	13	13	32	1	0	0	5
31 171 THOMAS COUNTY	2	2	13	13	21	1	0	0	2
31 173 THURSTON COUNTY	2	2	13	13	13	2	0	0	5
31 175 VALLEY COUNTY	1	1	13	13	23	2	0	0	2
31 177 WASHINGTON COUNTY	2	2	13	13	31	2	0	0	3
31 179 WAYNE COUNTY	2	2	13	13	32	1	0	0	3
31 181 WEBSTER COUNTY	1	1	13	13	21	1	0	0	5
31 183 WHEELER COUNTY	1	1	13	13		1	0	0	5
31 185 YORK COUNTY	2	2	13	13	33	1	0	0	5

NEW JERSEY

	County	EARTHQUAKE Aa Av	LANDSLIDE IE SE	EXPANSIVE SOIL DE	FLOOD Ia	STORM SURGE S	HURRICANE Pd	TORNADO Er
34 001	ATLANTIC COUNTY	1 2	13 13	13	2	2	4	1
34 003	BERGEN COUNTY	3 3	31 31	13	2	0	4	1
34 005	BURLINGTON COUNTY	2 2	13 21	13	2	2	4	1
34 007	CAMDEN COUNTY	2 2	13 13	13	1	0	4	1
34 009	CAPE MAY COUNTY	1 2	13 13	13	2	3	4	1
34 011	CUMBERLAND COUNTY	2 3	13 13	13	3	2	4	1
34 013	ESSEX COUNTY	3 3	21 31	13	3	1	4	1
34 015	GLOUCESTER COUNTY	2 2	13 13	13	2	0	4	2
34 017	HUDSON COUNTY	3 3	32 32	13	2	1	4	1
34 019	HUNTERDON COUNTY	3 3	13 31	13	2	0	3	2
34 021	MERCER COUNTY	3 3	13 13	13	4	0	3	1
34 023	MIDDLESEX COUNTY	3 3	13 13	13	3	2	4	2
34 025	MONMOUTH COUNTY	2 2	13 31	13	3	2	4	1
34 027	MORRIS COUNTY	3 3	21 31	13	3	0	3	1
34 029	OCEAN COUNTY	3 3	13 13	13	5	2	4	2
34 031	PASSAIC COUNTY	3 3	13 13	13	2	0	3	1
34 033	SALEM COUNTY	2 2	13 21	13	3	2	4	1
34 035	SOMERSET COUNTY	3 3	13 13	13	4	0	3	1
34 037	SUSSEX COUNTY	3 3	21 31	13	2	0	3	2
34 039	UNION COUNTY	3 3	21 31	13	4	1	3	1
34 041	WARREN COUNTY	3 3	13 13	13	3	0	3	2

NEW MEXICO

	County	EARTHQUAKE Aa Av	LANDSLIDE IE SE	EXPANSIVE SOIL DE	FLOOD Ia	STORM SURGE S	HURRICANE Pd	TORNADO Er
35 001	BERNALILLO COUNTY	3 3	31 31	23	5	0	0	1
35 003	CATRON COUNTY	3 3	31 31	31	1	0	0	1
35 005	CHAVES COUNTY	2 2	13 21	13	2	0	0	3
35 007	COLFAX COUNTY	2 2	31 32	22	1	0	0	4
35 009	CURRY COUNTY	1 1	13 13	31	1	0	0	2
35 011	DE BACA COUNTY	2 2	13 13	21	2	0	0	1
35 013	DONA ANA COUNTY	2 2	31 31	13	2	0	0	2
35 015	EDDY COUNTY	1 2	31 31	31	2	0	0	1
35 017	GRANT COUNTY	3 3	31 31	31	2	0	0	2
35 019	GUADALUPE COUNTY	2 2	13 21	21	1	0	0	3
35 021	HARDING COUNTY	2 1	13 23	32	2	0	0	1
35 023	HIDALGO COUNTY	3 3	13 13	13	2	0	0	1
35 025	LEA COUNTY	1 1	13 13	13	1	0	0	1
35 027	LINCOLN COUNTY	3 3	31 31	23	2	0	0	1
35 028	LOS ALAMOS COUNTY	2 2	31 31	31	1	0	0	3
35 029	LUNA COUNTY	2 2	13 32	32	2	0	0	4
35 031	MCKINLEY COUNTY	2 2	31 31	31	1	0	0	1
35 033	MORA COUNTY	2 2	31 31	22	2	0	0	2
35 035	OTERO COUNTY	2 2	13 13	13	2	0	0	1
35 037	QUAY COUNTY	1 1	13 22	21	3	0	0	1
35 039	RIO ARRIBA COUNTY	3 3	31 32	13	2	0	0	1
35 041	ROOSEVELT COUNTY	1 1	13 13	13	1	0	0	1
35 043	SANDOVAL COUNTY	3 3	31 31	31	1	0	0	1
35 045	SAN JUAN COUNTY	2 2	31 31	31	2	0	0	2
35 047	SAN MIGUEL COUNTY	2 3	31 31	32	3	0	0	1
35 049	SANTA FE COUNTY	3 3	31 31	22	3	0	0	1
35 051	SIERRA COUNTY	3 3	31 31	22	2	0	0	1
35 053	SOCORRO COUNTY	3 3	31 31	22	3	0	0	1
35 055	TAOS COUNTY	3 3	31 31	31	1	0	0	1
35 057	TORRANCE COUNTY	1 1	13 13	21	1	0	0	1
35 059	UNION COUNTY	3 3	31 31	31	1	0	0	1
35 061	VALENCIA COUNTY	3 3	31 32	23	2	0	0	3

NEW YORK

		EARTHQUAKE		LANDSLIDE		EXPANSIVE SOIL	FLOOD	STORM SURGE	HURRICANE	TORNADO
		Aa	Av	IE	SE	DE	Ia	S	Id	Er
36	001	ALBANY COUNTY	3 3	21	31	13	2	0	2	1
36	003	ALLEGANY COUNTY	2 3	21	21	13	2	0	2	1
36	005	BRONX COUNTY	2 2	23	13	13	1	2	4	-
36	007	BROOME COUNTY	2 2	23	23	13	5	0	2	1
36	009	CATTARAUGUS COUNTY	2 2	13	21	13	2	0	2	-
36	011	CAYUGA COUNTY	2 2	21	21	13	2	0	2	2
36	013	CHAUTAUQUA COUNTY	1 2	13	13	13	4	0	2	1
36	015	CHEMUNG COUNTY	2 2	13	21	13	4	0	2	2
36	017	CHENANGO COUNTY	2 3	21	31	13	3	0	3	1
36	019	CLINTON COUNTY	3 3	13	13	13	1	0	2	1
36	021	COLUMBIA COUNTY	3 3	31	31	13	2	0	3	2
36	023	CORTLAND COUNTY	2 2	21	31	13	3	0	2	1
36	025	DELAWARE COUNTY	3 3	31	31	13	3	0	3	1
36	027	DUTCHESS COUNTY	3 3	31	31	13	2	0	2	2
36	029	ERIE COUNTY	2 3	22	22	13	3	2	3	1
36	031	ESSEX COUNTY	3 3	22	32	13	1	0	2	1
36	033	FRANKLIN COUNTY	3 3	21	31	13	1	0	2	1
36	035	FULTON COUNTY	3 3	13	22	13	2	0	2	1
36	037	GENESEE COUNTY	3 3	31	32	13	2	0	2	1
36	039	GREENE COUNTY	3 3	13	13	13	3	0	2	1
36	041	HAMILTON COUNTY	3 3	13	22	13	1	0	2	1
36	043	HERKIMER COUNTY	3 3	13	13	13	2	0	2	1
36	045	JEFFERSON COUNTY	3 3	13	13	13	2	2	2	1
36	047	KINGS COUNTY	2 2	13	13	13	2	2	4	1
36	049	LEWIS COUNTY	3 3	13	21	13	2	0	2	1
36	051	LIVINGSTON COUNTY	2 2	21	21	13	2	0	2	1
36	053	MADISON COUNTY	2 2	13	21	13	2	0	2	1
36	055	MONROE COUNTY	2 3	23	23	13	3	2	3	1
36	057	MONTGOMERY COUNTY	3 3	21	31	13	2	0	2	1
36	059	NASSAU COUNTY	2 2	32	31	13	1	2	4	1
36	061	NEW YORK COUNTY	2 2	31	31	13	2	2	4	1
36	063	NIAGARA COUNTY	2 2	21	21	13	2	2	3	1
36	065	ONEIDA COUNTY	3 3	21	31	13	3	0	2	1
36	067	ONONDAGA COUNTY	2 2	21	23	13	3	0	2	1
36	069	ONTARIO COUNTY	2 2	32	32	13	1	0	2	2
36	071	ORANGE COUNTY	3 3	31	31	13	1	2	3	1
36	073	ORLEANS COUNTY	3 3	13	13	13	2	4	4	1
36	075	OSWEGO COUNTY	3 3	32	32	13	2	2	4	1
36	077	OTSEGO COUNTY	3 3	13	31	13	2	0	2	1
36	079	PUTNAM COUNTY	3 3	31	31	13	2	0	2	2
36	081	QUEENS COUNTY	3 3	32	32	13	1	2	4	1
36	083	RENSSELAER COUNTY	3 3	31	31	13	3	2	3	1
36	085	RICHMOND COUNTY	3 3	13	13	13	1	2	4	1
36	087	ROCKLAND COUNTY	3 3	31	31	13	1	2	4	-
36	089	ST. LAWRENCE COUNTY	3 3	31	31	21	1	2	3	1
36	091	SARATOGA COUNTY	3 3	31	13	13	2	0	2	1
36	093	SCHENECTADY COUNTY	3 3	13	13	13	2	0	2	1
36	095	SCHOHARIE COUNTY	1 2	13	13	13	2	0	2	1
36	097	SCHUYLER COUNTY	1 2	21	21	13	2	0	2	1
36	099	SENECA COUNTY	1 2	21	21	13	2	0	2	1
36	101	STEUBEN COUNTY	1 2	13	13	13	4	0	2	1

		EARTHQUAKE		LANDSLIDE		EXPANSIVE SOIL	FLOOD	STORM SURGE	HURRICANE	TORNADO
		Aa	Av	IE	SE	DE	Ia	S	Id	Er
36	103	SUFFOLK COUNTY	3 3	13	31	13	2	2	5	1
36	105	SULLIVAN COUNTY	3 3	22	22	13	3	0	3	1
36	107	TIOGA COUNTY	1 2	21	21	13	3	0	2	1
36	109	TOMPKINS COUNTY	2 2	21	21	13	3	0	2	1
36	111	ULSTER COUNTY	3 3	31	32	13	2	0	2	2
36	113	WARREN COUNTY	3 3	13	13	13	1	0	2	1
36	115	WASHINGTON COUNTY	2 2	21	22	22	3	0	2	1
36	117	WAYNE COUNTY	3 3	31	31	13	2	2	4	1
36	119	WESTCHESTER COUNTY	3 3	31	31	13	3	0	2	1
36	121	WYOMING COUNTY	3 3	13	13	13	2	0	2	1
36	123	YATES COUNTY	2 2	21	21	13	2	0	2	1

NORTH CAROLINA

	County	EARTHQUAKE Aa	Av	LANDSLIDE IE	SE	EXPANSIVE SOIL DE	FLOOD Ia	STORM SURGE S	HURRICANE Id	TORNADO Er
37 001	ALAMANCE COUNTY	1	2	13	23	22	1	0	3	2
37 003	ALEXANDER COUNTY	3	3	22	32	23	1	0	2	2
37 005	ALLEGHANY COUNTY	3	3	33	33	13	1	0	2	1
37 007	ANSON COUNTY	3	3	13	23	32	1	0	3	2
37 009	ASHE COUNTY	3	3	33	33	13	1	0	2	1
37 011	AVERY COUNTY	3	3	23	33	13	1	0	2	2
37 013	BEAUFORT COUNTY	1	1	13	13	23	2	2	6	2
37 015	BERTIE COUNTY	1	1	13	13	22	1	2	5	1
37 017	BLADEN COUNTY	2	2	13	13	21	2	0	4	3
37 019	BRUNSWICK COUNTY	2	2	13	13	21	1	3	5	1
37 021	BUNCOMBE COUNTY	3	3	31	33	13	3	0	2	2
37 023	BURKE COUNTY	3	3	31	31	22	2	0	2	2
37 025	CABARRUS COUNTY	3	3	32	32	32	1	0	2	2
37 027	CALDWELL COUNTY	3	3	23	33	22	3	0	2	2
37 029	CAMDEN COUNTY	1	1	13	13	13	1	2	5	1
37 031	CARTERET COUNTY	1	1	13	13	13	1	2	6	2
37 033	CASWELL COUNTY	1	2	23	23	23	1	0	3	2
37 035	CATAWBA COUNTY	3	3	32	32	23	1	0	2	2
37 037	CHATHAM COUNTY	2	2	23	23	22	1	0	3	3
37 039	CHEROKEE COUNTY	3	3	32	33	13	1	0	2	2
37 041	CHOWAN COUNTY	1	1	13	13	22	1	2	5	1
37 043	CLAY COUNTY	3	3	23	33	13	1	0	2	2
37 045	CLEVELAND COUNTY	3	3	31	31	23	1	0	2	2
37 047	COLUMBUS COUNTY	2	2	13	13	21	1	0	5	2
37 049	CRAVEN COUNTY	1	1	13	13	22	2	2	5	3
37 051	CUMBERLAND COUNTY	2	2	13	13	22	3	0	4	3
37 053	CURRITUCK COUNTY	1	1	13	13	21	1	2	5	1
37 055	DARE COUNTY	1	1	13	13	21	1	2	6	1
37 057	DAVIDSON COUNTY	2	2	13	23	31	1	0	3	2
37 059	DAVIE COUNTY	2	2	13	23	23	1	0	2	2
37 061	DUPLIN COUNTY	1	2	13	13	21	2	0	5	3
37 063	DURHAM COUNTY	1	2	22	23	32	1	0	3	2
37 065	EDGECOMBE COUNTY	1	1	13	13	13	3	0	4	2
37 067	FORSYTH COUNTY	2	2	21	23	31	2	0	2	2
37 069	FRANKLIN COUNTY	1	1	13	13	22	1	0	3	2
37 071	GASTON COUNTY	3	3	33	33	23	1	0	2	2
37 073	GATES COUNTY	1	1	13	13	22	1	2	4	1
37 075	GRAHAM COUNTY	3	3	33	33	13	2	0	2	2
37 077	GRANVILLE COUNTY	1	1	13	23	31	1	0	3	2
37 079	GREENE COUNTY	1	1	13	13	13	1	0	4	3
37 081	GUILFORD COUNTY	2	2	22	23	31	2	0	3	2
37 083	HALIFAX COUNTY	1	1	13	13	22	2	0	4	2
37 085	HARNETT COUNTY	2	2	13	13	21	2	0	3	3
37 087	HAYWOOD COUNTY	3	3	33	33	13	3	0	2	2
37 089	HENDERSON COUNTY	3	3	21	33	21	2	0	2	2
37 091	HERTFORD COUNTY	1	1	13	13	22	1	2	4	1
37 093	HOKE COUNTY	2	2	13	13	13	1	0	3	3
37 095	HYDE COUNTY	1	1	13	13	21	2	2	6	1
37 097	IREDELL COUNTY	3	3	31	31	31	1	0	2	2
37 099	JACKSON COUNTY	3	3	33	33	13	2	0	2	2
37 101	JOHNSTON COUNTY	1	2	13	13	22	1	0	4	3

	County	EARTHQUAKE Aa	Av	LANDSLIDE IE	SE	EXPANSIVE SOIL DE	FLOOD Ia	STORM SURGE S	HURRICANE Id	TORNADO Er
37 103	JONES COUNTY	1	1	13	13	22	1	2	5	3
37 105	LEE COUNTY	2	2	22	23	31	1	0	3	3
37 107	LENOIR COUNTY	1	1	13	13	13	2	0	5	3
37 109	LINCOLN COUNTY	3	3	31	31	23	1	0	2	2
37 111	MCDOWELL COUNTY	3	3	13	33	22	1	0	2	2
37 113	MACON COUNTY	3	3	32	32	13	2	0	2	2
37 115	MADISON COUNTY	3	3	33	33	13	1	0	2	2
37 117	MARTIN COUNTY	1	1	13	13	22	1	2	5	2
37 119	MECKLENBURG COUNTY	3	3	32	32	31	3	0	2	2
37 121	MITCHELL COUNTY	3	3	23	33	13	1	0	2	2
37 123	MONTGOMERY COUNTY	2	2	13	23	31	1	0	3	2
37 125	MOORE COUNTY	2	2	21	23	32	1	0	3	3
37 127	NASH COUNTY	1	1	13	13	22	1	0	4	3
37 129	NEW HANOVER COUNTY	2	2	13	13	22	1	2	5	1
37 131	NORTHAMPTON COUNTY	1	1	13	13	22	1	0	4	1
37 133	ONSLOW COUNTY	1	2	13	13	13	2	2	6	2
37 135	ORANGE COUNTY	1	2	21	23	21	1	0	3	2
37 137	PAMLICO COUNTY	1	1	13	13	21	2	2	6	2
37 139	PASQUOTANK COUNTY	1	1	13	13	13	1	2	5	1
37 141	PENDER COUNTY	2	2	13	13	21	2	2	5	2
37 143	PERQUIMANS COUNTY	1	1	13	13	22	1	2	5	1
37 145	PERSON COUNTY	1	2	23	23	21	1	0	3	2
37 147	PITT COUNTY	1	1	13	13	21	2	0	5	3
37 149	POLK COUNTY	3	3	23	33	23	1	0	2	2
37 151	RANDOLPH COUNTY	2	2	22	23	31	1	0	3	3
37 153	RICHMOND COUNTY	3	3	13	21	31	2	0	3	3
37 155	ROBESON COUNTY	2	2	13	13	13	3	0	4	3
37 157	ROCKINGHAM COUNTY	2	2	22	31	23	1	0	2	2
37 159	ROWAN COUNTY	3	3	13	23	31	1	0	2	2
37 161	RUTHERFORD COUNTY	3	3	21	33	23	1	0	2	2
37 163	SAMPSON COUNTY	2	2	13	13	21	1	0	4	3
37 165	SCOTLAND COUNTY	2	2	13	13	13	2	0	3	3
37 167	STANLY COUNTY	3	3	33	33	31	1	0	2	2
37 169	STOKES COUNTY	2	2	22	32	23	1	0	2	2
37 171	SURRY COUNTY	3	3	23	33	22	1	0	2	1
37 173	SWAIN COUNTY	3	3	33	33	13	1	0	2	2
37 175	TRANSYLVANIA COUNTY	3	3	23	33	13	2	0	2	2
37 177	TYRRELL COUNTY	1	1	13	13	13	1	2	6	1
37 179	UNION COUNTY	3	3	13	23	31	2	0	3	2
37 181	VANCE COUNTY	1	1	13	13	23	1	0	3	2
37 183	WAKE COUNTY	1	2	21	21	31	2	0	3	3
37 185	WARREN COUNTY	1	1	13	13	23	1	0	3	2
37 187	WASHINGTON COUNTY	1	1	13	13	21	1	2	5	1
37 189	WATAUGA COUNTY	3	3	31	33	13	1	0	2	2
37 191	WAYNE COUNTY	1	2	13	13	13	1	0	4	3
37 193	WILKES COUNTY	3	3	23	33	23	1	0	2	2
37 195	WILSON COUNTY	1	1	13	13	21	1	0	4	3
37 197	YADKIN COUNTY	2	2	21	31	21	1	0	2	2
37 199	YANCEY COUNTY	3	3	32	33	13	1	0	2	2

NORTH DAKOTA

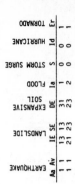

Code	County	EARTHQUAKE		LANDSLIDE		EXPANSIVE SOIL	FLOOD	STORM SURGE	HURRICANE	TORNADO
		Aa	Av	IE	SE	DE	Ia	S	Id	Er
38 001	ADAMS COUNTY	1	1	13	13	23	2	0	0	2
38 003	BARNES COUNTY	1	1	13	13	23	2	0	0	1
38 005	BENSON COUNTY	1	1	13	21	32	2	0	0	2
38 007	BILLINGS COUNTY	1	1	13	31	31	2	0	0	1
38 009	BOTTINEAU COUNTY	1	1	13	13	31	4	0	0	1
38 011	BOWMAN COUNTY	1	1	13	11	23	3	0	0	1
38 013	BURKE COUNTY	1	1	13	23	32	3	0	0	1
38 015	BURLEIGH COUNTY	1	1	13	13	23	1	0	0	2
38 017	CASS COUNTY	1	1	13	13	31	1	0	0	1
38 019	CAVALIER COUNTY	1	1	13	13	23	3	0	0	1
38 021	DICKEY COUNTY	1	1	13	13	31	2	0	0	1
38 023	DIVIDE COUNTY	1	1	13	13	23	4	0	0	2
38 025	DUNN COUNTY	1	1	13	13	31	2	0	0	1
38 027	EDDY COUNTY	1	1	13	13	22	1	0	0	2
38 029	EMMONS COUNTY	1	1	13	13	31	1	0	0	2
38 031	FOSTER COUNTY	1	1	31	31	23	3	0	0	2
38 033	GOLDEN VALLEY COUNTY	1	1	13	13	23	1	0	0	2
38 035	GRAND FORKS COUNTY	1	1	13	23	31	4	0	0	2
38 037	GRANT COUNTY	1	1	13	13	23	2	0	0	1
38 039	GRIGGS COUNTY	1	1	13	13	23	1	0	0	1
38 041	HETTINGER COUNTY	1	1	13	13	23	2	0	0	1
38 043	KIDDER COUNTY	1	1	13	13	23	1	0	0	1
38 045	LA MOURE COUNTY	1	1	13	13	31	4	0	0	2
38 047	LOGAN COUNTY	1	1	13	13	22	1	0	0	2
38 049	MCHENRY COUNTY	1	1	13	23	23	2	0	0	2
38 051	MCINTOSH COUNTY	1	1	13	13	31	1	0	0	2
38 053	MCKENZIE COUNTY	1	1	21	23	23	2	0	0	2
38 055	MCLEAN COUNTY	1	1	13	23	23	1	0	0	1
38 057	MERCER COUNTY	1	1	13	13	23	1	0	0	1
38 059	MORTON COUNTY	1	1	31	31	31	1	0	0	1
38 061	MOUNTRAIL COUNTY	1	1	21	31	23	4	0	0	2
38 063	NELSON COUNTY	1	1	13	13	23	1	0	0	1
38 065	OLIVER COUNTY	1	1	13	13	32	2	0	0	1
38 067	PEMBINA COUNTY	1	1	13	13	23	1	0	0	1
38 069	PIERCE COUNTY	1	1	13	13	31	2	0	0	1
38 071	RAMSEY COUNTY	1	1	31	31	31	1	0	0	2
38 073	RANSOM COUNTY	1	1	13	13	23	2	0	0	2
38 075	RENVILLE COUNTY	1	1	13	13	31	1	0	0	2
38 077	RICHLAND COUNTY	1	1	13	22	31	1	0	0	1
38 079	ROLETTE COUNTY	1	1	13	13	31	1	0	0	1
38 081	SARGENT COUNTY	1	1	13	13	23	2	0	0	1
38 083	SHERIDAN COUNTY	1	1	31	31	31	1	0	0	1
38 085	SIOUX COUNTY	1	1	13	31	31	2	0	0	1
38 087	SLOPE COUNTY	1	1	13	13	23	2	0	0	1
38 089	STARK COUNTY	1	1	31	31	31	3	0	0	1
38 091	STEELE COUNTY	1	1	13	21	31	1	0	0	1
38 093	STUTSMAN COUNTY	1	1	13	13	23	2	0	0	1
38 095	TOWNER COUNTY	1	1	13	13	32	1	0	0	1
38 097	TRAILL COUNTY	1	1	13	13	31	2	0	0	1
38 099	WALSH COUNTY	1	1	13	13	31	3	0	0	1
38 101	WARD COUNTY	1	1	31	31	23	3	0	0	2
38 103	WELLS COUNTY	1	1	13	13	31	1	0	0	1
38 105	WILLIAMS COUNTY	1	1	21	23	23	2	0	0	1

OHIO

FIPS	County	EARTHQUAKE Aa	Av	LANDSLIDE IE	SE	EXPANSIVE SOIL DE	FLOOD La	STORM SURGE S	HURRICANE Id	TORNADO Er
39 001	ADAMS COUNTY	2	2	31	31	13	5	0	1	2
39 003	ALLEN COUNTY	2	2	31	31	13	2	0	2	2
39 005	ASHLAND COUNTY	2	2	13	13	13	1	0	2	2
39 007	ASHTABULA COUNTY	2	2	31	31	21	3	0	2	2
39 009	ATHENS COUNTY	2	2	33	33	13	4	0	1	1
39 011	AUGLAIZE COUNTY	2	2	31	31	13	4	0	2	2
39 013	BELMONT COUNTY	2	2	33	33	22	3	0	1	3
39 015	BROWN COUNTY	2	2	31	31	13	3	0	2	4
39 017	BUTLER COUNTY	2	2	31	31	13	2	0	2	4
39 019	CARROLL COUNTY	2	2	31	31	21	2	0	1	2
39 021	CHAMPAIGN COUNTY	2	2	13	13	13	3	0	2	3
39 023	CLARK COUNTY	2	2	31	31	13	3	0	1	3
39 025	CLERMONT COUNTY	2	2	32	32	13	3	0	2	3
39 027	CLINTON COUNTY	2	2	13	13	13	2	0	2	2
39 029	COLUMBIANA COUNTY	2	2	33	33	21	3	0	1	2
39 031	COSHOCTON COUNTY	2	2	13	13	13	3	0	2	2
39 033	CRAWFORD COUNTY	2	2	13	13	13	3	0	2	2
39 035	CUYAHOGA COUNTY	2	2	31	31	21	1	0	1	2
39 037	DARKE COUNTY	2	2	31	31	13	4	0	2	3
39 039	DEFIANCE COUNTY	2	2	13	13	13	2	0	1	2
39 041	DELAWARE COUNTY	2	2	31	31	13	2	0	2	2
39 043	ERIE COUNTY	2	2	21	21	21	2	0	1	2
39 045	FAIRFIELD COUNTY	2	2	13	13	13	3	0	2	3
39 047	FAYETTE COUNTY	2	2	13	13	13	2	0	1	3
39 049	FRANKLIN COUNTY	2	2	13	13	13	2	0	1	3
39 051	FULTON COUNTY	2	2	22	22	21	1	0	1	4
39 053	GALLIA COUNTY	2	2	33	33	13	4	0	2	1
39 055	GEAUGA COUNTY	2	2	13	13	13	1	0	1	2
39 057	GREENE COUNTY	2	2	31	31	13	2	0	2	3
39 059	GUERNSEY COUNTY	2	2	22	22	21	2	0	1	2
39 061	HAMILTON COUNTY	2	2	33	33	13	2	0	2	3
39 063	HANCOCK COUNTY	2	2	31	31	13	2	0	2	3
39 065	HARDIN COUNTY	2	2	13	13	13	2	0	2	2
39 067	HARRISON COUNTY	2	2	32	32	21	1	0	1	2
39 069	HENRY COUNTY	2	2	13	13	13	3	0	2	2
39 071	HIGHLAND COUNTY	2	2	32	32	13	2	0	1	2
39 073	HOCKING COUNTY	2	2	33	33	13	5	0	2	1
39 075	HOLMES COUNTY	2	2	13	13	13	2	0	2	2
39 077	HURON COUNTY	2	2	13	13	13	2	0	1	3
39 079	JACKSON COUNTY	2	2	33	33	13	4	0	2	1
39 081	JEFFERSON COUNTY	2	2	22	22	21	2	0	1	2
39 083	KNOX COUNTY	2	2	13	13	13	2	0	2	3
39 085	LAKE COUNTY	2	2	31	31	21	1	0	1	2
39 087	LAWRENCE COUNTY	2	2	31	31	13	5	0	2	1
39 089	LICKING COUNTY	2	2	13	13	13	2	0	2	2
39 091	LOGAN COUNTY	2	2	31	31	13	3	0	1	3
39 093	LORAIN COUNTY	2	2	31	31	21	2	0	1	2
39 095	LUCAS COUNTY	2	2	21	21	21	2	0	1	3
39 097	MADISON COUNTY	2	2	13	13	13	2	0	2	3
39 099	MAHONING COUNTY	2	2	13	13	13	2	0	1	2
39 101	MARION COUNTY	2	2	13	13	21	2	0	2	2

FIPS	County	EARTHQUAKE Aa	Av	LANDSLIDE IE	SE	EXPANSIVE SOIL DE	FLOOD La	STORM SURGE S	HURRICANE Id	TORNADO Er
39 103	MEDINA COUNTY	2	2	13	13	13	1	0	2	2
39 105	MEIGS COUNTY	2	2	31	31	13	4	0	1	1
39 107	MERCER COUNTY	2	2	13	13	21	2	0	2	2
39 109	MIAMI COUNTY	2	2	33	33	13	3	0	2	2
39 111	MONROE COUNTY	2	2	33	33	22	2	0	1	2
39 113	MONTGOMERY COUNTY	2	2	22	22	13	5	0	2	2
39 115	MORGAN COUNTY	2	2	33	33	13	2	0	1	2
39 117	MORROW COUNTY	2	2	13	13	13	1	0	2	2
39 119	MUSKINGUM COUNTY	2	2	33	33	21	4	0	1	2
39 121	NOBLE COUNTY	2	2	31	31	13	1	0	1	2
39 123	OTTAWA COUNTY	2	2	31	31	13	2	0	1	2
39 125	PAULDING COUNTY	2	2	13	13	13	2	0	1	3
39 127	PERRY COUNTY	2	2	31	31	13	3	0	2	2
39 129	PICKAWAY COUNTY	2	2	23	23	13	3	0	2	2
39 131	PIKE COUNTY	2	2	31	31	13	5	0	1	2
39 133	PORTAGE COUNTY	2	2	13	13	13	2	0	2	2
39 135	PREBLE COUNTY	2	2	13	13	13	3	0	2	3
39 137	PUTNAM COUNTY	2	2	13	13	13	2	0	2	4
39 139	RICHLAND COUNTY	2	2	32	32	13	2	0	1	2
39 141	ROSS COUNTY	2	2	31	31	13	3	0	2	2
39 143	SANDUSKY COUNTY	2	2	22	22	21	2	0	1	2
39 145	SCIOTO COUNTY	2	2	31	31	13	5	0	2	2
39 147	SENECA COUNTY	2	2	13	13	13	2	0	1	2
39 149	SHELBY COUNTY	2	2	13	13	13	3	0	2	3
39 151	STARK COUNTY	2	2	32	32	21	2	0	1	2
39 153	SUMMIT COUNTY	2	2	13	13	13	2	0	2	2
39 155	TRUMBULL COUNTY	2	2	13	13	13	2	0	1	2
39 157	TUSCARAWAS COUNTY	2	2	33	33	21	3	0	1	2
39 159	UNION COUNTY	2	2	13	13	13	2	0	2	3
39 161	VAN WERT COUNTY	2	2	13	13	13	2	0	2	3
39 163	VINTON COUNTY	2	2	31	31	13	5	0	1	1
39 165	WARREN COUNTY	2	2	33	33	13	2	0	2	3
39 167	WASHINGTON COUNTY	2	2	33	33	13	2	0	1	2
39 169	WAYNE COUNTY	2	2	31	31	22	2	0	2	2
39 171	WILLIAMS COUNTY	2	2	13	13	13	1	0	1	2
39 173	WOOD COUNTY	2	2	13	13	13	2	0	1	2
39 175	WYANDOT COUNTY	2	2	13	13	21	1	0	2	3

OKLAHOMA

Code	County	Aa	Av	IE	SE	DE	Ia	S	Pd	Er
40 001	ADAIR COUNTY	2	2	13	13	13	2	0	1	5
40 003	ALFALFA COUNTY	2	2	13	13	13	2	0	1	5
40 005	ATOKA COUNTY	3	2	13	13	32	1	0	1	3
40 007	BEAVER COUNTY	2	2	13	13	13	2	0	1	5
40 009	BECKHAM COUNTY	2	2	13	13	13	1	0	1	5
40 011	BLAINE COUNTY	2	2	13	13	32	1	0	1	5
40 013	BRYAN COUNTY	3	2	13	13	13	4	0	1	4
40 015	CADDO COUNTY	2	2	13	13	32	1	0	1	5
40 017	CANADIAN COUNTY	3	2	13	21	13	1	0	1	5
40 019	CARTER COUNTY	3	2	13	13	13	2	0	1	5
40 021	CHEROKEE COUNTY	3	2	13	31	13	2	0	1	4
40 023	CHOCTAW COUNTY	3	2	13	13	32	3	0	2	2
40 025	CIMARRON COUNTY	1	1	13	31	21	1	0	1	6
40 027	CLEVELAND COUNTY	3	3	13	31	13	1	0	1	5
40 029	COAL COUNTY	3	2	13	32	13	1	0	1	5
40 031	COMANCHE COUNTY	2	2	13	13	21	2	0	1	4
40 033	COTTON COUNTY	2	2	13	13	21	1	0	1	4
40 035	CRAIG COUNTY	2	2	13	13	13	2	0	1	5
40 037	CREEK COUNTY	3	2	13	13	13	2	0	1	5
40 039	CUSTER COUNTY	2	2	13	13	31	3	0	1	5
40 041	DELAWARE COUNTY	2	2	13	13	13	2	0	1	4
40 043	DEWEY COUNTY	2	2	13	13	13	1	0	1	5
40 045	ELLIS COUNTY	2	2	13	13	13	1	0	1	5
40 047	GARFIELD COUNTY	2	2	13	13	22	2	0	1	5
40 049	GARVIN COUNTY	3	2	13	13	21	2	0	1	5
40 051	GRADY COUNTY	3	3	13	13	31	2	0	1	6
40 053	GRANT COUNTY	2	2	13	13	13	2	0	1	5
40 055	GREER COUNTY	2	2	13	13	21	1	0	1	5
40 057	HARMON COUNTY	2	2	13	13	13	1	0	1	5
40 059	HARPER COUNTY	2	2	13	13	13	3	0	1	5
40 061	HASKELL COUNTY	3	2	13	32	31	1	0	1	5
40 063	HUGHES COUNTY	3	2	13	23	13	2	0	1	6
40 065	JACKSON COUNTY	2	2	13	13	13	1	0	1	4
40 067	JEFFERSON COUNTY	3	2	13	21	13	3	0	1	5
40 069	JOHNSTON COUNTY	3	2	13	13	31	1	0	2	5
40 071	KAY COUNTY	2	2	13	13	23	2	0	1	6
40 073	KINGFISHER COUNTY	2	2	13	13	22	2	0	1	6
40 075	KIOWA COUNTY	2	2	13	31	13	3	0	1	5
40 077	LATIMER COUNTY	3	3	13	31	21	1	0	1	4
40 079	LE FLORE COUNTY	3	3	13	32	31	2	0	1	6
40 081	LINCOLN COUNTY	2	2	13	13	13	1	0	1	6
40 083	LOGAN COUNTY	2	2	13	13	13	2	0	1	6
40 085	LOVE COUNTY	3	2	13	21	13	2	0	1	4
40 087	MCCLAIN COUNTY	3	3	13	13	31	1	0	1	5
40 089	MCCURTAIN COUNTY	3	3	13	13	31	2	0	2	5
40 091	MCINTOSH COUNTY	3	2	13	13	13	1	0	1	6
40 093	MAJOR COUNTY	2	2	13	13	13	2	0	1	5
40 095	MARSHALL COUNTY	3	3	13	31	32	3	0	1	5
40 097	MAYES COUNTY	3	2	13	13	13	1	0	1	4
40 099	MURRAY COUNTY	3	3	13	13	13	3	0	1	6
40 101	MUSKOGEE COUNTY	3	3	13	31	31	2	0	1	5

Code	County	Aa	Av	IE	SE	DE	Ia	S	Pd	Er
40 103	NOBLE COUNTY	2	2	13	13	13	3	0	1	6
40 105	NOWATA COUNTY	2	2	13	22	21	3	0	1	5
40 107	OKFUSKEE COUNTY	2	2	13	13	13	2	0	1	6
40 109	OKLAHOMA COUNTY	3	3	13	13	31	3	0	1	6
40 111	OKMULGEE COUNTY	2	2	13	13	13	3	0	1	5
40 113	OSAGE COUNTY	2	2	13	13	13	3	0	1	5
40 115	OTTAWA COUNTY	2	2	13	13	13	3	0	1	5
40 117	PAWNEE COUNTY	2	2	13	13	13	1	0	1	6
40 119	PAYNE COUNTY	3	3	13	31	33	2	0	1	6
40 121	PITTSBURG COUNTY	3	3	13	13	13	1	0	1	6
40 123	PONTOTOC COUNTY	3	3	13	21	13	2	0	2	5
40 125	POTTAWATOMIE COUNTY	3	3	13	13	13	1	0	1	4
40 127	PUSHMATAHA COUNTY	3	2	13	13	13	2	0	1	4
40 129	ROGER MILLS COUNTY	2	2	13	13	13	1	0	1	6
40 131	ROGERS COUNTY	3	3	13	31	31	3	0	1	4
40 133	SEMINOLE COUNTY	3	3	13	23	31	2	0	1	6
40 135	SEQUOYAH COUNTY	3	2	13	13	13	2	0	1	4
40 137	STEPHENS COUNTY	3	2	13	13	13	1	0	1	5
40 139	TEXAS COUNTY	2	2	13	13	31	3	0	1	5
40 141	TILLMAN COUNTY	3	2	13	13	22	2	0	1	2
40 143	TULSA COUNTY	3	3	13	21	31	2	0	1	5
40 145	WAGONER COUNTY	2	2	13	32	32	5	0	1	5
40 147	WASHINGTON COUNTY	2	2	13	13	21	3	0	2	5
40 149	WASHITA COUNTY	2	2	13	13	13	1	0	1	5
40 151	WOODS COUNTY	2	2	13	13	13	2	0	1	5
40 153	WOODWARD COUNTY	2	2	13	13	13	1	0	1	4

OREGON

FIPS	County	EARTHQUAKE Aa	EARTHQUAKE Av	LANDSLIDE IE	LANDSLIDE SE	EXPANSIVE SOIL DE	FLOOD Ia	STORM SURGE S	HURRICANE Id	TORNADO Er
41 001	BAKER COUNTY	2	1	31	31	22	3	0	0	1
41 003	BENTON COUNTY	2	2	23	23	23	3	0	0	1
41 005	CLACKAMAS COUNTY	2	2	31	31	21	3	0	0	1
41 007	CLATSOP COUNTY	2	3	31	31	13	3	4	0	1
41 009	COLUMBIA COUNTY	2	1	31	31	13	2	0	0	1
41 011	COOS COUNTY	2	3	31	31	13	2	0	0	1
41 013	CROOK COUNTY	1	1	32	32	22	2	0	0	1
41 015	CURRY COUNTY	3	4	31	31	13	2	4	0	1
41 017	DESCHUTES COUNTY	2	1	31	31	22	3	0	0	1
41 019	DOUGLAS COUNTY	2	2	31	31	13	2	0	0	1
41 021	GILLIAM COUNTY	1	1	31	31	22	2	0	0	1
41 023	GRANT COUNTY	2	2	22	22	31	3	0	0	1
41 025	HARNEY COUNTY	2	3	31	32	21	2	0	0	1
41 027	HOOD RIVER COUNTY	2	2	31	31	22	3	4	0	1
41 029	JACKSON COUNTY	2	2	21	21	13	2	0	0	1
41 031	JEFFERSON COUNTY	2	2	31	31	21	2	0	0	1
41 033	JOSEPHINE COUNTY	2	2	23	23	13	2	0	0	1
41 035	KLAMATH COUNTY	2	2	31	31	31	2	0	0	1
41 037	LAKE COUNTY	2	2	31	31	31	2	0	0	1
41 039	LANE COUNTY	2	3	31	31	13	2	4	0	1
41 041	LINCOLN COUNTY	2	2	31	31	13	2	4	0	1
41 043	LINN COUNTY	2	2	32	32	31	2	0	0	1
41 045	MALHEUR COUNTY	1	3	31	31	31	2	0	0	1
41 047	MARION COUNTY	2	2	31	31	22	1	0	0	1
41 049	MORROW COUNTY	2	2	31	31	22	2	0	0	1
41 051	MULTNOMAH COUNTY	2	2	31	31	31	3	0	0	1
41 053	POLK COUNTY	2	2	22	22	13	2	0	0	1
41 055	SHERMAN COUNTY	2	2	31	31	31	3	0	0	1
41 057	TILLAMOOK COUNTY	2	3	31	31	13	3	4	0	1
41 059	UMATILLA COUNTY	2	2	31	31	21	2	0	0	1
41 061	UNION COUNTY	2	2	31	31	31	1	0	0	1
41 063	WALLOWA COUNTY	2	2	31	31	21	1	0	0	1
41 065	WASCO COUNTY	2	3	31	31	13	3	0	0	1
41 067	WASHINGTON COUNTY	2	2	31	31	22	2	0	0	1
41 069	WHEELER COUNTY	1	2	32	32	23	2	0	0	1
41 071	YAMHILL COUNTY	2	2	22	22	22	3	0	0	1

PENNSYLVANIA

FIPS	County	EARTHQUAKE Aa	EARTHQUAKE Av	LANDSLIDE IE	LANDSLIDE SE	EXPANSIVE SOIL DE	FLOOD Ia	STORM SURGE S	HURRICANE Id	TORNADO Er
42 001	ADAMS COUNTY	1	1	22	32	13	2	0	3	2
42 003	ALLEGHENY COUNTY	1	1	31	33	13	5	0	2	2
42 005	ARMSTRONG COUNTY	1	1	31	31	22	3	0	2	2
42 007	BEAVER COUNTY	1	1	31	31	21	1	0	2	1
42 009	BEDFORD COUNTY	1	3	23	33	13	2	0	3	2
42 011	BERKS COUNTY	2	1	23	33	13	2	0	2	1
42 013	BLAIR COUNTY	1	1	13	13	21	2	0	2	1
42 015	BRADFORD COUNTY	3	2	23	33	13	2	0	2	2
42 017	BUCKS COUNTY	3	2	32	32	13	3	0	2	2
42 019	BUTLER COUNTY	1	1	23	31	21	1	0	2	2
42 021	CAMBRIA COUNTY	1	1	23	31	13	2	0	2	2
42 023	CAMERON COUNTY	2	2	33	33	13	2	0	2	1
42 025	CARBON COUNTY	3	3	13	13	13	2	0	2	2
42 027	CENTRE COUNTY	1	1	13	13	22	4	0	2	1
42 029	CHESTER COUNTY	3	1	23	23	13	2	0	3	2
42 031	CLARION COUNTY	1	1	23	23	21	2	0	2	2
42 033	CLEARFIELD COUNTY	1	2	23	33	31	2	0	2	2
42 035	CLINTON COUNTY	1	2	13	13	13	4	0	2	2
42 037	COLUMBIA COUNTY	2	2	21	31	13	3	0	2	2
42 039	CRAWFORD COUNTY	2	2	31	31	21	3	0	2	1
42 041	CUMBERLAND COUNTY	2	1	13	13	13	3	0	2	2
42 043	DAUPHIN COUNTY	2	3	13	13	13	3	0	2	2
42 045	DELAWARE COUNTY	3	1	33	33	13	3	0	3	2
42 047	ELK COUNTY	2	2	21	21	13	2	0	2	1
42 049	ERIE COUNTY	2	1	31	31	13	2	0	2	1
42 051	FAYETTE COUNTY	1	2	13	13	21	2	0	2	2
42 053	FOREST COUNTY	1	1	33	33	13	1	0	2	1
42 055	FRANKLIN COUNTY	2	2	33	33	13	2	0	2	2
42 057	FULTON COUNTY	1	2	33	33	22	2	0	2	2
42 059	GREENE COUNTY	1	1	23	23	13	2	0	2	2
42 061	HUNTINGDON COUNTY	1	1	33	33	13	2	0	3	1
42 063	INDIANA COUNTY	1	1	33	33	21	2	0	3	2
42 065	JEFFERSON COUNTY	1	1	23	23	13	2	0	3	2
42 067	JUNIATA COUNTY	2	2	13	13	13	2	0	3	2
42 069	LACKAWANNA COUNTY	3	3	31	31	13	1	0	2	1
42 071	LANCASTER COUNTY	3	1	13	13	13	3	0	2	2
42 073	LAWRENCE COUNTY	3	3	13	13	22	3	0	2	2
42 075	LEBANON COUNTY	2	1	31	31	13	2	0	2	2
42 077	LEHIGH COUNTY	2	2	31	31	13	2	0	2	1
42 079	LUZERNE COUNTY	3	2	22	32	22	3	0	2	2
42 081	LYCOMING COUNTY	2	2	22	31	13	2	0	2	1
42 083	MCKEAN COUNTY	2	2	23	31	13	2	0	3	1
42 085	MERCER COUNTY	2	2	13	13	13	2	0	3	2
42 087	MIFFLIN COUNTY	3	3	13	13	13	3	0	3	1
42 089	MONROE COUNTY	3	3	13	13	13	2	0	2	1
42 091	MONTGOMERY COUNTY	3	2	23	23	13	2	0	2	2
42 093	MONTOUR COUNTY	2	2	33	33	13	2	0	2	2
42 095	NORTHAMPTON COUNTY	3	3	13	13	13	4	0	2	1
42 097	NORTHUMBERLAND COUNTY	2	2	23	23	13	2	0	3	2
42 099	PERRY COUNTY	2	2	13	13	13	2	0	3	2
42 101	PHILADELPHIA COUNTY	3	3	13	13	13	2	0	3	3

517

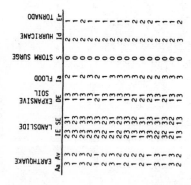

RHODE ISLAND

		EARTHQUAKE		LANDSLIDE		EXPANSIVE SOIL	FLOOD	STORM SURGE	HURRICANE	TORNADO
		Aa	Av	IE	SE	DE	Ia	s	Id	Er
44	001	BRISTOL COUNTY	3	3	13	13	13	1	2	4	1
44	003	KENT COUNTY	3	3	13	13	13	2	2	4	1
44	005	NEWPORT COUNTY	3	3	13	13	13	1	2	5	1
44	007	PROVIDENCE COUNTY	3	3	13	13	13	3	2	4	2
44	009	WASHINGTON COUNTY	3	3	13	13	13	1	2	5	1

		EARTHQUAKE		LANDSLIDE		EXPANSIVE SOIL	FLOOD	STORM SURGE	HURRICANE	TORNADO
		Aa	Av	IE	SE	DE	Ia	s	Id	Er
42	103	PIKE COUNTY	3	1	23	31	13	2	0	2	1
42	105	POTTER COUNTY	1	2	23	23	13	1	0	2	1
42	107	SCHUYLKILL COUNTY	3	3	23	33	13	3	0	2	2
42	109	SNYDER COUNTY	2	2	23	33	21	2	0	2	1
42	111	SOMERSET COUNTY	2	1	21	21	13	1	0	2	1
42	113	SULLIVAN COUNTY	2	2	21	23	13	3	0	2	1
42	115	SUSQUEHANNA COUNTY	3	1	22	23	13	3	0	2	1
42	117	TIOGA COUNTY	1	2	22	23	13	3	0	2	1
42	119	UNION COUNTY	3	2	22	23	13	2	0	2	1
42	121	VENANGO COUNTY	2	1	23	32	21	2	0	2	2
42	123	WARREN COUNTY	1	1	13	31	21	2	0	2	2
42	125	WASHINGTON COUNTY	2	3	32	31	13	3	0	2	1
42	127	WAYNE COUNTY	1	3	32	31	13	3	0	2	1
42	129	WESTMORELAND COUNTY	3	1	21	22	21	3	0	3	1
42	131	WYOMING COUNTY	1	3	21	22	13	3	0	2	1
42	133	YORK COUNTY	3	2	13	13	13	3	0	3	2

518

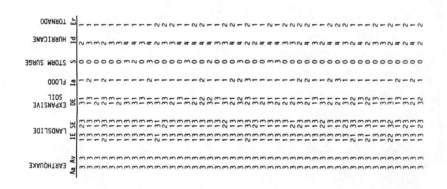

SOUTH DAKOTA

Code	County	EARTHQUAKE Aa	Av	LANDSLIDE IE	SE	EXPANSIVE SOIL DE	FLOOD Ia	STORM SURGE S	HURRICANE Id	TORNADO Er
46 003	AURORA COUNTY	1	1	13	13	21	1	0	0	3
46 005	BEADLE COUNTY	1	1	13	13	21	1	0	0	3
46 007	BENNETT COUNTY	2	2	21	32	31	2	0	0	3
46 009	BON HOMME COUNTY	1	1	13	13	22	2	0	0	4
46 011	BROOKINGS COUNTY	1	1	13	13	32	2	0	0	2
46 013	BROWN COUNTY	1	1	13	13	31	2	0	0	1
46 015	BRULE COUNTY	1	1	31	31	32	2	0	0	3
46 017	BUFFALO COUNTY	1	1	31	32	31	1	0	0	1
46 019	BUTTE COUNTY	2	2	31	33	31	2	0	0	1
46 021	CAMPBELL COUNTY	1	1	31	31	31	1	0	0	3
46 023	CHARLES MIX COUNTY	1	1	13	31	31	2	0	0	2
46 025	CLARK COUNTY	1	1	13	13	31	1	0	0	4
46 027	CLAY COUNTY	1	1	13	31	31	2	0	0	2
46 029	CODINGTON COUNTY	2	1	31	32	31	2	0	0	2
46 031	CORSON COUNTY	1	1	13	31	32	1	0	0	1
46 033	CUSTER COUNTY	2	2	31	31	31	1	0	0	1
46 035	DAVISON COUNTY	1	1	13	13	22	1	0	0	2
46 037	DAY COUNTY	1	1	13	13	31	2	0	0	2
46 039	DEUEL COUNTY	2	2	31	33	33	1	0	0	2
46 041	DEWEY COUNTY	1	1	13	13	13	1	0	0	1
46 043	DOUGLAS COUNTY	1	1	31	31	13	1	0	0	2
46 045	EDMUNDS COUNTY	1	1	13	13	13	2	0	0	1
46 047	FALL RIVER COUNTY	2	2	31	31	13	1	0	0	1
46 049	FAULK COUNTY	1	1	13	13	13	1	0	0	2
46 051	GRANT COUNTY	2	1	31	33	33	1	0	0	2
46 053	GREGORY COUNTY	1	1	13	13	13	2	0	0	2
46 055	HAAKON COUNTY	1	1	21	13	33	1	0	0	1
46 057	HAMLIN COUNTY	2	1	13	13	21	1	0	0	3
46 059	HAND COUNTY	1	1	13	13	13	1	0	0	2
46 061	HANSON COUNTY	1	1	31	31	32	2	0	0	3
46 063	HARDING COUNTY	2	2	31	31	13	1	0	0	1
46 065	HUGHES COUNTY	1	1	13	13	32	2	0	0	2
46 067	HUTCHINSON COUNTY	1	1	31	13	13	1	0	0	3
46 069	HYDE COUNTY	1	1	13	13	13	1	0	0	2
46 071	JACKSON COUNTY	2	1	21	33	32	1	0	0	2
46 073	JERAULD COUNTY	1	1	13	13	33	1	0	0	2
46 075	JONES COUNTY	1	1	21	32	33	1	0	0	1
46 077	KINGSBURY COUNTY	1	1	13	13	13	2	0	0	3
46 079	LAKE COUNTY	1	1	31	13	13	1	0	0	1
46 081	LAWRENCE COUNTY	2	2	31	31	31	1	0	0	4
46 083	LINCOLN COUNTY	1	1	13	13	31	2	0	0	3
46 085	LYMAN COUNTY	1	1	31	32	31	1	0	0	1
46 087	MCCOOK COUNTY	1	1	13	13	32	1	0	0	1
46 089	MCPHERSON COUNTY	1	1	13	13	13	1	0	0	1
46 091	MARSHALL COUNTY	1	1	31	31	31	1	0	0	3
46 093	MEADE COUNTY	2	1	13	13	33	2	0	0	4
46 095	MELLETTE COUNTY	2	2	21	32	32	1	0	0	3
46 097	MINER COUNTY	1	1	13	13	13	1	0	0	2
46 099	MINNEHAHA COUNTY	1	1	13	13	13	2	0	0	1
46 101	MOODY COUNTY	1	1	31	13	13	2	0	0	1
46 103	PENNINGTON COUNTY	2	2	31	32	33	2	0	0	2

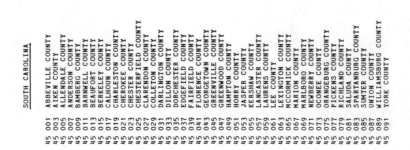

SOUTH CAROLINA

Code	County	EARTHQUAKE Aa	Av	LANDSLIDE IE	SE	EXPANSIVE SOIL DE	FLOOD Ia	STORM SURGE S	HURRICANE Id	TORNADO Er
45 001	ABBEVILLE COUNTY	3	3	13	13	31	1	0	2	1
45 003	AIKEN COUNTY	3	3	13	13	13	2	0	3	1
45 005	ALLENDALE COUNTY	3	3	13	13	23	1	0	3	1
45 007	ANDERSON COUNTY	3	3	23	33	31	2	0	3	1
45 009	BAMBERG COUNTY	3	3	13	13	21	1	0	3	1
45 011	BARNWELL COUNTY	3	3	13	13	31	2	0	4	1
45 013	BEAUFORT COUNTY	3	3	13	13	31	2	3	4	2
45 015	BERKELEY COUNTY	3	3	13	13	33	2	3	4	2
45 017	CALHOUN COUNTY	3	3	13	13	21	1	0	3	1
45 019	CHARLESTON COUNTY	3	3	21	31	13	2	3	4	1
45 021	CHEROKEE COUNTY	3	3	13	13	31	2	0	2	2
45 023	CHESTER COUNTY	3	3	13	13	13	1	0	2	1
45 025	CHESTERFIELD COUNTY	3	3	13	13	33	1	0	3	2
45 027	CLARENDON COUNTY	3	3	13	13	21	2	0	3	1
45 029	COLLETON COUNTY	3	3	13	13	31	2	3	4	1
45 031	DARLINGTON COUNTY	3	3	13	13	31	1	0	3	1
45 033	DILLON COUNTY	3	3	13	13	22	2	0	3	2
45 035	DORCHESTER COUNTY	3	3	13	13	13	2	2	4	1
45 037	EDGEFIELD COUNTY	3	3	13	22	13	1	0	3	1
45 039	FAIRFIELD COUNTY	3	3	13	13	21	2	0	3	2
45 041	FLORENCE COUNTY	3	3	13	13	23	2	0	3	2
45 043	GEORGETOWN COUNTY	3	3	33	33	32	3	3	4	2
45 045	GREENVILLE COUNTY	3	3	23	13	31	2	0	3	1
45 047	GREENWOOD COUNTY	3	3	13	13	21	1	0	2	1
45 049	HAMPTON COUNTY	3	3	13	13	21	2	0	4	1
45 051	HORRY COUNTY	3	3	13	13	31	2	3	4	2
45 053	JASPER COUNTY	3	3	13	13	21	2	3	4	1
45 055	KERSHAW COUNTY	3	3	13	13	21	1	0	3	1
45 057	LANCASTER COUNTY	3	3	13	13	31	2	0	2	2
45 059	LAURENS COUNTY	3	3	13	13	31	1	0	2	1
45 061	LEE COUNTY	3	3	13	13	21	2	0	3	1
45 063	LEXINGTON COUNTY	3	3	13	13	31	2	0	3	2
45 065	MCCORMICK COUNTY	3	3	13	13	32	1	0	2	1
45 067	MARION COUNTY	3	3	13	13	22	2	0	4	1
45 069	MARLBORO COUNTY	3	3	13	13	31	2	0	3	2
45 071	NEWBERRY COUNTY	3	3	21	33	13	1	0	2	1
45 073	OCONEE COUNTY	3	3	21	33	13	2	0	3	1
45 075	ORANGEBURG COUNTY	3	3	13	13	22	2	0	3	2
45 077	PICKENS COUNTY	3	3	22	32	31	2	0	3	1
45 079	RICHLAND COUNTY	3	3	13	13	31	2	0	3	1
45 081	SALUDA COUNTY	3	3	13	13	31	1	0	2	2
45 083	SPARTANBURG COUNTY	3	3	13	13	13	1	0	2	1
45 085	SUMTER COUNTY	3	3	13	13	21	2	0	3	1
45 087	UNION COUNTY	3	3	13	13	31	1	0	2	2
45 089	WILLIAMSBURG COUNTY	3	3	13	13	21	2	0	4	2
45 091	YORK COUNTY	3	3	13	23	32	1	0	2	2

TENNESSEE

FIPS	County	EARTHQUAKE Aa	EARTHQUAKE Av	LANDSLIDE IE	LANDSLIDE SE	EXPANSIVE SOIL DE	FLOOD Ia	STORM SURGE S	HURRICANE Pl	TORNADO Er
47 001	ANDERSON COUNTY	3	2	22	21	22	3	0	2	2
47 003	BEDFORD COUNTY	2	2	21	21	22	3	0	2	5
47 005	BENTON COUNTY	3	3	22	31	13	1	0	2	4
47 007	BLEDSOE COUNTY	3	3	22	23	22	2	0	2	4
47 009	BLOUNT COUNTY	3	3	21	23	23	2	0	2	2
47 011	BRADLEY COUNTY	3	2	23	23	21	2	0	2	2
47 013	CAMPBELL COUNTY	3	2	23	31	21	2	0	2	2
47 015	CANNON COUNTY	3	3	33	13	13	2	0	2	1
47 017	CARROLL COUNTY	3	2	33	13	21	2	0	2	4
47 019	CARTER COUNTY	3	2	33	31	23	1	0	2	4
47 021	CHEATHAM COUNTY	3	2	13	13	22	3	0	2	2
47 023	CHESTER COUNTY	3	3	13	13	13	1	0	2	3
47 025	CLAIBORNE COUNTY	3	2	23	23	21	1	0	2	1
47 027	CLAY COUNTY	3	3	23	23	23	3	0	2	3
47 029	COCKE COUNTY	3	3	32	32	22	2	0	2	1
47 031	COFFEE COUNTY	4	2	13	13	13	5	0	2	3
47 033	CROCKETT COUNTY	3	3	13	13	21	1	0	1	4
47 035	CUMBERLAND COUNTY	3	3	21	21	21	2	0	2	4
47 037	DAVIDSON COUNTY	2	2	13	23	13	1	0	2	4
47 039	DECATUR COUNTY	2	2	13	13	23	3	0	2	4
47 041	DE KALB COUNTY	2	2	13	13	13	1	0	2	4
47 043	DICKSON COUNTY	2	2	23	23	23	2	0	2	4
47 045	DYER COUNTY	5	5	13	13	22	2	0	1	4
47 047	FAYETTE COUNTY	4	4	33	33	23	3	0	2	5
47 049	FENTRESS COUNTY	2	2	31	31	22	1	0	2	3
47 051	FRANKLIN COUNTY	3	2	33	33	23	3	0	2	5
47 053	GIBSON COUNTY	3	3	13	13	23	1	0	2	5
47 055	GILES COUNTY	3	3	21	21	23	1	0	2	1
47 057	GRAINGER COUNTY	3	3	21	21	21	3	0	2	1
47 059	GREENE COUNTY	3	3	32	32	13	1	0	2	1
47 061	GRUNDY COUNTY	3	3	22	22	13	1	0	2	1
47 063	HAMBLEN COUNTY	3	3	23	23	23	1	0	2	5
47 065	HAMILTON COUNTY	2	2	21	21	23	1	0	2	1
47 067	HANCOCK COUNTY	3	3	32	32	21	1	0	2	1
47 069	HARDEMAN COUNTY	4	3	32	32	23	2	0	1	1
47 071	HARDIN COUNTY	3	3	22	22	13	2	0	2	1
47 073	HAWKINS COUNTY	3	3	32	32	13	1	0	2	1
47 075	HAYWOOD COUNTY	3	3	13	13	23	1	0	2	5
47 077	HENDERSON COUNTY	2	2	13	13	21	1	0	2	1
47 079	HENRY COUNTY	2	2	13	13	21	1	0	2	1
47 081	HICKMAN COUNTY	2	2	23	23	13	2	0	2	1
47 083	HOUSTON COUNTY	2	2	13	13	23	2	0	2	1
47 085	HUMPHREYS COUNTY	3	3	31	31	21	2	0	2	1
47 087	JACKSON COUNTY	3	3	33	33	23	3	0	2	2
47 089	JEFFERSON COUNTY	5	5	13	13	13	1	0	1	4
47 091	JOHNSON COUNTY	5	5	33	33	23	2	0	1	5
47 093	KNOX COUNTY	3	2	13	13	21	2	0	2	5
47 095	LAKE COUNTY	5	5	22	22	23	2	0	1	5
47 097	LAUDERDALE COUNTY	5	5	32	32	21	3	0	2	4
47 099	LAWRENCE COUNTY	2	2	13	13	13	2	0	2	1
47 101	LEWIS COUNTY	2	2	13	13	13	1	0	2	2

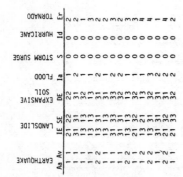

FIPS	County	EARTHQUAKE Aa	EARTHQUAKE Av	LANDSLIDE IE	LANDSLIDE SE	EXPANSIVE SOIL DE	FLOOD Ia	STORM SURGE S	HURRICANE Id	TORNADO Er
46 105	PERKINS COUNTY	1	1	21	22	22	1	0	0	2
46 107	POTTER COUNTY	1	1	31	31	31	2	0	0	2
46 109	ROBERTS COUNTY	1	1	13	13	32	1	0	0	1
46 111	SANBORN COUNTY	1	1	13	13	13	1	0	0	3
46 113	SHANNON COUNTY	2	2	13	13	31	2	0	0	2
46 115	SPINK COUNTY	1	1	13	13	33	2	0	0	2
46 117	STANLEY COUNTY	1	1	31	31	32	1	0	0	3
46 119	SULLY COUNTY	1	1	13	13	13	1	0	0	3
46 121	TODD COUNTY	2	2	21	21	32	1	0	0	3
46 123	TRIPP COUNTY	1	1	31	31	13	1	0	0	4
46 125	TURNER COUNTY	2	2	13	13	32	3	0	0	4
46 127	UNION COUNTY	2	2	31	31	31	2	0	0	1
46 129	WALWORTH COUNTY	2	2	21	21	31	1	0	0	1
46 135	YANKTON COUNTY	2	1	31	32	31	3	0	0	2
46 137	ZIEBACH COUNTY	1	1	21	33	32	2	0	0	

	EARTHQUAKE		LANDSLIDE		EXPANSIVE SOIL	FLOOD	STORM SURGE	HURRICANE	TORNADO
	Aa	Av	IE	SE	DE	la	S	Id	Er
47 103 LINCOLN COUNTY	2	2	13	13	13	2	0	2	5
47 105 LOUDON COUNTY	3	3	13	13	23	3	0	2	2
47 107 MCMINN COUNTY	3	3	22	23	22	1	0	2	3
47 109 MCNAIRY COUNTY	2	2	13	13	22	2	0	2	4
47 111 MACON COUNTY	2	2	13	13	21	1	0	2	4
47 113 MADISON COUNTY	2	2	13	13	13	2	0	2	5
47 115 MARION COUNTY	2	2	22	32	22	3	0	2	3
47 117 MARSHALL COUNTY	2	2	13	13	23	3	0	2	3
47 119 MAURY COUNTY	3	3	21	21	23	1	0	2	3
47 121 MEIGS COUNTY	3	3	32	32	22	1	0	1	2
47 123 MONROE COUNTY	3	3	13	13	13	3	0	2	3
47 125 MONTGOMERY COUNTY	2	2	13	13	13	1	0	2	4
47 127 MOORE COUNTY	2	2	13	13	13	2	0	2	3
47 129 MORGAN COUNTY	3	3	23	33	13	3	0	2	3
47 131 OBION COUNTY	5	5	22	31	13	2	0	2	4
47 133 OVERTON COUNTY	2	2	31	31	13	2	0	2	3
47 135 PERRY COUNTY	2	2	13	31	21	1	0	2	3
47 137 PICKETT COUNTY	2	2	32	32	13	1	0	2	3
47 139 POLK COUNTY	3	3	23	31	13	3	0	2	4
47 141 PUTNAM COUNTY	2	2	22	31	21	2	0	2	3
47 143 RHEA COUNTY	3	3	13	13	13	3	0	2	3
47 145 ROANE COUNTY	3	3	21	32	21	1	0	2	4
47 147 ROBERTSON COUNTY	3	3	22	32	22	3	0	2	4
47 149 RUTHERFORD COUNTY	5	5	13	13	21	1	0	2	5
47 151 SCOTT COUNTY	2	2	31	31	13	1	0	2	2
47 153 SEQUATCHIE COUNTY	2	2	23	32	22	1	0	2	4
47 155 SEVIER COUNTY	3	3	22	32	21	3	0	2	2
47 157 SHELBY COUNTY	5	5	21	21	13	3	0	2	5
47 159 SMITH COUNTY	2	2	13	13	22	1	0	2	3
47 161 STEWART COUNTY	2	2	21	21	23	2	0	2	2
47 163 SULLIVAN COUNTY	3	3	21	31	23	2	0	1	2
47 165 SUMNER COUNTY	2	2	13	31	22	2	0	2	4
47 167 TIPTON COUNTY	5	5	22	32	13	3	0	2	5
47 169 TROUSDALE COUNTY	2	2	13	13	13	1	0	2	2
47 171 UNICOI COUNTY	3	3	33	33	13	1	0	2	2
47 173 UNION COUNTY	3	3	22	32	21	2	0	2	2
47 175 VAN BUREN COUNTY	2	2	22	32	22	1	0	2	3
47 177 WARREN COUNTY	2	2	21	31	21	2	0	1	2
47 179 WASHINGTON COUNTY	3	3	21	31	31	3	0	2	4
47 181 WAYNE COUNTY	2	2	13	13	13	1	0	2	1
47 183 WEAKLEY COUNTY	4	4	13	22	22	2	0	2	5
47 185 WHITE COUNTY	2	2	22	31	31	1	0	2	3
47 187 WILLIAMSON COUNTY	2	2	21	21	21	2	0	2	4
47 189 WILSON COUNTY	2	2	13	13	23	1	0	2	4

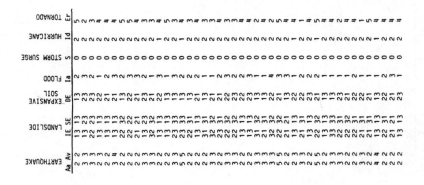

TEXAS

	EARTHQUAKE		LANDSLIDE		EXPANSIVE SOIL	FLOOD	STORM SURGE	HURRICANE	TORNADO
	Aa	Av	IE	SE	DE	la	S	Id	Er
48 001 ANDERSON COUNTY	1	1	13	13	31	2	0	2	3
48 003 ANDREWS COUNTY	1	1	13	13	31	1	0	1	2
48 005 ANGELINA COUNTY	1	1	13	13	31	2	0	3	4
48 007 ARANSAS COUNTY	1	2	13	13	32	1	2	3	1
48 009 ARCHER COUNTY	1	1	13	13	33	2	0	1	3
48 011 ARMSTRONG COUNTY	1	1	13	13	32	1	0	1	5
48 013 ATASCOSA COUNTY	1	1	13	13	33	2	0	3	5
48 015 AUSTIN COUNTY	1	1	13	13	13	1	0	4	3
48 017 BAILEY COUNTY	1	1	13	13	33	1	0	1	5
48 019 BANDERA COUNTY	1	1	13	13	32	2	0	2	3
48 021 BASTROP COUNTY	1	1	13	13	13	3	0	3	3
48 023 BAYLOR COUNTY	1	1	13	16	31	5	0	1	3
48 025 BEE COUNTY	1	1	13	13	32	1	0	3	2
48 027 BELL COUNTY	1	1	13	13	33	3	0	2	2
48 029 BEXAR COUNTY	1	1	13	13	33	3	0	2	2
48 031 BLANCO COUNTY	1	1	13	13	32	2	0	2	2
48 033 BORDEN COUNTY	1	1	13	13	33	1	0	1	4
48 035 BOSQUE COUNTY	1	1	13	13	33	2	0	2	2
48 037 BOWIE COUNTY	2	2	13	13	33	3	0	5	4
48 039 BRAZORIA COUNTY	1	1	13	13	33	3	2	5	3
48 041 BRAZOS COUNTY	1	1	13	13	13	1	0	3	1
48 043 BREWSTER COUNTY	1	1	13	13	32	1	0	1	2
48 045 BRISCOE COUNTY	1	1	13	13	31	2	0	1	4
48 047 BROOKS COUNTY	1	1	13	13	13	1	0	2	1
48 049 BROWN COUNTY	2	2	13	13	33	3	0	2	3
48 051 BURLESON COUNTY	1	1	13	13	33	1	0	3	1
48 053 BURNET COUNTY	1	1	13	13	33	3	0	2	2
48 055 CALDWELL COUNTY	1	1	13	13	33	2	0	3	1
48 057 CALHOUN COUNTY	1	2	13	13	33	1	2	5	2
48 059 CALLAHAN COUNTY	1	1	13	13	33	3	0	2	3
48 061 CAMERON COUNTY	1	1	13	13	32	2	2	5	2
48 063 CAMP COUNTY	2	2	13	13	31	2	0	4	2
48 065 CARSON COUNTY	1	1	13	13	31	1	0	1	4
48 067 CASS COUNTY	2	2	13	13	33	2	0	5	4
48 069 CASTRO COUNTY	1	1	13	13	31	1	0	1	4
48 071 CHAMBERS COUNTY	1	1	13	13	33	3	2	5	4
48 073 CHEROKEE COUNTY	1	1	13	13	31	2	0	3	1
48 075 CHILDRESS COUNTY	1	1	13	13	31	1	0	1	4
48 077 CLAY COUNTY	1	1	13	13	23	3	0	1	3
48 079 COCHRAN COUNTY	2	2	13	13	13	1	0	1	4
48 081 COKE COUNTY	1	1	13	13	32	2	0	1	3
48 083 COLEMAN COUNTY	2	2	13	13	33	3	0	2	3
48 085 COLLIN COUNTY	1	1	13	13	13	1	0	3	3
48 087 COLLINGSWORTH COUNTY	1	1	13	13	31	2	0	1	4
48 089 COLORADO COUNTY	1	1	13	13	33	1	0	3	2
48 091 COMAL COUNTY	2	2	13	31	33	3	0	2	1
48 093 COMANCHE COUNTY	2	2	13	13	31	2	0	2	2
48 095 CONCHO COUNTY	1	1	13	13	32	1	0	1	4
48 097 COOKE COUNTY	1	1	13	13	33	2	0	2	2
48 099 CORYELL COUNTY	2	2	13	21	33	3	0	2	2
48 101 COTTLE COUNTY	1	1	13	13	22	2	0	1	4

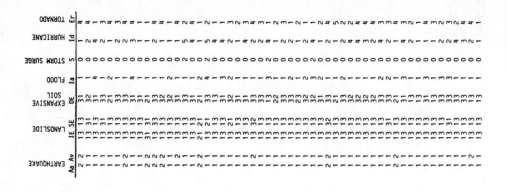

	TORNADO (Er)	HURRICANE (Id)	STORM SURGE (S)	FLOOD (Ia)	EXPANSIVE SOIL (DE)	LANDSLIDE (IE SE)	EARTHQUAKE (Aa Av)
48 211 HEMPHILL COUNTY							
48 213 HENDERSON COUNTY							
48 215 HIDALGO COUNTY							
48 217 HILL COUNTY							
48 219 HOCKLEY COUNTY							
48 221 HOOD COUNTY							
48 223 HOPKINS COUNTY							
48 225 HOUSTON COUNTY							
48 227 HOWARD COUNTY							
48 229 HUDSPETH COUNTY							
48 231 HUNT COUNTY							
48 233 HUTCHINSON COUNTY							
48 235 IRION COUNTY							
48 237 JACK COUNTY							
48 239 JACKSON COUNTY							
48 241 JASPER COUNTY							
48 243 JEFF DAVIS COUNTY							
48 245 JEFFERSON COUNTY							
48 247 JIM HOGG COUNTY							
48 249 JIM WELLS COUNTY							
48 251 JOHNSON COUNTY							
48 253 JONES COUNTY							
48 255 KARNES COUNTY							
48 257 KAUFMAN COUNTY							
48 259 KENDALL COUNTY							
48 261 KENEDY COUNTY							
48 263 KENT COUNTY							
48 265 KERR COUNTY							
48 267 KIMBLE COUNTY							
48 269 KING COUNTY							
48 271 KINNEY COUNTY							
48 273 KLEBERG COUNTY							
48 275 KNOX COUNTY							
48 277 LAMAR COUNTY							
48 279 LAMB COUNTY							
48 281 LAMPASAS COUNTY							
48 283 LA SALLE COUNTY							
48 285 LAVACA COUNTY							
48 287 LEE COUNTY							
48 289 LEON COUNTY							
48 291 LIBERTY COUNTY							
48 293 LIMESTONE COUNTY							
48 295 LIPSCOMB COUNTY							
48 297 LIVE OAK COUNTY							
48 299 LLANO COUNTY							
48 301 LOVING COUNTY							
48 303 LUBBOCK COUNTY							
48 305 LYNN COUNTY							
48 307 MCCULLOCH COUNTY							
48 309 MCLENNAN COUNTY							
48 311 MCMULLEN COUNTY							
48 313 MADISON COUNTY							
48 315 MARION COUNTY							
48 317 MARTIN COUNTY							

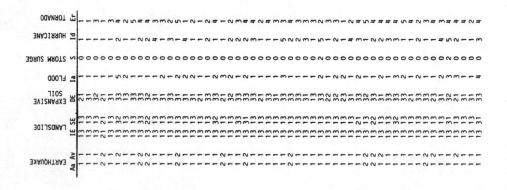

	TORNADO (Er)	HURRICANE (Id)	STORM SURGE (S)	FLOOD (Ia)	EXPANSIVE SOIL (DE)	LANDSLIDE (IE SE)	EARTHQUAKE (Aa Av)
48 103 CRANE COUNTY							
48 105 CROCKETT COUNTY							
48 107 CROSBY COUNTY							
48 109 CULBERSON COUNTY							
48 111 DALLAM COUNTY							
48 113 DALLAS COUNTY							
48 115 DAWSON COUNTY							
48 117 DEAF SMITH COUNTY							
48 119 DELTA COUNTY							
48 121 DENTON COUNTY							
48 123 DE WITT COUNTY							
48 125 DICKENS COUNTY							
48 127 DIMMIT COUNTY							
48 129 DONLEY COUNTY							
48 131 DUVAL COUNTY							
48 133 EASTLAND COUNTY							
48 135 ECTOR COUNTY							
48 137 EDWARDS COUNTY							
48 139 ELLIS COUNTY							
48 141 EL PASO COUNTY							
48 143 ERATH COUNTY							
48 145 FALLS COUNTY							
48 147 FANNIN COUNTY							
48 149 FAYETTE COUNTY							
48 151 FISHER COUNTY							
48 153 FLOYD COUNTY							
48 155 FOARD COUNTY							
48 157 FORT BEND COUNTY							
48 159 FRANKLIN COUNTY							
48 161 FREESTONE COUNTY							
48 163 FRIO COUNTY							
48 165 GAINES COUNTY							
48 167 GALVESTON COUNTY							
48 169 GARZA COUNTY							
48 171 GILLESPIE COUNTY							
48 173 GLASSCOCK COUNTY							
48 175 GOLIAD COUNTY							
48 177 GONZALES COUNTY							
48 179 GRAY COUNTY							
48 181 GRAYSON COUNTY							
48 183 GREGG COUNTY							
48 185 GRIMES COUNTY							
48 187 GUADALUPE COUNTY							
48 189 HALE COUNTY							
48 191 HALL COUNTY							
48 193 HAMILTON COUNTY							
48 195 HANSFORD COUNTY							
48 197 HARDEMAN COUNTY							
48 199 HARDIN COUNTY							
48 201 HARRIS COUNTY							
48 203 HARRISON COUNTY							
48 205 HARTLEY COUNTY							
48 207 HASKELL COUNTY							
48 209 HAYS COUNTY							

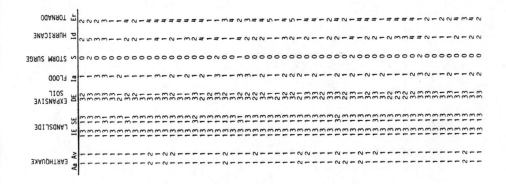

Code	County	EARTHQUAKE Aa	Av	LANDSLIDE IE	SE	EXPANSIVE SOIL DE	FLOOD la	STORM SURGE s	HURRICANE Id	TORNADO Er
48 319	MASON COUNTY	1	1	13	13	32	1	0	2	2
48 321	MATAGORDA COUNTY	1	1	13	13	33	3	2	5	2
48 323	MAVERICK COUNTY	1	1	13	31	33	1	0	3	3
48 325	MEDINA COUNTY	1	1	13	13	33	1	0	2	1
48 327	MENARD COUNTY	1	1	13	13	31	1	0	1	1
48 329	MIDLAND COUNTY	1	1	13	13	32	2	0	2	2
48 331	MILAM COUNTY	1	1	13	31	32	1	0	2	1
48 333	MILLS COUNTY	1	1	13	13	31	1	0	1	1
48 335	MITCHELL COUNTY	1	1	13	13	31	1	0	1	1
48 337	MONTAGUE COUNTY	2	2	13	13	33	2	0	2	4
48 339	MONTGOMERY COUNTY	2	2	13	13	32	2	0	3	3
48 341	MOORE COUNTY	1	1	13	13	13	1	0	1	2
48 343	MORRIS COUNTY	1	1	13	13	33	1	0	1	1
48 345	MOTLEY COUNTY	1	1	13	13	31	1	0	1	1
48 347	NACOGDOCHES COUNTY	1	1	13	13	31	2	0	2	2
48 349	NAVARRO COUNTY	1	1	13	13	21	2	0	2	1
48 351	NEWTON COUNTY	1	1	13	32	32	1	0	3	2
48 353	NOLAN COUNTY	1	1	13	13	31	1	0	1	2
48 355	NUECES COUNTY	2	2	13	31	32	3	2	3	5
48 357	OCHILTREE COUNTY	1	1	13	13	13	1	0	1	1
48 359	OLDHAM COUNTY	1	1	13	13	33	1	0	1	1
48 361	ORANGE COUNTY	1	1	13	13	32	2	2	5	1
48 363	PALO PINTO COUNTY	1	1	13	13	33	2	0	2	1
48 365	PANOLA COUNTY	1	1	13	31	21	1	0	2	2
48 367	PARKER COUNTY	1	1	13	13	31	2	0	2	1
48 369	PARMER COUNTY	1	1	13	13	21	1	0	1	3
48 371	PECOS COUNTY	2	2	13	13	31	1	0	1	2
48 373	POLK COUNTY	1	1	13	13	33	1	0	3	2
48 375	POTTER COUNTY	2	2	13	13	33	1	0	1	1
48 377	PRESIDIO COUNTY	2	2	13	13	33	2	0	2	1
48 379	RAINS COUNTY	1	1	13	13	33	2	0	2	1
48 381	RANDALL COUNTY	1	1	13	13	21	1	0	1	1
48 383	REAGAN COUNTY	1	1	13	13	33	1	0	1	1
48 385	REAL COUNTY	1	2	13	32	22	1	0	2	1
48 387	RED RIVER COUNTY	1	1	13	13	33	2	0	2	1
48 389	REEVES COUNTY	2	2	13	13	33	1	0	1	1
48 391	REFUGIO COUNTY	1	1	13	13	33	2	2	5	1
48 393	ROBERTS COUNTY	1	1	13	13	13	1	0	1	1
48 395	ROBERTSON COUNTY	1	1	13	13	31	2	0	3	2
48 397	ROCKWALL COUNTY	1	1	13	13	32	2	0	2	2
48 399	RUNNELS COUNTY	1	1	13	13	31	1	0	1	2
48 401	RUSK COUNTY	1	1	13	13	33	1	0	2	2
48 403	SABINE COUNTY	1	1	13	13	33	1	0	3	1
48 405	SAN AUGUSTINE COUNTY	1	1	13	13	33	1	0	3	1
48 407	SAN JACINTO COUNTY	1	1	13	13	33	1	0	3	2
48 409	SAN PATRICIO COUNTY	2	2	13	13	33	3	2	3	2
48 411	SAN SABA COUNTY	1	1	13	13	31	1	0	1	3
48 413	SCHLEICHER COUNTY	1	1	13	13	33	1	0	1	1
48 415	SCURRY COUNTY	1	1	13	13	31	1	0	1	3
48 417	SHACKELFORD COUNTY	1	1	13	13	31	1	0	1	2
48 419	SHELBY COUNTY	1	1	13	13	33	1	0	2	2
48 421	SHERMAN COUNTY	2	2	13	13	13	1	0	1	3
48 423	SMITH COUNTY	2	2	13	13	32	2	0	2	2
48 425	SOMERVELL COUNTY	1	1	13	13	33	1	0	2	2

Code	County	EARTHQUAKE Aa	Av	LANDSLIDE IE	SE	EXPANSIVE SOIL DE	FLOOD la	STORM SURGE s	HURRICANE Id	TORNADO Er
48 427	STARR COUNTY	1	1	13	13	31	2	0	2	2
48 429	STEPHENS COUNTY	1	1	13	13	31	1	0	1	1
48 431	STERLING COUNTY	1	1	13	13	31	1	0	1	2
48 433	STONEWALL COUNTY	1	1	13	13	33	1	0	1	5
48 435	SUTTON COUNTY	1	1	13	13	33	2	0	2	2
48 437	SWISHER COUNTY	1	1	13	22	31	1	0	1	1
48 439	TARRANT COUNTY	1	1	13	13	31	2	0	2	1
48 441	TAYLOR COUNTY	1	1	13	13	31	1	0	1	3
48 443	TERRELL COUNTY	1	1	13	13	13	1	0	1	2
48 445	TERRY COUNTY	1	1	13	13	33	1	0	1	1
48 447	THROCKMORTON COUNTY	1	1	13	13	33	1	0	1	1
48 449	TITUS COUNTY	1	1	13	13	33	2	0	2	1
48 451	TOM GREEN COUNTY	1	1	13	32	32	1	0	1	1
48 453	TRAVIS COUNTY	1	1	13	13	33	2	0	2	1
48 455	TRINITY COUNTY	1	1	13	13	31	2	0	2	1
48 457	TYLER COUNTY	1	1	13	13	31	1	0	2	1
48 459	UPSHUR COUNTY	1	1	13	13	33	1	1	3	1
48 461	UPTON COUNTY	1	1	13	13	31	1	0	1	2
48 463	UVALDE COUNTY	1	2	13	13	33	1	0	2	1
48 465	VAL VERDE COUNTY	2	2	13	13	33	1	0	2	2
48 467	VAN ZANDT COUNTY	1	1	13	13	13	2	0	2	1
48 469	VICTORIA COUNTY	1	1	13	13	32	3	2	3	1
48 471	WALKER COUNTY	1	1	13	13	33	1	0	3	1
48 473	WALLER COUNTY	1	1	13	13	33	2	0	3	3
48 475	WARD COUNTY	1	1	13	13	13	1	0	1	1
48 477	WASHINGTON COUNTY	2	2	13	13	33	2	0	3	1
48 479	WEBB COUNTY	2	2	13	13	33	1	0	2	3
48 481	WHARTON COUNTY	1	1	13	13	31	3	2	5	1
48 483	WHEELER COUNTY	1	1	13	13	32	1	0	1	1
48 485	WICHITA COUNTY	1	1	13	13	33	1	0	1	4
48 487	WILBARGER COUNTY	1	1	13	13	32	1	0	1	4
48 489	WILLACY COUNTY	1	1	13	32	33	1	2	7	1
48 491	WILLIAMSON COUNTY	1	1	13	21	33	2	0	3	1
48 493	WILSON COUNTY	1	1	13	13	31	1	0	2	1
48 495	WINKLER COUNTY	1	1	13	13	13	1	0	1	1
48 497	WISE COUNTY	1	1	13	13	32	1	0	1	3
48 499	WOOD COUNTY	2	2	13	13	32	2	0	2	2
48 501	YOAKUM COUNTY	1	1	13	13	31	1	0	1	3
48 503	YOUNG COUNTY	1	1	13	13	31	2	0	2	1
48 505	ZAPATA COUNTY	1	1	13	13	32	1	0	1	1
48 507	ZAVALA COUNTY	1	1	13	13	33	1	0	3	2

UTAH

FIPS	County	EARTHQUAKE Aa Av	LANDSLIDE IE SE	EXPANSIVE SOIL DE	FLOOD Ia	STORM SURGE S	HURRICANE Id	TORNADO Er
49 001	BEAVER COUNTY	4 5	31 31	21	1	0	0	1
49 003	BOX ELDER COUNTY	5 5	31 31	31	2	0	0	1
49 005	CACHE COUNTY	5 5	21 31	31	1	0	0	1
49 007	CARBON COUNTY	3 3	31 31	13	1	0	0	1
49 009	DAGGETT COUNTY	2 4	13 13	21	1	0	0	1
49 011	DAVIS COUNTY	5 5	31 31	21	2	0	0	1
49 013	DUCHESNE COUNTY	3 3	31 31	31	1	0	0	1
49 015	EMERY COUNTY	3 4	31 31	22	1	0	0	1
49 017	GARFIELD COUNTY	4 4	31 31	21	1	0	0	1
49 019	GRAND COUNTY	2 2	31 31	21	2	0	0	1
49 021	IRON COUNTY	5 5	31 31	21	1	0	0	1
49 023	JUAB COUNTY	5 5	31 31	21	1	0	0	1
49 025	KANE COUNTY	5 5	22 22	31	1	0	0	1
49 027	MILLARD COUNTY	5 5	31 31	31	3	0	0	1
49 029	MORGAN COUNTY	5 5	13 13	23	2	0	0	1
49 031	PIUTE COUNTY	5 2	31 31	31	1	0	0	1
49 033	RICH COUNTY	5 5	31 31	21	1	0	0	1
49 035	SALT LAKE COUNTY	5 5	32 32	22	1	0	0	1
49 037	SAN JUAN COUNTY	5 5	31 31	31	3	0	0	1
49 039	SANPETE COUNTY	2 2	13 13	21	1	0	0	1
49 041	SEVIER COUNTY	5 5	31 31	31	2	0	0	1
49 043	SUMMIT COUNTY	5 5	31 31	22	1	0	0	1
49 045	TOOELE COUNTY	5 2	31 31	31	1	0	0	1
49 047	UINTAH COUNTY	2 5	31 31	21	2	0	0	1
49 049	UTAH COUNTY	5 5	31 31	31	1	0	0	1
49 051	WASATCH COUNTY	3 3	21 21	21	1	0	0	1
49 053	WASHINGTON COUNTY	4 4	31 31	21	2	0	0	1
49 055	WAYNE COUNTY	5 5	21 21	31	1	0	0	1
49 057	WEBER COUNTY	5 5						

VERMONT

FIPS	County	EARTHQUAKE Aa Av	LANDSLIDE IE SE	EXPANSIVE SOIL DE	FLOOD Ia	STORM SURGE S	HURRICANE Id	TORNADO Er
50 001	ADDISON COUNTY	3 3	22 32	22	1	0	2	2
50 003	BENNINGTON COUNTY	3 3	22 32	13	2	0	2	1
50 005	CALEDONIA COUNTY	3 3	23 33	13	3	0	2	1
50 007	CHITTENDEN COUNTY	3 3	13 13	13	2	0	2	1
50 009	ESSEX COUNTY	3 3	22 32	21	2	0	2	1
50 011	FRANKLIN COUNTY	3 3	13 31	21	1	0	2	2
50 013	GRAND ISLE COUNTY	3 3	21 31	13	1	0	2	1
50 015	LAMOILLE COUNTY	3 3	21 31	21	1	0	2	2
50 017	ORANGE COUNTY	3 3	21 31	21	3	0	2	1
50 019	ORLEANS COUNTY	3 3	21 31	13	3	0	2	2
50 021	RUTLAND COUNTY	3 3	21 31	13	3	0	2	1
50 023	WASHINGTON COUNTY	3 3	21 31	13	4	0	2	2
50 025	WINDHAM COUNTY	3 3					2	2
50 027	WINDSOR COUNTY	3 3						

524

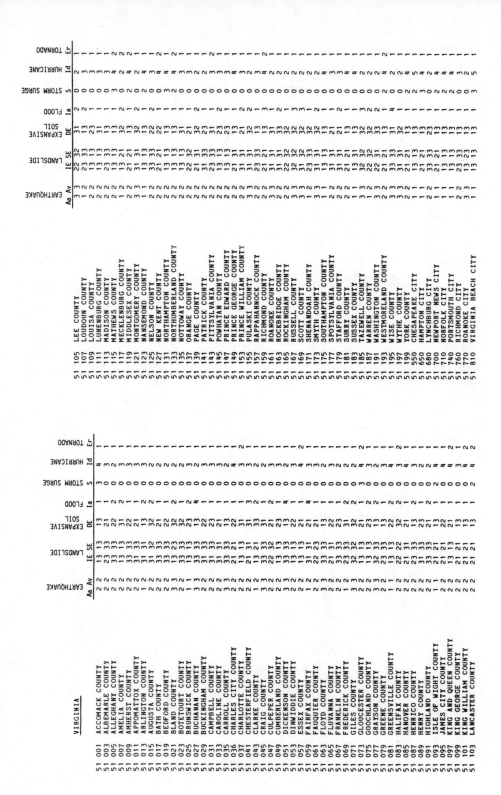

WEST VIRGINIA

		EARTHQUAKE (Aa Av)	LANDSLIDE (IE SE)	EXPANSIVE SOIL (DE)	FLOOD (Ia)	STORM SURGE (S)	HURRICANE (Id)	TORNADO (Er)
54 001	BARBOUR COUNTY	1 2	22 32	21	1	0	2	1
54 003	BERKELEY COUNTY	1 2	33 32	13	3	0	2	1
54 005	BOONE COUNTY	1 2	33 33	22	2	0	2	1
54 007	BRAXTON COUNTY	1 1	33 33	13	2	0	2	2
54 009	BROOKE COUNTY	1 2	33 33	22	2	0	2	1
54 011	CABELL COUNTY	2 2	33 33	21	4	0	2	1
54 013	CALHOUN COUNTY	1 1	33 33	13	2	0	2	1
54 015	CLAY COUNTY	2 2	33 33	13	3	0	2	1
54 017	DODDRIDGE COUNTY	1 2	33 33	13	2	0	2	1
54 019	FAYETTE COUNTY	2 2	31 31	13	5	0	2	1
54 021	GILMER COUNTY	1 2	33 33	13	2	0	2	1
54 023	GRANT COUNTY	2 2	23 31	13	4	0	1	2
54 025	GREENBRIER COUNTY	2 2	31 31	13	5	0	2	1
54 027	HAMPSHIRE COUNTY	2 2	33 33	21	1	0	2	1
54 029	HANCOCK COUNTY	1 1	33 33	13	5	0	2	1
54 031	HARDY COUNTY	2 2	33 33	23	2	0	2	2
54 033	HARRISON COUNTY	1 1	33 33	13	5	0	2	1
54 035	JACKSON COUNTY	2 2	33 33	23	5	0	2	1
54 037	JEFFERSON COUNTY	2 2	13 33	22	4	0	2	1
54 039	KANAWHA COUNTY	2 2	33 33	22	5	0	2	1
54 041	LEWIS COUNTY	1 1	33 33	13	2	0	2	2
54 043	LINCOLN COUNTY	2 2	33 33	21	4	0	2	1
54 045	LOGAN COUNTY	2 2	33 33	13	4	0	1	1
54 047	MCDOWELL COUNTY	2 2	33 33	13	5	0	2	1
54 049	MARION COUNTY	2 1	33 33	13	4	0	2	2
54 051	MARSHALL COUNTY	1 1	33 33	21	4	0	2	1
54 053	MASON COUNTY	2 2	32 33	13	5	0	2	1
54 055	MERCER COUNTY	2 2	31 31	13	2	0	2	1
54 057	MINERAL COUNTY	2 1	33 33	13	1	0	2	1
54 059	MINGO COUNTY	3 2	33 33	13	4	0	1	1
54 061	MONONGALIA COUNTY	1 1	33 33	13	1	0	2	2
54 063	MONROE COUNTY	2 2	31 31	13	2	0	2	1
54 065	MORGAN COUNTY	2 2	32 32	13	3	0	2	1
54 067	NICHOLAS COUNTY	2 2	33 33	13	2	0	2	1
54 069	OHIO COUNTY	1 1	33 33	13	4	0	2	1
54 071	PENDLETON COUNTY	2 2	33 33	13	2	0	2	1
54 073	PLEASANTS COUNTY	2 1	33 33	23	4	0	2	1
54 075	POCAHONTAS COUNTY	2 2	31 31	13	1	0	2	1
54 077	PRESTON COUNTY	1 1	33 33	13	1	0	2	2
54 079	PUTNAM COUNTY	2 2	33 33	22	5	0	2	1
54 081	RALEIGH COUNTY	2 2	33 33	13	3	0	2	1
54 083	RANDOLPH COUNTY	2 1	33 33	13	1	0	2	2
54 085	RITCHIE COUNTY	2 2	33 33	23	2	0	2	1
54 087	ROANE COUNTY	1 1	31 31	13	2	0	2	1
54 089	SUMMERS COUNTY	3 2	31 32	13	4	0	2	2
54 091	TAYLOR COUNTY	1 1	33 33	13	2	0	2	1
54 093	TUCKER COUNTY	2 1	33 33	13	4	0	2	1
54 095	TYLER COUNTY	1 1	33 33	23	4	0	2	1
54 097	UPSHUR COUNTY	1 1	33 33	21	2	0	2	1
54 099	WAYNE COUNTY	2 2	33 33	22	4	0	2	1
54 101	WEBSTER COUNTY	1 2	33 33	13	2	0	2	1

WASHINGTON

		EARTHQUAKE (Aa Av)	LANDSLIDE (IE SE)	EXPANSIVE SOIL (DE)	FLOOD (Ia)	STORM SURGE (S)	HURRICANE (Id)	TORNADO (Er)
53 001	ADAMS COUNTY	2	13 31	13	1	0	0	1
53 003	ASOTIN COUNTY	2	31 31	32	2	0	0	1
53 005	BENTON COUNTY	2	31 31	13	3	0	0	1
53 007	CHELAN COUNTY	5	31 31	13	2	0	0	1
53 009	CLALLAM COUNTY	5	31 31	13	4	4	0	1
53 011	CLARK COUNTY	3	31 31	13	3	0	0	1
53 013	COLUMBIA COUNTY	2	31 31	13	2	0	0	1
53 015	COWLITZ COUNTY	3	31 31	21	4	0	0	1
53 017	DOUGLAS COUNTY	4	31 31	13	2	0	0	1
53 019	FERRY COUNTY	2	31 31	13	1	0	0	1
53 021	FRANKLIN COUNTY	2	31 31	21	4	0	0	1
53 023	GARFIELD COUNTY	2	31 31	22	2	0	0	1
53 025	GRANT COUNTY	3	31 31	13	3	0	0	1
53 027	GRAYS HARBOR COUNTY	5	32 32	13	5	4	0	1
53 029	ISLAND COUNTY	5	31 31	13	1	4	0	1
53 031	JEFFERSON COUNTY	5	31 31	13	4	4	0	1
53 033	KING COUNTY	5	31 31	13	4	4	0	1
53 035	KITSAP COUNTY	5	31 31	13	2	4	0	1
53 037	KITTITAS COUNTY	2	32 32	13	2	0	0	1
53 039	KLICKITAT COUNTY	2	31 31	13	3	0	0	1
53 041	LEWIS COUNTY	3	31 31	13	3	0	0	1
53 043	LINCOLN COUNTY	1	31 31	13	1	0	0	1
53 045	MASON COUNTY	5	31 31	13	4	4	0	1
53 047	OKANOGAN COUNTY	5	31 31	13	2	0	0	1
53 049	PACIFIC COUNTY	5	31 31	13	2	4	0	1
53 051	PEND OREILLE COUNTY	3	31 31	13	1	0	0	1
53 053	PIERCE COUNTY	5	31 31	13	4	4	0	1
53 055	SAN JUAN COUNTY	5	13 13	13	1	4	0	1
53 057	SKAGIT COUNTY	5	31 31	13	4	4	0	1
53 059	SKAMANIA COUNTY	3	31 31	13	2	0	0	1
53 061	SNOHOMISH COUNTY	5	31 31	13	3	4	0	1
53 063	SPOKANE COUNTY	2	31 31	13	2	0	0	1
53 065	STEVENS COUNTY	2	31 31	21	1	0	0	1
53 067	THURSTON COUNTY	5	31 31	13	3	4	0	1
53 069	WAHKIAKUM COUNTY	5	13 13	13	2	4	0	1
53 071	WALLA WALLA COUNTY	2	13 13	21	2	0	0	1
53 073	WHATCOM COUNTY	1	13 13	22	2	4	0	1
53 075	WHITMAN COUNTY	2	31 32	13	4	0	0	1
53 077	YAKIMA COUNTY	3			4	0	0	1

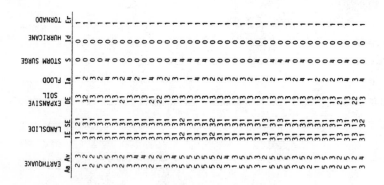

WISCONSIN

		EARTHQUAKE		LANDSLIDE		EXPANSIVE SOIL	FLOOD	STORM SURGE	HURRICANE	TORNADO
		Aa	Av	IE	SE	DE	Ia	S	Pd	Er
55 001	ADAMS COUNTY	1	1	13	32	21	1	0	0	4
55 003	ASHLAND COUNTY	1	1	13	13	21	4	0	0	3
55 005	BARRON COUNTY	1	1	13	13	13	2	0	0	3
55 007	BAYFIELD COUNTY	1	1	21	21	23	2	0	0	3
55 009	BROWN COUNTY	1	1	21	31	21	2	0	0	4
55 011	BUFFALO COUNTY	1	1	21	31	13	1	0	0	4
55 013	BURNETT COUNTY	1	1	13	13	13	1	0	0	4
55 015	CALUMET COUNTY	1	1	21	31	21	1	0	0	4
55 017	CHIPPEWA COUNTY	1	1	13	13	13	4	0	0	4
55 019	CLARK COUNTY	1	1	13	13	13	2	0	0	4
55 021	COLUMBIA COUNTY	1	1	21	31	21	1	0	0	4
55 023	CRAWFORD COUNTY	1	1	13	13	23	2	0	0	4
55 025	DANE COUNTY	1	1	13	13	13	2	0	0	4
55 027	DODGE COUNTY	1	1	31	31	13	1	0	0	4
55 029	DOOR COUNTY	1	1	13	13	21	2	0	0	1
55 031	DOUGLAS COUNTY	1	1	21	32	13	3	0	0	4
55 033	DUNN COUNTY	1	1	13	13	13	1	0	0	4
55 035	EAU CLAIRE COUNTY	1	1	21	31	21	1	0	0	1
55 037	FLORENCE COUNTY	1	1	13	13	22	1	0	0	4
55 039	FOND DU LAC COUNTY	1	1	13	32	23	2	0	0	2
55 041	FOREST COUNTY	1	1	13	13	13	2	0	0	4
55 043	GRANT COUNTY	1	1	21	31	23	2	0	0	4
55 045	GREEN COUNTY	1	1	13	13	13	1	0	0	4
55 047	GREEN LAKE COUNTY	1	1	13	32	23	1	0	0	4
55 049	IOWA COUNTY	1	1	21	31	21	2	0	0	2
55 051	IRON COUNTY	1	1	13	13	13	2	0	0	4
55 053	JACKSON COUNTY	1	1	13	13	13	2	0	0	4
55 055	JEFFERSON COUNTY	1	1	13	32	21	1	0	0	3
55 057	JUNEAU COUNTY	1	1	13	13	13	3	0	0	3
55 059	KENOSHA COUNTY	1	1	21	31	23	1	0	0	3
55 061	KEWAUNEE COUNTY	1	1	13	13	22	1	0	0	4
55 063	LA CROSSE COUNTY	1	1	21	31	23	3	0	0	4
55 065	LAFAYETTE COUNTY	1	1	13	13	13	1	0	0	1
55 067	LANGLADE COUNTY	1	1	13	13	13	1	0	0	3
55 069	LINCOLN COUNTY	1	1	21	21	21	2	0	0	4
55 071	MANITOWOC COUNTY	1	1	13	13	23	2	0	0	3
55 073	MARATHON COUNTY	1	1	13	13	13	2	0	0	4
55 075	MARINETTE COUNTY	1	1	13	13	21	1	0	0	3
55 077	MARQUETTE COUNTY	1	1	13	13	13	1	0	0	3
55 078	MENOMINEE COUNTY	1	1	21	31	21	3	0	0	3
55 079	MILWAUKEE COUNTY	1	1	13	13	13	1	0	0	3
55 081	MONROE COUNTY	1	1	13	32	23	1	0	0	4
55 083	OCONTO COUNTY	1	1	13	13	13	1	0	0	4
55 085	ONEIDA COUNTY	1	1	13	13	21	1	0	0	4
55 087	OUTAGAMIE COUNTY	1	1	21	31	22	2	0	0	4
55 089	OZAUKEE COUNTY	1	1	22	33	22	2	0	0	4
55 091	PEPIN COUNTY	1	1	13	13	13	1	0	0	4
55 093	PIERCE COUNTY	1	1	13	13	13	1	0	0	4
55 095	POLK COUNTY	1	1	13	13	13	1	0	0	4
55 097	PORTAGE COUNTY	1	1	13	13	13	1	0	0	3
55 099	PRICE COUNTY	1	1	13	13	13	1	0	0	3

		EARTHQUAKE		LANDSLIDE		EXPANSIVE SOIL	FLOOD	STORM SURGE	HURRICANE	TORNADO
		Aa	Av	IE	SE	DE	Ia	S	Pd	Er
54 103	WETZEL COUNTY	1	1	33	33	23	3	0	1	1
54 105	WIRT COUNTY	1	1	33	33	23	4	0	1	1
54 107	WOOD COUNTY	1	1	33	33	23	4	0	1	1
54 109	WYOMING COUNTY	2	2	33	33	13	3	0	2	1

WYOMING

		Aa	Av	IE	SE	DE	Ia	S	Id	Er
56	001	ALBANY COUNTY	2	2	13	21	13	3	0	0	1
56	003	BIG HORN COUNTY	2	3	31	31	32	1	0	0	1
56	005	CAMPBELL COUNTY	2	2	31	21	23	1	0	0	1
56	007	CARBON COUNTY	2	2	21	21	21	2	0	0	1
56	009	CONVERSE COUNTY	2	2	13	31	22	1	0	0	1
56	011	CROOK COUNTY	1	1	32	31	31	2	0	0	1
56	013	FREMONT COUNTY	5	5	22	31	13	3	0	0	1
56	015	GOSHEN COUNTY	2	2	13	21	31	2	0	0	1
56	017	HOT SPRINGS COUNTY	2	3	31	31	31	1	0	0	1
56	019	JOHNSON COUNTY	2	2	31	31	22	2	0	0	1
56	021	LARAMIE COUNTY	2	#	13	21	21	2	0	0	1
56	023	LINCOLN COUNTY	5	5	21	31	31	2	0	0	1
56	025	NATRONA COUNTY	2	2	31	31	31	1	0	0	1
56	027	NIOBRARA COUNTY	2	5	13	31	13	1	0	0	1
56	029	PARK COUNTY	2	2	21	21	31	2	0	0	1
56	031	PLATTE COUNTY	2	2	31	31	22	1	0	0	1
56	033	SHERIDAN COUNTY	2	2	31	31	31	2	0	0	1
56	035	SUBLETTE COUNTY	5	3	31	31	22	1	0	0	1
56	037	SWEETWATER COUNTY	2	#	31	31	13	2	0	0	1
56	039	TETON COUNTY	5	4	31	31	21	1	0	0	1
56	041	UINTA COUNTY	5	#	31	31	13	1	0	0	1
56	043	WASHAKIE COUNTY	#	3	31	31	31	2	0	0	1
56	045	WESTON COUNTY	1	2	31	32	32	1	0	0	1

		Aa	Av	IE	SE	DE	Ia	S	Id	Er
55	101	RACINE COUNTY	1	1	21	13	13	2	0	0	3
55	103	RICHLAND COUNTY	1	1	13	13	22	2	0	0	=
55	105	ROCK COUNTY	1	1	13	13	13	2	0	0	=
55	107	RUSK COUNTY	1	1	13	13	13	1	0	0	=
55	109	ST. CROIX COUNTY	1	1	13	32	13	2	0	0	=
55	111	SAUK COUNTY	1	1	13	13	21	1	0	0	=
55	113	SAWYER COUNTY	1	1	13	13	13	1	0	0	=
55	115	SHAWANO COUNTY	1	1	13	31	22	1	0	0	3
55	117	SHEBOYGAN COUNTY	1	1	13	21	13	2	0	0	=
55	119	TAYLOR COUNTY	1	1	13	31	21	3	0	0	=
55	121	TREMPEALEAU COUNTY	1	1	21	31	23	1	0	0	2
55	123	VERNON COUNTY	1	1	13	13	13	1	0	0	=
55	125	VILAS COUNTY	1	1	13	13	13	1	0	0	=
55	127	WALWORTH COUNTY	1	1	13	13	13	2	0	0	=
55	129	WASHBURN COUNTY	1	1	13	13	13	2	0	0	=
55	131	WASHINGTON COUNTY	1	1	13	13	13	1	0	0	=
55	133	WAUKESHA COUNTY	1	1	13	13	13	1	0	0	=
55	135	WAUPACA COUNTY	1	1	13	13	21	2	0	0	=
55	137	WAUSHARA COUNTY	1	1	13	13	21	1	0	0	=
55	139	WINNEBAGO COUNTY	1	1	33	13	23	1	0	0	=
55	141	WOOD COUNTY	1	1	13	13	13	1	0	0	=

APPENDIX B

Bibliography on Natural Disasters

Bibliography on Natural Disasters

Ambraseys, Nicholas N. "Bibliography of Dissertations and Theses on Disaster Phenomena." Unscheduled Events. Volume 2, 1968.

Ambraseys, Nicholas N. Earthquake Engineering Reference Index. London: Cementation Company, 1963.

Ambraseys, Nicholas N. Bibliography on Seismic Sea Waves and Associated Phenomena I. London: Department of Civil Engineering, Imperial College of Science, 1960.

Andriese, Pamela D., Compiler. Earthquake Predicting Information. U.S.G.S. Open-File Report No. 8-843. Washington, D.C.: U.S. Geological Survey, 1980.

Benjamin, Aaron L. and Michelle Swallow. U.S. Earthquake Reconstruction Program for Managua, Nicaragua. Monticello, Illinois: Vance Bibliographies No. P193, March 1979.

Berlin, G. Lennis. Earthquake Hazards and the Urban Environment. Monticello, Illinois: Council of Planning Librarians. Bibliography No. 390, 1973.

Burr, Nelson R., Compiler. Safeguarding Our Cultural Heritage: A Bibliography on the Protection of Museums. Works of Art. Monuments, Archives, and Libraries in Time of War. Washington, D.C.: The Library of Congress, General Reference and Bibliography Division, 1952.

Cochran, Anita L. Annotated Bibliography on Natural Hazards. Working Paper No. 22. Boulder, Colorado: University of Colorado, Natural Hazards Research and Applications Information Center, 1972.

Cochran, Anita L. Bibliography on Floodproofing. Prepared for the Conference on Floodproofing and Floodplain Management, Pacific Grove, California, March 20-25, 1977. Boulder, Colorado: University of Colorado, Natural Hazards Research and Applications Information Center, March 1977.

Cochran, Anita and Kathleen Torres. Flash Flood Warnings Bibliography. Prepared for Flash Flood Aareness Conference. April 1977. Phoenix, Arizona. Boulder, Colorado: University of Colorado Institute of Behavioral Sciences, Natural Hazards Research and Applications Information Center, April 1977.

Coffman, Jerry L. Catalog of Earthquake Photographs. Boulder, Colorado: National Oceanic and Atmospheric Administration. Environmental Data and Information Service. Key to Geophysical Records Documentation 7, 1976.

Computerized Information Retrieval Services Containing Natural Hazards Literature. Boulder, Colorado: University of Colorado, Natural Hazards Research and Applications Information Center, 1976.

Connors, Edward F., III, Compiler. Bibliography for Public Safety and Environmental Protection for Recreation and Park Areas. McLean, Virginia: PRC Public Management Services, Inc., September 1974.

531

Cunha, George Martin. Conservation of Library Materials: A Manual and Bibliography on the Care, Repair and Restoration of Library Materials. 2nd Edition. Metuchen, N.J.: Scarecrow Press, 1971 and 1972.

Debelius, JoAnne R., Editor. Building Technology Publications Supplement 2: 1977. Washington, D.C.: U.S. Department of Commerce, National Bureau of Standards, Center for Building Technology, 1978.

Dunne, Thomas. Directory of Disaster-Related Technology. Washington, D.C.: Federal Disaster Assistance Administration. U.S. Government Printing Office, 1975.

Earthquake Engineering Research Center. Library Printed Catalog. Berkeley, California: University of California, Earthquake Engineering Research Center, 1975.

Earthquake Engineering Research Institute. Bibliography of Earthquake Engineering. 3rd Edition. Compiled by Edward H. Hollis. Oakland, California: Earthquake Engineering Research Institute, 1971.

Earthquake Research for the Safer Siting of Critical Facilities. Washington, D.C.: National Academy of Sciences, National Research Council, Committee on Seismology, 1980.

Evans, Frank B. Modern Archives and Manuscripts: A Select Bibliography. Chicago: Society of American Archivists, 1975.

Gold, John R. Natural Hazards and Disasters: A Selected Bibliography of Behavioral Literature. Monticello, Illinois: Vance Bibliographies, No. P361, November 1979.

Harshbarger, D. and G. Moran. "A Selective Bibliography on Disaster and Human Ecology." Omega. Volume V, 1974, pp. 89-95.

Hunter, John E. Emergency Preparedness for Museums, Historic Sites and Archives: An Annotated Bibliography. Nashville, Tennessee: American Association for State and Local History, Technical Leaflet No. 114, September 1978.

Hunter, John E. Security for Museums and Historic Houses: An Annotated Bibliography. Nashville, Tennessee: American Association for State and Local History, Technical Leaflet No. 83.

Kemp, Toby. "Disaster Assistance Bibliography: Selected References for Cultural/Historic Facilities." Conservation Administration News, Number 11, October 1982. Reprinted in Technology and Conservation, Volume 8, Number 2, Summer 1983, pp. 25-7.

King, Richard G., Jr. A Guide to the Literature on Deterioration, Conservation and Preservation of Library Material. Berkeley, California: University of California, August 1981.

Larson, Peter T. and Frank Evangelista, Eds. NOAA Products and Services of the National Weather Service, National Environmental Satellite Service, Environmental Data Service, and the Environmental Research Laboratories. Washington, D.C.: U.S. Department of Commerce, November 1977.

Lee, W. H. World-Wide Earthquake Research Data Bases. Menlo Park, California: U.S. Department of the Interior, U.S. Geological Survey, Geological Division, Office of Earthquake Studies, to be published.

Manning, Diana H. Disaster Technology: An Annotated Bibliography. New York: Pergamon Press, 1976.

Mayes, R. L. and R. W. Clough. A Literature Survey: Compressive, Tensile, Bond and Shear Strength of Masonry. Berkeley, California: University of California, Earthquake Engineering Research Center, Report No. EERC 75 15, 1975.

Meyers, H. M. and C. A. Von Hake. Earthquake Data File Summary. Boulder, Colorado: U.S. Department of Commerce, National Oceanic and Atmospheric Administration, National Geophysical and Solar-Terrestrial Data Center, 1976.

Moe, Christine E. Earthquakes. Monticello, Illinois: Vance Bibliographies No. P512, June 1980.

Morton, David, Compiler. Selected Bibliography on Disaster Planning and Simulation. Boulder, Colorado: Natural Hazards Research and Applications Informations. Boulder, Colorado: University of Colorado, Natural Hazards Research and Applications Information Center, 1981.

Morton, David, Compiler. A Selected, Partially Annotated Bibliography of Recent Natural Hazards Publications. Boulder, Colorado: University of Colorado, Natural Hazards Research and Applications Information Center, published annually.

Nelson, John B. Catalog of Tsunami Photographs. Boulder, Colorado: U.S. Department of Commerce. National Oceanic and Atmospheric Administration, Key to Geophysical Records Documentation No. 13, 1980.

Petty, Geraldine, Lilita Dzirkals and Margaret Krahenbuhl. Economic Recovery Following Disaster: A Selected, Annotated Bibliography. Santa Monica, California: The Rand Corporation, 1977.

Quarantelli, E. L. and Verta A. Taylor. An Annotated Bibliography on Disasters and Disaster Planning. 3rd Edition. Disaster Research Center Miscellaneous Reports, Vol. 16. Columbus, Ohio: Ohio State University, Disaster Research Center, 1978.

Rayner, Jeanette. "Studies of Disasters and Other Extreme Situations—An Annotated Selected Bibliography." Human Organization. Volume 16, No. 2, 1957, pp. 30–40.

Richner, Mark E. The Application of Remote Sensing to Flood Inundation. Monticello, Illinois: Vance Bibliographies No. P535, 1980.

Robertson, George W., et al. An Annotated Bibliography of Coastal Zone Management Work Products. Washington, D.C.: U.S. Department of Commerce. National Oceanic and Atmospheric Administration, 1980.

Rodriquez, Thelma, et al. National Earthquake Hazards Reduction Program: Summaries of Technical Reports: Volume 10. USGS Open-File Report 80-842. Washington, D.C.: U.S. Geological Survey, 1980.

Rothe, J. P. Annual Summary of Information on Natural Disasters 1966-73. Paris, UNESCO, annual.

Torres, Kathleen and Penny Waterstone. Information Sources for Natural Hazards Research—Organizations, Periodicals, Newsletters and Reference Sources. Boulder, Colorado: University of Colorado, Natural Hazards Research and Applications Information Center, May 1977.

U.S. Department of Housing and Urban Development. Federal Disaster Assistance Administration. Directory of Disaster-Related Technology. Washington, D.C.: U.S. Government Printing Office, 1975.

U.S. Department of the Interior. U.S. Geological Survey. Scientific, Technical, Spatial and Bibliographic Data Bases of the U.S. Geological Survey, 1979. Washington, D.C.: U.S. Geological Survey, 1980.

U.S. National Fire Prevention and Control Administration. Fire Safety Reference 1977. Washington, D.C.: U.S. Department of Commerce, 1977.

Vance, Mary. Earthquakes and Buildings: A List of Books. Monticello, Illinois: Vance Bibliographies No. 276, 1980.

Vance, Mary. Floods, Flood Control and Flood Damage Prevention: A Bibliography. Monticello, Illinois: Vance Bibliographies, No. P999, July 1982.

Weathers, John W., Editor. Flood Damage Prevention: An Indexed Bibliography. Knoxville, Tennessee: Tennessee Valley Authority and University of Tennessee, Water Resources Research Center, October 1976.

Weeks, Ellen J. and Barclay G. Jones. The Social and Economic Aspects of Earthquakes and Other Natural Disasters: Risk Assessment, Hazard Mitigation, Emergency Management, Reconstruction and Recovery. Monticello, Illinois: Vance Bibliographies, Number P1260, August 1983.

Westgate, Kenneth. A Bibliography of Precautionary Planning for Disaster. Disaster Research Unit Occasional Paper No. 12. Bradford, England: University of Bradford, Disaster Research Unit, 1976.

White, Anthony G. A Problem in Public Management—Allocation of Emergency Services. Monticello, Illinois: Vance Bibliographies, No. P279, July 1979.

World Data Center A for Solid Earth Geophysics. Catalog of Significant Earthquakes from 2000 B.C. to 1979. Washington, D.C.: National Academy of Sciences, July 1981.

Young, Mary E. Disasters: Effects and Countermeasures—Volume I: 1964-75. A bibliography with abstracts. Springfield, Va.: National Technical Information Service, 1977.

Young, Mary E. Disasters: Effects and Countermeasures—Volume II: 1976-Present. A bibliography with abstracts. Springfield, Va.: National Technical Information Service, 1978.

APPENDIX C

Seminar Program

PROGRAM

Seminar on the Protection of Historic Architecture and Museum Collections from Earthquakes and Other Natural Disasters

March 29-30, 1982
Auditorium
National Academy of Science
2100 C Street, N.W.
Washington, D.C.

SPONSORING ORGANIZATIONS

AAM-ICOM

Advisory Board on the Built Environment
National Academy of Sciences

American Association of Museums

American Institute of Architects

American Institute for Conservation of Historic and Artistic Works

Association for Preservation Technology

Committee on the History and Heritage of American Civil Engineering
American Society of Civil Engineers

Historic House Association of America

National Park Service

National Trust for Historic Preservation

Smithsonian Institution

US-ICOMOS

**Seminar on the Protection of Historic Architecture
and Museum Collections from Earthquakes
and Other Natural Disasters**

March 29-30, 1982
Auditorium
National Academy of Sciences
2100 C Street, N.W.
Washington, D.C.

MONDAY, March 29

8:00 - 9:00 a.m. **Registration**

9:00 - 9:15 **Opening Remarks**

Chair: Michael L. Joroff, President
Architectural Research Centers Consortium,
Inc.

"Opening Statement"
Dr. Barclay G. Jones, AIA, AICP, Professor
Department of City and Regional Planning,
Cornell University

"Research Issues"
Dr. Frederick Krimgold
Civil Engineering Division, Engineering
Directorate, National Science Foundation

9:15 - 10:30 **Session I Opening Address**

Chair: Paul N. Perrot, Assistant Secretary
Museum Programs, Smithsonian Institution

Protection of our Cultural Heritage Against Natural
Disasters
Dr. Bernard M. Feilden, C.B.E., F.R.I.B.A.
Architect, Norfolk, England

10:30 - 11:00 Coffee

11:00 – 12:30	**Session II Recent Losses from Earthquakes and Natural Disasters**
11:00 – 11:45	A. Structures Chair: Russell V. Keune, AIA, Senior Vice President National Trust for Historic Preservation
	"On Earth as It Is: Recent Losses of Historic Structures from Earthquakes and Natural Disasters" W. Brown Morton, III Historic Preservation Consultant, Leesburg, VA
11:45 – 12:30	B. Artifacts Chair: Dr. Craig Black, President American Association of Museums AAM/ICOM
	"Lessons to be Learned from Friuli" Paul M. Schwartzbaum ICCROM, Rome Italy
12:45 – 2:00	Lunch
2:00 – 3:30 p.m.	**Session III Assessment of Hazards and Vulnerability**
2:00 – 2:45	A. Multi-Hazard Assessment of a Locale and a Site Chair: Dr. John Eberhard, AIA, Executive Director Advisory Council on the Built Environment National Research Council/National Academy of Sciences
	"Multi-Hazard Assessment of Localities and Sites" L. Neal FitzSimons, Chairman Committee on the History and Heritage of American Civil Engineering American Society of Civil Engineers
2:45 – 3:30	B. Vulnerability Assessment of a Structure Chair: Dr. Frederick Krimgold Civil Engineering Division, Engineering Directorate National Science Foundation
	"Assessing the Vulnerability of Historic and Museum Structures to Earthquakes" Eric Elsesser Forell/Elsesser, Consulting Engineers, San Francisco, CA

3:30 – 4:00	Coffee
4:00 – 5:30	**Session IV Vulnerability Reduction**
4:00 – 4:45	A. Making Structures Less Vulnerable Chair: Terry B. Morton, Chairman US–ICOMOS

"Reducing Vulnerability"
Melvyn Green
Melvyn Green & Associates, Inc., Consulting
Engineers
El Segundo, CA

4:45 – 5:30	B. Protective Storage and Display of Artifacts Chair: Elliott Carroll, President Association for Preservation Technology

"The Mitigation and Prevention of Earthquake
Damage to Artifacts"
Dr. John A. Blume
John A. Blume & Associates, Engineers, San
Francisco, CA

6:30	Reception National Building Museum Old Pension Building 440 G Street, N.W.
7:30	Dinner
8:30	**Session V Policy Issues**

Chair: Dr. Ernest Allen Connally
National Park Service, US Department of
Interior

"Welcoming Remarks"
Dr. Bates Lowry, Director
National Building Museum

"Disaster Preparedness and Response Policy"
Robert Garvey, Executive Director
Advisory Council on Historic Preservation

TUESDAY, March 30

9:00 – 10:30 a.m. **Session VI Preventive Measures**

9:00 – 9:45   A.   Emergency Preparedness Planning
                     Chair: Hugh C. Miller, AIA
                                  Chief Historical Architect
                                  National Park Service, US Department of
                                  Interior

                     "Museum Emergency Preparedness Planning"
                                  John Hunter, Regional Curator
                                  National Park Service
                                  US Department of Interior
                                  Lincoln, NB

9:45 – 10:30   B.   Documentation and Recording
                     Chair: Robert Kapsch, Chief
                                  HABS/HAER Division
                                  National Park Service, US Department of
                                  Interior

                     "Use and History of Traditional Recording Techniques
                     for Documentation of Sites and Monuments in
                     Disaster Prone Areas"
                                  Dr. John C. Poppeliers, Head
                                  Cultural Heritage Division, UNESCO, Paris,
                                  France

                     "Photogrammetry and Remote Sensing in Recording
                     Sites, Structures, and Cultural Objects"
                                  Professor Perry E. Borchers
                                  Department of Architecture, Ohio State
                                  University

10:30 – 11:00   Coffee

11:00 – 12:30   **Session VII Emergency Measures: Structures**

11:00 – 11:45   A.   Earthquake Damage to Structures
                     Chair: Tomas Spiers, AIA
                                  Committee on Historic Resources
                                  American Institute of Architects

                     "Emergency Protection to Damaged Structures"
                                  Donald del Cid, Architect
                                  Sutter & Sutter Architects, Ltd.,
                                  Libertyville, IL

11:45 – 12:30	B.	Water Damage to Structures
	Chair:	James C. Massey, President
		Historic House Association of America

"Wind and Water Damage to Historic Structures"
Nicholas H. Holmes, Jr., FAIA
Architect, Mobile, AL

| 12:45 – 2:00 | Lunch |

| 2:00 – 3:30 | **Session VIII Emergency Measures: Artifacts** |

2:00 – 2:45	A.	Earthquake Damage to Artifacts
	Chair:	Perry C. Huston, President
		American Institute for Conservation of
		Historic and Artistic Works

"Emergency Conservation of Earthquake-Damaged
Objects of Polychromed Wood in Friuli, Italy"
Bernard Rabin
Painting Conservator, Cranbury, NJ
and
Constance S. Silver
Conservator, Brattleboro, VT

"Preparedness for Natural Disasters for Monuments
and Artifacts"
Lawrence J. Majewski
Conservation Center, Institute of Fine Arts
New York University

2:45 – 3:30	B.	Water Damage to Artifacts
	Chair:	Ann Hitchcock, Chief Curator
		National Park Service, US Department of
		Interior

"Recovery of Water Damaged Books and Documents"
Mildred O'Connell, Field Service Director
Northeast Document Conservation Center
Andover, MA

| 3:30 – 4:00 | Coffee |

| 4:00 – 5:30 | **Session IX Public and Private Response Measures** |

	Chair:	Dr. Henry A. Millon, Dean
		Center for Advanced Study in the Visual Arts
		National Gallery of Art

A.　　International

"International Programs for the Rescue of
Cultural Properties"
　　Dr. Hiroshi Daifuku, Former Head
　　Sites and Monuments Division, UNESCO

B.　　Federal Government

"Federal Response Measures to Natural
Disasters"
　　Richard W. Krimm, Assistant Associate
　　Director
　　Office of Natural and Technological
　　Hazards, Federal Emergency Management
　　Agency

C.　　State and Local Government

"Applying Earthquake Safety Measures to the
Protection of Historic Architecture and
Museum Collections: Lessons from
California"
　　Robert Olson, Executive Director
　　California Seismic Safety Commission
　　　　　　and
　　Karl V. Steinbrugge
　　Consulting Structural Engineer
　　El Cerrito, CA

D.　　Private

"Mobilization of Private Philanthropy in
Responding to Damages Resulting from
Earthquakes and Other Natural Disasters"
　　Harold L. Oram
　　The Oram Group

5:30 – 5:45　　**Closing Session**

Chair: Dr. Barclay G. Jones, AIA, AICP, Professor
　　Department of City and Regional Planning,
　　Cornell University

"Closing Remarks"
　　Dr. Frederick Krimgold
　　Civil Engineering Division, Engineering
　　Directorate National Science Foundation

5:45　　Adjourn

APPENDIX D

List of Authors

List of Authors

Dr. John A. Blume, Chairman
URS/John A. Blume and Associates, Engineers
130 Jessie Street
San Francisco, California   94105

Prof. Perry E. Borchers
Department of Architecture
Ohio State University
189 Brown Hall
190 West 17th Avenue
Columbus, Ohio   43210

Dr. Hiroshi Daifuku
Former Head, Sites and Monuments Division
United Nations Educational, Social and Cultural Organization
4201 Cathedral Avenue, N.W.
Washington, DC   20016

Donald del Cid
Sutter and Sutter Architects, Ltd.
631 E. Park Avenue
Libertyville, Illinois   60048

Eric Elsesser
Forell/Elsesser, Consulting Engineers
631 Clay Street
San Francisco, California   94111

Dr. Bernard M. Feilden, C.B.E., F.R.I.B.A.
Architect
Stiffkey Old Hall
Wells-Next-the-Sea
Norfolk, NR23 1QJ, England

L. Neal FitzSimons
Engineering Counsel
10408 Montgomery Avenue
Kensington, Maryland   20795

Robert Garvey
Executive Director
Advisory Council on Historic Preservation
1100 Pennsylvania Avenue, N.W.
Washington, DC   20004

Melvyn Green
Melvyn Green and Associates, Inc.
Consulting Engineers
690 North Sepulveda Boulevard, Suite 120
El Segundo, California   90245

Nicholas H. Holmes, Jr., FAIA
Architect
257 South Conception Street
P.O. Box 864
Mobile, Alabama   36603

John C. Hunter
Regional Curator
National Park Service
Federal Building, Room 474
700 Centennial Mall North
Lincoln, Nebraska   68508

Richard W. Krimm
Assistant Associate Director
Office of Natural and Technological Hazards
Federal Emergency Management Agency
500 C Street, S.W.
Washington, DC   20472

Lawrence J. Majewski, Chairman
Conservation Center, Institute of Fine Arts
New York University
14 East 78th Street
New York, New York   10021

Arch. Riccardo Mola
Soprintendente per i Beni Ambientali,
   Archittettonici, Artistici e Storici
Bari, Italy

W. Brown Morton, III
Historic Preservation Consultant
4 East Loudoun Street
Leesburg, Virginia   22075

Mildred O'Connell
Field Service Director
Northeast Document Conservation Center
Abbot Hall, 28 School Street
Andover, Massachusetts   01810

Harold L. Oram
The Oram Group
777 Hunterbrook Road
Yorktown, New York   10598

Dr. John C. Poppeliers, Head
Cultural Heritage Division
UNESCO
7 Place de Fontenoy
75700 Paris, France

Bernard Rabin
Conservator
260 A Monroe Road
Cranbury, New Jersey   08512

Ralph W. Rose
Research Assistant
Program in Urban and Regional Studies
109 West Sibley Hall
Cornell University
Ithaca, New York   14853

Anne Russell, Director
Northeast Document Conservation Center
Abbot Hall, 28 School Street
Andover, Massachusetts   01810

Paul M. Schwartzbaum
ICCROM
13 Via di S. Michele
00153 Rome, Italy

Constance S. Silver
Conservator
500 Riverside Drive
New York, New York   10027

Peter H. Smith
Former Special Assistant for Urban Affairs
Advisory Council on Historic Preservation
1100 Pennsylvania Avenue, N.W.
Washington, DC   20004

Delbert B. Ward, Architect
Structural Facilities, Inc.
648 South 900 East
Salt Lake City, Utah   84102

David G. Westendorff
Research Assistant
Department of City and Regional Planning
106 West Sibley Hall
Cornell University
Ithaca, New York   14853

Index

552

553

Tuscania, 6; Valvano, [9] ; Venice, 18, 21, 105, 424-426; Villuzza of Ragogna, [54] , [56]

Jamaica, Port Royal, earthquake and tsunami, 1692, 110
Jamestown, Virginia, hurricane, 1667; 112
Japan, 83, 99, [101]
Japanese vibration tests, 18
Jefferson Davis Shrine, Biloxi, Mississippi, 6
Jerash, Jordan, undisturbed ruins, 4; 8th century destruction of, 19
Jewish Synagogue, Florence, 6
Johnstown, Pennsylvania, Johnstown Flood Museum, damage, 8
Jordan, 4, 19
Jordan valley, high risk area, 19

Kariye Paraecclesion, Istanbul, earthquake damage, 343
Keck, Caroline, water damage emergency treatment guidelines, 366-367
Kinetic damage, 93
Kotor, Yugoslavia, earthquake, 1667, 1979, 8, 419
Kouros, photogrammetric drawing, [259]
Krakatoa Island, Sumatra, volcanic eruption and tsunami, 1883; 110
Kursumli Han, Skopje, Yugoslavia, damage, 1963, 4

Lake Nasser, floodwaters, 3
La Libertad, Ecuador, sea surge, 1981; [109]
Landslides, 99, 103, 480-481, 487
Landslides, Anchorage, Alaska, 1964, [101] ; Guatemala City, Guatemala, [102] ; Lituya Bay, Alaska, 1958, 99, [102] ; Mount Hirascaran, Peru, 1970, 99; Vaiont Dam, Piave River, Italy,1963, 4
Laussedat, Aimé, 246, 254, [255]
League of Red Cross Societies, 398
le-Duc, Viollet, Chateau de Pierrefonds, 244
LeRoy, Julien-David, Les Ruins, 241, Les Edifices, 239
Lexsan, usefulness, 330
Libraries, Albany, New York, New York State Library, 1911, 371, [372] ; Andover, Massachusetts, Oliver Wendell Holmes Library, Phillips Academy, 1981, 378-381; Fairbanks, Alaska, Fairbanks Library, 1967, [98]; Florence, Italy, Biblioteca Nazionale, Gabinello Vieusseux, Geography Academy, Jewish Synagog, Opera di Duomo, 1966, 6; National Personnel Records Center, Missouri, 1973, 293; Palo Alto, Stanford University Meyer Library, 1978, 183; Philadelphia, Pennsylvania, Temple University, Charles Klein Law Library, 1972, 181; Pleasant Valley, New York, Arlington High School

Library, [375] ; Washington, D.C., Library of Congress, 1814, 116; Wilkes-Barre, Pennsylvania, Wyoming Historical and Geological Society, 1972
Library of Congress, fire, 116, 404
Library union registries, 400
Lice, Turkey, earthquake damage, 1975, [100]
Lightning, hazard of, 20, [125]
Lightning conductor, assessing need, 20-21
Lime mortar, 31, vs. Portland cement mortar, 35; weaknesses, 334, 339-342
Lisbon, Portugal, reconstruction, 11; tsunami, 1755; 110
Lituya Bay, Alaska, earthquake and landslide, 1958; 99, [102]
Local predisaster planning, 439-440
Lock Haven, Pennsylvania, Clinton County Historical Society, 6
Locke, California, Wooden Structures, 132, [137]
London, England, flood risk protection 3; lowering water table, 21; great fire, 1666; 11, 394
Lorenzetti, frescoes, 6
Los Angeles, California, Forest Lawn Memorial Park, statue of David, 1971, [5] ; Villa Adobe, 1971, 6
Los Angeles City Earthquake Safety Ordinance, 136
Los Angeles City Hazardous Building Code, 159
Louisville, Kentucky, tornado, 1890; 116
Lowry, Bates, 344

Maiano, Friuli, Italy, Chiesa di S. Giovanni, tabernacle, 360-363
Martini, frescoes, 6
Managua, Nicaragua, earthquake and fire, 1972, 6; Presidential Palace and Cathedral, 6; Ruben Dario bust damage, [7]
McKee, Harley J., 237-238
Measured drawings, 231-246
Mediterranean Sea, tsunami, 110
Mercalli Scale, 94, 199
Mercalli, Giuseppe, 94
Mesa Verde National Park, 80
Mesopotamia, Nippur, 232
Messbildanstalt, Berlin, 246
Mestre, Italy, 424-425
Metrophotography, Deneux de Montburn, [259] , 261
Mexico, earthquake damage, 1973, Puebla, Veracruz, Oaxaca, 6
Mexico City, Mexico, underground lake, 104
Meyderbaer, Albrecht, 246, 254
Micro-geographical risk analysis, 478
Military, at a disaster, 21; damage prevention, 197

Mitchell, John, 11
Mitigation, defined, 443; design, 195-196
Mixco Viejo, Guatemala, Mayan site damage, 1976, [9]
Mobile, Alabama, 6; Hurricane Frederick, 1969; 321-342
Monge, Gaspard, 243
Montbrun, Deneux de, [259], 261
Monophotogrammetry, 257
Montenegro, Yugoslavia, earthquake, 1979, 8, [40], 419-421
Monterey, California, Cooper-Molera Adobe Complex, 132, [135]
Montgomery, Alabama, State Capitol, repairs, 334, [337], [338]
Mosque of Mustapha Pasha, Skopje, Yugoslavia, 4
Mount Hirascaran, Peru, landslide, 1970; 99
Mount Tambora, volcanic eruption, tsunami, 1815; 110
Moveable sea barrier, Thames River at Woolwich, 3
Multi-Hazard ratings, U.S., 477-528
Murphysboro Tornado, 1925; 116
Museo Archeologico, Florence, Etruscan collection, 6
Museo delle Scienze, Florence, losses, 6
Museum quarterly, 408
Museums, artifact mounting systems, [157]; assets, criteria, 213-215; conceptual solutions, [163]; non-structural components, [157]
Museums, Athens, Greece, Acropolis Museum, 1979, 8; National Museum, 1979, 8; Biloxi, Mississippi, Jefferson Davis Shrine, 1969, 6; Bucharest, Romania, National Museum, 8; Cambridge, Massachusetts, Harvard Semetic Museum, 1970, 289; Corning, New York, Corning Museum of Glass, 1972, 6, 83, 107, [373], [375], [376]; Florence, Italy, Bardini Museum, Bargello, Museo Archeologico, Museo delle Scienze, Uffizi Gallery, 1966, 6; Houston, Texas, Contemporary Art Museum, 1976, 106, 399; Huaras, Peru, archaeological museum, 1970, 6; Johnstown, Pennsylvania, Johnstown Flood Museum, 1977, 8; New York, New York, Museum of Modern Art, 1958, 76, 399, State Maritime Museum, 256; Pittsburgh, Pennsylvania, Fort Pitt Museum, 1972, 6; Rio de Janeiro, Brazil, Museum of Modern Art, 1978, 395; Sacramento, California, State Railroad Museum, 132, [134]; Wichita Falls, Texas, museum, 1979, 182
Museums and Historic Buildings, seismic protection, 162
Music Conservatory, Florence, Italy, 6
Mycenean Age, aseismic building techniques, 11

NEH Field Service project, 374
NOAA Environmental Data and Information Service, 43
Nantucket, Rhode Island, Historic American Buildings Survey Project, 181
Naples-Bari, Italy, earthquake, 1930; 8
Natchez, Mississippi, tornado, 1840; 116
National Archives, 404; Registry of Paintings and Works of Art, 400
National Climatic Center, 124
National Comprehensive Emergency Management, [431]
National Disaster Assistance System, 438
National Endowment for the Arts, 399
National Endowment for the Humanities, 404
National Fire Protection Association, 193
National Flood Insurance Program, 439
National Geophysical and Solar Terrestrial Data Center, map, 39, 41
National Historic Preservation Act, amendments, 84
National Hurricane Center, 81
National Institute for Museum Services, 404
National Microfilm Association, 29
National Museum, Athens, Greece, 8
National Park Service, 404
National Personnel Records Center, Missouri, fire, 1973; 293
National Severe Storm Laboratory, 124
National Trust for Historic Preservation, 82, 399
National Weather Service, 124
Natural disaster, damage recording, 260-262; private response, 459-462
Natural disaster committee, function of, 60
Natural disaster policy, 72-73
Neapolitan earthquake of 1857, 8
Netherlands, sea surges, 108
Newberry, Massachusetts, tornado, 1743; 116
New Jersey, hurricane, 1938, 114
New Madrid, Missouri, earthquake, 1811, 95
New Mexico, Arroyodel Tajo Pictograph Site, photogrammetric record, 257
New York Museum of Modern Art, fire, 1958, 76, 399
New York, New York, photogrammetric records, Schermerhorn Block, 256, State Maritime Museum, 256; Villard Houses, 256
New York State Historical Society, 399
New York State Library, Albany, fire, 1911, 371, [372]
New York University, Conservation Center, 399
Nicaragua, 6, [7]
Niigata, Japan, earthquake, 1964, 99, [101]
Nippur, Mesopotamia, dwelling representation, 232
Northeast Document Conservation Center, 369, 399

558